THE GLOBALIZED LIBRARY

American Academic Libraries and International Students, Collections, and Practices

Edited by
Yelena Luckert
with Lindsay Inge Carpenter

Association of College and Research Libraries
A division of the American Library Association
Chicago, Illinois 2019

The paper used in this publication meets the minimum requirements of American National Standard for Information Sciences–Permanence of Paper for Printed Library Materials, ANSI Z39.48-1992. ∞

Cataloging-in-Publication data is on file with the Library of Congress.

Printed in the United States of America.
23 22 21 20 19 5 4 3 2 1

Contents

INTRODUCTION

The Globalized Library:

American Academic Libraries and International Students, Collections, and Practices

Perspectives on Globalization of American Libraries

When reflecting on libraries in the United States, we almost never think of them as being international in nature. We view them as "American" institutions, serving our "American" patrons and our "American" organizations. But academic libraries, like institutions of higher education at large, are key players in the effort to educate a diverse student body to be globally conscious members of our communities. In this volume, practitioners from America and Canada reflect on how their work is globalized, addressing themes including collection practices, professional development opportunities, outreach efforts, instructional strategies, and international partnerships.

From their inception, private and public, American academic and special libraries and archives have been in the forefront of building general and special collections in a multitude of languages, produced and acquired from all over the world. For some countries of the world, materials held in US libraries surpass what might be available to their citizens in their own libraries due to hostile governments, censorship, wars, economic hardships, or natural disasters. The federal government and many state governments have directly or indirectly supported acquisitions of foreign materials at colleges and universities, particularly after the passing of the Higher Education Act of 1965 (Title VI), which transformed academic institutions by allowing international studies to grow. Several papers in this volume talk in more detail about Title VI and its effects on libraries' collections, including chapters by Browndorf and Pappas (chapter 14), Celik (chapter 15), and Díaz and Espinosa de los Monteros (chapter 17). Collections were also put together through acquisitions of important private collections, monetary gift giving and endowments, and donations in-kind from libraries of scholars working in the field, private individuals, and local emigre communities. For example, the University of Maryland's impressive Judaica collection was acquired through a combination of these means, with only relatively modest support from the state. Chapters from Vargas-Betancourt, Hawley, and Jefferson (chapter 18), Des Jardin and Williams (chapter 16), Tatsumi (chapter 21), Necas (chapter 20), and Margolis and Zeter (chapter 19) address these approaches to collection development, illustrating how unexpected discoveries and partnerships can result in fascinating collections.

Establishing strong working relationships with vendors in and outside the country who could supply foreign-published materials was one of the most important tasks of librarians who worked with these collections. Whether through firm orders or approval plans, these were very labor-intensive tasks, which required a lot of skill from those who worked in the libraries. These professionals had to have mastery of the languages, cultural literacy, and sensitivity of the area studies they worked in to perform these duties as each country or region has its own political, historical, and cultural norms that are not readily apparent to outsiders even with good language skills. Working in these environments, it is easy to misunderstand, make a costly mistake, offend without realization, and sometimes even create an unintended international incident. Even seemingly simple tasks, like paying an invoice to a foreign business, can quickly become rather difficult and frustrating. Thus, librarians in these positions had to be very creative and adaptive, thinking outside the box. When available—and especially when libraries do not offer appropriate skills—vendors based in the United States specializing in foreign acquisitions have been often favored over those that are overseas. And there has been a big proliferation of those vendors, covering Europe, Latin America, Russia and the former Soviet states, and, more recently, the Middle East. In addition, some libraries that could afford it, like Harvard, were able to have scouts in the countries of their specific interest to select and purchase materials directly, particularly during times of an unstable publishing industry—for example, Russia during perestroika.

Materials published overseas were often printed on highly acidic paper of inferior properties and over time became a preservation nightmare for libraries. Progressively, preservation, and now digital preservation, have become a critical part of collection development and management of international materials. If nothing is done about the physical state of these items, quite quickly they simply will be unusable. But as libraries have been losing funding for all operations, including materials budgets, it has become more and more difficult to care for these collections. In this effort, the archival materials often fare better than general collections; their unstable properties make them more likely to be taken care of. Government- and non-government-sponsored organizations, private individuals, and corporations have provided additional resources via grants and donations to manage and preserve these treasures. Libraries get grants from big players such as the National Endowment for the Humanities, the Andrew W. Mellon Foundation, Institute of Museum and Library Services, as well as from smaller foundations, organizations, businesses, and even private donors with very specific interests in mind. International governments have also, at times, supported American collections of interest to them. (See articles by Necas and Yukako.) This, of course, requires a lot of development work of which librarians and curators of these collections are an integral part and play an active role.

There have been many commercial companies, groups, and individuals who have been trying to save general collections for the future as well. At first they microfilmed them, and as technology has evolved, these materials are now being digitized. K. G. Saur Verlag (which no longer exists), with its massive microform collections, such as *Hebrew Books from the Harvard College Library* (1989), the Yiddish Book Center, and best-known to everyone, Google, are just a few such companies and organizations. The creation of these massive microform or online resources has led to other issues for the libraries, including prohibitive costs of some of these products, dealing with unfriendly and outdated technology like microforms (which in turn pose serious preservation issues), the rights to access, the poor quality of mass digitization, and sometimes even some questionable practices that librarians have been debating about and struggling with. In response, large academic libraries collaborate with their own large-scale cooperative repositories, like the HathiTrust digital library, but unfortunately these too have many issues to overcome. On a smaller scale, despite all the difficulties and costs, many American libraries have also been trying to digitize for preservation some of their general collections of special interest materials, especially if outside funding is available. For example, the University of Maryland Jewish Studies department is currently supporting the library's project to digitize the backlog of unprocessed, highly brittle Judaica that has not yet been digitized elsewhere to ensure preservation and access to these materials, and which will only be available online.

With the changes in libraries from collection to service models, the instability of budgets, the need for student spaces, the lack and cost of storage, technology pressures, changes in how research is being conducted, shortages of positions, devaluation of humanities including the lack of support for language learning, and other important and difficult issues, in recent years foreign acquisitions as we know them have been threatened as well. Chapters of this book allude to this phenomenon. This situation is further exacerbated due to the fact that ebook publishing is in its infancy at best in many other countries, contributing to space issues, especially when the circulation of physical materials is declining, as evidenced by circulation statistics collected by the Association of Research Libraries (ARL).[1] The bright light here is the development of foreign digital collections, detailed in chapters by Browndorf and Pappas (chapter 14), Des Jardin and Williams (chapter 16), Necas (chapter 20), Vargas-Betancourt, Hawley, and Jefferson (chapter 18), and others. Thus, academic libraries seem to be moving away from general to either special or highly specialized collections in area studies.

Although collections might be the most obvious area initially where people think of libraries as international in nature, it is not the only area by any means. All types of libraries and archives in the United States (public, academic, school, special, etc.) hire staff for whom English is a second language for all sorts of jobs and responsibilities. Academic, museum, and government libraries have traditionally hired specialists with appropriate credentials, both heritage and non-heritage speakers, to select, acquire, manage, and preserve area studies collections at huge costs to institutions and American taxpayers. For these types of jobs, an MLS degree is often overlooked in favor of much-needed foreign language and related skills. And it does make sense. We can teach and train in "librarianship" but do not have the resources for teaching foreign-language skills.

Those who speak English as a second language find the library environment very welcoming, reassuring, and safe. In turn, they influence the dynamics of their organizations, internationalizing them from within and making our libraries even more accessible for non-English speakers. This phenomenon will only continue to grow as the world is becoming more and more globalized.

In recent years, many academic institutions count globalization or internationalization among their most important strategic goals and priorities. The realization that in order for America to be globally competitive we need to produce globally conscious graduates has pushed campuses—and thus libraries—in several new directions. In addition

to their hiring practices and the traditional role of libraries collecting foreign acquisitions, new trends are emerging. This volume is full of such examples. These chapters address many acute needs in international student education and highlight library initiatives that can make a huge difference. Reflective of our daily environments, these chapters talk about information literacy for international students on US campuses, efforts to make these students feel welcome and included, programs to develop satellite campuses overseas, initiatives for participation in education abroad, and development and growth of library professionals to support these efforts. These cases are very creative and inspiring. They give hope.

American higher education is experiencing a global boom. It is well known and highly prized around the world for its academic rigor, diversity of majors, use of emerging technology, flexibility, independent thinking, problem-solving, and the abundance of schools and programs to choose from in different geographic locations and with a range of tuition levels.[2] According to the Institute of International Education's *Open Doors Report on International Educational Exchange*, in 2017, 903,127 international (nonimmigrant) students were enrolled in American colleges and universities.[3]

Librarians are responding to these students' academic needs by investigating a range of pedagogical techniques. Chapters from Hodge (chapter 4) and Avery and Feist (chapter 2) offer best practices for teaching English-language learners and international students. Alwan, Doan, and Garcia (chapter 1) and Riley and Davis (chapter 6) present methods for addressing American academic values with international students, with a particular emphasis on conversations about expectations for the ethical use of information. Chen and Mastel (chapter 7) and Fu and Duque (chapter 3) highlight strategies for engaging with international students outside of traditional one-shot sessions, with approaches ranging from library orientations and materials offered in students' native languages to the creation of peer tutoring programs. Interestingly, many of the authors found that these practices are also beneficial for domestic students as well, suggesting that attention to international students' needs has broader benefits for the entire student population.

In addition to providing academic support, librarians are also leading initiatives to warmly welcome international students to the campus community. Chapters from Bordonaro (chapter 9) and Bohuski (chapter 8) offer case studies of successful outreach initiatives implemented at their institutions. Contributions from Gant, Amsberry, Su, Munip, and Borrelli (chapter 10), Stewart and Haggerty (chapter 11), Wu (chapter 13), and Wu and Hoffman (chapter 12) represent original research in international students' perceptions of libraries. These studies are especially welcome since recent literature on international students suffers from a lack of original research.[4] It is interesting to note that it was difficult to organize these chapters into purely "academic" and "non-academic" initiatives; this suggests to us that academic librarians are approaching their international students as whole people with a host of emotional, social, and intellectual concerns that intersect to inform students' experiences on American campuses.

At the same time, our academic institutions are investing in global programs, such as education abroad, which can be academic or non-academic in nature, student exchange programs, and international research opportunities. According to the Institute of International Education's *Open Doors Report on International Educational Exchange*, in 2014, 304,467 American students were studying abroad.[5] These impressive numbers are steadily growing. Although this has been an uncharted area for librarians, they have responded with enthusiasm and ingenuity, finding ways to address the new needs in line with their institutional goals. Some things are simply a given, including providing uninterrupted access to the institution's online materials and online research support through a general online information service such as CHAT or AskUs. Others are as varied and creative as they come—for example, providing students with direct contact with their subject librarian remotely, developing the online teaching tools for specific study-abroad classes, providing an information literacy class before the students' departure, having a librarian accompany a class on their international trip in a supporting role, and even developing and teaching study-abroad classes themselves. (See Kutner, chapter 24, and Luckert and Inge Carpenter, chapter 25.)

Global education goes far beyond education-abroad programs and libraries are following in step. Enabled by the development of technology and the open educational resources movement, and in competition with for-profit higher education among other things, colleges and universities have been developing platforms for online courses and programs that are accessible all over the world. Massive open online courses (MOOC) is one such example in which many colleges and universities in the United States have invested and are participating. Although we do not have an example in this book, libraries and librarians are looking into and figuring out the ways they can contribute to their campuses' efforts in this area. For example, at the University of Maryland, subject librarians are informed when faculty from their assigned departments are offering a MOOC so they can provide support for that course. Although often nothing comes of it, sometimes the librarians end up helping in the development of materials for the course or they participate in the interactive user forums, answering reference questions as the course's librarian.

Another major development in American higher education has been the growth of satellite campuses and programs in other countries. Many of these campuses are being developed in the Middle East, Southeast Asia, and East Asia, where universities believe that they will be profitable in terms of recruitment, research opportunities, and academic influence. To support these programs and their faculty and students, libraries of these institutions must build satellite libraries, programs, collections, and services, often from scratch and in environments very different from their home institutions. There are many obstacles in such efforts, including language and cultural differences, issues of accessing, purchasing and processing materials, information literacy needs, freedom of information, and many others. However, there are many wonderful examples of successes, as seen in chapters from Daniel (chapter 22), Martin and Parrott (chapter 27), McGivney, Costello, and Clarke (chapter 5), and Oberlies (chapter 26). Finally, there are other very creative and unique programs that allow American librarians to share their expertise with international colleagues, such as an African poetry program developed by Dawes and Maxey-Harris (chapter 23).

One of the most cherished qualities of American academic librarianship is the strong commitment to the profession at large and personal growth within it. Sharing of practices, materials and services, and mentoring of personnel have always been a part of this ideal. Libraries developed and perfected many different ways of cooperation and working together. Just think of the InterLibrary Loan systems, consortial agreements, large and small library-centered organizations and their many committees (for example, ALA), internships, and more. As we are working diligently on furthering these relationships, we also find ourselves looking outward, sharing our experience and knowledge with our international colleagues and at the same time learning from them. As in all other areas of librarianship, there is an amazing variety of unique and meaningful programs set up by ordinary librarians responding to local requests and needs.

This book provides several such examples, including a personnel exchange program (Pfander, Humphreys, and Joshipura, chapter 32), visiting librarian programs (Kuchi, chapter 30, and Law, chapter 31), virtual peer mentoring program (Corlett-Rivera and Kangas, chapter 29), contributions to international digital projects and the development of new cadres (Barcyzk, Britz, and Ponelis, chapter 33), and some helpful hints for those who are interested in doing international work (Boyd and Cramer, chapter 28). It is important to note that everyone who participates in these programs sees them as quite valuable and rewarding for everyone involved and hopes to continue them in the future.

As we can see in this book, American academic libraries are deeply involved in all aspects of the globalization of our institutions and community at large, whether it is apparent or not to those outside our walls. We continue to build international collections in many formats so our users are always connected with the bigger world. Through campus partnerships, we create specially designed programs and learning opportunities for international students, such as training in academic integrity and information literacy. We provide support to our education-abroad students by providing them access to our online resources, creating online teaching tools, and, in some cases, leading or accompanying classes on their trips. In a number of cases, librarians are involved in setting up satellite campuses, including establishing American-type libraries with American-type collections and services, often in countries where access to information is highly restricted.

Throughout these chapters, several common themes emerge. First, patience is a necessity when embarking on any project; this is true of almost all projects in academia but is especially true when initiatives require navigating complex legal and cultural considerations. Second, none of these projects can be undertaken alone. All of the authors emphasized the importance of partnerships, whether they are sustained, multi-year collaborations or short-term exchanges. Third, the role of both intensive planning and serendipity in the success of these projects is noted. Finally, the authors in this volume urge us to call upon the expertise of our local communities. Contacting international services units for statistics about the local international student body, asking legal offices for assistance in navigating tricky visa questions, and, most important, consulting with international staff and students themselves. All of these strategies are essential in contributing to the success of this type of work.

Globalization affects all aspects of our lives and everyone in our communities. As new immigrants come and settle, local public libraries respond to new populations by providing vernacular collections and services to newcomers centered on technology, citizenship, economic integration, and language acquisition. School media centers and their librarians, challenged by students who often do not speak English and might not have had much of formal education prior to their arrival, are creating programs and services that help these youngsters succeed.

Thus, it is not just about international or "foreign" students. The fabric of American society is changing with the largest immigration ever from all over the world. "Dreamers," immigrants, and refugees from war- or natural disaster-stricken countries all hope for better lives and see education as the key. American colleges and universities are brimming with individuals for whom English is a second language, who might be completely unfamiliar with the American educational system and cultural norms, feeling somewhat disenfranchised, displaced, and maybe even homesick for their own cultures, just as international students do.

Academic institutions have an obligation to these individuals, foreign or domestic, in helping them succeed academically and in helping them integrate into the overall American society. This starts with making them feel welcome and wanted on campuses. As the center of campus life, academic libraries carry this responsibility and are deeply involved in developing new and innovative approaches to shoulder it, from teaching information literacy to a variety of outreach programs so well detailed in this book. In short, academic libraries are finding their unique place in the education of students in a holistic sense, becoming a true campus partner in this enterprise.

Our world is getting smaller. Technology, migrations, and political and economic realities bind us in ways we never knew were possible. For libraries, it translates into always scarce and competing resources, both human and budgetary. Yet, American libraries and librarians are in a unique position to positively affect these changes. Our traditional roles as equalizers, providers of secure and non-threatening environments, and disseminators of knowledge and information provide us with a unique opportunity to bring all these threads together and act as unifiers and valuable partners, be it on our campuses, in our local communities, or in the world at large.

The involved and labor-intensive work described in this book often happens under the radar of our administrators, benefactors, and constituencies. Yet it is another opportunity for us to demonstrate our value to our communities at a time when some openly debate the need for the very existence of the library in the future. We need to be proactive not only by doing but also by putting our accomplishments front and center for everyone to see. We need to create a vocabulary of value which others outside the library field can easily understand and relate to.

So here is the purpose of this book: to take the pulse of what has been done recently in the area of international librarianship, put it together in one volume for easy access, inspire and share ideas to more libraries and librarians, and hopefully start developing the vocabulary that we can present to our administrators, politicians, and communities at large to communicate our value, and to elevate the image, need, and importance of libraries and those who work in them.

Notes

1. "Initial Circulation," ARL Statistics, accessed January 12, 2018, https://www.arlstatistics.org/analytics.
2. Partially from "International Students Choose American Colleges for Higher Education," https://www.campusexplorer.com/college-advice-tips/D2EA2098/International-Students-Choose-American-Colleges-for-Higher-Education/.
3. *Open Doors Report on International Educational Exchange*, Institute of International Education, 2017, https://www.iie.org/en/Research-and-Insights/Publications/Open-Doors-2017.
4. Amanda B. Click, Claire Walker Wiley, and Megan Houlihan, "The Internationalization of the Academic Library: A Systematic Review of 25 Years of Literature on International Students," *College & Research Libraries* 78, no. 3 (March 2017): 328–58. Of the 147 publications the authors reviewed, they considered only 48 percent representative of original research, which they defined as articles including a clear methods or methodology section (337).
5. *Open Doors Report on International Educational Exchange*, Institute of International Education.

Bibliography

Click, Amanda B., Claire Walker Wiley, and Megan Houlihan. "The Internationalization of the Academic Library: A Systematic Review of 25 Years of Literature on International Students." *College & Research Libraries* 78, no. 3 (March 2017): 328–58.

"Initial Circulation." ARL Statistics. Accessed January 12, 2018. https://www.arlstatistics.org/analytics.

"International Students Choose American Colleges for Higher Education." *Campus Explorer*. https://www.campusexplorer.com/college-advice-tips/D2EA2098/International-Students-Choose-American-Colleges-for-Higher-Education/.

Open Doors Report on International Educational Exchange, New York: Institute of International Education, 2017. https://www.iie.org/en/Research-and-Insights/Publications/Open-Doors-2017.

SECTION I

Information Literacy

CHAPTER ONE

Academic Librarians at the Forefront of IL Efforts with International Students in Higher Education

Ahmed Alwan, Joy M. Doan, and Eric P. Garcia

Introduction

Throughout institutions of higher education in the United States, recruitment and retention of international students has become a priority and strategy for enhancing global education, enriching the cultural environment, and generating additional income. However, literature in the field of international education has demonstrated that now more than ever academic institutions must continue to increase efforts to deal with issues around academic integrity among international students.[1] Instruction on academic integrity is all the more essential as cultural, educational, and linguistic hurdles can inhibit international students from understanding US academic dishonesty and fair-use guidelines.[2]

Academic librarians, as experts in information literacy and fair use, are poised to play a central role in providing international students with instruction on academic integrity. Using research on information literacy and the new Association of College & Research Libraries' (ACRL) Framework for Information Literacy for Higher Education, librarians can work with international students to emphasize the threshold concepts of Information Has Value and Scholarship is Conversation. Instruction on academic integrity can no longer be developed in the vacuum of traditional approaches geared to domestic students.

In an effort to promote academic integrity and support for California State University, Northridge's (CSUN) international student community, a workshop was developed in partnership with various entities on campus. This resulted in the development of a unique workshop anchored in the ACRL's Framework for Information Literacy. This chapter aims to provide a practical model for how librarians can engage with international students about the consequences of plagiarism, cultural differences regarding attribution and the emphasis in the US on independent scholarship, and the importance of critical thinking and analysis of resources.

Literature Review

As the campus culture continues to diversify, librarians have stepped forward to ease or eliminate the various barriers that impeded student learning. There has been a general hesitancy, for a variety of factors, on the part of international students to engage or interact with library services.[3–5] The growth of the international student population on college and university campuses has required a reevaluation of how library personnel conduct outreach efforts and create, develop, and promote library resources. This reevaluation of services and programs not only helps ensure that information literacy is provided to international students but that international students become lifelong learners.

The academic success of international students is contingent on their ability to utilize library services.[6,7] Unfortunately, many of the services academic libraries provide, such as reference services, interlibrary loan, and online-library web pages, may be unfamiliar to international students.[8] For many international students, the use of academic library services may not have been required in the past.[9] In supporting international students academically, librarians need to break away from the belief that these students will automatically seek out assistance from the library. Mu notes that international students tend "to view the library as a place to study and librarians as bookkeepers rather than information providers."[10] Librarians can play an active role in reaching out to international students by offering tailored support services, a web presence, and face-to-face contact, and by establishing a welcoming environment that attracts international students.[11,12]

It is also crucial for colleges and universities to avoid focusing solely on the academic needs of international students; they should not ignore other factors that could negatively affect the academic goals of these students. Such a singular focus will only work to undermine the university's ability to aid international students.[13] The establishment of cultural centers, specific programs, clubs, and associations could aid with international students' unique needs.[14] In building "bridges of tolerance and respect for other cultures," institutions aid in relieving the anxiety and isolation expressed by international students.[15] Student clubs and organizations create a culturally heterogeneous environment.[16] Student involvement benefits international students' cognitive skills and helps them develop socially.[17,18]

Gisela Lin and Jenny Li suggest a tertiary model—before, during, and after academic study—of support programs for international students.[19] They posit that such social support is most effective when carried out in bicultural environments (e.g., campus international student center, Phi Beta Delta Honor Society, and international student associations) that collaboratively engage international students with faculty, students, and staff.[20] However, it should be noted that the involvement of librarians within such social support groups or clubs tends to be very limited. In light of this, librarians must find ways to engage and interact with international students in these settings.

Library discovery systems tailored to international students should not add to the layers of institutional jargon these students encounter.[21] These systems should iterate examples and explanations and not dwell on punitive language.[22] Additionally, introducing international students to plagiarism detection software (e.g., Turnitin) and reference/citation management systems (e.g., EndNote, RefWorks, Zotero) may bolster their confidence, dissuade acts of plagiarism, and assist them in managing information.[23] Exposure to such tools should occur as part of library orientation, instruction, and/or supplemental workshops.

The promotion of online resources and tools can help to a certain degree; however, the promotion of information literacy skills and knowledge demands the appointment of a library liaison dedicated to international students.[24] An ideal liaison model will require a librarian who is genuinely interested in international students' success, which "will go a long way towards improving communication, and building a positive relationship between the library and the international student body."[25] By identifying the concerns of international students and seeking ways to improve the relationship, the liaison serves as a conduit and can assist in easing the "internal communication barriers and provide a friendly face and act as a bridge to this unfamiliar world."[26]

Academic Integrity and International Students

There are numerous reasons why a student would plagiarize.[27] Students may see an opportunity to receive a grade without having to participate in the learning process, wanting instead to focus their attention on other matters of importance. A 1996 study by Newstead, Stephen, Franklyn-Stokes, and Armstead demonstrated that the need or want to obtain a desired grade was a primary concern for students who had admitted to plagiarism.[28] Compounding the issue is the influence of peer pressure on international students. Policies that universities implement to curb plagiarism are only effective if students have an intrinsic motivation.[29] If international students perceive that academic plagiarism is occurring within an institution, there may be a greater desire to participate in such behavior.[30–32] Stone et al. determine that students have an influence on how their peers view academic integrity and dishonesty.[33] The temptation to plagiarize may stem from a variety of factors, including: poor planning, ineffective classroom management, poor preparation, mindless work, opportunities and cultural background.[34]

Consistently international students have been thought of as 'at risk' because of their lack of English skills,[35] or "persistent plagiarizers."[36] Yet, if educators recognize plagiarism as a Western construct, this will go a long way in breaking the stereotype or misconception that international students are inherently plagiarizers. When designing pedagogy, it is imperative that instructors not approach the process with assumptions and preconceived notions on a student's knowledge of academic integrity. Curriculum for international students focused on academic integrity cannot begin from the same baseline as it would for domestic students, as international students may be less familiar with the western idea of academic integrity.

Regardless of whether international students plagiarize more than domestic students, it is crucial for institutions to account for why international students continue to plagiarize. International students may understand what constitutes plagiarism, but they may not be aware of how or why the behavior is not condoned. International students are particularly vulnerable because they may be unfamiliar with the behavioral standards in

Western institutions, and often do not share the same fear of punishment as our domestic students.[37]

There is a striking similarity between international students and domestic students when considering the adaptation issues both encounter in acquiring a post-secondary degree. However, international students tend to encounter stressors which are more pronounced than domestic students.[38] They must contend with the challenges of a culture that is foreign to them, the stigma of being stereotyped, and overcoming language barriers.[39] The adjustment period coupled with the need to perform well academically, creates significant pressure on international students, which domestic students do not encounter. These cultural factors can have a profound impact on international students' performance. Students from particular cultures may rely on text memorization (i.e., rote learning) and can fail to provide attribution within their work.[40] It is vital that educators be receptive to the "broad understanding of how overseas students were taught."[41]

International students are placed at a further disadvantage because they may assume that the American educational system functions similarly to what they encountered in their home country and often experience a cultural shock when they learn that this is not the case. This is intensified by existing prejudices stemming from stereotypes that undermine their ability to be academically successful. Some faculty members' negative perception of international students can truly undermine their success.

The lack of sensitivity by faculty "concerning other cultures …can affect foreign students in subtle or explicit ways."[42] Some faculty view international students as an asset, as they can offer various perspectives on any given topic.[43] Although there is a level of insight that is contributed to the conversation by international students, some faculty have indicated that there is a greater need to handhold, which requires more time and effort from the instructor.[44,45] English language skills are important to be academically and socially successful.[46] Unfortunately, a lack of English proficiency may place international students at a disadvantage within the classroom.[47] The additional time needed for dealing with international students can contribute to faculty's unwillingness to support international students in the classroom.[48,49] The racism, and to a degree sexism, experienced by international students may contribute to unfair treatment and hostility that can erode the confidence of international students[50–53] and result in the erosion of the student-faculty relationship.[54–56]

Advocating for Recognition of Librarians' Role in Teaching Academic Integrity

Despite the increased awareness of issues surrounding plagiarism and international students, there is little consensus about the roles librarians can play in remedying the problem.[57] The overarching question remains: What part can librarians play without overstepping the boundaries of their existing roles and responsibilities within academia? Lynn Lampert, who has written extensively on the role of librarians as related to plagiarism, has identified a variety of directions in which librarians and libraries may want to proceed, including developing curricular and instructional solutions, teaching techniques to students and faculty on ways to avoid plagiarism within library instructional sessions, and developing online self-paced tutorials on citation styles.[58] However, Lampert concedes that some within academia believe that it is the role of writing instructors, discipline faculty, or even tutoring centers and not librarians to work with students on issues related to plagiarism.[59]

The reality on the ground is that librarians often serve as little more than guides on how to correctly use a citation style or act as "plagiarism detectives" who are approached by faculty to confirm suspicions of academic integrity.[60] In addition to playing a minor role when collaborating with faculty, librarians are also rarely consulted on university or college-wide policy or procedural issues related to academic integrity.[61] In spite of this, however, it seems that there is a growing call for librarians to seek a more active role in combatting academic dishonesty.[62]

Peterson and Lampert assert that instruction on academic integrity can no longer be the sole domain of teaching faculty.[63,64] The call for librarians to play a larger and more active role is echoed by others outside the field of librarianship, including Donald McCabe, the founder of the Center for Academic Integrity and renowned scholar on plagiarism and academic integrity in higher education. In an email interview with Lampert, McCabe explains that libraries and librarians can play a major role through "educational campaigns designed to help young people understand the 'proper' research uses of the internet…."[65]

Grounded in the theory and practice of information literacy, it seems only natural that librarians can play a central role in providing international students with instruction on academic integrity. Now more than ever, the new ACRL Framework for Information Literacy for Higher Education has provided librarians with a real opportunity to take a proactive role in addressing academic integrity issues on college and university campuses. The ACRL Framework has made it possible for librarians to update their pedagogy on teaching about academic integrity.[66] Librarians can shift from simply showing students how to use a citation style or where to go to find resources on citation styles to instructional sessions that involve more engaging and interactive discussions on the topic.

The new ACRL Framework has provided librarians with an opportunity to expand the conversation around academic integrity and allow international students to play an active role in their own learning. The threshold concepts of Information Has Value and Scholarship as Conversation are especially important as they allow librarians to shift from basic conversations to higher-order thinking that involves reasoning. Until recently, with the old ACRL standards, librarians continued to emphasize prescribed and rigid competencies, skills, and outcomes geared to developing information-literate students. In such cases, students were often passive participants in the learning process.

During a typical library instruction session, the conversation about using information and academic integrity would usually focus on search techniques and the use of a specific type of citation style. With the advent of the new ACRL Framework, the possibilities for how librarians can involve international students in discussions on critically engaging with scholarship and academic integrity has increased exponentially. Librarians can now have students participate in a richer, broader, and more complex conversation about why information has value. This is especially important in an age "where 'free' information and related services are plentiful."[67] Such discussions force students to think critically and proactively about academic integrity.

The International Student Population at CSUN

At CSUN, the international student population is a combination of students on F-1 and J-1 visa status. The CSUN International and Exchange Student Center (IESC) reports that as of fall 2016, the vast majority of students at CSUN (99.31 percent or 2,321) held F-1 visas. These are typically the most common visas issued by US Customs to international students looking to study in the US. With F-1 visas, any form of financial support is acceptable. Additionally, on-campus employment does not require a work permit and curricular practical training and post-degree optional practical training is permissible. In comparison, a much smaller minority (0.0068 percent or 16) international students at CSUN held a J-1 visa status. With this type of visa, international students must demonstrate substantial financial support provided specifically for the selected educational program. Any form of employment requires students to acquire a work permit.

In terms of a regional breakdown, in the fall of 2016, the majority of international students (88.37 percent or 2,051) arrived at CSUN from Asia, with the second largest group (6.68 percent or 155) being European nationals. The top five countries of origin, in order from highest to lowest, were Kuwait, China, India, Saudi Arabia, and South Korea. Students gravitated toward three specific colleges within the institution. The two largest groups could be found in the College of Engineering and Computer Science (43 percent or 998) followed by the College of Business (28.57 percent or 663).

The primary resource for international students at CSUN is the IESC, which is tasked with providing a variety of services and resources to newly admitted and continuing international students. Additionally, the IESC develops and deploys a variety of cultural and social events that allow students to share their heritage and get involved with the campus community.

Case Study: The Workshop

As summer library orientations and tours occurred, we recognized a gap in library outreach to CSUN's international student population. We began thinking of outreach methods that would provide meaningful exposure to library services and create greater student success in the areas of information literacy and academic integrity. By combining efforts with campus entities, particularly the IESC, we developed a 100-minute active learning workshop that utilized two threshold concepts of the ACRL Framework—Scholarship as Conversation and Information Has Value—to creatively introduce international students to the consequences of plagiarism, the cultural differences and the emphasis in the US on independent scholarship, and to encourage critical thinking and analysis of resources.

Campus Partners

In an effort to dispel international students' hesitancy or discomfort in approaching the library, we sought out partnerships with campus offices that work directly with international students.[68] Our intention was to garner feedback and gain buy-in on library outreach to international students. While multiple departments contribute to international student success at CSUN, the IESC is responsible for coordinating social and cultural events that assist international students in getting academically and socially involved with the campus community. In order to consociate active student learning modules with students' idiomatic norms, we determined that partnering with the IESC for an event would best yield favorable retention of our intended student learning outcomes (SLOs). During our initial meeting with the IESC staff, they provided valuable insight about international students at CSUN and ways in which the library could support these students. It was determined that a workshop on academic integrity would be most valuable to the students and that embedding the workshop in the IESC's Coffee Hour event series would yield the greatest international students' participation.[69] The decided-upon title of the workshop was "Oviatt Library: Helping International Students Succeed @ IESC Coffee Hour." The workshop was held approximately a quarter of the way through the fall semester (mid-October).

The Workshop

When planning the workshop, we focused on creating active learning exercises and activities that iterated and reinforced the two threshold concepts selected (i.e., Scholarship as Conversation, Information Has Value). Specifically, our SLOs for the workshop focused on the following "knowledge practices" from the ACRL Framework:[70]

From Scholarship as Conversation:

> Contribute to scholarly conversation at an appropriate level.
>
> Recognize that they are often entering into the midst of a scholarly conversation, not a finished conversation.

From Information Has Value:

> Give credit to the original ideas of others through proper attribution and citation.
>
> Understand that intellectual property is a social construct that varies by culture.

Our objective was to be informative while not overwhelming the students with regulative language. The team chose social media as the theme to tie together discussions and activities for the workshop, as we determined that social media would best connect to the student's prior knowledge. We primarily utilized think-pair-share activities[71] in order to build the students' confidence with non-rote learning settings and to accustom them to the idea that their contributions are part of a larger conversation that does not occur in an insular vacuum. The outline for the workshop was as follows:

Icebreaker (10 min.)

Library Orientation (10 min.)

Activity 1 (7 min.)

- o Students were placed in groups of up to four individuals. Students are assigned four apps (WhatsApp, Instagram, Twitter, and Snapchat) that are similar to each other and have similar functionality.

- Students were expected to act as experts and discuss which app is the best and why.
  - What do they share in common and/or differences?

Scholarship as Conversation discussion (5 min.)

Activity 2 (3–4 min.)

- Students were numbered off 1–4 and placed in groups.
- Students then selected a social media app with which they felt they had knowledge or experience.
- Students had to identify how apps (e.g., Facebook) parallel scholarly conversation.

Activity 3 (5 min.)

- Students were provided with an example of fake news. A group discussion followed in which students discussed how putting up inaccurate information on social media can get them conversationally "trapped" or poorly judged by their peers.
- The facilitators then explained the importance of knowing where the information or conversation it is originating from.

Information has Value Discussion (5 min.)

Interactive teaching activity (45 min.)

- Students were divided into two teams.
- Students participated in a *Family Feud*-style game where the answers focused on academic integrity and CSUN policies.

Q&A (10 min.)

Opportunity Drawing (5–7 min.)

In addition to active learning, the team noted the need to incentivize participation as this was a voluntary Friday midday workshop. Several prize structures were built into the workshop. Thanks to the generous support of the Delmar T. Oviatt Library Dean, the event had a full catered meal. The first forty participants to sign in received a gift bag that included candy and an assortment of school supplies (e.g., notebooks, highlighters, pens). Additionally, the end of each group activity was interspersed with raffled door prizes, including water bottles and stress balls. Finally, a grand prize that included a twenty-five-dollar campus money card was raffled after the team game.[72]

Assessment

The workshop consisted of fifty participants. A short six-question quantitative assessment was given toward the end of the session before the grand prize drawing in order to ensure maximum participation. The following questions were asked:

1. Are you familiar with the Academic Dishonesty[73] (i.e., cheating, fabrication, plagiarism) policies at CSUN?
2. Are you familiar with the penalties for Academic Dishonesty at CSUN?
3. Have you ever used the library's resources (e.g., databases, OneSearch[74]) for an assignment, project, or paper?
4. Have you ever talked with a librarian at the Oviatt Library (online, email, in-person, phone)?
5. Since you have been at CSUN, have you ever had a library lecture as part of one of your classes?

6. Has anyone working at CSUN (e.g., advisor, professor, counselor) talked to you about plagiarism or its consequences?

50 participants/ 30 surveys = 60% response rate	#1	#2	#3	#4	#5	#6
Yes	26 (87%)	22 (73%)	17 (57%)	13 (43%)	14 (47%)	20 (67%)
No	4 (13%)	8 (27%)	13 (43%)	17 (57%)	16 (53%)	10 (33%)

Of the fifty participants,[75] thirty completed the survey,[76] which yielded a 60 percent response rate. The data indicate that 87 percent (26) of the participants were familiar with CSUN's Academic Dishonesty policies, and that 73 percent (22) of the participants were familiar with the penalties for Academic Dishonesty. Questions three and four indicated an inverse relationship in which 57 percent (17) of the participants had used the library's resources, but 43 percent (13) had spoken with librarians. A little under half, 47 percent (14) of the participants had previously had a library instruction session. Finally, 67 percent (20) of participants had a conversation with an employee at CSUN about plagiarism and its consequences. The quantitative data indicates that while the majority of the participants reported some knowledge of CSUN's academic integrity policies and/or familiarity with library's resources, this is an area of potential growth for outreach.

Anecdotal feedback on the session in the form of verbal communication and email indicated that the session was well received. Additionally, we have been invited to repeat this workshop as part of the IESC Coffee Hours in subsequent terms. It is hoped that the continuation and growth of the "Oviatt Library: Helping international students Succeed @ IESC Coffee Hour" workshop will better assist CSUN's international students to acclimate to the US standards on academic integrity.

Conclusion

Discussions surrounding academic integrity and international students are improving in institutions of higher learning. The ACRL Framework as a pedagogical tool provides an opportunity to improve international students' information literacy skills. Active learning modules and the ACRL Framework help to better situate academic librarians as the "go-to" experts on fair use and academic integrity. Through campus partnerships, academic librarians can work with international students to emphasize the threshold concepts of Information Has Value and Scholarship is Conversation to better promote international students' success.

The "Oviatt Library: Helping international students Succeed @ IESC Coffee Hour" workshop utilized active learning modules based on the threshold concepts from the ACRL Framework that promoted academic integrity and supported California State University, Northridge's international students community. Moreover, it represents an effort to develop instruction on academic integrity that accounts for the specific and unique needs of international students. This case study serves as a practical example for librarians to engage international students about academic integrity and provides a roadmap for librarians to emphasize critical thinking and analysis of resources among international students.

Acknowledgments

We would like to express gratitude to the students that participated in the workshop, the Oviatt Library dean, Dr. Mark Stover, and the IESC director, Dr. Marta Lopez.

Notes

1. Jenny Gunnarsson, Wlodek J. Kulesza, and Anette Pettersson, "Teaching International Students How to Avoid Plagiarism: Librarians and Faculty in Collaboration," *The Journal of Academic Librarianship* 40, no. 3-4 (2014): 413–17.
2. Andrea H. Duff, Derek P. Rogers, and Michael B. Harris, "International Engineering Students—Avoiding Plagiarism Through Understanding the Western Academic Context of Scholarship," *European Journal of Engineering Education* 31, no. 6 (2006): 673–81.
3. Ann Curry and Deborah Copeman, "Reference Service to International Students: A Field Stimulation Research Study," *The Journal of Academic Librarianship* 31, no. 5 (2005): 409–20.
4. Cuiying Mu, "Marketing Academic Library Resources and Information Services to International Students from Asia," *Reference Services Review* 35, no. 4 (2007): 571–83.
5. Beth Ann Patton, "International Students and the American University Library" (doctoral dissertation, Biola University, 2002), http://files.eric.ed.gov/fulltext/ED469810.pdf.
6. Lorrie Knight, Maryann Hight, and Lisa Polfer, "Rethinking the Library for the International Student Community," *Reference Services Review* 38, no. 4 (2010): 581–605.
7. Cuiying, "Marketing Academic Library Resources," 571–83.
8. Pamela A. Jackson, "Incoming International Students and the Library: A Survey," *Reference Services Review* 33, no. 2 (2005): 197–209.
9. Cuiying, "Marketing Academic Library Resources," 571–83.
10. Ibid., 573.
11. Kiran Kaur, "Marketing the Academic Library on the Web," *Library Management* 30, no. 6 (2009): 454–68.
12. Seda Sümer, Senel Poyrzli, and Kamini Grahame, "Predictors of Depression and Anxiety Among International Students," *Journal of Counseling & Development* 86, no. 4 (2008): 429–37.
13. Romeria Tidwell and Shideh Hanassab, "New Challenges for Professional Counsellors: The Higher Education International Student Population," *Counselling Psychology Quarterly* 20, no. 4 (2007): 313–24.
14. Doreen Anne Rosenthal, Jean Russell, and Garry Thomson, "Social Connectedness Among International Students at an Australian University," *Social Indicators Research* 84, no. 1 (2007): 71–82.
15. Claire Kramsch, "In Search of the Intercultural," *Journal of Sociolinguistics* 6, no. 2 (2002): 275.
16. Betty Leask, "Using Formal and Informal Curricula to Improve Interactions Between Home and International Students," *Journal of Studies In International Education* 13, no. 2 (2009): 205–21.
17. Alexander W. Astin, *What Matters in College?: Four Critical Years Revisited* (San Francisco: Jossey-Bass, 1993).
18. Jee-Sook Lee, Gary F. Koeske, and Esther Sales, "Social Support Buffering of Acculturative Stress: A Study of Mental Health Symptoms among Korean International Students," *International Journal of Intercultural Relations* 28, no. 5 (2004): 399–414.
19. Jun-Chih Gisela Lin and Jenny K. Yi, "Asian International Students' Adjustment: Issues and Program Suggestions," *College Student Journal* 31, no. 4 (1997): 473.
20. Ibid.
21. Philip C. Howze and Dorothy M. Moore, "Measuring International Students' Understanding of Concepts Related to the Use of Library-Based Technology," *Research Strategies* 19, no. 1 (2003): 57–74.
22. Dawn Amsberry, "Deconstructing Plagiarism: International Students and Textual Borrowing Practices," *Reference Librarian* 51, no. 1 (2010): 31–44.

23. Lynn Lampert, *Combating Student Plagiarism: An Academic Librarian's Guide* (Oxford, U.K., Chandos, 2008).
24. Suhasini L. Kumar and Raghini S. Suresh, "Strategies for Providing Effective Reference Services for International Adult Learners," *Reference Librarian* 33, no. 69/70 (2000): 327.
25. Ibid., 333.
26. Ibid.
27. Bob Perry, "Exploring Academic Misconduct: Some Insights into Student Behaviour," *Active Learning in Higher Education 11*, no. 2 (2010): 97–108.
28. Stephen E. Newstead, Arlene Franklyn-Stokes, and Penny Armstead, "Individual Differences in Student Cheating," *Journal of Educational Psychology* 88, no. 2 (1996): 229.
29. Thomas H. Stone, I. M. Jawahar, and Jennifer L. Kisamore, "Using the Theory of Planned Behavior and Cheating Justifications to Predict Academic Misconduct," *Career Development International* 14, no. 3 (2009): 221–41.
30. Verity J. Brown and Mark E. Howell, "The Efficacy of Policy Statements on Plagiarism: Do They Change Students' Views?," Research in Higher Education 42, no.1 (2001): 103–18.
31. Donald L. McCabe, Kenneth D. Butterfield, and Linda Klebe Treviño," Academic Dishonesty in Graduate Business Programs: Prevalence, Causes, and Proposed Action," *Academy Of Management Learning & Education* 5, no. 3 (2006): 294–305.
32. Stone, Jawahar, and Kisamore, "Using the Theory of Planned Behavior," 221–41.
33. Ibid.
34. David A. Thomas, "How Educators Can More Effectively Understand and Combat the Plagiarism Epidemic," *Brigham Young University Education and Law Journal* (2004): 421–30.
35. Glenn D. Deckert, "Perspectives on Plagiarism from ESL Students in Hong Kong," *Journal of Second Language Writing* 2, no. 2 (1993): 131–48.
36. Chris Park, "In Other (People's) Words: Plagiarism by University Students—Literature and Lessons," *Assessment & Evaluation in Higher Education* 28, no. 5 (2003): 471–88.
37. Tricia Bertram Gallant, Nancy Binkin, and Michael Donohue, "Students at Risk for Being Reported for Cheating," *Journal of Academic Ethics* 13, no. 3 (2015): 217–28.
38. Chrisitne J. Yeh and Mayuko Inose, "International Students' Reported English Fluency, Social Support Satisfaction, and Social Connectedness as Predictors of Acculturative Stress," *Counselling Psychology Quarterly* 16, no. 1 (2003): 15–28.
39. Joanne W. McClure, "International Graduates' Cross-Cultural Adjustment: Experiences, Coping Strategies, and Suggested Programmatic Responses," *Teaching in Higher Education* 12, no. 2 (2007): 199–217.
40. Yu-Hui Chen and Mary K. Van Ullen, "Helping International Students Succeed Academically through Research Process and Plagiarism Workshops," *College & Research Libraries* 72, no. 3(2011): 209–35.
41. Niall Hayes and Lucas D. Introna, "Cultural Values, Plagiarism, and Fairness: When Plagiarism Gets in the Way of Learning," *Ethics & Behavior* 15, no. 3 (2005): 229.
42. Munir Fasheh, "Foreign Students in the United States: An Enriching Experience or a Wasteful One?," *Contemporary Educational Psychology* 9, no. 3 (1984): 315.
43. Andrea G. Trice, "Navigating in a Multinational Learning Community: Academic Departments' Responses to Graduate International Students," *Journal of Studies in International Education* 9, no. 1 (2005): 62–89.
44. Chen Zhuojun, "International Students' Preparation for and Adaptation to the American Higher Education System: A Study of Cross-Cultural Communication," *World Communication* 29, no. 2 (2000): 25–48.
45. Yeh and Inose, "International Students' Reported English Fluency," 15–28.
46. Maureen Snow Andrade, "International Students in English-Speaking Universities: Adjustment Factors," *Journal of Research in International Education* 5, no. 2 (2006): 131–54.
47. Erlenawati Sawir, "Language Difficulties of International Students in Australia: The Effects of Prior Learning Experience," *International Education Journal* 6, no. 5 (2005): 567–80.
48. Philip Altbach, "The Foreign Student Dilemma," *Teachers College Record* 39, no. 3–4 (1986): 236–37.

49. William Z. Nasri, "International Students: What Do We Owe Them? An Educator's Reflections," *Journal of Education for Library and Information Science* 34, no. 1 (1993): 75–78.
50. Jenny J. Lee, "International Students' Experiences and Attitudes at a US Host Institution: Self-Reports and Future Recommendations," *Journal of Research in International Education* 9, no. 1 (2010): 66–84.
51. Jenny J. Lee and Charles Rice, "Welcome to America? International Student Perceptions of Discrimination," *Higher Education* 53, no. 3 (2007): 381–409.
52. Chavella T. Pittman, "Race and Gender Oppression in the Classroom: The Experiences of Women Faculty of Color with White Male Students," *Teaching Sociology* 38, no. 3 (2010): 183–96.
53. Senel Poyrazli and Marcos Damian Lopez, "An Exploratory Study of Perceived Discrimination and Homesickness: A Comparison of International Students and American Students," *The Journal of Psychology* 141, no. 3 (2007): 263–80.
54. Arthur W. Chickering and Linda Reisser, *Education and Identity. The Jossey-Bass Higher and Adult Education Series* (San Francisco, CA: Jossey-Bass Inc., 1993).
55. George D. Kuh and Hu Shouping, "The Effects of Student-Faculty Interaction in the 1990s," *Review Of Higher Education* 24, no. 3 (2001): 309–32.
56. Ernest T. Pascarella and Patrick T. Terenzini, "Predicting Freshman Persistence and Voluntary Dropout Decisions from a Theoretical Model," *The Journal of Higher Education* 51, no. 1 (1980): 60–75.
57. Lampert, *Combating Student Plagiarism.*
58. Ibid.
59. Ibid.
60. Nancy Snyder Gibson and Christina Chester-Fangman, "The Librarian's Role in Combating Plagiarism," *Reference Services Review* 39, no. 1(2011): 132–50.
61. Ibid.
62. Ibid.
63. Lorna Peterson, "Teaching Academic Integrity: Opportunities in Bibliographic Instruction," Research Strategies 6, no. 4 (1988): 168–76.
64. Lampert, *Combating Student Plagiarism.*
65. Ibid., 58.
66. Colleen Burgess, "Teaching Students, Not Standards: The New ACRL Information Literacy Framework and Threshold Crossings for Instructors," *Partnership: The Canadian Journal of Library and Information Practice and Research* 10, no. 1 (2015): 1–7.
67. The Association of Research and College Libraries, "Framework for Information Literacy for Higher Education," January 11, 2016, http://www.ala.org/acrl/sites/ala.org.acrl/files/content/issues/infolit/Framework_ILHE.pdf.
68. Karen Bordonaro, "We All Have an Accent: Welcoming International Students to the Library," Feliciter 52, no. 6 (2006): 240–41.
69. The IESC Coffee Hour event series occurs each Friday afternoon during fall and spring semesters in the IESC office. A campus department or a series of speakers are invited to discuss relevant academic and/or campus life topics with international students. Coffee and snacks are typically served.
70. The Association of Research and College Libraries, "Framework for Information Literacy for Higher Education," January 11, 2016, http://www.ala.org/acrl/sites/ala.org.acrl/files/content/issues/infolit/Framework_ILHE.pdf.
71. Think-pair-share is a collaborative discussion technique that allows students to meaningfully consider a question(s) in small groups with their peers before addressing the larger group and/or instructor.
72. Participants had to be present at the time of the drawing to receive a prize.
73. Academic Dishonesty is the current terminology used by CSUN.
74. OneSearch is the Oviatt Library's resource discovery tool.
75. That is approximately 1.8 percent of CSUN's currently enrolled student population (2,837).
76. The survey was completed by all remaining participants.

Bibliography

Altbach, Philip. "The Foreign Student Dilemma." *Teachers College Record* 39, no. 3-4 (1986): 236–37.

Amsberry, Dawn. "Deconstructing Plagiarism: International Students and Textual Borrowing Practices." *Reference Librarian* 51, no. 1 (2010): 31–44.

Andrade, Maureen Snow. "International Students in English-Speaking Universities: Adjustment Factors." *Journal of Research in International Education* 5 (2) (2006): 131–54.

Association of Research and College Libraries, The. "Framework for Information Literacy for Higher Education." January 11, 2016. http://www.ala.org/acrl/sites/ala.org.acrl/files/content/issues/infolit/Framework_ILHE.pdf.

Astin, Alexander W. *What Matters in College?: Four Critical Years Revisited.* San Francisco: Jossey-Bass, 1993.

Bordonaro, Karen. "We All Have an Accent: Welcoming International Students to the Library." *Feliciter* 52, no. 6 (2006): 240–41.

Brown, Verity J., and Mark E. Howell. "The Efficacy of Policy Statements on Plagiarism: Do They Change Students' Views?" *Research in Higher Education* 42, no.1 (2001): 103–18.

Burgess, Colleen. "Teaching Students, Not Standards: The New ACRL Information Literacy Framework and Threshold Crossings for Instructors." Partnership: *The Canadian Journal of Library and Information Practice and Research* 10, no. 1 (2015): 1–7.

Chen, Yu-Hui, and Mary K. Van Ullen. "Helping International Students Succeed Academically through Research Process and Plagiarism Workshops." *College & Research Libraries* 72, no. 3 (2011): 209–35.

Chickering, Arthur W., and Linda Reisser. *Education and Identity. The Jossey-Bass Higher and Adult Education Series.* San Francisco, CA: Jossey-Bass Inc., 1993.

Curry, Ann, and Deborah Copeman. "Reference Service to International Students: A Field Stimulation Research Study." *Journal of Academic Librarianship* 31, no. 5 (2005): 409–20.

Deckert, Glenn D. "Perspectives on Plagiarism from ESL Students in Hong Kong." *Journal of Second Language Writing* 2, no. 2 (1993): 131–48.

Duff, Andrea H., Derek P. Rogers, and Michael B. Harris, "International Engineering Students Avoiding Plagiarism through Understanding the Western Academic Context of Scholarship." *European Journal of Engineering Education* 31, no. 6 (2006): 673–81.

Fasheh, Munir. "Foreign Students in the United States: An Enriching Experience or a Wasteful One?." *Contemporary Educational Psychology* 9, no. 3 (1984): 313–20.

Gallant, Tricia Bertram, Nancy Binkin, and Michael Donohue. "Students at Risk for Being Reported for Cheating." *Journal of Academic Ethics* 13, no.3 (2015): 217–28.

Gibson, Nancy Snyder, and Christina Chester-Fangman. "The Librarian's Role in Combating Plagiarism." *Reference Services Review* 39, no. 1 (2011): 132–50.

Gunnarsson, Jenny, Wlodek J. Kulesza, and Anette Pettersson. "Teaching International Students How to Avoid Plagiarism: Librarians and Faculty in Collaboration." *The Journal of Academic Librarianship* 40, no. 3–4 (2014): 413–17.

Hayes, Niall, and Lucas D Introna. "Cultural Values, Plagiarism, and Fairness: When Plagiarism Gets in the Way of Learning." *Ethics and Behavior* 15, no. 3 (2005): 213–31.

Howze, Philip C., and Dorothy M. Moore. "Measuring International Students' Understanding of Concepts Related to the Use of Library-Based Technology." *Research Strategies* 19, no. 1 (2003): 57–74.

Jackson, Pamela A. "Incoming International Students and the Library: A Survey." *Reference Services Review* 33, no. 2 (2005): 197–209.

Kaur, Kiran. "Marketing the Academic Library on the Web." *Library Management* 30, no. 6 (2009): 454–68.

Kramsch, Claire. "In Search of the Intercultural." *Journal of Sociolinguistics* 6, no. 2 (2002): 275.

Kuh, George D., and Hu Shouping. "The Effects of Student-Faculty Interaction in the 1990s." *Review of Higher Education* 24, no. 3 (2001): 309–32.

Kumar, Suhasini L., and Raghini S. Suresh. "Strategies for Providing Effective Reference Services for International Adult Learners." *Reference Librarian* 33, no. 69/70 (2000): 327.

Knight, Lorrie, Maryann Hight, and Lisa Polfer. "Rethinking the Library for the International Student Community." *Reference Services Review* 38, no. 4 (2010): 581–605.

Lampert, Lynn. *Combating Student Plagiarism: An Academic Librarian's Guide.* Oxford, U.K., Chandos, 2008.

Leask, Betty. "Using Formal and Informal Curricula to Improve Interactions between Home and International Students." *Journal of Studies in International Education* 13, no. 2 (2009): 205–21.

Lee, Jee-Sook, Gary F. Koeske, and Esther Sales. "Social Support Buffering of Acculturative Stress: A Study of Mental Health Symptoms among Korean International Students." *International Journal of Intercultural Relations* 28, no. 5 (2004): 399–414.

Lee, Jenny J. "International Students' Experiences and Attitudes at a US Host Institution: Self Reports and Future Recommendations." *Journal of Research in International Education* 9, no. 1 (2010): 66–84.

Lee, Jenny J., and Charles Rice. "Welcome to America? International Student perceptions of discrimination." *Higher Education* 53, no. 3 (2007): 381–409.

Lin, Jun-Chih Gisela, and Jenny K. Yi. "Asian International Students' Adjustment: Issues and Program Suggestions." *College Student Journal* 31, no. 4 (1997): 473.

McCabe, Donald L., Kenneth D. Butterfield, and Linda Klebe Treviño. "Academic Dishonesty in Graduate Business Programs: Prevalence, Causes, and Proposed Action." *Academy of Management Learning & Education* 5, no. 3 (2006): 294–305.

McClure, Joanne W. "International Graduates' Cross-Cultural Adjustment: Experiences, Coping Strategies, and Suggested Programmatic Responses." *Teaching in Higher Education* 12, no. 2 (2007): 199–217.

Mu, Cuiying. "Marketing Academic Library Resources and Information Services to International Students from Asia." *Reference Services Review* 35, no. 4 (2007): 571–83.

Nasri, William Z. "International Students: What Do We Owe Them? An Educator's Reflections." *Journal of Education for Library and Information Science* 34, no. 1 (1993): 75–78.

Newstead, Stephen E., Arlene Franklyn-Stokes, and Penny Armstead. "Individual Differences in Student Cheating." *Journal of Educational Psychology* 88, no. 2 (1996): 229.

Park, Chris. "In Other (People's) Words: Plagiarism by University Students—Literature and Lessons." *Assessment & Evaluation in Higher Education* 28, no. 5 (2003): 471–88.

Pascarella, Ernest T., and Patrick T. Terenzini. "Predicting Freshman Persistence and Voluntary Dropout Decisions from a Theoretical Model." *The Journal of Higher Education* 51, no. 1 (1980): 60–75.

Patton, Beth Ann. "International Students and the American University Library" (doctoral dissertation, Biola University, 2002). http://files.eric.ed.gov/fulltext/ED469810.pdf.

Perry, Bob. "Exploring Academic Misconduct: Some Insights into Student Behaviour." *Active Learning in Higher Education 11*, no. 2 (2010): 97–108.

Peterson, Lorna. "Teaching Academic Integrity: Opportunities in Bibliographic Instruction." *Research Strategies* 6, no. 4 (1988):168–76.

Pittman, Chavella T. "Race and Gender Oppression in the Classroom the Experiences of Women Faculty of Color with White Male Students." *Teaching Sociology* 38, no. 3 (2010): 183–96.

Poyrazli, Senel, and Marcos Damian Lopez. "An Exploratory Study of Perceived Discrimination and Homesickness: A Comparison of International Students and American Students." *The Journal of Psychology* 141, no. 3 (2007): 263–80.

Rosenthal, Doreen Anne, Jean Russell, and Garry Thomson. "Social Connectedness Among International Students at an Australian University." *Social indicators Research* 84, no. 1 (2007): 71–82.

Sawir, Erlenawati. "Language Difficulties of International Students in Australia: The Effects of Prior Learning Experience." *International Education Journal* 6, no. 5 (2005): 567–80.

Stone, Thomas H., I. M. Jawahar, and Jennifer L. Kisamore. "Using the Theory of Planned Behavior and Cheating Justifications to Predict Academic Misconduct." *Career Development International* 14, no. 3 (2009): 221–41.

Sümer, Seda, Senel Poyrzli, and Kamini Grahame. "Predictors of Depression and Anxiety Among International Students." *Journal of Counseling & Development* 86, no. 4 (2008): 429–37.

Thomas, David A. "How Educators Can More Effectively Understand and Combat the Plagiarism

Epidemic." *Brigham Young University Education and Law Journal* (2004): 421–30.

Tidwell, Romeria, and Shideh Hanassab. "New Challenges for Professional Counsellors: The Higher Education International Student Population." *Counselling Psychology Quarterly* 20, no. 4 (2007): 313–24.

Trice, Andrea G. "Navigating in a Multinational Learning Community: Academic Departments' Responses to Graduate International Students." *Journal of Studies in International Education* 9, no. 1 (2005): 62–89.

Yeh, Chrisitne J., and Mayuko Inose. "International Students' Reported English Fluency, Social Support Satisfaction, and Social Connectedness as Predictors of Acculturative Stress." *Counselling Psychology Quarterly* 16, no. 1 (2003): 15–28.

Zhuojun, Chen. "International Students' Preparation for and Adaptation to the American Higher Education System: A Study of Cross-Cultural Communication." *World Communication* 29 no. 2 (2000): 25–48.

CHAPTER TWO

Unlocking the Door:

Adapting Information Literacy Instruction for International Students

Susan Avery and Kirsten Feist

Introduction

The growth in international students at colleges and universities in the United States necessitates librarians address these changing numbers in their library instruction. The library is uniquely situated to respond to the implications of this growth through fostering meaningful learning experiences for international students, many of whom are new to the academic research process. In this chapter, the authors focus on adapting existing instructional content and learning objects and creating new materials that address the learning needs of international students. We also share strategies for working with international students in the various instructional settings they are likely to encounter in the library. The emphasis in this chapter is undergraduate students and, more specifically, first-year students for whom academic research is likely to be a new and often intimidating process. In this context, the role of the librarian in the instruction classroom takes on added meaning for the international student embarking on academic experiences at American colleges or universities.

The University of Illinois at Urbana-Champaign (Illinois) has one of the largest populations of international students in the United States. There are more than 10,000 international students, more than 5,400 of whom are undergraduates. They come from 112 countries with the largest population, 5,200, coming from China. Other countries represented in large numbers include India, South Korea, and Taiwan.[1] With a population of this size, the libraries at Illinois work with international students in many capacities during the course of the year. International students are present in library instruction classes at all levels and are users of other library services and spaces. Striving to meet their needs is an important part of the mission of both the library and the campus.

The setting in which new, first-year international students are likely to be introduced to the library and academic research varies greatly, largely dependent on the size of the institution they are attending. Larger institutions frequently teach international students in the context of English as a Second Language classes. Such a setting presents a mostly homogenous mix of students, all facing similar challenges of acclimating themselves to learning in a language that is not their native tongue. Smaller institutions rarely have this opportunity, and international students are often integrated into first-year writing classes with other freshmen.

While the needs of international students in each of the settings are similar, the approaches in each classroom will differ. At Illinois, international students are placed into first-year writing courses that fulfill the university's Composition 1 requirement dependent on entrance test scores. While most international students will take an English as a Second Language (ESL) class, students who have greater English abilities are placed into Rhetoric courses in which they are integrated with students who attended high school in the United States or another English-speaking country. While this chapter is focused specifically on undergraduate students, many of the recommendations can also be adapted to graduate students as well.

Literature Review

Regardless of the setting, be it a homogenous classroom of international students or an integrated classroom of international students and students educated in the United States, the learning objectives remain the same. It is the teaching methods and support provided for international students that must be adapted to meet educational needs. An awareness of the needs of international students in the classroom is a first step in creating effective learning experiences.

Recently published literature regarding both international students' formative educational experiences and perceptions of, and experiences in, higher education and academic libraries illustrate certain core concepts and trends that instruction librarians should be aware of when preparing to make such modifications to information literacy instruction sessions.

In their 2011 article, Mary Stuart, Catherine Lido, and Jessica Morgan conducted educational life history interviews with undergraduate students in the UK that reaffirmed the idea that a student's experience impacts his or her engagement with their university, with particular attention paid to those of minority ethnic backgrounds. Specifically, the authors highlight the importance of Pierre Bourdieu's research surrounding "cultural capital," which they describe as being rooted in the concept of "habitus" or "people's patterns in thought, beliefs, behavior, or taste."[2] As an individual has a habitus, so too do institutions, which may be at odds with an individual's.[3] This can lead to significant discrepancies between higher education experiences of the dominant cultural group and minority ethnic students in higher education, particularly in regards to issues surrounding "entitlement and sense of belonging."[4]

Beyond a student's experience in higher education, more broadly, habitus also impacts an international student's perception of academic libraries. In Illka Datig's 2014 article, a diverse sample of international students at NYU Abu Dhabi provided feedback via an online survey and individual interviews with freshman students, as the author wanted to gain feedback prior to students gaining too much exposure to the institution's library.[5] Some general impressions that emerged from the students' feedback included viewing libraries primarily as a home for books, academic pursuit, and quiet study. As the author states, "For many students, maintaining quiet is a moral issue, with clear right and wrong behavior," with one student poignantly describing the library as "a sanctuary."[6] Though librarians were not specifically asked about, those that did mention them had limited views of them as book keepers, unless their previous experience with libraries provided a richer understanding of the complexity of a librarian's role, such as previous instruction in database use.[7] As Datig explains, part of this limited understanding of libraries and librarians may stem from the fact that "several students explained that there was no 'culture of libraries' in their home countries."[8]

Depending on an institution, the majority of international students may hail from specific countries or regions, which may impact the approach an academic library takes to target or modify information literacy instruction to reflect the habitus of these dominant groups within the international student population. As noted previously, at the authors' institution, the majority of international students are from China, India, South Korea, and Taiwan respectively, with the habitus of these student populations taken into account when making instructional modifications.

In Xiaojie Duan's 2016 article, certain commonalities among international Chinese students' information-seeking behavior is explored. Duan highlights known challenges found in the existing literature, such as students lacking "adequate English vocabulary, including library terminology," finding that students were similarly not familiar with translation services embedded within interfaces but might use them if aware.[9] Moreover, lack of adequate English vocabulary in this regard can impact students in terms of research tool selection. Duan's research found that English language search engines (including Google) were used at some point in research by 79 percent of students, whereas 15 percent preferred Chinese language search engines for familiarity.[10]

Challenges with the English language extend to other international student populations as well. As Mark Sherry, Peter Thomas, and Wing Hong Chui note in their 2010 article, "English proficiency may be the single greatest barrier experienced by international students, since it affects both their ability to academically succeed ...but also it impacts their ability to engage socially with other students."[11] Furthermore, in Olivia Halic, Katherine Greenberg, and Trena Paulus' 2009 study, it was emphasized that participants faced difficulties in understanding spoken American English, such as specific dialects (in particular the Southern American accent), as written skills may have been favored over spoken skills when learning English in the students' home countries.[12]

Given the reality of English language barriers as academic challenges, Sherry, Thomas, and Hong Chui found that students who responded to their survey had positive views of writing center services.[13] Similarly, Duan found that surveyed students greatly valued reference librarians and related services, such as online chat features.[14] From a librarian perspective, this willingness by international students to use research and writing services could present exciting possibilities for collaboration.

In addition to language barriers, perhaps the largest barrier when considering how to modify information literacy instruction for international students comes back to past educational experience. As Duan notes, "most of the students answered that they have not gone to a library frequently in their home countries because they did not have to; one Chinese student responded that her Chinese university focused mostly on final exams and she did not have many weekly assignments to do."[15] Furthermore, as David Koenigstein notes in his 2012 article, depending on the culture of origin, international

students may have learned that "plagiarizing a source without appropriate assignation can be considered an honor to the original author," noting in particular that some students in mainland China, for example, may be taught that "information cannot be owned by any individual" but rather "belong to the collective society."[16]

Other challenges extend beyond purely academic concerns to personal experience. As Sherry, Thomas, and Hong Chui note, these may include challenges such as financial vulnerability, subsequent pressures as a result of this, as well as fears of social isolation due to barriers presented by the English language.[17]

In planning to address these challenges, Koenigstein highlights the importance of a student-centered approach. This may be as simple as avoiding excessive library jargon and American idioms or as complex as avoiding making a cultural faux pas that could prove an obstacle to learning.[18] Similarly, Halic, Greenberg, and Paulus emphasize the necessity "for educators who work with non-native English speaking international students to address not just the academic but also relational and affective issues of these students," particularly through "learner-centered instructional design."[19]

Perhaps the most impactful takeaway from the review of the existing literature is this: while the methods implemented to conduct studies of international students, the country in which the research was conducted, or even the disciplines of the authors varied greatly, most articles had one thing in common—they developed a tool to ask the international student population themselves what their experiences were. This serves as an important reminder that international student bodies on any given campus are not monolithic and that how an international student body is comprised on campuses across the US varies greatly. As such, the elements that make up the habitus of an individual or group should be considered when modifying information literacy instruction.

Adapting Instructional Content

The need to adapt existing instructional content for international students is likely to be a concern for many libraries. While libraries should strive to have instructional resources and learning objects that are understandable and accessible to all students, meeting the needs of international students may require some adaptations. As materials are adapted, it is important to keep a learner-centered instructional experience at the core of any changes. The resources students will use, whether in the classroom or out, must reflect their needs. Several questions can serve as guidance when adapting materials. These include:

- Who is the intended audience? Is this specifically for international students? Resources created specifically for international students will benefit from the expertise of those who work with international students daily.
- What is the purpose of the content? For example, is it intended to teach a basic library concept or skill, such as searching a database or evaluating information? In such cases, it is best to create resources that can be used by students in multiple settings.
- Is the content tied to a specific class assignment? The assignment should serve to guide the creation of resources. Specific elements of resources are likely to be reflected in similar assignments.
- Would students best be served by recreating the content or making some changes to the existing content? Reviewing content with the purpose and learning objectives for that content in mind will inform the need to revise or recreate.

In summer 2014, a large project was undertaken in the Undergraduate Library at Illinois to adapt and create new online instructional content for inclusion in a library guide that would complement first-year ESL courses. Crucial to the success of undertaking this project was the presence of someone who served in a supportive role for international students. The initial work at Illinois included a teaching assistant who taught first-year ESL classes. The input she provided was invaluable in helping better understand the specific needs of international students, modifying existing resources and learning objects, and creating new materials specifically targeting those needs. Having the expertise of someone with the ability to look at existing resources and make subsequent recommendations for adaptation through the lens of an international student provided us with the focus necessary to move forward. For smaller institutions without a similar academic unit on campus, it is vital to reach out to the faculty or instructors who have international students in their classes to gather similar information prior to modifying information literacy curricula.

In the process of creating the revisions at Illinois, the authors began by discussing specific assignments in first-year ESL classes, aspects of the research process instructors found were most difficult for students, and existing knowledge gaps international students exhibited regarding basic concepts such as defining topics, identifying keywords and alternatives, and plagiarism. Through our collaboration, the authors adapted many existing learning objects and created new ones to support the needs identified by the ESL program. Incorporating language that is commonly used by instructors and topic examples that were already being used in the classroom helped establish a higher degree of consistency for the students. While this project began in 2014, the resources continue to be revised on an annual basis to reflect any changes in the curriculum for the ESL courses and needs identified by the instructors in that program.

Two examples of specific changes include: (1) demonstration topics that are used in library instruction and the sample concept map were updated to reflect those used in the student course manual; and (2) in response to instructors expressing concerns that students did not fully understand the concept of plagiarism or its ramifications, the library created an infographic that served to illustrate these points.

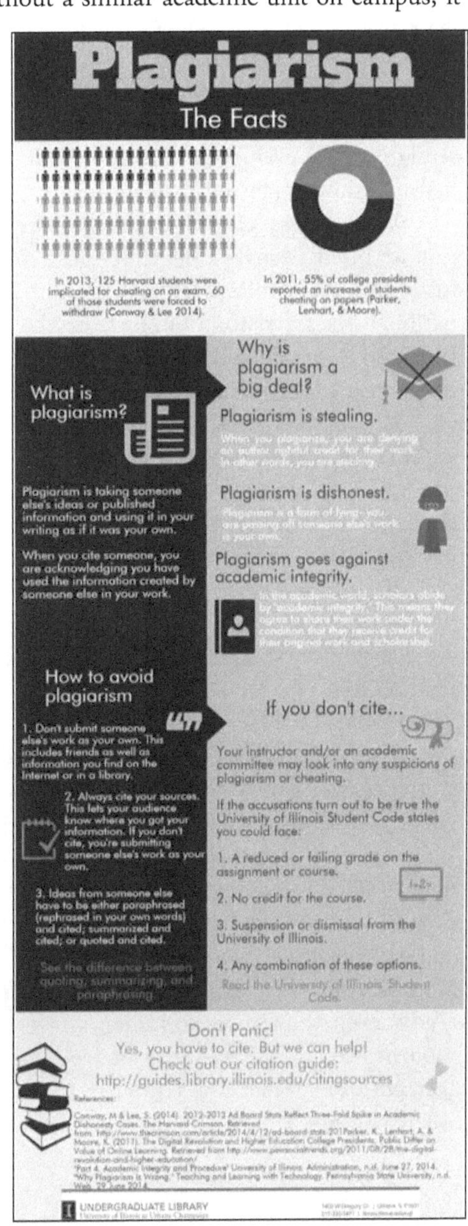

Figure 2.1. Plagiarism Facts

Creating Instructional Elements for International Students

In making revisions for international students, such as those previously noted at Illinois, instructional design models can provide a useful roadmap for retrofitting an existing information literacy curriculum and supporting materials for classes that are either solely or partially comprised of international students. While there are several instructional design models that instruction librarians can use depending on task and need, Angiah Davis' 2013 article highlights the particular usefulness of the ADDIE model. ADDIE, which stands for analyze, design, develop, implement, and evaluate, is cyclical in nature and lends itself well to collaboration with outside stakeholders because of the intentionality of its design.[20] Furthermore, because ADDIE is not a linear model, if an existing information literacy curriculum is in place that needs moderate updating to ensure responsiveness to international student need, it is possible to jump straight to the evaluative and analytical stages of the model to make necessary tweaks before re-implementing.

When using such instructional design models to update information literacy instruction for international students, it is also important to consider the importance of seeking input from, and collaborating with, units or individuals on campus that support international student instruction. Because the composition of the international student body is unique to each institution, these units and individuals can paint the clearest picture of their students' research needs beyond generalizations.

As noted previously, the English as a Second Language (ESL) department at the authors' institution provides standardized first-year instruction to international students that involves a research component. While the authors' close collaboration with the ESL department found that the basic information literacy skills ESL instructors want their first-year international students to learn are not all that different from those of the general student population, the ESL department's particular emphasis on skills, such as the importance of developing strong search terminology and close evaluation of sources, received the greatest attention when using instructional design elements to modify library instruction.

A final consideration when modifying elements of information literacy curricula, specifically for international students who are integrated into classes with the general student population, is the use of Universal Design for Learning (UDL). While often framed in terms related to students' physical abilities, the idea is that if a curriculum is designed in such a way that responds to the diversity of learning needs, no one student is at a disadvantage when receiving library instruction. A notable example of the degree to which students appreciate efforts to implement UDL in library instruction comes from a 2012 study conducted by Ying Zhong at the Walter W. Stiern Library at California State University, Bakersfield. As Zhong notes in the discussion of the study, even though most students in the class didn't require particular curriculum modifications, "the majority of students reported benefitting from UDL-integrated instruction."[21] That is to say, when a class is designed to meet the needs of all, no one is left behind.

Classroom Strategies for Teaching Homogenous Classes

In many ways, teaching a class that is made up solely of international students is more straightforward than teaching a class that contains a mix of international and domestic students. Students in an ESL class are likely to face many of the same challenges and the instruction provided can specifically target their needs. These courses are often provided at institutions that have a larger population of international students and are likely to mirror other first-year writing and composition courses in terms of the requirements they fulfill and the expected learning outcomes. In some cases, there may be additional general education classes that limit specific sections to international students only. At Illinois, for example, there are numerous sections of a public speaking course that are restricted to international students.

When teaching a class that is made up solely of international students, librarians should communicate with the instructor prior to the library instruction session to learn more about the students in that section. Are the students from a variety of countries or regions of the world? Are a significant number from the same country? A university may have an agreement or partnership with an institution in another country or have a particularly strong recruiting base in a country that results in a significant number of students from that country. Knowing this prior to a class and understanding the cultural and academic practices that students are likely to be familiar with can help engage students in the class and/or understand their willingness to participate. In many cases, these students arrive with very different cultural experiences and expectations, coming from settings where they have "learned classroom decorum that involves saving face, respecting the hierarchical position of the teacher above the students, and a receptive—rather than active—engagement."[22] Students are accustomed to a classroom where the instructor may be the only one who speaks and students remain silent.

Begin each class by creating a welcoming setting that is conducive to learning. Meet students at the door and welcome them into the classroom. Creating a truly participatory classroom is likely to be a challenge. Sharing such an expectation with the instructor prior to class can set up this expectation and the instructor can encourage students to participate. As noted in the literature review, language will be a challenge for many students. Moores and Popadiuk (2011) observed difficulties of students in their study: "Adjusting to a new educational system and the rigors of studying in a second language are considerable challenges."[23] An awareness of the use of metaphors and analogies during a class is particularly important, as many will not be understood by international students. Not unlike working with any class, librarians must be attentive to what strategies work best when encouraging student participation and putting these into practice on a regular basis. However, it should be noted that the prior educational experiences of international students are likely to impact class participation.

Classroom Strategies for Teaching Mixed Classes

While some institutions may offer a limited number of classes for international students only, it is simply not feasible for most institutions to do so. Regardless of institution or international student population, it is likely that the bulk of the classes an international student will take during their college years will be in an integrated classroom. For some international students, this is a preference. Yan and Sendall's 2016 study found that mixed classes of American and international students were preferred, noting such a setting gave international students an "opportunity to understand the DS (domestic student) and American culture."[24] While international students should be acknowledged in an integrated classroom, care should be taken not to completely change one's teaching style. Librarians need to keep in mind that students enter an instruction classroom with a variety of library and research experiences. This includes both domestic and international students. A first step is creating a presence in the classroom that welcomes and acknowledges all students.

Many of the strategies previously shared in this chapter, such as the use of universal design and remaining attentive to successful teaching strategies during a class session, should continue to be employed. Learning to navigate the culture in a new country and academic setting is something of which international students may be acutely aware. Focus groups in Young's 2011 study observed the "extensive exchange between teacher and students ...as well as the informality of the relationship between teacher and students."[25] Instructors in her study indicated making special efforts to encourage the participation of international students as well as efforts to "incorporate diverse learning activities."[26] As with any class setting, librarians must be cognizant of the needs of all students and avoid teaching to specific students in a class. Sharing the availability of librarians outside of the classroom is crucial. Students should be made aware of reference services and research assistance, whether in the format of drop-in assistance, scheduled appointments, or chat. The authors strongly feel an awareness of such services is one of the most valuable outcomes of any library instruction session.

Conclusion

Whether adapting library instruction curriculum and supporting materials for homogenous ESL classes or mixed classes in which ESL students are integrated, there are a variety of resources to consult and approaches to take that will simplify the process and ensure successful implementation. First and foremost, gaining an understanding of your institution's specific international student population and their needs and collaborating with the units on campus that support them is the most important step in adapting a responsive library instruction curriculum. In addition, consulting current literature on serving an international student population and following best practices for instructional design and Universal Design for Learning will ensure instructional sessions and supporting materials that meet the needs of all students and are amenable to future tweaks. Such responsiveness of library instruction curricula is essential because neither student body demographics nor library instruction trends are static. Moving forward in such a manner will result in the greatest benefits to our international student populations.

Notes

1. "Fall 2015 International Statistics," University of Illinois at Urbana-Champaign, http://isss.illinois.edu/download_forms/stats/fa15_stats.pdf
2. Mary Stuart, Catherine Lido, and Jessica Morgan, "Personal Stories: How Students' Social and Cultural Life Histories Interact With the Field of Higher Education," *International Journal of Lifelong Education* 30, no. 4 (July 2011): 490, doi:10.1080/02601370.2011.588463.
3. Ibid.
4. Ibid., 506.
5. Ilka Datig, "What is a Library?: International College Students' Perceptions of Libraries," *The Journal of Academic Librarianship* 40, no. 3/4 (May 2014): 351, doi:10.1016/j.acalib.2014.05.001.
6. Ibid., 353.
7. Ibid., 353–54.
8. Ibid., 354.
9. Xiaojie Duan, "How They Search, How They Feel, and How to Serve Them? Information Needs and Seeking Behaviors of Chinese Students Using Academic Libraries," *International Information & Library Review* 48, no. 3 (July 2016): 159, doi:10.1080/10572317.2016.1204179.
10. Ibid., 163.
11. Mark Sherry, Peter Thomas, and Wing Hong Chui, "International Students: A Vulnerable Population," *Higher Education: The International Journal of Higher Education and Educational Planning* 60, no. 1 (July 2010): 34, doi:10.1007/s10734-009-9284-z.
12. Olivia Halic, Katherine Greenburg, and Trena Paulus, "Language and Academic Identity: A Study of the Experiences of Non-Native English Speaking International Students," *International Education* 38, no. 2 (March 2009): 79.
13. Sherry, Thomas, and Hong Chui, "International Students: A Vulnerable Population," 37.
14. Duan, "How They Search, How They Feel, and How to Serve Them," 164, 166.
15. Ibid., 159.
16. David Koenigstein, "Alleviating International Students' Culture Shock and Anxiety in American Academic Libraries: Welcome, Ahlah We Sahlan, Anyeong Hae Sae Yo, Bievenidos, Huan Ying, Sanu Da Zuwa, Shalom, Swaagat Hai," *Library Philosophy and Practice* (May 2012): 80.
17. Sherry, Thomas, and Hong Chui, "International Students: A Vulnerable Population," 40–44.
18. Koenigstein, "Alleviating International Students' Culture Shock," 79–80.
19. Halic, Greenburg, and Paulus, "Language and Academic Identity," 91–92.
20. Angiah L. Davis, "Using Instructional Design Principles to Develop Effective Information Literacy Instruction," *College & Research Library News* 74, no. 4 (April 2013): 207.
21. Ying Zhong, "Universal Design for Learning (UDL) in Library Instruction," *College & Undergraduate Libraries* 19, no.1 (January 2012): 44, doi:10.1080/10691316.2012.652549.
22. Waneen Aden White and Caleb Rosado, "How Can International Students Overcome Their Biggest Obstacle in an American University?," *Journal of International Education Research* 10, no. 3 (Third Quarter 2014): 242.
23. Lisa Moores and Natalee Popadiuk, "Positive Aspects of International Students Transitions: A Qualitative Inquiry," *Journal of College Student Development* 52, no. 3 (May-June 2011): 295, doi:10.1353/csd.2011.0040.
24. Zi Yan and Patricia Sendall, "First Year Experience: How We Can Better Assist First-Year International Students in Higher Education," *Journal of International Students* 6, no. 1 (2016): 43.
25. Arlene Shorter Young, "First Time International College Students' Level of Anxiety in Relationship to Awareness of Their Learning-Style Preferences," *Journal of International Students* 1, no. 2 (Fall 2011): 47.
26. Ibid.

Bibliography

Datig, Ilka. "What is a Library?: International College Students' Perceptions of Libraries." *The Journal of Academic Librarianship* 40, no. 3/4 (May 2014): 350–56. doi:10.1016/j.acalib.2014.05.001.

Davis, Angiah L. "Using Instructional Design Principles to Develop Effective Information Literacy Instruction." *College & Research Library News* 74, no. 4 (April 2013): 205–207.

Duan, Xiaojie. "How They Search, How They Feel, and How to Serve Them? Information Needs and Seeking Behaviors of Chinese Students Using Academic Libraries." *International Information & Library Review* 48, no. 3 (July 2016): 157–68. doi:10.1080/10572317.2016.1204179.

Halic, Olivia, Katherine Greenburg, and Trena Paulus. "Language and Academic Identity: A Study of the Experiences of Non-Native English Speaking International Students." *International Education* 38, no. 2 (March 2009): 73–93.

Koenigstein, David. "Alleviating International Students' Culture Shock and Anxiety in American Academic Libraries: Welcome, Ahlah We Sahlan, Anyeong Hae Sae Yo, Bievenidos, Huan Ying, Sanu Da Zuwa, Shalom, Swaagat Hai." *Library Philosophy and Practice* (May 2012): 78–83.

Moores, Lisa, and Natalee Popadiuk. "Positive Aspects of International Students Transitions: A Qualitative Inquiry." *Journal of College Student Development* 52, no. 3 (May-June 2011): 291–306. doi:10.1353/csd.2011.0040.

Sherry, Mark, Peter Thomas, and Wing Hong Chui. "International Students: A Vulnerable Population." *Higher Education: The International Journal of Higher Education and Educational Planning* 60, no. 1 (July 2010): 33–46. doi:10.1007/s10734-009-9284-z.

Stuart, Mary, Catherine Lido, and Jessica Morgan. "Personal Stories: How Students' Social and Cultural Life Histories Interact with the Field of Higher Education." *International Journal of Lifelong Education* 30, no. 4 (July 2011): 489–508. doi:10.1080/02601370.2011.588463.

White, Waneen Aden, and Caleb Rosado. "How Can International Students Overcome Their Biggest Obstacle in an American University?" *Journal of International Education Research* 10, no. 3 (Third Quarter 2014): 241–48.

Yan, Zi, and Patricia Sendall. "First Year Experience: How We Can Better Assist First-Year International Students in Higher Education." *Journal of International Students* 6, no. 1 (2016): 35–51.

Young, Arlene Shorter. "First Time International College Students' Level of Anxiety in Relationship to Awareness of Their Learning-Style Preferences." *Journal of International Students* 1, no. 2 (Fall 2011): 43–49.

Zhong, Ying. "Universal Design for Learning (UDL) in Library Instruction." *College & Undergraduate Libraries* 19, no.1 (January 2012): 33–45. doi:10.1080/10691316.2012.652549.

CHAPTER THREE

Language and Information Literacy:

A Case Study of Library Orientation Taught in the Chinese Language

Liangyu Fu and Gabriel Duque

Introduction

The ACRL Cultural Competency for Academic Libraries Diversity Standards states that "librarians and library staff shall develop collections and provide programs and services that are inclusive of the needs of all persons in the community the library serves."[1] In recent years, the campuses of United States universities have seen an influx of international students and scholars. In this context, how to best serve this population has become a challenge and an opportunity for academic librarians.

Recently at the University of Michigan (U-M), a group of librarians from different units—and with different skillsets—collaborated to pilot and implement a successful and innovative project to offer library orientation in Chinese for new international students and scholars. Designed with the cultural background of the audience in mind, these orientation sessions address the audience's attitude toward academic libraries in general and meet the needs of a previously underserved community. In this chapter, we discuss how orientation sessions conducted in non-English languages enhance library services on a global campus and how using students' and scholars' native language helps improve their information literacy at an early stage of their new adventure in the United States.

Literature Review

In the library literature, much has been written about international students and scholars in academic libraries and their challenges and needs. These needs are identified mostly as related to language skills and adjusting to a new educational culture and system. A great deal of older literature presents these topics in terms of issues and problems to be corrected. Some of the most recent publications present a more complex and holistic approach and see differences and multilingualism more as assets and not necessarily as problems to be overcome.[2] Among them, some refer to virtual orientations or translation of websites and handouts and videos.[3] Our focus here is to concentrate on articles that specifically explore library orientation for international students in their native languages.

Liestman and Wu relate how the Rutgers University Libraries started a program to offer library orientations in Chinese and Korean.[4] Although attendance was low, pre- and post-tests indicated the effectiveness of native-language library orientation in familiarizing these new students with US academic libraries. Similarly, Lopez describes an effort at SUNY Buffalo to offer library tours given by bilingual students in various languages.[5] One of the stated goals was to lessen culture shock, and attendees were appreciative and engaged.

Spanfelner describes a course-integrated library instruction session, taught in English and Spanish, where most attendees were international students (native Spanish speakers).[6] An evaluation and conversations with students indicated that they appreciated the bilingual aspect of the class as well as the translated materials. Bosch and Molteni present a similar model and express that these types of sessions can help lower anxiety and foster a sense of inclusion.[7] They also emphasize the instructors' cultural background and language skills as important resources. A challenge they encountered was the proper translation of library terminology. More recently, the East Asian Library at the University of Pittsburgh Library has been offering library orientation sessions as well as course-integrated information literacy sessions in Chinese, Japanese, and Korean. Some of these sessions are scheduled and some are provided upon request.[8]

In some studies, orientation in non-English languages was briefly mentioned as something that authors recommended or that students requested. Mundava and Gray recommend that native language instruction be implemented based on a review of needs.[9] Puente, Gray, and Agnew conducted a study about library perception and use at the University of Tennessee.[10] Over 50 percent of survey respondents, who were multicultural and international faculty, students, and staff, indicated the usefulness of library resources or workshops in languages other than English.

Ideation

Traditionally, the U-M Library, partnering with the U-M International Center, has offered multiple library orientation sessions in English for new international students and scholars every August and September. These sessions are part of a large and comprehensive orientation program that covers many different topics to help newcomers adjust to a new country and educational system. English had been the only language used in library instruction until the summer of 2015, when Susan Go, the librarian for Southeast Asia, Australia, New Zealand, and the Pacific Islands, suggested offering one of these sessions to new international students and scholars in Chinese. Inspired by this idea, a few formal and informal conversations were held among library stakeholders to explore the necessity and feasibility of teaching in a non-English language.

Interested units at U-M Library—Asia Library, International Studies, and Learning Programs and Initiatives—saw the value of pioneering this new service to reach out to the Chinese-speaking community on campus, partly because of the significant size of this community. According to the *International Center 2016 Statistical Report*, 46 percent (3,099) of U-M's international students come from China and they constituted the largest group of international students on campus. Moreover, 58 percent (310) of the university's visiting scholars are affiliated with Chinese institutions. Besides providing research materials in more than four hundred languages, the U-M Library was dedicated to building a global and culturally diverse campus by initiating new projects and events for international students. It was time to take into consideration the diversity of native languages of our patrons.

There were some concerns about the idea at the beginning. The main concern was whether teaching in Chinese would be counterproductive to helping students and scholars adapt to the English environment. After careful consideration, two major U-M Library stakeholders—the Chinese studies librarian and the learning librarian (the authors)—agreed that in this specific case, non-English instruction would not go against cultural adaptation efforts that the university and the city have made to help international students and scholars. Primarily, this orientation session was intended to be a welcoming gesture and a quick overview of library resources, which are among the first resources that students need to start using immediately upon arrival on campus. Native language is a very effective medium when lending practical help to those newcomers to a different country. It is especially useful when explaining terms of art used in Chinese and American library systems. Overall, the Chinese session was intended to be a one-shot and elective event, not to replace any English-language orientations already offered to international students and scholars. It is worth noting that librarians who are non-native speakers of English played a pivotal role in championing this initiative. As native speakers of Chinese and Spanish and themselves former international students at US universities, the authors understood what this newer generation of international students and scholars had to face. In addition, they appreciated the value of native language to reinforce local community in a college town like Ann Arbor, Michigan.

Implementation

After the ideation phase, the authors consulted with the U-M International Center, the main unit that provides services and programs for the international population on campus. The Center appreciated this partnership and suggested that we try a pilot session after the new semester started in the fall of 2015. The authors volunteered to coordinate the effort and lead the instruction.

The implementation phase comprised three major tasks.

Team formation. A team of librarians was formed that summer to focus on the implementation of this instructional initiative. The team membership represented a cross-unit collaboration consisting of two subject specialists (Chinese studies librarian and chemistry librarian), two technical services staff (Chinese language catalogers), and one instruction librarian. All except the instruction librarian are native Chinese speakers.

A few preparation meetings were held, during which all the team members worked together on brainstorming the content and developing strategies for communication with stakeholders and instruction in Chinese. In the meantime, each team member had his or her own responsibilities. As the main presenters, the two subject specialists designed the presentation content, basing it upon the already existing English-language orientation materials; the two catalogers, as the tour leaders, worked on adjusting the tour itineraries for simultaneous groups; the instruction librarian, as the facilitator, helped with overall coordination and logistics, including booking and setting up the instruction space.

Content design. As noted, the main content of the Chinese orientation was based on already existing materials that were used in the English-language orientations for new international students and scholars, but the content was adapted to the cultural background of the audience and their previous experiences with academic libraries. For instance, they may have considered "resources" more as materials for research and teaching purposes but less as human resources from whom they can seek research support. They may not have understood the many services that subject specialists can provide them at the U-M Library because the subject librarian model is still being developed in most research libraries in China. Therefore, in the orientation, we emphasized the importance of becoming familiar with the subject specialists' role and encouraged the audience to contact their own subject librarians for field-specific questions.

We also designed content that addressed the differences of libraries and library services in China and the United States to help attendees adjust their expectations of the U-M Library. For example, figure 3.1 shows a slide that we used in our presentation to discuss the differences between the Chinese Library Classification (CLC) and the Library of Congress Classification (LCC), especially the classification letters, which may affect the way they locate materials and browse the shelves. Figure 3.2 introduces the interlibrary loan service and purchase recommendation service that are not as common in China as in the US. This information is covered in all orientations but it was emphasized more during the Chinese sessions to encourage the audience to try these likely "unfamiliar" services. The Chinese studies librarian's background and expertise contributed to the comparative perspective of the orientation content. Her library science education and library research experiences in China afforded her the perspective necessary to know that this kind of information should be disseminated.

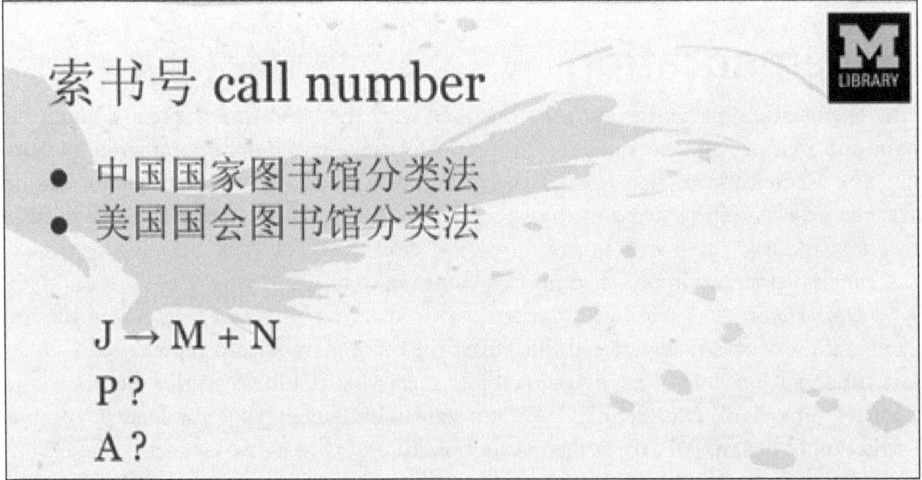

Figure 3.1. Presentation slide on differences between CLC and LCC.

若本馆尚未收藏，你可以：

- 利用馆际互借 (Interlibrary loan)
  - 遍及北美的合作学校
  - 免费服务
  - http://www.lib.umich.edu/interlibrary-loan
- 向我们推荐你需要使用的资料 (Suggesting purchases)
  - 写信告诉你的学科馆员
  - 使用线上表格 https://www.lib.umich.edu/mlibrary-collections/purchase-request-form

Figure 3.2. Presentation slide on likely "unfamiliar" services.

Logistics planning and coordination. The instruction librarian took charge of overall coordination and communication between the library and the International Center, which also helped promote the orientation to the new international students and scholars. As mentioned above, he was also responsible for logistics such as reserving and setting up the instruction space. In addition, the two presenters translated the existing "10 Things to Know about the MLibrary" English handout into Chinese and included it in the folder of selected promotional materials of the library distributed to all attendees.

The Sessions

At the beginning of this process, the authors were not certain that this session would be something that our international population would find valuable. As reflected in the literature review, few academic libraries had offered orientation in Chinese, so team members had few examples and case studies from which to learn.

The first session took place one week into the fall semester and several weeks after all the English-language orientations had been offered. We developed a registration page and publicized the session mostly through email sent out by the International Center. Before the session, the large number of people who signed up (seventy-eight) indicated that we were on the right track. The actual attendance for this session was sixty-eight.

The attendees were engaged and asked many questions. The session consisted of a one- hour presentation followed by a thirty-minute library tour that most students attended. Careful planning was important, given the large numbers of participants. We divided the attendees into three groups for the tour. Previously, we had designated tour leaders and different tour itineraries with different starting and ending places so that the groups would not run into each other too frequently. Attendees taking the tours especially appreciated the Asia Library, where the Chinese-language collection is located, and were also interested in the rest of the stops of the tour at the Hatcher Graduate Library and Shapiro Undergraduate Library.

After the success of this first Chinese-language orientation session, we debriefed and decided to offer two simultaneous orientation sessions focusing on different areas of knowledge (one for STEM fields and one for humanities and social sciences). We scheduled these two simultaneous sessions for late January. We allocated two hours for these sessions because the presentation had felt a bit rushed during the pilot. We again had to tweak the logistics: planning a thirty-minute introduction for all in our larger instruction space, dividing the group to attend a one-hour presentation by areas of knowledge in two different locations, and then taking each group on a library tour. However, we had to fall back into our previous plan of offering just one session and not two due to unforeseen circumstances that caused one presenter's absence. This session was attended by thirty-four people.

At the beginning of the new academic year, we again offered a session in September but this time a little earlier—September 9. Unexpectedly, the library suffered an electrical outage and had to be closed that day. We communicated with all attendees using email gathered in our registration system and re-scheduled for October 11. By this time, the chemistry librarian/co-presenter had accepted a job at another institution. With only one presenter remaining, we could no longer offer two sessions for different audiences, so we again offered one general orientation. The session was attended by sixty-six people. The fourth orientation session, held in January, drew an audience of nineteen people.

Assessment

The team members developed a short, simple survey for attendees to gather feedback (see Appendix 3A). We administered this survey after each of the sessions. To date, these four sessions have been attended by 187 students and scholars, and 41 percent of the attendees (seventy-seven people) have completed the survey so far. Three of the four surveys were bilingual (English and Chinese). Figure 3.3 to figure 3.6 show consolidated results for questions that we find especially meaningful.

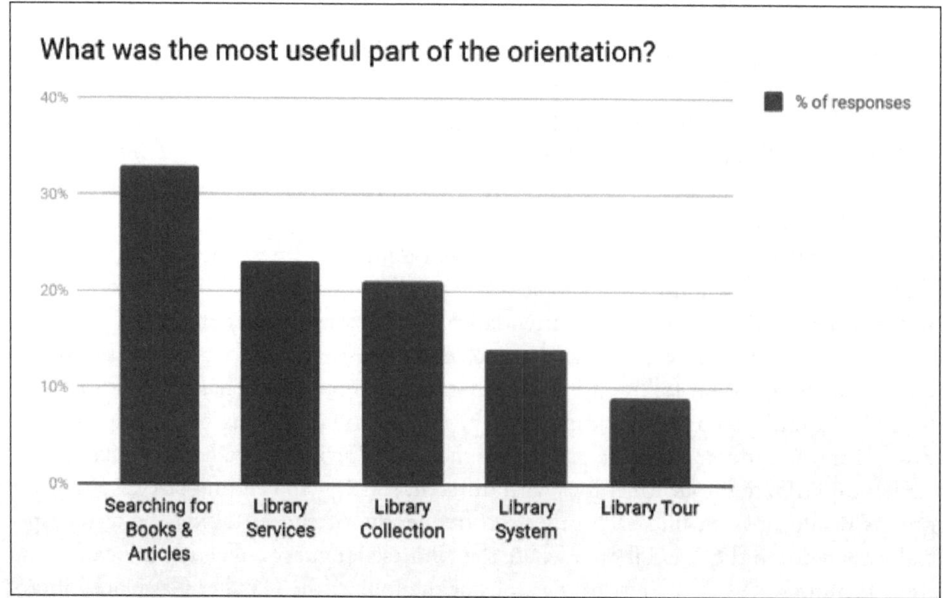

Figure 3.3. Consolidated Results: Orientation

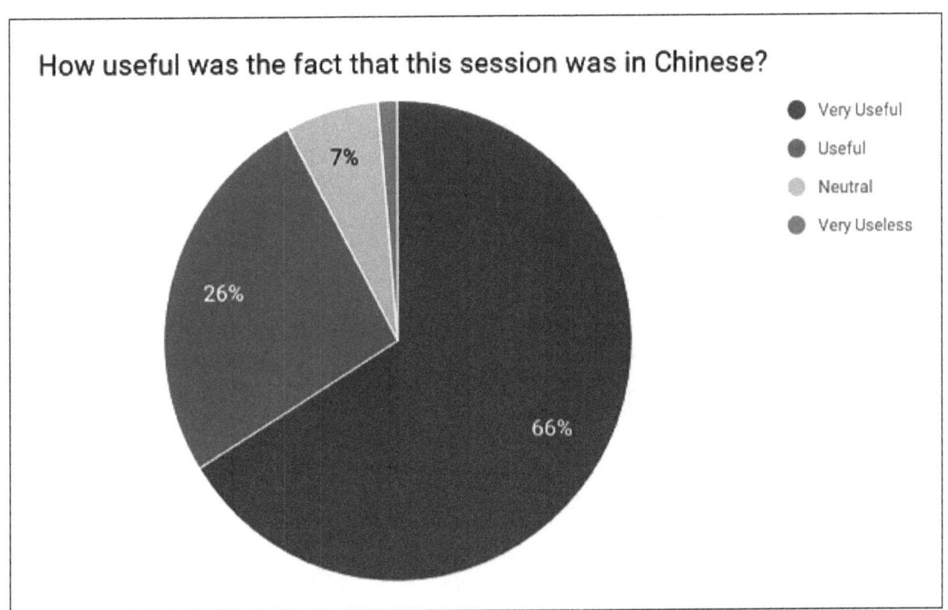

Figure 3.4. Consolidated Results: Sessions in Vernacular

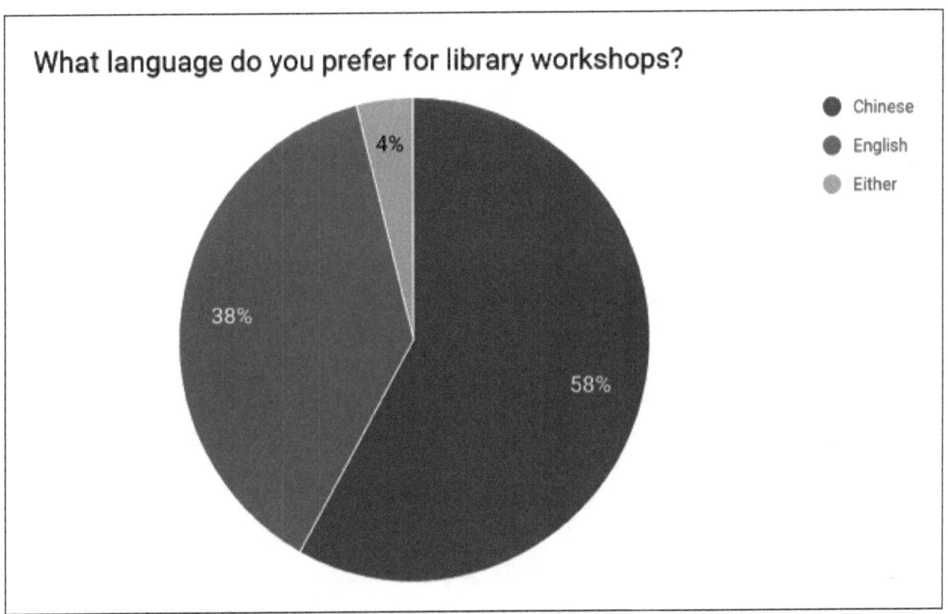

Figure 3.5. Consolidated Results: Preferred Language

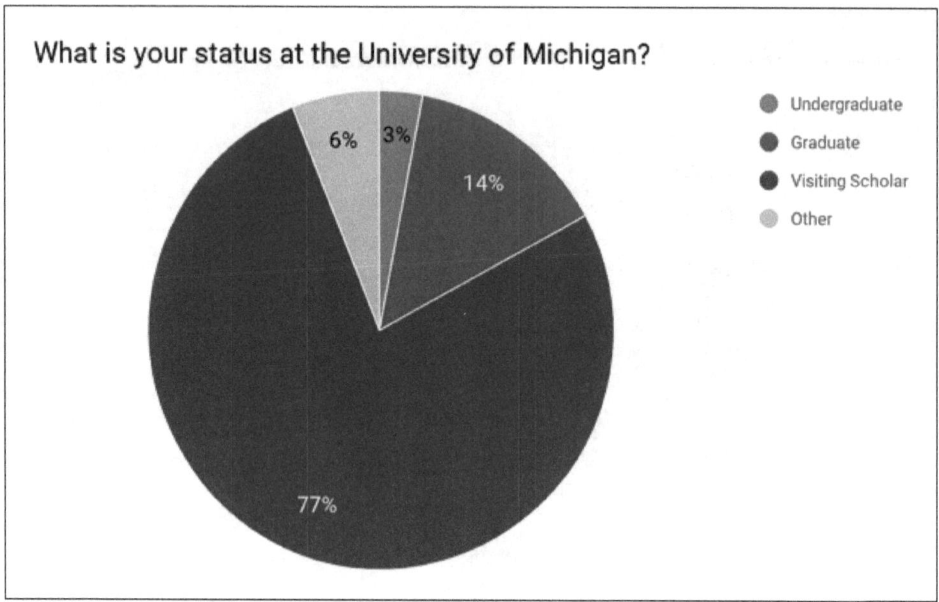

Figure 3.6. Consolidated Results: Demographics

Additionally, we asked the open-ended question, "Is there anything else you would like to let us know about the session?" There were numerous instances of people writing down "Great job!" or similar responses. Other entries included suggestions to better organize our tours (this applied to the first session). Specifically, attendees suggested that we reserve rooms at the different tour locations beforehand. Although this is not always possible, we did take this into account, subsequently alerting colleagues to be ready for the sometimes-large tour groups. Other comments were related to providing more information on "library rules," advanced searching skills (including searching in Chinese), and subject-specific resources (especially in STEM fields). This resulted in smoother tours and an opportunity for different library departments to welcome attendees and promote their specific services and programs.

Shortly after the pilot session was offered in 2015, the U-M Library communication office contacted us expressing their desire to cover this instructional project. It was featured in the Fall 2015 issue of the *News for Donors and Friends* newsletter published by the U-M Library Development Office. In the following year, 2016, the team received a U-M Library Learning and Teaching Collaboration Award.

Lessons Learned

The group is eager to apply the various lessons they have learned, with the objective of making an already successful program even better.

Location. To date, we have taught the sessions only on the U-M central campus, where the Hatcher Graduate Library and Shapiro Undergraduate Library are located. The survey findings suggest that perhaps moving the class closer to the School of Engineering on the north campus, approximately 2.5 miles from the central campus, is something to consider. The school receives a large number of Chinese students and scholars every year, so that location would be more convenient and perhaps increase participation numbers. The team has been discussing ways of fulfilling this need while also finding opportunities for attendees to tour the main library on central campus.

Session dates. We have only held sessions during the regular semester, later than most orientation and training programs. The demographic data we collected indicated that the sessions attracted more visiting scholars than undergraduate and graduate students, perhaps because the students are already ensconced in their busy class schedules at that point, whereas the scholars have more flexibility. Thus, we are now considering offering an August session because most international students are on campus ahead of the start of classes.

Application in Other Settings

Not every library has the language and/or subject expertise to enable the easy assembly of a team of librarians or other staff members who can devote time and energy to preparing and providing similar orientation sessions. Nonetheless, we believe that with some flexibility and creativity there are many takeaways from our experience that other types of libraries can use and apply.

Communicate with stakeholders from the beginning. In our case, we communicated with the U-M International Center. The Center shared suggestions with us on when to run a pilot session and helped us promote the session. We also talked with the heads of various library units to gain their support.

Leverage human resources. Be creative and think outside the box when considering who to include in a project like this. Language and instruction expertise are probably the most important. Our team was able to leverage non-public services staff to lead the tours and a non-Chinese speaker to organize the sessions. As mentioned in the literature review, training student assistants to offer tours can be useful as well. We were constrained by the number of librarians who had both the language expertise and instruction experience, however, and librarians at other institutions should approach an initiative like this with a realistic understanding of the human resources available to them.

Creatively reuse existing materials. To prepare for the presentation, the team translated a handout titled "10 Things to Know About U-M Library" and adapted the slideshow used in the English-language orientation sessions. We also included a Chinese-language brochure already available from the U-M Asia Library.

Make sure it is working. As with any instruction program, assessment is crucial. Through the surveys, we found out that our Chinese student and scholar audience really values and appreciates these sessions. They make them feel welcomed, recognized, and appreciated. This assessment also allowed us to make specific improvements based on respondents' comments and suggestions.

Communicate again. It is always a good idea to follow up not only with attendees to share presentation materials but also with stakeholders to inform them of attendance numbers and survey results or other assessment outcomes.

Conclusion

This creative and collaborative instructional initiative has provided a much-needed service to new bilingual students and scholars. It demonstrated innovative approaches of outreach to our international communities on campus and attested to the capacity of native language in building an inclusive community. It also set a model of collaboration in promoting intercultural understanding through library instruction. In the future, we will explore the possibilities of conducting additional sessions in other languages to serve more of our international students and scholars.

Acknowledgment

The authors would like to thank Dawn Lawson and Theresa Stanko for their editorial assistance.

Appendix 3A: Bilingual Online Survey

Hello! Thank you for attending the U-M Library Basics in Chinese workshop on mm/dd/yyyy .

Below are a few questions about this workshop. This information will let us improve the services we provide to international students. This electronic survey will take you about 5 minutes to complete. Participation in this study is completely voluntary. All the information you share with us will remain confidential and we will report only combined results, not individual ones. Your participation is greatly appreciated!
亲爱的读者，您好！感谢您参与 年 月 日举办的"密歇根大学图书馆资源与服务"中文讲座。此次问卷调查旨在帮助我们根据调查结果有针对性地改进，更好地为您服务。填写这份问卷大约需要5分钟。参加问卷调查完全基于个人自愿，本问卷不涉及个人隐私，您的回答将会受到严格保密。问卷所得结果只做综合分析而不进行任何个体呈现。希望获得您的支持和协助，感谢您在百忙之中填写本问卷。

Q1 Did you attend one of the three "U-M Library Basics" sessions that the library offered earlier this summer (date 1, date 2, or date 3)?
您之前是否参加过在（日期1、日期2或日期3）举办的关于密歇根大学图书馆资源与服务的英文讲座？

- o Yes
- o No

Q2 Below are the topics covered during this workshop. Please rank (drag up or down) these topics from most useful (1), to least useful (5)
关于讲座中涉及到的以下几项主题，请上下拖拽数字，排列出您认为最重要的主题。(1)为最重要，(5)为完全不重要。

______ General Information about the Library or Library System 图书馆概况
______ Library Collections 馆藏信息资源
______ Library Services 图书馆服务项目及使用权限
______ Searching for Books and Articles 馆藏资源检索功能
______ Library Tour 参观图书馆设施

Q3 Were there topics that were not covered that you would like to know more about?
本讲座涉及的内容以外，您是否还想了解图书馆其它方面的信息？

- o Yes
- o No

Q4 Which topic or topics that were not covered would you like to know more about?
您还想了解哪些在讲座中没有涉及的图书馆信息？

____

____

____

Q5 How useless/useful was the fact that this session was in Chinese?
本次讲座使用中文对您有用吗？

- o Very Useless 毫无用处
- o Useless 没有用
- o Neutral 中立
- o Useful 有用
- o Very Useful 非常有用

Q6 What language do you prefer for library workshops?
您希望图书馆使用哪种语言举办讲座？

- o Chinese 中文
- o English 英文
- o Either Language 没有偏好

Q7 Is there anything else you would like to let us know about this session?
您对图书馆资源建设与服务还有其它意见和建议吗？

____

____

____

Q8 What is your status at the University of Michigan?
您在密歇根大学的身份是？

- o Undergraduate Student 本科生
- o Graduate Student 研究生
- o Visiting Scholar 访问学者
- o Other 其他（请注明） ________________________

Notes

1. Racial and Ethnic Diversity Committee, "Diversity Standards: Cultural Competency for Academic Libraries (2012)," ACRL, accessed May 8, 2017, http://www.ala.org/acrl/standards/diversity.
2. Alison Hicks, "Reframing Librarian Approaches to International Student Information Literacy through the Lens of New Literacy Studies," in *Critical Literacy for Information Professionals,* ed. Sarah McNicol (London: Facet Publishing, 2016), 43.
3. Xiang Li, Kevin McDowell, and Xiaotong Wang, "Building Bridges: Vernacular Language Videos and Library Outreach to International Students," paper presented at the annual meeting of the Council on East Asian Libraries, Chicago, Illinois, March 23–27, 2015.
4. Daniel Liestman and Connie Wu, "Library Orientation for International Students in Their Native Language," *Research Strategies* 8.4 (1990): 191–96.
5. Manuel D. Lopez, "Chinese Spoken Here: Foreign Language Library Orientation Tours," *College and Research Libraries News* 44.8 (1983): 265–69.
6. Deborah L. Spanfelner, "Teaching Library Skills to International Students," *Community & Junior College Libraries* 7.2 (1991): 69–76.

7. Eileen K. Bosch and Valeria E. Molteni, "Connecting to International Students in Their Languages: Innovative Bilingual Library Instruction in Academic Libraries," in *International Students and Academic Libraries: Initiatives for Success*, ed. Pamela A. Jackson and Patrick Sullivan (Chicago: Association of College and Research Libraries, 2011), 135.
8. University Library System, "East Asia Library Instruction," University of Pittsburgh, accessed May 12, 2017, http://www.library.pitt.edu/eal-instruction.
9. Maud C. Mundava and LaVerne Gray, "Meeting Them Where They Are: Marketing to International Student Populations in US Academic Libraries," *Technical Services Quarterly* 25.3 (2008): 35–48.
10. Mark A. Puente, LaVerne Gray, and Shantel Agnew, "The Expanding Library Wall: Outreach to the University of Tennessee's Multicultural/International Student Population," *Reference Services Review* 37.1 (2009): 30–43.

Bibliography

Bosch, Eileen K., and Valeria E. Molteni. "Connecting to International Students in their Languages: Innovative Bilingual Library Instruction in Academic Libraries." In *International Students and Academic Libraries: Initiatives for Success*, edited by Pamela A. Jackson and Patrick Sullivan, 135–50. Chicago: Association of College and Research Libraries, 2011.

Hicks, Alison. "Reframing Librarian Approaches to International Student Information Literacy through the Lens of New Literacy Studies." In *Critical Literacy for Information Professionals*, edited by Sarah McNicol, 43–56. London: Facet Publishing, 2016.

Li, Xiang, Kevin McDowell, and Xiaotong Wang. "Building Bridges: Vernacular Language Videos and Library Outreach to International Students." Paper presented at the annual meeting of the Council on East Asian Libraries, Chicago, Illinois, March 26, 2015.

Liestman, Daniel, and Connie Wu. "Library Orientation for International Students in their Native Language." *Research Strategies* 8.4 (1990): 191–96.

Lopez, Manuel D. "Chinese Spoken Here: Foreign Language Library Orientation Tours." *College and Research Libraries News* 44.8 (1983): 265–69.

Mundava, Maud C., and LaVerne Gray. "Meeting Them Where They Are: Marketing to International Student Populations in US Academic Libraries." *Technical Services Quarterly* 25.3 (2008): 35–48.

Puente, Mark A., LaVerne Gray, and Shantel Agnew. "The Expanding Library Wall: Outreach to the University of Tennessee's Multicultural/International Student Population." *Reference Services Review* 37.1 (2009): 30–43.

Racial and Ethnic Diversity Committee. "Diversity Standards: Cultural Competency for Academic Libraries (2012)." ACRL. Accessed May 8, 2017. http://www.ala.org/acrl/standards/diversity.

Spanfelner, Deborah L. "Teaching Library Skills to International Students." *Community & Junior College Libraries* 7.2 (1991): 69–76.

U-M International Center. *University of Michigan 2016 Statistical Report: International Students, Scholars, Faculty, Staff and Education Abroad.* Ann Arbor: University of Michigan International Center, 2016.

CHAPTER FOUR

The Information-Fluent English Language Learner:

Cultural and Pedagogical Considerations

Megan Hodge

Introduction

Many of the students who wish to study in America have insufficient command of the English language to pass the TOEFL or IELTS examinations required for enrollment at U.S. institutions of higher education, and as a result, programs designed to teach proficiency in the English language have been developed at some of these universities. In addition to English grammar and vocabulary, some programs also seek to acculturate students to Western academic norms such as critical thinking, academic integrity, and the paper-writing process.

As many of the international students in the US first experience American education through these English language programs, the cultural norms taught by the programs are vital to the academic success of these students; without them, students struggle to recognize plagiarism in their writing, find reliable sources, and more. Librarians are uniquely equipped to meet this instructional need, a fact increasingly recognized by university ESL faculty and reflected in the recent creation and growth of ACRL's Academic Library Services to International Students Interest Group.

In my role as library liaison to Virginia Commonwealth University's English language program, I provide course-integrated instruction to around a dozen classes each semester. This instruction takes the form of interactive introductions to library spaces and resources as well as the teaching of content including evaluating sources, avoiding plagiarism, developing a search strategy, searching in library databases, and preparing for oral debates. This chapter describes the pedagogical practices I've found to be most effective in my own experience as well as from my research into ESL pedagogy for adult learners. These best practices also extend to building sensitivity to different academic backgrounds into your lessons.

Cultural Differences in Classroom Behaviors

While international students can, of course, come from almost any country, over 60 percent of international students in the United States come from just four countries: China, India, Saudi Arabia, and South Korea.[1] Regardless of a student's country of origin, however, it is advisable to become aware of cultural differences which may affect your lesson planning process.

First, be prepared for many students to arrive ten minutes or more after the official class start time. As Moeckel and Presnell note, "Egyptians and other Arabs may view appointment times as relative, not exact," and students often apply this conception of time to their classes once in the United States.[2] Later start times may be more common in lower-level language classes, where faculty are still acculturating their students to Western academic and cultural norms, than in upper-level classes. It is therefore advisable to check with the professor of record to learn whether students are likely to arrive on time, whether the professor generally starts class punctually, and to develop a lesson plan flexible enough to adapt to varying start times.

Not surprisingly, English language learners tend to sit with classmates who hail from the same country of origin. While this propensity can increase comfort in the classroom, it often leads to students speaking their native language with each other rather than English. Such native-language chatting may not always be inappropriate, even in the ESL classroom; for example, stronger students may serve as informal tutors by translating difficult concepts for their classmates. If assessment of individual students' language skills is desired, consider redistributing students around the classroom. Before attempting such a redistribution, however, consider that in some cultures, women are not permitted to socialize with men outside of their families and may therefore feel uncomfortable if asked to work with men. This is, again, a circumstance upon which the professor of record will be able to advise you.

When incorporating motivational and game-like elements into instruction for English language learners, consider consulting with the TESOL faculty member to ensure they will be comprehended and have the desired motivational effect. Pop culture references and humor based on idiom need to be carefully selected, if used at all, though funny GIFs and references to blockbuster movies such as those made by Disney and Marvel reliably draw smiles of recognition. Muslim students may not find candy a desirable bribe or reward for class participation due to religious guidelines about food preparation. Finally, some cultures value communal rather than individual efforts. In-class competitions, such as *Jeopardy*-style review games, may therefore be off-putting and even demotivating to students from such cultures. Putting students into groups to compete as teams will often alleviate feelings of demotivation that might be generated from competitive activities.

While English language learners (ELLs) and domestic students alike tend to learn more when the lecture is limited in favor of active learning and class discussion, small amounts of lecture are generally unavoidable. It is important to regularly pause, even during a short lecture, to check student comprehension of what you are discussing because ELLs often will not let you know that they do not understand or have a question. However, simply asking "Any questions?" or "Does that makes sense?" may not suffice. As Howze and Moore note, "In order to save face, many international students may say they understand, when in truth they may be more confused than ever."[3] Additionally, in some cultures, "head nodding can indicate a negative rather than an affirmative response."[4] Taking the time to administer a formative assessment—whether this takes the form of students writing a one-minute paper on a sticky note or completing a brief and fun online quiz in Kahoot or PollEverywhere—allows the instructor to check comprehension and clarify as needed.

Finally, anyone learning a new language, international student or no, may feel shy or uncertain about using that language in front of an unknown native speaker (i.e., you or the librarian guest-lecturer) who cannot yet be trusted not to judge or ridicule their pronunciation and diction.[5] In the interests of scaffolding learning (the students are enrolled in an English language program to learn to write and speak English, after all) but in a way that reduces student discomfort, several strategies can be employed. When possible, provide time for students to collect their thoughts before answering a question; this can be done via methods such as think/pair/share and group presentations. Audience response boards, as in figure 4.1 below, have the dual benefit of increasing participation in students nervous about speaking in front of the librarian and preventing the more confident students from dominating a class discussion. Above all, avoid putting individual students on the spot by asking them to extemporaneously answer a question; the one exception to this guideline is that such questioning is an effective classroom management technique if students are off-task.

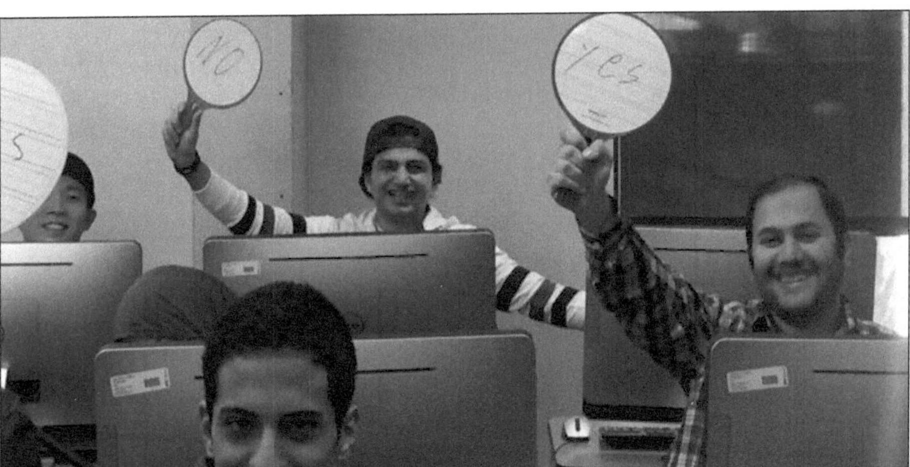

Figure 4.1. Audience using response boards

Pedagogical Strategies

Many of the strategies outlined in this section will be familiar to anyone who has gone through a teacher education program or is familiar with the literature on instruction, whether inside or outside libraries and higher education. These best practices are often especially effective with English language learners in library classrooms.

Scaffolding student learning

To help students be successful learners, it is important for instructors to provide the support, or scaffolding, that makes learning possible. As defined by Mu, "Scaffolding procedures in the library include: breaking down library tasks into subtasks, modeling the strategies needed to complete the tasks, and engaging students in activities that ensure a gradual shift in responsibility from the reference librarian or subject specialist to the students."[6] As mentioned above, a vital part of supporting English language learners is equipping them with the skills needed to thrive in an American university classroom.

One such skill is effective note-taking. Knowing when and how to take notes is a strategy proven to result in dramatically greater retention, yet it is a skill that students both domestic and international often lack.[7] Providing explicit cues to students about when to write something down—for example, when a new vocabulary word is introduced—can therefore be very helpful. An additional strategy is the use of repetition; one librarian "reminds students that his use of repetition is on purpose as a reminder to study the material."[8] Another method is the use of advance organizers, where students are given incomplete notes and are asked to fill them in over the course of the lesson. Teaching and repeating these cues help students learn a behavior which will hopefully become instinctive after enough practice.

Similarly, modeling practices, such as creating an organization mechanism for newly learned knowledge, helps students develop practices that will aid their studies in the present as well as throughout the rest of their academic studies. Thinking metacognitively about organizing new information is another study skill that studies have shown over and over again to be effective in increasing retention.[9] In the library classroom, this can take the form of creating a table to visualize the differences between scholarly and popular sources, or of organizing the reasons an example website is not trustworthy into the five Ws: who, what, when, where, and why.[10] Explaining why you are organizing the information this way makes explicit some of the knowledge that you have as a subject expert and, again, models an academic practice that can be used in other contexts.

Another method is to use analogies and comparisons to activate students' prior knowledge about a subject and help them more readily incorporate new modes of thinking into pre-existing mental frameworks.[11] For example, Western ideas about citation can be new to some international students. It can be helpful to begin a discussion on this topic by first exploring a similar idea that is shared across cultures: stealing a home-cooked meal. While the scenario of someone stealing a meal you have cooked to claim it as their own at a potluck may seem silly and often evokes grins from students, they universally agree that they would feel upset, annoyed, or hurt should someone do it to them. From a discussion of these feelings, the topic of academic integrity and citation can be eased into, with the disclaimer that Westerners feel the same way about someone using their written work without attribution. Such comparisons enable students to step more easily into frameworks that are otherwise alien.

Increasing student comprehension

For any lesson to be effective, students must understand what their teacher is communicating. With English language learners, students are already operating within the frameworks of a new language and a new academic culture to which library jargon is an added layer. Without understanding your vocabulary, it will be increasingly difficult for students to understand the concepts that those words describe. Taking a few additional measures to ensure maximal comprehension is therefore advisable.

Several studies have demonstrated that American undergraduates often do not understand library terminology and that a single library session is generally insufficient for long-term retention of such terminology.[12] Avoiding library jargon with English language learners is even more essential; use "search engine" for "database," "article" or "publication" for "source," and so on. However, keep in mind that even non-library words, such as "bias," may be unfamiliar to students and require definition. Conducting a comprehension check upon first using these words (e.g., "what does 'trustworthy' mean?") not only ensures that students do not miss important pieces of information but can also be used to break up even short lectures and introduce elements of interactivity. Students could, for example, be asked to work with a partner or small group to determine their definition of "trustworthy" and to identify a website or publication that they believe is trustworthy. Other strategies include rephrasing, using images, and using new vocabulary words in differing contexts.[13] Finally, all newly introduced words should be written out on a whiteboard/blackboard in addition to being spoken aloud, so students can see how the word is spelled as well as pronounced.

Even if the vocabulary you use while teaching is familiar, the speed of your speech may pose a barrier to student understanding. Enunciate longer words and try to speak more slowly. This doesn't mean you need to emulate Dory speaking whale in *Finding Nemo*, but be aware of the speed of your speech and "use longer pauses between semantic groups so that students can process the whole meaning and not spend too much time deciphering individual words or sentences."[14] If using an audio or video clip in class, turn on closed captioning and moderate the speed. On YouTube, this can be done by clicking the gear icon on any video and changing the speed from Normal to 0.75. Internet browser extensions like Transpose and Video Speed Controller enable you to slow down videos that don't have that functionality built in.

To mitigate the cognitive overload of following directions and learning new concepts/vocabulary at the same time, students often find it very helpful to have step-by-step instructions written out on the whiteboard/on your slides. Leaving these instructions up while students work together is also useful to keep students focused during longer activities as they can check whether they have, in fact, completed all tasks.

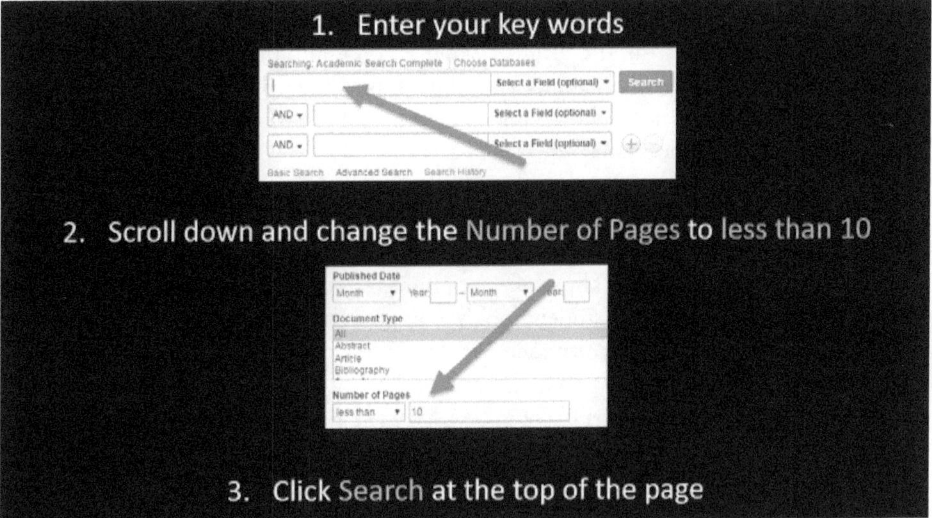

Figure 4.2. Step-by-Step Instructions

Finally, English language learners often appreciate the ability to listen to a longer text as well as read it. This helps them learn how to pronounce words they may have only seen in written form and helps the reading process go more quickly. A useful tool is TTSreader.com, a website as well as Chrome extension that reads aloud any text selected by a patron. TTSreader highlights each sentence as it is being read and offers British as well as American accents. Some databases, such as Opposing Viewpoints, offer this functionality as well.

Handling the Unexpected

The experienced teacher realizes that even the most thoughtfully prepared lesson plan can be diverted from its course for reasons entirely beyond human control: an unusually energetic or torpid class, current events such as the death of a celebrity, or an internet outage. The habits of building flexibility into your plans, as well as regularly checking the time to gauge whether your subsequent activities need to be modified to account for earlier parts of your lesson taking more or less time than you anticipated, will serve you well. Additionally, it may be beneficial to prepare for some other scenarios in the English language learner library classroom.

Anticipate that you probably will not get through your entire lesson plan. Discussions and activities both often take longer than expected; students often have questions about what they are supposed to be doing, questions about vocabulary, and questions about technical issues if, for example, they end up lost in a database. Reading may also take longer than expected, so use shorter articles if students need to read in class—to evaluate a source, for example. EBSCO databases include the functionality of limiting search results by number of pages, which is convenient both for in-class activities as well as a tip for students to keep in mind as they search for sources for their assignments. This slower pace has the additional benefits of reducing library anxiety and feeling like a luxury to librarians accustomed to the frenetic pace of a traditional fifty-minute session.

A related consideration is whether to use websites or other technology. Websites like PearDeck and Kahoot, which can turn presentations into active learning opportunities, often require that several steps be followed in order for students to log in as well as instructions on how to use them. If you are teaching in the context of a one-shot or have only an hour for your lesson, the minutes spent walking around to ensure everyone has logged in and explaining how the activity will work may use up precious time that would be better spent on your intended learning objectives, among which comfort with instructional tools is probably not included.

A common challenge in the twenty-first-century classroom is digital distraction, whether in the form of students texting their friends on their phones or checking Facebook on the classroom computers. Like their American counterparts, English language learners are not immune to the allure of their phones. Be aware, however, that what looks like off-task behavior may be a student looking up an unfamiliar word in an app on their phone. Consider asking the faculty member what their classroom phone policy is; some collect them at the beginning of class and return them at the end; others encourage their use during lessons where there is likely to be a lot of new vocabulary.

Conclusion

In closing, it is important to note that the most effective resource in being successful in the ELL library classroom is the faculty member. The professor can tell you ahead of time how many students there will be, whether they are mostly at the same level of proficiency or of widely varying abilities, if there is one student who tends to monopolize class discussions, and whether mobile phones are allowed in their classroom. As Polger and Sheidlower note, "an engaged professor is the best ally."[15] Faculty help extends to the classroom as well: they can circulate around the room, helping to answer questions and keep students on task, point out words that you did not realize were unfamiliar to students, and increase student engagement and buy-in by contributing judiciously to class discussions. Together, professor and librarian can ensure that English language learners get the most from their library instruction.

Notes

1. Institute of International Education, "A Quick Look at International Students in the U.S.," accessed May 1, 2017, https://www.iie.org/Research-and-Insights/Open-Doors/Fact-Sheets-and-Infographics/Infographics.
2. Nancy Moeckel and Jenny Presnell, "Recognizing, Understanding, and Responding: A Program Model of Library Instruction Services for International Students," *Reference Librarian* 24, no. 51/52, (1995): 313.
3. Philip C. Howze and Dorothy M. Moore, "Measuring International Students' Understanding of Concepts Related to the Use of Library-Based Technology," *Research Strategies* 19, no. 1 (2003): 63.
4. Moeckel and Presnell, "Recognizing, Understanding, and Responding," 312.
5. Allen Natowitz, "International Students in U.S. Academic Libraries: Recent Concerns and Trends," *Research Strategies* 13, no. 1 (1995): 4–16.
6. Cuiying Mu, "Marketing Academic Library Resources and Information Services to International Students from Asia," *Reference Services Review* 35, no. 4 (2007): 580.
7. Tamas Makany, Jonathan Kemp, and Itiel E. Dror, "Optimising the Use of Note-taking as an External Cognitive Aid for Increasing Learning," *British Journal of Educational Technology* 40, no. 4 (2009): 619–35; Deborah K. Reed, Hillary Rimel, and Abigail Hallett, "Note-Taking Interventions for College Students: A Synthesis and Meta-Analysis of the Literature," *Journal of Research on Educational Effectiveness* 9, no. 3 (2016): 307–33.
8. Mark Aaron Polger and Scott Sheidlower, *Engaging Diverse Learners: Teaching Strategies for Academic Librarians* (Santa Barbara, CA: Libraries Unlimited, 2017), 52.
9. Susan A. Ambrose, et al., *How Learning Works: Seven Research-Based Principles for Smart Teaching* (San Francisco: John Wiley & Sons, 2010), 192.
10. Candice Benjes-Small, et al., "Teaching Web Evaluation: A Cognitive Development Approach," *Communications in Information Literacy* 7, no. 1 (2013): 44–45.
11. Ulrich Boser, *Learn Better: Mastering the Skills for Success in Life, Business, and School, or, How to Become an Expert in Just About Anything* (New York: Rodale, 2017), 164–65; Andrea Malone, "Say This, Not That: Library Instruction for International Students in Intensive English Programs," *Brick and Click Libraries* (2010): 140.
12. Norman B. Hutcherson, "Library Jargon: Student Recognition of Terms and Concepts Commonly Used by Librarians in the Classroom," *College & Research Libraries* 65, no. 4 (2004): 349–54; Gayle Schaub, et al., "The Language of Information Literacy: Do Students Understand?," *College & Research Libraries* 78, no. 3 (2017): 283–96.
13. Lia D. Kamhi-Stein and Alan Paul Stein, "Teaching Information Competency as a Third Language: A New Model for Library Instruction," *Reference & User Services Quarterly* 38, no. 2 (1998): 174.

14. Mu, "Marketing Academic Library Resources," 579–80.
15. Polger and Sheidlower, *Engaging Diverse Learners*, 68.

Bibliography

Ambrose, Susan A., Michael W. Bridges, Michele DiPietro, Marsha C. Lovett, and Marie K. Norman. *How Learning Works: Seven Research-Based Principles for Smart Teaching.* San Francisco: John Wiley & Sons, 2010.

Benjes-Small, Candice, Alyssa Archer, Katelyn Tucker, Lisa Vassady, and Jennifer Resor. "Teaching Web Evaluation: A Cognitive Development Approach." *Communications in Information Literacy* 7, no. 1 (2013): 39–49.

Boser, Ulrich. *Learn Better: Mastering the Skills for Success in Life, Business, and School, or, How to Become an Expert in Just About Anything.* New York: Rodale, 2017.

Howze, Philip C., and Dorothy M. Moore. "Measuring International Students' Understanding of Concepts Related to the Use of Library-Based Technology." *Research Strategies* 19, no. 1 (2003): 57–74.

Hutcherson, Norman B. "Library Jargon: Student Recognition of Terms and Concepts Commonly Used by Librarians in the Classroom." *College & Research Libraries* 65, no. 4 (2004): 349–54.

Institute of International Education. "A Quick Look at International Students in the U.S." Accessed May 1, 2017. https://www.iie.org/Research-and-Insights/Open-Doors/Fact-Sheets-and-Infographics/Infographics.

Kamhi-Stein, Lia D., and Alan Paul Stein. "Teaching Information Competency as a Third Language: A New Model for Library Instruction." *Reference & User Services Quarterly* 38, no. 2 (1998): 173–79.

Makany, Tamas, Jonathan Kemp, and Itiel E. Dror. "Optimising the Use of Note-taking as an External Cognitive Aid for Increasing Learning." *British Journal of Educational Technology* 40, no. 4 (2009): 619–35.

Malone, Andrea. "Say This, Not That: Library Instruction for International Students in Intensive English Programs." *Brick and Click Libraries* (2010): 138–41.

Moeckel, Nancy, and Jenny Presnell. "Recognizing, Understanding, and Responding: A Program Model of Library Instruction Services for International Students." *Reference Librarian* 24, no. 51/52 (1995): 309–27.

Mu, Cuiying. "Marketing Academic Library Resources and Information Services to International Students from Asia." *Reference Services Review* 35, no. 4 (2007): 571–83.

Natowitz, Allen. "International Students in U.S. Academic Libraries: Recent Concerns and Trends." *Research Strategies* 13, no. 1 (1995): 4–16.

Polger, Mark Aaron, and Scott Sheidlower. *Engaging Diverse Learners: Teaching Strategies for Academic Librarians.* Santa Barbara, CA: Libraries Unlimited, 2017.

Reed, Deborah K., Hillary Rimel, and Abigail Hallett. "Note-Taking Interventions for College Students: A Synthesis and Meta-Analysis of the Literature." *Journal of Research on Educational Effectiveness* 9, no. 3 (2016): 307–33.

Schaub, Gayle, Cara Cadena, Patricia Bravender, and Christopher Kierkus. "The Language of Information Literacy: Do Students Understand?" *College & Research Libraries* 78, no. 3 (2017): 283–96.

CHAPTER FIVE

Globalizing Library Instruction:

Engaging Students at International Branch Campuses

Claudia McGivney, Laura Costello, and Janet Clarke

Introduction

Today's academic libraries must be able to communicate efficiently the depth of their resources to all campus communities, and Stony Brook University Libraries have worked to apply instructional methods to a broad spectrum of users. Our library has been using emerging technology, open access resources, and innovative teaching methods to engage with our local and global student and faculty community. Using our campus in South Korea as an example, we will highlight a number of strategies developed for delivering equitable information instruction sessions to our international students at satellite campuses across the world.

The current era in American academic libraries is one of globalized teaching and learning. As academia expands into new learning markets, libraries must be prepared and appropriately situated to support student success in these courses. The learning experience we provide for our international campus is designed to capitalize on the diversity of our resources and engage students on many levels of the research process. Our chapter discusses the adaptations we have made to our instruction practices and our tailoring of resources and services to online delivery for international students.

Many academic institutions have satellite campuses, and libraries are increasingly called upon to support these global initiatives. This chapter lays a framework for libraries developing instruction practice to include international branch campuses (IBC). Our mission as librarians is to increase access to scholarly resources, promote information exchange, contribute to student learning of effective information use, and provide support to all researchers across the university.

Today's libraries must be able to engage patrons using a variety of means, and this includes possessing the technological creativity to deliver instruction outside of the traditional brick-and-mortar classroom setting. In this chapter, we discuss a number of technological practices to engage students and collaborate with faculty across traditional boundaries. The goal of any information session is for students to be become better equipped to access the information they need, evaluate what they find, and seek additional help in navigating those resources. Our forward-facing liaison model coupled with creative applications of technology in our information sessions has allowed our library to proactively serve diverse populations.

Librarians must be ready to experiment and adapt in order to provide the most comprehensive instruction possible. We can only engage our users if we are able to connect with them, and globalization has necessitated that we expand our reach to academic communities across the world. In this essay, we demonstrate methods for developing a holistic and meaningful approach to information instruction practices for academic librarians teaching remotely.

Literature Review

Embracing diversity in information literacy has been a significant topic of interest and concern for many years in academic libraries. As the work of our researchers, departments, and institutions develops globally, this topic must come to the forefront of our practice. This international context inspired the Association of College & Research Libraries (ACRL) Student Learning and Information Literacy Committee, Global Perspectives on Information Literacy Working Group to develop a framework and understanding of information literacy concepts around the world. The group worked with librarians from different regions to explore similarities and differences in the way we understand and teach information literacy in order to form a more global understanding of best practices.[1] They found a shared difficulty in most of the narratives with communicating the discipline of information literacy but also a shared understanding of the importance of this work not just for scholarship but for social justice, citizenship, and communication.

Though information literacy teaching is an essential part of librarianship around the world, there are factors US-based librarians should consider when reaching out to their international communities. Jennifer Congyan Zhao and Tara Mawhinney[2] compared the information literacy skills and challenges of native English-speaking students and Chinese international students at McGill University and found that both groups needed help selecting, evaluating, and synthesizing sources. The Chinese international students needed additional assistance with culturally specific items like locating items in the library, citation and plagiarism, and awareness of library services. This is an important consideration for IBCs but equally important for international students on an institution's main campus. Information literacy classes can adapt to international audiences by providing more foundational knowledge about the ways to seek help in the library and the services and resources that students are able to access.

One of the best ways to provide this culturally specific library information is to reach out to groups of international students early and often, whether they are on main campus or a satellite campus. California State University, Fresno, began an effort to reach out to international students during their orientation and invited them to a more intensive library event early in the semester where they could see the space and learn about library services.[3] Outreach like this to international students on satellite campuses may have more challenges, since these campuses may not have access to the full range of resources and services that the main campus has.

The lessons from global undertakings can also be applied closer to home. There are several examples of US-based libraries working with IBC students and colleagues abroad to develop and enhance information literacy teaching. Mount Saint Vincent University in Nova Scotia, Canada, and Bermuda College in Hamilton, Bermuda, share several dual enrollment programs. Librarians at both institutions collaborated to use web conferencing software to provide online information literacy training to both sites. It was important to conduct shared information literacy courses because the sites share library resources and many students who begin their studies at Bermuda College go on to finish their degrees at Mount Saint Vincent, with full access to onsite and online resources.[4] Long Island University's Brooklyn campus took a similar approach to US students studying in their four-year Global College program, which takes place entirely abroad in several different countries. Though this program focuses on American students, the types of outreach and instruction are similar to reaching satellite campus students because the Global College students spend only four days orienting to the main campus before beginning their international journey.[5] For these students, it is imperative to be able to access and effectively use the library's online resources.

The relationships that US campus libraries have with their IBCs are just as diverse as the outreach efforts to international students. Harriett Green conducted a study of librarians working with international branch campuses and found that most of these campuses had few onsite staff members and relied on the electronic resources and virtual services of the main campus.[6] Outreach to these satellite campuses is vital for sharing both access to library resources and culturally specific library services with international students.

Background of SUNY Korea and Library

SUNY Korea is the first American university and one of the founding universities of the Incheon Global Campus in Incheon, South Korea, along with Ghent University, George Mason University, and the University of Utah. Like Qatar Foundation's Education City,[7] these institutions share a single campus but are separately administered by their home institutions. These institutions were invited by the South Korean government to establish and offer American- and European-style higher education experiences that allow students from the Northeast Asia region to earn international degrees without going abroad. The Incheon Global Campus is located in the Incheon Free Economic Zone and is being developed as a global hub for international business, research and development, and education in Northeast Asia. Instruction is in English and graduates will be poised for entering multinational and/or globally focused careers. Other institutions preparing to offer degree programs at the Incheon Global Campus includes, among other US and European universities, the Fashion Institute of Technology, another SUNY institution.

Designed to extend the academic strengths and educational model of Stony Brook University, SUNY Korea was launched in 2012 with graduate programs in computer science and technology and society. Today, it offers bachelor's, master's, and/or doctoral degrees in computer science, mechanical engineering, technological systems management, business management, and applied mathematics and statistics, and has an enrollment of about 350. Undergraduate students complete three years of coursework on the

Incheon campus, spending their sophomore year on the Stony Brook campus in New York. During their immersive year in New York, they take courses to meet the Stony Brook curriculum requirements and experience the full range of cultural and extracurricular events and activities that other Stony Brook University students have. Graduate students also have the option to study at the Stony Brook, New York, campus.

Like the Qatar instance, each university at the Incheon Global Campus administers its own suite of library resources and services. A central library shared by all the institutions is part of the vision for the campus at steady state, and its services and resources are currently under development. SUNY Korea students and faculty have 24/7 access to all the electronic resources that Stony Brook University provides. These resources and services are supplemented by the central library and consortial arrangements.

SUNY Korea Case Study

Personalized learning within a global community calls for academic librarians to create customized spaces for engagement. Such spaces may be as coordinated as a synchronous online session, a specialized subject guide acting as a portal for a specific population, or just the flexibility to offer specialized help on request. There are no librarians on site at the Incheon campus. Resources for these students include custom appointments for virtual reference at a time conducive to both parties' time zones. We have also created a research guide that is meant to act as a gateway into the Stony Brook University Libraries for our SUNY Korea students.

When our liaisons coordinate instruction for SUNY Korea, these sessions are carefully planned to account for the thirteen-hour time difference as well as the interdisciplinary resources most of these courses engage with. In the case of one such session, liaisons provided introductory information literacy instruction to two upper-level undergraduate courses that were taught by the same instructor at SUNY Korea. These courses focused on data science management and methods of socio-tech decision-making. Because of the time difference, the course instructors agreed to combine the session into one. The session was held at 2 a.m. (EST), and for this reason the liaisons teaching the session decided to limit the conferencing to audio, with opportunity for live Q&A as well as the chat feature. Adobe Connect is the platform for online sessions at Stony Brook University. We were able to share librarians' screens, and due to the interdisciplinary focus of both courses, a variety of resources were demonstrated, including Academic Search Complete, Business Source Complete, IEEE, and JSTOR. Plagiarism and citation management were covered and Endnote was demonstrated to students.

Survey Data

A survey was sent out to student participants of the session held in October 2016. The session addressed ways to contact liaison librarians, ensuring access to library materials, types of resources available, as well as search methods and evaluative criteria. When the open-ended question "What did you find most helpful about the library session?" was asked, student responses generally fell into four categories: access and use of databases (57.1 percent), critical thinking skills (19.2 percent), communication and library liaison contact (14.3 percent), or new knowledge (9.5 percent). In the broadest category, the library databases, student responses indicated that instruction on "how to access the library database" or "how to limit the number of articles" was the most helpful aspect of the session.

Presenters informed students that due to the significant time difference, neither librarian instructors nor students would be visible on screen. Adobe Connect was used to share the presenters' screens but neither presenter was visible to the students over the course of the session. When students were asked if it would be helpful to use video conference during the library instruction session, 81.5 percent of respondents indicated that it would be. Despite no visuals of the presenters, students' self-reported willingness to reach out to librarians on their own was not impacted and 85.2 percent indicated they would be "comfortable emailing a librarian." This is especially important for our SUNY Korea students as initial contact and the majority of communication will be through email.

When asked to provide suggestions for other topics and resources that liaison librarians might cover in future sessions, student responses again fell into a discernible pattern. Responses could be categorized as either additional help with topics covered in the session (53.8 percent), questions not specific to library resources (15.4 percent), or an indication that they had no suggestions (30.8 percent). Suggestions for additional help included advanced search techniques, strategies for constructing a search, or evaluation of subject-specific databases. Students were also asked to share their feedback on how to expand the libraries' engagement with our students at SUNY Korea.

Students were given the opportunity to write a narrative response on how the library might improve these sessions to address the needs of future students at SUNY Korea. Again, responses varied but overall they can be classified into several emergent themes. The desire for a variety of workshops to be offered in future (30.8 percent) received a number of topic suggestions, including one that asked for a library workshop paired with their orientation. Students also made requests for additional help in the form of video conferencing (15.4 percent) and requests for on-site help due to the significant time difference (15.4 percent).

Conclusion

Assessment is a vital component in evaluating the impact of instruction and is of particular significance when sessions are delivered remotely. In the case of SUNY Korea, student feedback greatly informs our liaisons' instructional practices and provides insight on how to shape our engagement with these students in the future. Based on survey responses, we will be adjusting and exploring opportunities for combining multiple course sections to attend information literacy sessions. Our liaisons will also be preparing workshops and other online tutorials to best prepare these students for a seamless transition to their immersive year in New York. We will continue to expand our synchronous sessions online and explore methods for deepening engagement with our students regardless of their physical location.

Notes

1. ACRL Student Learning and Information Literacy Committee, *Global Perspectives on Information Literacy: Fostering a Dialogue for International Understanding*, 2017, http://www.ala.org/acrl/

sites/ala.org.acrl/files/content/publications/whitepapers/GlobalPerspectives_InfoLit.pdf.

2. Jennifer Congyan Zhao and Tara Mawhinney, "Comparison of Native Chinese-Speaking and Native English-Speaking Engineering Students' Information Literacy Challenges," *Journal of Academic Librarianship* 41, no. 6 (2015): 712–24, doi:10.1016/j.acalib.2015.09.010.
3. Chris Langer and Hiromi Kubo, "From the Ground Up: Creating a Sustainable Library Outreach Program for International Students," *Journal of Library Administration* 55, no. 8 (2015): 605–21, doi:10.1080/01930826.2015.1085232.
4. Jiselle Maria Alleyne and Denyse Rodrigues, "Delivering Information Literacy Instruction for a Joint International Program: An Innovative Collaboration Between Two Libraries," *College & Undergraduate Libraries* 18, no. 2–3 (2011): 261–71, doi:10.1080/10691316.2011.577697.
5. Zhonghong Wang and Paul Tremblay, "The Global Library: Providing Resources and Services to International Sites," *College & Undergraduate Libraries* 16, no. 1 (2009): 26–52, doi:10.1080/10691310902754239.
6. Harriett Green, "Libraries Across Land and Sea: Academic Library Services on International Branch Campuses," *College & Research Libraries* 74, no. 1 (2013): 9–23, doi:10.5860/crl-259.
7. Qatar Foundation, *Education City*, 2017, https://www.qf.org.qa/enroll.

Bibliography

ACRL Student Learning and Information Literacy Committee. *Global Perspectives on Information Literacy: Fostering a Dialogue for International Understanding*, 2017. http://www.ala.org/acrl/sites/ala.org.acrl/files/content/publications/whitepapers/GlobalPerspectives_InfoLit.pdf.

Alleyne, Jiselle Maria, and Denyse Rodrigues. "Delivering Information Literacy Instruction for a Joint International Program: An Innovative Collaboration Between Two Libraries." *College & Undergraduate Libraries* 18, no. 2–3 (2011): 261–71. doi:10.1080/10691316.2011.577697.

Green, Harriett. "Libraries Across Land and Sea: Academic Library Services on International Branch Campuses." *College & Research Libraries* 74, no. 1 (2013): 9–23. doi:10.5860/crl-259.

Langer, Chris, and Hiromi Kubo. "From the Ground Up: Creating a Sustainable Library Outreach Program for International Students." *Journal of Library Administration* 55, no. 8 (2015): 605–21. doi:10.1080/01930826.2015.1085232.

Qatar Foundation, *Education City*, 2017, https://www.qf.org.qa/enroll.

Wang, Zhonghong, and Paul Tremblay. "The Global Library: Providing Resources and Services to International Sites." *College & Undergraduate Libraries* 16, no. 1 (2009): 26–52. doi:10.1080/10691310902754239.

Zhao, Jennifer Congyan, and Tara Mawhinney. "Comparison of Native Chinese-Speaking and Native English-Speaking Engineering Students' Information Literacy Challenges." *Journal of Academic Librarianship* 41, no. 6 (2015): 712–24. doi:10.1016/j.acalib.2015.09.010.

CHAPTER SIX

Acculturating International Students to the Ethical Use of Information and American Values:

A Case Study

Cheryl A. Riley and Marian G. Davis

Colleges and universities began to consider ways to increase enrollment when state aid to public higher education institutions began to drop in the late 1990s and 2000s.[1] One strategy institutions adopted to offset the decrease in state aid was to strengthen international recruitment efforts. Since the Institute of International Education began tracking international student enrollment at United States academic institutions in 1948/1949, enrollment has increased every year, achieving a 10 percent increase between 2013/14 and 2014/15.[2] The University of Central Missouri (UCM), a mid-sized comprehensive master's university, outpaced the national trend during the past five years. The total international student population at UCM increased 386 percent between 2012 and 2016 with a 1,425 percent increase in students from India (see table 6.1).

TABLE 6.1
Indian and International Student Enrollment at the University of Central Missouri

Semester	Indian Students	Total International Students
Fall 2016	2,319	2,638
Fall 2015	2,429	2,786

TABLE 6.1
Indian and International Student Enrollment at the University of Central Missouri

Semester	Indian Students	Total International Students
Fall 2014	1,506	1,899
Fall 2013	454	863
Fall 2012	152	542

Source: UCM Fact Book.

The majority of these students are graduate students majoring in computer science, computer information systems, or industrial management. Such a rapid influx of new students has presented challenges not only for the affected academic departments but also for support services including the library.

Lampert indicated that librarians had the ability to play a key role in educating students about research and strategies for avoiding plagiarism.[3] Librarians working on the UCM library's strategic plan were aware of this concept and saw an opportunity to incorporate it into the strategic plan while working to increase student use of the library and library resources. The FY 2014–2017 strategic plan included outreach to various student populations as one marketing strategy to increase the visibility of the library. The international students at UCM were identified as a campus population that would benefit from specific library outreach efforts.

During a routine, single-shot library instruction session for an industrial management class, the classroom instructor and students indicated a desire for additional training in the American Psychological Association (APA) citation style. As we discussed this request, it became obvious we could use this opportunity to partially fulfill the outreach goal in the strategic plan. Because this industrial management class consisted of predominantly international students, we felt the first step should be to consult with the director of the Intensive English Program (IEP). We discovered that the focus of the IEP curriculum was on writing style and content; APA style was secondary to this instruction. Further conversation with the IEP faculty revealed that some academic programs had requested additional assistance with helping their international majors acclimate to the writing, theories, and mechanics of the ethical use of information in the United States. Industrial management was one of the programs making this request and we decided to develop our materials around this program.

Practicing the Ethical Use of Information

Our first strategy to meet the strategic plan objective was to develop a video addressing the ethical use of information in the United States. We took this step because the ethical use of information is an important issue within higher education and we know all students can benefit from a deeper understanding of this concept. We focused the video content on the idea of joining a community of scholars and how to ethically use information because "good referencing is an indication of worthy membership of the academic community."[4] Experts in second-language learning suggest that source-use instruction, in supportive environments where plagiarism is not the central issue, is critical to increasing student understanding of why writers cite and why citations are important.[5]

The video script began with a statement from the university president and provost welcoming students into our community of scholars. It was hoped that including this introduction from a very popular and charismatic president would both increase student "buy-in" and brand the product. After an introduction to the concept of belonging to a community of scholars, we explain that all college students write papers and that a critical consideration when writing a paper is to give credit to others' ideas. The importance of correct, complete citations when practicing academic integrity and honesty is stressed throughout the video. We explain that every citation includes similar pieces of information: author name, title of the work, date of publication, and publication information. The video includes examples that show (1) the number of in-text citations in one paragraph of an academic article, (2) paraphrasing, and (3) direct quotations. We acknowledge that paraphrasing is difficult and provide some strategies that will reduce the incidence of accidental plagiarism. The relationship between the in-text citations and the reference page is highlighted throughout the video. After completion, the video was posted on the library website and sent to faculty, alerting them of the resource via an email blast. We also encouraged librarians to embed the video in their subject guides.

We then returned to the initial request for assistance with APA style and developed a tutorial on formatting APA citations, which we titled "APA Boot Camp." It consists of three PowerPoint presentations on APA style (figure 6.1). Students may choose either slides with note pages or a narrated option. One PowerPoint focuses on authors and in-text citations, one on journal citations, and one on other types of citations, such as a chapter in an edited book, a book review, and a video. MS Word formatting tips for a hanging indent, block quotation, title page, running head and page numbers, dot leader tabs, and information on figures and tables were added as a result of specific questions asked by students using the product. We also included a link to the APA Style Blog. Finally, we used LibWizard to build a tutorial to assess understanding of the information presented in the boot camp. SpringShare LibGuides and LibWizard were used to produce the boot camp.

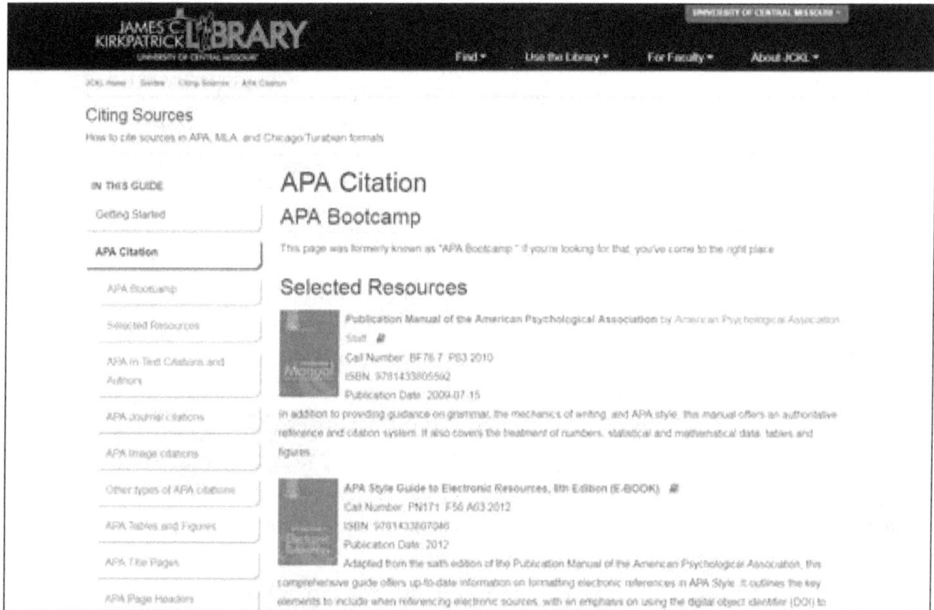

Figure 6.1. APA Boot Camp LibGuide (http://guides.library.ucmo.edu/apabootcamp)

As we were providing one-shot instruction sessions at our satellite facility, faculty began asking for our assistance with the acculturation process for our growing population of international students. Because most instruction requests again came from faculty teaching in the industrial management program, we began to address acculturation activities during our presentations to this population. Although international students receive an orientation when they arrive at the university, faculty determined that a reminder in individual classes was important. We reworked our instruction sessions to include approximately twenty minutes dedicated to American culture and American values.

American Culture and Values

Our conversations with industrial management faculty indicated attendance, punctuality, adherence to deadlines, and academic integrity were issues that appeared to present barriers to learning for their graduate students. We revised our instruction sessions by including information about conforming to American academic standards. Our goal is to help the students realize that such conformance is critical to their success as they pursue a degree from a US institution. We discuss the values of time, friendship, directness, informality, equality, and independence.[6] We note that Americans often appear to be very friendly because "such behavior is a social ritual in America"[7] but that this friendliness does not necessarily lead to friendship. We summarize the American communication style as being informal, direct, and assertive and emphasize that constructive criticism and mistakes are seen as learning opportunities. We address the individualistic and independent nature of American culture—the idea that Americans are expected to be self-reliant and not dependent on a group or family as much as in some cultures. Unlike some cultures, Americans often talk openly about their accomplishments. We briefly discuss the American concept of time—a discussion that begins with the concept that "time is money" and means that many Americans do not like to waste time. We also address the importance of punctuality in American culture, letting the students know that if you are not on time (or even slightly early) to an event, you may be perceived as being late. We emphasize that Americans are accustomed to scheduling appointments and that students should plan to keep appointments and be prompt. (And when that isn't possible, it is appropriate to let others know about the change in plans.) We point out that a consistent record of arriving late will likely annoy others, as Americans typically expect people to be on time and prepared.

After discussing the cultural differences regarding promptness and preparedness, we try to gain some understanding of other cultural differences that may present difficulties. Hofstede defined four dimensions of cultural differences: (1) individualism versus collectivism, (2) power distance, (3) masculinity/femininity differences, and (4) uncertainty avoidance.[8] These dimensions help practitioners consider their teaching and invite cultural considerations regarding teacher/student patterns of interaction.[9] We introduce topics such as perceived power distances in the classroom, the importance of knowing the correct answer versus developing and supporting an opinion, and the value placed on independent learning, ambiguity, and unpredictability. This discussion helps students, librarians, and instructors begin to appreciate the many differences and potential obstacles to their success in an unfamiliar setting. It also helps us gain an understanding of an individual class and often allows us to find common ground for discussion. Finally, we congratulate all the students on the initiative and determination it takes to pursue an education in a new country.

Academic Integrity

Once we have used American culture and values to establish a basic rapport with the group, we move on to the topic of academic integrity by using an online plagiarism quiz (http://en.writecheck.com/plagiarism-quiz)[10] that consists of ten questions. We ask everyone to answer the questions individually on paper, then we lead class discussion and collectively decide on an answer. Once the class has agreed to their collective answer, we look at the answer provided by the quiz developers. The rationale for the answers generates additional class discussion. After the class is over, the individual answer sheets are collected and the instructor is provided with an aggregate of the answers from the class. We have found that providing this information helps inform the instructor of an individual class's understanding and acceptance of American attitudes about plagiarism. After completing the plagiarism quiz, we emphasize the high value placed on avoiding plagiarism in this country. We acknowledge that other countries have different views and definitions of plagiarism but by choosing to study in America, a student has agreed to comply with the American understanding of plagiarism.

At this point, the instruction session segues into attribution and how it can be used to avoid plagiarism. Sometimes we show the library-developed video on the culture of scholarship and the ethical use of information; other times, we move on to the APA Boot Camp. Although both of these strategies have provided important dialogue with students, faculty reported to us that students still need additional assistance adapting to Western educational requirements. The next strategy was to develop course-specific LibGuides. We have developed LibGuides for four industrial management classes, including the research and capstone courses as well as some introductory-level graduate courses.

LibGuides

Each LibGuide is tailored to specific course assignments and requirements. Students in the Industrial Management graduate program are required to either write a paper for publication or complete a thesis. The majority of students write a paper for publication. The LibGuide for Industrial Management Seminar (figure 6.2) focuses on writing for

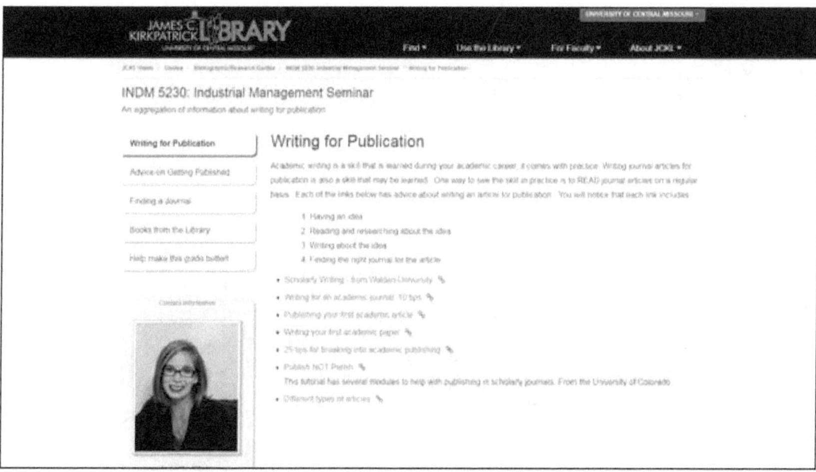

Figure 6.2. Course Guide for Industrial Management Seminar (http://guides.library.ucmo.edu/indm5230).

publication. It advises students to read scholarly publications regularly and links to articles about scholarly writing. A second page of the guide includes advice from publishers and professionals and provides tips for finding a journal in which to publish. We end the guide with a list of items available from the university library that may help in writing and publishing a scholarly article.

The LibGuide for Applied Research for Technology begins by defining a prospectus and introduces students to the DISCOVER method of developing a paper (Define, Inquire, Select, Collect, Organize, Verify, Express, Review). A link to the university *Thesis Manual* is provided, with specific pages on formatting the document highlighted. Another section of the guide covers the steps of writing a paper as some research indicates that students from other cultures do not have experience writing papers.[11] The next portion of the guide explains scholarly resources and provides lists of library-provided databases that can be used to locate information on their topics. Both technology and business databases are highlighted. We also include a discussion of dissertations and theses and explain the differences between the two. Finally, we include a link to the APA Boot Camp guide.

The LibGuide for Organization Dynamics (figure 6.3) suggests approaches to course assignments; specific approaches are vetted with the faculty member before the guide is published. It includes the general elements of a research paper, the DISCOVER process, how to write an outline, and a suggested outline for completing the assignment.

Figure 6.3. Course Guide for INDM 4260 Organizational Dynamics (http://guides.library.ucmo.edu/indm4260).

A LibGuide was created to help faculty with their frustration with the international student's ability to adapt to the Western educational system (figure 6.4). This LibGuide provides advice and strategies for working with international students and supplements information provided at the semi-annual professional development days sponsored by the university.

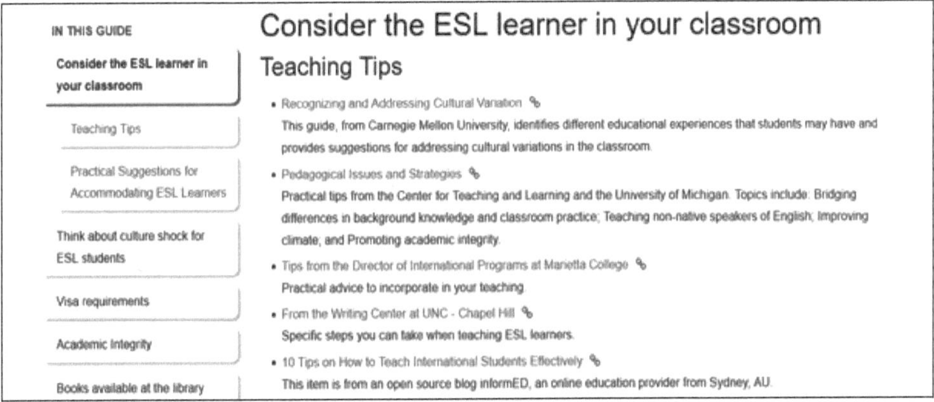

Figure 6.4. Working with International Students—Tips for Faculty LibGuide (http://guides.library.ucmo.edu/workingwithinternationalstudents).

Each of these LibGuides has been well received, with the APA Boot Camp being one of the most viewed subject guides at UCM. The Applied Research for Technology guide is the most popular of the guides prepared for the industrial management program. The Tips for Working with International Students has been viewed 379 times and is the forty-sixth most accessed guide (as of December 7, 2017)—without any marketing or promotion.

Conclusion

We believe our efforts to promote the ethical use of information in our particular community of scholars has been worthwhile. We asked those faculty who invited us into their classrooms to complete a survey rating the effectiveness of the librarian instruction session; our response rate was 80 percent. The results indicated 100 percent of respondents rated student performance as somewhat or greatly improved as a result of each of our outreach strategies: the face-to-face teaching sessions, the video, and the APA Boot Camp presentations. The respondents who requested the American Culture and Values discussion ranked their students' performance as somewhat improved. Specific course guides were utilized by 75 percent of the instructors surveyed; of those that encouraged use of the guides, 75 percent indicated student performance as showing some or great improvement. This same pattern held true with the guide dedicated to instructors who teach international students; 25 percent did not use the guide and 75 percent ranked their own improvement as somewhat or greatly improved. Faculty have, on the whole, been very appreciative of the video and several faculty rely on our APA Boot Camp. We view our work as an important contribution to information literacy. We will continue to work on marketing these products to students and updating the resources to remain current and relevant as assignments change.

Notes

1. Jennifer Ma and Sandy Baum, "Trends in Tuition and Fees, Enrollment, and State Appropriations for Higher Education by State," *College Board Advocacy & Policy Center Analysis Brief*, July 2012, accessed July 12, 2017, https://trends.collegeboard.org/sites/default/files/analysis-brief-trends-by-state-july-2012.pdf.

2. "International Student and U.S. Higher Education Enrollment Trends, 1948/2016/16," Institute of International Education, accessed July 12, 2017, https://www.iie.org/Research-and-Insights/Open-Doors/Data/International-Students/Enrollment/Enrollment-Trends.
3. Lynn D. Lampert, *Combating Student Plagiarism: An Academic Librarian's Guide* (Oxford: Chandos Publishing, 2008), 60–61.
4. Mike Hart and Tim Friesner, "Plagiarism and Poor Academic Practice—A Threat to the Extension of e-Learning in Higher Education?," *Electronic Journal on e-Learning* 2 (2004): 93, accessed July 12, 2017, http://ancasta.net/pubs/papers/ppap.pdf.
5. Diane Pecorari and Bejona Petrić, "Plagiarism in Second-Language Writing," *Language Teaching* 47 (2014): 276.
6. "American Values," Princeton University, Davis International Center, last modified July 21, 2013, accessed July 12, 2017, https://davisic.princeton.edu/guide-living-princeton/about-us-culture.
7. Ibid, para. 2.
8. Geert Hofstede, "Cultural Differences in Teaching and Learning," *International Journal of Intercultural Relations* 10 (1986): 307–8.
9. Patricia McLean and Laurie Ransom, "Building Intercultural Competencies: Implications for Academic Skills Development," in *Teaching International Students: Improving Learning for All,* ed. Jude Carroll and Janette Ryan (London: Routledge, 2005), 48.
10. "How Well Do You Know Plagiarism: Take This Quick 10-Question Quiz to Find Out," Turnitin, LLC, http://en.writecheck.com/plagiarism-quiz.
11. Diane Pecorari, *Teaching to Avoid Plagiarism: How to Promote Good Source Use* (Maidenhead, England: McGraw-Hill Education, 2013), 36.

Bibliography

Hart, Mike, and Tim Friesner. "Plagiarism and Poor Academic Practice—A Threat to the Extension of e-Learning in Higher Education?" *Electronic Journal on e-Learning* 2 (2004): 89–96. Accessed July 12, 2017. http://ancasta.net/pubs/papers/ppap.pdf.

Hofstede, Geert. "Cultural Differences in Teaching and Learning." *International Journal of Intercultural Relations,* 10 (1986):301-320.

Institute of International Education. "International Student and U.S. Higher Education Enrollment Trends, 1948/49-2015/16." *Open Doors Report on International Educational Exchange* (2016). https://www.iie.org/Research-and-Insights/Open-Doors/Data/International-Students/Enrollment/Enrollment-Trends.

Lampert, Lynn D. *Combating Student Plagiarism: An Academic Librarian's Guide.* Oxford: Chandos Publishing, 2008.

Ma, Jennifer, and Sandy Baum. "Trends in Tuition and Fees, Enrollment, and State Appropriations for Higher Education by State." *College Board Advocacy & Policy Center Analysis Brief* (2012). https://trends.collegeboard.org/sites/default/files/analysis-brief-trends-by-state-july-2012.pdf.

McLean, Patricia, and Laurie Ransom. "Building Intercultural Competencies: Implications for Academic Skills Development. In *Teaching International Students: Improving Learning for All,* edited by Jude Carroll and Janette Ryan, 45–62. London: Routledge, 2005.

Pecorari, Diane. *Teaching to Avoid Plagiarism: How to Promote Good Source Use.* Maidenhead, England: McGraw-Hill Education, 2013.

Pecorari, Diane, and Bejona Petrić. "Plagiarism in Second-Language Writing." *Language Teaching,* 47 (2014): 269–302.

Princeton University. Davis International Center. "American Values." Last modified July 21, 2013. Accessed July 12, 2017. https://davisic.princeton.edu/guide-living-princeton/about-us-culture.

Turnititn, LLC. "How Well Do You Know Plagiarism: Take This Quick 10-Question Quiz to Find Out." http://en.writecheck.com/plagiarism-quiz.

University of Central Missouri. *Fact Book 2016* (2016). https://www.ucmo.edu/ir/documents/factbook.pdf.

CHAPTER SEVEN

A Full Range of Support for Improving International Students' Experience in Higher Education:

A Case Study from the University of Minnesota Libraries

Yao Chen and Kristen Mastel

The University of Minnesota has nearly 6,000 international students, making up 13 percent of the total undergraduate and graduate student population, with students mostly from China, India, and Korea. The University of Minnesota Libraries engages international students through our year-round endeavor of a wide variety of programs and activities with the hope to ensure their academic and personal success. These activities include early interventions, such as orientation events and Introduction to Library Research tutorials. To ensure continued outreach during the academic year, the English-language learning librarians collaborate with subject experts to create Library Course Pages and scaffolded library instruction throughout the academic program. More importantly, the library actively participates in building a campus community to better serve international students. Together, this series of resources and services aims to help students and staff achieve success throughout the academic year. These programs and activities not only enrich international students' learning and cultural experiences, they also provide staff with opportunities to develop professionally and become diversity leaders and advocates.

Many libraries may not have a designated librarian for international students who could be the key person in the library to serve as their advocate. The work with international students has so many dimensions that it cannot be accomplished by a single person or even just a few individuals. At the University of Minnesota, the Diversity Leadership Committee, in collaboration with the English-language librarians and undergraduate services librarian, coordinates international student services internally and works closely with other campus departments and units to serve our international students and to collaborate on other diversity- and inclusion-related matters. Committee members, coming from different library units, volunteer to form subgroups and take on different projects. The committee guarantees that there is always a library representative to participating in different campus initiatives, programs, and events. Members rotate off the committee at different years to ensure the work will not be impacted by the reposition or vacancy of individuals. Committee members from different library units also bring information back and serve in an advisory capacity to the whole library.

Outreach to International Students

New Students Orientation is the first chance for students to get a glimpse of campus life and is an opportunity for the University of Minnesota Libraries' initial interaction with the students. As new international students orientation programs are probably mandatory in most universities, this is a great way to meet and get connected with international students. Since 2010, the University of Minnesota Libraries has been a key supporter of a variety of international students' orientation programs and activities hosted by the university's International Student and Scholar Services (ISSS). In addition to tabling at resource fairs during the new students' orientation events each fall semester, the new transfer students' orientation each spring semester, and some mid-term refresher programs, the libraries also provides open workshops and library tours to help international students navigate the physical and virtual library. Due to the voluntary nature of the workshops and tours and the fact students are usually overwhelmed at the beginning of a semester, we also tried to create materials that could be used by students at their own pace. In 2010, the libraries created a library brochure to introduce basic library resources and services to international students. Along with this English-language brochure, a Chinese version was also released, since about 50 percent of our international students came from China. A Korean version was created in 2013. The three versions of the brochure were uploaded to the library's website and were distributed to thousands of international students. After years of effort, the university's ISSS office now includes our brochures in the information package sent to all students prior to their travel to the US. This resource is also included in the annual ISSS adviser resource guide for new undergraduate international students. This brochure familiarizes new international students with the library and serves as a useful tool for academic advisors.

Audio-visual materials have been utilized in library orientations and instructions since the 1970s.[1] Today, advancements in technology makes it much easier and less costly to create streaming videos. Considering the popularity and effectiveness of audio-visual materials in learning, we created a welcome video for all new and transfer students in 2015. The video was originally planned to target the international student population. During a conversation with our undergraduate services librarian, we realized that all students could benefit from this video. Instructional design staff and the library's Communication Office were invited to participate in this project. In this welcome video, viewers are presented with a virtual tour of the library with a voiceover narration as well as an introduction to major services. One of our librarians welcomes and says goodbye to students at the beginning and end of the video to offer a friendly and approachable image of the library. Still images were used for most parts of the video, along with a transcript for easy captioning, allowing the content to be updated easily.

Building on orientation events, the English-language librarians are connected through academic units that primarily serve this student population. Housed under the College of Continuing Education, the Minnesota English Language Program (MELP) provides both credit-bearing and non-credit courses in English as a Second Language (ESL) at the University of Minnesota. The courses are designed to help non-native English speakers improve their listening, reading, writing, and speaking skills for success in the university classroom or in the workplace. MELP's coursework is based on skill and practical knowledge, such as pronunciation, grammar, listening, and speaking skills. Two main opportunities the library has that tie into the courses are in the Academic Writing and Speaking for Academic Purposes courses. In the Academic Writing course, students are expected to write an eight-page research paper. Throughout the course, students are guided through the process, from topic development to outlining and writing. Our library instruction mirrors this incremental approach. Often, the librarians are able to come into the course twice. During the first visit, we tour the library in small groups and discuss topic development and what is appropriate for an eight-page paper through mind mapping. From this, we distill the main concepts and how to apply keywords. Then we search the discovery tool to find books and articles for their paper. In the second session, we build on previous knowledge by introducing citation management tools and more specialized databases by subject. For the Speaking for Academic Purposes course, the librarians often give presentations on slide design, presentation techniques, and where to find copyright-free images. Many of the courses require students to practice their speeches in the library's 1:Button Studio, which is a plug-and-play recording studio. In addition, the library purchased a subscription to Lynda.com and various other streaming videos about public speaking that faculty use and require for students to view as part of their courses. Through these two courses, we begin to introduce a wide variety of resources and services the library provides that include hands-on experiences. By teaming up with subject librarians to create library support pages designed for specific courses with ESL-designated sections, we can reach more students across a variety of disciplines. ESL 3007 English for Physics is one example of a collaborative Library Course Page. We worked with the physics librarian to include physics foundation texts, reference materials, and links to videos that go along with each course week. This collaboration is beneficial because the English-language librarians know how to organize the information in a meaningful way while the physics librarian brings the subject expertise for reference resources.

The majority of MELP courses are not research-focused, and students may not have opportunities to use the library's extensive research resources and services. To explore new ways to reach out to MELP and raise awareness of a breadth of library services, the English-language librarians contributed an APP column in *Just for Fun*, a bi-weekly MELP newsletter distributed to all MELP students and instructors. The column introduces mobile applications that facilitate English-language learning. The higher education edition of the *2014 New Media Centers (NMC) Horizon Report* predicted that social media would be one of the "driving changes in higher education over the next one to two years."[2] In the 2017 report, NMC confirms the importance of social media technology and describes it as an integral part of our lives that will continue to "evolve at a rapid pace."[3] This exploration of mobile applications for learning purposes is a great way to reach out to students in an effective and relaxed manner. Mobile devices are playing an increasing role in both informal and formal education. It is a perfect place to teach information and media literacy. During one academic semester, seven applications were introduced to MELP students. The applications were selected based on certain criteria and had to meet several requirements, including low storage space needs, adequate privacy and security settings, and that they would not slow down the speed of devices. New features of mobile device software were also introduced. The Google Translate mobile application, for instance, allows instant text translation by focusing on the text with the device camera. The applications were selected to make students' learning and life easier and fun. The column was well received by the students and we were approached to contribute a new series of columns that introduce library research strategies.

In addition to MELP, the first-year writing courses became another great opportunity to engage students. This course is mandated for all new and transfer international undergraduate students, and librarians are usually invited to conduct a one-shot library instruction session. Library staff, who teach the sessions, are provided with a pre-formatted, standard syllabus, which is used to teach all first-year writing students, both domestic and international. It has been challenging to deliver the pre-formatted information to international students during a short period of time, and course instructors reported that the sessions were helpful but too overwhelming for the students. Some course instructors tried to break library instructions into smaller chunks and teach them in their own classroom but risked providing students with incorrect library information or concepts. For example, one instructor tried to introduce the concept of subject headings and explained that by selecting "subject" instead of "any" with a keyword in the library catalog search box, the user would receive more relevant results. This illustrates that ongoing collaboration with instructors and coordination of research skills both in the classroom and supplemented with online tutorials are needed in most courses.

Collaborating with faculty to teach information literacy has been well documented in library literature. In a few cases, librarians also partner with non-faculty specialists, such as writing specialists,[4] teaching assistants,[5] tutors,[6] and peer mentors.[7] As much as we would like to seek meaningful collaborations, in reality, that is not always easy. For example, many instructors request that the English-language librarians teach databases and the mechanics of searching, rather than the different dimensions of information literacy and the complexity of the research process. We attempted to strategically foster a deeper collaborative relationship by creating a list of self-paced modules to introduce information literacy skills. Rather than a replacement for the one-shot library instruction sessions, these modules serve as a complementary resource for students and instructors, allowing instructors to focus on their priorities in the classroom and giving students the opportunity to systematically study research skills on their own. While the modules cover common stumbling blocks that students encounter during their assignments, they help enrich both the faculty's teaching experience and improve students' learning experience. First-year writing program administrators commented that this resource substantially complements the work they have done to support international student writers across the university.

Studies have shown that students frequently turn to their friends and classmates when needing assistance.[8] Keeping this in mind, we created the Peer Research Consultant (PRC) program in 2009. With the creation of the SMART Learning Commons in the mid-2000s—a program that offers peer tutoring and media project support—there was an opportunity for library-led, peer-delivered academic support services. The PRC program was envisioned to help students with the library research process. Another PRC program goal is to support and hire students from traditionally underrepresented groups. We consider diversity training and experience as a requirement for peer-research consultants and try to include international students in the hiring. Information literacy techniques and strategies instruction are provided by our undergraduate services librarian, and day-to-day supervision and operational management are performed by our SMART Learning Commons coordinator. These peer consultants are not tutors in subject disciplines but rather are research consultants who provide one-on-one assistance to develop strategies and locate resources for research papers. They host drop-in hours in several libraries and are located where a lot of MELP students visit, the International Student and Scholar Services and Multicultural Center for Academic Excellence offices. In the 2016–2017 academic year, we provided more than 150 one-on-one consultations through the program, supporting mostly writing studies courses but also psychology and a variety of other courses. Student feedback has been very positive, including: "My experience with my peer research consultant went very well. She was willing to help me narrow my research topic and guided me in finding the appropriate sources for it. Overall, my peer research consultant boosted my confidence in exceeding in this paper." "The PRC helped simplify my search for articles. She was very knowledgeable in many resources. She was also great at being mindful of my particular style of brainstorming, which I really appreciated."

The libraries have also been making efforts to actively participate in existing national and university-wide initiatives and projects to engage international students. Since 2008, we have been celebrating the annual International Education Week, a joint initiative of the US Department of State and the US Department of Education that aims to celebrate the benefits of international education and exchange worldwide. This event is usually celebrated in November, and we find it is a perfect platform to bring both domestic and international students together to enhance their mutual understanding. American students are prepared for a global environment on campus through our diverse collection and staff expertise. International students are invited to exchange their experiences. In the past nine years, our library has been inventively exploring different approaches to enhance programs that integrate our resources and services into academic and non-academic programs and activities on campus. One year, the international studies librarians, area studies librarians, and other library experts from the arts and humanities and social sciences (e.g., journalism, history, political science, linguistics, etc.) hosted a one-stop consultation panel to provide research and non-research assistance to participants. Another year, we teamed up with archivists to stage a pop-up library in a busy student hub building to introduce and showcase our diverse collections and answer questions on site. Also, a library scavenger hunt was designed to encourage students to explore valuable collections located in lesser-known locations. For example, students were introduced to the only stand-alone South Asian collection in an academic library in the United States, one of the world's leading repositories of research materials on South Asia. In addition to hosting events for external users, we sent out one email every day to all library staff during this week with background information about the internationalization initiatives on campus and in the library field, including tips on open-mindedness and serving a diverse group of patrons. This series of events highlights the indispensable role the library plays in higher education and increases the visibility and presence of the library on campus.

In another highly visible interaction, librarians participated in the New International Student Seminar Moodle course, coordinated by the university's ISSS office. This online course is designed to help new and transfer international students adjust to the US and university culture, classroom etiquette, and academic expectations after they have been enrolled for a month or so. All new and transfer students are required to attend this online forum in order to register for their next semester's courses. There are five categories in which students could post their questions and share their experiences: writing papers, English language, classroom success, cultural adjustment, and health and safety. Staff from different campus units volunteered to moderate their preferred topic(s). This forum offers a relaxing mode in which moderators can interact with students about their university life, both academic and non-academic. Volunteer moderators do not grade students but rather have a conversation about topics they are interested in. In this forum, librarians can highlight our resources, services, and campus connection expertise to international students at their points of need on a daily basis. The participation in this program establishes an approachable image for the library. More importantly, it strengthens the collaboration between the library and the other student-supporting units, fostering future collaboration opportunities. This participation and collaboration arose out of conversations that took place in Academic Resources for International Students, an informal international student academic support group initiated by the former chair of the Diversity Leadership Committee.

Outreach to Staff Across Campus

International students often turn to the library for assistance with everything from research support to referrals to additional support that may be offered elsewhere across our campus. Since the University of Minnesota serves 60,000 students, there are many offices spread across two cities, and often they are in siloes that do not talk to one another. In addition, academic support units may have competing priorities, with each trying to promote their unique services to support teaching and learning. This is why the libraries initiated a group to coordinate campus-wide services and referrals. In 2013, the Academic Resources for International Students group was formed with the intention of bringing together groups on campus that offer academic support-related services to better serve our international students. Twelve key units that participate in this group meet bi-monthly, including the Office for Student Conduct and Counseling Services, SMART Learning Commons, the Department of Writing Studies, and the Center for Education Innovation, to name a few. As the initiator, the libraries have been a part of this group from the very start.

This group coordinates the Global Gopher event every spring to bring awareness of our services to international students via tours and an exhibit fair. However, this was not enough; we needed a resource geared not just to students but also to the front-line staff, such as advisors and faculty that might not get questions on a regular basis. The team of departments created the informal Academic Resources for International Students site (http://z.umn.edu/internationalstudents). The Google Sites-hosted platform was selected because it is easy to navigate, update, and suited our needs for this pilot project. Content was developed by all areas of campus, and rather than organizing items by department, resources and tools are integrated to support students' needs, such as adjusting to US culture, stress management, and paper-writing resources. Helpful icons were developed so a student or advisor could look through the resources easily and know if they were available by drop-in or by appointment, or if they were meant to be one-on-one assistance or in a group setting. This tool has proved helpful for library service desk staff, who often are approached by students looking for assistance with writing a paper or needing guidance on what services are provided across campus. Serving on cross-campus working groups allows us to reach out to all campus units to promote our resources and services and integrate them into the workflow of the campus.

We believe that an increased awareness of international students' backgrounds, their needs, and challenges will enhance our understanding of their information-seeking behaviors and our ability to offer tailored services. Our library is committed to exploring ways to empower and support our staff to in turn support international students. In addition to the email message sent out to all library staff members during the International Education Week, we host other events to learn about international students. For example, we invited an international student panel to have a conversation with public services staff and non-public-facing employees. We also invited ISSS to come in for a tailored training session to equip staff with knowledge and skills on working effectively with international students, scholars, and colleagues. We encourage staff to attend programs and activities on campus, such as the biannual Internationalizing the Curriculum and Campus Conference, to engage with a diverse group of scholars and students.

All these resources aim to help students and staff find success throughout the academic year. These programs and activities enrich international students' learning and cultural experiences; they also provide staff with opportunities to develop professionally and become diversity leaders and advocates. The Diversity Leadership Committee plays a key role in delivering and coordinating library services to international students. In addition to annual reflection on the work with international students, the committee is currently conducting a more systematic assessment to evaluate our existing services and identify areas for potential improvement.

Internationalizing campuses across the United States has been an ongoing mission of American higher education. Our library continues to work with collegiate units to ensure international students have a memorable and beneficial stay at the University of Minnesota.

Notes

1. Necia Parker-Gibson, "Reference and Media-Instruction by Any Means Necessary," *The Reference Librarian* 31, no. 65 (1999): 65.
2. New Media Centers, "NMC Horizon Report 2014 Higher Education Edition," 2014: 8, accessed February 20, 2017, http://www.nmc.org/publication/nmc-horizon-report-2014-higher-education-edition/.
3. New Media Centers, "NMC Horizon Report 2017 Higher Education Edition," 2017: 37, 2017), accessed February 20, 2017, http://www.nmc.org/publication/nmc-horizon-report-2017-higher-education-edition/.
4. Peggy A. Pritchard, "The Embedded Science Librarian: Partner in Curriculum Design and Delivery," *Journal of Library Administration* 50, no. 4 (2010): 376.
5. Sue Samson and Michelle S. Millet, "The Learning Environment: First-Year Students, Teaching Assistants, and Information Literacy," *Research Strategies* 19, no. 2 (2003): 84.

6. Laura Brady, Nathalie Singh-Corcoran, Jo Ann Dadisman, and Kelly Diamond, "A Collaborative Approach to Information Literacy: First-year Composition, Writing Center, and Library Partnerships at West Virginia University," *Composition Forum* 19 (2009): 1.
7. Rachel Callison, Dan Budny, and Kate Thomes, "Library Research Project for First-year Engineering Students: Results from Collaboration by Teaching and Library Faculty," *The Reference Librarian* 43, no. 89–90 (2005): 99.
8. Alison J. Head, "Project Information Literacy: What Can Be Learned about the Information-Seeking Behavior of Today's College Students?," paper presented at the ACRL Conference, Indianapolis, Indiana, April 10–13, 2013.

Bibliography

Brady, Laura, Nathalie Singh-Corcoran, Jo Ann Dadisman, and Kelly Diamond. "A Collaborative Approach to Information Literacy: First-year Composition, Writing Center, and Library Partnerships at West Virginia University." *Composition Forum* 19 (2009): 1–18.

Callison, Rachel, Dan Budny, and Kate Thomes. "Library Research Project for First-Year Engineering Students: Results from Collaboration by Teaching and Library Faculty." *The Reference Librarian* 43, no. 89–90 (2005): 93–106.

Head, Alison J. "Project Information Literacy: What Can Be Learned about the Information-seeking Behavior of Today's College Students?" Paper presented at the ACRL Conference, Indianapolis, Indiana, April 10–13, 2013.

New Media Centers. "NMC Horizon Report 2014 Higher Education Edition" (2014). Accessed February 20, 2017. http://www.nmc.org/publication/nmc-horizon-report-2014-higher-education-edition/.

New Media Centers. "NMC Horizon Report 2017 Higher Education Edition" (2017). Accessed February 20, 2017. http://www.nmc.org/publication/nmc-horizon-report-2017-higher-education-edition/.

Parker-Gibson, Necia. "Reference and Media-Instruction by Any Means Necessary." *The Reference Librarian* 31, no. 65 (1999): 61–78.

Pritchard, Peggy A. "The Embedded Science Librarian: Partner in Curriculum Design and Delivery." *Journal of Library Administration* 50, no. 4 (2010): 373–96.

Samson, Sue, and Michelle S. Millet. "The Learning Environment: First-Year Students, Teaching Assistants, and Information Literacy." *Research Strategies* 19, no. 2 (2003): 84–98.

SECTION II

Outreach & Inclusion

CHAPTER EIGHT

Faraway Flix:

Connecting to International Students through Film

Laura Bohuski

WKU has, at any given time, about 20,000 students enrolled in university programs across four campuses. WKU is a campus that is actively engaged in making international connections, so much so that its current vision statement asserts that WKU is "a leading American university with international reach."[1] Western's drive to establish and maintain international connections has been successful: of the 20,000 students currently attending WKU, 1,300 are international students from 70 seventy different countries.[2] With such a diverse student population, many of the departments at Western are actively engaged in developing programs to help connect our extensive international population with the rest of the student body. The library program that was developed out of this vision would become the film series called Faraway Flix.

Development

In the early 2010s, the library at Western's main campus was trying to develop a way to connect with the international student population. While many international students frequently visited the library to study, many of them were also student workers for the library. The director of the International Student Office, or the ISO, together with employees at the library, first attempted to put together a video representing the international student's experiences in the library. This video was developed with the idea of attracting new international students to use the library, to make those students feel welcome, and to promote the library as another place on campus where the international student population could come and develop a relationship with the campus community.

Unfortunately, this video, when finished, did not convey the welcoming feeling that either the International Student Office or the library wished to express. The video, meant to invite the international students into the library and into the community, wound up feeling more like an advertisement or promotional video. The video was scrapped but both the library and the International Student Office still wanted to make international students feel more comfortable on and connected to campus.

Even though the video failed, the idea of outreach through the medium of videos or film was still favored by both departments. The idea was then broached for an international film series. This proposal was backed from multiple sides because of the personal experience of the program's developers and from input from international students within the library. Most notably, one of the library staff members that spearheaded the development of the Faraway Flix program immigrated to the United States with her family. When dealing with her culture shock, films about her home country were comforting reminders of the culture she had left behind.

International students struggle with feeling disconnected from their community and their surroundings, even if other students from their country or ethnicity are in their program with them. The idea of a film program was appealing because, if developed correctly, the program could provide students with a feeling of home and an opportunity to share their culture with others. With these concepts in mind, the library created a committee of staff and faculty members from multiple departments, along with a representative from the International Student Office, with the thought of launching a new film program in the 2013–2014 school year.

The committee was drawn from three different departments to try and create a well-balanced committee. Since the library had initiated the idea and would be staffing the events, three to four members of the committee came from within different library departments. The other members of the committee were each drawn from different departments to help support the film series. The other members of the committee consist of one member from the film department to help with the film selections, one member from the International Student Office to help keep the committee up to date on the needs of the international students, and one committee member from the Student Activities Office (SAO) in a supporting role to make sure that the Faraway Flix event nights worked within the student activities events schedule—a total of about seven committee members at any given time.

In the beginning, one of the main purposes of the International Student Office was to supply the libraries with information about the demographics of the international student population—mainly, which countries were most heavily represented on campus. For WKU, these countries were Saudi Arabia, Brazil, and China. While the demographics helped the committee select which countries to choose films from initially, the library didn't want to limit themselves to showing films from the same three countries every year. Beyond wanting diversity in their film selections, the committee also wanted to be sure that the chosen films were comforting and welcoming to international students. This decision limited the type of film that the committee was willing to show, as both the library and the ISO did not want to hold viewings for films that focused on controversial topics, such as religion or politics.

For example, one of Western Kentucky's largest international student populations comes from Saudi Arabia, but this country is steeply divided along many different cultural, political, and religious lines. For these and other reasons, the Faraway Flix committee resolved early in their development that they wanted to choose films that were more about an aspect of culture or the society of the country described in the film. The committee decided to not show films that focused on high-tension issues, as these topics would likely bring tension into the international community present at the viewings instead of providing a safe and welcoming space. Because of this reasoning, in 2012 there were no films from Saudi Arabia that the committee was comfortable showing to the campus community, even though students from Saudi Arabia are one of Western's largest international populations. Instead, they chose to show a Middle Eastern film called *Caramel* in the film series' second year to help represent an aspect of Middle Eastern culture while still maintaining a fun and welcoming atmosphere.

Once the committee had decided on what kind of films to show, it had to make other decisions on the series. The committee decided that one film per full semester month, or three films per semester, was a good disbursement of films, without draining too many resources from the committee members, the library, and the ISO. Other initial committee decisions included the decision to provide culturally or ethnically appropriate food as related to the film, that Friday nights were the best evenings on which to host the events, and the best location to show the films.

2013–2014 Academic Year: Year One

For the first year, the committee chose to show the following films: *A Simple Life* (China), *The Lives of Others* (Germany), *Kahaani* (India), *Whale Rider* (New Zealand), *A Separation* (Iran), and *First Grader* (Kenya). The first film in the series was chosen in part because of the large Chinese student population that existed at WKU. To continue to attract students in following years, and to give the committee time to find culturally appropriate films, movies for the other two large international populations were delayed for subsequent years. The film *Caramel*, from Lebanon, was shown in the 2014–2015 academic year as a look into aspects of Saudi Arabian culture until the committee found a film they were comfortable showing. Two years later, in the 2016–2017 academic year, *Wadjda* was a newly released Saudi Arabian film that the committee was finally able to comfortably show. A Brazilian film, *The Way He Looks*, was shown in the intervening 2015–2016 academic year and appealed to the other large international population on campus.

Another incentive the committee provided to attract domestic as well as international students to the event was the offer of free food. The choice to provide themed food for the students was not a difficult decision, though it proved difficult to execute. In the first year, funding for Faraway Flix was solely provided by the library and the International Student Office. With these budgetary restrictions, funds for food and other additions, such as door prizes, were scarce. So, in the first year of Faraway Flix, people on the committee or members of the international community who volunteered brought ethnically appropriate food to each of the six films. While bringing in food worked, it was also a bit disorganized and could be both time-consuming and expensive.

Providing food as part of the session also influenced where the films were to be screened. The committee wanted a space that was easily accessible, had both a comfortable atmosphere and comfortable seating, had the technology available to show a film (a projector and a film screen), allowed food, and was routinely available on a Friday night. While these restrictions might not seem like they would severely limit where these events could be held, there were very few spaces left to the committee that met all their requirements and did not require a fee to use.

Eventually, the committee was able to reserve the Faculty House, a wooden house that was formerly a student center and had now become a venue for a variety of WKU events. The building has a rustic, cozy charm and is stocked with chairs and couches that can be configured in a variety of ways. There is also technology available to project a movie and food is allowed inside the building. The only big issue with the space is the problem of having to both arrange and breakdown the furniture for every event. Because the Faculty House is used consistently for events, the committee had to set up the chairs and couches at the beginning of the evening and then take them down before leaving, which added an hour to the time the committee had to spend at the events.

The main problems that Faraway Flix dealt with in its first year narrowed down to funding and working out issues that developed in the course of launching a new film series, including event location, the timing of food and the arrival of guest speakers, and making sure that the films shown were appropriate for the audience while being engaging enough so that students would them and return. These were all issues that Faraway Flix faced during its first year and, to some extent, still face even now. Then, because of the creation of a campus-wide initiative during Faraway Flix's second year, some of these issues were mitigated or changed.

2014–2017: Year Two to Present

During Faraway Flix's first year, another program, as a part of international outreach and growth, was being launched. This program is known at Western as IYO or the International Year Of. The IYO website states that:

> "The International Year Of... program is intended to provide the WKU campus and surrounding community with a rich, complex sense of place and interconnectedness through a year-long celebration of a single country. Throughout the school year, exploration of and interaction with the country occurs in multiple ways—including, but not limited to: enhanced course work featuring country-specific content; co-curricular activities; research projects; education abroad program offerings; visiting scholars, performers, and specialists; new institutional partnerships; campus and community events with a country-specific focus; cultural events, exhibits, and lectures."[3]

This program is a part of Western's goal to be an internationally relevant and inclusive university, and it has encouraged and led to the development of many new and interesting events on WKU's campus each year.

With the initialization of the first IYO event series, the Faraway Flix committee decided that aligning their content with the International Year Of... could only improve Faraway Flix. When deciding on films for the 2014–2015 academic year, the committee decided that one of those films should come from Ecuador, the first International Year Of... country. The committee could apply for a grant from the IYO office to fund both the specific IYO film that year and to help support the rest of the series as the funds provided by the IYO grant had to be matched by departmental support. With these funds, along with those provided by the Student Activities Office, Faraway Flix could make some changes. The funds were used to support both a new food service for the film and more door prizes for the students.

After receiving the grant from IYO, Faraway Flix could afford an agreement with Western's food vendor, Aramark. For every event, Aramark caters a selection of ethnically appropriate food; this lifted some of the time and monetary commitment from the committee members. This grant also freed up funds previously used to support the "catering" of the film events to improve the type of door prizes available to the students.

While some of the door prizes offered to students for attending these events were Western or community-specific, such as gift cards to local restaurants or WKU water bottles, with additional funds the committee could provide film and country-specific prizes as well. The larger prizes of the evening reflect the event itself by representing the two different aspects promoted by each event: film studies and international culture. The first door prize is a book. This book is usually about the film industry of the country or maybe the history of or the influences of film within the country being explored.

The second main door prize is a basket of food that comes from the represented country. The committee works carefully to select products made in or by the country to which the film corresponds. Because the budget is still low, around twenty-five to thirty dollars for each film including the cost of the book, getting a variety of products that match our specifications is sometimes difficult. Shopping at online outlets like Amazon or going to world markets both locally and in Nashville, Tennessee, helps us keep bringing in good door prizes while staying within budget.

Another change during this time was the room. The Faculty House, while providing a sufficient space to host the event, did have some problems. It took an hour for the committee to set up and break down the seating for the event, and though there were sofas and a few large comfy chairs, most of the seating was hard wooden chairs. Also, we had to continually bring a laptop to the room to show the film, even though there was a projector and a screen provided. The committee decided that if a better situation could be found, it would be useful to move the event and may attract more students if it was in a better location. Fortunately, one of our committee members is associated with the film department, which has a theater/auditorium room in Cherry Hall—one of the campus' original historical buildings that houses the English, History, and Film departments—that has built-in theater seating, allows food, and includes a projector, a DVD player, and a screen to show the film. The shift to this room reduced the strain on the committee members on event nights and made the event run smoother.

Over the course of this three-year span, 2014–2017, Faraway Flix aired eighteen films from eighteen different countries. Combined with the films from its first year, Faraway Flix has held twenty-four events over the course of four years. Each event has averaged

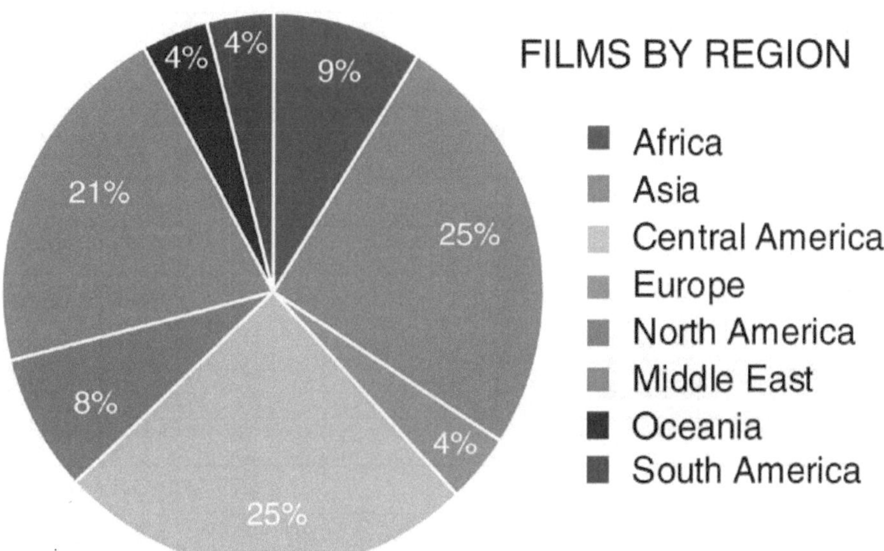

Figure 8.1. Films by Region

about twenty attendees, with some event participation as low as four (an outlier) and some as high as fifty. The following tables show a breakdown of the films chosen by region, country, and the number of attendees. Unfortunately, the attendance numbers for most of the first year's films are unavailable. *First Grader*, the Kenyan film, had an attendance of twenty-six people, and photos from other events show a similar attendance level, though no official counts exist.

TABLE 8.1
Faraway Flix Master List 2013–2017

COUNTRY	FILM	# of Attendees	CONTINENT/ REGION
Kenya	*First Grader*	26	Africa
South Africa	*Tsotsi*	17	Africa
China	*A Simple Life*	[Unavailable]	Asia
India	*Kahaani*	[Unavailable]	Asia
Japan	*Dark Water*	29	Asia
Thailand	*Uncle Boonmee Who Can Recall His Past Lives*	23	Asia
Philippines	*That Thing Called Tadhana*	16	Asia
South Korea	*A Brand New Life*	28	Asia
Ecuador	*Que Tan Lejos*	49	Central America
Czech Republic	*Autumn Spring*	20	Europe
Germany	*The Lives of Others*	[Unavailable]	Europe
France	*Une Hirondelle a Fait le Printemps*	11	Europe
Italy	*Suspiria*	37	Europe
Ireland	*Once*	28	Europe
Sweden	*The 100 Year Old Man*	15	Europe
Mexico/ Germany	*Guten Tag, Ramon*	4	Europe & North America
Iran	*A Separation*	[Unavailable]	Middle East
Lebanon	*Caramel*	15	Middle East
Saudi Arabi	*Wadjda*	28	Middle East
Iran	*A Girl Walks Home Alone at Night*	17	Middle East
Israel	*Footnote*	14	Middle East
Native America	*Smoke Signals*	18	North America
New Zealand	*Whale Rider*	[Unavailable]	Oceania
Brazil	*The Way He Looks*	36	South America

Future

Going forward, Faraway Flix is facing some new challenges. Over the past few years, Kentucky has greatly reduced spending on higher education and the university is having to drastically reduce its extraneous spending. One of the programs taking a cut is Faraway Flix, and this means the committee will also lose the grant funding from IYO. As stated above, a committee or event can only apply for funding from the International Year Of... if there is a department that will match IYO's grant. Since the library can no longer provide funds to Faraway Flix, we cannot apply for the grant.

Without the grant and the library funds, the extras that Faraway Flix can provide are drastically reduced. There will be no more catered food brought by Aramark to the events, and if no other funding is received, it is possible that the food door prizes will have to be removed as well. Fortunately, the library may be willing to donate the film books for door prizes for each event instead of providing monetary funds.

To compensate for the lack of food and other funding, the committee has decided to provide popcorn at each event along with a reusable plastic cup. Each time a student comes to an event, they will get a sticker or mark on the cup. The people at the end of the year/semester with the most marks or stickers will be entered into a drawing for a grand door prize, which we hope to get with funds provided by the Student Activities Office, which has been a partner of Faraway Flix since its inaugural year.

Running Faraway Flix

Committee work on Faraway Flix is generally light throughout the year. The first commitment is the six nights a year that committee members attend the film events, though consideration is given to personal schedules, and not all committee members are required to attend every event. Besides the event nights, the committee usually meets three to four times a year to discuss next year's movies and any new issues that might have arisen over the course of the academic year.

Early in the spring semester, the committee members meet to determine which countries the film series is going to highlight next year and which movies to select from those countries. Since the committee wants to provide a comforting environment for international students but also attract an audience for the events, the committee tries to pick recent films, typically nothing over ten years old and preferably nothing older than five years, if appropriate movies can be found. The only other requirement for these films, currently, is that these films should highlight a cultural theme.

It is the committee's responsibility to find and maintain contact with faculty and other campus community members to be able to find a speaker to come and talk about the international and cultural aspect of these films. Speakers have included faculty, staff, international students, as well as friends from the Bowling Green community. While this program is focused on both international and domestic students, WKU faculty, staff, and other members of the campus community are welcomed and encouraged to attend. On the other hand, while people from the community outside of Western can come to the event if they hear about the films from friends or colleagues, the library and the committee are not allowed to promote the event to the off-campus community to adhere to legal requirements.

Once the films have been chosen and the speakers contacted, then the other tasks for the committee are given out to individuals. The first task is to request that the WKU library order those films chosen for the following year, as the films become a part of Western's leisure film collection after they are used for the Faraway Flix events. Simultaneously, a different committee member is the contact for Aramark and orders the menus for each event and confirms that Aramark will be arriving the night of the event. Another two members oversee the acquisition of door prizes, ordering books from Amazon and going to local world grocery stores to buy the culturally appropriate foods. Other members go out to local restaurants and stores to see if they could provide door prizes for event nights. Overall, event nights make up the bulk of the committee work but they are also the best part.

A Routine Event Night

A routine event night begins in the weeks before the event happens with the advertising of the event through email, digital and physical posters, and social media. The committee also sends a faculty-all email requesting that faculty members inform their students about the opportunity to view our film, as it is an event that can be counted for credit in some courses. Though we do not advertise outside of the Western community, we advertise through as many WKU avenues as possible.

On the night of the event, there is no longer much set up required by the committee members. With the change of location to the film room in Cherry Hall, the committee should arrive about half an hour before the set time of the event. This allows the members time to open the room, set up the door prizes, and set out slips for students to fill out to sign up for the door prizes. These slips also serve to create an email list for future Faraway Flix events. At the same time, Aramark is setting up the food outside of the room so that audience members can get a plate of food as they enter the room.

At the set start time of the event, the committee chair or another member introduces our speaker for the evening. The speaker then introduces the film and some topics for consideration for the audience to contemplate as they view the film. This introduction usually only lasts a few minutes, and then the film begins. It is after the film has ended that the main discussion begins. The duration and depth of the discussion depend entirely on the audience. The more audience members there are, the more engaged they are and the better the discussion. We also seem to have better discussions on the nights of the annual International Year Of… events. The reasons these discussions are better have not been extensively studied, though we do usually have more people at the IYO events than on other nights.

After the film and discussion are completed, the night ends quickly. Students are given the opportunity to swipe their cards through a swiper, or an identification reader, so that their participation in the event is recorded. There is some lingering discussion among the remaining audience members and the committee checks the room for any spare plates or food left behind. The room is locked up and Aramark returns to remove any leftover food. Overall, the events are easy to set up, not time-consuming, and can pull in anywhere from twenty to fifty audience members.

Conclusion

Faraway Flix began in 2013 as a way to encourage international students to become more involved with the campus community and to give domestic students a look at cultures different from their own. Since its inception, Faraway Flix has grown through support from Western Kentucky University and is still a successful event series heading into its fifth year. As an educational event, with discussions about both the film and the country being represented, the films are free for viewing. The attraction of a free movie, food, and door prizes help bring students to the events, and the welcoming atmosphere brings back both international and domestic students. The time needed to plan and host these events is fairly low, with most of the time commitment limited to attending the six event nights. But with good food, good movies, and interesting discussions, these events are often a fun night out.

Notes

1. "About WKU," the website for Western Kentucky University, last modified January 14, 2016, http://www.wku.edu/about/.
2. "International Enrollment Management," the website for Western Kentucky University, last modified February 15, 2017, https://www.wku.edu/international/.
3. "International Year Of…," the website for Western Kentucky University, last modified October 10, 2016, http://www.wku.edu/iyo/aboutiyo.php.

Bibliography

"About WKU." Website for Western Kentucky University. Last modified January 14, 2016. http://www.wku.edu/about/.

"International Enrollment Management." Website for Western Kentucky University. Last modified February 15, 2017. https://www.wku.edu/international/.

"International Year Of…" Website for Western Kentucky University. Last modified October 10, 2016. http://www.wku.edu/iyo/aboutiyo.php.

CHAPTER NINE

Forging Multiple Pathways:

Integrating International Students into a Canadian University Library

Karen Bordonaro

This chapter will describe five different projects undertaken at the Brock University Library in St. Catharines, Ontario, Canada, which represent different pathways toward integrating international students into academic libraries. These projects were designed to welcome and introduce international students to the library as well as to support their extended learning by the library. Each of them represents a different type of pathway toward that goal of integration.

The five projects described in this chapter include the creation of a special welcome sign, the provision of a staff development workshop for student peer assistants, the construction of a specialized LibGuide, the development and use of an online library English as a Second Language (ESL) workbook and general online library tutorials, and the deployment of a self-access cart. These projects can easily be adapted to an American college context.

Brock University is a mid-sized university in Ontario, Canada with approximately 18,000 students, out of whom about 2,400 are international students. Of the total number of international students, about 1,800 are undergraduate students and about 600 are graduate students. Most of the students come from China (1,200), followed by students from India (150), Nigeria (130), the United States (50), Pakistan (50), Germany (40), and Saudi Arabia (40).

This chapter begins with a short foray into the library literature that deals with international students. It cites some examples in the literature of the many ways in which academic libraries have tried to integrate international students. This brief literature review is followed by descriptions of the five projects that form the main content of this chapter. Following these descriptions, the chapter ends with a consideration of how these projects offer multiple pathways for integrating international students into academic libraries.

Background Literature

The library literature on international students continues to grow. Although a recent systematic review[1] notes that it is not as prevalent as might be expected, it is still a topic that seems to be of more interest in recent literature than was the case in the past.[2]

Some of this literature offers examples of different ways that academic libraries have tried to integrate international students into their campuses. These ways include offering specialized library programming for international students, such as orientation workshops,[3] library instruction/information literacy sessions,[4] stand-alone online library tutorials,[5] and online video tours in different languages.[6]

Engaging in outreach efforts to international student groups on campus[7] is an additional method of integration found in the literature. This could also include direct marketing of library information to international students about available library resources and services.[8,9]

Other ways to integrate international students into academic libraries focus on librarians' abilities to work more effectively with them. Examples include broadening librarians' linguistic and cultural knowledge when working with non-native speakers of English[10–14] and offering tips for enhancing one-on-one interactions with these students in library settings.[15]

Librarians working with other campus partners is another way found in the literature that can serve to better integrate international students into North American libraries. Examples here include librarians working with international and multicultural student services staff[16] as well as with ESL instructors.[17]

A final method of integration worth highlighting in the literature is the attempt by librarians to better understand library experiences from the international students' own perspectives. This literature offers librarians insights into understanding the information-seeking behavior of international students[18] as well as diverse cultural perspectives on academic educational issues such as plagiarism[19] and class participation.[20]

The descriptions of the five projects offered in this chapter seek to bolster the library literature examples cited above. These projects offer further examples of ways in which academic librarians can try to integrate international students into their libraries. This chapter also offers the framework of multiple pathways as a more encompassing way to consider the importance of all these different ways to integrate international students.

Pathway One: Welcome Sign

The first pathway is an example of how librarians can broaden their awareness of the linguistic diversity that international students bring to campus. Its purpose is to promote the integration of international students into libraries through this heightened awareness.

This pathway took the form of a direct welcome. It involved the creation of a physical sign of welcome from the library to new international students, and it was created with direct input from the international students themselves. This project asked new international students to write "My name is _ and I come from _" in their native languages at an orientation program at the start of an academic year. The new international students were asked to do this in their own handwriting with a pen on paper in order to give the resulting poster a very authentic, individualized, and personal feel.

Once the poster was designed, it was printed and posted at the front door of the library; it also appeared in digital form on monitors inside the library. Many international

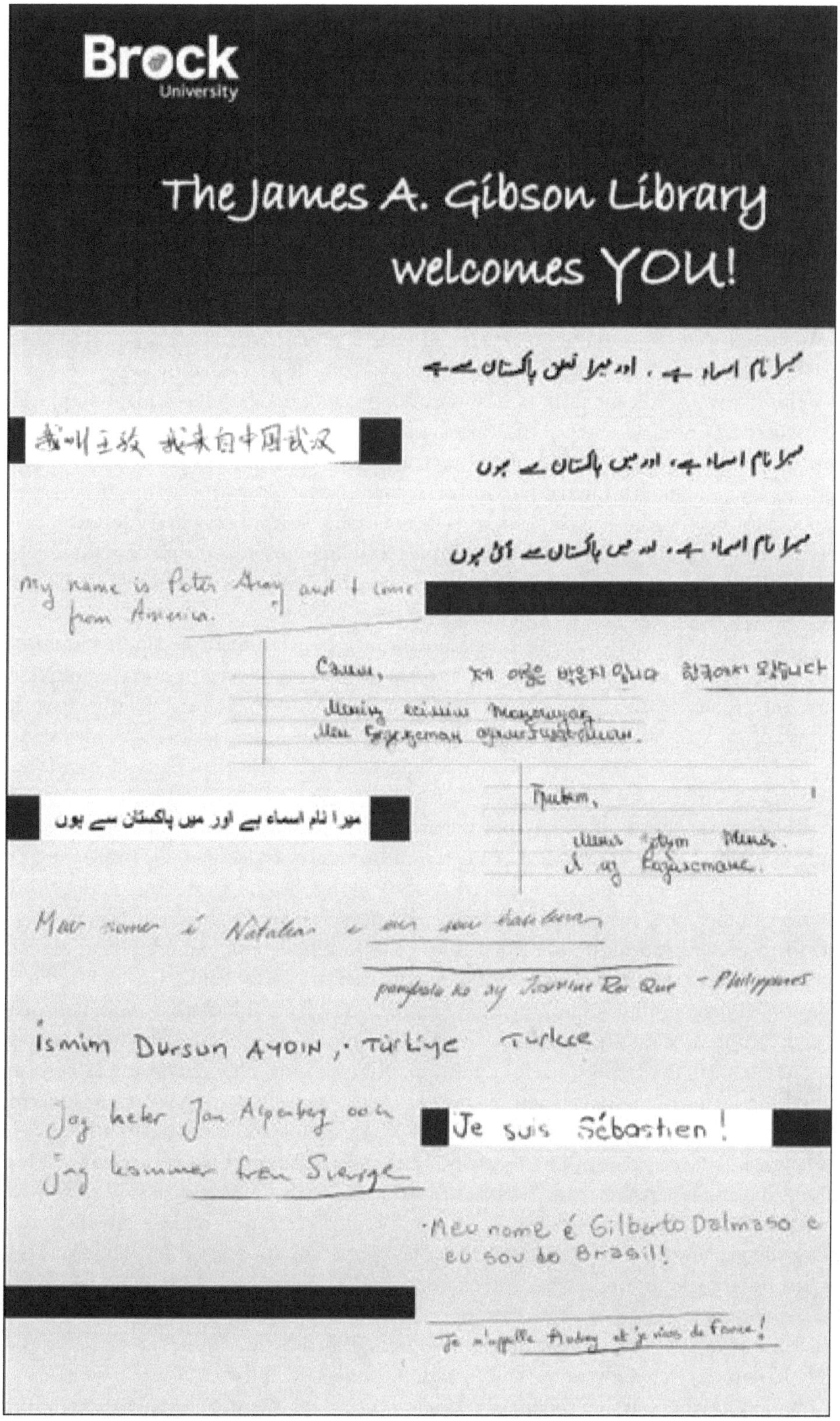

Brock University

The James A. Gibson Library welcomes YOU!

میرا نام اسماء ہے اور میں پاکستان سے ہوں

Je suis Sébastien!

Meu nome é Gilberto Dalmaso e eu sou do Brasil!

Figure 9.1. Welcome Sign.

students, both students who had signed as well as students who had not, appreciated the friendly gesture of welcome. They all expressed pleasure at seeing their native languages on display. This simple and small gesture from the library paid off large dividends in public goodwill from all international students on campus.

Pathway Two: Student Worker Development Workshop

The second pathway is an example of employing student peers to help librarians integrate international students into the library. Its purpose is to promote the integration of international students into libraries through student-to-student peer learning.

This pathway took the form of a staff development workshop for student employees who worked as peer assistants in the library. These library student peer assistants staff their own reception desk within our library and they often interact with international students on campus. An interactive workshop was conducted with them to discuss best practices for one-on-one interactions with international students at library service desks. The workshop began with each peer assistant receiving a paper slip that contained a tip or a statement about working with international students who are non-native speakers of English. The list of tips and statements appear below.

The workshop ran by having each student peer assistant read the tip or statement, then indicate if it made sense to them, and then had them add a personal example or experience if they wished. A short group discussion followed each tip. In this way, the content of each tip was covered by going around the table in a circle. Discussions were supplemented by my own experiences working with non-native speakers of English in libraries.

The tips and questions came from my own personal experience as an ESL instructor being applied to a library context. ESL teaching focuses on communicative strategies coming out of the four language skill areas of speaking, listening, reading, and writing. So, tip number one, for example, stresses the need for communication flowing back and forth between speaking partners. In another example, comprehensibility refers to a person making themselves understood, as opposed to comprehension, which refers to a person understanding something that someone else has said. Both comprehensibility and comprehension are important in a communication exchange. Further examples include stressing the importance of circumlocution—using different words to describe something if the original explanation was not clear. Another is using recasting, offering feedback indirectly in the form of a question—for example, saying, "In the stacks?" if a student asks for something "in the sticks." The most important tip is probably asking, "Does that make sense to you?" instead of asking, "Do you understand?" because the first question puts the responsibility for a successful interaction mainly on the person doing the explaining (i.e., the person at the service desk) as opposed to the person asking the question who might equate not understanding something with being personally deficient.

The conversation at this workshop was then guided by my inserting those types of explanations as given above into the discussion. I only added these further comments after the tip was read and the student peer offered their own interpretation, understanding, or experience with the particular tip.

This workshop was well received by the student peer assistants who added plenty of experiences of their own with international students to the discussion. It also underscored the important role that student peer assistants can make in helping international students adapt to a new academic climate.

The result of this workshop on peer assistants was a heightened sense of awareness when dealing with international students at the service desk. A copy of the tips was kept at the desk for referral. International students seemed to feel more comfortable coming up to this desk to ask individual questions of the peer assistants.

TIP SHEET FOR SUCCESSFUL INTERACTIONS

Working with International Students: Tips for Peer Assistants

Tip 1: Remember that every interaction is a two-way street. Both parties must participate and work with each other to make it successful.

Tip 2: Understand what comprehensibility is.

Tip 3: Understand what comprehension is.

Tip 4: Use circumlocution ("talking around").

Tip 5: Attitude makes a difference.

Tip 6: Use multiple learning styles.

Tip 7: Show sympathy, but practice empathy.

Tip 8: Be open to working with a third person.

Tip 9: Use conversation repair techniques: using fillers and pauses.

Tip 10: Another conversation repair technique: speaking more slowly. (How can you do this without sounding patronizing?)

Tip 11: Another conversation repair technique: admitting you did not understand what was asked.

Tip 12: Use recasting (offering feedback in the form of a question).

Tip 13: Don't correct people's grammar mistakes. (Why not?)

Tip 14: Observe successful interactions.

Tip 15: Learn from your own mistakes.

Tip 16: Read more about working with international students.

Tip 17: Attend lectures or programs on working with people from different cultures.

Tip 18: Make international students feel welcome. (How might you do this?)

Tip 19: Solicit feedback. ("Does that make sense to you?" is better than "Do you understand?")

Tip 20: Brainstorm with other staff members.

Tip 21: Try to learn another language yourself.

Tip 22: Smile.

Pathway Three: LibGuide

The third pathway is an example of developing online library material that international students can access individually on their own as a learning aid. Its purpose is to promote the integration of international students into libraries through online library support that points them to language-learning resources.

This pathway took the form of a LibGuide created for both international students who are non-native speakers of English and for domestic students who are learning a foreign language (http://researchguides.library.brocku.ca/international). Its intent was to show international students that other students on campus were language learners as well and that the library wanted to support them all equally.

The content of this LibGuide contains links to books, websites, online tutorials, writing guides, and other sites deemed helpful for both second- and foreign-language learners. The welcome section offers a link to "welcome" in many different languages and email contacts of library staff members who speak languages other than English. Contact information also includes my personal identification as a liaison librarian to international students and foreign language students as well as access to an online "book me" link tied to my personal meeting calendar.

Links to locally held language learning material available in and through our own library offer access to ESL material such as our library's collection of easy readers for English-language learners, the IELP (Intensive English Language Program) collection (http://catalogue.library.brocku.ca/search~S0?/tIELP+readers/tielp+readers/-3%2C-1%2C0%2CB/exact&FF=tielp+readers&1%2C529%2C), and books in our collection, such as *Succeeding as an International Student in the United States and Canada*[21] and *Study Skills for Speakers of English as a Second Language*.[22] Links to local ESL material also include access to the Accent Coach, a pronunciation program developed by a professor of Applied Linguistics at the university (http://www.englishaccentcoach.com/index.aspx). Local foreign-language learning material includes links to the Chinese book collection of the local Confucius Institute on campus (https://brocku.ca/confucius-institute/) as well as directions for finding further foreign-language learning material in specific foreign languages in our catalogue.

Links to websites outside of the library's holdings include, once again, both ESL and foreign-language sites, including Randall's ESL Cyber Listening Lab (http://www.esl-lab.com/), *Writing in North American Higher Education: A Primer for International Students* produced by OWL (the Online Writing Lab) at Purdue University (https://owl.english.purdue.edu/owl/resource/683/01/), and such sites as *Foreign Language Newspapers* (http://www.onlinenewspapers.com/) and *Ethnologue: Languages of the World* (https://www.ethnologue.com/).

Outcomes from making use of this LibGuide can be seen from increased statistics on page views. After the LibGuide was made available, its usage steadily increased over the course of time. Beginning with fewer than ten hits during the week when it first appeared, usage numbers gradually increased into the hundreds as time went on. At last check, the usage was more than 1,100 hits. Its direct impact on student work has not been formally measured to date but anecdotal accounts from both faculty and students have included "thank you"s for making it available; it has also been placed into course management systems pages for students to make use of as a language-learning resource.

The purpose of this LibGuide is to serve the language-learning needs of both non-native speakers of English as well as domestic students learning foreign languages.

Its uniqueness lies in serving both of those student populations through one vehicle in a stand-alone way. This represents another way for integrating international students into libraries by emphasizing that other students on campus are language learners as well and that the library supports them all.

Pathway Four: Online Library ESL Workbook and General Online Library Tutorials

The fourth pathway is another example of posting library material online for international students that they can refer to again and again as a means of extending their learning. Its purpose is to promote the continued integration of international students into libraries through ongoing online library support.

The online library workbook and tutorials described in this section also appear on the LibGuide described above. They are being considered as a separate pathway because they were created specifically to support the library needs of non-native English speakers rather than their language-learning needs, and because they flowed from a structured environment toward open individual use later on.

This pathway took the form of both an online library ESL workbook and general online library tutorials for international students who are non-native speakers of English. The online library ESL workbook was created as a supplemental tool for in-person ESL library workshops, and the general online library tutorials were made available in a specifically targeted way for international students, through a certificate program established by the campus office for international student services.

The online library ESL workbook (http://researchguides.library.brocku.ca/c.php?g=210701&p=2233745) was designed as a visual aid for in-person library instruction workshops for ESL student writing classes. It consists of a series of multiple-choice, true-false, and fill-in-the-blank questions. The questions are meant to be worked on by groups of students in library workshops, who then share their answers with the rest of the class until all the content is covered. The content appearing in the questions includes selecting good starting places, choosing keywords, using searching tips, evaluating results, and finding more good sources. Library skills that are meant to be identified and practiced through the use of this workbook encompass constructing effective search statements, using phrase searching, identifying subject headings, understanding what relevance means, and learning how to limit, sort, and evaluate results.

The utility of this online library ESL workbook lies in its simplicity. It is easy to access, follow, and share in classes where the content is being introduced, demonstrated, discussed, and applied. It serves an anchor function in these library instruction classes as the basis for shared classroom discussion.

The general online library tutorials, in contrast to the online library ESL workbook, were not created for a particular class or specifically for international students. Instead, they were created and made available on the main library website for anyone interested in taking them. Their targeted use for international students came about through a voluntary certificate program created by the international student services office called the "Certificate for Success." This certificate was a program developed to introduce new international students to the services offered by many departments and units across campus, including the library (https://brocku.ca/international-services/certificate-for-success).

The library component of the Certificate for Success program directed any interested international student to complete these general online library tutorials within the course management system used by the university. The library created a new course called Library Research Skills in which to house the general online library tutorials and to add an accompanying short, ten-question multiple-choice quiz. The reason for constructing a separate course in the course management system and adding a quiz component in this way was to give interested international students evidence to show that they had completed the tutorials for the certificate. Their general use on the open library website would otherwise not have tracked their identifiable personal use or successful completion.

The general online library tutorials were comprised of two separate tutorials, one called "Getting Started" and the other called "Beyond the Basics." Both take the form of a series of sequential pages that include definitional text passages along with embedded videos and interactive quizzes. Pages can be read, videos can be viewed, and embedded quizzes along with the quiz at the end can be taken as many times as a student wishes, with no time limit. Getting Started covers using keywords to search effectively, finding books and articles using our discovery tool, and understanding the differences between popular and scholarly articles. Beyond the Basics covers learning how to use citations to expand a search for articles on a subject, using Google Scholar more effectively to find resources, evaluating information that is found online, and understanding key concepts such as peer review and plagiarism.

Outcomes related to student learning from the online ESL workbook are connected to general library abilities of the upper-level writing students who had a library assignment in their classes. Instructors for those writing classes continue to request the answer sheet from me, both before and after library workshops have been offered. This means that the use of this workbook is being reinforced in these classes outside of the physical library presence of in-person one-time-only workshops. This usage of the workbook stems mainly from word-of-mouth communication between the ESL writing coordinator and me, the ESL instructors and me, and among the ESL instructors themselves. As for the general online library tutorials, usage comes from international students choosing to use this module as an elective in the certificate program. Uptake numbers in the program have been minimal, perhaps due to recent staff changes in the international student services offices, but its continued availability still offers a library component choice to future certificate students.

The purpose of both the online library ESL workbook and the targeted general online library tutorials are to offer online learning support to international students that begins in structured environments but remains available for ongoing future individual use. The online library ESL workbook does this through its use as an in-class tool created to introduce international students to library research strategies; it is also posted publicly for later referral. The general online library tutorials do this by offering an avenue for more in-depth library learning by any interested international student within a structured certificate program that can then be accessed and taken at any time. Both represent a pathway that aims to integrate international students into academic libraries through ongoing online support and availability.

Pathway Five: Self-Access Cart

The fifth pathway is an example of supporting one-on-one interactions with international students outside the library as a way to integrate them into the library. Its purpose is to promote the integration of international students into libraries through individualized personal support outside the physical confines of the library.

This pathway took the form of a self-access cart. A self-access cart is a physical cart full of resources that is attended by a person with the ability to help students in an informal one-on-one manner to extend their learning outside the classroom. This cart represents a mini and mobile version of a self-access center, a place originally designed to support language learning outside a language classroom.[23] Its use here as a library mechanism represents the adaption of a language-learning vehicle into a library learning one. The use of this self-access cart was unique in the library environment as the library does not have self-access carts for any other population.

The creation, stocking, and deployment of a self-access cart that could also include a library purpose was first initiated by ESL instructors at the university. The cart contained print resources such as books, puzzles, vocabulary games, and decks of playing cards, as well as laptops that could easily connect to online university resources and information. It also had a large welcome banner stationed nearby. Figure 9.2 shows what the cart looked like.

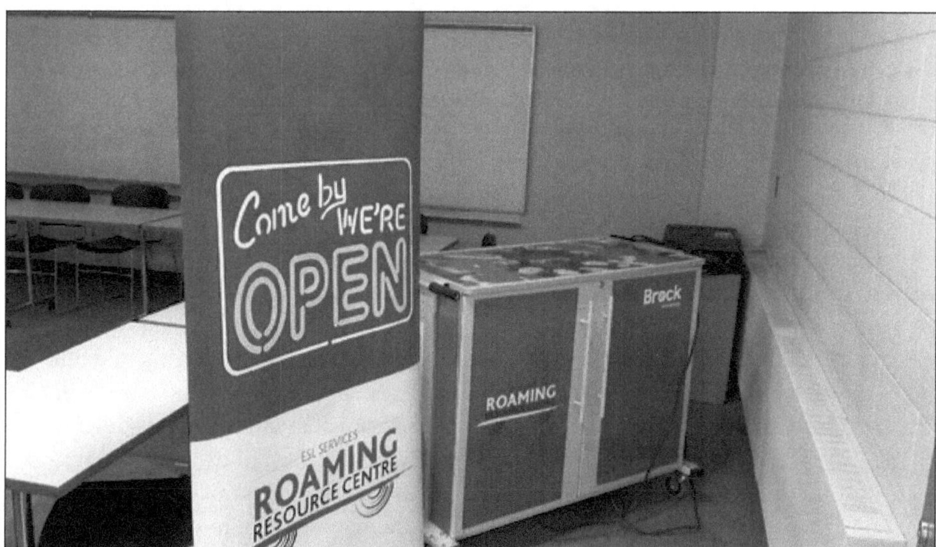

Figure 9.2. Self-access cart.

This cart offered ESL students many ways to extend their English-language learning beyond their language classrooms. University employees staffing it included ESL instructors, staff nurses, and librarians. The library component fits easily with the mandate to extend the learning of the ESL students beyond the classroom in an informal, self-directed, non-mandatory way. It was placed inside the international services building, where people staffing it could easily be seen, approached, and talked to by all international students. The international student center is a separate physical building on campus apart from the library. This is the place were ESL students take ESL classes and where staff and instructors in ESL Services have their offices. The self-access cart was placed in the main student lounge on the first floor of the international services building. This lounge was a comfortable room with couches, tables and chairs, a microwave, and large open windows on the main floor of the building. When not in use, the self-access cart was kept in a corner of the lounge. And in the case of the library, its staffing coincided with due dates of library research assignments for papers.

As a physical manifestation of out-of-classroom learning, the self-access cart serves a useful purpose. Participating in this initiative can give librarians an excellent opportunity to come out of the library and into the international students' own physical spaces. In this way, it can operate as both a mini reference desk and as an outreach vehicle. Librarians can answer questions from ESL students about library policies and direct them to useful sources of information for their assignments.

The use of a self-access cart by librarians can offer another way to integrate international students into academic libraries. This way reverses the normal entrance pattern of international students coming to the library by having a librarian instead go out to them. It offers a novel form of integration. In addition, it can offer the library a wider form of integration by presenting the library as a place on campus where international students can extend both their language learning and their library learning simultaneously.

Benefits of Multi-Pronged Approach

The five pathways described in this chapter offer multiple ways for librarians to help integrate international students into university libraries. Interested librarians could probably replicate most of these projects in their own home library settings without undue stress, effort, time, expertise, or high cost.

These avenues represent different ways to reach out to and support the needs of international students in academic libraries. The strategies include reaching out to individual international students as well as to groups of international students. In addition, they include ways to work directly with international students in person and to support them online. Finally, they include ways to reach international students both inside and outside the library.

- **Individuals and groups.** Reaching out to individual international students can be accomplished in the creation of a welcome sign in various native languages and through student library workers being educated in ways to better support communication with these students. Reaching out to groups of international students can be beneficial as well in integrating them into academic libraries. This could take place in a class environment, such as using an online ESL library workbook in library instruction classes or through making general online library tutorials available to all interested students in a certificate program.
- **In person and online.** In-person engagement can occur with the welcome sign and with the ESL workbook inside writing classes. Online contact and support can be offered through the creation of a specialized language LibGuide or the promotion of general online library tutorials to international students.
- **Inside and outside the library.** The welcome sign can reach them inside the library, for example, while the self-access cart can reach them outside the library. Both provide an avenue for librarians to connect with international students but they make use of different spaces to accomplish the same goal.

The five pathways described in this chapter offer many benefits for librarians wanting to connect international students to their libraries.

- Creating a welcome sign in different native languages fosters awareness of the linguistic diversity that international students bring to campus.
- Running a staff development workshop for library student workers empowers peer-to-peer student interactions in the library.
- Creating a LibGuide that includes both ESL and foreign-language learning material helps integrate international students by showing that there are other language learners on campus, too.
- Using an online library ESL workbook in a classroom and targeting general online library tutorials through a certificate program offers international students both initial and ongoing online library support.
- Staffing a self-access cart in an international services building offers librarians a way to support international students in their own physical spaces.

Deepening or establishing relationships with other campus partners can also offer ways to reach out to and connect with international students on campus. Librarians working with ESL instructors is one way, as seen above with the ESL workbook, as is working with general offices that deal with international students already placed in degree programs, as seen above with the general online library tutorials being made part of a certificate program. Other campus partnerships to explore could come from reaching out to academic support services to potentially offer joint programming on writing effective research papers, managing citations, and using citation styles appropriately. Plagiarism workshops could be another joint venture with academic support services, such as writing centers. It also benefits the library as an organization, making the library more visible on campus and putting the library on par with other departments. It also fulfills the university's strategic goal of internationalization.

Integrating international students into academic libraries can take place in many ways. Offering multiple avenues to international students underscores the message that the library is interested in helping them become successful, just as it is for domestic students. Librarians have many options at their disposal for exploring and creating multiple pathways to support international student success.

Notes

1. Amanda B. Click, Claire Walker Wiley, and Meggan Houlihan, "The Internationalization of the Academic Library: A Systematic Review of 25 Years of Literature on International Students," *College & Research Libraries* 78 (2017): 328–58, doi:10.5860/crl.78.3.328.
2. Diane E. Peters, *International Students and Academic Libraries: A Survey of Issues and Annotated Bibliography* (Lanham, MD: Scarecrow Press, 2010).
3. Daniel Liestman and Connie Wu, "Library Orientation for International Students in Their Native Language," *Research Strategies* 8 (1990): 191–96.
4. Miriam Conteh-Morgan, "Empowering ESL Students: A New Model for Information Literacy Instruction," *Research Strategies* 18 (2001): 29–38.
5. Betty Braaksma, Kathy Drewes, George Siemens, and Peter Tittenberger, "Building a Virtual Learning Commons: What Do YOU Want to Do?," *IFLA Conference Proceedings* (2007): 1–17.
6. Xiang Li, Kevin McDowell, and Xiatong Wang, "Building Bridges: Outreach to International Students via Vernacular Language Videos," *Reference Services Review* 44 (2016), 324–40.
7. John Hickok, "Exciting New Information Literacy Outreach Efforts to International Students,"

Proceedings of the 35th National LOEX Library Instruction Conference (2007): 89–91.
8. Mu Cuiying, "Marketing Academic Library Resources and Information Services to International Students from Asia," *Reference Services Review* 35 (2007): 571–83.
9. Maud C. Mundava and La Verne Gray, "Meeting Them Where They Are: Marketing to International Student Populations in U.S. Academic Libraries," *Technical Services Quarterly* 25 (2008): 35–48.
10. Karen Bordonaro, "We All Have an Accent," *Feliciter* 52 (2007): 240–41.
11. Karen Bordonaro, *The Intersection of Library Learning and Second-Language Education: Theory and Practice* (Lanham, MD: Rowman and Littlefield, 2014).
12. Jian Wang and Donald. G. Frank, "Cross-Cultural Communication: Implications for Effective Information Services in Academic Libraries," *portal: Libraries and the Academy* 2 (2002): 207–16.
13. Dawn Amesbury, "Using Effective Listening Skills with International Patrons," *Reference Services Review* 37 (2009): 10–19.
14. Miriam Conteh-Morgan, "Connecting the Dots: Limited English Proficiency, Second Language Learning Theories, and Information Literacy Instruction," *The Journal of Academic Librarianship* 28 (2002): 191–96.
15. Ignacio J. Ferrer-Vinent, "For English, Press 1: International Students' Language Preference at the Reference Desk," *The Reference Librarian* 51 (2010): 189–201.
16. Emily Love and Margaret B. Edwards, "Forging Inroads between Libraries and Academic, Multicultural and Student Services," *Reference Services Review* 37 (2009): 20–29.
17. Julia A. Martin, Kathleen M. Reaume, Elaine M. Reeves, and Ryan D. Wright, "Relationship Building with Students and Instructors of ESL: Bridging the Gap for Library Instruction and Services," *Reference Services Review* 40 (2012): 352–67.
18. Yan Liao, Mary Finn, and Jun Lu, "Information-Seeking Behavior of International Graduate Students vs. American Graduate Students: A User Study at Virginia Tech 2005," *College & Research Libraries* 68 (2007): 5–25.
19. Dawn Amesbury, "Deconstructing Plagiarism: International Students and Textual Borrowing Practices," *Reference Librarian* 51 (2009): 31–44.
20. David Koenigstein, "Alleviating International Students' Culture Shock and Anxiety in American Academic Libraries: Welcome, Ahlan Wa Sahlan, Anyeong Hae Sae Yo, Bienvenidos, Huan Ying, Sanu Da Zuwa, Shalom, Swaagat Hai," *Library Philosophy & Practice* (2012): 78–83.
21. Charles Lipson, *Succeeding as an International Student in the United States and Canada* (Chicago: University of Chicago Press, 2008).
22. Marilyn Lewis, *Study Skills for Speakers of English as a Second Language* (Basingstoke: Palgrave Macmillan, 2003).
23. Brian Tomlinson, "Principles and Procedures for Self-Access Materials," *Studies in Self-Access Learning* 1 (2010): 72–86, https://sisaljournal.org/archives/sep10/tomlinson/.

Bibliography

Amesbury, Dawn. "Deconstructing Plagiarism: International Students and Textual Borrowing Practices." *Reference Librarian* 51 (2009): 31–44.

———. "Using Effective Listening Skills with International Patrons." *Reference Services Review* 37 (2009): 10–19.

Bordonaro, Karen. *The Intersection of Library Learning and Second-Language Education: Theory and Practice*. Lanham, MD: Rowman and Littlefield, 2014.

———. "We All Have an Accent." *Feliciter* 52 (2007): 240–41.

Braaksma, Betty, Kathy Drewes, George Siemens, and Peter Tittenberger. "Building a Virtual Learning Commons: What Do YOU Want to Do?" *IFLA Conference Proceedings* (2007): 1–17.

Click, Amanda B., Claire Walker Wiley, and Meggan Houlihan. "The Internationalization of the Academic Library: A Systematic Review of 25 Years of Literature on International Students." *College & Research Libraries* 78 (2017): 328–58. doi:10.5860/crl.78.3.328.

Conteh-Morgan, Miriam. "Connecting the Dots: Limited English Proficiency, Second Language Learning Theories, and Information Literacy Instruction." *The Journal of Academic Librarianship* 28 (2002): 191–96.

———. "Empowering ESL Students: A New Model for Information Literacy Instruction." *Research Strategies* 18 (2001): 29–38.

Cuiying, Mu. "Marketing Academic Library Resources and Information Services to International Students from Asia." *Reference Services Review* 35 (2007): 571–83.

Ferrer-Vinent, Ignacio J. "For English, Press 1: International Students' Language Preference at the Reference Desk." *The Reference Librarian* 51 (2010): 189–201.

Hickok, John. "Exciting New Information Literacy Outreach Efforts to International Students," *Proceedings of the 35th National LOEX Library Instruction Conference* (2007): 89–91.

Koenigstein, David. "Alleviating International Students' Culture Shock and Anxiety in American Academic Libraries: Welcome, Ahlan Wa Sahlan, Anyeong Hae Sae Yo, Bienvenidos, Huan Ying, Sanu Da Zuwa, Shalom, Swaagat Hai." *Library Philosophy & Practice* (2012): 78–83.

Lewis, Marilyn. *Study Skills for Speakers of English as a Second Language.* Basingstoke: Palgrave Macmillan, 2003.

Liao, Yan, Mary Finn, and Jun Lu. "Information-Seeking Behavior of International Graduate Students vs. American Graduate Students: A user Study at Virginia Tech 2005." *College & Research Libraries* 68 (2007): 5–25.

Liestman, Daniel, and Connie Wu. "Library Orientation for International Students in Their Native Language." *Research Strategies* 8 (1990): 191–96.

Lipson, Charles. *Succeeding as an International Student in the United States and Canada.* Chicago: University of Chicago Press, 2008.

Love, Emily, and Margaret B. Edwards. "Forging Inroads between Libraries and Academic, Multicultural and Student Services." *Reference Services Review* 37 (2009): 20–29.

Martin, Julia A., Kathleen M. Reaume, Elaine M. Reeves, and Ryan D. Wright. "Relationship Building with Students and Instructors of ESL: Bridging the Gap for Library Instruction and Services." *Reference Services Review* 40 (2012): 352–67.

Mundava, Maud C., and La Verne Gray. "Meeting Them Where They Are: Marketing to International Student Populations in U.S. Academic Libraries." *Technical Services Quarterly* 25 (2008): 35–48.

Peters, Diane E. *International Students and Academic Libraries: A Survey of Issues and Annotated Bibliography.* Lanham, MD: Scarecrow Press, 2010.

Tomlinson, Brian. "Principles and Procedures for Self-Access Materials." *Studies in Self-Access Learning* 1 (2010): 72–86. https://sisaljournal.org/archives/sep10/tomlinson/.

Wang, Jian, and Donald G. Frank. "Cross-cultural Communication: Implications for Effective Information Services in Academic Libraries." *portal: Libraries and the Academy* 2 (2002): 207–16.

Xi, Li, Kevin McDowell, and Xiatong Wang. "Building Bridges: Outreach to International Students via Vernacular Language Videos." *Reference Services Review* 44 (2016); 324–40.

Themes from Interviews (Lib. staff)

- Cross-cultural comm.
- Customer service
- Physical space
- Challenges
- Future plans

= Student Focus Group

Common Theams

- Physical Environment
- Soft environment (surroundings)
- Staff + Librarians
- Resources

CHAPTER TEN

International Undergraduate Students and a Sense of Belonging:

A Case Study at Penn State University Libraries

Alia Gant, Dawn Amsberry, Chao Su, Lana Munip, and Steve Borrelli

Introduction

International students in higher education come from around the world to attend American colleges and universities where they may encounter a new culture, new behavioral norms, and linguistic challenges. Navigating this new ecosystem can be unsettling for students as they look for ways to fit in and feel at home. At Penn State University, international students seem drawn to the library as a place where they feel welcome and can find a private niche for studying or meeting with friends to work on a project. In interviews, many international students described the library as a kind of home away from home. This chapter explores this sense of belonging and describes the results of interviews with both students and library employees about how the library provides a welcoming environment for international students.

The impetus for this study came from an Ithaka S+R survey on undergraduate students' experiences in the library conducted by the Assessment Department at Penn State University Libraries in spring 2016. The survey showed no difference between undergraduate international and domestic students' feelings of inclusivity or sense of belonging in the library. Intrigued by these results, the authors set out to explore Penn State University Libraries' practices for inclusion of international undergraduate students and to present the perspective of international students as to what can further enrich the feeling of belonging. The major research questions in this case study are: (1) What factors contribute to international undergraduate students' sense of belonging in the Penn State libraries? (2) How can Penn State libraries further enrich that sense of belonging?

Literature Review

There are numerous studies that explore sense of belonging among college students. The definition of "sense of belonging" used in this study comes from Strayhorn, who describes it as "a feeling that members matter to one another and to the group, and a shared faith that members' needs will be met through their commitment together."[1] Strayhorn offers an extensive critique and review of the current literature on sense of belonging and demonstrates how sense of belonging differs based on factors such as race and sexual identity. Johnson et al. surveyed first-year college students of varied backgrounds and concluded that African-American, Hispanic/Latino, and Asian-Pacific students reported a weaker sense of belonging than white students.[2] Meeuwisse, Severiens, and Born also studied sense of belonging in both ethnic minority and majority students, observing that ethnic minority students' sense of belonging, unlike that of their majority peers, did not help contribute to their overall academic success.[3] Morrow and Ackermann[4] and O'Keeffe[5] both explore the relationship between sense of belonging and student retention among first-year college students.

A few studies focus exclusively on sense of belonging and international college students. Curtin, Stewart, and Ostrove conducted a climate survey with international and domestic graduate students in PhD programs and found that international students reported a stronger sense of belonging than their domestic peers.[6] Sawir et al. discuss loneliness and international students, noting that stronger bonds between international and domestic students can help create a sense of belonging and alleviate feelings of isolation.[7]

In the library literature, only a few studies address sense of belonging and academic libraries. Bodaghi, Cheong, and Zainab describe the importance of librarians' empathy in contributing to a sense of belonging for students who are visually impaired.[8] While no studies in the library field specifically discuss sense of belonging and international students, many authors have written about various aspects of international students and academic libraries. Amsberry[9] surveyed academic libraries in the United States about practices for working with international students, including orientations, programming, multilingual materials, and staff training. Click, Wiley, and Houlihan provide a systematic review of literature related to international students and academic libraries published between 1990 and 2014, listing more than two hundred works.[10]

A number of recent works report on surveys designed to assess international students' perceptions and usage of academic libraries. In a study of international students at two Australian libraries, Hughes found that international students were often unfamiliar with aspects of academic libraries, such as call numbers.[11] Shaffer, Vardman, and Miller surveyed both domestic and international students at an American university and found that international students seemed to be more dependent on the library than their domestic peers and thus wanted longer library hours as well as more computers.[12] In Datig's study of perceptions of libraries, international students indicated that they saw their academic library as primarily a quiet place for books as well as a place for independent study or study in groups.[13]

Method

Penn State University is made up of twenty-four commonwealth campuses located throughout the state as well as the World Campus for online students. The commonwealth campuses range in size from approximately four hundred students at the smallest campus to approximately 47,000 students at the University Park campus.[14] With the World Campus, the university is host to nearly 100,000 students, including about 6,700 international undergraduates.[15]

Both Penn State and the University Libraries have a strong commitment to diversity and inclusion. Within the University's Strategic Plan for 2016 to 2020, two major foundations are (1) fostering and embracing a diverse world and (2) enhancing global engagement—both illustrating how the university advocates for a culturally competent community and supports an inclusive climate on campus.[16] Diversity and inclusion are also foundational values in the University Libraries' strategic plan, highlighting the libraries' commitment to creating a welcoming environment and to providing collections and programs that reflect the diversity of the community and raise cultural awareness.

To address the research questions in this study, the authors interviewed library employees and conducted focus groups with international undergraduate students. Because the distribution of international students varies widely across the Penn State campuses, the research team interviewed library employees only from campuses where the undergraduate international student enrollment was at least 2 percent of the overall student population. The team selected employees to interview who were heads of campus libraries, library unit heads at the main University Park campus, and other librarians and staff who were known to have an active role in engaging with international students. The team conducted phone or in-person interviews with twenty-seven library employees at seven campuses. The interview questions are included in Appendix 10A.

To recruit international students for the focus groups, the research team partnered with the Office of Global Programs to send out a call for participants on a listserv for international students. As an incentive, students were offered twenty dollars to participate, and more than two hundred students responded. To obtain a diverse representation of the international undergraduate population, thirty-two students (eight for each focus group) were selected based on major, gender, and nationality. A total of twenty-seven students, representing fourteen countries, participated in the focus groups. Student demographics are given in Appendix 10B. The research team conducted four focus groups at three Penn State campuses with high enrollments of international undergraduate students. Two were held at University Park, which has approximately 4,800 international undergraduate students, one at Penn State Harrisburg (608 international undergraduates) and one at Penn State Abington (220 international undergraduates). Each focus group consisted of five to eight students and lasted approximately one hour. Two members of the research team were present during each focus group; one led the discussion while the other recorded the session and took notes. The focus group questions are included in Appendix 10C.

Library Personnel Interviews

The research team interviewed librarians and staff at the University Park campus in the Architecture Library, Business Library, Earth and Mineral Sciences Library, Life Sciences Library, News and Microforms Library, Social Sciences Library, Physical and Mathematical Sciences Library, Knowledge Commons, Library Learning Services, Adaptive Technology and Services, Special Collections, and User Services. Additionally, the research team contacted library heads and staff at the Abington, Harrisburg, Erie, Altoona, Berks, Greater Allegheny, and York campuses. Comments collected during the interviews can be categorized as cross-cultural communication issues, customer service, environment and physical space, challenges, and future plans.

Cross-cultural communication

Nearly every interviewee commented on linguistic and cultural issues that may arise during interactions with international students. Since for many international students English is not their first language, library employees have thought of creative ways to assist with communication. For example, some welcome desks have handouts showing common library terms translated into multiple languages. In addition, some library locations have displayed a poster welcoming students to the library as an inclusive place for everyone in several languages (see figure 10.1).

Many interviewees commented on the importance of avoiding library jargon. According to one head librarian, "Terminology, especially library jargon, can be challenging. I once referred a student to the circulation desk and realized that he was puzzled. He told me that circulation implies movement and was wondering if we had a desk that moves from one location to another."

Customer service

Many interviewees discussed their unit's emphasis on customer service for international and domestic students alike. As one librarian said, "We take their education personally, and we try to send that message out to everybody." Several librarians noted that they strive to provide the same high level of service for all students. A librarian stated, "We don't try and separate out our clientele. Anyone who walks in the door is going to receive the same service." Another head librarian noted that her library does not have programming specific to international students because they believe that students don't want to be singled out based on their country of origin.

Figure 10.1. "We Are Penn State" Poster[17]

Physical space

In addition to a high level of customer service, physical space also plays an important role in how international undergraduate students feel welcomed in the library. For example, in many of the campus libraries, there are group study spaces where collaborative work can occur and where talking is accepted, but there are also designated quiet zones. "I think the space itself is useful to our students," stated one library employee. "I see a large number of them come into the library, use the computers, socialize, because on our campus there aren't many places for students to be if they are not in class."

Library employees also describe how international undergraduate students utilize the libraries as a means to socialize. For example, a head librarian stated, "I think they are very much at home in the library. Many of these students live on or near the campus and many are very busy students who spend a lot of time studying, so they're in the library all the time. I think they feel comfortable here. They hang out here, they study here, and it's also just a part of the situation on this campus as well: there aren't a lot of things to do in the Middletown area, and also if you don't have a car that limits you, so many of them hang out in the library."

Challenges

Although librarians and staff perceive many positives related to international students, there are still existing challenges. Some interviewees commented that international undergraduate students may not understand the library system or how to navigate the library stacks. Another challenge is the lack of knowledge that some international undergraduate students have of what the library may offer. As one librarian noted, "A student may come in with different life and library experiences that translate into a different set of expectations than what we are used to aiming for. Figuring out how to negotiate these situations and provide the appropriate balance of education and service can be challenging."

Another example of differing expectations about libraries can be seen in the way international students may perceive the use of public spaces. For example, the head of the Knowledge Commons noted that one student approached him wondering why she could not work in a study group room when there only were two people in the room. As he commented, "She didn't understand why students might be uncomfortable if she worked alongside them." Library personnel have also noticed that some international undergraduate students may act in a way that seems contrary to the norms in the United States. While libraries in the US are often seen as places for quiet study, some international students may engage in boisterous discussions as part of their learning process.

Future plans

Many interviewees mentioned ideas they had for future plans related to international students. As one head librarian noted, "We're really at the beginning of the growth of a lot of what we can do with international students. We've done a lot to reach out, but I think there's more we can do." Some of the specific future initiatives include: Providing copies of library policies in multiple languages, attending mixers/coffee hours on campus for international students, hosting conversation groups that have an international focus, organizing globally focused exhibits such as international cookbooks, holding a speed-networking event with international and domestic students, and purchasing international bestsellers in their original languages. Some library staff also mentioned providing more activities during holiday times or times during the year that are designated breaks, in particular for international students who are not able to travel or return home. A librarian described, "Even having some kind of reception here during the holidays when students do not have a place to go. It is cultural and beneficial to them."

Student Focus Groups

After completing the focus group sessions, a multi-phase thematic coding process was devised to ensure inter-rater reliability, where each transcript was coded twice: once by each researcher and again as a group with all five researchers. Despite the differences among these three campus libraries in terms of size and available services, consistent needs and similar perceptions of a sense of belonging were found among the focus group participants. The following are the common themes that emerged from the focus groups.

Physical environment

The physical environment of the library, including its location on campus and the way in which the interior space is configured, plays an important role in students' usage. Most University Park focus group participants reported that they spent substantial portions of their days in the library, and some even perceived the library as their home. In contrast, students from Abington and Harrisburg visited the library less frequently and spent less time in the library building. Furthermore, students were not only looking for a well-configured, visually appealing library but also the ownership of a personal space. University Park students discussed being in the library for extended periods of time and desired personal space that they could "own" for the day. Therefore, crowded spaces, intimidating stacks, and lack of available workspace, particularly during finals week, would diminish their feelings of belonging.

Conversely, students appreciated properly equipped spaces that met their needs for productivity. Computer software, furnishings, comfortable chairs for rest, and proximity to food and a café all played a role in meeting their needs and making them feel welcome. At University Park, where there are multiple options for quiet or group study, participants reacted positively to the physical spaces available. Additionally, participants from all campuses were excited about the high-tech equipment like one-button studios and 3-D printers in the library.

Soft environment

Participants at University Park generally spent many hours every day in the library. They said the surroundings made them feel motivated and productive, and they felt as if they belonged there. As one female student said, "…this is pretty much a third home. If America is a second home, this is third home." Although students from Harrisburg and Abington did not visit the library as often as their University Park counterparts, they did visit the library frequently before exams, which indicated that the library was a preferred location to get work done. Furthermore, most participants reported feeling obligated to work and motivated when seeing other students working.

> There is this kind of like unspoken obligation, you know, like once you come to the library, you kind of like have to study. You know because everyone else is, even if you don't like actually are studying, you have to at least pretend you are study. —A female undergraduate international student, University Park

Another aspect of the facilities that contributed to international students feeling welcome was that the library provided multiple environments to accommodate different work needs so that students could find the place that matched what they wanted to do, whether it was to study quietly or work in groups. Participants at University Park appreciated being able to work in different environments within the building depending on their preferences and needs, and liked being able to move from one environment to another.

Focus group participants, particularly those at University Park, described the library as providing opportunities to connect with others socially. When asked what made them, as international students, feel welcome, one participant said, "I think it's the people, like you see people from all these nationalities just studying; it's a very international library." Furthermore, it was apparent that the participants shared a sense of pride when they noted that working hard late at night with other international students made them feel good.

> You feel welcome with these people around. They are from all over the world, from different countries but with one purpose. —A female undergraduate international student, University Park

Another example that illustrates how the social role of the library made the environment more inclusive came from a female Muslim student.

> The library has that environment, you know, it's just approachable people.... I remember so well, for a class I was studying for my exam, and this guy I would always see his face in class but we never talked in class, but he came up to me in the library and said oh are you studying for that. Because the environment is very suitable. —A female undergraduate international student, University Park

In addition to social spaces, the participants appreciated seeing international elements on display in the library. For example, multicultural collections, exhibits, and international newspapers were highly valued by the focus group participants as they provided connections to home countries and made them feel welcome. One Japanese student shared that she came to the library every day only to read a Japanese newspaper, which was the same newspaper she read daily back in Japan. International students were excited to see their cultures highlighted in the library and would like to see them integrated with greater frequency.

> In Turkey, wherever you go, like in the streets, everyone is selling newspapers, and when I see it here in Pattee Library it is very interesting. —A female undergraduate international student, University Park

This was reiterated by a Chinese male student who shared:

> This one time …I saw some Chinese authentic fiction. Actually, it was all in Chinese, traditional Chinese. I was amazed by that. I mean, you can't find the same type of library back in my home.… It's pretty amazing. —A male undergraduate international student, University Park

From conducting the focus groups, researchers were made aware of the importance of meeting the needs of international students as both academic and social beings. While the environment might be more daunting for international students than their domestic counterparts, it was evident that they welcomed and appreciated efforts made by the library to create environments that were conducive to both learning and socializing, and that reflected the local international student population.

Staff and librarians

Most of the participants said that they came to Penn State with limited or no previous experience interacting with library personnel. Nearly all the participants spoke highly of Penn State librarians and staff in terms of their helpfulness and expertise, and they regarded these interactions as an important contributor to their sense of belonging in the library.

> They are very helpful. One lady, she came up with me and she was helping me find a book and she couldn't find the book here so she went down, she called the other library on a Penn State Campus …to send the book here. Then she gave me a personal call the other day to say that the book was here. So, she just went out of her way. She didn't need to do that. —A male undergraduate international student, Harrisburg

Several participants mentioned that they felt they were treated the same as domestic students, which is consistent with the efforts of the librarians as mentioned in the interviews.

> In my opinion, I think it is pretty welcome. I don't think that they treat us any different than locals. —A male undergraduate international student, University Park

However, one participant also shared a poor customer service experience where she was made to wait for a half-hour to speak to a librarian only to be told to send an email to schedule a meeting. This experience resulted in her reluctance to seek further assistance from library staff.

Resources and services

The perception of services and resources provided by the libraries was another important topic that emerged from the focus groups. The participants' comments provided insight into the importance they placed on available services, ranging from the hours the library was open to the availability of group study rooms. There was almost universal demand among focus group participants for a 24/7 library. While the University Park campus is open 24/5, both Abington and Harrisburg have more limited hours, although Harrisburg does have a 24/7 space called the Cyber Café. Additionally, the students wanted the library to be open during the semester breaks as they were more likely to remain on campus than domestic students. While the University Park library offers a limited schedule during breaks, the Harrisburg and Abington libraries cannot fulfill this social role.

Overall, the focus group participants perceived most of the resources and services as welcoming, but there was room for improvement. First, they liked services that saved them money, such as textbooks on reserve and interlibrary loan. However, they rationalized per the availability that textbooks should be available in the library for all students and complained about the limited number of copies available and the short loan period for reserves. They also appreciated the variety of equipment and resources available for checkout, describing how they had checked out karaoke machines but asked that these resources be better promoted as many were not aware of equipment available. Second, they wanted more activities such as games, passive distractors like meditation and Yoga, and simple things like free coffee and cookies in the library during finals week. Overwhelmingly, the participants wanted to build an effective connection with the library. While instruction sessions were perceived as valuable, the students wanted more than just an initial session with a librarian. Students reported that the skills taught to be successful in the library—and applying what they learned—contributed to their feeling of belonging. As shared by a Chinese female student, feeling successful helped her get a better library user experience.

> Because, like, with my major art history, we have to do a lot of research and, like, the resources that are out there. And I feel, like, the more my classes talk about the importance of the library and giving us the steps of how to do things. That kind of makes me step outside of my comfort zone and actually try them out. Like, I was able to find my first book in the stacks the other day. [group laughter] I got to get a book from, like, a different campus. I forget what that's called, like, where you can, I don't know where you can request a book from a different university [Inter Library Loan]. So, we did that and so the more I got to do it, the more I was comfortable, and so I think that made it feel very welcoming. —A female undergraduate international student, University Park

In addition, library orientation was described as too rudimentary. Some participants suggested having an additional orientation in their second year, when they were more acclimated to the library environment and campus in general. Last but not least, international students are unfamiliar with US libraries' policies and practices, such as noise policies, strict no-food policy (in Abington library), and shushing librarians, which can be off-putting.

Discussion

International and domestic students alike want to be successful in their academic pursuits. Academic libraries in the US have evolved from being resource providers to partners in attaining academic outcomes, providing services around the resources targeted toward academic success. Providing the facilities and services, however, is not sufficient in presenting a culturally open and welcoming environment. As resources and services provided by academic libraries around the world differ, it's also important to assist international students to develop the situational context of the library to further enable their success.

Historically, US academic libraries are rules-based facilities. Noise policies, shushing librarians, strict no-food-and-drink policies are often in place designed to protect the collections, equipment, and general noise levels aimed at accommodating quiet study. Although well-intentioned, these traditional aspects of US academic libraries are not particularly welcoming to anyone. Some international students may be familiar with restrictive attitudes in their home libraries toward noise levels and overall access to materials[18] and bring with them a negative perception toward libraries that hold these policies. Participants in focus groups discussed the noise policy and shushing librarians as diminishing their sense of belonging. Students are coming to the libraries for different purposes—for quiet study, group work, or to socialize. They are in our spaces for extended periods of time. Relaxing policy and practice related to expected behavior within library spaces acknowledges the many ways that students desire to use available resources, creating more welcoming spaces for all students.

Participants in focus groups discussed the library as intrinsically motivating per the critical mass of other students engaged in academic study. Also discussed was the impact of the design and aesthetics of a space as motivating factors impacting their choice of where to study. If students perceive a space designed such that it meets their social or academic needs, they are more likely to situate themselves there. As noted by Shaffer, Vardman, and Miller, international students are more dependent on the library for providing facilities and resources than domestic students.[19] As such, hours of availability, ample seating, available workspaces, and appropriately equipped computers with software to accommodate course projects play a strong role in providing a welcoming environment for international students.

The varied environments libraries provide to accommodate quiet individual study and group study are valued by international students. Private spaces created by carrels, reading nooks, study rooms, or even lockers allow for feeling ownership of a space, an issue discussed across focus groups as important to their feeling welcome. Group-study rooms accommodate the kind of lively, boisterous discussion that is part of the learning process for some international students that domestic students or library personnel may find aggressive and intimidating, per a lack of cultural reference. The privacy of group-study spaces provides the freedom to approach learning from a culturally comfortable perspective while minimizing the impact on others.

Providing an environment that meets the productivity needs of the international student population plays a substantial role contributing to developing a sense of belonging. However, addressing academic productivity and success alone is insufficient for creating an intercultural environment where students, regardless of country of origin, feel they belong. Focus group participants discussed the value of international collections, particularly newspapers from outside the US, and multi-cultural exhibits reflective of the cultures of the international student population as providing connections to the familiar, to home. Integrating internationally themed exhibits throughout a library is a low-cost avenue toward projecting inclusiveness to a multi-cultural student body.

Through interviews with library personnel and in focus groups, examples of the library as a social connector were discussed. Library personnel at a commuter campus discussed how having few comfortable places on campus for students to "hang out" results in international students using the library as a social gathering place. On that campus, international and domestic students socialize in the library between classes. Libraries can accommodate by providing social spaces integrating couches and lounge chairs in areas where noise is accepted and encouraged. Board games, puzzles, or other activities that promote interaction further communicate group activity is welcome. Situating these areas near entrances or cafés communicates that interaction and moderate noise are acceptable and welcome without infringing on others who desire quiet study. Focus group participants from the University Park campus discussed unplanned encounters with classmates of different genders and ethnicities while in the library. These interactions enriched their sense of belonging while in the library, with multiple focus group participants referring to the library as their "home."

Facilities, equipment, and policies all contribute to projecting an open and welcome library. Not every library, however, has the physical or monetary resources to optimize their facility to accommodate the somewhat broader needs of international students. Every library can, however, strive to provide excellent customer service regardless of patron country of origin, experience, or familiarity with library services provided.

Focus group participants discussed positive customer service experiences as important contributors to building a sense of belonging and described how negative experiences resulted in one student's reluctance to seek further support from library staff. International students want to be successful, however; as noted by Hughes, international students often lack a familiarity with the services and resources provided by academic libraries in the US. This lack of familiarity is often an impeding factor to their success.[20] Library staff can provide support by assisting international students to develop the situational context of operating in their spaces, increasing the likelihood of a student's success.

International students have different life experiences and arrive with different expectations for academic libraries. Many international students have few interactions with library personnel, which can result in different expectations and misunderstandings. Focus group participants misinterpreted textbooks available as course reserves as a rationale that the library is obligated to provide copies of texts for all enrolled students and that the library was somehow failing to meet that obligation. Staff trained in cultural awareness and sensitivity are better equipped to accommodate misunderstandings. Cultural awareness training is a low-cost, high-impact practice that most libraries can afford in some form. Nearly every library can afford to invite international students from their campus to discuss what library services are like in their country and what they've found different in their experience in the US. When executed strategically, the event can play a dual role of orientating student participants to library services while teaching library personnel about differences in services across countries.

Staff properly trained to accommodate a multi-cultural clientele approach interactions with international students from a position of patience, recognizing the need to explain what services and resources are available. Focus group participants described that they don't know what library services and resources are available to them until they've been introduced to them. By taking the time to explain what is available or demonstrating that staff is here to support students, staff can create a personal connection valued by international students.

Nearly every interviewee discussed linguistic and cultural challenges as barriers to providing good customer service. Low-cost approaches to reducing these barriers and increasing the success of international students were suggested, including providing policies and handouts with common terms translated into multiple languages and avoiding library jargon. Libraries without the in-house expertise to develop these resources can benefit from partnering with other units on campus.

Focus group participants discussed instructional services received as an important facilitator of their success. Library instruction equips students with multiple contexts and strategies for operating in an otherwise unfamiliar environment. The success found through applying what was learned contributes to a feeling of belonging. As academic libraries in the US operate differently than those in many countries, a strong argument can be made as to the importance of a meaningful orientation experience.

Although library personnel interviewed indicated that they don't provide programming specifically targeting international students, and focus group participants didn't show much interest in general library programming, a role for inclusive programming exists. Generally, all students find finals to be stressful, and many spend substantial periods of time preparing in the library. During times like this, events such as "Destress-fest," where snacks, coffee, and games are provided for students to use during study breaks, provide relatively low-cost programming that may be particularly attractive to international students per the novelty alone when contrasted with library services in their home countries. International students are often unable to travel home during breaks in the semester. During these times, many look to the library to fulfill a social role or to make use of computers. Providing programming during breaks in the academic calendar that aim to promote socializing is an additional way a library can enhance a sense of belonging among its international undergraduate population.

Recommendations and Conclusions

Recommendations

1. All students want to feel successful. Adopt practices that aim at their success in library environments.
2. Relax policies relating to expected behaviors; allow library space to be used to meet the needs of users.
3. Provide enough seating, workspaces, and computer hardware and software to meet demand.
4. Accommodate the learning styles of people of different cultures by providing spaces to accommodate groups, individuals, and various noise levels.
5. Integrate multicultural exhibits reflective of the student population.
6. Facilitate the social connector role of the library through combinations of programming, spatial design, and policy.
7. Train employees in cultural differences, awareness, and sensitivity.
8. Invite international students to provide their perspective on the differences between services provided by libraries in their country and American libraries.
9. Be patient when working with international students. They don't know what's available until they're exposed to it.
10. Ensure international students receive library instruction.
11. Provide programs that aim to reduce stress and promote socialization.
12. Acknowledge the role of the library for the international student population and adapt to accommodate.

Conclusion

Libraries aim to provide an open and inclusive environment where all users feel they belong. The needs of international undergraduate students are similar to those of domestic students; however, they may need additional support for developing the situational context of operating in a US academic library. A well-equipped and available space to accommodate the productivity and social needs meets the needs of all users. Well-trained staff empathetic to the challenge of studying in a country other than their own and open to taking the extra steps to accommodate will go a long way in furthering efforts to create an inclusive environment. This chapter discussed many low-cost ways to enrich the connection between the library and international students. Ultimately, a participant in the Abington campus focus group said it best: "I think if you just touched the hearts of the students, I think it would be just welcoming." Aim to touch the hearts of individual students and they'll feel they belong.

Appendix 10A: Interview Questions

1. Can you tell us some of the things you do to make students feel comfortable and welcome?
2. Do you offer programs or services that are targeted specifically at international students?
    - [If interviewee says No] Why not? Is it due to budget constraints? Do you feel that there is not a need for programs focused on international students? Have you tried in the past but not had success with these kinds of programs?
    - [If interviewee says Yes] Could you please talk about these programs, including both academic and non-academic programs (for example, a library orientation for international students, game night, an instruction session for international students, or other types of events), and talk about the history of these programs.
3. Do you collaborate with other services on campus for international students, and if you do, can you elaborate on these collaborations?
4. Do you have internationally focused collections? What are they? Do you have a sense of how well these collections are used by international students?
5. Is there anything in particular that you do in your library that is specifically targeted at making international students feel welcome and included?
6. Have library employees ever received training related to working with international students?
7. How would you describe the interactions between international students and library employees? Do you get a sense that international students feel comfortable approaching library staff?
8. Compared with domestic students, what specific kind of difficulties do international students usually have? Why do you think they have these questions? Because of language? Culture or something else?
9. What do international students seem to like most about your library, or the services or programs that you offer?
10. Are there things that they don't like? Are there programs or services that they have asked for that you don't currently offer?
11. Can you talk about a program or service that you've offered in the past that international students have really valued or appreciated?
12. Is there anything that you've done in the past for international students that hasn't worked? What would you do differently if you tried this again?
13. What would you like to do for international students that you haven't been able to yet? What is holding you back? Is it money? Staffing?
14. Have you heard about any interesting programming or service approaches that aim to make international students feel more welcome?

Appendix 10B: Demography of Student Participants

Participant	Nationality	Gender	Major	University Campus
1	Turkey	Female	Electrical Engineering	University Park
2	China	Female	Energy, Business and Finance	University Park
3	Korea	Male	Economics	University Park
4	India	Male	Petroleum Engineering	University Park
5	Brazil	Male	Aerospace Engineering	University Park
6	Saudi Arabia	Female	Finance	University Park
7	Swaziland	Male	Agribusiness Management & Information Systems Management	University Park
8	Japan	Female	Education and Public Policy	University Park
9	Iran	Female	Psychology & Labor Employment Relations	University Park
10	Malaysia	Male	Economics	University Park
11	China	Female	Art History, Communications Arts & Sciences	University Park
12	Thailand	Female	Energy Engineering	University Park
13	China	Male	Applied Statistics	University Park
14	India	Male	Information Sciences and Technology	University Park
15	Turkey	Male	Mechanical Engineering	Harrisburg
16	China	Female	Marketing	Harrisburg
17	Korea	Female	Biochemistry	Harrisburg
18	England	Male	Biology and Psychology	Harrisburg
19	India	Male	Management / Marketing	Harrisburg
20	India	Female	Life Science	Harrisburg
21	Saudi Arabia	Male	Cyber Security & Information Sciences and Technology	Harrisburg
22	China	Female	Accounting	Harrisburg
23	Malaysia	Female	International Politics	Abington
24	Indonesia	Male	Science	Abington
25	Korea	Male	Accounting	Abington
26	China	Female	Undecided	Abington
27	Russia	Female	Undecided	Abington

Note: N (Nationality) = 14; N (Female) = 14; N (Male) = 13

Appendix 10C: Focus Group Questions

Qu. #	Research Question Mapping*	Question Type	Primary/ Probing	Question
1.	1, 3	Engagement	Primary	How often do you come to the library and how long do you usually stay?
			Probing	Are you usually here to do work, or do you do other things while you're here?
2.	1, 3	Engagement	Primary	Do you have a favorite place in the library?
			Probing	Is there an area, part of a particular floor or nook where you usually go? Is this a place where you try to avoid friends and distractions? Or do you use the library as a place to meet up?
3.	1, 3	Exploration	Primary	There are a lot of places across campus or around town where you could choose to go. Why do you come to the library instead of someplace else (e.g. Hub, Student Enrichment Center [Harris.])?
			Probing	Do you come for the quiet? For the noise, the liveliness? The physical resources (computers, books, help)? What is it about the library that makes you want to come here?
4.	1, 3	Exploration	Primary	What are some things about the library that make you feel welcome?
			Probing	What do you like about being in the library? Do you talk with the people who work here? Have you ever asked for or received help from someone in the libraries that was really helpful/ useful? What kind of impact did that interaction have on your thoughts about the library? Do you engage with other students when you're in the library? With friends, classmates, students who work here? Do you have friends who work here? Do you have a preference asking for help between student employees and full-time library employees?
5.	1, 3	Exploration	Primary	What does the library do for you as an international student?

Qu. #	Research Question Mapping*	Question Type	Primary/ Probing	Question
			Probing	Does it help you in any way? Is the library someplace to be other than where you live or is it more than that? Explain? How are our libraries different from those in your home country?
6.	1, 3	Exploration	Primary	Do you ever check out books or movies in a language other than English?
			Probing	Do the libraries have much in [language] (books, or movies)? Do you read the international newspapers the libraries subscribe to? Do they help connect you to home?
7.	1,2, 3	Exploration	Primary	We try to provide environments that are welcoming to everyone at Penn State. Describe some things about the library that make it feel good to work/ be here from the perspective of an international student?
			Probing	Do you find being around other people being productive helpful? Is the signage helpful? Would you like to see them in additional languages? What about the staff, the people working here?
8.		Exploration	Primary	Have you ever attended an event at the library (distress fest, finals week recharge, concert, talk, movie)?
			Probing	Do these types of experiences contribute to you feeling connected as part of Penn State?
9.	2	Exploration	Primary	Where else besides the library do you go to study or do work?
			Probing	Why there? What is it about it that makes you want to be there to be productive?
10.	1, 3	Exploration	Primary	During breaks in the semester, most of the campus closes but the libraries stay open. Do you make use of the library during these times?
			Probing	What do you tend to do when you're here during breaks? Do you use the computers and Wi-Fi? 3-D printing? Read for fun? Watch videos? Play video games? Drink coffee? Just hang out?

Qu. #	Research Question Mapping*	Question Type	Primary/ Probing	Question
11.	2	Exploration	Primary	Is there anything that makes you feel like the library is not a welcoming space?
			Probing	Are there things about the library that you don't like? What would you do to make it better?
12.		Exit	Primary	Is there anything else you want to tell us about your experiences in the libraries?

*Note: The main research question:

1. What factors contribute to international students' sense of belonging in the Penn State University Libraries?
2. What can be done to further enrich that sense of belonging?
3. What are the current and past practices employed by Penn State University Libraries to ensure their services and facilities are welcoming and supportive to the international undergraduate student population?

Notes

1. Terrell L. Strayhorn, *College Students' Sense of Belonging* (New York: Routledge, 2012), 8.
2. Dawn R. Johnson, Matthew Soldner, Jeannie Brown Leonard, Patty Alvarez, Karen Kurotsuchi Inkelas, Heather T. Rowan-Kenyon, and Susan D. Longerbeam, "Examining Sense of Belonging Among First-Year Undergraduates From Different Racial/Ethnic Groups," *Journal of College Student Development* 48, no. 5 (2007): 525.
3. Marieke Meeuwisse, Sabine E. Severiens, and Marise Ph Born, "Learning Environment, Interaction, Sense of Belonging and Study Success in Ethnically Diverse Student Groups," *Research in Higher Education* 51, no. 6 (2010): 528.
4. Jennifer Morrow and Margot Ackermann, "Intention to Persist and Retention of First-Year Students: The Importance of Motivation and Sense of Belonging," *College Student Journal* 46, no. 3 (2012): 483.
5. Patrick O'Keeffe, "A Sense of Belonging: Improving Student Retention," *College Student Journal* 47, no. 4 (2013): 605.
6. Nicola Curtin, Abigail J. Stewart, and Joan M. Ostrove, "Fostering Academic Self-Concept: Advisor Support and Sense of Belonging Among International and Domestic Graduate Students," *American Educational Research Journal* 50, no. 1 (2013): 108.
7. Erlenawati Sawir, Simon Marginson, Ana Deumert, Chris Nyland, and Gaby Ramia, "Loneliness and International Students: An Australian Study," *Journal of Studies in International Education* 12, no. 2 (2008): 148.
8. Nahid Bayat Bodaghi, Loh Sau Cheong, and A. N. Zainab, "Librarians Empathy: Visually Impaired Students' Experiences Towards Inclusion and Sense of Belonging in an Academic Library," *The Journal of Academic Librarianship* 42, no. 1 (2016): 87.
9. Dawn Amsberry, "Engaging International Students with the Academic Library," *Student Engagement and the Academic Library,* edited by Loanne Snavely (Santa Barbara, CA: Libraries Unlimited, 2012), 71–72.

10. Amanda B. Click, Claire Walker Wiley, and Meggan Houlihan, "The Internationalization of the Academic Library: A Systematic Review of 25 Years of Literature on International Students," *College & Research Libraries* 78, no. 3 (2017): 328–29.
11. Hilary Hughes, "International Students' Experiences of University Libraries and Librarians," *Australian Academic & Research Libraries* 41, no. 2 (2010): 77–82.
12. Christopher Shaffer, Lisa Vardaman, and Donna Miller, "Library Usage Trends and Needs of International Students," *Behavioral & Social Sciences Librarian* 29 no. 2 (2010): 109.
13. Ilka Datig, "What Is a Library?: International College Students' Perceptions of Libraries," *The Journal of Academic Librarianship* 40, no. 3–4 (2014): 350–51.
14. The Pennsylvania State University, "Penn State University Budget Office Enrollment by Race/ Ethnicity Fall 2016," accessed August 5 2017, https://budget.psu.edu/factbook/StudentDynamic/MinorityEnrolbyEthnicity.aspx?YearCode=2016&FBPlusIndc=N.
15. Ibid.
16. The Pennsylvania State University, "The Pennsylvania State University's Strategic Plan for 2016 to 2020," last modified February 2016, http://strategicplan.psu.edu/the-plan/.
17. Created by Public Relations and Marketing, Penn State University Libraries.
18. Diane E. Peters, "A Survey of Issues," *International Students and Academic Libraries: A Survey of Issues and Annotated Bibliography* (Lanham, MD: Scarecrow Press, 2010), 10.
19. Shaffer et al., "Library Usage Trends and Needs of International Students," 110–11.
20. Hughes, "International Students' Experiences of University Libraries and Librarians," 78–82.

Bibliography

Amsberry, Dawn. "Engaging International Students with the Academic Library." In *Student Engagement and the Academic Library,* edited by Loanne Snavely, 71–83. Santa Barbara, CA: Libraries Unlimited, 2012.

Bodaghi, Nahid Bayat, Loh Sau Cheong, and A. N. Zainab. "Librarians Empathy: Visually Impaired Students' Experiences Towards Inclusion and Sense of Belonging in an Academic Library." *The Journal of Academic Librarianship* 42, no. 1 (2016): 87–96. doi:10.1016/j.acalib.2015.11.003.

Click, Amanda B., Claire Walker Wiley, and Meggan Houlihan. "The Internationalization of the Academic Library: A Systematic Review of 25 Years of Literature on International Students." *College & Research Libraries* 78, no. 3 (2017): 328–58. doi:10.5860/crl.78.3.328.

Curtin, Nicola, Abigail J. Stewart, and Joan M. Ostrove. "Fostering Academic Self-Concept: Advisor Support and Sense of Belonging Among International and Domestic Graduate Students." *American Educational Research Journal* 50, no. 1 (2013): 108–37. doi:10.3102/0002831212446662.

Datig, Ilka. "What Is a Library?: International College Students' Perceptions of Libraries." *The Journal of Academic Librarianship* 40, no. 3-4 (2014): 350–56. doi:10.1016/j.acalib.2014.05.001.

Hughes, Hilary. "International Students' Experiences of University Libraries and Librarians." *Australian Academic & Research Libraries* 41, no. 2 (2010): 77–89.

Johnson, Dawn R., Matthew Soldner, Jeannie Brown Leonard, Patty Alvarez, Karen Kurotsuchi Inkelas, Heather T. Rowan-Kenyon, and Susan D. Longerbeam. "Examining Sense of Belonging Among First-Year Undergraduates from Different Racial/Ethnic Groups." *Journal of College Student Development* 48, no. 5 (2007): 525–42. doi:10.1353/csd.2007.0054.

Meeuwisse, Marieke, Sabine E. Severiens, and Marise Ph Born. "Learning Environment, Interaction, Sense of Belonging and Study Success in Ethnically Diverse Student Groups." *Research in Higher Education* 51, no. 6 (2010): 528–45. doi:10.1007/s11162-010-9168-1.

Morrow, Jennifer, and Margot Ackermann. "Intention to Persist and Retention of First-Year Students: The Importance of Motivation and Sense of Belonging." *College Student Journal* 46, no. 3 (2012): 483–91.

O'Keeffe, Patrick. "A Sense of Belonging: Improving Student Retention." *College Student Journal* 47, no. 4 (2013): 605–13.

Peters, Diane E. "A Survey of Issues." In *International Students and Academic Libraries: A Survey of Issues and Annotated Bibliography*, 1–54. Lanham, MD: Scarecrow Press, 2010.

Sawir, Erlenawati, Simon Marginson, Ana Deumert, Chris Nyland, and Gaby Ramia. "Loneliness and International Students: An Australian Study." *Journal of Studies in International Education* 12, no. 2 (2008): 148–80. doi:10.1177/1028315307299699.

Shaffer, Christopher, Lisa Vardaman, and Donna Miller. "Library Usage Trends and Needs of International Students." *Behavioral & Social Sciences Librarian* 29, no. 2 (2010): 109–17. doi:10.1080/01639261003742231.

Strayhorn, Terrell L. *College Students' Sense of Belonging A Key to Educational Success for All Students.* New York: Routledge, 2012.

The Pennsylvania State University. "The Pennsylvania State University's Strategic Plan for 2016 to 2020." Last modified February 2016. http://strategicplan.psu.edu/the-plan/.

———. "Penn State University Budget Office Enrollment by Race/Ethnicity Fall 2016." Accessed August 5, 2017. https://budget.psu.edu/factbook/StudentDynamic/MinorityEnrolbyEthnicity.aspx?YearCode=2016&FBPlusIndc=N.

CHAPTER ELEVEN

International Student Perceptions of Libraries:

Experiences from the Middle East and North Africa

Kristine N. Stewart and Kenneth C. Haggerty

Introduction

Globalization has facilitated the movement of goods, services, people, and information across geographic borders once perceived too vast to cross. Technology has further assisted in the integration of economies and cultures, greatly changing the environment in which libraries and librarians operate. Libraries worldwide serve a more diverse population of patrons, both in-house and online with searching for, accessing, and using information. This is especially true for academic librarians in the United States, who are tasked with serving a patron population that is constantly changing due to visiting scholars and student exchange programs. The academic librarian of the twenty-first century plays a vital role in an increasingly diverse global university environment.

Cultural views toward libraries and information access may impact the way that international students and scholars use information for personal, academic, and professional purposes.[1] As such, it is important that librarians understand not only the cultural identity and experiences of their patrons but also their own so that they may question assumptions that underlie the collections and services offered by their libraries.[2] The United States has a public legacy of libraries, largely due to philanthropists, such as Andrew Carnegie and Bill Gates, who established libraries and library programs that have influenced "areas of education, research and development, and professional communications"[3] from the late 19th century to present day. As such, American librarians often come from backgrounds where libraries are established cultural institutions, however, this is not necessarily the case elsewhere in the world.

Differences between institutions in the West and Middle East are chronicled in an article by Wand,[4] which discusses the collectivist culture of the Middle East and its influence on how students learn and use the academic library. Considering linguistic and cultural differences that globally conscious librarians will encounter in serving diverse patrons, this chapter presents the findings of a qualitative case study of nine Arab students from the Middle East and North Africa (MENA) region studying abroad at a public university in the Midwestern United States.

The purpose of this study was to better understand the types of experiences which have contributed to Arab international students' perceptions and uses of information and libraries. In-depth, semi-structured interviews were conducted to understand how students from the MENA region perceive and use libraries and information as international students in the U.S. During interviews, participants were asked about their past and present experiences with seeking information and using libraries in both their home countries as well as during their time as students in the United States.

Literature Review

International students are a popular topic in library and information science (LIS) literature; as such, only a select few will be mentioned. Jackson and Sullivan and Koenigstein and Zimerman[5] provide an overview of challenges faced by international students (such as varying educational standards and language barriers) and methods which librarians may employ to better assist this group of students. Several studies have focused on outreach services for[6] and library instruction of international students.[7] Literature that provides some useful context to this study are those regarding international students' perceptions of libraries and the cultural and practice-based competencies required of librarians working with international students. Datig supplemented an online survey with interviews of international students to uncover perceptions students have of libraries.[8] Datig's findings revealed the broad spectrum of experiences students have with libraries, ranging from none to ongoing, regular use of libraries. Although not specific to the context of international students, additional relevant literature includes findings about students experiencing cross-cultural issues. These are issues well addressed in studies by Long[9] and Adkins and Hussey[10] regarding perceptions of libraries by Latino students as well as the role of these institutions in their lives as students.

At present, there is very little literature in the field regarding the issues and challenges faced by international students from the MENA region. However, a recent study conducted by Ibraheem and Devine investigated the academic and interpersonal experiences of Saudi Arabian students studying in the US.[11] This study revealed that many of these students struggle with language issues, the structure of American libraries, and communication with library staff.

As noted by Click et al., the field of LIS has a long and inspiring history in the Arab world; however, literature regarding LIS in the region is sparse and often outdated.[12] Relevant literature concerning libraries and library usage in the MENA region fall into two broad categories: information resources and instruction offered by libraries and qualifications required of librarians in the region.

Information resources and instruction offered by libraries in MENA varies greatly by country and by type of institution within each country. A study by AlQudsi-ghabra et al. found library services in private schools were better than in public schools in terms of the number, variety, and quality of library services.[13] In part, this was due to the influence of private, international schools with American or British backgrounds. Similarly, students in the United Arab Emirates (UAE) lack exposure to libraries prior to attending university as "few public schools have functioning school libraries" and because it wasn't until the twenty-first century when public libraries were planned and built in the UAE.

Library literature is rich with articles regarding library collaboration and cooperation; however, it is important to note that it is a relatively new phenomenon within MENA, dating back to the late 1990s and early 2000s. Several studies discuss initiatives for sharing resources electronically and via consortiums and interlibrary loan programs.[14] These studies emphasized the importance of library collaboration within the region due to the high cost of commercial vendors[15] and indicated there was a need to better market these resources to library users and provide more robust support for e-resources.[16] Obstacles to cooperation in the region vary by country but include budgetary concerns, discrepancies in staff training, and issues of safety and security due to civil unrest throughout the region.[17]

Linguistic obstacles are often faced by library users in the region and are a common theme addressed in the literature. Fahmy and Rifaat discussed the linguistic barriers that affect the information literacy (IL) skills of Arab students. Available information in Arabic, both print and electronic, is limited, often disorganized, outdated, of varying quality, hard to find, or absent entirely.[18] Along similar concerns regarding language, Kaba found in an analysis of academic library websites in the UAE that many library websites (80 percent) were unavailable in Arabic and often lacked live chat support.[19] Consequently, when students use the library online, they may encounter obstacles related not only to language but also the ability to ask for help. The use of the English language is used as a common denominator throughout the Gulf region and thus carries ramifications for information literacy instruction. As noted by Moyo and Mavodza, this requires deeper "pedagogical awareness to understand the way that IL messages are conveyed to culturally or linguistically varied student groups."[20] In an assessment of an online IL program, Martin, Burks, and Hunt emphasized the importance of student input on their online tutorial as the research team were from different cultural backgrounds than their students.[21] The lack of students' exposure to IL instruction prior to entering the university was also reported, although not necessarily unique to the UAE.

Lack of formal training or professional qualifications required of library professionals was frequently noted in the literature.[22] A study of health professional library users in Saudi Arabia by Khudair and Bawden found that very few library users had received any instruction or support from library staff and only half of users would ask for help.[23] Findings from this study suggested the lack of formal LIS training resulted in lower levels of confidence and knowledge of library professionals, elements critical to support library users. Similarly, Khurshid's study of non-degreed librarians in library management revealed the lack of professional qualifications of library management and the negative impact of this on the level and quality of services offered by libraries.[24] Contributing factors noted in this study include frequent turnover rates in management, lack of understanding of library policies and procedures, and superficial knowledge of library operations and services.

A review of LIS literature from the region reveals that students from MENA may have varying depths of experiences using libraries based on their country of origin and whether they attended public or private schools growing up. Although libraries and librarians in MENA experience similar challenges to libraries elsewhere, some of these issues are exacerbated by the inconsistency in professional qualifications required of librarians, language concerns that impact the use of collections, and the quality of information literacy instruction. We only discovered one study that focused specifically on library use by international students from MENA. Therefore, this study seeks to fill a gap in existing research by further exploring this issue as well as investigating how international students' past experiences using libraries and seeking information in their home countries have shaped or influenced how they perceive libraries while studying abroad in the United States.

Methodology

To learn more about the library and information-seeking experiences of Arab international students, in-depth, semi-structured interviews were conducted with participants. To recruit study participants, an email was sent out by the university's International Center (on behalf of the researchers) to students whose home country was identified as being one of the twenty-two Arabic-speaking countries of the Arab League. Nine students were recruited as participants in this study. The interview participants came from seven different countries within the MENA region and had spent anywhere from one to four years studying in the US. Each student included in this chapter is identified in table 11.1 by their level of education and home country.

TABLE 11.1
Participant Identification

Participant	Education Level	Country
Zeinab	Undergraduate	Lebanon
Amir	Graduate	Iraq (went to university in Jordan)
Awadh	Undergraduate	Saudi Arabia
Ahmed	Graduate	Kuwait
Abdul	Graduate	Saudi Arabia
Nourah	Undergraduate	Kuwait
Riham	Undergraduate	Palestine (also lived in Jordan)
Ayoub	Undergraduate	Morocco
Pancea	Undergraduate	Egypt

Interviews were audio-recorded and transcribed, verbatim, by the researchers. Interviews were semi-structured, but all included the following questions:

1. What is information? What is a library?
2. What are your experiences with libraries or other information centers in your home country? In the US?
3. Have you received any instruction on how to search for, retrieve or evaluate information in your home country? In the US?

4. What do library spaces look like in your home country? In the US?
5. Are there types of information or resources that you currently access or use in the US that you did not access before studying abroad?
6. How do your experiences accessing information and using libraries in your home country differ from your experiences in the US?
7. How do you feel your past experiences prior to coming to the US influenced how you think about information access and libraries?

Findings

Students did not limit their responses to academic libraries but also referenced their experiences using public and school libraries. Students did, however, primarily rely on their experiences with academic libraries in the US to illustrate similarities and differences between libraries in their home countries and their current experiences.

Collections and space

Students' perceptions of libraries were based heavily on the usefulness of their collections and resources to their information needs. The quality and composition of library resources available to students varied greatly based on the type of library. For example, every student in this study had used a public library in the past but indicated that public libraries were not well-used in their home countries due to the poor quality of resources and services. Several participants noted outdated library collections, containing materials focused primarily on "old Arabic"[25] materials such as Arabic poetry, literature, religion, and history. Language also plays a major role in the utility of library resources. Quotes from students revealed issues regarding the influence of colonizers' languages on library collections and the predominance of English as the language of scientific publication.

> Most of them [the books] are in Arabic and French since our system is based on the French since we were colonized by France. I don't speak French.[26]

> There are not many books translated from Arabic. This is the reason why most people don't use the library... it doesn't have a lot of sources about science or something, it's all in another language.[27]

Amir indicated that differences between the funding of higher education in his home country of Iraq and where he finished his bachelor's degree, in Jordan, influenced his need to use the library: "In Iraq, the education system is free, so they give you your books. In Jordan, you have to buy these.... I have to go to the library."[28] Amir's statement also reflects differences between educational systems, as it suggests that assigned textbooks are the only sources needed for a course. Amir also noted that his academic library in Iraq lacked Internet access, which greatly affected the value of the library as a resource. In contrast, Nourah, who attended a private, American high school in Kuwait, noted the similarities she saw between library resources at her private high school and the academic library she uses in the US. As opposed to the other students who referred primarily to books as library resources, she alluded to electronic resources accessible from her school library: "I did my library research online mostly. I'd just sit at home and do the research."[29]

Nourah's response not only addressed the type of resources she accessed through her school's library (i.e., e-resources) but the library as an online space where she could retrieve information needed for her studies. Nourah appreciated the convenience associated with being able to access library resources from home. Students in this study, however, primarily focused their responses on the physical library space.

> It's [US library] similar to the one in my private [school] but not in the public libraries in Kuwait.... Even the atmosphere and the way everything is set up. That's similar.[30]

> I think it [his library in Saudi Arabia] is larger than the library here [in the US] ...it has many tables and computers and you can print limited papers.[31]

> It's [speaking of his academic library in Kuwait] very formal. It is more of a learning-based facility while in the US it is more of an informal, casual thing. We can just use the Internet, read books, magazines, videos, or even just chat with your friends. There are more functions in the US [library] than what we have. The one we have is more of just books ...in the US it [the library] has more broader functions, more purposes.[32]

> They [libraries] are similar.... Here it [the library] is bigger with more technology, it's more organized.[33]

Library users

Participants indicated that university students appeared to be the most common patron of libraries, both public and academic. However, students from Kuwait and Saudi Arabia noted differences in the gender of library users in their countries. Ahmed experienced an academic library that was segregated by gender, with days of the week assigned as either "male" or "female" days at the library. "We had different days for women and different days for men. But I know there is some kind of separation so all of the collaboration is either male-based or female-based."[34] Abdul noted library policies did not allow children in libraries in Saudi Arabia; as a consequence, he saw fewer women in libraries in his home country. "Some women want to come to the library but they can't because of their children and because of the rule of the library that doesn't allow children. So, women can't come to the library because of her children."[35]

Role of librarians in research

During interviews with students, students explained how librarians in their home countries often play a different role in the research process.

> There are librarians there and, yeah, they teach, but they are not in the mood to teach. Like they are there to finish their mission every day and there is no helpful spirit. They will tell you maybe, "Ok, do you want this book? Just tell us its name and I will go and search for you." There's no, "Sit and I will give you this technique and you have to go and search for it." Like, even there is no spirit for helping.[36]

> There is like a counter and there is a guy ...you can't go access the library and look for a book. You have to tell him the name and then he's going to, like, bring you the book or whatever you need. It's not like here, you go and you look for the book you are interested in. They just give him the name and he accesses the computer and then he brings you the book you need.[37]

> The main difference is that we weren't exposed or taught these kind of information search techniques. Where I come from, people expect you to find information and that is it. You don't know where or how.[38]

The above statements from students reflect differences in librarians' approaches to helping students find information sources; in some cases, this may be due to a lack of formal training or qualifications required of librarians. The type of service provided by librarians may also be in response to the library design and may reflect the reality that the traditional "reference room" and closed library stacks that we, as American librarians, often think of as a thing of the past or a format relegated to special collections and archives are still a model of service elsewhere in the world. Students expressed appreciation for their librarians in the US who taught them how to search for and retrieve information on their own. One student indicated it made her research feel more like her own. "That makes your research more accurate.... It's how I want to make this research. I reached a conclusion. It's not about the people who gave you information."[39]

Approaches to education and research

As indicated by the student statements above, primary differences in participant experiences occur when seeking information and how they have been taught to look for information. Participants noted that although they may have had research classes in their home countries, these classes occurred during high school when research meant nothing to them. Those who had these classes while enrolled at a university in their home country felt they were not being pushed to perform research.

> Whatever you found on the Net, the professor would be like, "That's fine. That's okay." Here, you can see that the professor wants to know where you find it. Something from Wikipedia he would say, "Oh, that's not accurate." This is not the case back home. Back home you can bring whatever you want.[40]

> The way I write my papers now is completely different. I can go to the library and find books and use it. I used to write from literature on the

> Internet and that's it. Most students [in Egypt] are like, "Okay, I have a paper and I'm just going to copy and paste."[41]

The majority of participants spoke at length about the challenges they encountered when first starting out as students in the US due to different academic expectations.

> In Egypt, I work harder in reading my books and studying and memorizing, but here I'm more busy with papers and research and reading a book and discussing it in class. Education in Egypt is based on memorizing information. After I get out of exams, I completely forget everything.[42]

> It's based on only memorizing the thing, memorizing the idea.... But here there is kind of critical thinking. You have to read, you have to understand, and then you have a lot of choices that you have to choose the right thing from it. Or even ...your research paper would be based on what you understood, not what you memorized. So, it will be more about thinking, not about listing information.[43]

> My classes here, we have to write like four papers during the semester. It is nothing like that in Jordan.[44]

One student, Nourah, had attended a private, American school in her home country and experienced these challenges in Kuwait prior to coming to the US.

> In a public school, you are rarely asked to get research done or an essay about something that requires research. But when I went to a private school, it was an American school.... They expected me to have research done. It's not like writing from your mind, like from what you think from your mind. Because in a public school you just write it.... You don't need resources or something to prove anything. So when I went to private school, I had to learn this all over again. Like how to actually cite stuff and where to get information from and those useful tools [for citation]. I never used them before.[45]

Research and citation skills were something almost every student noted they had to adjust to quickly, but that their work had excelled as a result. Several students shared the stories of their "first paper" in the US and how they learned about issues regarding citation and plagiarism.

> I had never heard about the APA format or the MLA format. But, like, a couple of weeks ago when one of my teachers asked for a research paper, she told us it had to be in this format. I was, like, the only girl in the class who raised their hand and asked, "What is APA?" It was a new experience for me.... Maybe if I was, if I had been raised in an American school in Lebanon things would be different. But since it's public school we've never experienced this.[46]

> I didn't know. Here in US this plagiarism thing is a big thing. You have to cite your resources. It is not just copy and paste.... My first research paper I wrote my professor asked me to come to his office. I had written my paper the way I was used to back home so he made me do it over.[47]

> I do remember writing my first paper. I was, like, copying paragraphs from websites and pasting them on my paper, and my roommate and these friends of mine were like, "What are you doing?" They were like, "This is plagiarism ...you may get expelled from the university." They said at least I have to paraphrase the information and to cite it.... It's really different from back home.[48]

Discussion

As illustrated in the findings above, students had very different experiences accessing information, using libraries, and adjusting to academic expectations as students in the US. Students in this study had a broad range of experiences with libraries, from those who had experienced similar libraries in their home countries to those whose library lacked Internet access. Differences in students' experiences were based primarily on the student's country of origin and the type of education they had received—public or private. This was particularly evident in the responses of Nourah, who had attended a private American school. The library in her private school in Kuwait resembled her university library in the US. The most significant differences Nourah experienced occurred years prior to studying abroad in the US when she transitioned from a public school in Kuwait to a private school.

> In my private school, all my teachers were American. It's like mini-America inside ...for like a big portion of my life. We had a lot of problems with, like, conforming to the outside world [in Kuwait] ...like walking around. I would go outside and had my guy friends from school and we would just go to the mall and something like that and people look at us and are like, "What are they doing? Where do they think they are living?" You know you just don't sit with guys and girls, 'cause that's not our culture.[49]

As a student from a private school in Kuwait, Nourah adapted easily to life as a student in the US. It was when she left school at the end of the day that she experienced the differences between the culture of Kuwait and the culture of the American institution she attended in Kuwait. Nourah noted the segregation of genders in Kuwait, which was also noted by two other students in this study (from Kuwait and Saudi Arabia). Although students from MENA studying abroad in the US may come from a country with gender segregation, this is something that only students from the Gulf region of the Middle East indicated was a difference they adjusted to when they moved to the US.

Despite the rich history of libraries in the Middle East, the modern history of libraries in the region varies greatly. For example, Zeinab referenced the outdated collections of libraries in Lebanon and the influence of the French in the collection due to the colonization of Lebanon by France. As noted by Moulaison,[50] libraries built under colonization were not necessarily meant to support or foster learning but to serve the needs of those who established them. Oil-rich nations such as Saudi Arabia, however, have a very different modern history of libraries due to radical changes in the development and expansion of higher education in the country.

> We started building universities, like, forty or fifty years ago. That is maybe the oldest university, and since 2004 we had seven or eight universities. But after that, after the new king, we had maybe like thirty universities, public and private.[51]

Many countries in the region have experienced ongoing periods of civil unrest and other conflicts, which have affected not just the infrastructure of libraries and academic institutions but of the very country itself. As the student from Iraq noted, "There are different priorities. I'm talking about students, they don't have food, transportation, electricity."[52] Amir's academic library didn't provide access to the Internet; however, he's the only student in this study that indicated such an experience.

Other students referred to the culture of libraries in the US as an explanation of the differences between libraries in their home country and the US.

> A library in my country is completely different from here. I think that in Egypt we don't have the library culture. Especially for youth and college students. If I told my friend, "Let's go to the library." They would be like, "Oh my God, you are so weird." Here in the US, I come to the library a lot.[53]

As librarians, we hold a unique position within an academic institution. We interact with every level and type of user at the university with an information need. As professionals, it is important that we are mindful of any assumptions we may have regarding our patrons as these assumptions may impact the type and level of service we provide. As demonstrated in this study, students from MENA will arrive at the library with varying levels of experience. Be prepared to meet these students at their point of need and be proactive about outreach to international students because, as this study learned, student perceptions and expectations of the library may be influenced by their experiences elsewhere.

Conclusion

The purpose of this study was to better understand the types of experiences which have contributed to Arab international students' perceptions and use of information and libraries. Students who participated in this study have done an amazing job adapting to such radically different educational standards. They all demonstrated an awareness of the information resources available to them through their university and an appreciation for the library and the wealth of knowledge it holds for both their academic and personal lives.

The experiences these students encountered in their home countries while accessing information and using libraries have laid a foundation for how they relate to information resources in the present. Their past experiences offered a means for comparing the resources they had access to in their home countries with their current access as international students in the US. Findings from this research demonstrated the diversity of experiences coming from the MENA region and shed light on a variety of factors that impact how international students engage with libraries. Elements that were found to influence student perceptions of libraries include educational backgrounds, the history of libraries in their home countries, prior experiences using libraries and seeking information, and educational expectations and standards.

A limitation of this study is that it only included a small number of students from select Arab nations and is therefore not representative of the entire Middle East; it does, however, provide a sampling of the perceptions of library and information use that incoming international students from MENA may have. The descriptions that students provided of their experiences with libraries and information may assist librarians in understanding the difficulties and transitions that international students face when introduced to higher education and academic libraries in the US.

Notes

1. Dawn Amsberry, "Deconstructing Plagiarism: International Students and Textual Borrowing Practices," *The Reference Librarian* 51 (2009): 31–44.
2. Ester J. de Jong and Candace A. Harper, "Preparing Mainstream Teachers for English-Language Learners: Is Being a Good Teacher Good Enough?," *Teacher Education Quarterly* (2005):101–24.
3. Siobhan Stevenson, "The Political Economy of Andrew Carnegie's Library Philanthropy, with a Reflection on its Relevance to the Philanthropic Work of Bill Gates," *Library & Information History* 26 (2010): 237–57, accessed April 3, 2017, doi:10.1179/175834910X12816060984359.
4. Patricia A Wand, "Key Library Constituents in an International Context," *Journal of Library Administration* 51 (2011): 242–54, accessed April 22, 2017, doi:10.1080/01930826.2011.540555.
5. *International Students and Academic Libraries: Initiatives for Success*, ed. Pamela A. Jackson and Patrick Sullivan (Chicago: Association of College and Research Libraries, 2011); David Koenigstein, "Alleviating International Students' Culture Shock and Anxiety in American Academic Libraries: Welcome, Ahlan Wa Sahlan, Anyeong Hae Sae Yo, Bienvenidos, Huan Ying, Sanu Da Zuwa, Shalom, Swaagat Hai," *Library Philosophy and Practice* (May 2012): 1–6; Martin Zimerman, "Plagiarism and International Students in Academic Libraries," *New Library World* 113 (2012): 290–99, accessed March 27, 2017, doi:10.1108/03074801211226373.
6. Feng-Ru Sheu and Roman S. Panchyshyn, "Social Introduction to Library Services for International Students," *Library Review* 66 (2017): 127–43, accessed April 3, 2017, doi:10.1108/LR-08-2016-0072; Xiang Li, Kevin McDowell, and Xiaotong Wang, "Building Bridges: Outreach to International Students via Vernacular Language Videos," *Reference Services Review* 44 (2016): 324–40, accessed March 20, 2017, doi:10.1108/RSR-10-2015-0044; Chris Langer and Hiromi Kubo, "From the Ground Up: Creating a Sustainable Library Outreach Program for International Students," *Journal of Academic Librarianship* 55 (2015): 605–21, accessed April 3, 2017, do i:10.1080/01930826.2015.1085232.
7. Selenay Aytac, "Use of Action Research to Improve Information Literacy Acquisition of International ESL Students," *New Library World* 117 (2016): 464–74, doi:10.1108/NLW-03-2016-0017; Alison Lahlafi and Diane Rushton, "Engaging International Students in Academic and Information Literacy," *New Library World* 116 (2015): 277–88, accessed April 3, 2017, doi:10.1108/NLW-07-2014-0088; Yusuke Ishimura and Joan C. Bartlett, "Are Librarians Equipped to Teach International Students? A Survey of Current Practices and Recommendations for Training,"

The Journal of Academic Librarianship 40 (2014): 313–21, accessed April 10, 2017, doi:10.1016/j.acalib.2014.04.009.

8. Ilka Datig, "What is a Library?: International College Students' Perceptions of Libraries," *The Journal of Academic Librarianship* 40 (2014): 350–56, accessed April 22, 2017, doi:10.1016/j.acalib.2014.05.001.
9. Dallas Long, "Latino Students' Perceptions of the Academic Library," *The Journal of Academic Librarianship* 37 (2011): 504–11, accessed April 21, 2017, doi:10.1016/j.acalib.2011.07.007.
10. Denice Adkins and Lisa Hussey, "The Library in the Lives of Latino College Students," *The Library Quarterly: Information, Community, Policy* 76 (2006): 456–80, accessed January 3, 2017, doi:10.1086/513862.
11. Abiodun I. Ibraheem and Christopher Devine, "Saudi Students, American Academic Library: A Survey, *Library Review* 65 (2016): 267–80, accessed April 20, 2017, doi:10.1108/LR-11-2015-0112.
12. Amanda B. Click, Josiah Drewry, and Mahmoud Khalifa, "Library and Information Science Research in the Arab World: A Systematic Review 2004–2013," in *Library and Information Science in the Middle East and North Africa*, ed. Amanda B. Click, Sumayya Ahmed, Jacob Hill and John D. Martin III, 235–54 (Berlin: de Gruyter, 2016).
13. Taghreed M. AlQudsi-ghabra, Ammar H. Safar, and Nedaa M. Qabazard, "Comparison of Private and Public School Library Services in Kuwait: A Case Study," *School Libraries Worldwide* 19 (2013): 45–58.
14. Janardhanan K. Vijatakumar and Faten Al Barayyan, "The Role of the Document Delivery Service at an Evolving Research Library in Saudi Arabia," *Interlending and Document Supply* 43 (2015): 41–46, accessed April 30, 2017, doi:10.1108/ILDS-01-2014-0011; Mohammad S. Awwad and Sawsan M. Al-Majali, "Electronic Library Services Acceptance and Use: An Empirical Validation of Unified Theory of Acceptance and Use of Technology," *The Electronic Library* 33 (2015): 1100–120, accessed April 30, 2017, doi:10.1108/EL-03-2014-0057; K. N. Sheshadri et al., "Library Consortium, Resources Sharing and Networking in United Arab Emirates: A Study," *International Journal of Library Science* 3 (2011), accessed April 30, 2017; Heather Lea Moulaison, "Exploring Access in the Developing World: People, Libraries and Information Technology in Morocco," *Library Hi Tech* 26 (2008): 586–97, accessed April 30, 2017, doi:10.1108/07378830810920914.
15. Vijatakumar and Al Barayyan, "The Role of the Document Delivery Service"; Awwad and Al-Majali, "Electronic Library Services Acceptance and Use"; Sheshadri et al., "Library Consortium"; Moulaison, "Exploring Access in the Developing World."
16. Awwad and Al-Majali, "Electronic Library Services Acceptance and Use."
17. Jordan M. Scepanski and Yasar Tonta, "Library Collections in the Middle East and North Africa," in *Library and Information Science in the Middle East and North Africa*, ed. Amanda B. Click, Sumayya Ahmed, Jacob Hill, and John D. Martin III, 235–54 (Berlin: de Gruyter, 2016); Maysoon Saleem, "Use of Social Media by Academic Librarians in Iraq," *New Library World* 116 (2015): 781–95, accessed April 30, 2017, doi:10.1108/NLW-03-2015-0018.
18. Engy I. Fahmy and Nermine M. Rifaat, "Middle East Information Literacy Awareness and Indigenous Arabic Content Challenges," *International Information & Library Review* 42 (2010): 111–23, accessed April 30, 2017, doi:10.1080/10572317.2010.10762853.
19. Abdoulaye Kaba, "Marking Information Resources and Services on the Web: Current Status of Academic Libraries in the United Arab Emirates," *Information Development* 27 (2011): 58–65, accessed April 22, 2017, doi:10.1177/0266666910394625
20. Mathew Moyo and Judith Mavodza, "A Comparative Study of Information Literacy Provision at University Libraries in South Africa and the United Arab Emirates: A Literature Review," *Library Review* 65 (2016): 93–107, accessed April 30, 2017, doi:10.1108/LR-06-2015-0069.
21. Janet Martin, Jane Birks, and Fiona Hunt, "Designing for Users: Online Information Literacy in the Middle East," *portal: Libraries and the Academy* 10 (2010): 57–73, accessed April 30, 2017, doi:10.1353/pla.0.0086.
22. Ahmad Khudair and David Bawden, "Healthcare Libraries in Saudi Arabia: Analysis and Recommendations," *Aslib Proceedings: New Information Perspectives* 59 (2007): 328–41, accessed

April 30, 2017, doi:10.1108/00012530710817555; Husain Al-Ansari, "Application of Information and Communication Technologies in Special Libraries in Kuwait," *The Electronic Library* 29 (2011): 457–69, accessed April 30, 2017, doi:10.1108/02640471111156731; AlQudsi-ghabra, Safar, and Qabazard. "Comparison of Private and Public School Library Services in Kuwait: A Case Study."

23. Khudair, "Healthcare Libraries in Saudi Arabia: Analysis and Recommendations."
24. Ibid.
25. Zeinab.
26. Zeinab.
27. Abdul.
28. Amir.
29. Nourah.
30. Ibid.
31. Abdul.
32. Ahmed.
33. Awadh.
34. Ahmed.
35. Abdul.
36. Zeinab
37. Ayoub.
38. Ahmed.
39. Zeinab.
40. Ayoub.
41. Pancea.
42. Ibid.
43. Zeinab.
44. Riham.
45. Nourah.
46. Zeinab.
47. Pancea.
48. Ayoub.
49. Nourah.
50. Moulaison, "Exploring Access in the Developing World: People, Libraries and Information Technology in Morocco."
51. Awadh.
52. Amir.
53. Pancea.

Bibliography

Adkins, Denice, and Lisa Hussey. "The Library in the Lives of Latino College Students." *The Library Quarterly: Information, Community, Policy* 76 (2006): 456–80. Accessed January 3, 2017. doi:10.1086/513862.

Al-Ansari, Husain. "Application of Information and Communication Technologies in Special Libraries in Kuwait." *The Electronic Library* 29 (2011): 457–69. Accessed April 30, 2017. doi:10.1108/02640471111156731.

AlQudsi-ghabra, Taghreed M., Ammar H. Safar, and Nedaa M. Qabazard. "Comparison of Private and Public School Library Services in Kuwait: A Case Study." *School Libraries Worldwide* 19 (2013): 45–58.

Amsberry, Dawn. "Deconstructing Plagiarism: International Students and Textual Borrowing Practices." *The Reference Librarian* 51 (2009): 31–44. Accessed April 22, 2017. doi:10.1080/02763870903362183.

Awwad, Mohammad S., and Sawsan M. Al-Majali. "Electronic Library Services Acceptance and Use:

An Empirical Validation of Unified Theory of Acceptance and Use of Technology." *The Electronic Library* 33 (2015): 1100–120. Accessed April 30, 2017. doi:10.1108/EL-03-2014-0057.

Aytac, Selenay. "Use of Action Research to Improve Information Literacy Acquisition of International ESL Students." *New Library World* 117 (2016): 464–74. doi:10.1108/NLW-03-2016-0017.

Click, Amanda B., Josiah Drewry, and Mahmoud Khalifa. "Library and Information Science Research in the Arab World: A Systematic Review 2004–2013." In *Library and Information Science in the Middle East and North Africa*. Edited by Amanda B. Click, Sumayya Ahmed, Jacob Hill, and John D. Martin III, 235–54. Berlin: de Gruyter, 2016.

Datig, Ilka. "What is a Library?: International College Students' Perceptions of Libraries." *The Journal of Academic Librarianship* 40 (2014): 350–56. Accessed April 22, 2017. doi:10.1016/j.acalib.2014.05.001.

de Jong, Ester T., and Candace A. Harper. "Preparing Mainstream Teachers for English-Language Learners: Is Being a Good Teacher Good Enough?" *Teacher Education Quarterly* 32 (2005): 101–24.

Fahmy, Engy I., and Nermine M. Rifaat. "Middle East Information Literacy Awareness and Indigenous Arabic Content Challenges." *International Information & Library Review* 42 (2010): 111–123. Accessed April 30, 2017. doi:10.1080/10572317.2010.10762853.

Ibraheem, Abiodun I., and Christopher Devine. "Saudi Students, American Academic Library: A Survey. *Library Review* 65 (2016): 267–80. Accessed April 20, 2017. doi:10.1108/LR-11-2015-0112.

International Students and Academic Libraries: Initiatives for Success. Edited by Pamela A. Jackson and Patrick Sullivan. Chicago: Association of College and Research Libraries, 2011.

Ishimura, Yusuke, and Joan C. Bartlett. "Are Librarians Equipped to Teach International Students? A Survey of Current Practices and Recommendations for Training." *The Journal of Academic Librarianship* 40 (2014): 313–21. Accessed April 10, 2017. doi:10.1016/j.acalib.2014.04.009.

Kaba, Abdoulaye. "Marking Information Resources and Services on the Web: Current Status of Academic Libraries in the United Arab Emirates." *Information Development* 27 (2011): 58–65. Accessed April 22, 2017. doi:10.1177/0266666910394625.

Koenigstein, David. "Alleviating International Students' Culture Shock and Anxiety in American Academic Libraries: Welcome, Ahlan Wa Sahlan, Anyeong Hae Sae Yo, Bienvenidos, Huan Ying, Sanu Da Zuwa, Shalom, Swaagat Hai." *Library Philosophy and Practice* (May 2012): 1–6.

Khudair, Ahmad, and David Bawden. "Healthcare Libraries in Saudi Arabia: Analysis and Recommendations." *Aslib Proceedings: New Information Perspectives* 59 (2007): 328–41. Accessed April 30, 2017. doi:10.1108/00012530710817555.

Khurshid, Zahiruddin. "Non-Librarians as Managers: The Case of State University Libraries in Saudi Arabia." *International Federation of Library Associations and Institutions* 39 (2013): 214–20. Accessed April 30, 2017. doi:10.1177/0340035213497675.

Lahlafi, Alison, and Diane Rushton. "Engaging International Students in Academic and Information Literacy." *New Library World* 116 (2015): 277–88. Accessed April 3, 2017. doi:10.1108/NLW-07-2014-0088.

Langer, Chris, and Hiromi Kubo. "From the Ground Up: Creating a Sustainable Library Outreach Program for International Students." *Journal of Academic Librarianship* 55 (2015): 605–21. Accessed April 3, 2017. doi:10.1080/01930826.2015.1085232.

Li, Xiang, Kevin McDowell, and Xiaotong Wang. "Building Bridges: Outreach to International Students via Vernacular Language Videos." *Reference Services Review* 44 (2016): 324–40. Accessed March 20, 2017. doi:10.1108/RSR-10-2015-0044.

Long, Dallas. "Latino Students' Perceptions of the Academic Library." *The Journal of Academic Librarianship* 37 (2011): 504–11. Accessed April 21, 2017. doi:10.1016/j.acalib.2011.07.007.

Martin, Janet, Jane Birks, and Fiona Hunt. "Designing for Users: Online Information Literacy in the Middle East." *portal: Libraries and the Academy* 10 (2010): 57–73. Accessed April 30, 2017. doi:10.1353/pla.0.0086.

Moyo, Mathew, and Judith Mavodza. "A Comparative Study of Information Literacy Provision at University Libraries in South Africa and the United Arab Emirates: A Literature Review." *Library Review* 65 (2016): 93–107. Accessed April 30, 2017. doi:10.1108/LR-06-2015-0069.

Moulaison, Heather Lea. "Exploring Access in the Developing World: People, Libraries and Information Technology in Morocco." *Library Hi Tech* 26 (2008): 586–97. Accessed April 30, 2017. doi:10.1108/07378830810920914.

Saleem, Maysoon. "Use of Social Media by Academic Librarians in Iraq." *New Library World* 116 (2015): 781–95. Accessed April 30, 2017. doi:10.1108/NLW-03-2015-0018.

Sheshadri, K. N., K. Manjunatha, D. Shivalingaiah, and Natarajan Radhakrishnan. "Library Consortium, Resources Sharing and Networking in United Arab Emirates: A Study." *International Journal of Library Science* 3 (2011). Accessed April 30, 2017.

Sheu, Feng-Ru, and Roman S. Panchyshyn. "Social Introduction to Library Services for International Students." *Library Review* 66 (2017): 127–43. Accessed April 3, 2017. doi:10.1108/LR-08-2016-0072.

Scepanski, Jordan M., and Yasar Tonta. "Library Collections in the Middle East and North Africa." In *Library and Information Science in the Middle East and North Africa*. Edited by Amanda B. Click, Sumayya Ahmed, Jacob Hill and John D. Martin III, 235–54. Berlin: de Gruyter, 2016.

Stevenson, Siobhan. "The Political Economy of Andrew Carnegie's Library Philanthropy, with a Reflection on its Relevance to the Philanthropic Work of Bill Gates." *Library & Information History* 26 (2010): 237–57. Accessed April 3, 2017. doi:10.1179/175834910X12816060984359.

Vijayakumar, Janardhanan K., and Faten Al Barayyan. "The Role of the Document Delivery Service at an Evolving Research Library in Saudi Arabia." *Interlending and Document Supply* 43 (2015): 41–46. Accessed April 30, 2017. doi:10.1108/ILDS-01-2014-0011.

Wand, Patricia A. "Key Library Constituents in an International Context." *Journal of Library Administration* 51 (2011): 242–54. Accessed April 22, 2017. doi:10.1080/01930826.2011.540555.

Zimerman, Martin. "Plagiarism and International Students in Academic Libraries." *New Library World* 113 (2012): 290–99. Accessed March 27, 2017. doi:10.1108/03074801211226373.

CHAPTER TWELVE

Applying an Instructional Design Approach to International Student Outreach

Kimberly Davies Hoffman and Kathy Leezin Wu

Introduction

The University of Rochester (UR), like most other American universities, is facing a rapid increase in international student enrollment. From 2010 to 2015, the university's international student population increased by 69 percent.[1]

Statistics from the UR's International Services Office (ISO) indicate enrollment of 1,127 international undergraduate students, 1,561 international graduate level students, and 488 visiting scholars representing 134 countries in the 2016–2017 academic year.[2] Our highest percentage of international students and scholars hail from China, India, and (South) Korea, with fall 2016 enrollment statistics at 1,811, 306, and 153 respectively.

With an eye to lending support to the growing number of international students and scholars, Kathy Wu, our government information and economics librarian (gov econ librarian), took a strong interest in making sure international students were well-acclimated to their new academic library system. Once an international student herself (from Taiwan), she has a keen understanding of how tricky it can be to move from one country to another, from one perspective of what a library offers to another.

For many years, the gov econ librarian has been heavily involved with courses in the English for Academic Purposes Program (EAPP), she has collaborated with UR's ISO, and she connects frequently with student associations with a cultural mission (e.g.,

Chinese Student Association). At times, the gov econ librarian developed ideas, planned, and worked with several science librarians to implement a handful of events targeted to Chinese graduate students majoring in engineering and sciences. In 2015, the gov econ librarian formalized her efforts in the inception of a library-based group named the UR International Community, or URIC. This team of eight library staff and librarians served to create a new era of commitment to supporting and highlighting the needs and cultures of our growing international population. Each member held a personal interest in the support of international students:

- At the Sommerville Science & Engineering Libraries, where the bulk of UR international students study in the sciences, the director is a Persian-born American citizen.
- The head of Outreach, Learning, and Research Services and the modern languages and culture outreach librarian both studied and taught languages and cultures—French and Spanish respectively.
- The education outreach librarian and the head of the Art/Music Library serve many graduate-level students hailing from abroad.
- The humanities outreach librarian and a library assistant IV possess a strong cultural heritage—India and Greece, respectively—and were also very committed to resolving the academic challenges faced by international students.

As a team, they collectively brainstorm programs, build campus partnerships, and collaborate to offer programs and events to reach a much wider audience of international students across campus.

With new departmental leadership and support through the head of Outreach, Learning, and Research Services (OLRS) came experience and expertise in instructional design (ID). Sound pedagogical and organizational approaches to instruction and programming were introduced and began to be practiced throughout OLRS. While ID cannot be fully applied to the various strategies and outreach programs mentioned within this chapter, especially for the activities that occurred prior to 2015, the ADDIE model has allowed us to put retroactive and ongoing pieces of the programming process into an organized structure. ADDIE—an acronym for Analysis, Design, Develop, Implement, Evaluate—is a common instructional design framework used to design and develop educational and training programs.[3] In applying this method to our work with international students, we are able to clearly see the lines of progression of our work as well as look back to consider where we can improve our efforts. We encourage other librarians to engage a similar model of instructional design thinking, no matter where they are in the process, to streamline efforts and document a reasonable path for moving forward with outreach and programming for international students.

In this chapter, we lay out the process and various steps of ADDIE as they relate to background user needs research, plans created to meet those needs, how specific programs were developed and implemented, and finally, closing the loop to improve upon our programs based on evaluating the success and impact of our efforts.

Analysis

Many international students arriving in the US have little learning and research experience in an American academic institution. Upon enrollment, they are expected to do everything the same as American students—a daunting task, as international students face barriers including language and cultural misunderstandings that their domestic peers do not have to face.

As mentioned in the introduction, through our gov econ librarian's personal experience, she could put herself into newly arriving international students' shoes. She could easily recognize their language, cultural, and personal challenges because she had lived them. Prior to 2011, informal conversations and interactions with international students and scholars suggested that many had not heard of crucial services such as interlibrary loan or basic navigational to in-depth research assistance via a librarian.

Having such hunches of the struggles faced by international students led us to want to know "the true story" through a variety of assessment measures. We needed to make sure our actions toward supportive programming for international students were not based merely on assumptions, but on data gathered from essential stakeholders—international students and the professors who work with them.

Assessment

Between 2011 and 2016, three purposeful assessment techniques were applied to gather information that could help RCL determine the true barriers that international students considered problematic to their ultimate academic success.

One. In 2011 through 2013, RCL librarians conducted a series of interviews with the following goals and questions in mind:

- How do international students use library services and resources?
- How do librarians engage international students in the research process?
- How can RCL create a comfortable and welcoming environment for international students?

The first set of interviews ran from May through November 2011. Fourteen Chinese graduate students from the Electrical and Computer Engineering (ECE) program were interviewed, followed up with focus groups of one to three students during lunches that typically lasted sixty to ninety minutes. The second set of interviews ran from May 2012 to May 2013. Eleven additional international students were interviewed, each meeting lasting about sixty minutes.

Two. In March and April 2016, librarians sent out a survey regarding international students to all River Campus faculty. The survey contained four questions about workshops for international students. (See Appendix 12A.) Sixty-three faculty from the eighteen academic departments/programs returned a response.

Three. In June to July 2016, a survey was sent to all incoming fall international graduate students. One hundred fifty-two international students representing a combined twenty-seven departments/programs responded to the survey. (See Appendix 12B.)

Assessment Results

Based on the information gathered, we are able to make some general assertions in five different areas: services, collections, library space and locations of study, past library research experience, and workshops. As much as possible, we will attempt to focus only on challenges unique to international students.

Services

While some students were not familiar with library terms like "interlibrary loan" or "recall," others were completely unaware that RCL provided services such as these. For those students who were already familiar with ILL service, they learned of it through tips shared by their faculty advisors and/or lab mates.

An interesting point learned was that international students place a strong reliance on their classroom, lab, and cultural networks to find solutions to academically based problems they face. Answers regarding what services the library can provide were limited to peers' past experience and perceptions of what the library is and does. When one student interviewee took a selective course in American educational and linguistics practices, outside of her network, she discovered how to effectively navigate the libraries and become familiar with the services RCL could provide.

Collections

Through interviews, we found that ECE Chinese graduate students were meeting their research needs via IEEE Xplore, as journal articles are their primary source for more in-depth study. Other international students stated using Web of Science, Compendex, PubMed, or Google Scholar.

Most of the interviewees indicated that students mainly used the library collections for their research. In cases when they could not find sources from within the library, they turned to their departmental advisors/professors. Some advisors and professors would lend books from their private collections, thus circumventing the opportunity to learn about ILL. In one interesting conversation with ECE Chinese graduate students, we learned that the multi-article needs for a literature review—a common practice within ECE—caused much concern with the students that they were running up enormous costs for the library. It became obvious that students were not familiar with the acquisitions process within American libraries or how we provide access to our subscription-based journal articles.

Library space and locations of study

In one-on-one conversations, many Chinese students described a library as merely a building with space for students to study quietly. In general, they do not conceive of a library as a hub where academic activities and learning opportunities occur. From discussions between the gov econ librarian and ECE Chinese students, we learned that these students had very little, if any, experience wandering their Chinese libraries' stacks and retrieving books (due to closed stacks policies) before they came to the US. Furthermore, these Chinese students had not become familiar with the UR Libraries' stacks, even one year or more into their studies at UR.

Students liked RCL's atmosphere, with a mix of quiet study areas and collaborative workspaces. One student described the library as a "holy place" and only for professionals. International students stated constant usage of the library as a place to study from the moment they arrived on campus. They further used the library as a get-away, solitary space after the intense group work and confined spaces experienced in their labs. Despite Carlson Science & Engineering Library's prime location for science students, the main, iconic Rush Rhees Library tends to be the most frequented library on campus and a preferred location for workshops and special services offered to international students.

However, students stated especially appreciating the welcoming feel of Carlson Library. Furthermore, some students were astonished by the idea of a library hosting a party.[4] This was quite a revolutionary idea for them. International students taking courses in fields like anthropology are encouraged to observe and absorb American culture through events like RCL's annual Scare Fair.

Past library research experience

Through data collection, we gleaned that some students came to the United States without much library experience, while others had worked in previous libraries as student employees. The past working experience within libraries enhanced and eased those international students' ability to acquire knowledge about American libraries and effectively utilize our resources.

Perhaps harkening back to their own country-specific library experiences, students were under a stereotypical impression that librarians sit behind the desk reading books or simply retrieving materials and replacing them on the shelves. The librarian, in their mind, would have nothing to do with students' research and/or learning. A librarian would not visit a class nor would they consult students upon their requests for research assistance. As a result, Chinese students would not immediately consider a librarian to be a source of assistance. Repeatedly, international students shared that they did not want to "bother" the librarians, "cause trouble," or "add more workload to librarians." Beyond pure politeness, other reasons for such reticence could be that students were nervous about expressing themselves verbally and/or being embarrassed in front of others, as they exposed an academic "weakness."

Some Chinese students mentioned that subject librarians do not exist in their university libraries. To them, Chinese librarians serve more as generalists, sharing all subject responsibilities with their librarian colleagues. However, this impression could be inaccurate since the interviewed Chinese students had very little personal interactions with librarians when they were in China.

Workshops

The majority of international students responding to the 2016 survey consider themselves needing help in all types/areas of academic or scientific writing. Eighty-four percent of the respondents expressed interest in workshops targeting the research process. Workshops focused on citation management and/or academic honesty were ranked of least interest to international students among the four topics offered. We continue to discuss whether the low level of interest is due to a cultural unfamiliarity with issues of academic honesty and plagiarism and thus these topics do not register with international students as being something of key importance to their academic success.

In sharp contrast, faculty survey respondents considered citation management and academic honesty workshops to be of most potential benefit to their international students. A need for learning the research process ranked as the second top workshop focus for international students, but only with a small score. Most of the faculty responding to the 2016 survey said that they would encourage their international students to seek librarian assistance and would post a link or list of workshops on their syllabus and/or Blackboard course.

Design

From interview data and surveys across academic departments, we were able to identify areas in which we could begin planning outreach efforts to minimize students' feeling of isolation, confusion, and lack of confidence in tasks that are key to achieving academic success. With a cautious eye to offering programs specifically targeted to international students' needs without calling attention to particular populations, we opted for a one-size-fits-all model while being strategic in where and how publicity of the events was orchestrated.

Based on our findings, we were able to begin focusing our attention on a few key areas.

Communication

We learned that most international students miss important, library-relevant information for a number of reasons. We also discovered that many international students choose not to approach librarians or library staff unless specifically urged by their faculty/advisors. We were heartened to hear from so many professors that they would be willing to forward library-related announcements or offers of research assistance through the syllabus, Blackboard announcements, or word-of-mouth. Librarians within OLRS are working hard to build and strengthen relationships with their departmental faculty via instructional initiatives, targeted outreach on issues of collections, data, scholarly communications, etc., and learning more about our Blackboard Learning Management System so that we are better prepared to assist with faculty's technical questions and emboldened to become a partner within the e-version of their courses. Faculty also become a key collaborator in our effort to reach international students. A broad marketing approach (i.e., announcements sent to all students and not just those who are international) seems best to lessen the potential of mislabeling international students as the only ones in need of certain library services. That said, we continue to partner with campus groups focused on the needs of international students, as well as those essential to graduate students.

Timing of events/intervention

Knowing the best time to distribute important library-based information plays a significant role in helping international students meet their academic needs. We found that international students would most likely read everything passed to them during orientation, when they first arrived on campus. The window of time is short—starting from the first day on campus until the first day of class—and the competition with so many other offices vying for their attention (not to mention their own personal acclimation to a new country and culture) can be overwhelming. During this transitional time, students have free time to explore their new learning environment. Everything is new to the students, and we expect the students to be eager to absorb any helpful information or personal resource (i.e., a librarian) that comes their way. This seems to be a prime time to capture their attention. It is important to track the ebb and flow of semester projects within a department so that we can reach out when needs to use the library are especially high. Finally, if we are to help students feel at home, we must think about breaks and holidays when most domestic students leave campus but international students typically stay, despite drastic decreases in food or residential services.

Creation of tools/guides

Delivering important library-relevant information to international students while removing all the possible cultural and language barriers and making sure international students are aware of the information that will be most helpful has become a true challenge for librarians. The creation of tools and guides must strike a balance of not overwhelming students with too much information, especially in library-specific terms, with an emphasis on what services will be most crucial to their success as students and how to relate some of these services to ones they might be familiar with in their country's libraries. Furthermore, we have noticed that students of certain countries rely on consuming information in their native language, despite being immersed in American culture and the English language. Tools and guides in English that allow for the opportunity to digest and re-read (or re-listen) would be of benefit to international students. Finally, we must consider where and at what times students will notice and pick up on tools and guides we create for them, thus distribution location and mode (print versus digital) are factors to think about.

We frequently negotiate the need to craft tools and guides that are specific to the needs of international students without labeling them as "special needs." Developing a guide for all (also known as universal design[5]) is tricky when deciding how much and what content to incorporate. Resources like books on writing techniques, CDs for American accent training, or identified reserve materials in the Chinese language would obviously not appeal to a domestic student wanting a primer on the library but would be key for our international community.

Types of events to organize

International students mentioned in the interviews that they learned a lot about the American library through library tours. This standard programming format would be just as valuable for domestic students; thus, thinking about how to craft a script (or a variety of script options) that can speak to specific but widespread needs is essential. Interviewees' impressions of library buildings, librarians, library services, and resources were very different from past experiences in their home countries. Considering library tours that can engage participants in conversations about their past library experience can help enliven the tour, bring meaning and transition from one experience to another, and allow librarian and students to foster a new relationship.

Feedback from the faculty survey stated that nearly 50 percent of the respondents think citation management and academic honesty workshops can dramatically benefit their international students. Other recommended workshop topics included research topic development, finding/evaluating resources, and getting familiar with the scholarly publishing landscape. These topics are of key importance to all students and we would need to be mindful of balancing the key content with issues like introductory context (as in the case of academic honesty), pacing (both in speech and content), and use of jargon. Thinking about workshops in phases (e.g., introductory, intermediate, and advanced) could help address these issues so that it would be up to the individual student to decide the right level of content for them. Also, titling a workshop to be something like *Cultural Differences in Academic Honesty* could attract international students as well as domestic students who are curious about how such matters are addressed abroad. While the librarian does not have to be the expert in areas of international law, the conversation between international and domestic students could be enough for each to walk away with new knowledge gained.

Information gathering

It is crucial to identify the myriad offices and departments on campus that have a stake in international students' success and share information, services, and ideas for collaboration and/or complementary services. Also important is that the library maintains a list of these key resources so that as needs arise, we can serve as a reference and a bridge between departments and services.

Development

In an attempt to increase the probability that they would utilize the library, we develop engaging and low-stress events, informational brochures/web resources, and celebrations to honor and share traditions of international students. We meet frequently with student service offices on campus (e.g., International Student Office, Writing, Speaking, and Argument Program, Center for Excellence in Teaching and Learning) so that coordinated programs reduce redundancy and carve out unique niches of support.

Indirect outreach efforts

We developed a novel brochure for international students and scholars. In this brochure,[6] we share policies on due dates and ways of renewing and requesting needed materials, featured services (like ILL, online chat, and citation management training), and a directory of subject librarians. We offer a print and electronic version of the brochure. In addition to the e-brochure, we were able to translate the RCL dean's welcome message into Chinese, French, Spanish, Arabic, and Korean languages (http://www.library.rochester.edu/welcome).

An accompanying library web page (http://libguides.lib.rochester.edu/InternationalStudentsGuide) targeted at international students and scholars was designed with their unique needs in mind. We include information about books for ESL users, DVDs and videos in different languages, self-paced YouTube tutorials for understanding LC call numbers and locating books and journals, and a directory for other relevant university services.

Workshops

Library tours, orientations to the libraries' services and resources, workshops to guide students how to use databases with key searching tips, citation clinics, and programs on issues of academic honesty have been scheduled multiple times at perceived key points in the semester when students would have the most immediate need. (See Appendix 12C.)

Other, more sophisticated topics for workshops, as identified via faculty and graduate student surveys, continue to be discussed and shared with campus partners so we can make sure that the right departments are offering relevant services. UR's Writing,

Speaking, and Argument Program (WSAP) is one office with whom we communicate frequently. Both faculty and graduate students have identified the desire for more writing training—in general terms as well as for specialized scientific writing. Expressed interest in relating to and communicating with one's research advisor, along with the ability to find research mentors, can be developed within specific departments and/or through the Office of Graduate Studies. Assistance with reading speed and retention could be referred to our Center for Excellence in Teaching and Learning (CETL). Skills-based workshops on the evaluation of sources and locating then synthesizing information fall squarely into the wheelhouse of the library. We are currently debating whether to offer standalone programs for such things or, as we strengthen our presence within disciplinary courses, make sure these skills are integrated into departments where we see higher percentages of international students.

Making students feel at home

One of the library's first interactions with international students happens through group orientations, whether for all undergraduate students or through academic departments. It is important that we make a positive first impression, offering just enough information that students will retain in a sea of new details from many campus departments and offices. As long as we can convey to the students that the library is a place of refuge, resources, and assistance, and encourage them to ask questions no matter how simple they deem their question, we will feel successful. Through URIC planning, our undergraduate orientation for international students has morphed into a playful and competitive game of Bingo, utilizing information gleaned from League of Librarian cards[7] and other library resources. Graduate-level orientations focus more on the serious nature of research, teaching, and faculty relationships where we stress the idea of librarians as collaborators.

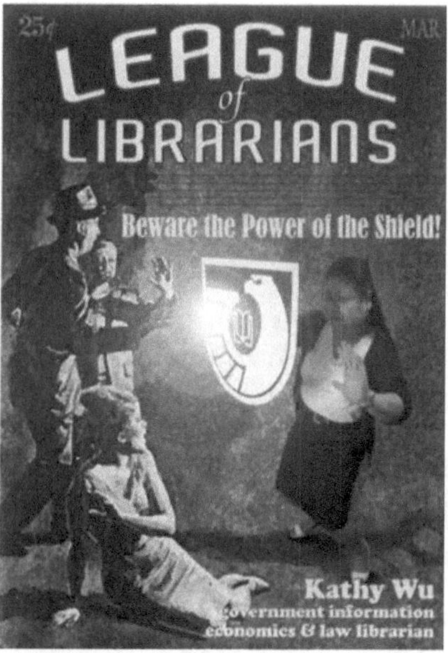

Figure 12.1. Example of a League of Librarians card

To promote diversity and inclusion on campus, URIC organized a series of cultural events meant to honor and share the traditions of our students. Offering these opportunities campus-wide provided a sense of place and pride to the students participating in the events. We were also able to expose new cultural traditions to students outside of the highlighted countries, sparking new conversations and bringing disparate populations together.

A few of our programs related to holiday traditions included the following:

- Diwali celebrations featuring students and faculty of India dressed in traditional costume who spoke of the region-specific ways in which they celebrate the Festival of Light (including in the United States) and showcased Indian treats.
- For Lunar New Year celebrations, students from China, South Korea, Vietnam, Hong Kong, and Taiwan organized stations where they could highlight how their country celebrates the new year, along with library collections, crafts, and food. The second year of this celebration focused on a university professor who shared his expertise in the traditional Chinese art of papercutting.
- Nowruz, the Persian New Year, was marked by a showcase of culture, music, dance, and food. An anthropology professor spoke to the crowd, sharing traditions of Nowruz, peppering in moments of music videos and dance, one most notably orchestrated by students of a World Dance course who prepared a performance specifically for the event.

Seeking greater opportunities to connect our programming with UR curricula, URIC sponsored a demonstration of Mukbang, a Korean food and social media phenomenon, and encouraged professors from a Writing About Food course and a Korean language course to embed elements of Mukbang into their curriculum. Both professors brought their students to the event so they could experience the phenomenon first hand and continue conversations they had been having in class.

Finally, to make our international students feel at home in the library, especially during semester breaks, URIC has hosted pizza parties with primarily American-style games. These informal events allow library staff to build relationships with some of our students in conversational language exchange. They serve to feed our students while the dining halls are closed, and in the case of a Mid-Day Countdown on December 31, to bring us together to ring in the new year.

Implementation

The UR International Community (URIC) emerged in 2015 as a small team of library staff dedicated to increasing the library's profile in support of student academic success. The delivery of multiple events and learning opportunities has become more numerous and varied and much better supported than what one librarian could do on her own.

The members of URIC, under the leadership of the gov econ librarian, continue to meet monthly to discuss international student needs (based on survey findings and anecdotally), look to the future to see what's possible, and plan for tools, workshops, and events.

Setting dates according to the ebb and flow of the semester, along with meeting greatest academic needs in a timely fashion, becomes priority #1. Finding conducive locations to sponsor the events, with an eye to highest visibility (for targeted audiences as well as those who might happen upon an event) and of benefit to meet the tailored program needs, takes some strategy and practical thinking. Where, when, to whom, and in what venues to publicize the events are thinking pieces crucial to getting the word out in order to attract the greatest audience. As mentioned earlier, a new direction we have taken is to think critically about what courses have an interest in the events we are planning. Can we inspire those professors and students to bring the content into their classroom before or after a program happens? Can we help professors develop meaningful assignments to expand the learning horizons of the students? The fact that an instructor committed to teaching her World Dance students a new style and choreography of dance in preparation for Nowruz exceeded our expectations and added a tremendous richness to both the program and the students' course experience.

Details involving how many volunteers are needed, what the room set-up will look like and who will move furniture, what supplementary materials are necessary to enrich the program, how to engage students in a program to provide ownership (and retention) in the learning, etc. are all necessary to consider in advance to ensure success of a program.

We've seen some big wins with our program efforts, along with others that elicited little to no response. The ability to observe, analyze, and reflect on our experiences help to keep us motivated, moving ahead, and improving to solidify successful growth. For a snapshot of attendance levels of our various programs, table 12.1 is divided among our series categories: orientations, workshops, holidays, and Global Village.

TABLE 12.1
URIC Sponsored Programs and Numbers of Participants

Orientations	**# of participants**
International Student Orientation (undergraduates), 2015 and 2016 combined	298
Orientation to the Simon School English Language & US Culture Program, 2015 and 2016 combined	80
Warner School International Student Orientations, 2015 and 2016 combined	65
Workshops	**# of participants**
Library Tours, 2015 and 2016 combined	20
Workshops for the ISO's ESL classes	57
Introduction to the Library Services & Resources	10
Ethics in Academic Honesty	4
Citation Clinic, 2015-2017 combined	20
Research Support to the International Summer Immersion Program (ISIP), 2015 and 2016 combined	54
Support and showcasing ISIP student presentations on the final project	32
Seminars on brief histories of UR in 12 objects and 24 buildings	18
Introduction to Reference Managers	1

TABLE 12.1
URIC Sponsored Programs and Numbers of Participants

Holidays	# of participants
Diwali celebration, 2015 and 2016 combined	83+
Lunar New Year celebration, 2016	80+
Japanese Sakura Celebration with a demonstration on the Tea Ceremony and showcasing the Doll Festival and Children's Day, 2016	20
Chinese New Year celebration with a focus on papercutting, 2017	57
Persian New Year celebration, 2017	85
Global Village	**# of participants**
Book display for the International Community, 2015	n/a
Book display on Third Culture Kids, 2015	n/a
Book display on International Education Week, 2016	n/a
International Game Day and Pizza Party, 2015	38
Pizza Party and Mid-Day countdown on Dec. 31, 2015	27
Mukbang highlighting Korean food and culture, 2017	84

In sum, through all of URIC's activities and events dating 2015–2017, we have reached 1,133 international students and scholars. Additionally, we have calculated 274 views of our International Students & Scholars' Libguide from February 2016–May 2017, with countless "shares" of the material within the guide from librarian to librarian.

Evaluation

URIC continues to monitor the progress of our efforts to support students and make adjustments where necessary. Some of our bigger successes include 164 incoming students representing numerous countries attending a lively library orientation session in 2016 and 325 attendees between the holiday celebrations in 2015–2017. Conversely, we must still work on finding the best topics, times, and marketing venues to attract a greater number of program participants. Through an overall evaluation of how our library programs as a whole were functioning, we've been able to identify some themes of areas we need to focus more attention on and develop helpful worksheets/checklists that guide the way to a successful program. Attention to planning for the following themes have helped to increase participation:

- **Bring an audience with you.** Specifically seek campus groups and academic courses you can identify as potential audiences of interest; either extending a special invitation to attend or suggest ways in which the coursework can benefit from the upcoming program.
- **Timing is everything.** Whether following the ebb and flow of the semester and project due dates or coordinating with a special day, week, or month, "hitching your horse" to a timeline that's meaningful and will attract the attention of those most in need can pay off in terms of audience numbers and impact.

- **Make it interactive.** We have experimented with offering programs in a myriad of formats (large lecture hall orientations, library tours, closed room workshops, formal events with guest speakers, and open-space pop-up programs), but one thing we have learned as a way to draw an audience and have them remember the experience is to get them involved.
- **Plan, plan, and plan some more.** One of our most valued checklists right now is a comprehensive list of publicity methods, main contacts for sending out announcements, and deadlines to be sure we don't miss opportunities to communicate our events.

Now that we have offered programs in a one-size-fits-all universal design model with varying success, we are turning our attention to outreach librarians assigned to specific departments to take a more subject-oriented approach. The pivot came to us in a spark as librarians assigned to the sciences were sharing their success delivering chemistry-focused workshops and stating how many (presumably) international students were in attendance. If general workshops on academic honesty don't call to international students at large, perhaps we will have more success working with faculty and department research councils to offer programs that are in direct need of students' academic priorities. This way, we develop a captive audience and continue with the idea of universal learning design—in this case, at least, for students in the sciences.

Our latest focus is to interview all RCL outreach librarians to find out more about the student composition of their subject areas, the most obvious resource and research-related needs, and the ways in which the librarians are already reaching out to their students, whether international or not. Once an analysis of each area is done, URIC can begin brainstorming ideas with the subject librarians, offering up gained knowledge about the needs of international students who could potentially be studying within their assigned departments. We could work with the outreach librarians to develop methods of instructional approach that could address specific needs of international students while engaging domestic students in the cultural diversity of their discipline. Playing off international and domestic students' strengths and academic contributions would be a huge win for everyone.

Conclusion

With our latest round of interviews with librarians and data gathered from recent survey results of international graduate students, a new cycle of ADDIE begins. We are currently at the point of embarking on analysis of the data, solidifying numbers of international students per academic department, discovering trends across librarian approaches and needs of our constituents, sharing best practices, and then moving into plans for the future—a continuous, cyclical process that will ensure progress, refinement, and success, especially as projections of international student enrollment are due to increase.

Furthermore, practices in outreach and in the classroom have already manifested themselves. Our most recent international student orientation focuses on gathering students' stories of their past library experiences to open the door for informal conversations about what the River Campus Libraries will offer them. A summer bridge program engaged African students, many of whom will attend American universities in fall 2017, in the differences between their past library experiences to what they can expect at the university library they visit and utilize next.

As we reflect back to our gov econ librarian's inspirational start to assuring that UR international students were looked after to all that we have accomplished since URIC's beginnings in 2015 and beyond, we feel confident that our efforts will continue to grow and strengthen as demographics on campus shift. While overall strategies and committee participation may adjust to ongoing needs and priorities of the library, our dedication to serving international students, among all segments of our diverse campus population remains firm.

Appendix 12A: Faculty Survey about International Students' Needs (http://goo.gl/MEBLCF)

Survey about International Students

Dear Professors,

The River Campus Libraries recognize that international graduate and undergraduate students often need extra support because of their relative unfamiliarity with the American academic system. As the liaison librarians for your departments, we want to understand the gaps in academic preparation that you may notice in your international graduate and undergraduate students. Based on your feedback, we will work to design, offer, and/or coordinate (with relevant campus services) workshops that will support your international students in their academic success. By completing the following four-question survey, please let us know which workshops you believe will benefit your students most.

Thank you very much,

River Campus Outreach Librarians

1. Please identify your department

2. Do you think international students will benefit from workshops on the following? (Please rank the workshops from 1 (most useful) to 7 (least useful) to indicate the usefulness of the workshops.)

- Research process (developing topic, finding and evaluating resources)
- Funding opportunities (finding venues and writing grant proposals)
- Conference opportunities (finding venues, writing proposals, and developing engaging presentation)
- Scholarly publishing landscape (finding journals, writing reviews, Open Access, copyright/author agreements)
- Introduction to data management, preservation, and UR Research Institutional Repository
- Citation management and academic honesty
- Academic skills like time management or note taking when researching

3. Do you have suggestions for other workshops?

4. In what ways do you foresee encouraging your students to seek out assistance from the librarians?

	Graduate Students	Undergraduate Students
Offer extra credit		
Encourage students during office hours		
Encourage students during class		
Offer a link or list of workshops on my syllabus		
Announcements via Blackboard, etc.		

Other (please specify)

Appendix 12B: International Graduate Student Survey (http://goo.gl/1mUVng)

International Graduate Student Survey

The River Campus Libraries recognize that as an international graduate student, you bring your cultural and learning experience to University of Rochester community, and contribute to the university's global experience. We also recognize that it is a brand new academic experience for you. As the liaison librarians for your departments, we want to offer workshops that will support your academic careers at the University of Rochester. By completing the following five-question survey, please let us know which workshops will benefit you most.

Thank you very much,

River Campus Outreach Librarians

1. Please identify your department

2. Do you need help with academic/scientific writing for:

	Select all that apply
Research paper/course assignments	
Thesis	
Dissertation	
Conference paper	

Other (please specify)

3. If workshops on the following topics are offered at Rush Rhees Library and Carlson Library, which ones would you attend?

	Select all that apply
Research process (developing topic, finding and evaluating resources)	
Citation management and academic honesty	
Introduction to data management, preservation, and UR Research Institutional Repository	
Academic skills like time management or note taking when researching	

4. Do you have suggestions for other workshops?

5. Location wise, which library will work best for you to attend workshops?

- Rush Rhees Library
- Carlson Library
- Physics-Optics-Astronomy Library (POA)

Appendix 12C: Schedule of 2016-2017 workshops (http://goo.gl/LJ9aPS)

Library Tour (The tour is about 15 to 30-minute long. Participating students may stay in the tour as long as they want according to their schedule.)

Date	Time	Participating Librarian
9-9-16	3 pm	
9-13-16	3 pm	
9-14-16	11:30 am	
9-16-16	11:30 am	
9-21-16	3 pm	
9-23-16	3 pm	

Workshops (provided by the Citation Management Tool Team) - Intro to **what a Reference Manager is**

Fall 2016

Date	Time	Location	Participating Librarian
Oct 26, 2016	1 pm – 2 pm	Rush Rhees	
Nov. 3, 2016	1 pm – 2 pm	Carlson	
Nov. 10, 2016	4 pm – 5 pm	Rush Rhees	
Nov. 15, 2016	4 pm – 5 pm	Carlson	

Spring 2017

Date	Time	Location	Participating Librarian
March 29, 2017	1 pm – 2 pm	Rush Rhees	
April 5, 2017	1 pm – 2 pm	Carlson	
April 12, 2017	4 pm – 5 pm	Rush Rhees	
April 19, 2017	4 pm – 5 pm	Carlson	

Workshops on Library Services and Resources

Date	Time	Location	Participating Librarian
Oct. 28, 2016	3 pm – 3:30 pm	Rush Rhees	
Oct. 28, 2016	3 pm – 3:30 pm	Carlson	
Nov. 4, 2016	4:30 pm – 5 pm	Rush Rhees	
Nov. 4, 2016	4:30 pm – 5 pm	Carlson	

Workshops on Using Databases & Searching Tips - Bring Your Own Topics (Each session needs two librarians)

Date	Time	Location	Participating Librarian # 1	Participating Librarian # 2
(Humanities/Social Sciences) Nov. 11, 2016	4 pm – 5 pm	Rush Rhees		
(Science) Nov. 11, 2016	4 pm – 5 pm	Carlson		
(Humanities/Social Sciences) Nov. 18, 2016	4 pm – 5 pm	Rush Rhees		
(Science) Nov. 18, 2016	4 pm – 5 pm	Carlson		

Workshops on Ethical Writing Process in Academic Honesty

Date	Time	Location
Oct. 19, 2016	6 pm – 7 pm	Rush Rhees
Nov. 2, 2016	6 pm – 7 pm	Carlson

Notes

1. Office of the Provost, "Past Factbooks," University of Rochester, accessed August 22, 2017, http://www.rochester.edu/provost/ir/pastfactbooks.html.
2. International Student Office, "All UR Sponsored Students and Scholars," University of Rochester, accessed August 22, 2017, https://rochester.box.com/shared/static/izm9c41f0z9vj80ur9ng96hbzqfcnhvf.pdf.
3. Ed Forest, "ADDIE Model: Instructional Design," *Educational Technology*, January 29, 2014, http://educationaltechnology.net/the-addie-model-instructional-design/.
4. River Campus Libraries, "Scare Fair 2016," University of Rochester, October 2016, https://www.library.rochester.edu/event/scare-fair-2016.
5. National Center on Universal Design for Learning, "What is UDL?," July 31, 2014, http://www.udlcenter.org/aboutudl/whatisudl.
6. River Campus Libraries, "Are You Library Smart?," Fall 2016, https://www.library.rochester.edu/files/pdf/survival_tips_international_students.pdf.
7. Kathleen McGarvey, "In a league of their own," *Rochester Review* 72, no. 3 (2010), http://www.rochester.edu/pr/Review/V72N3/feature2.html.

Bibliography

Forest, Ed. "ADDIE Model: Instructional Design." *Educational Technology*. January 29, 2014. http://educationaltechnology.net/the-addie-model-instructional-design/.

International Student Office. "All UR Sponsored Students and Scholars." University of Rochester. Accessed August 22, 2017. https://rochester.box.com/shared/static/izm9c41f0z9vj80ur9ng96hbzqfcnhvf.pdf.

McGarvey, Kathleen. "In a League of Their Own." *Rochester Review* 72, no. 3 (2010). http://www.rochester.edu/pr/Review/V72N3/feature2.html.

National Center on Universal Design for Learning. "What is UDL?" July 31, 2014. http://www.udlcenter.org/aboutudl/whatisudl.

Office of the Provost. "Past Factbooks." University of Rochester. Accessed August 22, 2017. http://www.rochester.edu/provost/ir/pastfactbooks.html.

River Campus Libraries. "Are You Library Smart?" Fall 2016. https://www.library.rochester.edu/files/pdf/survival_tips_international_students.pdf.

———. "Scare Fair 2016." University of Rochester. October 2016. https://www.library.rochester.edu/event/scare-fair-2016.

CHAPTER THIRTEEN

Developing Effective Integration Services:

Learning from Asian International Graduate Students Academic-Striving Experiences

Yi-Chin Sarah Wu

Introduction

Although the number of international students has increased each year in the US, recent studies[1,2] have highlighted several caveats for the future competitiveness of American higher education. The Canadian government aims to double the number of international students by the year 2022.[3] China has also developed a plan to become an education hub in the near future.[4] Meanwhile, scholars have paid attention to the mobility of international students, the numerous benefits for institutions, and immigration policies around the world. However, the learning experiences of international students have not been fully examined in the US. Research on enhancing students' retention, graduation, or academic performance has focused on assisting at-risk students or non-traditional students as well as increasing their involvement in diverse activities during their studies. For many years, international students were often found to be isolated from the host society or suffered from loneliness.[5,6] Therefore, it is valuable to explore students' experiences from their perspectives to improve current services or programs and fill their needs.

Literature Review

Acculturation

Traditionally, anthropologists widely study the impact of culture variation among different societies. In recent years, social scientists and educators have endeavored to explore the influence of culture on learning.[7,8] Limited studies have shown that culture as a factor is tied to students' academic performance. Schwartz[9] asserted that culture is a critical factor that affects the determinants of goal setting and goal completion. Researchers have also identified learning patterns among Asian Americans,[10,11] African Americans,[12,13] and Native Americans.[14,15] Scholars indicated that Western learning culture values private and public questioning of knowledge while Eastern culture values the effortful, respectful, and pragmatic acquisition of knowledge.[16] People from individualistic cultures, such as Americans, are taught the concept of being independent. As a result, they tend to express their own needs and personal rights.[17] By contrast, people from less independence-focused cultures, such as Chinese, tend to avoid drawing attention to themselves and their personal opinions.[18,19]

International students on US campuses can be seen as a vulnerable group. Most of them previously studied primarily in their home countries and relocated to the US to pursue advanced degrees.[20] When these students make the adjustments necessary to succeed in their new culture, this can be life-changing. Scholars call this change "acculturation."[21] Berry defined acculturation as "the dual process of cultural and psychological change that takes place as a result of contact between two or more cultural groups and their individual members."[22] As they interact with different cultures, individuals' experiences change their behavior or values, or both.

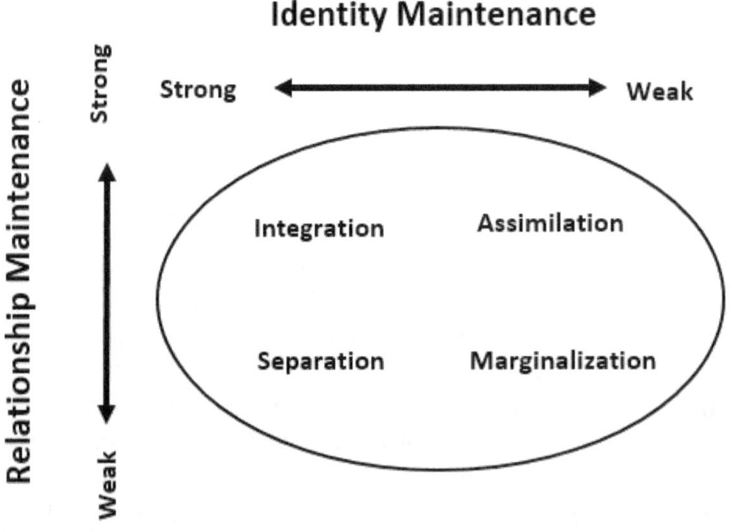

Figure 13.1. Four Acculturation Tendencies.
Adapted from "Immigration, Acculturation and Adaptation," by J. W. Berry, 1997, *Applied Psychology: An International Review*, 46, p. 10.

Berry's[23–25] bi-dimensional model of acculturation (see figure 13.1) has been widely used in immigration studies and will be used as the theoretical framework of this study. In this model, four acculturation tendencies—integration, assimilation, separation, and marginalization—are cultivated by exploring people's perceptions regarding two main topics. The first topic examines the level at which people maintain their identity and characteristics (identity maintenance), and the second examines the level at which they maintain relationships within the host society (relationship maintenance). In this model, people with weak identity maintenance but strong relationship maintenance with the host society are categorized as having an *assimilation* tendency of acculturation. People with strong identity maintenance and relationship maintenance with the host society are categorized as having an *integration* tendency of acculturation. People with strong identity maintenance but weak relationship maintenance with the host society are categorized as having a *separation* tendency of acculturation. And finally, weak relationships with both dimensions are categorized as the *marginalization* tendency of acculturation.

To be clear, using Berry's acculturation model as the basic framework with which to identify an international student's acculturation tendencies does not imply that students have no other acculturation characteristics; rather, it simply identifies the strategies of acculturation students prefer to use in most contexts. In this study, I adopted Berry's acculturation model as a lens through which to investigate Asian international graduate students' acculturation tendencies.

Academic striving

Selecting classes or activities that advance skills, trying to reach educational goals, having conversations with people from diverse backgrounds, and completing multiple academic tasks in college or university can be a tough journey for many students. It can be even more strenuous for international students since they often experience more culture shock or adaptation issues than domestic students.

Social cognitive theory, motivation theory, self-determination theory, and attribution theory have developed frameworks for researchers to understand the impact of students' motivation, goals, and beliefs on their academic performance.[26–28] Tinto[29] has developed a theoretical model that identifies the various factors that influence students' academic persistence. Students' engagement in academic and social activities has a positive impact on their persistence in completing their education. Correspondingly, Kuh[30] asserted that engagement in educationally purposeful activities was also associated with desired college outcomes. The importance of grit—determination and resilience—in successful college experiences has gained the attention of educational researchers in recent years. Duckworth and Quinn[31] found that grit predicted students' academic performance in US military academies. Researchers found that Black male college students who had higher grit levels had higher grade performance than students with lower grit levels.[32] However, Tewell, Berg, and Galvan[33] have argued that educators labeling students with higher or lower resilience could overlook efforts students are making and therefore miss opportunities to engage with them.

Few studies have examined how the motivations, beliefs, or goals of international students are linked to their academic performance, although recent research has provided greater insights into their learning challenges, such as English deficiency[34] and lack of academic socialization.[35] In their studies of international students, Poyrazli and Kavanaugh[36] found that Asian students experienced more overall adjustment strain and lower levels of English proficiency than European students. Even though many higher education institutions provide such services as orientations and diverse culture events to help international students adjust to US campuses, research indicates that these students are unlikely to use those services or do not see the services as meeting their needs.[37–39]

Despite the growing body of studies on the predictors of successful academic performance in college, research on international students' learning experiences accompanied by a cultural perspective of academic performance has been limited. To date, Severiens and Wolff[40] found that academic integration had a positive effect on learning and grades among domestic students. However, they also found that academic integration had a positive impact on the quality of learning for international students but negatively affected their grades. Glass and Westmont[41] affirmed that a sense of belonging enhanced international students' grades. Although grades are usually seen as a gauge of students' academic performance, looking solely at an international graduate students' GPA might be problematic due to the nature of the graduate program. Without applying GPA as students' academic performance, Wu[42] examined the relationship among acculturation, academic, and social integration and found that both identity maintenance and relationship maintenance of acculturation predicted students' academic integration, but identity maintenance of acculturation alone did not predict social integration.

Because international students' learning issues have attracted educators' attention more and more, it is worth exploring the reasons and strategies used by Asian international graduate students to fulfill their needs and achieve their goals.

Purpose

The study is primarily guided by the acculturation framework and literature on college students' learning outcomes, with particular attention to students' goals, beliefs, motivations, and learning experiences. The purpose of this study is to explore academic-striving experiences among Asian international graduate students with regard to their acculturation tendencies, the challenges associated with their relationships with American students, faculty, or co-national peers, and strategies they used to address their concerns.

Methodology

First, acculturation scores from 116 Asian international graduate students were collected from two research universities in the spring of 2016. Fifty-three of these students who agreed to participate in follow-up interviews were then categorized into the four acculturation tendencies, based on their acculturation scores. Then, in the summer of 2016, twelve Asian international students were purposefully selected for further interviews—three participants for each acculturation tendency. To gain insight into students' lived experiences and explore their perspectives, an interview protocol (see Appendix 13A) was developed that asked open-ended questions and used some prompts. The goal of the interview was to encourage "students to make sense of their experience rather than the educator making sense of it for them."[43] The interview protocol included five open-ended questions, which were composed to elicit students' feelings, the reasons for their engagement in their home culture and American culture, their strategies for conquering difficulties, and suggestions for their institutions. In general, the interviews lasted about sixty minutes. All of the interviews were transcribed. Cross-case analysis[44] was applied to explore the connections and dissimilarities across cases and the four acculturation tendencies.

The following table presents the descriptive analyses of the background characteristics of the twelve interviewees. Each acculturation tendency had three Asian international graduate students. Pseudonyms were assigned to provide anonymity to every participant.

TABLE 13.1.
Interviewee demographic information

Acculturation	Name	Nationality	Gender	Degree Status	Discipline
Assimilation	Adam	China	Male	3rd year, Doctoral	STEM
	Austin	South Korea	Male	2nd year, Master	Social Science
	Angel	Malaysia	Female	2nd year, Master	Business
Integration	Ian	China	Male	3rd year, Doctoral	Humanities
	Isaac	South Korea	Male	2nd year, Doctoral	STEM
	Ida	China	Female	2nd year, Master	Social Science
Separation	Sam	India	Male	4th year, Doctoral	Social Science
	Scott	Taiwan	Male	3rd year, Doctoral	STEM
	Sally	Vietnam	Female	2nd year, Doctoral	Social Science
Marginalization	Mary	South Korea	Female	4th year, Doctoral	Art
	Mona	Taiwan	Female	5th year, Doctoral	Social Science
	Ming	China	Male	2nd year, Master	Social Science

Seven males and five females participated in this study, and all of them were pursuing their degrees as full-time students in the US for the first time. All of the students had been in their programs for at least one year.

Results

Assimilation

Students with assimilation tendencies scored high on maintaining a relationship with American society but low on maintaining their Asian cultural identity. Students with an assimilation tendency revealed that improving their English was the most important goal before they came to the US. When these students started school, they realized that interacting with students from their own countries could edge out their time spent interacting with American students. Therefore, they preferred to spend most of their time interacting with domestic students. Even though they missed their home culture, they did not see it as harming their academic performance. In this study, Angel and Austin both chose to have American students as roommates during their first year. Angel, a second-year master's student from Malaysia, said:

I went back to my country for a short visit during summer. When I come back to the US, I found that my English was not [as] fluent as before. I guess it is because I spend too much time on speaking my mother language. For me, it was terrible. I was scared because this situation can change my academic performance, right? I try to speak English as much as I can. I try to participate [in] all kinds of events that my college host[s]. I feel I learn more American culture than other international students.

Austin, who came from South Korea, said:

> I don't like to say I like to hang out with Americans more than Korean[s]. I feel that it is more like a necessary thing. I live in the US, so I

> need to know them. It would help me get along well. But I only have twenty-four hours and I have work to do. I have to read; I have to do experiments. Do I have extra time talk with other Koreans? No, but if yes, I would love to talk with them, but I don't have that extra [time].

Adam, a third-year doctoral student from China, said:

> Now I am here, I want to know the culture. It's about the life you choose. I know people say [the] international students who like to hang out with Americans are hypocritical, worship foreign things, and fawn on foreign powers or forget my origin, so on and so on. But I don't care. I feel sad, but I won't change my decision.

When following up on a question regarding his efforts to maintain his academic performance, Adam said:

> Building my social network with other Americans is critical for my future career. Although my American friends did not really help my GPA, the interactions with them did help me in understanding their culture. I did not know what to talk [about] in a social event; however, I feel now I have more confidence to work with them, talk with them, or have deeper conversations.

Integration

Students with an integration tendency scored high on both maintaining a relationship with

American society and in maintaining their Asian cultural identity. Like students with assimilation tendencies, students with integration tendencies often participated in American curricular or co-curricular activities; however, they also revealed their challenges and limitations in making friends with domestic students. For example, Isaac said:

> It's necessary to understand American culture if I live here. This is also a learning process that I won't avoid. I know I cannot become them [Americans]. I know I would never belong to them. I like to experience their homecoming, and I like their meaning of Thanksgiving. But there is some part of American culture that I did not get used to it, or I will never be proficient at, such socializing in public—that's my weakness. They can talk a lot [laugh], really, everything! I listen; that's also part of my culture.

Like Isaac, Ian showed that things had changed from his first year to his third year in his program:

> My first year, I tried to get as many American friends as I can. But at the same time, my English was terrible at first year. I guess I ruined many friendships that might be able to go further.

Ian occasionally participated in some social events but did not push himself to have strong relationships with domestic students. Making friends with domestic students could be challenging for international students. Like Isaac, Ida mentioned her efforts to immerse herself in American culture. She said:

> No matter, my American classmates invite me to whatever parties, I always said yes in the first year; however, I am really not a party girl. I often feel isolated in those events. And I have so many school work need to be finished. So, now, I decline their invitations more often. I don't know what they think of me, but I think it will be fine.

Compared to the assimilation students with "strong ties" to American society, the "weak ties" of students with integration tendencies adjust their goals and behaviors when their attempts to make friends were unsuccessful or not as satisfying as they had expected. When asking these students about their efforts to maintain their academic performance, Ida said:

> I always like to ask my classmates if they want to have lunch or dinner together. At that situation, it is more casual, we have same interests. At least we are from same program [laugh]. And I can control the conversation topic: faculty, homework, stress ...etc. I do the same thing with friends from my countries. We talk about finding a job here, how to give good impression, sometimes some visa issues. They have more experiences than I do. Some are doctoral students. So, I get lots of benefits from talking with different people.

Separation

Students with separation tendencies scored low on maintaining a relationship with American society but high on maintaining their Asian cultural identity. Scott mentioned that opportunities for immersion did not exist, even though he lived in the US, because of the characteristics of his program. He said:

> The most challenging part during my doctoral career so far is having barely chance to interact with native students. In physics program, over 90 percent [of] students are international students. Only less than three are native students in my lab. Plus, graduate students are always busy for experiments. We spend more than eight hours in our lab. Unless there are some experimental issues, we rarely have a chat even with colleagues in the same lab, not to mention talk to native people. At the beginning—the period with less burden of research—speaking and listening are the most difficult things to me. I could hardly talk to native people fluently, leading to me being shy before. This also caused me to lose some opportunities to know new friends.

When asking Scott about his interactions with co-nationals, he said:

> I was elected to be a president in Taiwanese Student Association, so I was actively involved in many Taiwanese activities. It's really nice to have someone speak your own language and share learning experience together. I often received some good advices from them.

Like Scott, Sally revealed that her program requires great volumes of reading and writing, which made her unable to engage much in nonacademic activities.

> Maybe I can find a study partner, but I realized I find a study partner too late in this semester. So, it takes me a lot of my time to finish a report or prepare exams. I read English paper or watch talk show to make sure my English ability can be maintained at a certain level. I hang out with friends from my countries more often; they know how to survive.

In terms of the strategies they used to persist in their learning, Sally said:

> I hope you don't see I am pathetic [laugh]. I often stay in the library and finish my homework there. Besides going to the class, I spend lots of time there. The library in my school provide a very friendly environment—you can eat, you can book a room to have group discussion. It is prohibited in my country; I mean, in the library in my country, it is always too quiet to study. But here I feel I am—in America, I am one of them, just like other Americans, I study there. Even though I don't know them. But I like the feeling that I am living in their life; I am not isolated from them.

Sam, a fourth-year doctoral student in the dissertation-writing stage, said:

> My family are still in my country, so finish my study as soon as possible is my ultimate goal. They are great support—I Skype with them every weekend. I also have great advisor. He is very supporting me in terms of giving more flexible time to complete some tasks or providing me more office hours to discuss my research results. If I have something that I want to share, I can go to his office. Just like friends. I enjoy that! Without his encouragement or support, I really don't know how to survive.

Marginalization

Students with marginalization tendencies scored low on both maintaining a relationship with American society and on maintaining their Asian cultural identity. Ming, a second-year master's student, said:

> I feel nervous every time when I talk to my professor or people from my program. Just always worried about my English is not good enough. And sometimes, I didn't know what they were talking about. So, it is hard to build relationship with them. I did not know many friends from my country in my program. Sometimes, I regret coming to US. It

> was much harder than I thought. But I need to get through this. I often watch Chinese TV shows; it helps me feel not alone.

Mona felt that her doctoral program was not what she thought it would be.

> When I applied to this program, I imagined the environment would be friendly. Yes, they are friendly but not that supportive. You just can feel it. I'm alone. And every time I seek some help, I always heard, "I'm sorry to hear that," but they do nothing. Like, I know I am the only international student in my program. I posted an information in the discussion board about seeking a partner, like a study group. No one responded. I asked some staffs, professors. They didn't know what to do, but they wish me good luck on searching. Things like this made me feel frustrated. So, I walk alone on the hallway. I eat my lunch alone.

When asking Mona about her interactions with students from her country, she said:

> No time. Really, if I really want to relax for a while from my intense study life, I would go to see movies and watch TV.

Mary pointed out that she had less pressure to socialize with people because she was currently at the dissertation-writing stage. In addition, she believed that social skills would not make her stand out from other Americans in the job market.

> Since I am writing dissertation, writing and reading occupy all my daily life. At this stage, I don't need to attend Americans' activities or Koreans' activities often. There are too many scandals there. I don't want to involve in it. Doctoral study is also not like undergraduate study. I believe social activities is important, but doctoral study, hey, publication, publication, and publication. And I don't want to work in the US after graduation. Even I choose to work in the US; I believe I could never compete with other Americans with their social skills. They learn how to socialize since they are kids.
>
> I realized how important of social life after I came to US. So, research publication is a way or maybe the only way to persuade people hire me as long as you don't have big personality issue.

When asking these students about their efforts to maintain their academic performance, Ming said:

> I think of dropping out sometimes, but I can't. I don't know how to face my family, friends, if I go back. So, I stay; at least, I need to finish my degree. Although studying here is such a hard mission, I try my best, presenting in conference, making some professional networks, turning my work on time with high quality. I actually like to make friends, but just don't know it could be this hard in the US.

Mary also mentioned:

> Although I didn't know attending some social activities can help me in what ways, but I guess that's why school life here can be so different from my previous experiences in my country.

One common thing among Ming, Mona, and Mary was that they kept telling themselves that they had to graduate from their doctoral programs for specific reasons. However, they also talked more about their perceived strengths and weaknesses than the other interviewees.

Discussion

Acculturation scores were obtained by asking the students about the level at which they maintained their own identity and characteristics as well as the level at which they maintain their relationships with American society. This study explored the strategies international students with different acculturation tendencies used to cope with challenges, providing a picture of how these students reacted to what they experienced in their programs.

Although many students in this study perceived that improving their English and making friends with domestic students were their goals, students with the integration, separation, and marginalization tendencies all encountered difficulties in interacting with domestic students. Some students' programs did not even have many domestic students in their learning environment. In addition, one student found that reading English and collaborating with faculty were much more effective ways to enhance their learning experiences. This finding supports a comparison study between domestic students and international students' performance on the National Survey of Student Engagement and the Multi-Institutional Study of Leadership.[45] The study found that international students scored the quality of interaction with faculty higher than domestic students did, whereas domestic students scored higher on co-curricular engagement, communication with diverse others, and major leadership characteristics. Due to the challenges of making friends with domestic students, some international students decided to study English materials by themselves, including reading the daily news, to make sure that they were more comfortable in their English environment.

Libraries can play a critical role in enhancing international students' learning by providing English learning resources, for example. When students realized that American students were not the majority population in their doctoral programs, speaking to other international students was also an alternative approach to practicing conversations in English. The libraries can be a safe station on campus where these students meet.

Like students with the integration tendency, students with the separation tendency were inclined to maintain their relationship with their home culture. The feeling of home when they met people from the same country was satisfying enough for them to enjoy their doctoral studies. For that reason, library resources in students' mother languages may create a sense of home for students, and students may also feel that their schools care about them.

Some researchers have also found that students who were less engaged in academic or social activities tended to have lower academic achievement. The findings from our study did not fully support these results and showed that lower levels of engagement behavior in international graduate students resulted from their difficulties in entering academic or social circles at the beginning of their studies. Once students clarify their strengths and weaknesses within the larger society, however, they tend to build the perseverance to pursue their degrees.

The findings of this study reflect that Asian international students are motivated by their sense of personal accomplishment, which aligns with Niles's[46] findings that Asian international students are more likely to perceive themselves as engaged in their program to achieve social approval. Interestingly, the students in this study attempted to engage in American culture or make friends during the first year in their programs; however, due to the challenges or reality they faced, they adjusted their goals and behaviors after multiple attempts.

Supporting international students' academic achievement requires thoughtful programs or services designed with an understanding of their needs and expectations. Often, this requires the collaboration of multiple units within the institution. Scholars from the NAFSA Association of International Educators Region VI conference strongly encourage collaboration among different offices to support international students in a more comprehensive way.

Conclusion

The findings from this study provide insights into Asian international graduate students' concerns regarding different acculturation tendencies as well as the strategies they developed in their studies to accomplish their goals. The interview protocol can be applied to other international students for similar research interests. Future research is needed to find ways to help these students overcome the challenges and fears they have of interacting with domestic students—and how to provide services for international graduate students with intense study schedules.

Appendix 13A. Interview Protocol

Thank you for your willingness to be interviewed. In this interview, I want to follow-up to gain a better understanding of your learning experiences in the US. Please feel free to be candid with your responses. Everything you say will be confidential, and all written transcripts and summaries of your responses will be composed in a fashion that do not identify you or your school. Please feel free to ask me any questions at any time during the interview.

Questions:

WARM-UP

Could you tell me a little bit about yourself and why you came to the US to study?

MAIN QUESTIONS

1. Why did you decide to pursue a master/doctorate degree?
2. During your study, can you remember a time where you experienced a challenging situation or difficult circumstance where your Asian background played a role?
    a. What happened? What was the most challenging thing about this situation?
    b. How did you deal with this situation?
    c. How did this experience change how you viewed yourself?
    d. How did you see yourself before this experience?
    e. How does your culture, being Asian, affect how you viewed the experience you described?
    f. How did this experience change how you applied learning strategies during your study?
3. What other experiences have you had, especially interacting with other students or faculty during your study, that you would like to share?
4. Do you think you would like to maintain a certain level of interaction with other Asian students for the rest of your study? Why or why not?
5. Do you think you would like to maintain a certain level of interaction with other American students for the rest of your study? Why or why not?

CLOSING QUESTIONS

Is there anything else you would like to share?

Notes

1. Myrna R. Olson, "Issues and Trends of International Students in the United States," *International Journal of Education* 4, no. 1 (2016).
2. Hang Gao and Hans de Wit, "China and International Student Mobility," *International Higher Education* 90 (2017).
3. Keith Nuthall, "As Part of New International Strategy, Canada Aims to Double Foreign Students," *The Chronicle of Higher Education*, January 22, 2014, http://www.chronicle.com/article/As-Part-of-New-International/144139.
4. Yojana Sharma, "Asia: Countries Vying to Become Education Hubs," *University World News*, March 20, 2011, http://www.universityworldnews.com/article.php?story=20110318130607540.
5. Andrea G. Trice, "Faculty Perspectives Regarding Graduate International Students' Isolation from Host National Students," *International Education Journal* 8, no. 1 (2007): 108–117.
6. Kun Yan, "Chinese International Students in the United States: Adjustment Problems and Coping Behaviors," in *Chinese International Students' Stressors and Coping Strategies in the United States* (Singapore: Springer, 2017), 19–32.
7. Lori D. Patton, "Black Culture Centers: Still Central to Student Learning," *About Campus* 11, no. 2 (2006).
8. Elizabeth J. Tisdell, *Exploring Spirituality and Culture in Adult and Higher Education* (John Wiley & Sons, 2003).
9. Shalom H. Schwartz, "A Theory of Cultural Value Orientations: Explication and Applications," *Comparative Sociology* 5, no. 2 (2006): 137–182, doi:10.1163/156913306778667357.
10. Bolanle A. Olaniran, "Social Skills Acquisition: A Closer Look at Foreign Students on College Campuses and Factors Influencing Their Level of Social Difficulty in Social Situations," *Communication Studies* 47, no. 1–2 (1996): 72–88, doi:10.1080/10510979609368465.
11. Ranjani Selvadurai, "Problems Faced by International Students in American Colleges and Universities," *Community Review* 12 (1992): 27–32, https://eric.ed.gov/?id=EJ469274.
12. Gloria Ladson-Billings, "Fighting for Our Lives: Preparing Teachers to Teach African American Students," *Journal of Teacher Education* 51, no. 3 (2000), doi:10.1177/0022487100051003008.
13. Carla R. Monroe, "Understanding the Discipline Gap through a Cultural Lens: Implications for the Education of African American Students," *Intercultural Education* 16, no. 4 (2005): 317–330, doi:10.1080/14675980500303795.
14. Karen L. Davidson, "A Comparison of Native American and White Students' Cognitive Strengths as Measured by the Kaufman Assessment Battery for Children," *Roeper Review* 14, no. 3 (1992): 111–115, doi:10.1080/02783199209553403.
15. Jacqueline F. Nuby and R. L. Oxford, "Learning Style Preferences of Native American and African American Secondary Students," *Journal of Psychological Type* 44 (1998): 5–19, http://files.eric.ed.gov/fulltext/ED406422.pdf.
16. Roger G. Tweed and Darrin R. Lehman, "Learning Considered within a Cultural Context: Confucian and Socratic Approaches," *American Psychologist* 57, no. 2 (2002).
17. Yoojung Kim, Dongyoung Sohn, and Sejung Marina Choi, "Cultural Difference in Motivations for Using Social Network Sites: A Comparative Study of American and Korean College Students," *Computers in Human Behavior* 27, no. 1 (2011): 365–372.
18. Wendi L. Gardner, Shira Gabriel, and Angela Y. Lee, "'I' Value Freedom, but 'We' Value Relationships: Self-Construal Priming Mirrors Cultural Differences in Judgment," *Psychological Science* 10, no. 4 (1999): 321–326.
19. Masaki Yuki, "Intergroup Comparison versus Intragroup Relationships: A Cross-Cultural Examination of Social Identity Theory in North American and East Asian Cultural Contexts," *Social Psychology Quarterly* (2003): 166–183.
20. Institute of International Education, "Open Doors 2013: Fast Facts" (2014), http://www.iie.org/Research-and-Publications/Open-Doors/Data/Fast-Facts.
21. John W. Berry, "A Psychology of Immigration," *Journal of Social Issues* 57, no. 3 (2001): 615–631.
22. John W. Berry, "Acculturation: Living Successfully in Two Cultures," *International Journal of*

Intercultural Relations 29, no. 6 (2005): 698.
23. John W. Berry, "Psychological Aspects of Cultural Pluralism: Unity and Identity Reconsidered," *Topics in Culture Learning,* 2 (1974): 17–22.
24. John W. Berry, "Acculturation as Varieties of Adaptation," in *Acculturation: Theory, Models and Some New Findings*, ed. A. M. Padilla (Boulder, CO: Westview, 1980), 9–25.
25. John W. Berry, "Immigration, Acculturation, and Adaptation," *Applied Psychology* 46, no. 1 (1997): 5–34.
26. Aaron E. Black and Edward L. Deci, "The Effects of Instructors' Autonomy Support and Students' Autonomous Motivation on Learning Organic Chemistry: A Self-Determination Theory Perspective," *Science Education* 84, no. 6 (2000): 740–56.
27. Paul R. Pintrich and Akane Zusho, "Student Motivation and Self-Regulated Learning in the College Classroom," in *Higher Education: Handbook of Theory and Research* (Netherlands: Springer, 2002), 55–128.
28. Hasan Afzal, Imran Ali, Muhammad Aslam Khan, and Kashif Hamid, "A Study of University Students' Motivation and Its Relationship with Their Academic Performance," International *Journal of Business and Management,* no. 4 (2010): 80–88, doi:10.5539/ijbm.v5n4p80.
29. Vincent Tinto, *Leaving College: Rethinking the Causes and Cures of Student Attrition* (Chicago: University of Chicago Press, 1987).
30. George D. Kuh, "What Student Affairs Professionals Need to Know About Student Engagement," *Journal of College Student Development* 50, no. 6 (2009): 683–706.
31. Angela Lee Duckworth and Patrick D. Quinn, "Development and Validation of the Short Grit Scale (GRIT–S)," *Journal of Personality Assessment* 91, no. 2 (2009): 166–74.
32. Zorana Ivcevic and Marc Brackett, "Predicting School Success: Comparing Conscientiousness, Grit, and Emotion Regulation Ability," *Journal of Research in Personality* 52 (2014): 29–36.
33. Angela Galvan, Jacob Berg, and Eamon Tewell, "Resilience, Grit, and Other Lies-Academic Libraries and the Myth of Resiliency," paper presented at the Association of College and Research Libraries (ACRL), Baltimore, MD, March 22-25, 2017.
34. Christine J. Yeh and Mayuko Inose, "International Students' Reported English Fluency, Social Support Satisfaction, and Social Connectedness as Predictors of Acculturative Stress," *Counselling Psychology Quarterly* 16, no. 1 (2003): 15–28.
35. Susan Kristina Gardner and Pilar Mendoza, eds. *On Becoming a Scholar: Socialization and Development in Doctoral Education* (Stylus, 2010).
36. Senel Poyrazli and Philip R. Kavanaugh, "Marital Status, Ethnicity, Academic Achievement, and Adjustment Strains," *College Student Journal* 40, no. 4 (2006): 767–80.
37. Pius L. D. Ang and Pranee Liamputtong, "'Out of the circle'": International Students and the Use of University Counselling Services," 108–30.
38. Adam Raunic and Sophia Xenos, "University Counselling Service Utilisation by Local and International Students and User Characteristics: A Review," *International Journal for the Advancement of Counselling* 30, no. 4 (2008): 262–67.
39. Jenny Hyun, Brian Quinn, Temina Madon, and Steve Lustig, "Mental Health Need, Awareness, and Use of Counseling Services Among International Graduate Students," *Journal of American College Health* 56, no. 2 (2007): 109–18.
40. Sabine Severiens and Rick Wolff, "A Comparison of Ethnic Minority and Majority Students: Social and Academic Integration, and Quality of Learning," *Studies in Higher Education* 33, no. 3 (2008): 253–66.
41. Chris R. Glass and Christina M. Westmont, "Comparative Effects of Belongingness on the Academic Success and Cross-Cultural Interactions of Domestic and International Students," *International Journal of Intercultural Relations* 38 (2014): 106–19.
42. Yi-Chin Wu, "Exploring the Relationships among Self-Regulation, Acculturation, and Academic and Social Integration for Asian International Doctoral Students," PhD diss. (The Florida State University, 2015).
43. Marcia B. Baxter Magolda and Patricia M. King, "Toward Reflective Conversations: An Advising Approach that Promotes Self-Authorship," *Peer Review* 10, no. 1 (2008): 8.
44. Robert E. Stake, *Multiple Case Study Analysis* (Guilford Press, 2013).

45. Yi-Chin Wu, "A Comparison of International Students and Domestic Students: Findings from National Survey of Student Engagement and Multi-Institutional Study of Leadership," paper presented at the NAFSA: Association of International Educators Conference Region VI, Columbus, OH, April 2017.
46. F. Sushila Niles, "Cultural Differences in Learning Motivation and Learning Strategies: A Comparison of Overseas and Australian Students at an Australian University," *International Journal of Intercultural Relations* 19, no. 3 (1995): 369–85.

Bibliography

Afzal, Hasan, Imran Ali, Muhammad Aslam Khan, and Kashif Hamid. "A Study of University Students' Motivation and Its Relationship with Their Academic Performance." International *Journal of Business and Management*, no. 4 (2010): 80–88. doi:10.5539/ijbm.v5n4p80.

Ang, Pius L. D., and Pranee Liamputtong. "'Out of the Circle'": International Students and the Use of University Counselling Services." *Australian Journal of Adult Learning*, no.1, (2008): 108–30.

Berry, John W. "A Psychology of Immigration." *Journal of Social Issues* 57, no. 3 (2001): 615–631.

———. "Acculturation as Varieties of Adaptation." In *Acculturation: Theory, Models and Some New Findings*, edited by A. M. Padilla, 9–25. Boulder, CO: Westview, 1980.

———. "Acculturation: Living Successfully in Two Cultures." *International Journal of Intercultural Relations* 29, no. 6 (2005): 697–712. https://doi.org/10.1016/j.ijintrel.2005.07.013.

———. "Psychological Aspects of Cultural Pluralism: Unity and Identity Reconsidered." *Topics in Culture Learning*, 2 (1974): 17–22.

———. "Immigration, Acculturation, and Adaptation." *Applied Psychology* 46, no. 1 (1997): 5–34.

Black, Aaron E., and Edward L. Deci. "The Effects of Instructors' Autonomy Support and Students' Autonomous Motivation on Learning Organic Chemistry: A Self-Determination Theory Perspective." *Science Education* 84, no. 6 (2000): 740–56.

Davidson, Karen L. "A Comparison of Native American and White Students' Cognitive Strengths as Measured by the Kaufman Assessment Battery for Children." *Roeper Review* 14, no. 3 (1992): 111–15. doi:10.1080/02783199209553403.

Duckworth, Angela Lee, and Patrick D. Quinn. "Development and Validation of the Short Grit Scale (GRIT–S)." *Journal of Personality Assessment* 91, no. 2 (2009): 166–74.

Galvan, Angela, Jacob Berg, and Eamon Tewell. "Resilience, Grit, and Other Lies-Academic Libraries and the Myth of Resiliency." Paper presented at the *Association of College and Research Libraries (ACRL)*, Baltimore, MD, March 22–25, 2017.

Gao, Hang, and Hans de Wit. "China and International Student Mobility." *International Higher Education* 90 (2017): 3–5.

Gardner, Susan Kristina, and Pilar Mendoza, eds. *On Becoming a Scholar: Socialization and Development in Doctoral Education*. Stylus, 2010.

Gardner, Wendi L., Shira Gabriel, and Angela Y. Lee. "'I' Value Freedom, but 'We' value Relationships: Self-Construal Priming Mirrors Cultural Differences in Judgment." *Psychological Science* 10, no. 4 (1999): 321–26.

Glass, Chris R., and Christina M. Westmont. "Comparative Effects of Belongingness on the Academic Success and Cross-Cultural Interactions of Domestic and International Students." *International Journal of Intercultural Relations* 38 (2014): 106–19.

Hyun, Jenny, Brian Quinn, Temina Madon, and Steve Lustig. "Mental Health Need, Awareness, and Use of Counseling Services among International Graduate Students." *Journal of American College Health* 56, no. 2 (2007): 109–18.

Institute of International Education. "Open Doors 2013: Fast Facts." (2014). http://www.iie.org/Research-and-Publications/Open-Doors/Data/Fast-Facts.

Ivcevic, Zorana, and Marc Brackett. "Predicting School Success: Comparing Conscientiousness, Grit, and Emotion Regulation Ability." *Journal of Research in Personality* 52 (2014): 29–36.

Kim, Yoojung, Dongyoung Sohn, and Sejung Marina Choi. "Cultural Difference in Motivations for Using Social Network Sites: A Comparative Study of American and Korean College

Students." *Computers in Human Behavior* 27, no. 1 (2011): 365–72. https://doi.org/10.1016/j.chb.2010.08.015.

Kuh, George D., "What Student Affairs Professionals Need to Know About Student Engagement," *Journal of College Student Development* 50, no. 6 (2009): 683–706. http://dx.doi.org/10.1353/csd.0.0099.

Ladson-Billings, Gloria. "Fighting for Our Lives: Preparing Teachers to Teach African American Students." *Journal of Teacher Education* 51, no. 3 (2000): 206–14.

Magolda, Marcia B. Baxter, and Patricia M. King. "Toward Reflective Conversations: An Advising Approach that Promotes Self-Authorship." *Peer Review* 10, no. 1 (2008): 8–11.

Monroe, Carla R. "Understanding the Discipline Gap through a Cultural Lens: Implications for the Education of African American Students." Intercultural Education 16, no. 4 (2005): 317–30. https://doi.org/10.1080/14675980500303795.

Niles, F. Sushila. "Cultural Differences in Learning Motivation and Learning Strategies: A Comparison of Overseas and Australian Students at an Australian University." *International Journal of Intercultural Relations* 19, no. 3 (1995): 369–85.

Nuthall, Keith. "As Part of New International Strategy, Canada Aims to Double Foreign Students." *The Chronicle of Higher Education*. January 22, 2014. http://www.chronicle.com/article/As-Part-of-New-International/144139.

Nuby, Jacqueline F., and R. L. Oxford. "Learning Style Preferences of Native American and African American Secondary Students." *Journal of Psychological Type* 44 (1998): 5–19. http://files.eric.ed.gov/fulltext/ED406422.pdf.

Olaniran, Bolanle A. "Social Skills Acquisition: A Closer Look at Foreign Students on College Campuses and Factors Influencing Their Level of Social Difficulty in Social Situations." *Communication Studies* 47, no. 1–2 (1996): 72–88. doi:10.1080/10510979609368465.

Olson, Myrna R. "Issues and Trends of International Students in the United States." *International Journal of Education* 4, no. 1 (2016): 1–14.

Patton, Lori D. "Black Culture Centers: Still Central to Student Learning." *About Campus* 11, no. 2 (2006): 2–8.

Pintrich, Paul R., and Akane Zusho. "Student Motivation and Self-Regulated Learning in the College Classroom." In *Higher Education: Handbook of Theory and Research*. Netherlands: Springer, 2002, 55–128.

Poyrazli, Senel, and Philip R. Kavanaugh. "Marital Status, Ethnicity, Academic Achievement, and Adjustment Strains." *College Student Journal* 40, no. 4 (2006): 767–80.

Raunic, Adam, and Sophia Xenos. "University Counselling Service Utilisation by Local and International Students and User Characteristics: A Review." *International Journal for the Advancement of Counselling* 30, no. 4 (2008): 262–67.

Schwartz, Shalom H. "A Theory of Cultural Value Orientations: Explication and Applications." *Comparative Sociology* 5, no. 2 (2006): 137–82. doi:10.1163/156913306778667357.

Selvadurai, Ranjani. "Problems Faced by International Students in American Colleges and Universities." *Community Review* 12 (1992): 27–32. https://eric.ed.gov/?id=EJ469274.

Severiens, Sabine, and Rick Wolff. "A Comparison of Ethnic Minority and Majority Students: Social and Academic Integration, and Quality of Learning." *Studies in Higher Education* 33, no. 3 (2008): 253–66.

Sharma, Yojana. "Asia: Countries Vying to Become Education Hubs." *University World News*. March 20, 2011. http://www.universityworldnews.com/article.php?story=20110318130607540.

Stake, Robert E. *Multiple Case Study Analysis*. Guilford Press, 2013.

Tinto, Vincent. *Leaving College: Rethinking the Causes and Cures of Student Attrition*. Chicago: University of Chicago Press, 1987.

Tisdell, Elizabeth J. *Exploring Spirituality and Culture in Adult and Higher Education*. John Wiley & Sons, 2003.

Trice, Andrea G. "Faculty Perspectives regarding Graduate International Students' Isolation from Host National Students." *International Education Journal* 8, no. 1 (2007): 108–17.

Tweed, Roger G., and Darrin R. Lehman. "Learning Considered within a Cultural Context: Confucian and Socratic Approaches." *American Psychologist* 57, no. 2 (2002): 89.

Wu, Yi-Chin. "Exploring the Relationships Among Self-Regulation, Acculturation, and Academic and Social Integration for Asian International Doctoral Students." PhD diss. The Florida State University, 2015.

Yan, Kun. "Chinese International Students in the United States: Adjustment Problems and Coping Behaviors." In *Chinese International Students' Stressors and Coping Strategies in the United States.* Singapore: Springer, 2017, 19–32.

Yeh, Christine J., and Mayuko Inose. "International Students' Reported English Fluency, Social Support Satisfaction, and Social Connectedness as Predictors of Acculturative Stress." *Counselling Psychology Quarterly* 16, no. 1 (2003): 15–28.

Yuki, Masaki. "Intergroup Comparison versus Intragroup Relationships: A Cross-Cultural Examination of Social Identity Theory in North American and East Asian Cultural Contexts." *Social Psychology Quarterly* (2003): 166–83.

SECTION III

Collections & Digital Humanities

CHAPTER FOURTEEN

Local, Global, Digital?: Digital Humanities and Slavic Area Studies

Megan Browndorf and Erin Pappas

Introduction

In the past ten years, the work done in area studies—that is, the interdisciplinary study of regional topics—has changed dramatically. As such, the nature of the support that librarians need to provide scholars has similarly changed. This change has been particularly acute for librarians supporting Slavic area scholarship as research in the region has continued to lose US federal funding since the dissolution of the Soviet Union.[1] And it has been particularly acute in terms of reactions to new technologies for research, including what has come to be referred to as the digital humanities (DH). This chapter looks at the intersections of digital humanities and Slavic studies, focused specifically on Title VI centers. We examined twenty-one centers, important now and historically, for evidence of projects and support for Slavic work in DH. Many projects have already been written about by librarians. Our goal here is to develop an overview of the last decade, with a specific focus on the overlap of Slavic area studies and digital humanities, in order to help librarians looking for ways to support this work at their home institutions.

We explore ways that area studies librarians can continue to support new methods of scholarship without losing the international expertise that defines our field. We provide background on area studies centers, the digital humanities, and the conceptual (as well as practical) linkages between them. While this chapter has a fairly narrow purview, we hope it will be indicative of larger trends and concerns. It is intended primarily as a survey of former and current national resource centers; a list of the institutions included can be found in this endnote.[2] Although the specific geographic areas covered may vary from institution to institution, most of these resource centers include some permutation of Russia, Eastern Europe, and Central Asia. We then turn our attention to three themes which emerged in our survey of Title VI centers: support and development of tools and methods, digital pedagogy support, and digitization/digital collections. Finally, we bring the discussion back to what librarians trying to support this work can do. We speak specifically from our experiences as Slavic librarians and so do not touch upon the other regions covered by Title VI funding, though these may share our concerns with vernacular languages, funding, and historically deep institutional collections. As such, we focus here only on programs housed at R1 institutions in the United States with dedicated Slavic area studies centers.[3] While some DH work at these centers dates from the 1990s and early 2000s, we have limited the scope of this study to projects from the last decade. This means we focus only on projects that were begun in 2006 or later. While many digital projects have clear antecedents that reach back much further, to include them here would provide less a current "state of the field" and more a retrospective.

Area Studies: Centers, Libraries, and Support

Since their formal codification in the Higher Education Act of 1965 (Title VI), which provided the federal funding for language centers, area studies has been a bastion of internationalism within American research universities.[4] Federal allocations provided resources to ensure that library collections could support deep and sustained research for world regions as defined by the federal government.[5] As area studies departments appeared in universities, area studies librarianship developed to support them.[6] Large, diverse collections in foreign languages that were built using interdisciplinary, international expertise defined this new approach to librarianship. With regard to university libraries, area studies provided justification for collecting materials in regional vernaculars as well as being potential sources of funding to allow for purchases in foreign scholarship, newspapers, ephemera, and language education.

Yet today these programs are in jeopardy. Plagued by the loss of deep collections budgets, local constraints on foreign purchasing, and the loss of federal funding for specific regions, libraries are finding it increasingly difficult to acquire vernacular materials.[7] Under the auspices of austerity, streamlining, and consolidation, disparate collections and programs are now being replaced with a more generic "international" or "global" studies focus.[8] Librarians continue to support geographically focused interdisciplinary programs as they have since the heyday of area studies in the 1960s but with increasingly less latitude for acquisitions. While the impulse to think beyond the regions predates the current funding contraction, it does point to a trend that sidelines vernacular languages in favor of English-only. The reasons for this are many, but among them may be counted declining support for the humanities in favor of skills-based education and training, as well as a generic "global" focus that encourages colleges and universities to consolidate small departments, especially those with regional language and literature focus, to eliminate waste.

Digital Humanities and the Library

Other changes to this and related fields can be viewed in a more positive light, such as the development and growth of the digital humanities. Although the current political climate remains astonishingly hostile to the humanities, still the digital humanities flourish. Naturally, these are not without their detractors, and for good reason. Attention has been drawn to the Anglocentrism and whiteness of DH, but these critiques do not in and of themselves ameliorate the underlying issues, including limitations on language.[9] For example, many projects come out of American colleges and universities using English-language resources, having been developed for undergraduate courses. We ask: Where do area studies, rich in cultural and linguistic diversity, fit in this new environment?

While many advancements were crucial to the development of DH, underpinning them all were computing technologies that allowed work to be done at scale.[10] Yet, digital humanities is much more than simply tools and platforms. It strives for an ethos of transparency, collaboration, iteration, and sharing that stands in marked contrast to a humanities tradition of singularity—one scholar, one field, one monograph. Matthew Kirschenbaum sums up the paradigm quite succinctly:

> Whatever else it might be then, the digital humanities today is about a scholarship (and a pedagogy) that is publicly visible in ways to which we are generally unaccustomed, a scholarship and pedagogy that's bound up with infrastructure in ways that are deeper and more explicit than we are generally accustomed, a scholarship and pedagogy that is collaborative and depends on networks of people and that lives an active, 24/7 life online.[11]

When looking at the programs, projects, and DH work being done in Slavic centers, this ethos of public collaboration is apparent, particularly when we look beyond digital or digitized collections.

Especially important for our analysis is this distinction between digital/digitized collections and digital humanities proper. Libraries are often providers of digital collections and may have contributed to digitization in whole or part. These collections have fundamentally enabled the digital turn in the humanities but are not in and of themselves practices, methods, or theoretical orientations. In other words, DH work often depends on the existence of (mostly static) digital collections, but the mere existence of digital collections in certain libraries or centers does not in and of itself indicate any particular affinity for DH work being done there.[12]

In addition to a distinction between digital/digitized collections and the digital humanities, there is also the distinction between digital humanities and traditional humanities to consider. While humanities departments seem under siege—administratively under-supported, derided by policy makers, and faced with declining enrollments—DH has robust support structures, from federal NEH and NEA grants to local monies in the form of innovation or teaching grants. DH is now supported "on a growing number of campuses by a level of funding, infrastructure, and administrative commitments that would have been unthinkable even a decade ago."[13] Here we may see a parallel between the "traditional" humanities and area studies, which are presumed to be outmoded, in decline, and no longer relevant, in contrast to the growing presence of DH and catch-all "global studies" department and initiatives. Among graduate students, in particular, digital humanities are seen as a necessary skill to be acquired before matriculating or going onto the job market. Digital methodologies, tools, and teaching are seen as in-demand in the academic marketplace, which may explain why graduate students and early-career scholars gravitate toward them.[14]

All twenty-one institutions we examined have some kind of DH presence on campus, though this may manifest differently depending on the local environment. Many institutions have large DH centers which act as hubs for academic departments across the campus. Others have this support distributed throughout academic departments or centrally located in the library. These differences in paradigms for developing research projects and tools—DH center, distributed support model, and library-based model—similarly affect how DH and area studies co-exist on campuses.

A number of institutions, such as UCLA, Stanford University, and the University of Virginia, have dedicated DH Centers that support most (or all) of the DH work on a campus. These institutions have dedicated digital humanities centers that steward specific projects and initiatives. At these types of institutions, the library plays a minimal role in supporting the digital humanities because that work is being done in a center. However, the library may be working at cross-purposes with that center, duplicating work or failing to capitalize on local or national initiatives.

A second model centers support for DH work in the departments and colleges which do that work. In these institutions, departments and colleges support DH work, sometimes with the support of campus technology centers and the library, but sometimes on their own. In these situations, library support is often conducted through a departmental subject liaison. Examples of institutions that use models like this include Duke University and the University of Texas-Austin.

The last model places DH support squarely in the library. In these institutions, the library is the center for DH work and scholarship and has individuals hired to support DH work on campus. They may work with subject liaisons to support the work. Examples of institutions with models like this include Kansas University and Indiana University. While an institution generally focuses their support in one of these three directions, support for DH throughout the university can include pieces of all three models.

To complicate the issue still further, individuals with what we would consider "library" expertise and knowledge may actually be housed in a separate DH center, while the library pursues initiatives and projects on its own. In other words, library DH and campus DH may be working at cross-purposes, duplicating efforts, or trying to tap into the same limited pool of resources. Returning to area studies faculty and students, we did not find any clear reasons why one model would be preferred over another for DH projects. However, as with all research, it seems likely that scholars would naturally gravitate toward one of these based either on reputation, past experiences, or word-of-mouth. As a matter of course, they may bypass local infrastructures and institutions entirely, the better to collaborate with colleagues across institutions.

Area Studies Today: The State of the Field

To return to area studies, many Title VI-funded centers lost their federal support in the 2013 and 2015 rounds of awards.[15] Of the twenty-one institutions we identified in our initial survey, seven lost their federal funding completely, while the others saw a reduction in the amount distributed. However, all are important historically and at present; federal grant money is not the only metric for impact. These institutions house major area studies collections, employ specialist librarians, catalogers, and bibliographers, and are regular destinations for researchers and visiting scholars. It seems increasingly unlikely that those monies will be recouped in future rounds of funding, making it incumbent on the institutions themselves to make area studies a continuing priority. Some have met this challenge through shared collections and collection development policies, while others have chosen to severely limit their vernacular expenditures or purchases from foreign presses.[16] Along with high-level language training, interdisciplinarity is a hallmark of area studies. A typical area studies center, for instance, will function as a touchstone for political scientists, language instructors, historians, anthropologists, linguists, economists, and literature scholars. To bring this back to the growth of DH, this means that area studies librarians already possess a sought-after capability within that field—namely, the ability to move fluidly between various disciplines.

We are broadly interested in the ways that digital humanities presumes a globalizing universality—if not Anglophone in nature, then almost unfailingly written in Roman script—that stands in stark contrast to the inherent particularity of area studies in which the world is comprised of discrete and bounded "regions." Presumably, we have similarly limited time in which to build cultural competence and interdisciplinarity within the digital humanities, thus ensuring that it is truly global in its purview. We would like to push the conversation further and ask how we can ensure that deep, particular knowledge is not glossed over. Even more specifically, what do digital projects offer the Slavic scholarly community, and how can they raise awareness beyond our field? In the following pages, we examine places where the digital humanities and area studies have already intersected and identify three sites of continuing cooperation: digital tools and research, pedagogy, and digitization and exhibition.

Digital Tools and Research

While many different types of digital projects and research have taken place on these twenty-one diverse campuses, two are of particular interest for Slavic research. These are mapping/geospatial/GIS (Global Information Systems) and text-based or linguistic analysis. In terms of the latter, issues that were identified in the 2000s included a dearth of full-run digital collections, poor or no OCR if digitized, and a lack of robust metadata, among others. Michael Neubert, former Slavic librarian and digital projects coordinator at the Library of Congress, edited a volume of *Slavic & East European Information Resources* devoted to digital libraries. This special issue was simultaneously released as a book entitled *Virtual Slavica: Digital Libraries, Digital Archives.*[17] In it, librarians discussed such problems as the Comintern Archives, "Making the Cyrillic OPAC a Reality," and providing digital reference for Slavists at the University of Illinois. Twelve years later, the Comintern Archives are accessible in another form, few of the Cyrillic OPAC problems identified remain to trouble scholarly research, and the University of Illinois is still doing Slavic digital reference. The only other piece to provide an overview of the digital Slavic landscape, Patricia Hswe's "What You Don't Know Will Hurt You" holds up only as a retrospective overview. It provides a mix of out-of-date projects and problems, each of which has outgrown their constraints from a decade ago.[18]

However, many of the technical problems that plagued scholars and researchers in the 2000s have now have been all but resolved. Vendors, most notably EastView, have taken the lead in making large corpuses of OCR-ed text available to scholars. We are only now beginning to witness the effects of the mass digitization of important collections, either done by vendors, universities and university presses, or some partnership thereof—particularly on text-based analysis projects.[19] The projects that result may reflect local holdings and concerns or address broader issues, such as rendering Slavic languages machine-readable. Representative projects range from explorations of Bulgarian and Czech dialects, topic modeling the Russian Primary Chronicle, text mining novels from the Russian Revolution, or encoding Cyrillic characters in Unicode.[20]

In our survey of research universities, GIS and geography-based projects appeared fairly frequently.[21] One possibility for their widespread distribution is that, depending on the software program being used, these projects can have a very low barrier to entry. Maps used as base layers for projects are widely and freely available through programs such as Google Earth. They also do not require specialized language skills, and may allow scholars to work well beyond their areas of linguistic expertise as well as tapping into student involvement. Geographic locations and toponyms are also easily translated between the vernacular language and English, with many programs having this functionality already built-in. For example, this means that scholars of the Silk Road—which historically stretched from Asia Minor through Central Asia—may work across languages as disparate as Turkish, Armenian, Georgian, Farsi, Russian, Uzbek, and Chinese, even if they know only one of these languages.[22] While the Electronic Cultural Atlas Initiative (ECAI) Silk Road Atlas project does not rely on GIS per se, it stands out as an early example of geographic work that crosses multiple boundaries: linguistic, spatial, and national.

Digital Pedagogy: Language Learning and Beyond

Many of the institutions we looked at leveraged digital approaches to the humanities for the education of graduate and undergraduate students, whether their own or visiting. Among these, three pedagogical tracks stood out as being particularly important: first, in technical and digital support for language training and language centers; second, in the translation of primary source materials (translation allows such material to be accessible to undergraduate students who may have little to no vernacular language capacity); and finally, in the development of courses with digital aspects. These classes may in and of themselves serve a pedagogical function, the better to train subsequent cohorts of digital humanists.

Early applications of digital technologies to Slavic arose from the study and teaching of regional languages and the sharing of pedagogical material to support those endeavors. Computer-mediated language learning for the languages of Eastern Europe and the former Soviet states grew throughout the 1990s along with the capability to render Cyrillic text digitally.[23] As the technology advanced, so did these projects become more complex. They developed from the straightforward sharing of audio-visual material on websites to online tutorials, interactive modules, and dynamic websites.

In keeping with the interdepartmental nature of area studies, many area studies centers partnered with language learning labs to develop these technologies, even without the guiding mandate of an overarching project or grant. Examples of institutions that have supported or currently support digital technologies in their methods of language instruction include Indiana University, Duke University, and UCLA. Both Indiana's and UCLA's programs are supported in conjunction with larger language-learning centers, which include non-Slavic languages, while Duke's program is developed through its Slavic Language Resource Center.[24]

As the digital humanities have matured, the classroom has become one of the key sites for their development. This includes the creation of lessons, tools, and archives for use by undergraduates and graduate students. As mentioned previously, it also encompasses training advanced students to employ digital humanities methods in their research and teaching. A forerunner among peers, Harvard's Davis Center hired an individual to coordinate curriculum and use of digital projects and to maintain a list of "pedagogical resources" on its website, including digital artifacts and videos on teaching.[25]

Teaching DH in the Slavic classroom is particularly developed as part of the training for graduate students, who may then utilize these tools and techniques in their own teaching. It may also reflect the desire of early career scholars and doctoral students to add DH to their skillsets and thus increase their prospects on the academic job market.

For instance, Yale's Marjeta Bozovic has been experimenting with the Joseph Brodsky Digital Humanities lab. This is a seminar that aims both to teach students about Brodsky and to "introduce students to new ways of conducting and presenting research, using digital tools."[26] Here she partners with DH, library, and IT staff, including the Slavic librarian, and notes:

As early adopters and "digital natives," graduate students are taking leading roles in many DH projects—as are librarians and specialized technical staff. By pulling different parts of the university into contact and into the open, such partnerships have the potential to forge strategic alliances with consequences beyond the research at hand.[27]

In much the same vein, Harvard and Stanford both have courses that combine learning about Slavic area studies with learning about DH work.[28]

Furthermore, these institutions have conferences, support groups, and trainings developed to enable graduate students to bring DH methods into their research. Some of these have been specific to the region: Harvard's Mapping Cultural Space Across Eurasia fellowship, Columbia's 2014 NEH Summer Institute on East Central Europe, and Stanford's "Russian Formalism and the Digital Humanities" conference.[29] As a rule, the audience for most DH graduate experiences goes beyond Russian and East European studies. Instead, graduate students doing work at some Title VI universities seek out Digital Humanities groups (such as those at Stanford), fellowships (such as those at Harvard), or conferences and trainings (such as DHSI: Digital Humanities Summer Institute, or HILT: Humanities Intensive Learning & Teaching). Only one or two graduate students associated with or funded by a Title VI center may have projects that rely heavily on digital humanities tools. However, as a rule, the support for learning the tools and applying them tends to originate outside their home departments, particularly at institutions which already have robust digital humanities centers and staffing.

Digitization and Exhibition

Even more than pedagogy or research, DH work in digitization and exhibition has tended to involve significant collaboration with the library, with known vendors, or a combination of the two. Much of the work that involves libraries and librarians has come out of this particular intersection. In our survey of the literature, it became obvious that this was the main instance where librarians were involved from the outset rather than being consulted after the fact—that is, when a project was already well underway. Librarians can and should be consulted early on, especially when metadata standards are necessary for the project to scale correctly. They are much better equipped to do this kind of work than scholars, who are able to "produce wonderful resources using creative combinations of technology to make a point, either for research or teaching, but sometimes the description of these projects, and how the pieces fit together, proves to be a huge challenge."[30] The entire digitization pipeline relies on library expertise, from recommending what collections should be digitized, to taking ownership of project management, to recommending and implementing metadata standards.[31]

This means that whole archival, paper, and microfilm collections have migrated to online, whether through vendor efforts, collaborations between research institutions, or partnerships between them. For instance, the Center for Research Libraries acquires, digitizes, and hosts files from member institutions, which are then made freely available to members of the CRL community. For area studies, these have been done under the auspices of the Slavic and East European Materials Project, which began in 1995 as a way to share regional collections between CRL member institutions.[32] Their digital Ukrainian Émigré Press Collection was drawn from libraries in Europe and North America and represents an excellent example of a fully interinstitutional collaboration.[33] Another example is Yale's legacy Slavic collection, 2.5 million pages of which was digitized by three separate vendors in 2010–2011. This was a collection of "indisputable historical value." Also in its favor was its "well-rounded coverage of Slavic philology," but of utmost importance was "the fact that the publications of the collection [were] no longer covered by copyright laws, and, last but not least, the idea that these titles published in the eighteenth and nineteenth centuries could finally become available worldwide to students of Slavic studies."[34]

No institution is free from dealing with the legacies of digital preservation. It is imperative that ongoing support is planned from the outset, though whether this should take place through the library remains an open question. Specifically, many older projects are now almost inaccessible due to changes in operating standards, upgrades, or ongoing maintenance. Existing exhibitions tend to date from the late 1990s to mid-2000s and, if still available, may be maintained only sporadically. Some are riddled with broken links or dependent on older technologies. If and when older projects are available, they may show their age to the point of being completely unusable, functioning as artifacts rather than learning objects. As Eileen Llona points out, "Lack of infrastructure from the beginning makes the lifetime of these kinds of projects questionable, even if the content value is high."[35] We follow that assessment and suggest that shared responsibility, whether this takes the form of project-specific communities or dedicated interinstitutional support (i.e., staffing, server space, ongoing maintenance), may mitigate these issues somewhat.

Most of the literature coming out of the Title VI affiliates relates to digitization and sometimes digital analysis. In this respect, they hew to a model that most large research libraries implicitly follow. That is to say, they produce and make available certain kinds of content but are not primarily concerned with how the content or collections are used.[36] In fact, the most up-to-date information about Slavic DH, including applications and pedagogy, relies on more informal and fast-moving channels of communication. Facebook, Twitter, and the ASEEES newsletter are all important for disseminating projects, calling for collaborators, and defining the parameters of the subfield.

DH and Slavic Area Studies: Looking to the Future

Despite the limitations we have laid out above—including rapidly aging projects and infrastructure, limited attention to maintenance, and lack of coordination among centers, disciplines, and scholars—the impact of DH on area studies is likely to continue. Thus, it is incumbent upon librarians to anticipate growth in DH scholarship and its specific demands, needs, and desired outcomes. For example, many of the institutions which we examined have pre-existing DH centers, either located within the library or elsewhere on campus, to help scholars build up the necessary skills to take on digital humanities projects.[37] Some institutions have no such center but nonetheless have a librarian with a job responsibility that addresses DH and/or digital projects more broadly. As librarians, we must ask ourselves: What support can we offer these scholars and what should the role of the library be in their work? To that end, what skills do we already have which allow us to play that role? What skills do we need to develop in ourselves and future area studies librarians?

One strategy might entail using the tools and expertise that area studies librarians have honed through physical collection support in the service of digital projects. Perhaps the "digital turn" can offer a way out of the perceived insignificance of area studies collections, casting them in the same positive light as the (Anglophone) digital humanities now receive. At the same time, developing regional digital resources, especially with international partners, raises a new set of concerns: lack of stability, differing standards, labor expenditures, and poor infrastructure, to name but a few.

Digital humanities differs from traditional scholarship in its explicit attention to and indeed championship of collaborative and distributed labor. This extends to every iteration of a project, which may require collaboration among institutions, and among scholars, researchers, and librarians with various skillsets. One course is for librarians to learn to identify the skills gaps in a project and be able to bring in the right people to fill those gaps. These roles may even be external to the organization—indeed, even to the institution. Institutions, even large R1s with a number of support staff, cannot reasonably expect that librarians can support faculty projects indefinitely. While this might be the case at a liberal arts college or even a four-year comprehensive, the technical demands of today's DH projects are likely to outstrip any single person's capacity for support.

In conclusion, we found the following to be generally true. As a rule, DH projects done in conjunction with area studies centers have tended to reflect the preexisting strengths of those centers: language, geography, and interdisciplinary regional analysis. We note that ad-hoc collaboration does exist between regional institutions and their American counterparts but that it has a tendency to be fleeting and project-based. Lasting connections, if they exist, are usually at the interpersonal rather than institutional level. This makes inter-departmental and -institutional collaborations even more vital, especially since Slavic generally has a small footprint in contrast to larger language and literature departments, especially English.

In 2016, the Association for Slavic, East European, and Eurasian Studies (ASEEES) chartered a Digital Humanities Interest Group.[38] This decision formalized a nascent community that began as a conversation at the 2015 ASEEES convention about DH practices and networks within the field. Their stated goal was to "advance a community of practice around digitally inclined scholarship and research projects, with a strong focus on the teaching, curation, and preservation thereof in Slavic, East European and Eurasian Studies."[39] As we have made clear above, DH undertakings often demand that individuals look beyond their own institutions for skills, interests, and funding. Affiliate groups and networks like Slavic DH can help fill those gaps. It remains, however, for area studies librarians to seek out these groups and figure out how to implement their initiatives locally.

Notes

1. In using the terms "Slavic" and "Slavic and East European," we follow the terminological conventions of the journal *Slavic & East European Information Resources*, wherein these terms are "to be understood as shorthand for the following Slavic and non-Slavic countries: Albania, Armenia, Azerbaijan, Belarus, Bosnia-Herzegovina, Bulgaria, Croatia, Czech Republic, Estonia, Georgia, (Modern) Greece, Hungary, Kazakhstan, Kosovo, Kyrgyzstan, Latvia, Lithuania, Macedonia, Moldova, Montenegro, Poland, Romania, the Russian Federation, Serbia, Slovakia, Slovenia, Tajikistan, Turkmenistan, Ukraine, and Uzbekistan. While we understand that these terms may not be those preferred by the citizens of some of the nations included, we chose them because they are generally understood in English-speaking countries and because the available alternatives are much too long. The list of countries is based on those recognized by the government of the United States, where the journal is based." (SEEIR, n.d.)
2. These are: Columbia University, Duke University-University of North Carolina-Chapel Hill (joint), Harvard University, Georgetown University, Indiana University, The Ohio State University, Stanford University, University of California-Berkeley, University of California-Los Angeles, University of Chicago, University of Illinois-Urbana-Champaign, University of Kansas, University of Michigan, University of Pittsburgh, University of Texas-Austin, University of Washington, University of Wisconsin, Cornell University, Syracuse University, and Yale University.
3. Many liberal arts institutions are doing exceptional work with digital humanities—Lafayette, Grinnell, Carleton, and Haverford, to name but a few; however, as these generally lack the extensive primary and secondary source collections associated with area studies, we have chosen to omit them.
4. Higher Education Act (HEA) of 1965 [P.L. 89-329], as amended; U.S. Department of Education, "About OPE—International and Foreign Language Education," accessed August 31, 2017, https://www2.ed.gov/about/offices/list/ope/iegps/index.html.
5. These have been defined with varying degrees of specificity in the twentieth and twenty-first centuries but currently correlate to: Latin America; the Middle East (typically in conjunction with North Africa); Sub-Saharan Africa; Europe, Eastern Europe, and Eurasia; and Asia-Pacific (whether Southern, Southeastern, or Eastern). The specific ways that regions map onto the current geo-political and military concerns of the United State are, unfortunately, beyond this scope of this chapter.
6. Joe Lenkart, "Current Trends in Research Resources from Russia, Eastern Europe, and Eurasia: Implications for Reference Services and Resource Sharing," *Slavic & East European Information Resources* 17 no. 4 (2016): 215–25.
7. In particular, Laura L. Adams, "The Crisis of U.S. Funding for Area Studies," *ASEEES Newsnet* 53, no. 2 (2013), https://aseees.org/sites/default/files/downloads/2013-03.pdf.
8. See further, Jonathan Z. Friedman and Cynthia Miller-Idriss, "The International Infrastructure of Area Studies Centers: Lessons for Current Practice From a Prior Wave of Internationalization," *Journal of Studies in International Education* 19 no. 1 (2015): 86–104, doi:https://doi.org/10.1177/1028315314536992.
9. Alexis Lothian and Amanda Phillips, "Can Digital Humanities Mean Transformative Critique?," *Journal of E-Media Studies* 3, no. 1 (2013); Tara McPherson, "Why is the Digital Humanities So White?, or, Thinking the Histories of Race and Computation," in *Debates in the*

Digital Humanities, ed. Matthew K. Gold, 138–60 (Minneapolis: Minnesota University Press, 2012).

10. Matthew Kirschenbaum, "What is Digital Humanities and What's It Doing in English Departments?" in *Debates in the Digital Humanities*, ed. Matthew K. Gold, 3–11 (Minneapolis: Minnesota University Press, 2012). See also "Forum: Text Analysis at Scale," in *Debates in the Digital Humanities*, ed. Lauren F. Klein and Matthew K. Gold (Minneapolis: Minnesota University Press, 2016).
11. Kirschenbaum, "What is Digital Humanities?," 11.
12. John Unsworth, "What Is Humanities Computing and What Is Not?" *Graduate School of Library and Information Sciences*, Illinois Informatics Institute, University of Illinois, Urbana, November 8, 2002, http://computerphilologie.uni-muenchen.de/jg02/unsworth.html.
13. Kirschenbaum, "What is Digital Humanities?," 9.
14. Leonard Cassuto, "The Job-Market Moment of Digital Humanities," *The Chronicle of Higher Education* (January 22, 2017), http://www.chronicle.com/article/The-Job-Market-Moment-of/238944.
15. The institutions that lost funding in these cuts include Duke University/University of North Carolina, Georgetown University, University of Michigan, and Columbia University. "84.015A National Resource Centers (NRC) and 84.015B Foreign Language and Area Studies (FLAS) Fellowships Programs Grantees and Funding for FY 2014, FY 2015, and Estimates for FY 2016-17," International Education Program Services, accessed December 1, 2017, https://www2.ed.gov/about/offices/list/ope/iegps/nrcflasgrantees2014-17.pdf; "84.015A National Resource Centers (NRC) and 84.015B Foreign Language and Area Studies (FLAS) Fellowships Programs Grantees and Funding for FY 2010 and Estimates FY 2011-13," International Education Program Services, accessed December 1, 2017, https://www2.ed.gov/about/offices/list/ope/iegps/nrcflasgrantees2010-13.pdf.
16. Lisa R. Carter and Beth M. Whitaker, "Area Studies and Special Collections: Shared Challenges, Shared Strength," *Portal* 15 no. 2 (2015): 357–58.
17. Michael Neubert, *Virtual Slavica: Digital Libraries, Digital Archives* (Binghampton, NY: Haworth Information Press, 2005). Co-published simultaneously as *Slavic & East European Information Resources* 6 no. 2–3 (2005).
18. Patricia Hswe, "What You Don't Know Will Hurt You: A Slavic Scholar's Perspective on the Practicality, Practicability, and Practice of Digital Scholarship," Slavic & East European Information Resources 7 no. 4 (2007): 3–15, http://dx.doi.org/10.1300/J167v07n04_02.
19. Jon Giullian, "'Seans chernoi magii' na Taganke: The Hunt for *Master and Margarita* in the Pravda Digital Archive," *Slavic & East European Information Resources (SEEIR)* 14 no. 2/3 (2013): 102–26, http://dx.doi.org/10.1080/15228886.2013.813374.
20. Digital Humanities at Berkeley, "Bulgarian Dialectology as a Living Tradition," 2016, http://bulgariandialectology.org/; Texas Czech Legacy Project (TCLP), "Texas Czech Dialect Archive" (TCDA), 2015, http://laits.utexas.edu/txczechproject/dialect-archive; Sean Griffin, "Visualizing Shakhmatov: An Experimental Data Visualization of the Textual History of the Kievan Primary Chronicle," http://slavic.ucla.edu/person/sean-griffin/; Sean Griffin, "Big Data and Big Novels: Text Mining the Prose of the Russian Revolution," http://slavic.ucla.edu/person/sean-griffin/; David J. Birnbaum, Ralph Cleminson, Sebastian Kempgen, and Kiril Ribarov, "Character Set Standardization for Early Cyrillic Writing after Unicode 5.1, with an Associated Table of Early Cyrillic characters in Unicode," *Scripta & e-Scripta 6* (2008): 161–93.
21. Examples include Harvard's *Imperiia Project* (http://dighist.fas.harvard.edu/projects/imperiia/), mapping the historical Russian Empire and sponsored GIS training; the Black Sea Networks project (http://blackseanetworks.org/) by Columbia, Yale, New York University, and Cambridge; Stanford's *Geographies of the Holocaust* (http://web.stanford.edu/group/spatialhistory/cgi-bin/site/project.php?id=1015); a UC Berkley course from Jewish Studies on "Mapping Diasporas" (https://mappingdiasporas.wordpress.com/).
22. For instance, both the University of Kansas and the University of Washington currently house Silk Road projects. See further, http://silkroad.ku.edu/ and https://depts.washington.edu/silkroad/.

23. Richard Robin, "Computers and Pedagogy in Russian: Where Have We Been? Where Are We Going?" *Slavic & East European Journal*, vol. 50, no. 1 (2006): 65–81.
24. "Center for Language Technology (CeLT)," Indiana University, accessed September 8, 2017, http://celt.indiana.edu/portal/; "UCLA Language Materials Project," UCLA, accessed September 8, 2017, http://www.lmp.ucla.edu/Default.aspx; "Slavic Language Resource Center," Duke University, accessed September 8, 2017, http://slaviccenters.duke.edu/.
25. "Anna Mudd: Curricular and Digital Projects Coordinator," *Davis Center*, accessed September 8, 2017, http://web.archive.org/web/20160923233248/http://daviscenter.fas.harvard.edu/about-us/people/anna-mudd.
26. Yale University Center for Teaching and Learning, "Joseph Brodsky Digital Humanities Lab," accessed June 4, 2018, https://ctl.yale.edu/showcase/joseph-brodsky-digital-humanities-lab.
27. Marijeta Bozovic, "Avant-gardes and Emigres: Digital Humanities and Slavic Studies," *ASEEES Newsnet* 55, no. 4(2015), http://aseees.org/avant-gardes-and-emigres-digital-humanities-and-slavic-studies-marijeta-bozovic-yale-university-0.
28. "Media, Method, and Practice," *Davis Center*, accessed September 8, 2017, https://daviscenter.fas.harvard.edu/student-resources/courses/media-method-and-practice.
29. "Themes We Explore," *Davis Center*, accessed September 8, 2017, https://daviscenter.fas.harvard.edu/research/individual-research/fellows-program/themes-we-explore; "America's East Central Europeans: Migration and Memory," *Columbia University*, accessed September 8, 2017, https://nehsummerinst.columbia.edu/; "Russian Formalism & the Digital Humanities," *Stanford Digital Humanities*, accessed September 8, 2017, https://digitalhumanities.stanford.edu/russian-formalism-digital-humanities.
30. Eileen Llona, "The Librarian's Role in Promoting Digital Scholarship: Development and Metadata Issues," *Slavic & East European Information Resources* 8 no. 2-3 (2007): 154.
31. Patricia Hswe, "Digitizing the Zdenka and Stanley B. Winters Collection of Czech and Slovak Posters, 1920–1991," *Slavic & East European Information Resources* 8, no. 2/3 (April 2007): 127–36; Tatjana Lorković, Graziano Krätli, and Carolyn Caizzi, "Yale University Library has Digitized its Legacy Slavic Collection Created by Joel Sumner Smith," *Slavic & East European Information Resources* 13, no. 2/3 (September 2012): 180–89; Ksenya Kiebuzinski, "Emigre Digital Collection at the Center for Research Libraries," *ASEEES Newsnet* 52, no. 4: 11; Bradley L. Schaffner, "A Public/Private Partnership for Digitization: The Russian Archives Database Project," *Slavic & East European Information Resources* 8, no. 4 (October 2007): 77–85; "Yale U. Press to Publish Stalin's Library," *Information Management Journal* 41, no. 5 (September 2007): 12.
32. Slavic and East European Materials Project [SEEMP], Center for Research Libraries Global Resources Network, accessed September 1, 2017, http://www.crl.edu/programs/seemp.
33. Specifically drawn from the Ukrainian Research Institute at Harvard University, the Ukrainian Free Academy of Sciences in New York City (under the sponsorship of Columbia University), and the Thomas Fisher Rare Book Library at the University of Toronto.
34. Lorković, Krätli, and Caizzi, "Yale University Library has Digitized its Legacy Slavic Collection," 183.
35. Llona, "The Librarian's Role," 154.
36. One notable exceptions here is Bozovic, "Avant-gardes and Emigres."
37. Tim Bryson, Miriam Posner, Alain St. Pierre, and Stewart Varner, *ARL SPEC Kit 326: Digital Humanities, Association of Research Libraries* (November 2011).
38. Association for Slavic, East European, and Eurasian Studies (ASEEES), "Affiliate Group Spotlight: Digital Humanities," *ASEEES Newsnet* 56, no. 3 (2016): 10–11; Slavic DH: Digital Humanities in the Slavic Field, "About," accessed September 1, 2017, https://www.aseees.org/sites/default/files/downloads/newsnet%20june%202016_0.pdf.
39. ASEEES, "Digital Humanities," 10.

Bibliography

Adams, Laura L. "The Crisis of U.S. Funding for Area Studies." *ASEEES Newsnet* 53 no. 2 (2013). https://aseees.org/sites/default/files/downloads/2013-03.pdf.

Association for Slavic, East European, and Eurasian Studies (ASEEES). "Affiliate Group Spotlight: Digital Humanities." *ASEEES Newsnet* 56 no. 3 (2016): 10–11. http://aseees.org/sites/default/files/downloads/newsnet%20june%202016_0.pdf.

Birnbaum, David J., Ralph Cleminson, Sebastian Kempgen, and Kiril Ribarov. "Character Set Standardization for Early Cyrillic Writing after Unicode 5.1, with an Associated Table of Early Cyrillic characters in Unicode." *Scripta & e-Scripta 6* (2008): 161–93.

Carter, Lisa R., and Beth M. Whitaker. "Area Studies and Special Collections: Shared Challenges, Shared Strength." *Portal* 15, no. 2 (2015): 353–73. https://doi.org/10.1353/pla.2015.0017

Cassuto, Leonard. "The Job-Market Moment of Digital Humanities." *The Chronicle of Higher Education.* January 22, 2017. http://www.chronicle.com/article/The-Job-Market-Moment-of/238944.

"Forum: Text Analysis at Scale." In *Debates in the Digital Humanities*, edited by Lauren F. Klein and Matthew K. Gold, 525–68. Minneapolis: Minnesota University Press, 2016.

Friedman, Jonathan Z., and Cynthia Miller-Idriss. "The International Infrastructure of Area Studies Centers: Lessons for Current Practice From a Prior Wave of Internationalization." *Journal of Studies in International Education* 19 no. 1 (2015): 86–104. doi:10.1177/1028315314536992.

Giullian, Jon. "'Seans chernoi magii' na Taganke: The Hunt for *Master and Margarita* in the Pravda Digital Archive." *Slavic & East European Information Resources (SEEIR)* 14 no. 2–3 (2013): 102–26. http://dx.doi.org/10.1080/15228886.2013.813374.

Higher Education Act (HEA) of 1965 [P.L. 89-329], as amended.

Hswe, Patricia. "Digitizing the Zdenka and Stanley B. Winters Collection of Czech and Slovak Posters, 1920–1991." *Slavic & East European Information Resources* 8 no. 2-3 (2007): 127–36.

———. "What You Don't Know Will Hurt You: A Slavic Scholar's Perspective on the Practicality, Practicability, and Practice of Digital Scholarship." *Slavic & East European Information Resources 7* no. 4 (2007): 3–15. http://dx.doi.org/10.1300/J167v07n04_02.

Kirschenbaum, Matthew. "What is Digital Humanities and What's It Doing in English Departments?" In *Debates in the Digital Humanities*, edited by Matthew K. Gold, 3–11. Minneapolis: Minnesota University Press, 2012.

Lenkart, Joe. "Current Trends in Research Resources from Russia, Eastern Europe, and Eurasia: Implications for Reference Services and Resource Sharing." *Slavic & East European Information Resources* 17 no. 4 (2016): 215–25.

Llona, Eileen. "The Librarian's Role in Promoting Digital Scholarship: Development and Metadata Issues." *Slavic & East European Information Resources* 8 no. 2 (2007): 151–63.

Lorković, Tatjana, Graziano Krätli, and Carolyn Caizzi. "Yale University Library has Digitized its Legacy Slavic Collection Created by Joel Sumner Smith." *Slavic & East European Information Resources* 13 no. 2–3 (September 2012): 180–89.

Lothian, Alexis, and Amanda Phillips. "Can Digital Humanities Mean Transformative Critique?" *Journal of E-Media Studies* 3 no. 1 (2013).

McPherson, Tara. "Why is the Digital Humanities So White?, or, Thinking the Histories of Race and Computation." In *Debates in the Digital Humanities*, edited by Matthew K. Gold, 138–60. Minneapolis: Minnesota University Press, 2012.

Neubert, Michael, ed. *Virtual Slavica: Digital Libraries, Digital Archives.* Binghampton, NY: Haworth Information Press, 2005. Co-published simultaneously as *Slavic & East European Information Resources* 6 no. 2-3 (2005).

Robin, Richard. "Computers and Pedagogy in Russian: Where Have We Been? Where Are We Going?" *Slavic & East European Journal*, vol. 50, no. 1 (2006): 65–81.

Schaffner, Bradley L. "A Public/Private Partnership for Digitization: The Russian Archives Database Project." *Slavic & East European Information Resources* 8, no. 4 (October 2007): 77–85.

Slavic & East European Information Resources [SEEIR]. "About This Journal." Accessed September 1, 2017. https://sites.google.com/site/seeirjournal/about.

Slavic and East European Materials Project [SEEMP]. Center for Research Libraries Global Resources Network. Accessed September 1, 2017. http://www.crl.edu/programs/seemp.

Slavic DH: Digital Humanities in the Slavic Field. "About." Slavic DH.

Unsworth, John. "What Is Humanities Computing and What Is Not?" *Graduate School of Library and Information Sciences*. Illinois Informatics Institute, University of Illinois, Urbana. November 8, 2002. http://computerphilologie.uni-muenchen.de/jg02/unsworth.html.

U. S. Department of Education. "About OPE - International and Foreign Language Education." Accessed August 31, 2017. https://www2.ed.gov/about/offices/list/ope/iegps/index.html.

U. S. Department of Education. "84.015A National Resource Centers (NRC) and 84.015B Foreign Language and Area Studies (FLAS) Fellowships Programs Grantees and Funding for FY 2010 and Estimates FY 2011-13." Accessed December 12, 2017. https://www2.ed.gov/about/offices/list/ope/iegps/nrcflasgrantees2010-13.pdf.

U. S. Department of Education. "84.015A National Resource Centers (NRC) and 84.015B Foreign Language and Area Studies (FLAS) Fellowships Programs Grantees and Funding for FY 2014, FY 2015, and Estimates for FY 2016-17 Accessed December 12, 2017." https://www2.ed.gov/about/offices/list/ope/iegps/nrcflasgrantees2014-17.pdf.

"Yale U. Press to Publish Stalin's Library." *Information Management Journal* 41, no. 5 (September 2007): 12.

CHAPTER FIFTEEN

Collection Development and Acquisitions for International and Area Studies Collections in Academic and Research Libraries

Osman Celik

Introduction

In an increasingly globalized world, change is experienced at multiple levels by individuals, organizations, and state-actors. American higher education and academic libraries have been always at the forefront of and directly influenced by the globalization process in multitude aspects of their operation. With the constant unfolding of new developments in numerous regions with global implications for all actors, scholarly interest in global affairs and international studies from various academic fields (particularly social sciences and humanities) continues to solidify its place across university and college campuses. Given interdisciplinary approaches as the preferred method of inquiry, the dynamic research landscape for international and area studies scholarship poses a welcoming challenge for academia which strive for better understanding, explanation, and, if possible, prediction of social, political, economic, and historical changes in different societies and regions.

The challenge for teaching and research communities in global and international studies in American higher education presents a parallel challenge in the development and management of international and area studies collections by academic and research libraries. In this regard, the challenge in supporting curricula and research activities in global affairs and international studies necessitates the deployment of multiple methods of collection development and acquisitions of materials in all formats from and about each global region, namely, Latin America, Africa, Middle East, Western Europe, Eastern Europe and Slavic countries, South Asia, Southeast East Asia, and East Asia.

This chapter presents an overview of collection development practices and acquisitions of teaching and research library materials in all formats for international and area studies. The chapter is organized as follows. It first discusses the state of publishing and scholarly regional interest for international and area studies within the US context. It then briefly discusses collection development practices and policies with respect to global and area studies from research libraries' perspectives. The third section discusses basics of technical services of international and area studies collections with special emphasis on various acquisitions methods such as blanket, approvals, firm orders, the Library of Congress Cooperation Acquisitions Program, gifts in-kind, and exchanges. The last section of the chapter touches upon area studies librarianship and its critical role.

The State of Publishing in International and Area Studies and Scholarly Interest

American academic and research libraries have been known for their impressive collection sizes, which represent hundreds of languages and dialects and myriad formats that have been increasingly and actively utilized in teaching, learning, and research activities on college and university campuses. Although there has not yet been a precise metric or reliable statistical measure of the analog-digital ratio of academic and research library collections, given advances in information technology and online availability of enormous information resources, one can confidently postulate that library collections will continue to be defined by increasing electronic and digital information resources.[1] However, one exception to such a trend is, arguably, library materials that are critical to teaching and research in international and area studies, particularly from Africa, Eastern Europe and Slavic countries, the Middle East, East Asia, South Asia, and Southeast Asia.

There is no doubt there are more materials available for collecting than ever before in international and area studies, which currently constitute a sizable portion of major academic and research library print collections. According to the Association of Research Libraries (ARL) survey of 126 member research libraries, sixty-four respondents indicated the presence of important research collections in at least one global region in their respective libraries. Similarly, sixty-four responding libraries reported that their libraries actively collect in at least one global region.[2] One of the most defining features of these collections, besides being "distinctive collections," is that print and other analog formats seem to dominate international and area studies collections.[3] The ARL survey on collecting global resources also presents some interesting descriptive statistics on format types. Accordingly, the majority of participating ARL libraries pointed out the predominantly print and analog nature of their international and area studies collections.[4]

In this regard, given the expansion of digital and electronic resources in English and for some Western European languages to some extent, American academic and research libraries collections are facing a "digital at home and print abroad" context with respect to their collection-building choices in global and area studies. For instance, a survey of ebook markets by Duke University librarians in 2012 showed that the development of ebook markets in most regions have been significantly lagging behind the US, Western Europe, Japan, China, and South Korea.[5] While numerous small ebook vendors and aggregators have emerged in multiple regions, there is still a significant lack of reliable electronic resources, particularly with respect to foreign monographs and periodicals, despite the plethora of independent online information resources from non-Western regions. One of the main reasons for this lack is that the economics and business models of, for instance, ebook packages and other electronic resources from global regions have not reached the level of the US and most Western European publishing industries. The development of electronic and digital information resources in those regions seems to be potentially impeded by uncertainty and noncompliance with respect to intellectual property rights and copyright laws and, thus, numerous unresolved licensing issues in local settings. Therefore, given such inadequacy in legal and institutional settings, there do not seem to be enough economic incentives for foreign and local publishers to provide electronic and digital resources for non-English-language teaching and research materials.

As to scholarly publication trends, a study undertaken by Kurzman indicates the increasing trend of books published outside the US in general and the steadily increasing number of non-English books held by American academic libraries between 1960 and 2010.[6] The same study, using the data from OCLC WorldCat database, looks at the international focus of social science books and articles published in the US between 1960 and 2010 (see figures 15.1 and 15.2). These two figures indeed reveal several trends in global and area studies scholarship. With the exclusion of books on Western Europe, up to 51 percent of US social science books published focused on Africa, Eastern Europe/Eurasia, East Asia, Middle East, and South and Southeast Asia. The percentage of social science articles for the same period and world regions approaches 28–30 percent with steadily increasing trends in both Africa and Middle East regions since the early 1990s. While the

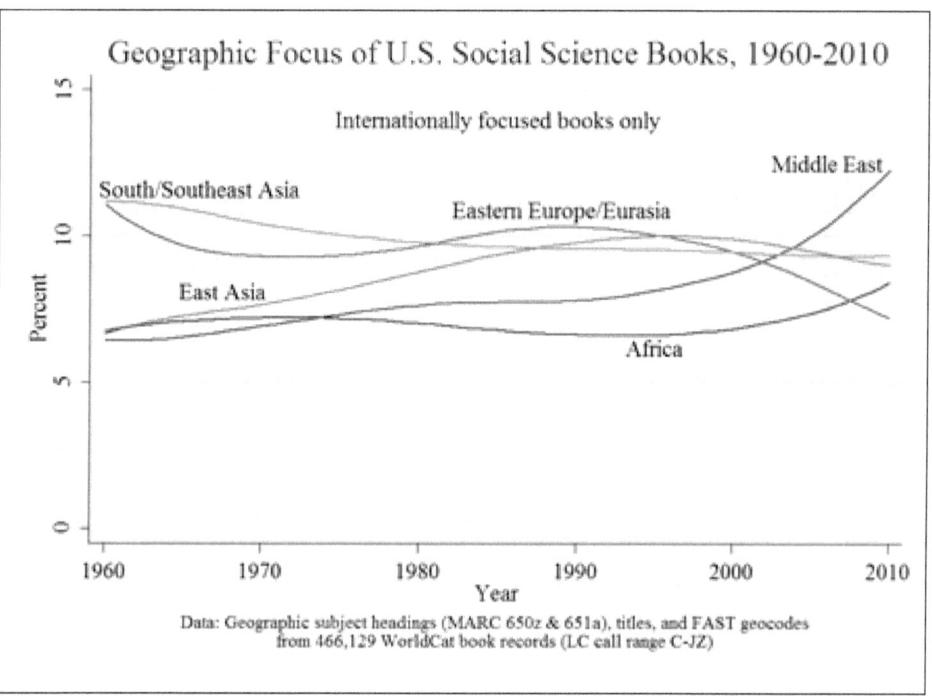

Figure 15.1. Geographic Focus of U.S. Social Science Books, 1960–2010

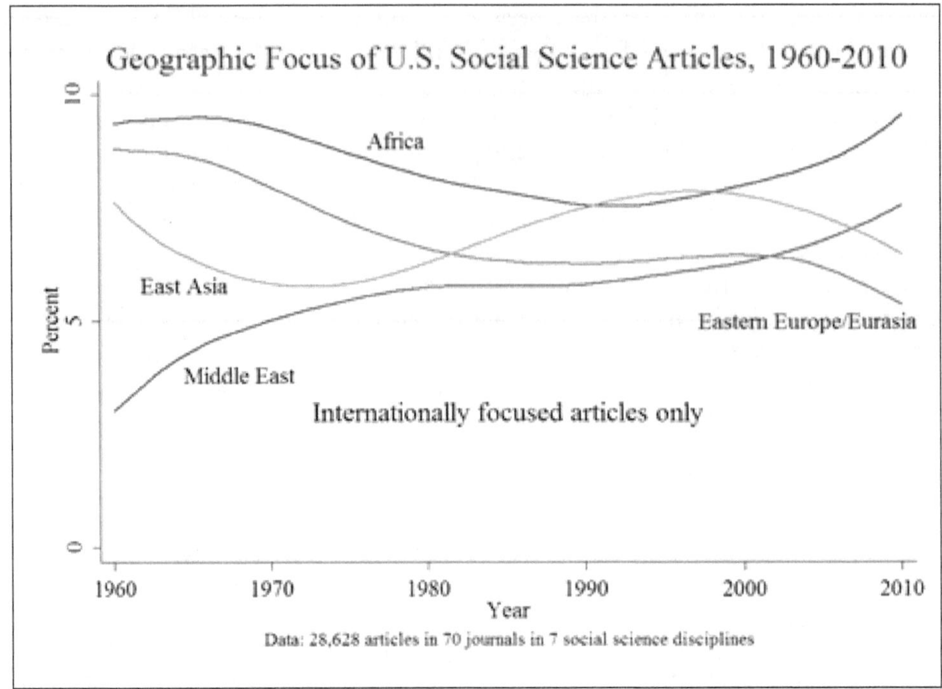

Figure 15.2. Geographic Focus of U.S. Social Science Articles, 1960–2010

author has not come across a similar study for humanities subjects on international and area studies, one can assuredly expect to see similar patterns of scholarly attention and publication trends with respect to these non-Western regions. In short, given the predominance of analog publications in non-Western regions as well as publications trends, area studies scholarship scholarly interests and the nature of collections would unlikely change in the immediate future of academia and American academic and research libraries.

Collection Development (CD) and CD Policies in Academic and Research Libraries

The challenge in supporting curricula and research activities in global affairs and area studies in American higher education necessitates the deployment of multiple methods of collection development and acquisitions of materials in all formats from and about each unique region. One of the first collection-building efforts in this direction was the Farmington Plan before WWII and the Library of Congress' Public Law 480 Program (PL480), which was established in 1962 in an effort to supply overseas publications selected by local agents in multiple regions and numerous countries to US libraries.[7]

Collection development efforts in area studies were not as systematic given the underlying uncertainties in the availability of foreign publications. Collection building in area studies can be found as early as the late 1920s, particularly in the humanities and social sciences with the basic interdisciplinary approaches.[8] With the emergence of the importance of area studies in the post-WWII period, American higher education saw the establishment of numerous academic programs and centers dedicated to various global regions along with faculty and student recruitment. Hence, it was after such development that academic and research libraries undertook more systematic collection development in international and area studies. While numerous research universities have continued to build international and area studies collections with significant depth and breadth with respect to all global regions, many other universities have been able to focus on a few specific regions and build significant area studies collections that not only serve their respective campus communities but also scholars and researchers from other regions.[9]

The use of collection development (CD) policies has been instrumental to build area studies collections more methodically, with more focus and direction that are corresponding with teaching and research interests in colleges and universities. The practice of CD policies and their content also varied across academic libraries. While some academic libraries have developed CD policies which present specific details, such as subjects, topics, country, regions, historical periods, and the type of formats a library has collected and continues to collect, other research libraries continue to utilize brief policies with broad collection parameters (see for instance the University of Chicago Library's and Michigan State University Libraries' CD policies with respect to Middle East Studies.[10])

There are many clear benefits of maintaining CD policies in international and area studies. First, the presence and maintenance of a policy can significantly inform faculty, graduate and undergraduate students, and researchers on and off campus about the historical and current content of specific area studies collections that can be potentially used in learning, teaching, and research activities. Second, the use of CD policy and its archive allows academic libraries to evaluate and assess accumulated collections in myriad formats and in various aspects that can determine the strengths and weaknesses of collections and future directions for collection development in a given area's studies.

Fundamentals of Technical Services in International and Area Studies Collections

Collection development in international and area studies in most academic libraries have converged on numerous collection-building methods and materials-acquisition practices over the years. To begin with, blanket and approval plans with vendors in foreign regions and countries have been effective and reliable acquisition methods for building global and area studies collections that ensure the incoming of core and current titles, mostly in print from various global regions. Additionally, approval plans are also the cost-effective way of receiving core and important titles from numerous countries and global regions.[11] However, there is also a caveat to establishing and relying on approval plans in area studies, which is that each approval plan from overseas needs to be very well-defined with subject parameters and frequently reviewed to ensure materials added to the collection are aligned with teaching curricula and research interests on campus.

Dozens of established vendors in almost every region also provide some essential technical services, such as bibliographic records, EDI purchase orders and invoices, and shelf-ready services with varying qualities at reasonable prices. Utilizing appropriate and desired technical services from foreign vendors can potentially minimize processing time for Roman- and non-Roman-language materials in acquisitions and cataloging departments. Such services can ultimately make teaching and research materials available for users in library stacks in a shorter period of time.

Firm orders are also frequently used as another method of acquisition which is deployed when published content from overseas can be identified by faculty and students in advance and can be supplied through blanket and approval vendors in each region. As with firm orders, most subscriptions for periodical titles and standing orders for area studies collections are also handled through established vendors in each region and major countries—similar to acquisitions practices in North American and Western European publications and vendors. In-kind gifts, exchanges, and institutional memorandum of understanding with academic libraries and institutions abroad are also complementary methods of acquisition and collection development for a prominent international and area studies collections in academic libraries. Gifts and exchanges are a particularly underutilized and laborious method of acquisition, in general, that can potentially enhance library collection unexpectedly and imaginatively.

The Library of Congress' PL 480 program was transformed into the Cooperative Acquisitions Program of the Library of Congress by the late 1990s, which continues to constitute an important method of acquisitions and collection development with its offices in Cairo, Islamabad, Jakarta, Nairobi, New Delhi, and Rio for over one hundred academic and research libraries and institutions.[12] With its six overseas offices, the Library of Congress' program has been instrumental in developing collections and supplying some critical teaching and research materials in numerous Roman and non-Roman languages from Africa, Middle East, South Asia, Southeast Asia, and South America, and particularly from geographies where it has been difficult to collect and library materials are not easily available through commercial vendors.[13]

Current Challenges in International and Area Studies Collections

Academic library services in general and collections in particular in international and area studies have been rather more collection-centric until recently. As indicated above, most area studies collections in academic and research libraries are still in print. This is particularly the case with respect to monographs and periodicals from and about regional studies in non-English languages. With the exception of monographs and periodicals published in North America and Western Europe in English and other Roman languages, almost all publications from Eastern Europe/Slavic regions, Middle East, South Asia, Southeast Asia, and East Asia in numerous languages are currently in print format. Aside from small ebook vendors and aggregators, there is still a significant lack of reliable digital resources in monographs and serials. This is in part due to uncertainty and noncompliance with respect to intellectual property and copyright laws and licensing issues. And most freely available online and open access information resources from most global regions tend to be less reliable and are not maintained regularly; hence, access can easily be disrupted.

One other feature that characterizes international and area studies collections across American academic and research libraries is, with a few exceptions, that there is little coordination among libraries in terms of cooperative and collaborative collection-building, maintenance, and preservation of these collections. Potentially high rates of duplication, particularly in monograph collections, and unknown complementarities of area studies collections among research libraries at regional and national levels can be seen as indications of such inadequate collaboration.

As print collections from and about each geographic area have been growing as an effort to increase depth and breadth of library collections, the storage, preservation, and overall long-term stewardship of these collections have emerged as important issues for collection managers and library administration with critical financial and staff implications for academic libraries. Lastly, a frequent oversight and unacknowledged challenge in collection development is the acquisitions method for international and areas studies. In this respect, heavy reliance on broad approval plans with an inadequate review of content relevance to current teaching and research needs of faculty and students can result in low circulation rates and underutilized area studies collections, which would eventually call for further attention in terms of storage, preservation, and stewardship issues.

International and Area Studies Librarianship, Technical Services, and Foreign Vendor Relations

For decades, area studies librarianship has been the critical component for the development and maintenance of international and area studies collections in all formats that support dynamic curricula and scholarly research at American higher education institutions. Performing liaison services, in addition to collection development, reference services, and information literacy instruction, area studies librarianship is engaged in their academic communities in international and area studies.[14] Given their regional and subject expertise as well as extensive language skills and knowledge of cultural contexts, these librarians are in positions to quickly become members of scholarly networks and connect to area studies centers, departments, faculty, and students from area studies regions.

Furthermore, with such regional and language expertise, area studies librarianship has also been instrumental in providing technical services for international studies collections in numerous languages and formats. The variety of language skills acquired by areas studies librarians for their respective regions have always been at the service of catalog librarians who try to provide discoverability and access to incoming unique materials from global regions. Area studies librarians' language skills have been also frequently utilized by acquisitions services in academic and research libraries. More specifically, area studies librarians have been critical in communicating with foreign vendors and are key actors in overseeing blanket and approval plans, firm orders, and serial subscriptions, and coordinating such activities with acquisitions departments and foreign vendors.

As to the budgetary aspects of building and managing international and area studies collections, funding for these collections has been more or less steady for most academic libraries. However, given the increasing importance and expansion of global studies in American higher education, some more critical regions, such as Africa and the Middle East, have registered increases in their materials budgets.[15] On the other hand, with the significant decline in Title VI funds for research libraries in recent years, most funds come from libraries' regular materials allocations and, to a lesser extent, specific endowments and grants.

Collection Strategy for International and Areas Studies Collections

With flat materials budgets and growing serials expenditures, academic and research libraries need to strategize their collection development for international and area studies, which will continue to increase their depth and breadth in serving their respective academic communities. Hence, it has become increasingly crucial and challenging to find a balanced and quickly adjustable mode of collection development and acquisitions that collection managers and area studies librarians can operate with.

An optimal operational strategy for building and maintaining area studies collections at academic libraries needs to be designed to ensure minimizing the cost associated with maintaining and preserving such collections for years to come. Collaborative and cooperative collection development has become a critical factor for sustainable research-level library collections in international and area studies. In this regard, the need for cooperation and collaboration in building area studies collections is highly desirable, since wide scholarly interest in global regions requires further improvement of the breadth and depth of research library collections, which becomes challenging in the face of limited budgets.[16] Therefore, a cost-minimizing strategy, first and foremost, would certainly require academic libraries' active participation in shared print projects, intensifying their efforts to pursue more regional and cross-regional shared print initiatives and projects in close cooperation and collaboration with other academic and research libraries and OCLC.

Since the bulk of print materials continue to be from overseas, the same strategy would require a reformulation of collection development policies to prioritize analog content acquisitions that would be less likely to be digitized in the near future. Additionally, there is also a constant need to reevaluate and re-prioritize collection development choices to meet the unique information needs of faculty, researchers, and students. The implementation of such a strategy would ensure cost-effective and efficient acquisitions and building of international and area studies collections for a prominent academic library. Finally, there is a critical need to continuously integrate and provide access to available online information resources from and about international and area studies, including governmental and non-governmental documents and data sources.

Concluding Remarks

There is no doubt that a globalized world has created increasingly globalized libraries in American higher education. One of the major implications of globalized American academic libraries, in addition to the increasing presence of international faculty, students, and area studies centers and academic departments on college and university campuses, is the increasing size and depth of area studies collections in academic libraries' stacks. Library collections in international and area studies have been one of the core collection development activities for academic and research libraries for decades. The collection development in this regard has been in response to supporting curricula and research activities in international and area studies, which in turn requires the deployment of multiple methods of collection development and acquisitions of materials in numerous languages and formats from and about each global region.

The future of collections in American higher education necessitates the deployment of unconventional and innovative models of sustainable collection-building. These models are strategically built on capitalizing on the network of academic and research libraries, considering the evolving scholarly record, shared print repositories, and sourcing and scaling of collection management at various levels.[17] Particularly, given the cost of long-term stewardship and storage and preservation commitments, the future of collecting in international and area studies critically hinges upon more cooperative collection development and shared print repositories among academic and research libraries locally as well as within and across multiple regions in North America. For instance, Triangle Research Libraries Network (TRLN) is a success story of cooperative collection development not only in non-English-language print materials from numerous global regions but also electronic resources and print retention.[18] The Big Ten Academic Alliance[19] and the 2CUL partnership[20] between Columbia and Cornell University Libraries are also impressive examples of institutionalized cooperative and collaborative undertakings that include collection development and maintenance of analog and electronic and digital resources, as well as shared professional and technical expertise across networked campus libraries.

To conclude, international and area studies librarians with their exemplar language and cultural expertise, the Library of Congress, a rich pool of foreign vendors in each global region, and technical services of academic libraries have been instrumental and are four key players enabling these important collections in terms of supply, discoverability, access, and usability for faculty, researchers, and students in American higher education. However, given the print format's current predominance, the economics of information for international and area studies collections will continue to be distinguished from that of most mainstream publications in English and Western European languages. These collections are clearly distinguished from North American and Western European collections with their more labor-intensive technical services and vendor relations. In moving forward, more automation with respect to mainstream library materials from global regions is critically needed so that the bulk of these materials will not enter the backlogs of technical services. Lastly, strategic cooperation and coordination among area studies librarians, foreign vendors, and technical services will remain one of the most important aspects of successful and sustainable collection development and acquisitions of international and area studies collections in American academic and research libraries for years to come.

Notes

1. Dan Chapin Hazen and Deborah Jakubs, "The Global Dimensions of Scholarship and Research Libraries: Finding Synergies, Creating Convergence," Harvard Library, 2013, http://nrs.harvard.edu/urn-3:HUL.InstRepos:28553796; Wookjin Cheun, Marion Frank-Wilson, Luis A. Gonzalez, Akram Khabibullaev, Wen-Ling Liu, Andrea Singer, and Noa Wahrman, *SPEC Kit 324: Collecting Global Resources* (Washington: Association of Research Libraries, September, 2011), https://doi.org/10.29242/spec.324.
2. Cheun et al., *Kit 324*.
3. 3. Lisa R. Carter and Beth M. Whittaker, "Area Studies and Special Collections: Shared Challenges, Shared Strength," *portal: Libraries and the Academy* 15, no. 2 (2015): 353–73, https://muse.jhu.edu/article/578273.
4. 4. J. Burgett., J. Haar, and L. L. Phillips, "The Persistence of Print in a Digital World: Three ARL Libraries Confront and Enduring Issue," proceedings ACRL Tenth National Conference,

March 15–18, 2004, Denver, Colorado: 75–80; see also Cheun et al., *SPEC Kit 324.*
5. *Global E-Book Snapshot,* Duke University Library, 2012, http://www.crl.edu/Events/8478/conf_papers.
6. 6. Charles Kurzman, "Shifts in Scholarly Attention Among World Regions," OCLC Research Briefing, June 2013, https://www.oclc.org/research/events/2013/06-07a.html.
7. 7. Mary F. Casserly, "A History of the Farmington Plan," *Library Collections, Acquisitions, and Technical Services* 27, no. 1 (2003): 132–33, http://www.tandfonline.com/doi/full/10.1080/14649055.2003.10765904; Dan C. Hazen and James H. Spohrer, eds., *Building Area Studies Collections,* Vol. 52 (Wiesbaden: Otto Harrassowitz-Verlag, 2007); Lesley Pitman, *Supporting Research in Area Studies: A Guide for Academic Libraries* (Waltham, MA: Chandos Publishing, 2015).
8. 8. Zachary Lockman, *Field Notes: The Making of Middle East Studies in the United States* (Stanford, CA: Stanford University Press, 2016).
9. 9. Hazen and Spohrer, eds. *Building Area Studies Collections,* 9–10.
10. 10. "Middle East," The University of Chicago Library, Collection Development Policy, http://guides.lib.uchicago.edu/c.php?g=297396&p=1992077#s-lg-box-6060818; "Collection Development Policy Statement: Muslim Studies and Middle East Studies," Michigan State University Libraries Guides, http://libguides.lib.msu.edu/c.php?g=300056&p=2003787.
11. 11. Pitman, *Supporting Research in Area Studies,* 33-35.
12. Ibid., 28–30.
13. Alice L. Kniskern, "Library of Congress Overseas Offices: Acquisition Programs in the Third World," *Library Acquisitions: Practice & Theory* 6, no. 2 (1982): 87–101, doi:10.1016/0364-6408(82)90034-5.
14. Hazen and Spohrer, eds., *Building Area Studies Collections,* 6–7.
15. Cheun et al., *SPEC Kit 324.*
16. Carolyn T. Brown, "The Changing Nature of Area Studies," International Collections and Development Workshop, Center for Research Libraries and Library of Congress, February 27–28, 2006, http://www.crl.edu/sites/default/files/d6/attachments/pages/Brown_CRL-LOC.pdf.
17. Lorcan Dempsey, Constance Malpas, and Brian Lavoie, "Collection Directions: The Evolution of Library Collections and Collecting," *portal: Libraries and the Academy* 14, no. 3 (2014): 393–423, https://muse.jhu.edu/article/549200.
18. Programic Councils, TRLN, http://www.trln.org/programmatic-councils/collections-council/.
19. B1G Academic Alliance, https://www.btaa.org/home.
20. "Cornell and Columbia Libraries to Build a Joint Technical Infrastructure," Cornell University Library, https://www.library.cornell.edu/about/news/press-releases/cornell-and-columbia-libraries-build-joint-technical-infrastructure.

Bibliography

B1G Academic Alliance. https://www.btaa.org/home.

Brown, Carolyn T. "The Changing Nature of Area Studies." International Collections and Development Workshop, Center for Research Libraries and Library of Congress. February 27–28, 2006. http://www.crl.edu/sites/default/files/d6/attachments/pages/Brown_CRL-LOC.pdf.

Burgett, J., J. Haar, and L. L. Phillips. "The Persistence of Print in a Digital World: Three ARL Libraries Confront and Enduring Issue." Proceedings ACRL Tenth National Conference, March 15–18, 2004, Denver, Colorado: 75–80.

Carter, Lisa R., and Beth M. Whittaker. "Area Studies and Special Collections: Shared Challenges, Shared Strength." *portal: Libraries and the Academy* 15, no. 2 (2015): 353–73. https://muse.jhu.edu/article/578273.

Casserly, Mary F. "A History of the Farmington Plan." *Library Collections, Acquisitions, and Technical Services* 27, no. 1 (2003): 132–33. http://www.tandfonline.com/doi/full/10.1080/14649055.2003.10765904.

Cheun, Wookjin, Marion Frank-Wilson, Luis A. Gonzalez, Akram Khabibullaev, Wen-Ling Liu, Andrea Singer, and Noa Wahrman. *SPEC Kit 324: Collecting Global Resources.* Washington:

Association of Research Libraries, September, 2011. https://doi.org/10.29242/spec.324.
Cornell University Library. "Cornell and Columbia Libraries to Build a Joint Technical Infrastructure." https://www.library.cornell.edu/about/news/press-releases/cornell-and-columbia-libraries-build-joint-technical-infrastructure.
Dempsey, Lorcan, Constance Malpas, and Brian Lavoie. "Collection Directions: The Evolution of Library Collections and Collecting." *portal: Libraries and the Academy* 14, no. 3 (2014): 393–423. https://muse.jhu.edu/article/549200.
Duke University Library. *Global E-Book Snapshot.* 2012. http://www.crl.edu/Events/8478/conf_papers.
Hazen, Dan Chapin, and Deborah Jakubs. "The Global Dimensions of Scholarship and Research Libraries: Finding Synergies, Creating Convergence." Harvard Library, 2013. http://nrs.harvard.edu/urn-3:HUL.InstRepos:28553796.
Hazen, Dan C., and James H. Spohrer, eds. *Building Area Studies Collections*, Vol. 52. Wiesbaden: Otto Harrassowitz-Verlag, 2007.
Kniskern, Alice L. "Library of Congress Overseas Offices: Acquisition Programs in the Third World." *Library Acquisitions: Practice & Theory* 6, no. 2 (1982): 87–101. https://doi.org/10.1016/0364-6408(82)90034-5.
Kurzman, Charles. "Shifts in Scholarly Attention Among World Regions." OCLC Research Briefing, June 2013. https://www.oclc.org/research/events/2013/06-07a.html.
Lockman, Zachary. *Field Notes: The Making of Middle East Studies in the United States.* Stanford, CA: Stanford University Press, 2016.
Michigan State University Libraries Guides. "Collection Development Policy Statement: Muslim Studies and Middle East Studies." http://libguides.lib.msu.edu/c.php?g=300056&p=2003787.
Pitman, Lesley. *Supporting Research in Area Studies: A Guide for Academic Libraries.* Waltham, MA: Chandos Publishing, 2015.
Programic Councils. TRLN. http://www.trln.org/programmatic-councils/collections-council/.
The University of Chicago Library. "Middle East." Collection Development Policy. http://guides.lib.uchicago.edu/c.php?g=297396&p=1992077#s-lg-box-6060818

CHAPTER SIXTEEN

Leveraging Local Networks and International Partnerships in Japanese Collection Development

Molly Des Jardin and Michael P. Williams

Introduction

The University of Pennsylvania's collection of unique Imperial Japanese Navy memorabilia began with a serendipitous discovery: Robert Hegwood, a PhD candidate in the History department at Penn, stumbled upon a scrapbook in a used bookstore in Tokyo. Sensing that it would be important to researchers, Robert purchased the scrapbook with its final home in the Penn Libraries' collection in mind. He then contacted the Japanese Studies librarian, Molly Des Jardin, from Tokyo and inquired about the possibility of the libraries acquiring the scrapbook for the wider research community to use.

Delighted with Robert's discovery, Molly decided to purchase the scrapbook from him for the libraries. When Molly and library specialist Michael P. Williams saw the scrapbook in person, they learned that it contained ephemera from all over North America that were collected on a 1936 cruise of the Imperial Japanese Navy Training Fleet (*Renshū Kantai* 練習艦隊) from Japan to the United States and the Caribbean.[1] As the training fleet is not well represented in library collections, both the librarian and the library specialist began to undertake research on the fleet and the multiple cruises of its ships, especially the *Asama*, *Iwate*, *Izumo*, and *Yakumo*, which predominated in the latter half of the training fleet's time. Fascinated with the global scope of the fleet's travels, they investigated what other materials might have been produced by the cruises, and this led them not only to the release of a blog post on the topic, but also to the development of a collection that served to contextualize the scrapbook with memorial cruise books, scientific documents produced by officers, ships' newspapers, and photo albums. The Penn Libraries now owns the most comprehensive collection of this kind—known locally as the Japanese Naval Collection—and has been engaged in digitizing and promoting it for researchers' free use worldwide.

This chapter details the development of the Penn Libraries' Japanese Naval Collection, from its inception in our student's scrapbook discovery to the iterative process of searching for and purchasing other Imperial Japanese Navy Training Fleet materials and related items, and encompasses promotion of the collection online by making digital facsimiles available and posting about its context and import on social media. Here, we re-envision the acquisitions, cataloging, digitization, and promotion process as the result of a network of individuals (both inside and outside the library) collaborating toward a shared vision of special collections. We have been integrating processes rather than functioning as a unidirectional assembly line in which component parts can be passed down a pipeline. Through this network of individuals, who share their complementary but unique skills and knowledge, formerly compartmentalized area studies materials can be more cohesively unified into a global collection and can enhance the value of the library's distinctive special and research collections in an increasingly international context.

Seeds of a Japanese Special Collection

Why build a collection around a single scrapbook, acquired by chance thanks to a student's discovery? With competing research demands on a necessarily limited budget, the decision to acquire more Imperial Japanese Navy materials required serious consideration. When taking into account the research interests of the Penn community in Japan's foreign relations in the early twentieth century, as well as the importance of these primary sources to researchers around the world, the librarian felt it was imperative to preserve them in a library context rather than leave them to languish in the hands of private sellers. Moreover, the Penn Libraries is in a special position to go beyond housing and preserving the materials: we are also able to digitize and make them available freely as well as promote their discovery in multiple languages.

Historically, the Japanese Studies department in the Penn Libraries has striven to acquire materials of relevance to the needs of members of the Penn community, with affiliations ranging among organizations such as the University's Department of East Asian Languages and Civilizations (EALC) and its Japanese Language Program, the Department of History, the Department of Art History, the Department of the History and Philosophy of Science, the Penn Museum of Museum of Archaeology and Anthropology, and the Joseph H. Lauder Institute of Management & International Studies. The Japanese Studies unit serves this diverse community, ranging from humanities to social sciences and contemporary to premodern topics, by purchasing materials directly requested by patrons or else by identifying materials advertised by publishers perceived to meet their needs.

This collecting strategy, coupled with an existing commitment to purchase items from Japanese publishers whose output is unambiguously scholarly, provided the Penn

Libraries with a strong research foundation for Japanese Studies, but it also limited the libraries' ability to purchase materials not mediated by academically oriented publishers and produced for the library marketplace. While the libraries would regularly acquire reproductions of popular, out-of-print magazines or series of newly reprinted documents, these circulating items—often owned by many academic libraries—are far from "special collections." Meanwhile, unconventional and ephemeral items, like our newly acquired naval scrapbook, would have been considered out of the scope of the Japanese collection in the past if it had even been discoverable in the first place. Only recently have we attempted to build true "special collections" composed of East Asian materials, especially Japanese.

Alice Prochaska notes that term *special collections* "is almost infinitely elastic" and can be stretched to include criteria such as "almost any library material ...more than 100 or 150 years old" and even area studies collections themselves "in their entirety or in respect of the nonstandard materials they contain."[2] She elaborates that "generally but not always, rare books and manuscripts are brought together as special collections."[3] Closely following that interpretation, the Penn Libraries have recently renewed a commitment to invest in their special collections through the establishment of the Kislak Center for Special Collections, Rare Books and Manuscripts, a state-of-the-art facility for the use and preservation of the Penn Libraries' most treasured and most vulnerable physical materials. The Penn Libraries' 2015–2017 Strategic Plan highlights its importance to the libraries:

Support for researchers involves a wide range of staff competencies and services. With the advent of the Kislak Center and the Schoenberg Institute for Manuscript Studies, we are building professional strength alongside a coordinated program supporting the digital humanities.[4]

While the Kislak Center does not explicitly denote how *special collections* differ from *rare books* and *manuscripts*, it describes its breadth of collections as spanning "from medieval manuscripts to twenty-first century artists' books."[5] The vast majority of these materials are the artifacts of European and American civilizations, with incunables and early printed books very well represented in addition to manuscripts. The collections also include items local to Philadelphia, such as the recent acquisition of Benjamin Franklin's first printing job in the area.[6] While area studies are far from absent in the Penn Libraries' special collections—notably, the Penn Libraries has a broad collection of rare Judaica and a small but significant collection of Indic manuscripts—these are largely the result of the acquisition of pre-existing private collections, and their characteristics hew closely to the traditional "rare books and manuscripts" definition of special collections.[7]

The Japanese rare collection, on the other hand, explicitly encompasses internationally focused materials beyond that definition that are deliberately sought out and curated by the librarian—thus enhancing the diversity of the collections at the Penn Libraries geographically and culturally as well as in terms of material type. Given the heightened prominence of the Kislak Center as both a highly trafficked physical space on campus and as a hub of scholarly instruction and collaboration, and the increasing importance of unique collections in an age of material abundance, the Japanese Studies department has worked diligently to assert its own relevance by actively acquiring materials that can coexist with and be co-contextualized by the Penn Libraries' other special collections. By way of functional definition for the Japanese Studies department, the term *special collections* considers the age of an item, its relative cost and replaceability, the damage or loss that it would sustain as a circulating item, and the ability to create a digital facsimile.

In the past, the Penn Libraries had rarely sought to accession Japanese material that fit these working criteria. Indeed, neither Tsuen-hsuin Tsien's 1977 list of "Rarities and

Specialties of East Asian Materials in American Libraries" nor Marra, Morimoto, and Yoshimura's 2003 "Directory of North American Collections of Old and Rare Japanese Books, Other Print Materials, and Manuscripts" attribute any special East Asian collections at all to the Penn Libraries.[8] (At the same time, given the lack of adherence to a traditional "old and rare books and manuscripts" definition, the Penn Libraries' rare Japanese collection may not even be listed in such directories now.) Seven years later, former Penn Libraries Chinese Studies librarian Jidong Yang narrated the loss of the McCartee Library, an extensive collection of Japanese and Chinese books formally accessioned into the Penn Libraries in November 1900 and which by 2007 had become subject to scatter, loss, and apparent deaccessioning. Yang concludes, "As a special collection the McCartee Library existed for only a short period of time. By the time Derk Bodde started to write about the origin of Penn's Chinese Collection [in 1944], the memory of the McCartee Library had long faded away."[9] While attempts to reclaim the long-dissolved McCartee Library have met with some limited success, this collection was notably not the result of a coordinated effort; instead, it was the wholesale acquisition of an individual's existing personal library. The decision to acquire a mélange of multilingual Americana reassembled in Japan in the form of a scrapbook, as well as a plethora of supporting and related materials, represents a shift in collection strategy and reflects both a growing commitment to expanding the global reach of special collections and spotlighting items that embody global and local ties.

Why this shift toward special collections comprising materials traditionally not collected by the Penn Libraries in area studies? Focusing on special and rare materials, while still growing the traditional research collection and secondary sources that contextualize the special collections, will allow institutions to make their area studies collections distinctive and relevant in new ways in the international academic community. Purchasing rare materials from the used market in places like Japan opens the way to acquiring unique holdings from otherwise private, closed collections inaccessible to researchers. It also circumvents the additional material costs imposed by Western dealers as well as their individual selection policies, which may favor foreign items for their aesthetic value as objects over their research value as resources. Area studies librarians' specialized language skills and knowledge of the book and publishing trades in their respective regions allow special collections to diversify and become more meaningful in an environment where, through digitization and promotion online, their collections need to relate more directly to patrons around the world, not just English speakers in the United States. Through acquiring area studies special collections with a cooperative arrangement of researchers, librarians, curators, and technical services specialists, American academic institutions can position themselves in an outward-looking, globally oriented way and dramatically increase their relevance to diverse international communities through unique holdings perhaps found nowhere else in the world.

Iterative Discovery and Contextual Material

The acquisition of the scrapbook was indeed a watershed moment for discovering a body of materials which largely has been uncollected by libraries both inside and outside of Japan. The identification of the scrapbook with the Imperial Japanese Navy Training Fleet provided significant information for further discovering related materials. The first wave of searching for *Renshū Kantai* in romanization on OCLC WorldCat, and in Japanese in Japan's primary online used book portal,[10] yielded a selection of twenty-two titles frequently employing the Japanese words *kinen* 記念 ("commemoration") and *shashinchō* 写真帖 ("photobook"). Extant English-language bibliographic records provided by Libraries Australia offered translated titles such as *1937 Memory to the Voyage of Training Squadron* and *Souvenir of the Cruise by the Training Squadron in Financial Year 1938*.[11] Eventual acquisition of these titles revealed them as exemplars of so-called "cruise books" produced by the training fleet. These yearbook-like souvenir books include rosters and portraits of recent Naval Academy graduates, photographic evidence of their journeys throughout the Pacific Ocean and beyond, and information about their global activities, including exchanges with locals.

In addition to cruise books, this first wave encompassed Japanese-language materials produced in the United States by Japanese immigrants and first-generation Japanese Americans, a body of literature that would be missed by English-language-driven attempts to document this minority population. None of these publications had been produced commercially and many are marked as *hibaihin* 非売品, or "not-for-sale," titles, which have historically been difficult to identify and collect for libraries of Japanese-language materials.[12] Each subsequent discovery provided keywords and concepts that helped us eventually expand the breadth and depth of the Japanese Naval Collection to include even more uncommon primary sources, encompassing items as diverse as colonial gazetteers, mimeographed military documents, souvenir postcards, and even an oil painting.[13] These materials are owned by few if any other libraries and provide important context for those studying the role of Japan and its military in the world. Beyond our PhD candidate who discovered the original scrapbook, Penn has several additional PhD students in EALC and history who are interested in Japan's international relations during this period and are excited to have such unique primary materials at hand for their research.

The ability to discover these materials was due in part to the close working relationship of the librarian and the library specialist, combining the full spectrum of library service expertise as well as a high degree of proficiency in Japanese. Molly, as librarian, and Michael, as library specialist, have leveraged their respective skills to collaborate on collection development activities through iterative feedback in the acquisitions and cataloging process. Generally, the librarian discovers materials through careful attention to faculty and student needs and from official sources like publisher catalogs and flyers, bibliographies, and vendor recommendations; meanwhile, in seeking bibliographic data for items, the library specialist uncovers companion materials, series information, and unique keywords and subject headings that provide the librarian with new sources of discovery for collection building.

Such iterative feedback would be markedly difficult without the steady globalization of bibliographic utilities and marketplaces mediated by the internet. The increased presence of Japanese bibliographic records in WorldCat provides additional opportunities for discovery during the acquisitions and cataloging process.[14] CiNii, the Japanese National Institute of Informatics' Japanese equivalent of WorldCat, provides additional bibliographic data from Japanese libraries outside of WorldCat's network.[15] Meanwhile, just as online marketplaces like eBay have increased the purchasing span of special collections libraries,[16] so too have Japanese-language markets for secondhand books grown with the Web's development. Diane Perushek's 2007 guide to building East Asian library collections notes how "smaller out-of-print bookstores, found by the dozen in the Kanda section of Tokyo, are rarely set up to handle overseas sales.... About thirty percent of the used books also appear online, thanks to an association of Kanda booksellers."[17] This association—the Japanese Association of Dealers in Old Books—has maintained a database of product listings called *Nihon no Furuhon'ya*, or "Japan's Used Bookstores," since 1997. As of January 2000, ninety-three stores had contributed their product listings; as of 2015, it boasts more than 2,300 affiliated stores across Japan nationwide.[18] *Nihon no Furuhon'ya* is, as of this writing, the predominant online marketplace for out-of-print and rare materials in Japan, including formerly classified government materials.[19] The growing participation of individual sellers on Amazon Japan,[20] and the increasing presence of these same sellers on Amazon.com localizing their listings for North American buyers, has created a robust online marketplace aimed at global audiences.

Vendor as Partner: From Discoveries to Acquisitions

While their listings are accessible globally through the internet, not all sellers on *Nihon no Furuhon'ya* are willing to accept foreign payments or ship overseas. Compounded by the scattering of Japanese naval materials among dozens of sellers, such barriers would be difficult to overcome without a purchasing agent in Japan. The Penn Libraries have been able to leverage a longstanding relationship with Japan Publications Trading Co., Ltd. (JPT) to circumvent this role. JPT is the Penn Libraries' primary vendor of Japanese-language materials, ranging from monographs to serials to visual materials, and they will extend their searches to used book markets and independent sellers outside of traditional distribution channels.

These extended searches do not, however, merely apply to out-of-print items formerly available through commercial publishers that have since only become accessible through second-hand stores. Many items sold on *Nihon no Furuhon'ya* have never been available as commercial products, and while we can rarely reconstruct in detail the provenance of specific items, many bear inscriptions and ownership stamps—the telltale evidence of having been in personal collections or in other libraries. In particular, manuscript items and unique aggregations of materials from diverse, unconnected creators exist as one-of-a-kind listings only available through this network of Japanese booksellers.

Just as the Penn Libraries' commitment to use JPT as its primary vendor has led to efficiencies in purchasing and consistency in product delivery, so has it engendered a cooperative relationship between the two organizations supported by near-daily email communication with our dedicated JPT representative through which the Penn Libraries are offered collection development insights and recommendations. JPT's annual library visits, generally coinciding with the Association for Asian Studies annual conference, allow for face-to-face meetings and a chance for the Penn Libraries to show JPT how the materials they brokered have become fully formed research collections. In one such visit to the Penn Libraries during the early development period of Penn's Japanese special collections, JPT customer representative Yōko Hayashi remarked, "You've sure been ordering a lot of weird stuff lately." Hayashi's unexpected words have become a badge of honor to us, and her frank delivery underscores our close working relationship and how willing JPT staff are to work with sellers to help the Penn Libraries acquire unlikely library resources.

This plenitude of resources and information is a far cry from the situation of the mid-twentieth century, in which the acquisitions of "retrospective materials" were "more difficult and expensive because of shortage of materials on the market, competitive buying among many libraries throughout the world, and the fact that the information received from overseas [was] usually not up to date."[21] This led publishers to instead employ "various technical devices, including photoduplication, microreproduction, and reprinting ...extensively introduced to make available many otherwise unobtainable materials," including "the selected archives of the Japanese army, navy, and other government agencies."[22] A library-oriented market has developed in Japan for materials, even now, based in physical reproductions and reprinting that are often quite expensive and can be of questionable quality, depending on the state of the original materials. Yet the majority of naval materials uncovered through the Penn Libraries' targeted searches have neither been acquired by any other identifiable library in any format nor are they available in commercial reproductions, making the collection even more rare and important to preserve both digitally and physically.

Digitizing Collections for Preservation, Discovery, and Access

As the growing collection of Imperial Japanese Navy materials includes many unique items in fragile condition and because of its promise to researchers around the world—including those whose distance and funding makes travel to Philadelphia unfeasible—the librarian took the opportunity to have the out-of-copyright items digitized in-house and put on *Print at Penn* and *Penn in Hand*, the Penn Libraries' homes for digital facsimiles of printed and manuscript items respectively. Her proposal to the library group Digital Penn, which manages the digitization workflow at the library's SCETI imaging facility,[23] was accepted with enthusiasm, and the scrapbook, cruise books, and various scientific and official documents were slotted into the imaging queue.

Some items, in particular the scrapbook that inspired the collection, involve dangerously acidic paper; due to the difficulty of rehousing them, however, it is doubtful that this problem can be rectified in the near future. This issue means that the digitization effort has had the double effect of promotion and preservation—it allows the materials to be used without physical handling and provides high-quality facsimiles of items that may deteriorate even without handling. Moreover, these images can be shared widely and used to promote Penn's special collections online. The items' housing in a climate-controlled facility in the Kislak Center, however, will mitigate against deterioration, and despite having been initially acquired by the Japanese Studies department, they are now part of the libraries' special collections holdings for storage purposes. This highlights the cooperative relationship that the librarian has established with the special collections staff, who welcome these additions to their area. Meanwhile, the library specialist is involved in a collaborative workflow with the special collections technical processing staff to create MARC records that conform to rare books cataloging standards and even EAD-compliant finding aids.[24] Without this close relationship involving specialists with varying expertise, the digitization, preservation, and complete cataloging of the Imperial Japanese Navy materials would never have been possible.

Social Media and the Power of Promotion

In 2012, Mitch Fraas, the curator for special collections in the Penn Libraries' Kislak Center, joined the Penn Libraries' blogosphere by launching *Unique at Penn*, dedicated to "descriptions and contextualization of items from the collections of the University of Pennsylvania Libraries . . .which are in some sense 'unique'—drawn from both our special and circulating collections."[25] This blog largely began with a focus on European materials and early Americana, though it had published posts on non-Western topics from Penn's South Asian Studies and Middle East Studies librarians. The library specialist's April 2013 post on our Japanese Juvenile Fiction Collection of early 1900s paperback pulp novels, discovered in the stacks in and rehoused in the Kislak Center that year, represented the first introduction of East Asian materials to the blog's readership as well as the first time the blog had featured a contribution from cataloging staff.[26]

This collaborative publishing arrangement between the curator and the library specialist has continued into the present, with six long-form posts published on *Unique at Penn* and one on the *Schoenberg Institute for Manuscript Studies* blog. These posts have created narrative-length collection profiles of the Penn Libraries' research collections, contextualized by items acquired through interlibrary loan, digital facsimiles in international libraries, and the expertise of local scholars and staff. The June 19, 2016, introduction of the training fleet materials entitled "Japanese Naval Cruise Books and the *Renshū Kantai*" features photographic material gathered by our scrapbook-hunting PhD candidate, Robert, from a research trip to California, as well as an animated GIF of the digitized scrapbook flipping page by page, provided by the Penn Libraries' library imaging assistant Chris Lippa.[27] As in the library specialist's previous posts, Japanese words are provided in both translated and original script versions to communicate the importance of global languages to our local readers while providing foreign-language keywords and tags that can be indexed by search engines and lead to discovery in Japanese. This strategy emphasizes the global contexts of the Penn Libraries' Japanese Collection rather than considering the objects as quaint, inscrutable artifacts. Additional social media advertising on platforms like Twitter, Facebook, Instagram, and Flickr similarly embrace Japanese-language access by including Japanese as well as English keywords and descriptions, taking advantage of the truly global nature of social media and the opportunities it presents for academic libraries' outreach efforts.

Building special collections with an underlying assumption that they will be actively promoted represents a shift in collection development attitudes identified by Penn Libraries curator Daniel Traister: "The historic attitude of 'get it, catalog it, preserve it' (the classic technical services functions) has become 'get it, catalog it, promote it.'"[28] Rachel Franks frames the latter part of this process as a cycle of "curation," "choreography," and "connection," in which librarians become "digital storytellers" who use digital media to stage their collections and solicit feedback.[29] By linking promotion with preservation, and by building on existing cataloging through expanded narratives that transcend the limitations of bibliographic records, the Penn Libraries' Japanese Studies department takes advantage of the library specialist's material expertise and the librarian's extensive knowledge of the academic landscape to create unique stories and connect them with a ready audience.

The digital outreach efforts for the Japanese Naval Collection spearheaded by the *Unique at Penn* posts have been successful, inviting interest from researchers locally, nationally, and globally, several of whom have been eager to see these materials in person. A

November 2016 Japanese-language symposium held in Philadelphia, "Road to the Pacific War in Recent Historiography," provided the opportunity to showcase a selection of the Penn Libraries' cruise books and other training fleet materials to a delegation of Japanese scholars; the library specialist's bibliographic tour conducted bilingually in English and Japanese further emphasized to visitors the Penn Libraries' commitment to supporting and enhancing global scholarship.

Our *Unique at Penn* posts have reached potential patrons who were not aware of the particular strengths of the Penn Libraries' Japanese Collection and special collections and have even sparked new research topics inspired by the materials. The librarian and the library specialist have each been contacted by researchers from places as varied as Japan, Australia, Montana, and Wisconsin, who are interested in having digital facsimiles of materials advertised first on *Unique at Penn* or through word of mouth. The Penn Libraries' digitization efforts for the Japanese Collection broadly serve both an outreach and access purpose in these cases. Through high-quality digitization and promotion, we have been able to increase our audience and number of patrons—virtual as well as in-person visitors to the libraries—and thus the usage of the collections; at the same time, we are proud to have been able to inspire new research and use of unique primary sources that are otherwise hidden in the hands of private collectors and used book shops.

International Collections and the Twenty-First Century Library

Twenty-first-century librarianship and library collections are already here, and both are proving to be increasingly global endeavors. This global need comes from numerous sources: international students on campus and international researchers accessing our collections and the need to distinguish ourselves in a profoundly interconnected environment. What makes libraries relevant, and what makes area studies collections important within academic libraries in the United States? And how can we leverage our library staff in building such collections?

It may be the case that, going forward, special collections and unique primary sources housed in American libraries will be key in distinguishing university libraries at the same time as making their holdings more directly relevant to researchers both on campus and around the world. If most prominent collections contain the same academic monographs and journals, what will make the Penn Libraries stand out in the global academic community? We propose that acquiring materials that appeal to researchers outside of the English-language sphere of research, including international on-campus scholars and students as well as those at other institutions, will invite further interest in American library collections and enhance the libraries' prestige in a global context. This is possible, however, only if libraries also engage in active outreach to patrons who may not yet know that these collections even exist. With engagement in social media and through digitization efforts that include high-quality, usable facsimiles of unique and especially non-Western materials, academic libraries can emphasize their commitment to global engagement and their services to the global community.

This process, of course, is far from simple. It requires collaboration and cooperation throughout the university library, including among staff with differing skills and positions and in disparate units, and encouraging those staff to learn from each other to enhance their own skill sets. In addition, it is imperative that libraries rely on their staff with the appropriate language and subject expertise, as well as international partnerships and connections, to prioritize and evaluate the materials that the libraries choose to focus on. Finally, it is those partnerships and connections—with researchers on- and off-campus as well as with international vendors and individual sellers, as the case may be—that allow collecting of unique and relevant materials to be inspired and undertaken in the first place. The library does not consist of only librarians, after all. It is embedded in an increasingly global community of scholars, students, online visitors, professional librarians, expert staff, curators, publishers, vendors, and dealers in a network that cannot be reasonably deconstructed. It is through this network of expertise and cooperation that academic libraries can truly become important players in the increasingly global world of twenty-first-century scholarship.

Notes

1. The primary focus of Penn's acquisitions has been materials relating to the Imperial Japanese Navy Training Fleet, *Teikoku Dai Nippon Kaigun Renshū Kantai* 大日本帝国海軍練習艦隊; several items relating to the postwar Training Fleet of the Japan Maritime Self-Defense Force, *Kaijō Jieitai Renshū Kantai* 海上自衛隊練習艦隊, have also been accessioned to emphasize the continuity of Japan's global presence on the seas.
2. Alice Prochaska, "Special Collections in an International Perspective," *Library Trends* 52, no. 1 (2003): 138–39.
3. Ibid.
4. Penn Libraries, "University of Pennsylvania Libraries Strategic Plan for 2015–2017," 11.
5. Kislak Center for Special Collections, Rare Books, and Manuscripts, "About the Kislak Center," http://www.library.upenn.edu/kislak/about.
6. Samuel Keimer's "An Elegy on the Much Lamented Death of the Ingenious and Well-Belov'd Aquila Rose, Clerk to the Honourable Assembly at Philadelphia, Who Died the 24th of the 6th Month, 1723, Aged 28." A facsimile of this item can be viewed at *Print at Penn*, http://dla.library.upenn.edu/dla/print/index.html.
7. Arthur Kiron, "The Professionalization of Wisdom: The Legacy of Dropsie College and Its Library," in *The Penn Library Collections at 250* (Philadelphia: University of Pennsylvania Library, 2000); David Nelson, "The Penniman-Gribbel Collection of Sanskrit Manuscripts," Ibid.
8. Tsuen-hsuin Tsien, "Current Status of the East Asia Collections in American Libraries," *The Journal of Asian Studies* 36, no. 3 (1977): 499–514; Toshie Marra, Hideyuki Morimoto, and Reiko Yoshimura, "Directory of North American Collections of Old and Rare Japanese Books, Other Print Materials, and Manuscripts," *Journal of East Asian Libraries* 131 (2003): 68–109.
9. Jidong Yang, "The McCartee Library and the East Asian Collection of the University of Pennsylvania," in *Collecting Asia: East Asian Libraries in North America, 1868-2008*, ed. Peter X. Zhou (Ann Arbor: Association for Asian Studies, 2010), 57. Yang traces the earliest mention of the McCartee Library to 1891 but concludes that it likely had been established between 1881–1888.
10. *Nihon no Furuhon'ya* 日本の古本屋, http://www.kosho.or.jp.
11. OCLC 222488612 and OCLC 222504216 respectively. These MARC records were in Romanized form only until the Penn Libraries acquired each of these titles and enhanced the records with Japanese script. It is crucial for specialists in libraries to be able to search flexibly for these reasons and to be able to Romanize Japanese, enter non-Romanized Japanese search terms, and translate those terms to likely English records to identify the full range of available materials.
12. Association of Research Libraries Office of Management Studies, Workshop for Japanese Collection Librarians in American Research Libraries: August 28–30, 1978, Washington, D.C. (Washington, DC: Association of Research Libraries Office of Management Studies, 1978).

13. While a complete hand list is beyond the scope of this writing, a few items in the collection may be highlighted: a 1928 "special issue" of the *Māsharu Shinpō* or "Marshall Islands Report" welcoming Prince Nobuhito (brother of the newly-crowned Emperor Hirohito), who had enlisted in the Navy (OCLC 959291462); *Jitsugyō Eigo Bunrei*, a compilation of English-language speeches, documents, and letters from the Renshu Kantai's 1927 cruise, published as examples of diplomatic English in action (OCLC 959387778); and the 1922 *Umi no Wakōdo*, a self-published memoir by Otohiko Inoue, a member of the 1920–1921 cruise (OCLC 957675198).
14. Particularly, records contributed by Waseda University Library, the National Diet Library of Japan (NDL), and the Japanese bibliographic network Toshokan Ryūtsū Center Co., Ltd.
15. http://ci.nii.ac.jp is searchable through both English- and Japanese-language interfaces.
16. Scott B. Pagel, "Building a Rare Book Collection from Scratch," *Trends in Law Library Management and Technology* 17, no. 1 (2007).
17. Diane Perushek, "Building Library Collections in East Asian Studies," in *Building Area Studies Collections*, eds. Dan Hazen and James Henry Spohrer (Wiesbaden: Harrassowitz, 2007): 140.
18. Jun'ichirō Kida, "'Denmō Kaikai' Koshoten no Hōmupēji," Hōsho Gekkan: Kosho o Meguru Jōhōshi 172 (2000); Japanese Association of Dealers in Old Books [JADOB], "Nihon no Furuhon'ya ni Tsuite" (January 19, 2015 version), https://www.kosho.or.jp/wppost/plg_WpPost_post.php?postid=82.
19. JADOB, "Nihon no Furuhon'ya ni Tsuite."
20. https://www.amazon.co.jp/.
21. Tsuen-hsuin Tsien, "East Asian Collection in America," *The Library Quarterly* 35, no. 4 (1965): 266.
22. Ibid., 267.
23. The Schoenberg Center for Electronic Text & Image.
24. EAD (Encoded Archival Description) is the Penn Libraries' standard for describing manuscript collections, as the original Training Fleet scrapbook was deemed. The description of archival materials is generally outside of the expertise of area studies staff at Penn, just as the processing of Japanese-language material is outside of the expertise of special collections staff.
25. Arthur Mitchell Fraas, "About," Unique at Penn (blog), Penn Libraries, accessed June 12, 2017, https://uniqueatpenn.wordpress.com/about/.
26. Michael P. Williams, "Early Taishō Japanese Juvenile Pocket Fiction: Tatsukawa Bunko and its Imitators," *Unique at Penn* (blog), Penn Libraries, April 23, 2013, https://uniqueatpenn.wordpress.com/2013/04/23/.
27. Michael P. Williams, "Japanese Naval Cruise Books and the Renshū Kantai," *Unique at Penn* (blog), Penn Libraries, June 9, 2016, https://uniqueatpenn.wordpress.com/2016/06/09/.
28. Beth M. Whittaker, "'Get It, Catalog It, Promote It': New Challenges to Providing Access to Special Collections," *RBM: A Journal of Rare Books, Manuscripts, and Cultural Heritage* 7, no. 2 (2006): 122.
29. Rachel Franks, "Establishing an Emotional Connection: The Librarian as (Digital) Storyteller," *Australian Library Journal* 62, no. 4 (2013).

Bibliography

Association of Research Libraries Office of Management Studies. *Workshop for Japanese Collection Librarians in American Research Libraries: August 28–30, 1978, Washington, D.C.* Washington, DC: Association of Research Libraries Office of Management Studies, 1978.

Fraas, Arthur Mitchell. "About." *Unique at Penn* (blog). Penn Libraries. Accessed June 12, 2017. https://uniqueatpenn.wordpress.com/about/.

Franks, Rachel. "Establishing an Emotional Connection: The Librarian as (Digital) Storyteller." *Australian Library Journal* 62, no. 4 (2013): 285–94.

Japanese Association of Dealers in Old Books. "*Nihon no Furuhon'ya* ni Tsuite" 日本の古本屋について [About *Nihon no Furuhon'ya*]. Last modified January 19, 2015. https://www.kosho.or.jp/wppost/plg_WpPost_post.php?postid=82.

Kida, Jun'ichirō 紀田順一郎. "'Denmō Kaikai' Koshoten no Hōmupēji" 《電網快々》古書店の ホームページ [Homepages of Secondhand Bookstores on the "Instant Internet"]. *Hōsho Gekkan: Kosho o Meguru Jōhōshi* 彷書月刊: 古書を巡る情報誌 172 (2000): 4–7.

Kiron, Arthur. "The Professionalization of Wisdom: The Legacy of Dropsie College and Its Library." In *The Penn Library Collections at 250*, 182–201. Philadelphia: University of Pennsylvania Library, 2000. Accessed June 14, 2017. http://www.library.upenn.edu/exhibits/rbm/at250/dropsie/ak.pdf.

Kislak Center for Special Collections, Rare Books, and Manuscripts. "About the Kislak Center." Accessed June 12, 2017. http://www.library.upenn.edu/kislak/about/about.html.

Marra, Toshie, Hideyuki Morimoto, and Reiko Yoshimura. "Directory of North American Collections of Old and Rare Japanese Books, Other Print Materials, and Manuscripts." *Journal of East Asian Libraries* 131 (2003): 68–109.

Nelson, David. "The Penniman-Gribbel Collection of Sanskrit Manuscripts." In *The Penn Library Collections at 250*, 202–17. Philadelphia: University of Pennsylvania Library, 2000. Accessed June 14, 2017. http://www.library.upenn.edu/exhibits/rbm/at250/southasia/dn.pdf.

Pagel, Scott B. "Building a Rare Book Collection from Scratch." *Trends in Law Library Management and Technology* 17, no. 1 (2007): 13–17.

Penn Libraries. "University of Pennsylvania Libraries Strategic Plan for 2015–2017." 2014. Retrieved from https://confluence.library.upenn.edu/display/libstratplan.

Perushek, Diane. "Building Library Collections in East Asian Studies." In *Building Area Studies Collections*, edited by Dan Hazen and James Henry Spohrer, 130–44. Wiesbaden: Harrassowitz, 2007.

Prochaska, Alice. "Special Collections in an International Perspective." *Library Trends* 52, no. 1 (2003): 138–50.

Tsien, Tsuen-hsuin. "Current Status of the East Asia Collections in American Libraries." *The Journal of Asian Studies* 36, no. 3 (1977): 499–514.

———. "East Asian Collection in America." *The Library Quarterly* 35, no. 4 (1965): 261–75.

Whittaker, Beth M. "'Get It, Catalog It, Promote It': New Challenges to Providing Access to Special Collections." *RBM: A Journal of Rare Books, Manuscripts, and Cultural Heritage* 7, no. 2 (2006): 121–33.

Williams, Michael P. "Early Taishō Japanese Juvenile Pocket Fiction: Tatsukawa Bunko and its Imitators." *Unique at Penn* (blog). Penn Libraries. April 23, 2013. https://uniqueatpenn.wordpress.com/2016/06/09/japanese-naval-cruise-books-and-the-renshu-kantai/.

———. "Japanese Naval Cruise Books and the Renshū Kantai." *Unique at Penn* (blog). Penn Libraries. June 9, 2016. https://uniqueatpenn.wordpress.com/2016/06/09/japanese-naval-cruise-books-and-the-renshu-kantai/.

Yang, Jidong. "The McCartee Library and the East Asian Collection of the University of Pennsylvania." In *Collecting Asia: East Asian Libraries in North America, 1868–2008*, edited by Peter X. Zhou, 54–64. Ann Arbor: Association for Asian Studies, 2010.

CHAPTER SEVENTEEN

Collections at Work:

Forming Global Citizens through Outreach and Engagement

José O. Díaz and Pamela Espinosa de los Monteros

> *"I have for a long time ...desired as you know to build a fine library—not of great size but choice and at the same time useful."*[1]
>
> –Andrew Dickson White, President Cornell University

Cornell University founders' Ezra Cornell and Andrew Dickson White set out to create the "truly American university"[2] and envisioned the library to be "the heart"[3] of their newly chartered land-grant institution. In 1868, with a book appropriation of $11,000, White traveled to Europe on university business and purchased books from Paris, Stuttgart, Frankfurt, Heidelberg, Berlin, and London[4] for the new University Library. White, a diplomat, scholar, university president, and bibliophile of the French Revolution, has long been recognized as the library's "founding collector."[5] His travels abroad together with his interest in rare books and manuscripts would lay the foundations for Cornell's first collections.[6] Cornell University's founding collections are an early example of academic libraries' longstanding commitment to the global dimension of information and scholarship.

The academic library and area studies collections are often overlooked as tools to support cross-cultural exchange, global awareness, and foreign-language literacy. For nearly 125 years, area studies collections have provided local gateways to the cultures, political systems, and languages of the non-Western world. The discipline and its habits of collecting, organizing, and interpreting materials have been described as a form of "translation."[7] Alan Tansman, a professor of Japanese literature, argued that "if area studies can be understood as an enterprise seeking to know, analyze, and interpret foreign cultures through a multi-disciplinary lens, translation may be the act par excellence of area studies." He went on to explain that area studies "is primarily an effort to make the assumptions, meanings, structures, and dynamics of another society and culture comprehensible to an outsider."[8] These efforts at translating the world developed a new sense of urgency following America's transition from an agrarian to an industrial and global power during the closing days of the nineteenth century. The two world wars that followed in rapid succession convinced US colleges and universities that if the nation meant to exercise global leadership, its long-held Eurocentric focus was inadequate. US universities had to move to teach, conduct research, and otherwise "translate" developing regions such as Africa, Asia, Latin America, the Middle East, and the Soviet Union.[9]

This new approach brought seismic changes to all aspects of the academic enterprise.

International programs and academic centers aimed at offering language and cultural training became available in all major American universities. Foreign-born scholars joined American faculty departments. Funding, mostly under the guise of Title VI and the Fulbright-Hays Act, flooded college campuses.[10]

These intellectual and budgetary changes affected academic libraries as well. They joined their parent institutions and internationalized their holdings by adding massive foreign collections centered on the history, geography, literature, and international relations of understudied nations and regions. They created the academic bibliographer position: a hybrid scholar/librarian job with language and cultural expertise and deputized to focus his/her scholarly endeavors on material selection and organization, teaching, and outreach[11] for a geographic region. Today, area studies collections and librarians are fixtures in the modern academic library landscape. Like other library collections, area studies holdings are wide-ranging, deep, and comprehensive. It is, however, their interdisciplinary nature and foreign language holdings that distinguishes them from traditional subject librarianship.[12] They serve as gateways for those seeking language and cultural instruction. They have become a focal point for American universities seeking new and effective ways to globalize their curriculum and enhance research opportunities for students and faculty.

The professionals who serve these collections are credentialed, skilled, and uniquely positioned to support interdisciplinary collaborations.[13] Advanced degrees, intensely rooted in these holdings, are regularly awarded. In short, area studies and their supporting collections and libraries have for decades attempted to translate and integrate the global and local dimensions of information.

Library Engagement in Area Studies

The distinctiveness of area studies collections and its myriad contributions to learning have not spared them or their practitioners from the many changes the library ecosystem is facing. Changes in information and technology continue to test how librarians interact with and support patrons. The emergent engagement model of librarianship has challenged area librarians to assume new roles that move away from a traditional collection-centered model. Instead, the engagement model offers area librarians the opportunity to immerse themselves in their users' workflows and become true partners in the research enterprise. By doing so, area studies librarians may assist their users to navigate the global and multilingual information landscape as well as utilize the information resources at their disposal. For area studies librarianship, the movement to deemphasize collections and embrace a vision of librarianship built on partnerships is fraught with both risks and opportunities.[14]

At first glance, engagement with area studies collections seems to present insurmountable barriers. Traditionally, area studies collections have been seen as the sole purview of scholars, regional experts, and graduate students ostensibly proficient in the language and the region. To engage other users, particularly undergraduate populations, with collections that demand language proficiency and considerable understanding of a region is a tenuous enterprise. These barriers parallel some of the common cross-cultural and linguistic challenges encountered by those engaged in foreign-language instruction or overseas service-learning activities.[15]

However, a closer look reveals an agreeable reality. Unlike foreign-language training, service-learning activities, or special/rare collection materials, engagement with area studies collections *could* be based on a degree of mediation/facilitation that could make them more approachable and less intimidating and reasonably remove access challenges. How could area studies librarians position themselves and put their collections to work in forming and shaping global citizens? The engagement model is one part of the answer.

The framework for the engaged librarian strategically places the library, librarian, and collection as an integral part of the research and instruction cycle while championing the library as an intellectual meeting place for programming, conversation, and inquiry. To do so, librarians are actively looking to engage users with their collections online, in the classroom, on campus, and in extracurricular activities. This model demands that librarians create learning environments that will incorporate the use and discovery of appropriate information sources into the activity flow of students and faculty.

However, there is risk involved in engagement. The comfortable predictability of routine tasks gives way to new demands that require new knowledge. As the forthcoming case studies show, The Ohio State University Libraries' Area Studies Department is heeding our institution's demand to employ our resources in the creation of globally competent citizens. It has also adopted engagement as the intellectual framework that governs its approach to service. In these demands and approaches some see a looming crisis; others see a treasure trove of prospects. Either way, area studies will not shy away from the challenge. After all, it was a global crisis and its accompanying demands that gave birth to our discipline and our collections. From crisis, we know full well, comes opportunity.

The Setting

The Ohio State University is a world-class public research university and the leading comprehensive teaching and research institution in the state of Ohio. With more than 63,000 students, the Wexner Medical Center, fourteen colleges, eighty centers, and 175 majors, the university offers its students uncommon breadth and depth of opportunity in the liberal arts, sciences, and professional programs. Students interested in international studies have access to five Area Studies Centers tasked with advancing the knowledge of international cultures and world regions by sponsoring and facilitating a wide range of academic activities. University Libraries support center faculty and staff via their area studies librarians and collections.

The Area Studies Centers engaged in these case studies are the East Asian Studies Center (EAS) and the Center for Latin American Studies (CLAS). They both strive to be catalysts for original thought and action in the study of Asian and Latin American cultures in Ohio, in the US, and around the world. They combine exceptional expertise with far-reaching partnerships at home and abroad.

The Center for Latin American Studies is home to 107 faculty members from thirty-three departments. It is a leading promoter of the university's efforts to internationalize the curriculum, foster multidisciplinary initiatives, and increase diversity of perspectives. CLAS works to increase the supply of Latin American specialists at all levels of the educational system for service in areas of national need, as identified by the US Department of Education, in government, education, business, and nonprofit sectors. An integral part of its mission is to advance and disseminate knowledge about Latin America among P-12 and postsecondary educators, the business community, the media, and the community at large.

The East Asian Studies Center connects seventy faculty, instructors, and postdoctoral researchers in nineteen disciplines for increased collaborations among various fields and specializations. The center, a Title VI-supported entity, seeds new courses in language and area studies, enabling students to explore new areas or deepen their knowledge in current ones. Additionally, it partners with university resources, such as the William Oxley Thompson Library, the Huntington Archives, the Billy Ireland Cartoon Library & Museum, and EASC Media Library, to provide access to unique tools for study. It also provides scholarships for language and disciplinary studies and encourages undergraduate student scholarship through research, writing, and translation competitions.

One of our most interesting and perhaps groundbreaking initiatives involved not a center but a department: geography. The Department of Geography at Ohio State is recognized as one of the top five geography departments in the nation and employs world-renowned faculty and researchers in the field to engage students at the graduate and undergraduate level. It uses critical analysis and innovative technologies to understand, among others, the challenges of urban growth and decline, regional population shifts and societal change, spatial patterns of human activity and the effects on the physical landscape, and the development of spatial models and mapping techniques. Its academic offerings include air transportation studies, atmospheric sciences, geography, and geographic information science.

The case studies that follow exemplify diverse models of engagement at our institution and the contribution of the library to the internationalization of the curriculum. Each case study demonstrates the expansion of the librarian role, the effectiveness of program development beyond the traditional single in-class sessions, and the impact of the librarians' role in supporting teaching faculty. Our librarians conceived and developed these programs with a full understanding that their success was far from certain. Their risk-benefit analysis, however, showed that in these cases their latent benefits clearly outweighed the risks.

The Library Has Left the Building: Engaging with Non-Library Collections

In 2015, the Center for Latin American Studies (CLAS), the Department of Spanish and Portuguese (SPPO), and the Interdisciplinary Working Group on the Andes & Amazonia (IWGAA) purchased the Andean and Amazonian Artifact Collection. The collection consists of hand-made artifacts and material culture items envisioned as instructional tools to support the units' interdisciplinary minor, the Quechua language studies program, and related courses. The program envisioned the development of a teaching collection available to foreign-language and Latin American Cultural Studies instructors.[16] The purchase had a worthy goal in mind: to develop curricula and integrated learning methods that would explore the language, culture, people, and context of the Andean and Amazonian region through active learning pedagogy.[17]

Translating the vision for the collection into practice presented a significant challenge. Issues of cataloging and circulation quickly arose, and the responsible departments approached the University Libraries for assistance. Resources and policy limitations prevented immediate integrating of the collection but the librarians sought alternative solutions. Further discussions led SPPO to turn the collection into a permanent exhibit housed in its building. The libraries, acting as a knowledge broker,[18] shared best practices ranging from curation and labeling to furniture and instructional design.

The collaboration worked. Today, the Andean and Amazonian Artifact Collection has become one of the most visible initiatives of the SPPO and, perhaps more critical, it opened a dialogue with SPPO faculty about the libraries' role in managing research collections. With the stewardship of the collection out of the library's purview, new opportunities to assist in the development of instructional tools and enhance the accessibility of the collection have taken a central role.[19] Throughout this initiative, the libraries did not ignore its traditional role. It actively collected Andes and Amazonian sources while also expanding its service role in new directions. To make these efforts more proactive, the libraries created an Andean and Amazonian LibGuide highlighting sources and original content developed for the collection. The guide emphasized locally available content, digitized collections, and online sources available through other libraries, museums, and cultural institutions.

Historically, Andean and Amazonian sources have not been one of the libraries' collection strengths. This gap provided an opportunity for librarians to address the role of different institutions in promoting access to information for this region.[20] The guide found an eager audience in two courses: Spanish-Alternative Literacies and Historiographies in the Andes and Amazonia: Reading and Writing Practices Beyond Text, Spanish-Honors Senior Seminar in Latin American Literatures and Cultures.[21] The guide's success led to instruction opportunities including a pre-orientation lecture for the Fulbright Hays Short-Term Seminar on "Teaching the Andes: Redefining the Common Good and Reclaiming the Public Square" provided to K-12 teachers in the Midwest and ongoing involvement with the courses' capstone assignments.

Recently, the Center for Languages, Literatures, and Cultures' Global Gallery[22] exhibit *Hidden Life of Things: Andean and Amazonian Artifacts and the Stories They Tell* made good use of the LibGuide and other library-provided materials, including reproductions of the bilingual Quechua/Spanish edition of *Don Quixote*, *Tercero catecismo* (an Aymara text), digital audio recordings of Quechua, and the Latin American Studies Collection and Andean/Amazonian LibGuide.[23] Exhibit organizers recognized the University Libraries as a leading partner for its contributions. The visibility of the LibGuide allowed students and faculty to discover available collection and online resources. In addition, this exhibit led faculty member to discover the LibGuide tool and ponder its possibilities.

The Extensive Reading Program (ERP): Engaging with Foreign Language Collections[24]

Frequently, area studies librarians encounter the challenge of making their collections discoverable to a novice language learner. The language challenge is often compounded by undergraduate students' dependency on online search engines as their primary search method.[25] Unsurprisingly, these factors limit the possibility of undergraduates discovering the richness of interdisciplinary area studies collections at their institution. The Extensive Reading Program (ERP) developed at Ohio State aimed to address these challenges by creating a user-friendly method that would allow collections to be discovered by novice foreign-language students.[26]

Area studies staff designed the ERP for a beginning foreign-language student in search of books suitable for their reading level. The goal of this program was to introduce first- and second-year undergraduate students to materials that would support their foreign-language education. To reach students, area studies librarians worked alongside Japanese-language faculty to develop the scope of the program. Department teaching faculty found value in the idea of a programmatic approach to enhance students' reading skills.

After recruiting interested faculty, area studies librarians organized a meeting with participating faculty to determine the scope of the program and its general workflow. This initial meeting led to programmatic decisions on whether the program would be virtual (allowing users to locate collection material on their own) or in-person (requiring a physical space in the library). Ultimately, the teaching faculty opted for a mixed approach: a virtual and in-person self-paced student instruction program to supplement their foreign-language curriculum. Librarians and teaching faculty also set clear expectations for their respective roles in the project. Librarians would be in charge of identifying collection materials, creating the discovery tools for the collection materials, and other logistical matters. Faculty would evaluate the proposed collection items, categorize them by language level, market the program among their students, and assess its impact.

Librarians then worked to identify suitable collection content that fit the project scope. For the initial program, they reviewed 450 potential titles and eventually selected 220 items to be categorized by faculty. Then they met with faculty to sort the items into their appropriate reading levels. To make the items discoverable, librarians created a LibGuide to organize the project's resources and provide a virtual hub. For ease of access, librarians embedded the guide into the library resource link available to the student through their course management system. Librarians and teaching faculty meet annually to review and sort new books suggested for the project.[27] Selected items are added to the guide on an annual basis.

Participation in the ERP is voluntary and supplemental. This has affected its format and effectiveness. Because no academic credit is given, the program is kept informal. Thus, the in-person reading event held in the spring resembles a social gathering where students discuss foreign-language books they have read or intend to read. The event also allows students to ask questions of the instructors who also participate in the program. The librarians promote the virtual and in-person program through area studies library blogs entries and other methods. However, librarians rely primarily on the department partners and faculty to promote the program directly to their students.

The face-to-face reading phase of the program is held every spring to allow new foreign-language students to gain a foundational base in their chosen language of study. The faculty partners are responsible for facilitating the event.[28] For this program, library staff members pull 200 items from the collection and organize them by reading level. This in-person component of the project complements the virtual service by allowing librarians to personally interact with students and faculty. Through this event, librarians receive the chance to recommend suggested titles that inform future acquisitions.

World Geography LibGuide: Engaging with Interdisciplinary Courses

The World Geography LibGuide project has both didactic and financial implications. In 2016, University Libraries partnered with Student Government, the Office of Distance Education and eLearning (ODEE), the Office of Academic Affairs (OAA), and the University Center for the Advancement of Teaching (UCAT) to develop three faculty grant programs intended to reduce the costs of textbooks. Additionally, ALX, as the initiative became known, nicely dovetailed with President Michael Drake's 2020 vision calling for affordability and "excellence in education."[29] The libraries and their ALX partners sponsored proposals designed to replace a conventional textbook with an open educational resource or low-cost alternative.[30]

In the fall of 2016, the Center for Latin American Studies approached the libraries' Area Studies Department with a request: a geography professor, teaching an online course, needed regional/area expertise on the development of an open-education resource intended to replace an undergraduate world geography textbook. Underlying the project's objective was the professor's experience directing the university's Service Learning Initiatives. The aforementioned enterprise integrated meaningful community service with instruction, often in locations abroad. Our geographer was also looking to restructure the course curriculum and to urge Ohio students to engage with contemporary global issues through the lens of geography.

The project proved challenging from its inception. Initially, the instructor sought to find regional experts on campus that could suggest contemporary and authoritative sources on global issues. To accommodate this request, the libraries' Area Studies Department recruited area studies librarians to select resources suitable for an undergraduate world geography course. One area studies librarian worked as project manager and tasked each participating librarian to select a variety of sources organized onto a regional page template. Unlike other LibGuides, this online textbook/guide would direct users to sources addressing an aspect of a general or broader topic identified by our professor.[31]

Access challenges proliferated through the project. Only electronically accessible sources were viable for an online course and included issues related to single-user licenses. In addition, the libraries' Area Studies Department lacked subject experts for Western Europe, South East Asia, and Africa. To bridge these gaps, the library invited area studies librarians from Ohio University and the University of Illinois Urbana-Champaign to join the project. Ohio State librarians created a template for each regional page, determined the guide's geographic and topical coverage, set criteria for each section, trained area and subject librarians to curate individual regions, edited the guide for consistency, and, if needed, added sources. Other library subject liaisons contributed their expertise as needed.[32]

By all accounts, the World Geography LibGuide was a success. One hundred and fifteen students enrolled in the course and used the guide. Each student saved an average of 140 dollars. Some of our successes, however, went beyond dollars and cents. The guide allowed area studies librarians to highlight its collections and monitor their usage, and it opened the door to future collaboration with colleagues from the field. Equally noteworthy, librarians and faculty understood and overcame hurdles centered on access and copyright limitation in an online environment. Perhaps more rewarding, area studies librarians showcased their expertise by selecting sources rather than tools, thus becoming true partners in the teaching endeavor.[33]

Collections at Work

This chapter demonstrates that building great collections centered on specific geographic regions and their cultural manifestations is a necessary condition in the education and formation of competent global citizens. Without collections, there can be no engagement and outreach. Without engagement and outreach, collections become at best dormant and ineffective, at worst an expensive luxury.

A common thread runs through these case studies: librarians need to be in "the flow."[34] To create opportunities for learning, support foreign-language literacy, and deliver content in new and imaginative ways requires more than subject expertise. It mandates initiative, enthusiasm, and commitment. It also requires acknowledgment that we, too, can and should play an important instructional role. To assume that role is to admit, and commit to the notion, that collections are but a tool. The rest is up to us.

Notes

1. Marg G. Dimunation and Elaine D. Engst, *A Legacy of Ideas: Andrew Dickson White and the Founding of the Cornell University Library* (Ithaca, NY: Cornell University Libraries, 1996), 6, http://rmc.library.cornell.edu/footsteps/exhibition/ADW.pdf.
2. Ibid., *preface.*
3. Cornell University Libraries, "Olin @ 50: Inspiration Since 1961: The Early Days of the University Libraries," Cornell University Libraries, accessed April 26, 2017, https://olinuris.library.cornell.edu/olinat50/early-days.
4. Ali Houissa, "History and Development of the Cornell University Library Collections on the Middle East," Cornell Middle East and Islamic Studies Collection, Cornell University Libraries, accessed April 18, 2017, https://middleeast.library.cornell.edu/content/about-collection.
5. Ibid, *preface.*
6. Modern-day librarianship recognizes the practice of traveling abroad and collecting foreign-language materials as foundational steps in the creation of area and international studies collections, see Dimunation and Engst, *preface;* Mara Thacker and Mary Rader, "Keeping the 'Area' in Area Studies: All about International Acquisitions Trips," paper presented at the International and Area Studies Collections in the 21st Century (IASC21) Conference, 2016, http://hdl.handle.net/2142/94657.
7. Alan Tansman, "Japanese Studies: The Intangible Act of Translation in Szanton," in *The Politics of Knowledge: Area Studies and the Disciplines,* ed. David Szanton (Berkeley, CA: University of California Press, 2004), 184.
8. Ibid., 184
9. Mark L. Grover, "Library Area Studies Organizations and Multidisciplinary Collection and Research: The Latin American Experience," paper presented at the International Federation of

Library Associations Conference, 2008, http://hdl.handle.net/2142/8845.

10. For more on these programs, see National Research Council, *International Education and Foreign Languages: Keys to Securing America's Future* (Washington, DC: The National Academies Press, 2002), 13–82. For a legislative history of the programs, see pages 267–83.
11. For more on bibliographers, see Kristine K. Stacy-Bates et al., "Competencies for Bibliographers," *Reference & User Services Quarterly* 42, no. 3 (2003): 235; Malgorzata M. Hueckel, "The Duties, Educational Backgrounds, and Intellectual Profiles of Slavic Bibliographers in Academic Libraries in the United States," master's thesis (University of North Carolina at Chapel Hill, 1990), 10–43; Dan C. Hazen, "Twilight of the Gods? Bibliographers in the Electronic Age," *Library Trends* 48, no. 4: 821, accessed Search Premier, EBSCOhost.
12. Masha Misco, "Disciplinary Points of Departure: How Area Studies Librarians Fit Within the Subject Paradigm," *College & Undergraduate Libraries* 18, no. 4 (2011): 386.
13. Ibid., 388.
14. For more on engagement see: José O. Díaz, "The Roles of Engagement at The Ohio State University Libraries: Thoughts from an Early Adopter," *The Reference Librarian* 55, no. 3 (2014): 224–33, doi:10.1080/02763877.2014.910741. The role of librarians in supporting and/or participating in classroom instruction continues to attract scholarly interest. See, for example, Nicholas J. Rowland and Jeffrey A. Knapp, "Engaged Scholarship and Embedded Librarianship," *Journal of Higher Education Outreach and Engagement* 19, no. 2 (2015): 15–33, doi:10.1080/02763877.2014.910741; José O. Díaz and Meris Mandernach, "Relationship Building One-Step at a Time: Case Studies of Successful Faculty-Librarian Partnership," *portal: Libraries and the Academy* 17, no. 2 (2017), 273–82, http://rave.ohiolink.edu/ejournals/article/346894538.
15. TyAnna Herrington, "Crossing Global Boundaries: Beyond Intercultural Communication," *Journal of Business and Technical Communication* 24, no. 4 (2010): 517, doi:10.1177/1050651910371303.
16. Materials included masks, children's dolls, musical instruments, ceremonial items.
17. Michelle Wibbelsman, "Andean and Amazonian Material Culture and Performance Traditions as Sites of Indigenous Knowledges and Memory," *TRANSMODERNITY: Journal of Peripheral Cultural Production of the Luso-Hispanic World* 7, no.2 (2017): 57–84. http://www.escholarship.org/uc/item/5223g28c.
18. Gavin Bennett and Nasreen Jessani, eds., *The Knowledge Translation Toolkit: Bridging the Know-do Gap: A Resource for Researchers* (Ottawa, ON: Sage Publications, 2011), http://www.deslibris.ca/ID/438562.
19. For example, the libraries' instructional librarian partner with a Quechua instructor to create audio recordings of Quechua poems, riddles, and short stories that are traditionally shared in conjunction with the artifacts. These sound recordings were disseminated on SoundCloud as an instructional tool and supplement understanding of the collection.
20. See introduction text and graphic courtesy of Robyn Ness: http://guides.osu.edu/Andean.
21. See the guide here: http://guides.osu.edu/Andean. The courses are Spanish 7650 Alternative Literacies and Historiographies in the Andes and Amazonia: Reading and Writing Practices Beyond Text graduate course.
22. *The Center for Languages, Literatures, and Cultures' Global Gallery* exhibits are on-site and online exhibits in Hagerty Hall of The Ohio State University. The rotating exhibits feature world media that promote the customs, cultures, artistic creations and cultural artifacts of other countries and peoples. For more information, see https://cllc.osu.edu/wmcc/global-gallery.
23. See reproductions and an excerpt of the exhibit panel here: http://guides.osu.edu/c.php?g=474915&p=3826560.
24. The authors wish to thank our former colleague, Amy Wang. She conceived this initiative and saw it to fruition. This portion of the papers is based on her presentation and remarks at the International and Area Studies Collections for the 21st Century held at the University of Illinois, Urbana-Champaign in October 2016.
25. Madeleine C. Shanahan, "Transforming Information Search and Evaluation Practices of Undergraduate Students," *International Journal of Medical Informatics* 77, no. 8 (2008): 519, doi:10.1016/j.ijmedinf.2007.10.004.

26. The literature on Japanese language acquisition is very extensive. See Amy Snyder Ohta, *Second Language Acquisition Processes in the Classroom: Learning Japanese* (Mahwah, NJ: Lawrence Erlbaum Associates, 2001); Jack Jinghui Liu and Shibata, Setsue, "Why College Students Want to Learn Asian Languages: A Comparative Study of Motivational Factors for the Selection of Chinese, Japanese, Korean and Vietnamese," *Journal of the National Council of Less Commonly Taught Languages*, 5 (2008): 33–55; Sin Yi. Tsang, "Learning Japanese as a Foreign Language in the Context of an American University: A Qualitative and Process-Oriented Study on De/Motivation at the Learning Situation Level," *Foreign Language Annals*, 45, no.1 (2012): 130–63; Van C. Gessel, "Teaching 'the Devil's Own Tongue': The Challenges of Offering Japanese in a College Environment," ADFL Bulletin 28, no. 2 (1997): 6–10. For more on undergraduate search habits, see Courtney Young, "Librarians Can Finish What Starts with Google," Reference Librarian 54, no. 4 (2013): 353–55, doi:10.1080/02763877.2013.816223; Helen Goergas, "Google vs. the Library: Student Preferences and Perceptions When Doing Research Using Google and a Federated Search Tool," *portal: Libraries & the Academy*, 13, no. 2 (2013): 165–85, http://rave.ohiolink.edu/ejournals/article/346757447; Michelle Dalton, "The Form of Search Tool Chosen by Undergraduate Students Influences Research Practices and the Type and Quality of Information Selected," *Evidence Based Library & Information Practice* 9, no. 2 (2014): 19–21.
27. A copy of the LibGuide can be viewed at guides.osu.edu/Tadoku.
28. On average, thirty-five students attend the in-person event.
29. Michael V. Drake, "2020 Vision: A Focus on Excellence," accessed August 14, 2017, https://president.osu.edu/presidents/drake/speeches-and-statements/state-of-the-university-address-january-21-2016.html.
30. For more on textbooks, open sources, and financial sustainability, see John Levi Hilton III and David Wiley, "Open Access Textbooks and Financial Sustainability: A Case Study on Flat World Knowledge," *The International Review of Research in Open and Distributed Learning* 12, no. 5 (2011): 18–26; John L. Hilton III and David A. Wiley, "A Sustainable Future for Open Textbooks? The Flat World Knowledge Story," *First Monday* 15, no. 8 (2010), https://firstmonday.org/ojs/index.php/fm/article/view/2800/2578.
31. A typical regional page included sources on the following broad topics: geography and natural environment, population, economic systems, geopolitics and conflict. Additional sources included a regional news database, a regional musical genre represented as an embedded audio/video file, and a link to local cultural events in Columbus representative of that region.
32. Ten area studies librarians and three subject specialists at three institutions, including The Ohio State University, Ohio University, and the University of Illinois, Urbana-Champaign, collaborated in the creation of this LibGuide. The Ohio State University Libraries' Teaching & Learning Department, Copyright Resources Center, and our electronic resource officer provided consultation on licensing, access, and overall design.
33. GEOG 2750 World Regional Geography can be found here: http://guides.osu.edu/c.php?g=463881.
34. Lorcan Dempsey, "Reconfiguring the Library System Environment," *portal: Libraries and the Academy* 8, no.2 (2008): 111–20.

Bibliography

Bennett, Gavin, and Nasreen Jessani. *The Knowledge Translation Toolkit: Bridging the Know-do Gap: A Resource for Researchers*. Ottawa, ON: Sage Publications, 2011. Ebook.

Cornell University Libraries. "Olin @ 50: Inspiration Since 1961: The Early Days of the University Libraries." Cornell University Libraries. https://olinuris.library.cornell.edu/olinat50/early-days.

Dalton, Michelle. "The Form of Search Tool Chosen by Undergraduate Students Influences Research Practices and the Type and Quality of Information Selected." *Evidence Based Library & Information Practice* 9, no. 2 (2014): 19–21.

Díaz, José O. "The Roles of Engagement at The Ohio State University Libraries: Thoughts from an Early Adopter." *Reference Librarian* 55, no. 3 (2014): 224–33. doi

10.1080/02763877.2014.910741.
Díaz, José O., and Meris A. Mandernach. "Relationship Building One Step at a Time: Case Studies of Successful Faculty-Librarian Partnerships." *portal: Libraries and the Academy* 17, no. 2 (2017): 273–82. http://rave.ohiolink.edu/ejournals/article/346894538.
Dempsey, Lorcan. "Reconfiguring the Library Systems Environment." *Portal: Libraries and the Academy* 8, no.2 (2008): 111–20.
Dimunation, Marg G., and Elaine D. Engst. *A Legacy of Ideas: Andrew Dickson White and the Founding of the Cornell University Library.* Ithaca, NY: Cornell University Libraries, 1996. http://rmc.library.cornell.edu/footsteps/exhibition/ADW.pdf.
Drake, Micheal V. "2020 Vision: A Focus on Excellence." *Office of the President.* Accessed August 14, 2017. https://president.osu.edu/presidents/drake/speeches-and-statements/state-of-the-university-address-january-21-2016.html.
Gessel, Van C. "Teaching 'the Devil's Own Tongue': The Challenges of Offering Japanese in a College Environment." *ADFL Bulletin* 28, no. 2 (1997): 6–10.
Goergas, Helen. "Google vs. the Library: Student Preferences and Perceptions When Doing Research Using Google and a Federated Search Tool." *portal: Libraries & the Academy,* 13, no. 2 (2013): 165–85. http://rave.ohiolink.edu/ejournals/article/346757447.
Grover, Mark L. "Library Area Studies Organizations and Multidisciplinary Collection and Research: The Latin American Experience." Paper presented at the International Federation of Library Associations Conference, August 2008. http://hdl.handle.net/2142/8845.
Hazen, Dan. "Twilight of the Gods? Bibliographers in the Electronic Age." *Library Trends* 48, no. 4 (2000): 821–41. Academic Search Premier, EBSCOhost.
Herrington, TyAnna. "Crossing Global Boundaries: Beyond Intercultural Communication." *Journal of Business and Technical Communication* 24, no.4 (2010): 516–39. doi:10.1177/1050651910371303.
Hilton III, John L., and David Wiley. "Open Access Textbooks and Financial Sustainability: A Case Study on Flat World Knowledge." *The International Review of Research in Open and Distributed Learning* 12, no. 5 (2011). http://www.irrodl.org/index.php/irrodl/article/view/960/1860.
———. "A Sustainable Future for Open Textbooks? The Flat World Knowledge Story." *First Monday* 15, no. 8 (2010). https://firstmonday.org/ojs/index.php/fm/article/view/2800/2578.
Houissa, Ali. "History and Development of the Cornell University Library Collections on the Middle East." Cornell Middle East and Islamic Studies Collection, Cornell University Libraries. https://middleeast.library.cornell.edu/content/about-collection.
Hueckel, Malgorzata M. "The Duties, Educational Backgrounds, and Intellectual Profiles of Slavic Bibliographers in Academic Libraries in the United States." Master's thesis. University of North Carolina at Chapel Hill, 1990.
Huth, B., M. Warren, and T. Burgess. "Guide to the Andrew Dickson White Papers, 1832–1919." Division of Rare and Manuscript Collections, Cornell University Library. http://rmc.library.cornell.edu/EAD/htmldocs/RMA00002.html#s3.
Jinghui Liu, Jack, and Setsue Shibata. "Why College Students Want to Learn Asian Languages: A Comparative Study of Motivational Factors for the Selection of Chinese, Japanese, Korean and Vietnamese." *Journal of the National Council of Less Commonly Taught Languages,* 5 (2008): 33–55.
Knapp, Jeffrey A. "Engaged Scholarship and Embedded Librarianship." *Journal of Higher Education Outreach and Engagement* 19, no. 2 (2015): 15–33. doi:10.1080/02763877.2014.910741.
Misco, Masha. "Disciplinary Points of Departure: How Area Studies Librarians Fit Within the Subject Paradigm." *College & Undergraduate Libraries* 18, no. 4 (2011): 385–90.
National Research Council. International Education and Foreign Languages: Keys to Securing America's Future. Edited by Mary Ellen O'Connell and Janet L. Norwood. Washington, DC: The National Academies Press, 2007. https://www.nap.edu/catalog/11841/international-education-and-foreign-languages-keys-to-securing-americas-future.
Ohta, Amy Snyder. *Second Language Acquisition Processes in the Classroom: Learning Japanese.* Mahwah, NJ: Lawrence Erlbaum Associates, 2001.
Shanahan, Madeleine C. "Transforming Information Search and Evaluation Practices of Under-

graduate Students." *International Journal of Medical Informatics* 77, no. 8 (2008): 518–26, doi:10.1016/j.ijmedinf.2007.10.004.

Stacy-Bates, Kristine K., Jan Fryer, Jeffrey D. Kushkowski, and Diana D. Shonrock. "Competencies for Bibliographers." *Reference & User Services Quarterly* 42, no. 3 (2003): 235–41.

Tansman, Alan. "Japanese Studies: The Intangible Act of Translation in Szanton." In *The Politics of Knowledge: Area Studies and the Disciplines*, edited by *David L.* Szanton, 184–216, Berkeley, CA: University of California Press, 2004.

Thacker, Mara, and Mary Rader. "Keeping the 'Area' in Area Studies: All about International Acquisitions Trips." Paper presented at International and Area Studies Collections in the 21st Century (IASC21) Conference, University of Illinois Library, Urbana-Champaign, IL. October 13-14, 2016. http://hdl.handle.net/2142/94657.

Tsang, Sin Yi. "Learning Japanese as a Foreign Language in the Context of an American University: A Qualitative and Process-Oriented Study on De/Motivation at the Learning Situation Level." *Foreign Language Annals*, 45, no.1 (2012): 130–63.

Wibbelsman, Michelle. "Andean and Amazonian Material Culture and Performance Traditions as Sites of Indigenous Knowledges and Memory." *TRANSMODERNITY: Journal of Peripheral Cultural Production of the Luso-Hispanic World* 7, no.2 (2017): 57–84. http://www.escholarship.org/uc/item/5223g28c.

Young, Courtney. "Librarians Can Finish What Starts with Google." *Reference Librarian* 54, no. 4 (2013): 353–55. doi:10.1080/02763877.2013.816223.

CHAPTER EIGHTEEN

Shared Global Heritage in Research Libraries

Margarita Vargas-Betancourt, E. Haven Hawley, and Rebecca J.W. Jefferson

Shared global heritage crosses boundaries and creates new communities. The Latin American and Caribbean Collection, the Isser and Rae Price Library of Judaica, and the Panama Canal Museum Collection at the George A. Smathers Libraries of the University of Florida (UF) are central to digital library projects and innovative instruction in a major academic library at a US research university. The Smathers Libraries at UF are highly collaborative, with shared global heritage activities embracing partnerships at UF, with other institutions, and internationally.[1]

The Special and Area Studies Collections Department in the Smathers Libraries is one of the very few units in an academic research library that completely integrates archives and special collections with area studies collections.[2] This provides an optimal environment for collaboration across curatorial boundaries and forming partnerships in distinctive ways.

The three collections have built deep and broad holdings, and their intersections of acquisitions and management build upon their mutual strengths rather than fostering competition. Personnel engage in partnerships across the boundaries of heritage professions and institutions, with specialists and generalists collaborating to manage library, archives, and museum materials. The structure of programs facilitates engagement with and sharing of resources by universities, national repositories, and small heritage organizations or communities. This chapter offers an overview of selected programs and projects that articulate the intersection of the three collections, offering specific models for multi-institutional activities designed to serve one or many campuses, as well as researchers around the world.

The Latin American and Caribbean Collection (LACC) is central to the department's boundary-crossing collections. LACC traces its preeminence to the Farmington Plan, close ties with UF's renowned Center for Latin American Studies, and exceptional manuscript collections on the Caribbean. The University of Florida is a founding partner of the Digital Library of the Caribbean, which through shared governance and the participation of more than forty institutions has established the largest open access Caribbean historical collection in the world. An LACC curator co-founded the *Desmantelando Fronteras/Breaking Down Borders* webinar series, which enables Latin American and Caribbean archivists to consult with colleagues in the Americas to increase awareness of projects worldwide. The award-winning series facilitates exchange rather than one-way instruction, with personnel from three US universities coordinating the webinars.

The Isser and Rae Price Judaica Library holds internationally distinctive Judaica from the nineteenth and twentieth centuries, with exceptionally rare *festschriften*, ephemera, and periodicals as the foundation for the foremost Jewish Studies research collection in the southeastern United States. The Jewish Diaspora Collection of the Price Library is a collaborative and cooperative digital library designed to preserve and provide wide access to Jewish heritage materials from Florida, Latin America, and the Caribbean. Price Library personnel developed the Beyond the Memory of the Holocaust course, connecting students with historical collections, UF faculty expertise, and a Holocaust survivor to stimulate an informed creative work of Holocaust memory.

The Panama Canal Museum Collection began as a community repository focused largely on American experiences but since then has been integrated into SASC as an international collection. LACC and Panama Canal Collection curators worked with digital humanities faculty on a multi-institutional Caribbean history course. In 2016, Panama Silver, Asian Gold: Reimagining Diasporas, Archives, and the Humanities was taught as a distributed online collaborative course with faculty and students from Amherst College, the University of Florida, the University of Miami, and the University of the West Indies.

The University of Florida looks to the future as a space of collaboration to advance global shared heritage. In 2016, UF signed an agreement with the Biblioteca Nacional de Cuba José Martí (BNJM) to coordinate collaborative international library digitization activities on behalf of BNJM. Digitization of monographs, newspapers and journals, maps, and legal documents will make available copies of BNJM materials not known to exist elsewhere. Importantly, this facilitation will aid in bringing together additional agreements in progress between specific institutions and the BNJM, with UF serving as facilitator and ensuring communication among many heritage partners. The exceptionally strong holdings of the Latin American and Caribbean Collection are a foundation upon which all of these activities build.

A Preeminent Collection on Latin America and the Caribbean

At the University of Florida (UF), the acquisition of Latin American material related to the Caribbean began in the 1930s with the creation of the School for Inter-American Affairs by UF president John J. Tigert. Tigert believed that the University of Florida had a special role because of its immediacy to the Caribbean.[3]

While UF served Latin American students, UF faculty developed extensive relationships with Latin American countries.[4] These partnerships through personal connections opened a pathway but did not allow UF to support the travel of students and faculty to Latin America. To address the need for support, in 1961 UF's Graduate School proposed the creation of the Center for Latin American Studies with the purpose of continuing service to Latin American students and preparing US students for careers related to Latin America.[5]

The Cold War provided the context for this development. In the aftermath of the Cuban Revolution, the United States sought to deter other Latin American countries from turning to Communist ideologies. The establishment of the center enabled many UF initiatives, including the strengthening of the existing library collection.

In 1948, US librarians developed the Farmington Plan, a collaborative agreement among select US libraries each of which specialized in collecting materials from specific regions. The Farmington Plan, too, reflected Cold War priorities. US librarians acknowledged that United States leadership in the post-WWII world required deepening national resources for understanding other regions. Extensive library collections aided this goal, but early on it was acknowledged that the Library of Congress could not collect all regions comprehensively. The Farmington Plan embodied a collaborative effort among many institutions.[6]

Archives, rare books, and artifacts came to be of strong interest as Latin America and the Caribbean became a battlefield of the Cold War. After acknowledging the significance of UF's Caribbean holdings, US librarians within the framework of the Farmington Plan assigned the mission to collect Caribbean content to the University of Florida Libraries in 1951. Two years later, the Farmington Plan recognized Latin America as a region in which material should be collected.[7] The Latin American and Caribbean Collection has worked to fulfill this mission. UF formed partnerships with Caribbean institutions in order to microfilm their holdings. One of the favorite stories of LACC librarians is that of a UF librarian who traveled by boat from country to country in the Caribbean in the 1950s and 1960s. The university gained materials with each stop at which the librarian microfilmed cultural and historical materials loaned by local owners. Library Director Stanley West and two UF presidents, John S. Allen and J. Wayne Reitz, wrote that the librarian's travel resulted in one of the most thorough collections of Caribbean newspapers possible and led toward strong partnerships with Caribbean repositories.[8]

Digital Library of the Caribbean (dLOC)

These existing relationships served as the foundation for the Digital Library of the Caribbean (dLOC). In 2004, nine founding partners officially established dLOC.[9] Under the leadership of Florida International University (FIU), the University of the Virgin Islands (UVI), and UF, the founding institutions, along with a growing number of partners, have contributed digital content from their holdings to the open access repository. dLOC is now "the largest open access collection of Caribbean materials with over 2 million pages of content, 39 institutional partners, and over 1 million views each month."[10] Florida International University (FIU) and the University of Florida facilitate the consortium, the former providing administrative support and the latter overseeing technical infrastructure.[11]

The Digital Library of the Caribbean (dLOC) is, on one hand, a digital repository for resources from and about the Caribbean and circum-Caribbean from archives, museums, libraries, academic institutions, and private collections. On the other, it is a platform that provides a scholarly cyberinfrastructure for Caribbean studies. As a research foundation, dLOC includes technical, social, governmental, and procedural supports, including open-source tools, executive and scholarly advisory boards, a permission-based rights model to support intellectual property as well as cultural and moral rights, and a core support team. As a scholarly resource, dLOC provides context, in addition to content, by placing Caribbean materials within academic discourse.[12]

dLOC's open access platform is a key element in partnerships with Caribbean and Latin American institutions because it provides equitable access to materials. This is essential in overcoming a potential lack of trust resulting from an historic, uneven, and for many years unregulated flow of Latin American and Caribbean cultural material to the United States. That flow began in the nineteenth century with US expansionist policy and continued during the Cold War era, for political and economic reasons, as explained above. The unequal relationship among US, Latin American, and Caribbean institutions reinforced the idea of US superiority instead of acknowledging institutions as partners. To counteract such a narrative, dLOC's partners participate in dlOC's governance through the executive board and scholarly advisory board. More importantly, partners retain rights over their material; they only give permission for the material to be made accessible online and to be preserved.

The funding model of dLOC is also designed to strengthen equity. dLOC members contribute funding for the sustainability of the project. Members are usually institutions from higher-income countries, like the United States, while Caribbean and Latin American institutions, known as partners, are expected only to provide content. Both members and partners participate equally in dLOC's governing structure.

Jewish Diaspora Collection (JDoC)

The Isser and Rae Price Library of Judaica comprises an internationally distinctive collection of more than 120,000 items, including approximately 10,000 scarce or rare items held in the library's unique set of reading rooms known as the "Judaica Suite."[13] Although the bulk of the collection hails from North America and Europe, the Price Library also holds significant Jewish resources from Latin America, particularly Argentina, Brazil, and Mexico. In 2014, the Price Library of Judaica applied for and won a National Endowment for the Humanities (NEH) Challenge Grant to reposition itself as a major repository of Jewish resources from Florida, Latin America, and the Caribbean.[14]

The impetus for this repositioning project resulted from a survey conducted by the library to examine its strengths and national standing. The survey also was motivated by a search for how the collection could align with other preeminent UF collections, such as the Latin American and Caribbean Collection and the P. K. Yonge Library of Florida History, to meet current and future scholarly needs.

The Judaica Library curator detected significantly increased interest among national and international scholars in the Jewish experience in Latin America and the Caribbean. Certain topics were of great interest but little supported by existing collections. Topics such as the impact of Jewish diasporic movements on global migration and settlement patterns, cultural and religious identities, and issues of politics, education, slavery, and civil rights had strong research potential. The library could play an important scholarly and cultural role by preserving and making accessible hidden or endangered Jewish materials from the region. Even in Florida, which has a strong Jewish population in a state considered a gateway to the Caribbean, a lack of continuity exists among efforts to collect and preserve the archives, records, and published accounts of such communities. In locations where a lack of resources or political upheavals endanger materials, Jewish historical materials are even more likely to be abandoned or overlooked.

With an NEH Challenge Grant, the Judaica Library has built the Jewish Diaspora Collection (JDoC), a cooperative, open access digital library modeled on and built in conjunction with the highly successful Digital Library of the Caribbean. The idea for JDoC also grew from the success of a project funded by the Library Services and Technology Act (LSTA) to digitize a long-standing Florida newspaper, the *Jewish Floridian.*[15] The paper holds a wealth of information about the history of the Jewish community of Florida from the 1920s to the 1990s. Despite its importance, the newspaper was available on microfilm at only two institutions in Florida: the Price Library of Judaica and the Jewish Museum of Florida. Converting the microfilm to digital format required a partnership of those two institutions and the public library system in South Florida, with the latter promoting the *Jewish Floridian* as a model for broadening access to Florida's ethnic newspapers.

The online *Jewish Floridian* newspaper quickly became the most popular viewed item among the library's digital collections of Judaica, resulting in more than one million hits to the website and with many other ethnic newspapers subsequently being added to the database. JDoC is now the partner site for most of Florida's Jewish news providers to host their digital content.[16] A similar joint project is underway with a long-running Jewish newspaper in Buenos Aires, *Nueva Sion,* established in 1948 and currently produced online (http://www.nuevasion.com.ar/). The project will enable *Nueva Sion* to digitize its historical printed issues. These older issues, which currently cannot be accessed for research, hold important information about the growth and development of Argentina's Jewish population after WWII.

To date, JDoC offers access to more than 600 items with more than 180,000 pages of content, including archives, photographs, newspapers, pamphlets, memoirs, and ephemera, many of which have been seen by very few researchers. Collaborative partnerships to provide content have been agreed upon or are being discussed for dLOC/JDoC with Jewish institutions and research groups from Barbados, Jamaica, Uruguay, Peru, El Salvador, Panama, and Cuba.

Many of these projects began as dLOC partnerships, with content added through dLOC to JDoC, allowing multiple points of discovery. For example, the Barbados Synagogue Restoration Project (BSRP) is a full dLOC partner with its own landing page within the dLOC partner pages (http://dloc.com/ibsrp). BSRP content also appears within the Caribbean Judaica section of JDoC (http://ufdc.ufl.edu/l/caribbeanjudaica). Whether accessing content through dLOC or JDoC, researchers gain access to BSRP's incredible archival documentation of the centuries-old synagogue and Jewish community of Barbados. A more complex relationship has been formed with a Jewish partnering institution in Mexico, the Center of Documentation and Research of the Jewish Communities in Mexico.

Centro de Documentación e Investigación Judío de México (CDIJUM)

Center of Documentation and Research of the Jewish Communities in Mexico (CDIJUM)

On May 10, 2017, the University of Florida and the Centro de Documentación e Investigación Judío de México (Center of Documentation and Research of the Jewish Communities in Mexico) signed a collaborative agreement. The framework for this collaboration is the UF Libraries' NEH grant project, Repositioning Florida's Judaica Library: Increasing Access to Humanities Resources from Florida, Latin America, and the Caribbean Communities, described above.

With support from UF's Center for Latin American Studies, the UF academic director of the collaborative agreement visited CDIJUM in July 2015. She invited the CDIJUM director to contribute content to the Jewish Diaspora Collection (JDoC). Based on the dLOC model, JDoC provides a digital repository for endangered Jewish holdings from Latin American and Caribbean repositories.[17] After initial contact, UF invited CDIJUM's director to campus to discuss projects that might be undertaken jointly.[18] Some of these projects include the digitization of Mexican Jewish newspapers like *Kesher* (1987–), *Der Weg* (1931–1977), *Di Shtime* (1939–1981), and *Prensa Israelita* (1945–1986). The Latin Americanist Research Resources Project (LARRP), a consortium of research libraries under the umbrella of the Center for Research Libraries (CRL), funded the digitization of UF's holdings of *Kesher*.[19]

In 2016 and 2017, LARRP also granted funding for the digitization of a wide range of Mexican Jewish newspapers. This second iteration of the project will allow the digitization of CDIJUM's complete newspaper holdings, which are considered by UNESCO as a World Memory Collection. The 2017 earthquake gave special significance to the project because it endangered the entire collection by causing irreparable damage to the CDIJUM building.[20] Other projects suggested are the digitization of UF's Mexican Jewish material not held by CDIJUM. Those projects included: making accessible the *festschrift* of the Colegio Israelita from the 1930s; the procurement of funds to digitize untapped sections of CDIJUM's archives, such as the Comité Central Israelita archive; an international symposium for Latin American Jewish collections to share knowledge about collecting and preserving Jewish heritage; and physical and online exhibits.

The Breaking Down Borders Project

The Desmantelando Fronteras/Breaking Down Borders online series is a webinar series launched by the Society of American Archivists' Latin American and Caribbean Cultural Heritage Archives Roundtable (LACCHA) in collaboration with the Digital Library of the Caribbean, the Association of Caribbean University, Research, and Institutional Libraries (ACURIL), and Latin American colleagues.[21] In 2012, LACCHA leadership developed two webinars on special collections for a Latin American audience through the US Department of State. The experience alerted them to the fact that Latin American and US archivists had great interest in the work of other colleagues in the Americas.[22] They formed the series' mission as showcasing archival projects of Latin America and the Caribbean and providing a collaborative space for Latin American and Caribbean archivists to share their projects, experiences, and takeaways. The project received the Society of American Archivists' Diversity Award in 2016.

Key to the success of the project was the partnership among LACCHA, dLOC, and ACURIL, as well as the support of the Asociación Latinoamericana de Archivos (Latin American Association of Archives, with the acronym ALA), Laura Kaspari Hohmann (the US Department of State's Information Resource Officer), and Benjamín Medina (director of the Benjamin Franklin Library in the US Embassy in Mexico). Such collaboration attracted the participation of the constituents of each association/institution.

Given their extensive work in Latin America and the Caribbean, the founders of the webinar acknowledged the technological barriers that their colleagues might face, such as unreliable internet connectivity. Consequently, the organizers asked presenters to pre-record their presentations. This gave presenters a greater feeling of control over their presentations. The six webinars produced during the 2015–2016 cycle have been preserved in the online scholarly repository at the University of Miami Libraries.[23] The team decided to archive the webinars in this way to provide an open access platform, which created equitable access to the materials and helped overcome potential distrust by Latin American institutions of US institutions.

The Panama Canal Museum Collection

The Panama Canal Museum Collection (PCMC) has become one of the signature collections at UF's Department of Area and Special Collections. In 1999, Canal Zone residents who retired to Florida opened the Panama Canal Museum in Seminole, Florida. Their objective was "to preserve the history of the American Era of the Panama Canal (1904–1999)."[24] The collection consists of artifacts, publications, and manuscripts that American Canal Zone residents or their descendants donated to the museum. In 2012, the Panama Canal Museum closed its doors and transferred its holdings to the UF libraries.

The transfer has already resulted in significant academic projects and has gained international recognition for the UF Libraries. In 2014, for example, Ernesto Pérez Mauri, producer at the major Panamanian TV company Telemetro, contacted UF to request that we connect him with the Panama Canal Society, which is based in the United States. He sought the contact as part of producing the seventh episode of *Espejo de Un País*, an eight-part documentary about the history of the Panama Canal, prepared to commemorate the centennial of the Panama Canal. Because personnel from the UF Libraries have attended the annual meeting of the Panama Canal Society since 2011, they were able to help Pérez Mauri coordinate interviews with former American residents of the Panama Canal Zone.[25] The episode was aired on August 14, 2014.[26]

Even though the collection highlights the perspective of American residents, it is possible to find the presence and impact of West Indians in the construction of the canal. As archivists and librarians locate this material, they are incorporating it into the Digital Library of the Caribbean to create a public archive of West Indians in Panama. The George A. Smathers Libraries were nominated in 2011 for UNESCO's Memory of the World Register as an institution that serves as a repository for records that document the presence of West Indians in the Panama Canal project.[27]

The West Indian presence in Panama and its effect in the development of Caribbean nationhood was highlighted in the course Panama Silver, Asian Gold: Migration, Money, and the Making of the Modern Caribbean taught simultaneously at UF, Amherst College, and the University of Miami in fall 2013.[28]

In October 2017, the three professors and one UF librarian presented a paper on their work with the PCMC collection at the 13th International Conference on Caribbean Literature (ICCL). During the trip to Panama, they also visited the West Indian Museum of Panama and established contact with the Society of Friends of the West Indian Museum of Panama (SAMAAP).[29] The UF librarian used those connections in the project Addressing Issues of Race, Class, and Gender Through Theatrical Literature Production and Community Discourse, 2014–2015, which included the writing of a play by Deborah Dickey that examined the racial, gender, and cultural relationships that constituted the reality of West Indian and American women's lives in the Panama Canal, a public staged reading of the play, and a post-show discussion.[30] The play was staged in Gainesville, Florida on February 20, 2015, and in Panama during the summer of 2016.

The syllabus for the course continues to evolve, reflecting the needs of each participating institution and emerging interests of faculty and students. A dynamic instructional partnership among the institutions has emerged through the pioneering efforts of faculty who embrace digital technologies to facilitate the shared co-creation of course content and access by students at each institution to unique local community and expert resources.

Similarly, in an effort to look at new ways of integrating the libraries' expanding global resources into curriculum, the Price Library of Judaica curators developed the Beyond the Memory of the Holocaust course, which brought students into the library to learn from curators and faculty about the Holocaust and use their knowledge to inform a literary or artistic creative work based on their studies.[31]

The course divided into three sections. The first section introduced students to the history of the Holocaust as it is recorded in the Price Library of Judaica collection. The students were given hands-on access to primary materials, such as documents, letters, photographs, and survivor testimonies, as well as creative works like film, sculpture, and art. Most of the resources shown were part of the Price Library's growing collection of Floridian, Latin American, and Caribbean Judaica.

Students in the second section were taught how discrimination against Jews and other groups led to persecution and transformed into genocide in the first half of the twentieth century. They were also instructed as to how this historical knowledge shapes current perspectives about politics, international law, and ethics and why and how we remember and memorialize acts of genocide. In the third part of the course, faculty introduced students to creative writing methods and to approaches for interviewing survivors, with encouragement to work on individual creative projects.

Students presented poems, artwork, a sculpture, a dance recital and an original martial arts routine in the culminating session of the semester. Selected materials became part of the historical collections of the Price Library of Judaica. A student interviewed a Holocaust survivor and produced an interpretative essay. His work was exhibited with that of other students in the class in the library during the final week of the spring semester. The student's interview and essay were added to JDoC as part of the library's growing collection of Floridian materials.[32] The course continues to evolve and this year will use the library's new José Moskovits Anti-Semitism Collection—a worldwide survey of opinions on anti-Semitism collected and compiled in Argentina—as a theme and thread running throughout the course.[33]

Looking to the Future

Creating access to collections is a foundation of collaborative scholarship and teaching, and the UF Libraries partner with many institutions to continue increasing access to shared global heritage collections.

The libraries and the University Press of Florida are engaged in an NEH/Mellon-funded grant to create open educational resources. *Books about Florida and the Caribbean: from the University Press of Florida to the World* is digitizing thirty out-of-print books about the Caribbean and Florida that were published from 1968 to 1992, making these scarce but important books available online without charge. The project includes creating an advisory board, securing permissions and rights, digitizing and distributing with Creative Commons licensing, marketing, and creating guidelines for similar efforts by other libraries and presses.[34]

The opening of relations between Cuba and the United States offers a compelling and rare opportunity to unite heritage institutions and their collections in a way that brings together the scholars and public of long-separated countries. The UF Libraries and the Biblioteca Nacional de Cuba José Martí (BNJM) have recently built upon the Florida institution's long-time collaborations with archives and libraries in Cuba to establish a profoundly broad and deep digital collection of Cuban heritage. The University of Florida and BNJM signed an agreement in 2016 to focus on digitization and the exchange of digital files for maps, legal materials, monographs, and serials. UF Libraries agreed to coordinate North American digitization efforts, complementing BNJM's digitization of sectors of its own holdings that were not held by North American institutions. The files will be uploaded to the Digital Library of the Caribbean and provided directly to collaborating institutions requesting complete files for local hosting.

Existing digitization projects and new agreements established by BNJM will be coordinated with the University of Florida commitment. Numerous institutions have expressed interest in being part of the project, which will define Cuban bibliographical scholarship for decades to come. Among the institutions included in initial discussions are Auburn University, Columbia University, Cornell University, Duke University, Harvard University, Queens University, Tulane University, UCLA, the University of California, the University of Miami, the University of North Carolina, the University of Texas, the University of Toronto, as well as the Center for Research Libraries and the New York Public Library. Importantly, the partnership with BNJM facilitates rather than restricts partnerships with US academic libraries. The UF Libraries have added personnel to coordinate the emerging consortial projects, reflecting the university's commitment to service, collaboration, and open access. A Cuban Heritage Coordinator was hired in spring 2017, and two multi-lingual graduate students were hired as one-semester Digital Cuban Bibliography interns in summer and fall of that year.[35]

Conclusion

Local collections and strengths can be shared as global heritage through collaboration. Collaborating with partners across a large university campus, among many institutions, and with communities and heritage organizations internationally creates collections, supports teaching, and generates digital access to materials formerly available only within a single institution's walls. Digital library projects and innovative instruction require a high level of collaboration and an understanding that the limits of one's own institution are a call for partnership. These partnerships create communities across professional divides, uniting institutional holdings, allowing faculty to broaden student horizons, and building bridges across disparities of resources and political divides. UF's multi-institutional activities can serve as a resource to stimulate academic libraries to identify their own strengths and to partner for ambitious projects that support research and teaching, as well as the public good, through a commitment to shared global heritage woven together through process and programs.

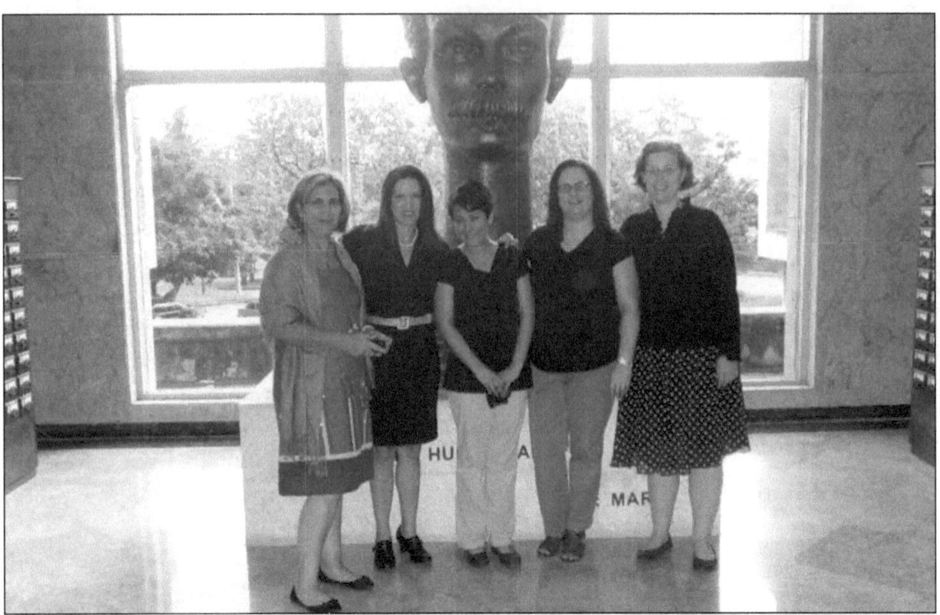

FIGURE 18.1.
Faculty and librarians in December 2012 with BNJM subdirector Nancy Machado. From left to right: Nancy Machado, Lillian Guerra, Margarita Vargas-Betancourt, Brooke Wooldridge, Laurie Taylor.

FIGURE 18.2.
Faculty and librarians in December 2012 with director Eduardo Torres Cuevas and subdirector Nancy Machado of Cuba's National Library. From left to right: Margarita Vargas-Betancourt, Lillian Guerra, Eduardo Torres Cuevas, Brooke Wooldridge, and Nancy Machado.

FIGURE 18.3.
The exhibition *Voices from the Panama Canal* displayed at the Panama Canal Centennial Celebration at University of Florida, August 2014.

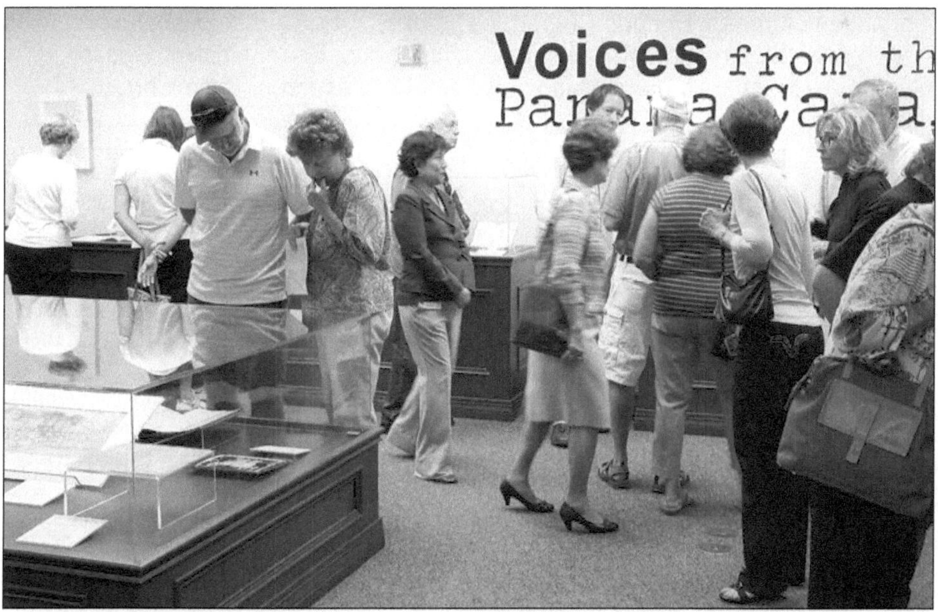

FIGURE 18.4.
The exhibition *Voices from the Panama Canal*, displayed at the Panama Canal Centennial Celebration at University of Florida in August 2014, brought together community members, librarians, and scholars.

FIGURE 18.5.
The NEH Challenge Grant for building collections of Judaica related to Florida, Latin America, and the Caribbean has produced partnerships between US and other institutions to created shared access to global heritage. From left to right, from a January 2016 meeting: Margarita Vargas-Betancourt, Latin American and Caribbean Librarian; Enrique Chmelnik, Director of the Center of Documentation and Research of the Jewish Communities in Mexico; Dean Judith C. Russell, George A. Smathers Libraries; and Rebecca J.W. Jefferson, Price Library of Judaica.

Notes

1. An overview of these collaborations is detailed in Laurie N. Taylor, et al., "Library Collaborative Networks Forging Scholarly Cyberinfrastructure and Enabling an Environment of Radical Collaboration," in *Handbook of Research on Academic Library Partnerships and Collaborations,* ed. Brian Doherty (Hershey, PA: IGI Global, 2016), 1–30, http://ufdc.ufl.edu/AA00030795/00001.
2. Lisa R. Carter and Beth M. Whittaker, "Area Studies and Special Collections: Shared Challenges, Shared Strength," *portal: Libraries and the Academy* 15.2 (April 2015): 353–73. Carter has continued research into the administrative structures and context of hybrid departments. She presented "Organizing Libraries: Area Studies & Special Collections" at the International and Area Studies Collections in the 21st Century Workshop, University of Illinois at Urbana-Champaign, October 14, 2016.
3. "History," Center for Latin American Studies at the University of Florida, last accessed May 12, 2017, http://www.latam.ufl.edu/about/history/.
4. The Graduate School, University of Florida, *Proposal for an Inter-American Cultural and Scientific Center* (Gainesville, FL: 1961), 1, last accessed May 12, 2017, http://ufdc.ufl.edu/AA00002847/00001.
5. Ibid., 2–3.
6. Ralph D. Wagner, *A History of the Farmington Plan* (Lanham, MD: Scarecrow Press, 2002), 86.

7. Ibid., 209, 210.
8. Laurie Taylor, "Librarian on a Boat or Digital Scholarship, Caribbean Studies, and the Digital Library of the Caribbean (dLOC): Alternative Sabbatical Proposal for 2016–2017," University of Florida Digital Collections (UFDC), last accessed May 12, 2017, http://ufdc.ufl.edu/AA00037232/00001.
9. Archives Nationales d'Haïti; Caribbean Community Secretariat (CARICOM); National Library of Jamaica; La Fundación Global Democracia y Desarrollo (FUNGLODE); Universidad de Oriente, Venezuela; University of the Virgin Islands; Florida International University; University of Central Florida; University of Florida, Digital Library of the Caribbean, "About dLOC," Digital Library of the Caribbean, last accessed May 12, 2017, http://dloc.com/dloc1/about.
10. Laurie Taylor, "Librarian on a Boat."
11. "About dLOC."
12. Laurie Taylor, Margarita Vargas-Betancourt, and Brooke Wooldridge, "The Digital Library of the Caribbean (dLOC): Creating a Shared Research Foundation," *Scholarly and Research Communication,* Simon Fraser University 4.3 (2013), last accessed May 12, 2017, doi:10.22230/src.2013v4n3a114.
13. Rebecca Jefferson, "A Priceless Collection," *Ha-Tanin,* Newsletter of the Center for Jewish Studies at the University of Florida 20 and 21 (Spring/Fall 2010): 9–12, last accessed August 15, 2017, http://web.jst.ufl.edu/haTanin/2009-10/2009-10.html.
14. Rebecca Jefferson et al., "Repositioning Florida's Judaica Library: Increasing Access to Humanities Resources from Florida, Latin America and the Caribbean Communities," University of Florida Digital Collections (UFDC), last accessed August 15, 2017, http://ufdc.ufl.edu/AA00022790/00001.
15. Rebecca Jefferson and Bess de Farber, "Florida Digital Newspaper Library: Broadening Access and Users (LSTA Grant Proposal)," University of Florida Digital Collections (UFDC), last accessed August 15, 2017, http://ufdc.ufl.edu/AA00010438/00001.
16. See, for example, the *Jewish Press of Pinellas County* (Clearwater, FL), University of Florida Digital Collections (UFDC), last accessed August 15, 2017, http://ufdc.ufl.edu/AA00032765/00162.
17. Jewish Diaspora Collection (JDoC), University of Florida Digital Collections (UFDC), last accessed May 12, 2017, http://ufdc.ufl.edu/judaica. The CDIJUM director at the time was Enrique Chmelnik.
18. The trip was funded through a travel grant from UF's Center for Latin American Studies.
19. For the proposal, see: Margarita Vargas-Betancourt, et al, "2016 LARRP Digitization Proposal," University of Florida Digital Collections (UFDC), last accessed May 12, 2017, http://ufdc.ufl.edu/AA00039438/00001. For the actual content, see *Kesher,* University of Florida Digital Collections (UFDC), last accessed May 12, 2017, http://ufdc.ufl.edu/l/AA00052698/00002/allvolumes.
20. Margarita Vargas-Betancourt and Bess de Farber, "Digitization of a UNESCO World Memory Collection: Mexico's Jewish Heritage Newspapers," University of Florida Digital Collections (UFDC), last accessed May 12, 2017, http://ufdc.ufl.edu/IR00009388/00001.
21. At the time, the co-chairs of LACCHA were Natalie Baur and Margarita Vargas-Betancourt, while George Apodaca was LACCHA's Online Communications Liaison.
22. George Apodaca, Natalie Baur, and Margarita Vargas-Betancourt, "Breaking Down Borders: LACCHA Launches New Webinar Series with Colleagues in the Caribbean and Latin America," *Archival Outlook* (May/June 2015): 14, 27, last accessed May 12, 2017, http://www.bluetoad.com/publication/?i=259343.
23. Latin American and Caribbean Cultural Heritage Archives (LACCHA) Society of American Archivists, "Desmantelando Fronteras/Breaking Down Borders Webinar Recordings," Scholarly Repository, University of Miami, last accessed May 12, 2017, http://scholarlyrepository.miami.edu/laccha_saa/.
24. Panama Canal Museum, last accessed August 15, 2017, http://cms.uflib.ufl.edu/pcm/Home.aspx.
25. American residents of the Panama Canal Zone identify themselves as Zonians.

26. Telemetro, "#7 El espejo de un país: El camino hacia la reversión," last accessed May 12, 2017, http://www.telemetro.com/nacionales/reportajes/espejo-pais-camino-reversion_3_724757566.html.
27. Memory of the World Register, Nomination Form "The Silver Men: West Indian Labourers at the Panama Canal, last accessed May 12, 2017, http://www.unesco.org/new/fileadmin/MULTIMEDIA/HQ/CI/CI/pdf/mow/nomination_forms/Panama%20silvermen.pdf.
28. The instructors of the course were Leah Rosenberg (University of Florida), Rhonda Cobham-Sander (Amherst College), and Donette Francis (University of Miami). "Panama Silver, Asian Gold: Migration, Money, and the Making of the Modern Caribbean; & Panama Silver, Asian Gold: Reimagining Diasporas, Archives, and the Humanities," Digital Library of the Caribbean, last accessed August 15, 2017, http://dloc.com/digital/panamasilver.
29. Society of Friends of the West Indian Museum of Panama, last accessed May 12, 2017, http://www.samaap.org/.
30. Deborah B. Dickey and Rebecca Fitzsimmons, "Addressing Issues of Race, Class, and Gender Through Theatrical Literature Production and Community Discourse," University of Florida Digital Collections (UFDC), last accessed May 12, 2017, http://ufdc.ufl.edu/IR00004963/00001.
31. The syllabus can be read online. Katalin Rac and Rebecca Jefferson, "IDH 3931 Beyond the Memory of the Holocaust Syllabus," University of Florida Digital Collections (UFDC), last accessed August 15, 2017, http://ufdc.ufl.edu/IR00009719/00001. Local writer, Stacey Goldring, co-teaches the course, and she has helped develop it through the inclusion of her Second Generation Holocaust Survivors Writing Workshop.
32. Mr. Morris Spiegler (the interviewee) and his family donated two born-digital photographs to provide visual context for the interview "Surviving Transnistria: Marcel Spiegler's Story" and the essay "A Gold Ring for a Loaf of Bread," JDoC Florida collections, last accessed August 16, 2017, http://ufdc.ufl.edu/AA00054854/00001.
33. "Library Acquires Major Anti-Semitism Collection," *Collectanea: the quarterly e-newsletter of the Isser and Rae Price Library of Judaica at the University of Florida* 1:2 (June 2017): 1, last accessed August 16, 2017, http://ufdc.ufl.edu/IR00010025/00002.
34. Laurie N. Taylor, et al, *Books about Florida and the Caribbean: from the University Press of Florida to the World*, University of Florida Digital Collections (UFDC), last accessed June 8, 2017, http://ufdc.ufl.edu/AA00032435/00001. Taylor and others have an important ARL SPEC Kit in progress titled *Organization of Libraries, Presses, and Publishing*, with anticipated 2017 publication date by Association of Research Libraries (Washington, D.C.). Proposal available at: http://ufdc.ufl.edu/AA00047744/00001.
35. E. Haven Hawley, "Cuban Heritage Digitization," last accessed June 8, 2017, http://www.uflib.ufl.edu/spec/cuba/; E. Haven Hawley, "Smathers Graduate Internships in Digital Cuban Bibliography," University of Florida Digital Collections (UFDC), last accessed June 8, 2017, http://ufdc.ufl.edu/AA00055782/00001.

Bibliography

Apodaca, George, Natalie Baur, and Margarita Vargas-Betancourt. "Breaking Down Borders. LACCHA Launches New Webinar Series with Colleagues in the Caribbean and Latin America." *Archival Outlook* (May/June 2015): 14, 27. Last accessed May 12, 2017. http://www.bluetoad.com/publication/?i=259343.

Carter, Lisa R., and Beth M. Whittaker. "Area Studies and Special Collections: Shared Challenges, Shared Strength." *portal: Libraries and the Academy* 15.2 (April 2015): 353–73.

Center for Latin American Studies at the University of Florida. "History." Last accessed May 12, 2017. http://www.latam.ufl.edu/about/history/.

Dickey, Deborah B., and Rebecca Fitzsimmons. "Addressing Issues of Race, Class, and Gender Through Theatrical Literature Production and Community Discourse." University of Florida Digital Collections (UFDC). Last accessed May 12, 2017. http://ufdc.ufl.edu/IR00004963/00001.

Digital Library of the Caribbean. "Panama Silver, Asian Gold: Migration, Money, and the Making of the Modern Caribbean; & Panama Silver, Asian Gold: Reimagining Diasporas, Archives, and the Humanities." Last accessed August 15, 2017. http://dloc.com/digital/panamasilver.

The Graduate School. University of Florida. *Proposal for an Inter-American Cultural and Scientific Center.* Gainesville, FL: 1961, 1. Last accessed May 12, 2017. http://ufdc.ufl.edu/AA00002847/00001.

Hawley, E. Haven. "Cuban Heritage Digitization." Last accessed June 8, 2017. http://www.uflib.ufl.edu/spec/cuba/.

Hawley, E. Haven. "Smathers Graduate Internships in Digital Cuban Bibliography." University of Florida Digital Collections (UFDC). Last accessed June 8, 2017. http://ufdc.ufl.edu/AA00055782/00001.

Jefferson, Rebecca. "A Priceless Collection." *Ha-Tanin,* Newsletter of the Center for Jewish Studies at the University of Florida 20 and 21 (Spring/Fall 2010): 9–12. Last accessed August 15, 2017. http://web.jst.ufl.edu/haTanin/2009-10/2009-10.html.

Jefferson, Rebecca, and Bess de Farber. "Florida Digital Newspaper Library: Broadening Access and Users (LSTA Grant Proposal)." University of Florida Digital Collections (UFDC). Last accessed August 15, 2017. http://ufdc.ufl.edu/AA00010438/00001.

Jefferson, Rebecca, et al. "Repositioning Florida's Judaica Library: Increasing Access to Humanities Resources from Florida, Latin America and the Caribbean Communities." University of Florida Digital Collections (UFDC). Last accessed August 15, 2017. http://ufdc.ufl.edu/AA00022790/00001.

Jewish Diaspora Collection (JDoC). University of Florida Digital Collections (UFDC). Last accessed May 12, 2017. http://ufdc.ufl.edu/judaica.

Jewish Press of Pinellas County (Clearwater, FL). University of Florida Digital Collections (UFDC). Last accessed August 15, 2017. http://ufdc.ufl.edu/AA00032765/00162.

Kesher. University of Florida Digital Collections (UFDC). Last accessed May 12, 2017. http://ufdc.ufl.edu/l/AA00052698/00002/allvolumes.

Latin American and Caribbean Cultural Heritage Archives (LACCHA) Society of American Archivists. "Desmantelando Fronteras/Breaking Down Borders Webinar Recordings." Scholarly Repository. University of Miami. Last accessed May 12, 2017. http://scholarlyrepository.miami.edu/laccha_saa/.

"Library Acquires Major Anti-Semitism Collection." *Collectanea: the quarterly e-newsletter of the Isser and Rae Price Library of Judaica at the University of Florida* 1:2 (June 2017): 1. Last accessed August 16, 2017. http://ufdc.ufl.edu/IR00010025/00002.

Memory of the World Register. Nomination Form, "The Silver Men: West Indian Labourers at the Panama Canal. Last accessed May 12, 2017. http://www.unesco.org/new/fileadmin/MULTIMEDIA/HQ/CI/CI/pdf/mow/nomination_forms/Panama%20silvermen.pdf.

Panama Canal Museum. Last accessed August 15, 2017. http://cms.uflib.ufl.edu/pcm/Home.aspx.

Rac, Katalin, and Rebecca Jefferson, "IDH 3931 Beyond the Memory of the Holocaust Syllabus." University of Florida Digital Collections (UFDC). Last accessed August 15, 2017. http://ufdc.ufl.edu/IR00009719/00001.

Society of Friends of the West Indian Museum of Panama. Last accessed May 12, 2017. http://www.samaap.org/.

Spiegler, Morris. *Surviving Transnistria: Marcel Spiegler's Story* and *A Gold Ring for a Loaf of Bread.* JDoC Florida collections. Last accessed August 16, 2017. http://ufdc.ufl.edu/AA00054854/00001.

Taylor, Laurie. "Librarian on a Boat or Digital Scholarship, Caribbean Studies, and the Digital Library of the Caribbean (dLOC): Alternative Sabbatical Proposal for 2016–2017." University of Florida Digital Collections (UFDC). Last accessed May 12, 2017. http://ufdc.ufl.edu/AA00037232/00001.

Taylor, Laurie N., et al. *Books about Florida and the Caribbean: from the University Press of Florida to the World.* University of Florida Digital Collections (UFDC). Last accessed June 8, 2017. http://ufdc.ufl.edu/AA00032435/00001.

———. "Library Collaborative Networks Forging Scholarly Cyberinfrastructure and Enabling an

Environment of Radical Collaboration." In *Handbook of Research on Academic Library Partnerships and Collaborations,* edited by Brian Doherty, 1-30. Hershey, PA: IGI Global, 2016. http://ufdc.ufl.edu/AA00030795/00001.

Taylor, Laurie, Margarita Vargas-Betancourt, and Brooke Wooldridge. "The Digital Library of the Caribbean (dLOC): Creating a Shared Research Foundation." *Scholarly and Research Communication.* Simon Fraser University 4.3 (2013). Last accessed May 12, 2017. doi:10.22230/src.2013v4n3a114.

Telemetro. "#7 El espejo de un país: El camino hacia la reversion." Last accessed May 12, 2017. http://www.telemetro.com/nacionales/reportajes/espejo-pais-camino-reversion_3_724757566.html.

University of Florida. Digital Library of the Caribbean. "About dLOC." Last accessed May 12, 2017. http://dloc.com/dloc1/about.

Vargas-Betancourt, Margarita, and Bess de Farber. "Digitization of a UNESCO World Memory Collection: Mexico's Jewish Heritage Newspapers." University of Florida Digital Collections (UFDC). Last accessed May 12, 2017. http://ufdc.ufl.edu/IR00009388/00001.

Vargas-Betancourt, Margarita, et al. "2016 LARRP Digitization Proposal." University of Florida Digital Collections (UFDC). Last accessed May 12, 2017. http://ufdc.ufl.edu/AA00039438/00001.

Wagner, Ralph D. *A History of the Farmington Plan.* Lanham, MD: Scarecrow Press, 2002, 86.

CHAPTER NINETEEN

Leveraging Connections to Build and Promote International Special Collections:

A Case Study

Mary Jo Zeter and Deborah J. Margolis

Michigan State University Libraries supports the research and teaching needs of a large campus with seventeen degree-granting colleges and more than 200 programs in undergraduate, graduate, and pre-professional study. Its collections include more than 7,339,706 titles and are global in scope. Michigan State (MSU) is a comprehensive research university but it does not have an Ivy League history; it was founded in 1855 as a land-grant college. While less rich in alumni resources, our history positions us to capitalize on local contacts and popular collections in building special collections. In the twenty-first century, MSU increasingly embraces a "World Grant Ideal," where high-quality, inclusive, and internationally connected research is central to the university's mission. Subject and area librarians with responsibility for international and foreign-language collecting are supported in their efforts to contribute to special collections by a receptive and congenial head and staff, a flexible and willing technical services unit, administrative support for international travel, and the freedom to work creatively to promote the use of these materials.

In this case study, we will describe elements of our library's successful program of building special collections of international materials from the perspectives and experiences of two MSU Libraries area studies specialists. We begin by describing our popular culture collection, a very large and significant category of MSU's special collections holdings, especially as it relates to the growth in international materials. Examples of international acquisitions and related activities follow, selected to illustrate some of the routes by which our special collections work has grown.

The Russel B. Nye Popular Culture Collection

Popular culture materials began to be collected in earnest in the late 1960s with the support of Michigan State University professor Russel B. Nye, a Pulitzer Prize-winning scholar and pioneer of popular culture studies. In his important historical overview, *The Unembarrassed Muse: The Popular Arts in America*, Nye defined the popular arts as those created for mass consumption by artists "using forms and media to which his audience has easiest access," namely television, movies, radio, paperback books, comic books, magazines, etc. Works of popular art "express the taste and understanding of the majority," free from "minority standards of correctness." Within MSU Special Collections, American western fiction and detective and dime novels formed the foundation of what later became the Russel B. Nye Popular Culture Collection. In consultation with Professor Nye and his English Department colleague, Professor Larry Landrum, plans were made in the mid-1970s for the growing collecting emphasis on popular culture to be focused on four categories of materials: comic art, popular fiction in many genres, popular informational materials, such as almanacs and etiquette manuals, and print materials related to the popular performing arts.

The popular culture collection in MSU Special Collections supports the institution's historically strong program in popular culture studies, but there is also a growing awareness of the value of these materials as primary sources in cultural and literary studies and for the study of foreign languages. For example, students may engage with questions related to the visual depiction of race and gender in comic books, and by extension in the popular culture writ large of a nation or of a society during a particular historical period. The stand-alone graphic novel (as opposed to serialized or stand-alone shorter format comic books) now predominates in the commercial comic art publishing landscape of some European countries such as Spain and has grown greatly in importance in many other countries, for example, Brazil. "Graphic novel" is a catch-all phrase and many, in fact, recount historical events or the lives of important political or cultural figures. In Brazil, a popular series of graphic novels presents adaptations of some of that country's literary classics. Second-language learners may be able to utilize graphic novels to build their language skills while gaining valuable cultural knowledge through a medium far more accessible than many other vernacular language resources available in the library.

Working with a Hebrew-language instructor, the Middle East Studies Librarian, Deborah Margolis, used graphic novels by Israeli writers and artists in a class visit to a library exhibition and in a bibliographic instruction/information literacy session. In the exhibition, *Interpreting the Interior: Israeli Writer and Filmmaker Etgar Keret*, students/viewers could read the entirety of a very short story of Keret's in Hebrew and English and compare it with a graphic novel version of the same story. The librarian developed questions that would engage students with the exhibit and the story, raising issues of culture and gender. This exhibit—including the Israeli graphic novels and comics—was made available to libraries and other cultural institutions as a traveling exhibit. In 2012, the exhibit traveled to the San Francisco Jewish Community Library and is available to any institution that can meet accepted loan standards. Many of the comics in the exhibit had been previously donated to the MSU Libraries Special Collections by an Israeli researcher who had come to MSU to use our comic art collection. Since the exhibition, the Middle East Studies librarian has further built the collection by visits to comics bookstores, festivals, and publishers in the region.

International Comic Art

MSU libraries' comic art collection, begun by Professor Nye in 1970, has grown to become the largest collection of its kind anywhere, with more than 250,000 cataloged items. American comic books make up by far the largest portion of the collection, with more than 200,000 items, 90 percent of which have come to MSU via donation. However, the purchase of a collection of 11,000 European comic books and albums in 1995 gave MSU "the most nearly comprehensive collection of European comics in any Western Hemisphere library," according to the MSU Libraries' comic art bibliographer, Randall W. Scott. Today, European comic art is one of the four major collecting foci within the panorama of materials that make up the collection, acquired with the goal of maintaining a representation of all artists and nationalities.

Recent years have seen an acceleration in the internationalization of the comic art collection at MSU, in particular with respect to comic art from Africa, Asia, and Latin America. Librarian area specialists have stepped up to increase the representation of comic art from nearly every country in these vast regions by choosing to spend some of their general materials allocations for comic art materials destined for special collections and through a willingness to pursue a variety of acquisition venues. When it comes to international popular culture materials, it is important that vendors of general materials, and not just specialty dealers, be aware of the library's collecting interests. In many cases, smaller vendors are willing to include newsstand comics purchases in their shipments of new books or journals. Cultivating good business relationships with vendors and highlighting niche areas of collecting interest can lead to out-of-the-ordinary acquisition opportunities. For example, by making country-based book vendors aware that MSU holds a world-class comics collection and is keenly interested in growing its international holdings, vendors are more likely to seek out the offerings of local collectors which can, in turn, be offered to the library. Valuable runs of comic books assembled by collectors have thus been acquired via vendors that usually provide only new academic monographs and journals.

MSU area librarians have frequently acquired popular culture materials as well as other special collections materials during foreign acquisitions trips or while traveling internationally for other reasons, such as conference attendance. For example, the Latin American studies librarian, Mary Jo Zeter, has purchased runs of comic books at the Santiago, Chile, international book fair and at stalls in the city's largest flea market, and to buy zines by making a trip to a small zine fair held in the outskirts of the city. Zines are seldom if ever offered by vendors, even those that are based in-country, as they are usually self-published and not distributed through the usual commercial channels.

Faculty Connections

MSU librarian-faculty connections have led to a number of valuable special collections acquisitions. One example is the Alfredo Levy Conservatory Collection, which was brought to the attention of the Latin American Studies librarian by MSU College of Music composition professor, Ricardo Lorenz, after he met with its then owner. The collection is valuable because as a reflection of the life of a Cuban conservatory it captures a very vibrant period in Cuban and Caribbean musical history, from the early to mid-twentieth century. This can be seen in the ownership markings and in dedications to important cultural figures—not only musicians but poets and writers. It consists primarily of 1920s and '30s published classical music, including some first edition scores, but there are also manuscripts and miscellanea. Significantly, a large number of women composers are represented. After receiving evidence of its provenance through signed statements by witnesses to its sale in Cuba in the 1990s, this 1,000-plus item collection was acquired for special collections in 2014. Items from the collection have been featured in exhibits, and Dr. Lorenz plans to co-author an article about the collection's history and content with a Cuban colleague.

A special faculty-related acquisition resulted from a connection with Saleem Alhabash, assistant professor in MSU's College of Communications. The Middle East Studies librarian was involved with an exhibition at the library of Arab-American middle school journalists' writings and photos. Dr. Alhabash spoke with them at the exhibit and talked about his time as the managing editor of a youth newspaper in Palestine when he was a teen. Thus was born the idea to acquire the newspaper for MSU Libraries' Special Collections. Dr. Alhabash introduced the librarian to the current editor of *The Youth Times*, and her organization (PYALARA) donated bound volumes of the newspaper to the MSU Libraries. The Middle East Studies librarian completed the donation by collecting the subsequent print issues on a trip to the region. The MSU Libraries now owns a complete run of this bilingual (primarily Arabic, some English) newspaper written by and for young people who live in Palestine. The newspaper and donor NGO were featured in the library exhibition, *States and Visions: Recent Library Acquisitions from Palestine and Israel.* This type of rare acquisition helps MSU to fulfill its mission as a "world-grant" university, preserving and making available popular expressions across political boundaries.

Community Connections

Serendipitous community contacts can lead to exciting outcomes not foreseeable from the start. When Christopher Beisel, co-owner of Libros San Cristobal, a fine arts press located in Antigua, Guatemala, first contacted the Latin American studies librarian while visiting family nearby in Michigan, little more was expected than a sales call for beautiful but expensive books. Indeed, the oversized folio he brought to the library, *Village Churches of Santiago de Guatemala, 1524–1773*, with its gorgeous twenty-two hand-colored reproductions of architectural drawings produced from zinc plate engravings printed on a Vandercook hand letterpress, was out of budgetary reach. However, the visit resulted in an immediate connection to the press and the work it carried out in a lovely compound at the end of a dirt road in Central America. That connection culminated in a 2013 visit and presentation by Mr. Beisel and two of the presses' Kachiquel artisans at MSU. Mr.

Beisel showed slides of the workshop in Guatemala and of the surrounding area and discussed the social and cultural context in which the press operates. The artisans explained elements of their work and demonstrated the weaving of hand-made amate bark paper, which they also produce. This memorable event was accompanied by the donation of *U Cayibal Atziak, Images in Guatemalan Weavings*, a comprehensive catalog of textile designs containing more than three hundred hand-letterpress-printed and illuminated zinc plate impressions, to Special Collections. A traditional backstrap woven textile in shades of MSU "Spartan green" was added to the covers of the leather binding of the copy given to MSU.

Eventually, several beautiful Libros San Cristobal editions were donated to Special Collections, including *Prosa de Antigua* (stories illustrated with original, illuminated woodblock prints), *Ancient Ceremonial Hachas of Southern Mesoamerica* (original art drawings of native sculptures printed from zinc photo-engraved plates; MSU's copy came in a slipcase covered in Michigan deer leather that was worked in Antigua!), and a version of the Mexican bingo game, Lotería, in book form accompanied by a deck of lotería cards with original images drawing on Guatemalan themes.

Faculty and community connections were also instrumental in the acquisition and discoverability of a truly international collection, the William G. Lockwood Collection of Romani Ethnology and Gypsy Stereotypes, with items from Europe, Asia, Africa, and the Americas. Anthropologist William G. Lockwood began collecting material about the Roma in the late 1950s, gathering scholarly works and documents, Roma music and poetry, and representations of Gypsies in the arts and popular culture. His spouse, Yvonne R. Lockwood, was a curator of folklife at MSU's Museum. The Lockwoods collected cookbooks as well, and we were fortunate that they offered their collections to MSU. The Roma collection includes several thousand books and periodicals, several hundred examples of sheet music, and around 1,200 records. The foreign-language monographs, in many languages our technical services staff did not have expertise in, were outsourced to Backstage for cataloging. The vinyl records have been made available not only through the library catalog but also through Discogs, a "user-built database of music." The library had recently acquired the Rovi Collection, a massive AV collection, and was looking for ways to enrich the metadata in an automated way. Our head of cataloging and metadata services knew a local woman who was an active Discogs community user. The library was able to hire her to work on the Lockwood Roma musical recordings as a test of using Discogs to pull metadata into our MARC records. Having the Roma albums in Discogs has increased their discoverability too; we have received requests from around the world for little-held recordings and in one case were able to digitize a song and share it with a user in Greece. Our technical services division, from acquisitions to cataloging, has been universally supportive and found creative solutions for making available international materials and collections.

Conclusion

None of the area studies librarians' collections activities would be possible without institutional support. We are supported to travel internationally, our acquisitions department facilitates the addition of new vendors and approval plans across the globe, and many other library staff helps us in our efforts to promote the use of special collections materials through exhibitions, instruction, and events.

For librarians at institutions which don't currently support international acquisitions trips, consider that funding from college or university departments or centers may be available and that foreign cultural ministries may sponsor attendance at national book fairs. MSU area studies librarians have combined international conference presentations with book-buying, thus getting more value for travel dollars. Moderately priced international popular culture materials and alternative or community-based press publications can often be acquired by working with vendors known to the area studies librarian community.

Tapping local connections for international special collections material and organizing successful outreach and instructional activities stemming from these acquisitions have provided evidence to administrators of the value in supporting international collecting. For the past two summers, our local summer camp for refugee kids has made a visit to MSU Libraries Special Collections where they interacted with comics from their region or country. Through collecting and outreach, we aim to fulfill our university's world-grant mission, making a diversity of beautiful materials available to researchers and the public alike.

Bibliography

Discogs. "About Discogs." Accessed December 15, 2017. https://www.discogs.com/about.

Margolis, Deborah J. "Etgar Keret Travelling Exhibit: A Guide to the Contents of the Travelling Exhibit Interpreting the Interior: Israeli Writer and Filmmaker Etgar Keret." Michigan State University Libraries. Accessed December 15, 2017. http://libguides.lib.msu.edu/travellingkeretexhibit.

———. "Interpreting the Interior: Israeli Writer and Filmmaker Etgar Keret: Research Guide Created in Conjunction with Library Exhibit." Michigan State University Libraries. Accessed December 15, 2017. http://libguides.lib.msu.edu/keret.

———. "States and Visions: Recent Library Acquisitions from Palestine and Israel: Exhibition on Display at MSU Main Library, January through March 2016." Michigan State University Libraries. Accessed December 15, 2017. http://libguides.lib.msu.edu/visions.

Michigan State University. "World Grant Ideal." Accessed December 15, 2017. http://president.msu.edu/advancing-msu/presidential-vision/world-grant-ideal.html.

Morris, Shaneka, and Gary Roebuck, eds., *ARL Statistics 2014–2015*. Washington, DC: Association of Research Libraries, 2017. http://publications.arl.org/ARL-Statistics-2014-2015/53.

Nye, Russel B. *The Unembarrassed Muse: The Popular Arts in America*. New York: Dial, 1970.

Scott, Randall W. "Collection Development Policy Statement." Michigan State University Libraries. Accessed December 15, 2017. http://comics.lib.msu.edu/devpol.htm.

CHAPTER TWENTY

International Collaborations at the Immigration History Research Center Archives (IHRCA)

Daniel Necas

The globe is increasingly interconnected on many different levels: denser and more frequent travel options, the multilayered exchange of personal messages among the world's populations, corporate and governmental collaborations and communications, and academic research projects. These research projects are often conducted by teams of members scattered across a number of institutions, often in multiple countries. It is not surprising that libraries and archives also explore the possibilities of linking the content in their holdings, combining efforts to advance projects and make information on related subjects more complete and easily accessible by anyone.

In 1963, the IHRC Archives—known then as the "Immigrant Archives" at the University of Minnesota's Walter Library, the main library on the Minneapolis campus[1]—began collecting documentation on immigrants to the United States. Since then, the archives has engaged in various projects involving international collaborations, even at times when some parts of the world relevant to the immigrant groups within the IHRCA's collecting scope were difficult to work with. These included countries with restricted travel and information exchange, dominated by the Soviet Union, from Estonia to Romania and Serbia, from Czechoslovakia to Belarus and Ukraine.

Migrants have always been among the most significant agents of information and material exchange among the world's cultures. Carrying their language and heritage with them as they seek a new place to live and adapt to new customs, values, and standards, they are forced to forge new connections and, at times, sever old ones. While maintaining relationships with their relatives and friends in their homelands, they stand as mediators between their original cultures and those into which they are trying to integrate. Our predecessors at the IHRC Archives were well aware that in order to fully understand the wide spectrum of immigrant experiences, it was necessary to keep learning about the immigrants' homelands, to know who was interested in the study of the emigration flows, and where documentation sent or brought by those who had left was archived.

During the first years of the IHRCA's existence, faculty members from the University of Minnesota with expertise and language skills related to migration from southern, central, and eastern Europe (the original focus of the IHRCA) traveled to Slovenia, Croatia, Hungary, and Greece to establish relationships that, in some cases, continue to this day. Exchanging duplicates and the microfilming of combined newspaper holdings from institutions on both sides of the Atlantic were among the earliest collaborative projects. The collecting scope expanded during the 1970s and 1980s to include other parts of Europe, from Finland to Italy and all the way to Armenia, Syria, and Lebanon, extending later to southeast Asia (following the refugee exodus after the Vietnam war), Latin America, and several parts of Africa. All were represented in the records of various refugee resettlement agencies, which has always been a strong component of the IHRCA's holdings. In these decades, a number of graduate students and fellows from Finland, Poland, and Italy helped process and describe the collections of personal papers and organizational records, which almost always contained large portions of materials in the original languages of the immigrants.

The 1990s changed the world in fundamental ways when millions of more people gained the ability to travel and migrate. The possibilities to further develop traditional ways of cooperation opened up, and the arrival and widespread utilization of the internet brought the previously distant content, colleagues, and institutional networks ever closer.

This chapter examines and compares two major projects developed at the IHRCA in the past eight years: (1) a more traditional international exchange of archival staff with specific language skills, which resulted in the processing of IHRCA's substantial holdings of materials in foreign languages, and (2) an innovative digitization project gathering archivists, librarians, faculty, students, and community volunteers who worked together to develop a thematic digital archive of migrant correspondence. By collaborating with a number of repositories and their staff in Europe, the project brings together pieces of trans-Atlantic communication that were scattered in archives on both sides of the ocean.

The aim is to explore a range of benefits (and challenges) the two types of collaboration can bring, both to the hosting or coordinating organization and to the visiting or participating partners, as well as to our users. The first project is the processing of the Estonian American collections that has so far enabled ten archivists from the National Archives in Tallinn to participate in the program. The second effort is made visible by the Digitizing Immigrant Letters (DIL) project, which has built a digital archive of migrant correspondence, making available online digitized letters written between 1850 and 1970 by and to immigrants; they were found in the IHRC Archives and collections held by partner repositories or private individuals.

Estonian Processing Project

The Estonian processing project began in 2009 and is now in its ninth year. Archivists have visited every year, with the exception of 2015. Up to that point, ten archivists have participated in the two-member teams from the National Archives of Estonia, and four colleagues from Tallinn have made two visits.

Until 2003, the Estonian American holdings at the IHRC Archives were among its smallest by volume—a handful of manuscript collections, a dozen or so periodical titles, and a few hundred books, altogether not exceeding twenty-five linear feet. By comparison, the largest sets of materials documenting the Finnish, Italian, Polish, or Ukrainian immigrants were all approaching 1,000 linear feet each. With the IHRCA's move in 2000 to a new, state-of-the-art facility in Minneapolis from an old coffee warehouse located in St. Paul, donors of materials became keen on transferring their treasures that were sometimes held in inadequate spaces to IHRCA's new home in the Elmer L. Andersen Library. Like other immigrant populations, Estonian Americans had created and cared for their own archive, which was reaching the limits of its capacity, and its custodians found it difficult to continue the work, particularly in making the rich collections accessible to a wider research audience. A thirty-year relationship between the IHRCA and the Estonian Archives in the US (established in Lakewood, New Jersey, in 1974[2]) resulted in an agreement to deposit close to 800 linear feet of archival collections, periodicals, and books in the recently completed cavernous storage spaces of the Archives and Special Collections department of the University of Minnesota Libraries in Minneapolis.

The creators and compilers of the materials were mostly refugees from Estonia who arrived in the United States as displaced persons in the late 1940s and early 1950s. Eventually, they found careers in a wide range of professions. Among them were construction company field inspector, music composer, gardener, teacher, Boy Scout instructor, actor, painter, graphic designer, librarian, journalist, chemist, and accountant. The materials often document the dramatic years of World War II and the flight of Estonians from their country occupied alternatively by Germany and the Soviet Union. They also document their lives in displaced-persons camps in the US, in British and French occupation zones after the war, and in their new adopted homelands. Many Estonians ultimately resettled in other parts of Europe, the United States, and Australia. Their movement around the world is reflected in the variety of languages in which the documents were written. While most of the documentation is in Estonian, other languages, including English, German, Swedish, French, Russian, Finnish, Hungarian, Danish, and Polish, are represented as well. The collections also provide a detailed picture of the rich cultural and social life of the Estonian diaspora maintained by many organizations established around the United States and the world.

The massive acquisition of materials—bringing the Estonian American collection to the ranks of the largest at the IHRC Archives in the course of less than two years between 2003 and 2005—was unusual and different from how most other IHRCA collections had been slowly accumulated over the four previous decades. Rather than processing one collection at a time as resources, staff time, and available language skills allowed, it became imperative to process and produce new descriptions for hundreds of individual sets of personal papers and organizational records, ranging from a couple of linear inches to dozens of linear feet. What made it even more challenging was the unusually high percentage of materials in the Estonian language, with smaller pockets of five or six additional languages (mostly German, Russian, Swedish, and French, in addition to English).

The IHRC Archives has always used the good services of international students at the University of Minnesota or local community volunteers to process its foreign-language materials. In this instance, though, given the rarity of Estonian-language skills on campus and the impossibility to accommodate large numbers of volunteers on a long-term basis, it was necessary to turn to Estonia for help. Thanks to the efforts of four key players—the BaltHerNet (Baltic Heritage Network) Foundation, the National Archives of Estonia, the Estonian Archives in the US, and the IHRC Archives—the funds they provide enable two archivists from Tallinn to work full-time for one month every year at IHRCA. Their expenses include airfare, lodging, continuing salaries, health insurance, and paperwork processing fees. The University of Minnesota's Office of the International Student and Scholar Services handles communications with the US State Department in arranging the appropriate visas and permits. The entire process, from the start of the negotiations for each year's visit to the arrival of the archivists, usually takes about five months, so planning ahead is essential.

Once on-site, the archivists from Tallinn get acquainted with the necessary local policies and procedures at the Andersen Library, familiarize themselves with IHRCA's collection management standards and system, and begin their task. In close collaboration with IHRCA staff members, they sort, weed out, de-duplicate, re-house, label, and, on varying levels, describe the prioritized collections to be processed. Utilizing a wealth of resources in Estonia, our colleagues always come equipped with detailed biographical and historical background information on the creators or subjects of the collections. This information is gathered in advance while the archivists are preparing for their Minnesota sojourn, which ultimately produces significant time savings and allows for more hours dedicated to actual processing and description of the materials.

The international cooperation of the IHRC Archives and the Estonian National Archives would not be possible without the generous support from the National Archives in Tallinn, the Estonian Archives in the US, the BaltHerNet Foundation, and the multi-faceted assistance from the staff of the IHRC Archives, the Archives and Special Collections Department of the University of Minnesota Libraries, the International Student and Scholar Services office at the University of Minnesota, and the local Estonian American community. This collaboration has resulted in more than 300 individual collections of personal papers and organizational records processed since 2009, significantly enhancing access to these collections and their usability for future on-site and off-site researchers.

Digitizing Immigrant Letters (DIL) Project

Immigrant correspondence has long provided valuable sources for researchers in the field of immigration history and migration studies. The letters included in the DIL archive have been utilized by students in history, sociology, and linguistics classes. Scholars have used them to study and create visualizations of migration networks or to illustrate narratives of migration. There have been exhibits and newspaper articles featuring selected content as well as expressed interest in exploring the text-mining possibilities of the corpus of the transcribed and translated text. The DIL project is defined by shared selection criteria to focus on letters exchanged among close relatives and by consistently supplying transcriptions of the handwritten text and translations into English. Another feature of the project has been the inclusion of representatives of many language and cultural groups (currently fourteen languages in four different scripts) that have one common denominator: migration.

The work on the project has been highly collaborative, benefiting from the contributions of individuals centered around the team at the University of Minnesota as well as collaborators, consultants, advisers, and supporters from other institutions in the United States and abroad. With the support of about half a dozen external funders, the IHRCA has hosted, organized, or participated in a number of workshops, symposia, and roundtables. These events attracted scholars of migration from around the world with research interests in migrant correspondence, archivists and librarians previously involved in work with collections of letters, computer programmers and developers, as well as students. Institutions that have been involved in the project thus far include archives, libraries, museums, and universities in Vienna, Prague, Ljubljana, Maribor, Koper, and Debrecen, to name a few. (For a complete list of institutions that have participated in the project so far, see Appendix 20A.)

Participants from other institutions, in addition to those above, gathered at numerous workshops and symposia over the past nine years (see Appendix 20B). A series of meetings and visits have taken place since 2011 to establish a network of individuals and institutions interested in contributing content or otherwise developing the project. Recently, efforts have begun to channel the content generated by the existing and new collaborations in Europe and the United States through the Europeana Digital Library and the Digital Public Library of America.

The IHRC and the IHRC Archives have been developing the Digitizing Immigrant Letters (DIL) project since 2009. With the advancement of digital technologies, the opportunity and need to create a digital archive of letters written and received by migrants, along with the interest and enthusiasm of several individuals at and around the Immigration History Research Center, facilitated the initial efforts in 2008 and 2009. Over the years, most participants have agreed that expanding the digital archive from holding about a hundred letters to becoming a collection of thousands and perhaps tens of thousands would be highly attractive to scholars of migration and other research fields. The possibility of multiple institutions in North America and Europe (and perhaps beyond) selecting and digitizing letters from their holdings within the framework of the project would enable this expansion. It is not unrealistic to expect that someday related content from both sides of correspondences between migrants and their homebound relatives, presently held by institutions located in different parts of the world, could be linked and re-united in a digital archive.

While there have been other letter digitization projects, the DIL project offers letters that share a set of selection criteria (see more details below), focusing on those written by close relatives that contain a significant emotional charge. Transcriptions and translations are consistently supplied. Another feature of the project has been the inclusion of as many languages as possible. Scholars of immigration history and migration studies have used migrant letters in the past to feature correspondence from an individual or a particular immigrant/ethnic group, often producing published volumes of correspondence. It is our hope that a large, fully searchable archive of letters in digital format gathering content from multiple repositories around the world for a number of varied migrant and cultural groups—and providing one convenient, online point of access—would facilitate new research and help form new perspectives on the effects migration can have on close human relationships, based on research across letters written by multiple authors from multiple language and cultural backgrounds.

Sometimes, a small collection of letters is practically all that is left after one's life. One such example is the set of letters from the IHRCA's collection of Mike Vukasinovich Papers. The Vukasinovich collection contains four letters written to (or dictated for) Mike Vukasinovich by his mother in Plavnice, a village near Bjelovar in northwest Croatia. There is also a bank deposit record book, a receipt for $5.00 (US dollars) made out to

Milko Vukasinovich dated December 29, 1920, for a deposit on a third-class steamship ticket (*SS Olympic*) for January 26 (1921?) signed by George Olson of the Merchants National Bank, Saint Paul, Minnesota, and a coroner's report listing the items found on the man at the time of his death—all of which were neatly put in the same envelope with the report. Mike (Mihailo) died in a St. Paul hospital at the age of 54 from coronary pneumonia in 1935. The four letters from his mother were what he had saved, apart from a few other items which are also reminiscent of his homeland in Croatia. Perhaps someone else wrote letters to him or he wrote to someone whose papers may become a source of another set of letters eventually contributed to the digital archive. A little additional information could add another small piece to the record of Mike Vukasinovich's life.

The project has so far been supported generously by several entities within the University of Minnesota and beyond, both by in-kind contributions (staff time and travel, technology) and financially: the Rudolph J. Vecoli Chair in Immigration History (IHRC), the American Latvian Association Fellowship (IHRC), College of Liberal Arts, IHRC Archives, Archives and Special Collections, University Libraries, Institute for Global Studies, the Center for Austrian Studies, Global Programs and Strategy Alliance. Institutions outside of Minnesota include the National Library and National Archives, the University, all in Ljubljana, Slovenia, and the University of Vienna.

External funding has been provided by the following organizations: the University of Maribor, Slovenia; the City of Vienna, Cultural Fund; the University of Vienna, Austria; the Botstiber Foundation, Pennsylvania; and Minnesota Historical and Cultural Grants (Minnesota Historical Society).

In 2011, the IHRC was selected by the Society of American Archivists to receive the Philip M. Hamer and Elizabeth Hamer Kegan Award

> in recognition of its outstanding efforts in promoting the knowledge and use of documentation of the immigrant experience through the Digitizing Immigrant Letters Project. Established in 1973, this award recognizes an archivist, editor, group of individuals or institution that has increased public awareness of archival documents for educational, instructional or other purposes.
>
> The award committee expresses its high regard for the team's efforts to promote access to immigrant letters through an inviting and useful website. We particularly recognize the stellar presentation of transcriptions and translations of letters in several languages, which makes the multilingual material accessible both in the original language and in English. The web access, together with the project's sponsorship of scholars, public talks and exhibits, increase public awareness of American immigrant history for scholars, family historians, and the general public.[3]

Summary of the Digital Archive's Content

There are currently 100 letters totaling approximately 420 pages of handwritten or typed text. Fourteen languages in four different scripts (Arabic, Cyrillic, Greek, and Latin) are represented in the digital archive. The content comes from seventeen individual archival collections, fourteen of which are held by the IHRC Archives. (More details about the letter sets can be found in Appendix 20C.)

One set of letters (Wehle) is physically located in a partner archival repository, the Sammlung Frauennachlaese (Collection of Women's Writings) at the University of Vienna, Austria. Digital copies of the original letters are included in the project with permission of the owning repository. Two sets of original letters are still in private hands (Petris in Canada and Kovac in Slovakia); digital copies are again used with permission of the owners. Additionally, two sets of letters are currently being digitized, transcribed, and translated from the National Archives and from the National Library, both in Ljubljana, Slovenia. This recent collaboration will bring the number of collections to nineteen and the number of non-IHRCA sets of letters to five. For the first time, the digital files and metadata will be added to the Digital Library of Slovenia and from there to the Europeana Digital Library (all others are now stored in and delivered by the University of Minnesota's U Media Archive from where they are systematically contributed to the Digital Public Library of America), enabling experimentation with aggregating the content from the two major digital repositories together in a new portal or user interface. IHRC Archives is currently also developing a new website or gateway for the project, which was scheduled to go live in the fall of 2017.

Content Selection

Based on input from scholars of migrant correspondence, preference is given to letters exchanged between immediate family members, close relatives, or others where a potential for a marked emotional charge exists (lovers, friends).[4] The archive thus helps document how close human relationships are affected by migration. So far, all letters pertain to transatlantic migrations during the period roughly between 1860 and 1960, most notably the labor migration of the latter part of the nineteenth and early twentieth centuries, as well as the displaced persons resettlement in the United States after WWII. The language and geographic scope of the digital archive have been determined and informed mainly by the collecting strengths of the IHRC Archives, funding sources requiring focus on central Europe (emigration from the former Austro-Hungarian Empire), and available language expertise. Additional funding from sources not limiting the work to specific geographic or cultural areas would enable a more broadly inclusive pool of developing content, adding immigrant groups not yet represented in the archive to possibly cover the entire continent of Europe (for which collaborations within the Europeana Digital Library would seem especially suitable) and beyond to create a representative sample of documentation that would reflect migrations to the US and North America more richly, completely, and accurately for the above time period. The timeframe coincides with the coverage of the IHRCA's holdings, which begin with documenting the post-1848 revolutionary movement emigration from Europe up to the present. While there are good reasons for moving that date back in history to include earlier immigrant groups from the early nineteenth and preceding century and cover more of what is known as the "postal era," privacy protection and copyright considerations determine the preference for pre-WWII materials, with the exception of those for which the rights owners can provide appropriate permissions. Another consideration is the availability of contextual information for each set of letters (biography of authors and recipients, photographs, historical background information, the provenance of materials, etc.).

As a rule, each letter is transcribed in the original language and typed into a machine-readable format. This work has so far been done by graduate and undergraduate students, faculty, and archivists. Each letter is also translated into English and the translations typed into a machine-readable format. As with transcription, this work has so far been done by graduate and undergraduate students, faculty, and archivists. Tables in Appendix 20D indicate what type of collaborator performed transcription and translation work on which sets of letters.

Translation and transcription have so far been the most labor- and time-intensive components of the project. Based on the experiences up to this point, it is clear that the best results are achieved when these two tasks are accomplished by highly qualified team members. That poses a difficulty as continuing to rely on (mostly) volunteer work would become impossible if the production of new content were to be scaled up significantly. Seeking funding sources specifically for these parts of the effort or exploring crowdsourcing opportunities are among the top priorities for further development of the project. Additionally, the plan is to cooperate regularly with interested faculty and their students in appropriate classes who could be credited for their transcription and translation assignments as part of their coursework. This model has proven to be successful in producing reliable results and in developing collaborative relationships between archivists and faculty members with their students, including internationally. An example is a translation studies class at the University of Koper in Slovenia which transcribes and translates letters from the local Slovenian repositories under the guidance of their professor, adding historical background information for the letters and their writers. The work is incorporated into the curriculum and is counted toward the fulfillment of the class requirements. A similar arrangement has been tested at the University of Minnesota.

Benefits and Challenges

Processing projects involving visiting staff from abroad tend to require long periods of planning, significant financial costs, dependence on government regulations, a large time commitment from both sides for the duration of the visit, overcoming or harmonizing differences in local practices and standards, and the availability of office and workspace. In the case of the Estonian program, the results have always justified the effort and expense. In a relatively short time, a sizeable amount of materials is processed without the need to have to go back and refine or redo the work. The new physical location and the improved and much-expanded aids for finding materials are very tangible and welcome enhancements for the access to the materials by researchers, and provide easier serviceability of the collections to both onsite and offsite researchers by the IHRCA staff members and student assistants. Much appreciated is the luxury of having two full-time professional staff members, who can for one month focus entirely on the task of processing and describing the materials at hand without the usual everyday distractions by unexpected patrons, tasks and projects, meetings, and what could be called "institutional noise" that many archivists experience while working at their institutions, often understaffed and requiring heroic multitasking.

It is also clear from the experiences of this program that collections benefit from being processed by someone who can understand the language and cultural and historical backgrounds of the materials and the human beings who created or compiled them in the given circumstances.

Then there are the intangible benefits of the interactions with colleagues from different working environments and cultures who can offer new perspectives on routinely accepted and unquestioned practices and habits. By spending significant amounts of time working together closely toward a common goal, all involved are fortunate to expand their networks of resource persons around the world. Work relationships and friendships established as a result of the visits, usually last for years and often lead to further opportunities for collaborative work on different projects. These human relationships naturally help form the inter-institutional webs of links enabling a more meaningful flow of ideas and information. By meeting varied staff members from the same partner institution, one acquires a much deeper understanding of the culture and functions of that institution, not to mention a more diverse picture of the city, country, and culture from which the visitors (and some of the concerned collections) originate. On the other side, it is hoped that for the almost one dozen staff members from the National Archives of Estonia the shared experience of visiting the same organization in the United States, the IHRC Archives, and the University of Minnesota, and living in Minneapolis for a month, has provided a chance to connect beyond the routine work-related levels.

The Digitizing Immigrant Letters project has taken advantage of the potentially indefinite, multifaceted collaborations happening often simultaneously among many different institutions, from archives, museums, and libraries to academic departments and institutes in a number of countries, as opposed to the bilateral nature of the processing projects focusing on one language area at a time. Working primarily with digital content allows for a more distributive nature of the work and flexibility in scheduling, dividing, and sharing the tasks. One could argue that in the future a processing project could perhaps be conducted long-distance after all items in a collection have been digitized, although digitization has so far seemed much easier and less costly when the digitized items have already been processed and described, at least on aggregate levels. Flexibility seems to be the key difference between the two types of projects. Flexibility is also needed when it comes to funding and the possibilities of incorporating the work into one's everyday duties over longer periods of time. Being flexible allows for a perhaps slower but more natural evolution of the project, requiring a reconsideration of one's assumptions and processes and adjusting them as priorities, external conditions, and available resources change.

It also appears that multi-institutional digitization projects that bring together a diverse pool of collaborators and target materials documenting multiple migrant populations and nationalities are preferred by funding agencies and certainly reach wider audiences. Their open-endedness and wider range of contributors with varied perspectives provide more space for innovation and unexpected or unintended enhancements. The longer timeframe facilitates the adoption of new technologies as they continue to evolve. The larger scale and geographic scope of the digitization project encourage the creation of regional alliances and subgroups that can synergize and utilize commonly shared resources. At the same time, the project is always open to the additions of new partners and collaborators who have the potential to rejuvenate and reenergize the effort (independent of government regulations or travel limitations). Given the current trends in the field, it is possible to integrate small-scale work, in most cases, into existing workflows; most project team members' home institutions encourage their employees to engage in digital arts, sciences, and humanities and to pursue inter-institutional and international collaborations.

Like many other efforts that make digitized content widely accessible, the DIL project relies on linked open data in bringing together on the Semantic Web items from multiple repositories and multiple archival collections in these repositories—and will do so increasingly in the future. It is crucial to ensure the maximum possible interoperability of the data to be able to create meaningful linkages and provide helpful context for the varied, often multilingual content.[5]

If we think of archivists (and other contributors) as data containers—human carriers of vast amounts of data who are varied, frequently multilingual, and of diverse cultural backgrounds—it is also necessary to imagine their interoperability. Among the main building blocks of such interoperability is cultural sensitivity, openness to different traditions, willingness to develop knowledge of the language (if not language competency), and the capacity to reference commonly shared information beyond one's own native environment. It is archivists as human beings who transform their repositories into functioning institutions capable of preserving archival records and making them available for research, contextualization, and interpretation. The more interoperable they are, the greater the potential is for the discovery of relevant connections to records scattered in multiple repositories, often in more than one country. Unlike data which must be manipulated externally by human operators, professionals in cultural heritage organizations and repositories have the option of finding ways to make themselves interoperable from within, by their own agency.

By moving between different cultural and physical environments, migrants by nature create international networks. Their correspondence often reflects and records in great detail their paths and networks. International collaborative projects, such as the Digitizing Immigrant Letters Project at the IHRC Archives, provide open multilateral spaces for bringing these records to light and reconstructing the flows of information, emotions, people, and cultural (sometimes also financial) capital around the world. It is crucial to understand these flows, especially in recent years when all parts of the world have to address ever-more challenging migrations brought about by the growing numbers of refugees displaced forcibly from their homelands by conflicts arising from the inability to build and maintain peaceful and prospering societies.

Conclusion

Given the widespread interconnectedness of academic libraries and archives, it is impossible to think of these institutions as working in isolation from the rest of the world. As the creators of archival collections move around the world generating the records of their own worldwide connections in the archival materials they create or compile, those who care for and provide access to these materials must be able to identify and understand the international and transnational dimensions of the records. International collaborations naturally growing out of work with such records can substantially enhance the resulting appraisal, processing, description, and digitization processes.

Of particular interest is the deepened ability to interpret and contextualize the records, to re-activate their potential for international connections that may have been hidden and dormant while stored in a donor's home or office or waiting to be processed and utilized by archivists and other scholars and researchers. By opening themselves to international partnerships and by offering their collections to users beyond their stacks and their own institutional computer networks, libraries will provide educational and creative spaces in which to help grow new generations of world citizens—citizens capable of understanding cultures beyond their own and who are well-equipped to tackle problems and issues left to us by the isolationist and xenophobic Cold War mentality still entrenched in the ruling structures on both sides of the divide. If libraries, archives, and museums can become major facilitators of international exchanges based on the collections they hold, it would also be a significant opportunity to lift the field to prominence away from lingering perceptions of irrelevance, powerlessness, and being a funding nuisance to which it is frequently relegated by some captains of politics and corporations. Gaining the recognition that our profession deserves would be a nice side benefit to the major contributions we make to the common good by facilitating international connections and by exposing library and archives users to the larger contexts through which we all must navigate our lives.

Acknowledgments

Thanks for reading and helpful comments to Ellen Engseth and John Butler of the University of Minnesota Libraries, as well as to the editors of this volume, Yelena Luckert and Lindsay Inge Carpenter of the University of Maryland Libraries. I would also like to acknowledge former IHRC Program Director Haven Hawley (currently at the University of Florida, Gainesville), Piret Noorhani (Tartu College, Toronto, Ontario) of the Baltic Heritage Network, for initiating the Estonian exchange processing program in 2008–2009, former IHRC Director Professor Donna Gabaccia (currently at the University of Toronto, Scarborough, Ontario), and Professor Sonia Cancian (then of Concordia University, Montreal, Quebec, currently at the Zayed University, Dubai) for their vision and groundbreaking work in establishing the Digitizing Immigrant Letters project during 2008–2012.

Appendix 20A. Participant institutions represented in DIL project and events

SLOVENIA:

University of Maribor: History Department, Sociology Department, International Relations Office, University Library; University of Koper; National Archives of Slovenia, National and University Library, Institute for Migration Studies of the Slovene Academy of Sciences, University of Ljubljana's Department of American Studies, Studia Slovenica library and archives, Institute for Ethnic Studies at the Museum of Ethnography, Ljubljana.

AUSTRIA:

Vienna City Archives (Gasometer), Komensky School Archives, Vienna; Sammlung Frauennachlässe (Collections of Women's Writing), University of Vienna, University of Salzburg

SLOVAKIA:

Institute of History of the Slovak Academy of Sciences, Emigration Museum of the Matica Slovenska, Bratislava; Archive of Matica Slovenska, Slovak National Library, Literary Archive, Martin; Catholic University of Ruzomberok, History Department

BOHEMIA:

Naprstek Ethnographic Museum, a branch of the National Museum of the Czech Republic, Charles University, Institute of Ethnology, Ministry of Foreign Affairs, Government of Czech Republic, Strategic Planning Department, Prague

POLAND:

Warsaw City Archives, Jagiellonian University of Krakow

HUNGARY:

Open Society Archives, Budapest; University of Debrecen

CROATIA:

Institute for Migration and Ethnic Studies, and State Archives, Zagreb

GERMANY:

Freie Universitaet Berlin, Bochum University

ITALY:

University of Genoa

CANADA:

Concordia University, Montreal; University of Montreal, University of Winnipeg, Mennonite Heritage Centre, Winnipeg, Tartu College, Toronto; University of Saskatchewan, Saskatoon; University of British Columbia, Vancouver; Canadian Museum of Civilization, Gatineau, Quebec

ESTONIA:

National Archives, Tallinn

NORWAY:

University of Bergen

FINLAND:

University of Turku

CHINA:

Wuyi University

IRELAND:

Trinity College Dublin

SCOTLAND:

University of Edinburgh

ENGLAND:

University of Birmingham

UNITED STATES:

University of Minnesota, Center for Hmong Studies, Concordia University, St. Paul; Minnesota Historical Society, St. Olaf College / Norwegian American Historical Association, Northfield, Minnesota; University of Alabama, University of Virginia, University of Wisconsin; Swenson Swedish Immigration Research Center, Augustana College, Illinois; National Czech and Slovak Museum and Library, Cedar Rapids, Iowa; Polish Museum of America, Chicago; Rutgers University; Idaho State University, Pocatello; Texas A&M University, College Station; Florida State University, Tallahassee; State University New York at Buffalo

Appendix 20B: Workshops, Conferences and Symposia

October 23, 2008: "Time in Migration History: Explorations through Various Media." Presidential panel at the Social Science History Association's Annual Meeting (Miami, Florida)

December 10–11, 2009: "Creating Digital Archive and Website about Letters, Literacy, Emotions and Migration." (Minneapolis, Minnesota)

May 17–18, 2010: "The Migration Letter: Archiving Intimacy in the Postal Era." (Minneapolis, Minnesota)

November 15, 2011: "Digitizing Immigrant and Homeland Letters: Problems and Opportunities." Round table at the annual meeting of the Social Science History Association (Boston, Massachusetts)

June 10–11, 2012: "Digitizing Immigrant Letters across the Atlantic." Workshop held in Vienna, Austria

May 15–16, 2013: "Digitising Experiences of Migration." Workshop organized by the Coventry University, England, held in Utrecht, The Netherlands

March 13–14, 2014: "Digitising Experiences of Migration." Workshop organized by the Coventry University, England, held in Omagh, Northern Ireland

April 28–29, 2015: "International Scholarly Conference Transatlantic Migrations—Immigrant Communications and the *National Homes* in the USA." Organized by and held at the University of Maribor, Slovenia

Appendix 20C: List of Letter Sets

1. America Letters (Finnish) (7 letters)
2. Callimachos (Greek) (5)
3. Delfino (Italian) (7)
4. Granovsky (Ukrainian) (7)
5. Grebenstchikoff (Russian) (13)
6. Hitti (Arabic) (5)
7. Kovac (Slovak) (7)
8. Lazar (Hungarian) (4)
9. Nemanich (Slovenian) (5)
10. Paikens (Latvian) (7)
11. Panucevich (Belarusian) (7)
12. Prebilic (Slovenian) (2)
13. Petris (Italian) (4)
14. Rypka/Kostlan (Czech) (2)
15. Sisca (Italian) (8)
16. Vukasinovich (Croatian) (4)
17. Wehle (German) (6)

Appendix 20D: Authors of Transcriptions and Translations

Transcription:

Graduate	Undergraduate	Faculty	Archivists	Community Members
America Letters	Grebenstchikoff	Delfino	Granovsky	Lazar
Callimachos	Hitti	Kovac	Rypka/Kostlan	
Nemanich	Prebilic	Petris	Wehle	
Paikens		Sisca		
Panucevich		Vukasinovich		

Translation:

Graduate	Undergraduate	Faculty	Archivists	Community Members
America Letters	Grebenstchikoff	Delfino	Granovsky	Lazar
Callimachos	Hitti	Kovac	Rypka/Kostlan	
Nemanich		Petris	Wehle	
Paikens		Sisca	Prebilic	
Panucevich		Vukasinovich		

Notes

1. The Immigrant Archives grew out of a research project conducted by a group of University of Minnesota History Department faculty in 1962–1963 on the Iron Range in northern Minnesota. While initially focusing primarily on the southern European immigrant groups present on the range (and under-represented in the existing archival repositories at the time), the collecting scope of the Archives eventually broadened to include most immigrant populations from central and eastern Europe, Armenia, Syria, and Lebanon, as well as records about refugees and immigrants from southeast Asia, Africa, and Latin America, created by resettlement agencies during the 1970s–1990s. In 1974, the Immigrant Archives merged with the Center for Immigration Studies (established in the College of Liberal Arts (CLA) in 1965) and became known as the Immigration History Research Center (IHRC). In 2012, the archives returned to the University Libraries as a new entity, IHRC Archives (IHRCA), separate from the research center (IHRC), which continues to operate within the University of Minnesota's College of Liberal Arts.
2. Efforts to catalogue and describe archival materials brought by Estonian displaced persons from Europe after WWII had commenced ten years earlier in New York, organized by the Estonian World Federation and the Estonian National Committee in the US ("The Custodian of Estonian American Heritage, Estonian Archives in the U.S., Inc.: A Short History" compiled by Evald Rink, in *Estonian Archives in the U.S., Inc. 1964–2004*, Lakewood, 2004.)
3. Letter from the Award Subcommittee Chair, Lisa Conathan, April 30, 2012.

4. For more on the significance of emotion in migrant letters and the potential of such letters for research by scholars of migration, see Donna Gabaccia and Sonia Cancian, "Migrant Letters Enter the Digital Age: The Digitizing Immigrant Letters Project at the IHRC," 2013, accessed December 20, 2017, https://drive.google.com/file/d/0B30XoT-5S7LMRjdSUG1ZN0VUREk/view.
5. The importance of interoperability of linked open data for publishing cultural heritage content is analyzed and described in detail by Eero Hyvönen, *Publishing and Using Cultural Heritage Linked Data on the Semantic Web* (San Rafael, CA: Morgan & Claypool Publishers, 2012).

Bibliography

Gabaccia, Donna, and Sonia Cancian. "Migrant Letters Enter the Digital Age: The Digitizing Immigrant Letters Project at the IHRC." 2013. Accessed December 20, 2017. https://drive.google.com/file/d/0B30XoT-5S7LMRjdSUG1ZN0VUREk/view.

Hyvönen, Eero. *Publishing and Using Cultural Heritage Linked Data on the Semantic Web*. San Rafael, CA: Morgan & Claypool Publishers, 2012.

Rink, Evald. "The Custodian of Estonian American Heritage, Estonian Archives in the U.S., Inc.: A Short History." In *Estonian Archives in the U.S., Inc. 1964–2004*. Lakewood, 2004.

CHAPTER TWENTY-ONE

Toward a Comprehensive Collection on the Allied Occupation of Japan:

A Partnership between the University of Maryland Libraries and the National Diet Library of Japan

Yukako Tatsumi

Introduction: International Digitization Projects

Technological change has opened limitless possibilities for libraries, archives, and museums to share access to unique and rare materials across institutions. These institutions have responded by creating a variety of opportunities for collaboratively integrating their isolated collection materials into unified systems of overarching common cultural and historical inheritance across the divisional or institutional borders.[1] These collaboration models, however, are circumscribed within single nations, mainly in North America,[2] Oceania,[3] or Europe,[4] and do not transcend national or regional borders. Although the digital world has grown increasingly transnational, few publications have documented international collaboration models for digital projects.[5]

This chapter outlines an international collaboration model for a digitization project between an American academic library and the Japanese national library. The University of Maryland Libraries (UMD) has partnered with the National Diet Library of Japan

(NDL),[6] the Japanese equivalent of the US Library of Congress. They are collectively pursuing a bilateral digitization initiative, the Book Reformatting Project, which aims to preserve and create digital access to the materials held in the Gordon W. Prange Collection (hereafter, the Prange Collection). The Prange Collection is one of the UMD's premier special collections; it comprehensively archives Japanese-language print publications issued during the first four years of the Allied Occupation of Japan, from 1945 to 1949.

The Book Reformatting Project, in terms of its scope and duration, stands out as quite distinct from the standard digitization program. In contrast to typical projects that selectively digitize collection materials,[7] the Book Reformatting Project intends to reformat *all* books in the Prange Collection, a total of 71,000 titles. The project is consequently in place for a long duration; it started in May 2005 and continues uninterrupted as of today in 2017.

Why does this project seek to reformat the entire collection? How are the UMD and the NDL able to collectively manage this large-scale project over such a long period of time? How do they overcome the inevitable obstacles, given the geographical barriers and organizational, linguistic, and cultural differences between them? To answer these questions, this chapter first illuminates the historical background of the NDL's postwar collection development policies and practices, which led to the emergence and evolution of the UMD-NDL partnership. The chapter then discusses how this partnership initiated and advanced the Book Reformatting Project by examining the activities, structure, and processes of the project. In so doing, the chapter seeks to uncover the project's "collaboration catalysts,"[8]—the specific circumstances that make it more likely for collaborations to flourish. It also explores the challenges of creating and expanding digital access to the Prange Collection materials across institutional barriers and national boundaries. Lastly, the chapter draws conclusions about the future of the project and its potential impact on scholarly research and public memory in the changing context of the digital environment and higher education.

Historical Background for the Evolution of the UMD-NDL Partnership: 1960s–2000s

The UMD-NDL partnership can be traced back to the NDL's initiative of collecting postwar primary source documents, which started in the late 1960s. After two decades of rapid recovery from the devastation of World War II, Japanese intellectuals became interested in exploring collective experiences and public memories of the Allied Occupation of Japan.[9] In search of primary source materials, researchers began flocking to the Washington National Records Center (WNRC) in Suitland, Maryland, which held the archives of the Supreme Commander for the Allied Powers (SCAP). These materials were declassified in March 1972 by Richard Nixon's Executive Order 11652, Classification and Declassification of National Security Information and Material.[10]

Noting the trend of Japanese researchers making the long journey to the WNRC, NDL officials became convinced of the urgent necessity of acquiring copies of SCAP documents. Individual collection efforts were neither organized nor systematic and seemed unlikely to build a comprehensive collection. To address this need, the NDL embarked, in March 1978, on an institutional project of SCAP collection development.[11] In pursuit of this ambitious project, it launched two specific programs. First, an annual budget of

36,561,000 yen[12] was allocated specifically to collect the documents related to the Allied Occupation of Japan. Second, the NDL assigned a representative to reside in Washington, DC and pursue the acquisition of the SCAP materials at the WNRC.

The NDL pursued these programs for over a decade, but in the early 1990s the project was obligated to face the challenges of changing the target materials. SCAP documents were rendered inaccessible from 1993 to 1996 when the WNRC was temporarily closed while its materials were relocated to a new archive, the National Archives and Records Administration (NARA),[13] which would be built on the site of the University of Maryland, College Park, MD. In response to this prospect, the NDL examined potential candidates of alternative target collections, such as the Presidential Libraries, Marine Corps Historical Center, and MacArthur Memorials,[14] and finally selected the Prange Collection as a primary alternative target for its postwar collection development.[15]

If the WNRC was a treasure trove of American occupiers' documents, the Prange Collection is a treasure trove of the documents of the occupied Japanese. It includes every single Japanese-language print publication issued during the first four years of the Allied Occupation of Japan, 1945–1949. It holds approximately 71,000 books, 18,000 newspaper titles, 13,800 magazine titles, 10,000 news agency photographs, and much more. Its vast holdings include materials of all kinds: literature from classical to modern, children's and juvenile fiction, education materials, academic and technical books in all disciplines, encyclopedias, recreational pamphlets, wall newspapers, maps, comic books, cartoons—not to mention national and local newspapers and magazines from all over Japan. These comprehensive materials collectively reveal the transformative contexts of homes, schools, workplaces, and communities during the revolutionary years and capture people's daily practices across regions, generations, and socio-economic status. They illuminate the ways Japanese people reinterpreted and reshaped their identities and how they imagined, interacted, and negotiated with unprecedented possibilities and constraints in the political, economic, industrial, social, and educational arenas of postwar Japan.

The NDL's early 1990s shift to the Prange Collection made perfect sense since it was the only collection that complements the NDL's collection of postwar Japanese language materials. The NDL lacked a serious number of Japanese publications for the immediate postwar years, from the defeat in August 1945 to February 1948, when the National Diet Library Law was enacted, which mandated the deposit of one copy of every Japanese print publication. The Prange Collection's holdings came precisely from this period and would therefore perfectly fill the gap in the NDL's postwar collection.[16]

As the only institution in a position to help the NDL fulfill its mission of postwar collection development, the UMD proudly seized on the opportunity to form a partnership. This partnership accelerated the UMD's pursuit of the lifelong goal of a collection donor, Dr. Gordon W. Prange (1910–1980). A history professor at the University of Maryland, Prange was dedicated to the establishment of Allied Occupation Studies at the University of Maryland. He joined the US Navy in 1943 and was transferred to the Allied Forces in Japan in November 1945, where he became Chief of the Historical Branch of SCAP's Intelligence Section. SCAP had an intelligence unit, the Civil Censorship Detachment (CCD), which reviewed all civilian communications, including personal correspondence, telephone calls, radio broadcasts, films, and publications. Immediately following the Allied landing on Japanese soil, the CCD began requiring Japanese publishers to submit a pre-release copy of every potential publication for CCD review. When Prange learned that SCAP planned to lift its censorship regime in November 1949, he immediately arranged for the CCD collection to be archived at the UMD. As a professional historian, he was convinced of the historical value of the CCD's collection and its great potential to become the best collection in the United States on the Occupation of Japan and the War in the Pacific.[17] In order to arrange for the physical transport of the vast number of materials, he hired carpenters to construct more than 500 wooden crates. It took two years for Prange to accomplish the process of sorting, boxing, and shipping them from Tokyo to College Park, Maryland.

Since the crates arrived in College Park in the early 1950s, the UMD provided dedicated stewardship for the collection. After the UMD's decade-long administrative struggle to deal with the space constraints, these crates were finally unpacked in the 1960s. The new interest was prompted by a change in the American political climate, specifically the war in Vietnam and the military and political crisis in Asia. The American redefinition of Japan, the former Axis enemy, as a vital Cold War ally rapidly raised scholarly interest in the region, which consequently advanced East Asian Studies curricula and relevant resources and systems—notably, library collections—at higher education institutions. In response to the growing interest in the unpacked materials both on and off campus, the UMD hired a librarian who was a Japan specialist and was therefore qualified to appraise the material values and create bibliographic records.[18] This librarian's and his successors' efforts successfully increased the visibility and accessibility of the materials, which consequently drew a number of celebrated scholars from both the United States and Japan beginning in the 1970s.[19] As users' demand for these materials increased in the 1980s, the UMD embarked on preservation efforts, gaining grant funding and forming a partnership with a Japanese publishing agency.[20] The UMD was convinced that partnership with the NDL would further intensify their preservation efforts, promote the accessibility of the materials, and benefit current and potential users in both nations.

In April 1992, one year after the NDL's assessment of the Prange materials, the UMD and NDL collectively launched a preservation and access creation initiative. The NDL contributed $1.5 million for this joint project,[21] which sought to microform the approximately 13,800 magazine title holdings, encompassing approximately four million pages. The first project was a great success: it was completed in August 1996,[22] generating a total of 63,000 microfiches. This successful completion was followed by a reformatting of the 18,000 newspaper titles encompassing approximately two million pages, which ended up with a total of 3,800 reels in 2002.[23]

This decade-long microforming project was the fruit of a bilateral partnership and achieved monumental outcomes. Every single magazine and newspaper held by the Prange Collection crossed over the Pacific Ocean in microform version and returned to Japan, five decades after those collections had originally made the reverse journey. Beginning in April 1997, these microforms were housed in the Modern Japanese Political Documents Division at the NDL's Main Library in Tokyo[24] and have been accessible there ever since.

The UMD-NDL Prange Book Reformatting Project: 2005–present

On May 2, 2005, NDL Librarian, Takao Kurosawa and UMD president, C. D. Mote, Jr. signed a Memorandum of Understanding (MOU) and entered a joint initiative of digital preservation and access creation of the Prange Collection's book holdings, named the Prange Book Reformatting Project.[25] The MOU states that this project aims to digitize Prange's entire book holdings, comprising an estimated 71,000 titles, or a total of seventeen million pages. The MOU also clarifies the institutions' agreement on an overview of the project, including the target materials and their volumes, the responsibilities of each party, the ownership of digitized products, institutional access to products, and so on.

Due to the collection's enormous scope, the Book Reformatting Project is divided into phases lasting several years each. Each phase targets specific subject areas of the materials to be reformatted. Prior to defining each phase, the UMD and the NDL together examine the crucial factors of selecting target materials, (e.g., the physical conditions of the targeted materials), users' potential demand for them, and the readiness of their bibliographic data. Any relevant information specific to each phase is stated in a supplemental agreement.

Phase 1: Children's literature (April 2006–March 2010)

The first phase of the Book Reformatting Project started with children's literature, which comprised approximately 8,000 titles. The UMD-NDL partnership had two reasons for selecting this collection. First, cataloged bibliographic information for children's literature had already been fully available before the beginning of the project. Second, the institutions anticipated a high potential demand for the use of these materials. The NDL analyzed public libraries' holdings of postwar children's literature and discovered the significantly low rates of holdings of this genre across the nation.[26]

The most unique feature of this phase was the production of color microfilms. Children's books were first digitized and then the digitized versions were converted to color microforms in order to capture the color graphics and censorship markings of the original copies, which CCD examiners had written directly on them with colored pencils.[27] These color microforms have been accessible since October 2006 at the International Library of Children's Literature (ILCL), which was one of the NDL's two branch libraries.[28] The ILCL provides a comprehensive inventory of the Prange Collection's children's literature, sorting the titles and related information about picture books, readers, manga, and other resources, along with galley proofs.[29] In 2013, the images of color microforms were integrated into the NDL's Prange Digital Collection, which are accessible at NDL's three institutions: the Main Library, ILCL, and Kansai-kan branch library in Osaka/Kyoto region.[30]

Phase II (April 2010–March 2016): School materials and censored newspaper articles (CNA)

The project's second phase focused on education materials, including textbooks, instructional manuals for teachers, supplemental materials, workbooks for pupils, and so on. They comprised approximately 6,500 titles and documents, totaling approximately 975,000 pages.[31] The reason the educational materials were chosen was the availability of a full inventory with their comprehensive bibliographic information.[32]

In March 2014, four years after the beginning of Phase II, the UMD and the NDL made a collective decision on changing the target materials. They agreed to switch from education materials to another significant collection materials, the Censored Newspaper Articles (CNA). The CNA collection consisted of approximately 15,755 items, including newspaper articles galley proofs, censorship documents, news releases, and photographs. These materials in the CNA collection consisted of pre-publication articles and, thus, were separately organized from the published version of the newspaper titles. Accordingly, when the newspaper titles had been microfilmed in the 1990s as discussed above, the CNA collection was not preserved in microform at that time due to the unpreparedness of its bibliographic data.[33] Both the UMD and the NDL were aware of the urgent necessity of preserving the CNA collection due to its fragility and contents and agreed to work on its preservation when its metadata became available. When the UMD informed the NDL of its readiness for digitization in the middle of Phase II, they decided to prioritize the CNA collection. CNA digitization took a year to complete and the project switched back to education materials after that. Phase II was successfully completed in March 2016, followed by the smooth transition to Phase III.

Phase III (April 2016–March 2023): Social sciences and humanities

Phase III started in April 2016 with a prospect of a seven-year-long enterprise. This phase targets the titles in the social sciences and the humanities disciplines, which comprises approximately 9,900 titles (11,000 volumes) totaling approximately 1,650,000 pages.[34] Reasons for targeting these subject areas are a good prospect of high demand for the materials in these genres and a well-developed inventory of these materials with bibliographic data. As of March 2017, after the first year of Phase III, a total of 1,400 titles have been digitized.

All of the digitized images produced by the project have been uploaded to the NDL's Digital Collections and accessible onsite. As of March 2017, NDL's Prange Digital Collection holds approximately 7,300 book titles related to the humanities and social sciences disciplines, 8,100 titles of children's literature, and 15,775 CNA items. The total access numbers below demonstrate high interest in and demand for the Prange book holdings.

TABLE 21.1
Total title/item numbers accessible with the NDL Prange Digital Collection

Year	General Books (title)	Children's Literature (Title)	Censored Newspaper Articles (Item)
2017	7,300 (1,400 added)	8,100	15,775
2016	5,900 (no addition)	8,100	15,775
2015	5,900 (800 added)	8,100	—
2014	5,100 (1,500 added)	8,100	—
2013	3,600	8,100	—

TABLE 21.2
Total numbers of off- and on-site search/access to the NDL Prange Digital Collection[35]

	Off-site Search/Access	Onsite Search/ Access	Total Off- and On-site Access
2016	61,837	37,124	98,961
2015	93,117	8,559	101,676
2014	52,889	7,675	60,564

Collaboration Catalysts for the Success and Sustainability of the Project

For over two decades, the UMD and the NDL have advanced their collaborative partnership for the successful pursuit of these projects. Zorich et al. address identifiable circumstances that make it more likely for collaborations to flourish; they theorize these factors as "collaboration catalysts."[36] Making use of this conceptual framework, this section discusses collaboration catalysts specific to the UMD-NDL partnership that have enabled the success of its Book Reformatting Project. The chapter ultimately aims to demonstrate the applicability of these catalysts to other partnerships that stretch beyond departmental, institutional, and international borders.

Vision

The two institutions share a common vision, one that makes their collective efforts to overcome the inevitable obstacles worthwhile and enables them to maintain their engagement and motivation. As discussed in the previous section, the NDL has a clear vision of collecting the materials issued under the Allied Occupation; this is stated in its collection development policy.[37] The Book Reformatting Project, which seeks to digitize the Prange holdings entirely rather than selectively, reflects this vision.

The NDL's dedication to enhancing its postwar collection is a perfect fit for the UMD's mission. The UMD aspires to institutional leadership by contributing to the worldwide research community through its mission to promote access, collaboration, creativity, diversity, and stewardship. The UMD believes that "with like-minded partners, we're leading efforts to deliver and preserve information in the digital age," in the words of its 2015–2017 strategic plan.[38]

Administrative home base unit

The Book Reformatting Project has been governed by a specific administrative base unit at each institution. At the NDL, the Modern Japanese Political Documents Division (*Kensei Shiryō-shitsu*), a unit of the Reader Services and Collections Department, administers the project as one of its divisional roles in managing collection development of modern Japanese political documents. The Division consists of approximately ten full-time staff members; one of them works at the Prange Collection as a representative in residence. S/he mediates bilateral communications and engages in project management in collaboration with the Prange Collection's staff members.

At the UMD, four full-time Prange Collection staff members are comprehensively involved in the project tasks, from daily communication to project management. The curator of the Prange Collection regularly communicates to manage administrative and operational support activities with the Modern Japanese Political Documents Division. Constant communication between the partnered units intensifies interconnectedness and enables them to coordinate consistent, cohesive, and efficient workflows and deal collectively with any emerging issue. The interconnectedness of the two institutions is exemplified in the smooth transition from one phase to another and the flexibility that they showed by substituting materials targeted for digitization in Phase II. This interconnectedness enables both institutions to overcome emerging and potential problems effectively and to grow the project collaboratively.

Embeddedness within the institutional structure

The administrative home base units in each country play a key role, not only mutually between the organizations but also internally. When a specific organizational unit oversees the project, its operation can be easily embedded within the institutional structure under its leadership and initiative. Consequently, the project can be constantly supported by other administrative and functional divisions at each institution.

At the NDL, four different units are involved in the project for financial and technological purposes. Finances are handled by the Reader Services and Collection Development Division (*Riyō Sābisu bu*), which allocates an annual budget. The Account Division (*Kaikei-ka*) is in charge of logistical processes, such as the issuance and approval of purchase contracts as well as payments to the vendor upon delivery of the scanned images. For the technical roles, the Digital Information Department (*Denshi Jōhō-ka)* undertakes the planning and execution of digital collections while the Digital Library Division (*Denshi Tosho-ka*) provides logistical stewardship for the same collections.

At the UMD, similarly, several departments provide extensive support for the project as well. The Department of Digital Systems and Stewardship (DSS) is crucial as a consultant for digital specifications, including file naming and answering technical questions from the Prange staff members or the NDL. It also administers the technological infrastructure of the Prange Digital Collection by maintaining workstation hardware and software for quality control of the scanned images. In addition, DSS provides training for library technicians to create directory listings of project images and any other technical assistance as needed. The head and conservator of the Preservation Department also provide consultation and preservation services for the original materials and of the archival images. They also advise on the procedures for selecting books to be disbound, the disbanding itself, and rehousing of the books.

The stable and close involvement of a third party

This project involves a third party, the contractor, which has been extensively involved in the entire digitization procedure since the microforming project started in the 1990s. This specific contractor is responsible for receiving and scanning the Prange materials, creating metadata, inspecting it, and delivering it. This contractor's responsibility is clearly stated as "mandatory requirements for vendor" in a supplemental agreement issued for each phase. Accordingly, both parties understand and agree on the contractor's responsibilities, which make the entire digital process smooth and easy to proceed. Guidelines for this vendor, such as the digitization specification, are adapted from published manuals for digitization projects for archival and cultural heritage materials.[39]

The most distinctive feature of this contractor's involvement is its scanning location. It is located next door to the Prange Collection on the fourth floor of the Hornbake Library North on campus. The UMD decided to do the scanning onsite due to the fragility, uniqueness, and excessive amount of the Prange Collection materials. Onsite scanning allows the UMD to constantly monitor the entire digitization process and provide further assistance and guidance as necessary. The immediate solution of any issues that arise and frequent interaction with the contractor is one of the significant elements for the smooth and successful implementation of the project operation. After completion of onsite scanning, the contractor delivers external hard drives that have saved the digital images to its office for file naming and post-processing.

Challenges

Two separate versions of the digital collection

The Prange Digital Collection is deposited in each institution's digital collection system. These systems are independently operated, making it unlikely that each version would be interoperated or merged into a single collection. This means that two separate versions of the Prange Digital Collection exist although both digital collections deposit identical images of the Prange Collection holdings. The unlikelihood of the interoperability and convergence of the two separate digital collections is likely confusing and makes it challenging to shape a coherent view of the Prange Collection among worldwide user communities.

To harmonize the two separate versions of Prange Digital Collection, Prange's social media posts disseminate the latest information on the NDL Prange Digital Collection. The digitized images are annually added to the NDL Prange Digital Collection every March, the last month of the Japanese fiscal year, and the Prange Collection then annually updates the public on social media as to the number of newly accessible titles. In addition, when the Prange Collection posts any digital image accessible with the UMD Prange Digital Collection, it provides a URL of the equivalents accessible in the NDL Prange Digital Collection. The UMD also publicizes any relevant information on the NDL's resources on the occupation-period materials to form a holistic view of any relevant primary source materials for this historical period and highlight the interrelationship of the collection materials held by the two institutions.

Copyright restrictions

The NDL and the UMD govern the accessibility of their materials in accordance with their respective nation's copyright and institutional policies. The UMD applies US copyright laws to the Prange holdings on a legal basis on the San Francisco Peace Treaty enforced in April 1952, which authorized US governmental ownership of any materials related to the US Army's activities under the Allied Occupation of Japan.[40] The NDL, on the other hand, applies Japanese copyright laws to the digital surrogates, which authorize limited access to duplicates of the copyrighted materials.[41]

In either case, a majority of the Prange materials are considered still under copyright, so both institutions limit digital derivatives to onsite access only. The NDL provides three access points to the Prange Digital Collection: the Tokyo Main Library, ILCL, and Kansai-kan branch library. In the United States, the UMD campus is the only access point of the Prange Digital Collection. Having only four access points worldwide arguably constitutes a disservice to global user communities in the twenty-first-century digital information environment.

The good news, however, is the Japanese government's awareness of the necessity of reforming its copyright laws. In March 2017, the Agency of Cultural Affairs of Japan conducted a public survey that sought international users' comments on a draft to change the relevant laws and regulations on Japanese copyright. This draft sought to achieve extended access to the NDL Digital Collections from abroad; such access is currently approved only for domestic information institutions.[42] The Japanese government's permission to allow full or even partial access to the NDL Digital Collection from overseas will undoubtedly accelerate users' access to Prange holdings and advance the scholarly works on postwar Japanese history and beyond.

Conclusion

The UMD-NDL Book Reformatting Project offers a model case of an international digitization project, demonstrating a range of successful catalysts for pursuing a collaborative program across national borders. First, having a shared vision of the project is a cornerstone for sustaining and expanding the project. The NDL is committed to building a comprehensive collection of the Allied Occupation period. The NDL's mission is well-aligned with the UMD's dedication to its leadership role in pursuing cultural endeavors, advancing digital accessibility, and supporting worldwide research communities. The home base unit is another key element for pursuing a bilateral project. It externally facilitates interconnectedness through constant and consistent communication between the partnered units and internally situates the project within the organizational support systems across the departmental divisions. Another key issue is having a stable relationship with the third-party contractor. Long-term collaboration makes it possible to benefit from the type of professional expertise and experience that the contractor has achieved through deep involvement in the project.

These collaboration catalysts have successfully nurtured this UMD-NDL partnership for over two decades and have made it possible to provide and promote trans-Pacific accessibility of the Prange materials. The unparalleled comprehensiveness of the Prange holdings provides limitless possibilities for expanding, advancing, and reshaping the scholarship on the Allied Occupation of Japan, which largely remains to be explored by English-language historiography. The growing body of the UMD-NDL Prange Digital Collection will play a crucial role in uncovering unknown historical narratives about this era for Japan, the United States, East Asia, and beyond. The Book Reformatting Project should be considered a leading transnational endeavor that continuously offers a hopeful example for the preservation of the world's cultural heritage, contributing to the scholarly and public understanding of local, national, and international history of postwar Japan, and enriching human civilization by increasing digital access to irreplaceable materials for a worldwide audience.

Notes

1. For example, Diane M. Zorich, Gunter Waibel, and Ricky Erway, "Beyond the Silos of the LAMs: Collaboration among Libraries, Archives and Museums," OCLC Redsearch, http://www.oclc.org/content/dam/research/publications/library/2008/2008-05.pdf; Helena Robinson, "'A Lot of People Going That Extra Mile': Professional Collaboration and Cross-Disciplinarity in Converged Collecting Institutions," *Museum Management and Curatorship* 31, no. 2 (2016): 143–44; Günter Waibel and Ricky Erway, "Think Globally, Act Locally: Library, Archive, and Museum Collaboration," *Museum Management and Curatorship* 24, no. 4 (2009): 323–24.
2. Wendy M. Duff et al., "From Coexistence to Convergence: Studying Partnerships and Collaboration among Libraries, Archives and Museums," *Information Research: An International Electronic Journal* 18, no. 3 (2013): 6–7; Zorich, Waibel, and Erway, "Think Globally, Act Locally," 17–19.
3. Duff et al., "From Coexistence to Convergence," 7–8.
4. Sanjica Faletar Tanackovic and Boris Badurina, "Collaboration of Croatian Cultural Heritage Institutions: Experiences from Museums," *Museum Management and Curatorship* 24, no. 4 (2009): 299–300; Zorich, Waibel, and Erway, "Think Globally, Act Locally," 16–18.
5. Only a few articles have been published on international collaborative digitization projects, including Hsiao-Ming Yu, "International Collaboration on Digitization of Rare Chinese Books at National Central Library: Models and Outcomes," *International Journal of Humanities and Arts Computing* 8, no. supplement (2014): 128–29; Hao Phan, "International Collaboration in Library Digitization: Experiences from the Southeast Asia Digital Library Project," *Journal of Electronic Resources Librarianship* 25, no. 4 (2013): 316–17.
6. The NDL was founded in 1947 with the assistance of political scientist, Luther Evans, the tenth US Librarian of Congress. The NDL is the successor agency to the two prewar imperial libraries governed by the Parliament and the Ministry of Education respectively. National Diet Library, "Purpose of Establishment and History," accessed on August 23, 2017, http://www.ndl.go.jp/en/aboutus/outline/purpose.html.
7. Selection of materials for digitization is apparently a common topic for library research. See, for example, Alexandra Mills, "User Impact on Selection, Digitization, and the Development of Digital Special Collections," *New Review of Academic Librarianship* 21, no. 2 (2015); B. Ooghe and D. Moreels, "Analysing Selection for Digitisation: Current Practices and Common Incentives," *D-Lib Magazine* 15, no. 9–10 (2009).
8. Zorich, Waibel, and Erway, "Think Globally, Act Locally," 21.
9. Akira Amakawa, "Special Lecture: Looking Back on My Research Around 1970, and the History of the Allied Occupation of Japan and Related Topics," *Sankō Shoshi Kenkyū [Reference Service and Bibliography]*, no. 77 (2016): 64–67.
10. Toshiyuki Yamada, "National Diet Library's Special Collection: The Documents on the Allied Occupation of Japan," *Intelligence*, no. 8 (2007): 61.
11. Ibid., 70.
12. National Diet Library, "Evolution of Collecting Initiative of the Allied Occupation Related Materials," *Sankō Shoshi Kenkyū [Reference Service and Bibliography]*, no. 77 (2016): 8. It is approximately $165,434 based on an exchange rate in April 1978, the starting month of the Japanese fiscal year, which was approximately 221 yen per dollar.
13. Yamada, "National Diet Library's Special Collection," 67.
14. Atsumi Kumata, Masaaki Chiyo, and Sakae Edamatsu, "Workshop Series (1): Activities During Preparatory and Early Phases of the GHQ/SCAP Records Microfilming Joint Project between the National Diet Library and the National Archives and Records Services (NARS)," *Sankō*

Shoshi Kenkyū [Reference Service and Bibliography], no. 77 (2016): 45.

15. In addition to the Prange materials, the NDL collected the Truman Library documents, the Eisenhower Library documents, the MacArthur Memorial documents, and the Marine Corps Historical Center documents from 1993 to 1996; Yamada, "National Diet Library's Special Collection," 68.
16. National Diet Library, "Purange Bunko Shūshū Jigyō No Genjō [Current Situation of Collecting the Prange Collection Materials]," *Kokuritsu Kokkai Toshokan Geppō [NDL Monthly Bulletin]*, no. 560 (2007): 2.
17. Gordon W. Prange, "Byrd, Harry C.—Correspondence, 1948–1950," (1949), faculty papers, Gordon W. Prange, Series 4, Box 2, University Archives, University of Maryland Libraries, College Park, MD.
18. Sara C. Snyder, "Odyssey of an Archives: What the History of the Gordon W. Prange Collection of Japanese Materials Teaches Us About Libraries, Censorship, and Keeping the Past Alive," master's thesis, University of Maryland, College Park, 2007: 51–63.
19. Frank Shulman, "Okuizumi Eizaburo at the University of Maryland Libraries, 1974–1984," *Research Bulletin of Education History of Postwar Japan*, no. 27 (2014): 8–9.
20. Snyder, "Odyssey of an Archives," 125–26.
21. Ibid., 132.
22. Yamada, "National Diet Library's Special Collection," 67.
23. Masato Fujimaki, "The Prange Collection Media Reformatting Projects," *Gekkan IM (Monthly IM)* 47 (2008): 16.
24. Yamada, "National Diet Library's Special Collection," 67.
25. National Diet Library and University of Maryland Libraries, "Memorandum of Understanding," (2005).
26. Fujimaki, "The Prange Collection Media Reformatting Projects," 16.
27. A full overview of Phase I can be found in Eiko Sakaguchi, Kenichiro Shimada, and Amy Wasserstrom, "A Cross-Pacific Partnership: The University of Maryland Libraries and the National Diet Library of Japan Jointly Reformat Children's Books," *OCLC Systems & Services* 26, no. 1 (2010).
28. International Library of Children's Literature Resources and Information Division, "Access to the Prange Collection's Children's Literature," *National Diet Library Monthly Bulletin*, no. 560 (2007): 14.
29. The International Library of Children's Literature, "Prange Collection's Children's Literature," accessed on August 23, 2017, http://www.kodomo.go.jp/search/collection/special01.html.
30. National Diet Library, "The Evolution of the NDL Digital Collection," accessed on August 23, 2017, http://dl.ndl.go.jp/ja/history.html.
31. National Diet Library and University of Maryland Libraries, "Supplemental Agreement Prange Book Reformatting Project: Phase Two," (2010).
32. Please refer to Eiko Sakaguchi and Akemi Noda, *Merirando Daigaku Toshokan Shozo Godon W. Purange Bunko Kyoiku Tosho Mokuroku: Senryoki Ken'etsu Kyoiku Kankei Tosho 1945–1949 [Bibliography Catalog of Education Books Held by the Gordon W. Prange Collection at the University of Maryland Libraries: Censored Education-Related Materials under the Occupation, 1945-1949]* (Tokyo: Bunsei Shoin, 2007).
33. Gordon W. Prange Collection, "Censored Newspaper Articles," accessed on August 23, 2017, https://prangecollection.wordpress.com/2014/04/20/censored-newspaper-articles/.
34. National Diet Library and University of Maryland Libraries, "Supplemental Agreement Prange Book Reformatting Project: Phase Three" (2016).
35. Reader Services and Collections Department, "Overview of Access to the Materials Housed in the Modern Japanese Political Documents Division" (2017).
36. Zorich, Waibel, and Erway, "Think Globally, Act Locally," 21.
37. National Diet Library, "Shiryō Shūshū Hōshin Sho [Collection Development Policy]," 14, accessed on August 23, 2017, http://www.ndl.go.jp/jp/aboutus/collection/pdf/housin.pdf.
38. University of Maryland Libraries, "Partnerships and Collaborations," accessed on August 23, 2017, http://www.lib.umd.edu/about/deans-office/partners.

39. The guidelines for the vendor referred to Anne R. Kenney, Oya Y. Rieger, and Group Research Libraries, *Moving Theory into Practice: Digital Imaging for Libraries and Archives* (Mountain View, CA: Research Libraries Group, 2000).
40. Snyder, "Odyssey of an Archives," 94.
41. NDL shows a procedure of copyright clearance to provide access to the digital surrogates. National Diet Library, "Dejitaruka Shirō No Intā Netto Kōkai Ni Tsuite [About Internet Access to the Digitized Resources]," accessed on August 23, 2017, https://openinq.dl.ndl.go.jp/search#3.
42. European Association of Japanese Resources Specialists, "Access to the NDL Digital Collections from Abroad," accessed on August 23, 2017, http://www.eajrs.net/access-ndl-digital-collections-abroad.

Bibliography

Amakawa, Akira. "Special Lecture: Looking Back on My Research around 1970, and the History of the Allied Occupation of Japan and Related Topics." *Sankō Shoshi Kenkyū [Reference Service and Bibliography]*, no. 77 (2016).

Duff, Wendy M., Jennifer Carter, Joan M. Cherry, Heather MacNeil, and Lynne C. Howarth. "From Coexistence to Convergence: Studying Partnerships and Collaboration among Libraries, Archives and Museums." *Information Research: An International Electronic Journal* 18, no. 3 (2013).

Fujimaki, Masato. "The Prange Collection Media Reformatting Projects." *Gekkan IM (Monthly IM)* 47 (2008): 14–17.

Gordon W. Prange Collection. "Censored Newspaper Articles." https://prangecollection.wordpress.com/2014/04/20/censored-newspaper-articles/.

Kenney, Anne R., Oya Y. Rieger, and Group Research Libraries. *Moving Theory into Practice: Digital Imaging for Libraries and Archives* [in English]. Mountain View, CA: Research Libraries Group, 2000.

Kumata, Atsumi, Masaaki Chiyo, and Sakae Edamatsu. "Workshop Series (1): Activities During Preparatory and Early Phases of the GHQ/SCAP Records Microfilming Joint Project between the National Diet Library and the National Archives and Records Services (NARS)." *Sankō Shoshi Kenkyū [Reference Service and Bibliography]*, no. 77 (2016).

Mills, Alexandra. "User Impact on Selection, Digitization, and the Development of Digital Special Collections." *New Review of Academic Librarianship* 21, no. 2 (2015): 160–69.

National Diet Library. "Dejitaruka Shirō No Intā Netto Kōkai Ni Tsuite [About Internet Access to the Digitized Resources]." https://openinq.dl.ndl.go.jp/search#3.

———. "Evolution of Collecting Initiative of the Allied Occupation Related Materials." *Sankō Shoshi Kenkyū [Reference Service and Bibliography]*, no. 77 (2016): 3–10.

———. "The Evolution of the NDL Digital Collection." http://dl.ndl.go.jp/ja/history.html.

———. "Purange Bunko Shūshū Jigyō No Genjō [Current Situation of Collecting the Prange Collection Materials]." *Kokuritsu Kokkai Toshokan Geppō [NDL Monthly Bulletin]*, no. 560 (November 2007).

———. "Purpose of Establishment and History." http://www.ndl.go.jp/en/aboutus/outline/purpose.html.

———. "Shiryō Shūshū Hōshin Sho [Collection Development Policy]." http://www.ndl.go.jp/jp/aboutus/collection/pdf/housin.pdf.

National Diet Library and University of Maryland Libraries. "Memorandum of Understanding." 2005.

———. "Supplemental Agreement Prange Book Reformatting Project: Phase Three." 2016.

———. "Supplemental Agreement Prange Book Reformatting Project: Phase Two." 2010.

Ooghe, B., and D. Moreels. "Analysing Selection for Digitisation: Current Practices and Common Incentives." *D-Lib Magazine* 15, no. 9–10 (2009).

Phan, Hao. "International Collaboration in Library Digitization: Experiences from the Southeast Asia Digital Library Project." *Journal of Electronic Resources Librarianship* 25, no. 4 (2013): 316–21.

Prange, Gordon W. "Byrd, Harry C.—Correspondence, 1948–1950." 1949.

Reader Services and Collections Department. "Overview of Access to the Materials Housed in the Modern Japanese Political Documents Division." 2017.

Resources and Information Division, International Library of Children's Literature. "Access to the Prange Collection's Children's Literature." *National Diet Library Monthly Bulletin*, no. 560 (November 2007).

Robinson, Helena. "'A Lot of People Going That Extra Mile': Professional Collaboration and Cross-Disciplinarity in Converged Collecting Institutions." *Museum Management and Curatorship* 31, no. 2 (2016): 141–58.

Sakaguchi, Eiko, and Akemi Noda. *Merirando Daigaku Toshokan Shozo Godon W. Purange Bunko Kyoiku Tosho Mokuroku: Senryoki Ken'etsu Kyoiku Kankei Tosho 1945–1949 [Bibliography Catalog of Education Books Held by the Gordon W. Prange Collection at the University of Maryland Libraries: Censored Education-Related Materials under the Occupation, 1945-1949]*. Tokyo: Bunsei Shoin, 2007.

Sakaguchi, Eiko, Kenichiro Shimada, and Amy Wasserstrom. "A Cross-Pacific Partnership: The University of Maryland Libraries and the National Diet Library of Japan Jointly Reformat Children's Books." [In English]. *OCLC Systems & Services* 26, no. 1 (2010): 18–28.

Shulman, Frank. "Okuizumi Eizaburo at the University of Maryland Libraries, 1974–1984." *Research Bulletin of Education History of Postwar Japan*, no. 27 (2014): 19–28.

Snyder, Sara C. "Odyssey of an Archives: What the History of the Gordon W. Prange Collection of Japanese Materials Teaches Us About Libraries, Censorship, and Keeping the Past Alive." Master's thesis. University of Maryland, College Park, 2007.

Tanackovic, Sanjica Faletar, and Boris Badurina. "Collaboration of Croatian Cultural Heritage Institutions: Experiences from Museums." *Museum Management and Curatorship* 24, no. 4 (2009): 299–321.

The International Library of Children's Literature. "Prange Collection's Children's Literature." http://www.kodomo.go.jp/search/collection/special01.html.

University of Maryland Libraries. "Partnerships and Collaborations." http://www.lib.umd.edu/about/deans-office/partners.

Waibel, Günter, and Ricky Erway. "Think Globally, Act Locally: Library, Archive, and Museum Collaboration." *Museum Management and Curatorship* 24, no. 4 (2009): 323–35.

Yamada, Toshiyuki. "National Diet Library's Special Collection: The Documents on the Allied Occupation of Japan." *Intelligence*, no. 8 (2007): 61–72.

Yu, Hsiao-Ming. "International Collaboration on Digitization of Rare Chinese Books at National Central Library: Models and Outcomes." *International Journal of Humanities and Arts Computing* 8, no. supplement (2014): 124–51.

Zorich, Diane M., Gunter Waibel, and Ricky Erway. "Beyond the Silos of the LAMs: Collaboration among Libraries, Archives and Museums." http://www.oclc.org/content/dam/research/publications/library/2008/2008-05.pdf.

SECTION IV

Establishing Libraries & Services Abroad

CHAPTER TWENTY-TWO

International Collaborations:

Development of the Duke Kunshan University Library

Linda Daniel

Academic librarians are often embedded in projects or courses but rarely are they asked to establish a library in a new university in a country as historically rich or as politically complicated as China. Duke University Libraries were asked to help build the services and collections for the Duke Kunshan University Library and have played an instrumental role in its setup and in making it an integral partner in the Sino-American partnership between Duke University, Wuhan University, the city of Kunshan, and Jiangsu Province. Duke Kunshan's mission is to create a world-class liberal arts and research university that will, "inspire students to master academically rigorous coursework, generate new ideas and develop creative solutions to the world's challenges, preparing them not just for careers in specific fields, but to become globally sophisticated leaders and citizens."[1] The university opened its doors to its first cohort of students in fall 2014. From its inception, the Duke Kunshan Library has endeavored to support the university's objective to address the changing needs of global higher education and global challenges.

Similar to the ambitious efforts that established this joint-venture university in China, an entrepreneurial spirit has been a key component of this library initiative. Librarians have been actively seizing opportunities to create meaningful programs; have collaborated with administrators, faculty, and students to implement creative solutions to problems encountered in the library's start-up; and have been persistent in efforts to integrate information literacy and critical thinking into the curriculum. These efforts have been personally rewarding for the Duke librarians secunded to Duke Kunshan. They also show how American librarians can be leaders in international education in China and how this work supports the development of globalization and international librarianship.[2]

The creation and development of Duke Kunshan University can be attributed to the coming together of three different aspirations: the desire by the Chinese government to educate its brightest students to be critical, innovative thinkers; Duke University's desire to be a leader in global education coupled with the opportunity to develop research projects with access to China-based sites, information, and resources; and the desire of the city of Kunshan to attract a world-class university to help solidify its economic growth and technological progress.[3]

China's educational history includes a strong willingness to experiment in order to create world-class institutions of higher education. William Kirby points out, in *Global Opportunities and Challenges for Higher Education Leaders: Briefs on Key Themes*, that involvement with international partnerships to reach this goal is not a new phenomenon in China. Wuhan University, founded in 1893, was influenced by European educational methods to become a "Self-Strengthening" institution,[4] and many state institutions, before 1949, were patterned after the model of the German university, which holistically integrated research and teaching.[5] Michael Roth, author of *Beyond the University: Why Liberal Education Matters*, describes his Chinese colleagues' admonition that liberal education in China goes back centuries and that it "was never a disconnected or remote theory ...but always had as its fundamental mission or *telos* the refinement of the student for the purpose of nurturing and guiding the nation as a whole."[6]

To understand why the building and funding of joint-venture universities with liberal arts curricula, such as Duke Kunshan, now appeals to the Chinese government, it is important to understand the trajectory of higher education in China since World War II. From 1949 to the late 1970s, the primary goal of Chairman Mao and the Chinese Communist Party was to reconstruct and modernize the country using the Soviet Union as its economic and social model. In higher education, Soviet teaching methods, administrative procedures, and textbooks were emulated, and most students received training in technical and vocational skills. In addition, from 1966–1976, Mao's Cultural Revolution purged the country of traditional and capitalist elements and, in effect, destroyed the Chinese educational system as many schools were closed and students were forced to migrate to rural areas to perform manual labor. The postwar period was a disastrous time for higher education in China and it took many years for the country's educational system to recover.[7]

In 1978, with Deng Xiaoping's Open Door Policy, the Chinese government focused on economic and educational reform and the country began to move from a Soviet model to a market economy with socialist characteristics. Students were trained for careers in the sciences and math while less attention was given to the humanities.[8] Implementation of the higher education curriculum focused on rote learning and test-based competence. Memorization of content became important and instruction to promote creativity skills and innovative thinking was de-emphasized.

In the late 1990s, another shift in Chinese higher education occurred. The goal became to improve the quality and availability of education for the whole country and to make China more economically competitive on a global level. To increase national and international competence, the national curriculum focused on educating the "whole person" with "cultural quality education."[9] Scientific and technological expertise and skills were developed, and the government invested in education to bring greater prosperity to the nation.

In July 2010, China's Ministry of Education released its comprehensive plan for modernizing its educational system, *The Outline of China's National Plan for Medium and Long-term Education Reform and Development 2010–2020,* commonly known as Blueprint 2020. This mandate called for higher education institutions in China to "open their best faculties to the world, and to participate in or set up collaborative international academic organizations."[10] Today, it is clear that China is dedicated to building a knowledge-based economy and access to world-class education is considered an essential element in the country's development. The success of Blueprint 2020 can be seen in the increase in the number of schools and students. By 2015, there were 2,560 regular Chinese institutions of higher education and thirty-seven million Chinese students enrolled in college or university.[11,12] China has the largest student population of any country in the world.[13]

Many policymakers in China see the American system of higher education as a way to provide programs that promote critical thinking, creativity, and innovation and to develop curricula that focus on liberal education. In response, many leading American universities are eager to become involved in the opportunities afforded by the rapid rise of Chinese higher education and to have a "China strategy" to give them a foothold in that growing market. By 2015, there were twenty-nine joint-venture universities in China. In addition to Duke Kunshan University, New York University has built a campus in Shanghai as part of its global network, Stanford has built a research center at Peking University, and other American universities are involved in a variety of academic engagements in China.[14] English is the language of instruction for all degree-granting programs at Duke Kunshan, so the university offers Chinese students the opportunity to prepare themselves for graduate education or employment in English-speaking countries.

Duke's 2006 strategic plan, "Making a Difference," clearly stated that the university gives a high priority to going beyond its campus to strengthen its international partnerships.[15] Under President Richard H. Brodhead, the university's vision was to become not only a more global university but a leader in global education. The plan to establish a joint-venture university in China offered the university the opportunity to achieve its objectives to further its international reputation and global impact, to develop innovative teaching models to extend the reach of its educational standards, and to strengthen its research capabilities and increase research funding in such areas as air and water quality, health inequities, economic development, and technological innovations.[16] An enticing incentive was the Chinese government's willingness to commit large amounts of money for scientific research and to build international partnerships.[17]

From its inception, the primary interest of the Chinese partners in Duke Kunshan has been the development of the four-year university. Access to world-class, innovative education is a top priority for Chinese higher education. Duke's status as a top-tier university with considerable name recognition, practical knowledge about innovative teaching methods and cutting-edge research, and significant intellectual capital made it a highly desirable partner.[18]

Jiangsu province, home to the city of Kunshan, is one of China's wealthiest areas. In 2016, Jiangsu had the highest per capita gross domestic product in China.[19] Kunshan is located approximately thirty-five miles from Shanghai. The two cities are connected by high-speed rail and the sixteen-minute trip makes Shanghai easily accessible. The Jiangsu province is known for its technical innovations and rapid growth, and the construction of a top-tier university was seen as critical to ensuring its continuing development. When it became known that Duke was looking for a campus site in China, Kunshan offered land and financial incentives to entice Duke to set up a joint-venture university in this location. After much negotiation, Duke University in partnership with the city of Kunshan and Wuhan University, formed Duke Kunshan University and received final approval from the Ministry of Education in 2013.[20]

In fall 2014, Duke Kunshan University opened its doors to its first class of students. The faculty, staff, and students in the first semester saw themselves as pioneers. They were intrigued by the opportunity to help set up and establish a new university in China and were ready to take on the challenge of the unexpected. Students were enrolled in master's degree programs in global health, medical physics, or management science, or in the Global Learning Semester (GLS), a program for undergraduate students from Chinese universities, Duke University, or other top-tier universities from around the world.[21] Faculty were from Duke and other US universities or had been hired for longer-term appointments by Duke Kunshan University.

In this first year, 2014–2015, the interim directors of the Duke Kunshan Library were secunded from Duke, and this direct partnership reinforced the strong ties between the two institutions. The expectation that the rigor of the academic mission of Duke University needed to be realized at Duke Kunshan was carried forward by the secunded librarians who worked closely with Duke Kunshan faculty and students and were responsible for providing them with the services and collections equal to the quality of a Duke education.

This startup required the cooperation and expertise of many departments within the Duke University Libraries (Duke's central university library system) and from three of Duke's independently administered professional school libraries, Goodson Law Library, the Medical Center Library, and Ford Library at the Fuqua School of Business. The secunded librarians did not have prior experience setting up a new library nor had they traveled to China. It was an experience they met with enthusiasm and with some trepidation. The support of Duke librarians and administrators made this feel like a team effort that offered many opportunities, and it allowed for risk-taking with the understanding that any difficulties encountered would be treated as lessons learned rather than failures.

All Duke Kunshan degree-granting programs entail the receipt of a Duke diploma, and consequently Duke Kunshan faculty and students have access to the electronic resources available to Duke affiliates, to the extent that purchase agreements and licenses permit. This access required Duke collection development librarians to contact vendors and explain the status of Duke Kunshan programs and students, in some cases negotiate with vendors for additional access. Duke information technology staff set up open source library management systems, discovery platforms, and web proxy servers so the resources could be used in China. The twelve-hour time difference between China and North Carolina required people to work outside normal business hours when in-person communication was needed to set up or troubleshoot services or access to collections. Due to the inherent difficulties of working in China, it has become clear that the development of an international library requires individuals to be dedicated to the mission of the university to ensure that technology can be used across the globe and within a country that can tightly control access to information.

Duke Libraries' electronic resources are available in China through a secure Virtual Private Network (VPN) that allows access to websites and other internet resources that would not normally be available in China. Duke Kunshan faculty, staff, and students have access to the Duke Kunshan wireless network and the VPN when they are on campus and it quickly connects them to Duke resources. Duke's Office of Technology (OIT) monitors this IT network to ensure its security.

The protection of academic freedom at Duke Kunshan, including access to information, has been one of the founding principles of the university and a clear expectation for Duke University's continued involvement in this joint venture. While faculty and students are expected to be respectful of Chinese laws and regulations, they are encouraged to be intellectually curious and are not deterred from tackling and openly discussing highly complex issues.[22] With the help of the VPN technology, Duke University Libraries' are able to provide students and faculty at Duke Kunshan access to relevant scholarly resources available at Duke.

The print collection at Duke Kunshan needs to provide copies of titles not available in electronic format or whose use would be preferred in print, and its size needs to meet Ministry of Education (MOE) requirements.[23] Duke Libraries' Technical Services staff has provided assistance with cataloging, acquisitions, and discovery. They established the initial procedures for ordering and importing print books, provided written documentation for specific cataloging procedures, helped troubleshoot cataloging and discovery problems, and created new modules within the Duke discovery tools for the Duke Kunshan Library. The use of Chinese import companies to acquire print books in the US for the Duke Kunshan Library is now the preferred method of acquisition. This process has worked well but can be slow as it may take ten to twelve weeks for a book to be delivered from the US to Kunshan. The use of ebooks, ordered and cataloged through Duke Libraries, shortens this acquisitions process and offers an attractive alternative since it eliminates customs screenings and makes texts more immediately accessible.

From the beginning, the Duke Kunshan Library has been a collaborative partner in the endeavors of the Duke Kunshan University. Librarians at Duke Kunshan have faculty status and the library director attends the weekly chancellor's meetings to discuss university strategies and policies. The opportunity for librarians to be an integral part of the establishment of this new university, to have a voice in setting priorities and developing its programs, increased clear communication and provided a greater understanding of the ways librarians can contribute to the mission of the university. The seat at the chancellor's meeting also affords the opportunity for the library to become blended into the fabric of the university. For example, a Duke librarian was one of the organizers of a key event held in fall 2014 in conjunction with the university's grand opening. Representatives from seventeen Chinese partner institutions attended Duke Kunshan classes, toured the library, and spoke with panels of students and faculty as part of this open house. Duke Kunshan used this opportunity to demonstrate the effectiveness of the liberal arts curriculum and interactive teaching methods. The visitors asked many questions about these American methods and how to assess mastery of content when rote learning and recitation are not emphasized.

Secunded librarians have served on the Global Learning Semester (GLS) admissions committees and have reviewed and made recommendations about international and Chinese students' applications for the program. This involvement has given librarians an increased understanding of incoming students' academic and language proficiencies and has integrated the library into the process that determines the success of the GLS program.

The lack of Mandarin language fluency by Duke secunded librarians encouraged the development of alternative ways to communicate with non-English speakers. As the keynote speaker at the Jiangsu Academic Library and Information System (JALIS) annual meeting, a Duke librarian used the translation assistance of a Duke Kunshan undergraduate student majoring in translation services at her home university to effectively present a program about the services and collections available through the Duke Kunshan Library. The student mentioned this experience as a highlight in her speech at the university's fall semester closing ceremony as she effectively used her skills to partner with faculty, and she was honored to be asked to talk with Chinese professionals about the accomplishments of the Duke Kunshan Library.

In collaboration with Chinese library staff, Duke librarians were able to work effectively with Chinese vendors and build relationships with library administrators at several Chinese universities. In spring 2016, three Chinese book vendors were invited to campus for a book fair. These vendors brought newly published books in English to campus so that students, faculty, and staff could choose the titles they would like to have added to the library's collections. The library provided the funds to purchase the selected books and this form of patron-driven acquisition has proved to be a popular way to involve the campus in building the print collection.

Research and instruction librarians at Duke Kunshan work closely with Duke subject librarians to provide services and resources needed for undergraduate and graduate students in China. Since the number of staff in the Duke Kunshan Library has been small—two librarians in 2014–2015 and three librarians in 2015–2017—this support has been essential. Duke librarians have provided assistance with research guides, course readings, assessment measures, focus groups, and the establishment of new graduate programs. As the new four-year undergraduate program is developed, additional librarians will be hired by Duke Kunshan. The depth of subject knowledge and understanding of specialized research tools and methods offered by Duke librarians will continue to be an important resource for the Duke Kunshan librarians.

Duke Kunshan University's website describes its commitment to problem-based learning that engages students to generate new ideas and creative solutions to real-world problems. This mission focuses on the development of students who can think critically and have key skills, such as creativity, independent thinking, and evidence-based reasoning. Duke secunded librarians and faculty, in conjunction with Duke Kunshan librarians, have focused efforts to incorporate information literacy skills and critical thinking into the curriculum. In 2016, a Duke secunded librarian partnered with faculty and administrators and successfully won an Education & Research Innovations in China (ERIC) grant to bring two instructors from the Center for Assessment & Improvement of Learning at Tennessee Technology University, the home of the Critical-thinking Assessment Test (CAT test), to the Duke Kunshan campus to hold a two-day workshop on critical thinking skills. Goals of the workshop were to

- meet the stated interest of Duke Kunshan professors to learn more about critical thinking;
- provide quantitative feedback on critical thinking skills for students through the CAT instrument and specific classroom training and evaluation;
- create a key element of the overall assessment landscape for Duke Kunshan;
- create a cohort of Duke professors who could potentially take the lessons learned in the workshop and associated activities back to their courses at Duke;
- open the potential to use Duke Kunshan-derived data for publications on cross-cultural/international comparisons of critical thinking skills and scores; and
- implement a trial approach to critical thinking training, teaching, and measuring that could inform a process in the four-year undergraduate degree program.[24]

Twenty-four professors and senior administrators attended the workshop to learn more about the philosophy of critical thinking, look closely at the CAT instrument, and learn how to score responses to the CAT test. Thirty-eight Duke Kunshan students took the CAT that semester and these tests, after being de-identified, were scored as part of the workshop. This exercise proved useful as it developed the critical thinking skills of the test scorers and gave faculty a chance to see how Duke Kunshan students reason through real-world problems. On the second day, the training sessions focused on how to develop lesson plans for specific classes to encourage the development of critical thinking skills.

The workshop was just one element in a broader plan to more fully integrate critical thinking skills into the culture of teaching at Duke Kunshan. A critical thinking study group discussed scholarly writings that focus on teaching critical thinking skills on international campuses and a bibliography of critical thinking resources was compiled. Other components of the plan include developing customized critical thinking exercises and analyzing the results of targeted critical thinking efforts in the classroom. Students who took the CAT received letters with their scores and met with secunded Duke faculty and librarians to discuss ways they could increase their critical thinking skills. This data collection at Duke Kunshan will continue so as to build a greater understanding of how Chinese and international students use critical thinking skills and where gaps in teaching may occur.

In tandem with critical thinking skills, the development of literacy skills is being built into the Duke Kunshan curriculum. A survey to assess GLS students' understanding of information literacies was developed and administered in fall 2016 to students before and after taking Duke Kunshan courses. The difficulties encountered by the students and identified by the pre-survey helped determine the content of library sessions and workshops. A credit-bearing information literacy course was developed and approved at Duke by the Ad Hoc Joint Duke Kunshan University Committee of the Arts & Science Council. The course is built around the learning outcomes of the 2015 ACRL Framework for Information Literacy for Higher Education and looks to address social justice within information literacy to prepare students to be active, informed citizens. The course lesson plans will use interactive teaching methods and will be co-taught by Duke and Duke Kunshan librarians in spring 2018 as part of the GLS program.

You Guo Jiang, author of *Liberal Arts Education in a Changing Society: A New Perspective on Chinese Higher Education*, points out that if the ultimate goal of a university education is to create global citizens who can transcend utilitarianism, then Chinese universities need to offer a liberal arts education that educates students in critical thinking.[25] Jiang discusses the many challenges for China's higher education system to provide this type of education: the difficulty of building world-class liberal arts universities in China that are recognized in global rankings; the need to give students a broad education that shapes their lives and enhances their roles as citizens while ensuring their competitiveness for jobs; the changes needed in recruiting and hiring practices in order to attract faculty who understand active learning and critical thinking methods; and the challenge of finding ways to revamp tenure and promotion structures so teaching is supported and rewarded as an equal to research and publishing.[26]

Because China's top-tier universities cannot easily or quickly change to address these challenges, Duke University's interest and willingness to use its talents to develop a liberal arts university in Kunshan holds great appeal. Duke University's Liberal Arts in China Committee has developed an interdisciplinary curriculum built on a culture of pedagogy that is immersive, in which teachers and students work closely together to approach open questions, articulate hypotheses, test out ideas, and challenge one another. It will be the type of education that builds critical thinking and problem-solving skills.[27] The campus' small size will offer opportunities for problem-based and team-based learning, close connections between faculty and students, and easy access to partnerships with Duke Kunshan's research centers. In turn, Duke's presence in China will open possibilities for collaboration and will secure its leadership role in helping to define the next frontiers of higher education.

Many scholars have written about the risks joint-venture universities take on by being involved in higher education in China. These risks include financial costs, reputational dangers to the rigor of the curriculum and the quality of the students and the faculty, and uncertainty about the possibility of creating a liberal education in a country that has an illiberal political system.[28] However, the opportunities outweigh the risks if universities can control specific factors that jeopardize success. The assurance from the Chinese government that academic freedom will be protected at joint-venture universities offers librarians an opportunity to play a major role in supporting and fostering intellectual freedom. The future and ultimate success of these joint-venture universities remain to be seen, but the support provided by American library partners has helped build their high-quality services and collections, encouraged the open sharing of information, and created collaborations and initiatives that foster intellectual freedom and critical thinking while striving to redefine librarianship in the global environment.

Notes

1. Duke Kunshan University, "Duke Kunshan University—Overview," 2017, accessed April 5, 2017, https://dukekunshan.edu.cn/en/about/duke-kunshan.
2. Linda Daniel, Research & Instruction Librarian, was secunded from Duke University to Duke Kunshan University, Aug.–Dec. 2014, to set up the Duke Kunshan Library and returned to Duke Kunshan as the Associate University Librarian, Aug. 2015–Dec. 2016. Danette Pachtner, Research & Instruction Librarian, was secunded from Duke to Duke Kunshan, Feb.–June 2015. In May 2014, Mengjie Zou was hired by Duke Kunshan as Senior Library Assistant and in 2017 was promoted to Instruction/Research and Collection Development Librarian. In Aug. 2015, Dr. Helen Xu was hired by Duke Kunshan as the University Librarian. Additional librarians will be hired by Duke Kunshan as the student population grows and the university prepares to launch the four-year undergraduate program in fall 2018.
3. Sally Kornbluth, "Memo to the Faculty from Provost Sally Kornbluth: Duke and the Development of Duke Kunshan University," emailed to the Duke University Academic Council, March 16, 2016, 5.
4. Jean-Marc F. Blanchard and Kun-Chin Lin, "Contemplating Chinese Foreign Policy: Approaches to the Use of Historical Analysis," *Pacific Focus* 28, no. 2 (2013): 158. The Self-Strengthening Movement was a Chinese military and political reform movement of the second half of the nineteenth century that attempted to adapt Western institutions and military innovations to Chinese needs.
5. William C. Kirby, "The World of Universities in Modern China," in *Global Opportunities and Challenges for Higher Education Leaders: Briefs on Key Themes*, ed. Laura E. Rumbley et al. (Rotterdam: Sense Publishers, 2014), 73.
6. Michael Roth, *Beyond the University: Why Liberal Education Matters* (New Haven: Yale University Press, 2014), 194.
7. You Guo Jiang, *Liberal Arts Education in a Changing Society: A New Perspective on Chinese Higher Education* (Leiden: Brill, 2015), 37–39.

8. Ibid., 39–40.
9. Ibid., 48.
10. China Government, "Outline of China's National Plan for Medium and Long-Term Education Reform and Development (2010–2020)," July 2010, accessed April 7, 2017, https://internationaleducation.gov.au/News/newsarchive/2010/Documents/China_Education_Reform_pdf.pdf, 21.
11. China Data Online, "Number of Schools by Level and Type--China Yearly Macro- Economics Statistics (National)," 2015, accessed April 22, 2017, http://chinadataonline.org.proxy.lib.duke.edu/member/macroy/macroytshow.asp?code=A1401.
12. National Bureau of Statistics of China, "Number of Students of Formal Education by Type and Level (2015)," in *China Statistical Yearbook-2016*, accessed April 24, 2017, http://www.stats.gov.cn/tjsj/ndsj/2016/indexeh.htm.
13. Zhao Xinying, "China Has 1 in 5 of All College Students in the World: Report," China Daily, April 8, 2016, accessed April 10, 2017, http://www.chinadaily.com.cn/china/2016-04/08/content_24365038.htm.
14. Kirby, "The World of Universities in Modern China," 75.
15. Duke University, "Making a Difference: The Strategic Plan for Duke University," Sept. 14, 2006, accessed April 20, 2017, https://provost.duke.edu/sites/all/files/DKU%20Phase%20II%20Curriculum%20Prospectus%20090616.pdf, 9.
16. Kornbluth, "Memo to the Faculty," 5.
17. Kirby, "The World of Universities in Modern China," 5.
18. Kornbluth, "Memo to the Faculty," 7.
19. eChinacities.com, "Jiangsu Is China's Wealthiest Province in Terms of Per Capita GDP 外国人网," Sept. 23, 2016, accessed April 23, 2017, http://www.echinacities.com/china-media/Jiangsu-is-Chinas-Wealthiest-Province-in-Terms-of-Per-Capita-GDP.
20. Kornbluth, "Memo to the Faculty," 7.
21. Duke Kunshan University, "DKU Granted Final Approval," Sept. 17, 2013, accessed April 20, 2017, https://dukekunshan.edu.cn/en/dku-granted-final-approval.
22. Ibid., 13–14.
23. The MOE's official policy for number of books required per student has not been officially updated since the late 1990s. The new library, to be built in Phase 2 of Duke Kunshan University, will use its agreements with Wuhan University and Duke University to help it meet MOE requirements.
24. Ken Rogerson et al., "ERIC Grant Proposal: Critical Thinking Skills at Duke Kunshan University: Workshop, Study Group, and Best Practices," Feb. 15, 2016.
25. Jiang, Liberal Arts Education in a Changing Society, 148.
26. Ibid., 147–51.
27. Duke University, Liberal Arts in China Committee, "Duke Kunshan University: Curriculum Prospectus," Sept. 6, 2016, accessed April 9, 2017, https://provost.duke.edu/sites/all/files/DKU%20Phase%20II%20Curriculum%20Prospectus%20090616.pdf, 5.
28. See Kirby, "The World of Universities in Modern China," 75; Kornbluth, "Memo to the Faculty," 12–16; Pun, "The Value of Intellectual Freedom in Twenty-First-Century China,"566–67; US Congress, House of Representatives, Committee on Foreign Affairs, Hearings before the Subcommittee on Africa, Global Health, Global Human Rights, and International Organizations: Is Academic Freedom Threatened by China's Influence on U.S. Universities?, 114th Cong., 1st sess., 2015, 61–63.

Bibliography

Blanchard, Jean-Marc F., and Kun-Chin Lin. "Contemplating Chinese Foreign Policy: Approaches to the Use of Historical Analysis." *Pacific Focus* 28, no. 2 (August 1, 2013): 145–69. doi:10.1111/pafo.12006.

China Data Online. "Number of Schools by Level and Type--China Yearly Macro-Economics Statistics (National)." 2015. http://chinadataonline.org.proxy.lib.duke.edu/member/macroy/macroyt-show.asp?code=A1401.

China Government. "Outline of China's National Plan for Medium and Long-Term Education Reform and Development (2010–2020)." July 2010. https://internationaleducation.gov.au/News/newsarchive/2010/Documents/China_Education_Reform_pdf.pdf.

Duke Kunshan University. "DKU Granted Final Approval." Sept. 17, 2013. https://dukekunshan.edu.cn/en/dku-granted-final-approval.

———. "Duke Kunshan University—Overview." 2017. https://dukekunshan.edu.cn/en/about/duke-kunshan.

Duke University. Liberal Arts in China Committee. "Duke Kunshan University: Curriculum Prospectus." September 6, 2016. https://provost.duke.edu/sites/all/files/DKU%20Phase%20II%20Curriculum%20Prospectus%20090616.pdf.

———. "Making a Difference: The Strategic Plan for Duke University." Sept. 14, 2006. https://provost.duke.edu/wp-content/uploads/stratPlan2006-plan.pdf.

eChinacities.com. "Jiangsu Is China's Wealthiest Province in Terms of Per Capita GDP (外国人)." Sept. 23, 2016. http://www.echinacities.com/china-media/Jiangsu-is-Chinas-Wealthiest-Province-in-Terms-of-Per-Capita-GDP.

Jiang, You Guo. *Liberal Arts Education in a Changing Society: A New Perspective on Chinese Higher Education*. Leiden: Brill, 2014.

Kirby, William C. "The World of Universities in Modern China." In *Global Opportunities and Challenges for Higher Education Leaders*, edited by Laura E. Rumbley, Robin Matross Helms, Patti McGill Peterson, and Philip G. Altbach. Sense Publishers, 2014. doi:10.1007/978-94-6209-863-3_16.

Kornbluth, Sally. "Memo to the Faculty from Provost Sally Kornbluth Duke and the Development of Duke Kunshan University." March 16, 2016.

National Bureau of Statistics of China. "Number of Students of Formal Education by Type and Level (2015)." In "China Statistical Yearbook-2016." China Statistics, 2016. Press. http://www.stats.gov.cn/tjsj/ndsj/2016/indexeh.htm.

Pun, Raymond. "The Value of Intellectual Freedom in Twenty-First-Century China: Changes, Challenges, and Progress." *Library Trends* 64, no. 3 (Winter 2016): 556–71. http://search.proquest.com/docview/1783939131/abstract/C625DA002F254AFFPQ/1.

Rogerson, Kenneth, Edith Allen, Linda Daniel, Li Hui, and Deedra McClearn. "ERIC Grant Proposal: Critical Thinking Skills at Duke Kunshan University: Workshop, Study Group, and Best Practices." February 15, 2016.

Roth, Michael S. *Beyond the University: Why Liberal Education Matters*. New Haven: Yale University Press, 2014.

US Congress, House of Representatives, Committee on Foreign Affairs, Hearings before the Subcommittee on Africa, Global Health, Global Human Rights, and International Organizations: Is Academic Freedom Threatened by China's Influence on U.S. Universities? 114th Cong., 1st sess., 2015.

Xinying, Zhao. "China Has 1 in 5 of All College Students in the World: Report." *China Daily*. April 8, 2016. http://www.chinadaily.com.cn/china/2016-04/08/content_24365038.htm.

CHAPTER TWENTY-THREE

African Poetry Libraries—

A Global Collaboration

Lorna Dawes and Charlene Maxey-Harris

Introduction

In 2014, the African Poetry Book Fund[1] (APBF) and the University of Nebraska-Lincoln (UNL) literary magazine, the *Prairie Schooner*, established African Poetry Libraries in five countries—Botswana, Gambia, Ghana, Kenya, and Uganda—to support the creativity of aspiring and established poets in their local communities. The UNL librarians were asked to serve as consultants on the initiative by working with local volunteers to set up the libraries and provide ongoing assistance and advice to the new libraries during the first three years of their operation. The goals of the libraries are to support the local community of poets through access to contemporary poetry and to serve as a resource for poets interested in publication in Africa and around the world. The collections are comprised of solicited donations from US and UK publishers, and each library receives 300–400 books annually for the first three years, after which the libraries become completely self-directed and self-sufficient. This chapter will describe the highlights of this innovative initiative and the development of the partnership between the APBF and the University of Nebraska University Libraries that has shaped a global connection between literary arts organizations and publishers in the US and UK, African libraries, writer's co-ops, cultural centers, and poets.

As academic libraries are aligning their priorities to the campus directives and strategic plans, they are focusing on intercultural exchanges, global experiences, and knowledge brokering in new and exciting ways. New themes, like knowledge transfer and knowledge exchange, express the need for libraries to add value not only to their college and university but also to the local, national, and international community. The University of Hong Kong refocused its direction to a knowledge exchange emphasis by distributing grants to eight universities to support programs that engaged in knowledge exchange activities, such as exhibitions, book talks, and other innovative professional exchanges.[2] Themes supporting community engagement and global exchanges between academic libraries and the community are increasingly popular and more present in library mission statements as scholarly activities are encouraged to bridge the gap between the scholars and the public.[3]

African public libraries play an important role in community development. Greying and Zulu outline the monumental responsibility that these libraries have to preserve indigenous knowledge and folklore, produce creative work that increases engagement, disseminate knowledge throughout the community, and provide spaces for discussion.[4] Unfortunately, however, in some African countries, it is the community libraries that are taking on a similar role in meeting the essential needs of the community. Mostert, outlining norms for community libraries, explains that these community libraries are managed through participative governance, are community funded, provide inclusive services, have self-determined membership, provide access to community-relevant information, provide collaborative interactions between users and librarians, and foster cooperative relationships between the library and community groups. The ultimate goals are for the library to be proactively inclusive, engaged with the needs and interest of the community.[5] Similarly, du Plessis expressed the need for the "retooling" of African libraries to take ownership and be active with information transfer and sharing of written and oral traditions based on African culture and values instead of relying on the passive Western model.[6]

Documenting the impact of poetry in a community, although difficult to quantify, is very important to the poets, organizers, and audience that interacts in that space. The Library as Incubator Project is an organization that is facilitating and promoting poetry collections and collaborations between artists and libraries. The project highlights numerous writing and poetry collections and collaborations that are taking place in libraries across the nation and reveals that there are a few academic libraries organizing and supporting these endeavors.[7] Sjollema and Hanley studied the qualitative impact of using poetry-writing groups in developing communities in Montreal,[8] and although poetry is most often associated with therapy, the study reported the benefits of developing community action skills to maintain consistent participation, relationship building, and the writing and sharing of poetry. Ultimately, there were benefits to the creators and organizers in learning to write and develop social action agendas and challenges related to sustainability of the program.[9]

An intriguing project among poets, zoos, and public libraries is documented in *The Language of Conservation*, as it chronicles the development and assessment of a model for a collaborative research project over three years.[10] In the study, The Poets House in New York, the New York Wildlife Conservation Society, and a select group of public libraries forged partnerships to increase access to poetry by making connections with nature and by leveraging the common desire to preserve stories and make poetry more accessible to the public through book donations and learning events. The project was designed to bring together these entities from five cities to enhance spaces in nature with poetry and provide a space for discussion, appreciation, and discovery. Poems strategically placed within zoos imprinted and expanded the educational experiences of the public.[11] The Poets House in New York was built in 1985 on the premise that poetry is to be shared, and it provides free access to a comprehensive open-stacks collection of poetry in addition to hosting and organizing poetry events and workshops.[12] It is from the Poets House model that the African Poetry Book Fund Library was developed.

Based on a personal relationship, Dr. Kwame Dawes, editor of the *Prairie Schooner* and an English professor at UNL, approached two members of the library faculty, Lorna Dawes and Charlene Maxey-Harris, about his work in the African Poetry Book Fund and the establishment of the African Poetry Libraries project. The libraries were born out of a need to support the local poets in their writing: "The project was prompted by the observation by our editorial board that much of the poetry we were seeing in our contests and in the submissions for publication, revealed a distinctive lack of exposure of the writers to contemporary poetry."[13] It is the hope that access to the work of contemporary poets will impact the writing of local poets that continues to energize this project. The goal of the partnership was to seek the expertise of the UNL library faculty to help with establishing the libraries, selecting suitable venues, consulting on the organization of the collection, and the training and management of the volunteers. A letter of memorandum with the *Prairie Schooner* was drafted, addressing scope, rationale, and responsibilities in the project, and the three-year pilot timeline was set. The UNL librarians consulted with the poets and volunteers to select suitable spaces, set up and manage the library collections, and plan events. The APBF Libraries Facebook page and website were set up and managed by the UNL librarians to facilitate communication between the African poetry libraries and to support and publicize the libraries' activities and events.

In the letter of memorandum, the UNL librarians committed time for managing and administrating the collection through consultation, working with APBF to identify the libraries, and assisting with the promotion of the project. Most of the work by the librarians involved selecting appropriate locations, organizing the collection, defining the process for book preparation, and mailing the contents to the respective libraries. Additional time was spent simplifying and documenting the library management procedures in a manual for the volunteers to use. The librarians work with the *Prairie Schooner* during the summer months to prepare and process the shipment of books for delivery. After the initial delivery, the librarians make monthly efforts via email to obtain consistent feedback from the volunteers about their programs and events, giving them opportunities to discuss problems and issues pertaining to the setting up and management of the library. After three years, the letter of memorandum will be revisited to evaluate the libraries' involvement and continued partnership. A change in the leadership of the *Prairie Schooner* will move the project elsewhere, but this will not sever the partnership that is already established among the UNL Libraries, APBF, and the African Poetry Libraries. If this occurs, the memorandum will be re-examined at that time and UNL librarians will continue to support the African Poetry Libraries. It is the intention of the librarians to establish connections with other academic libraries that would like to be involved in the project by adopting and supporting the poetry libraries as they become self-sufficient and are no longer officially supported by the APBF. This will ensure the viability of the poetry libraries and allow for continued UNL Libraries' involvement in the project.

Identifying Local African Partners and Selecting Library Locations

The African Poetry Libraries are reading libraries that serve poets, lovers of poetry, and new audiences. They are located in public spaces that are run by teams of writers and art supporters. Identifying suitable local partners was imperative if the libraries were going to have an impact on the community and were going to remain and thrive after the initial support from the African Poetry Book Fund. The most efficient way of identifying poets willing to take on such responsibilities was through a combination of actively pursuing connections in specific countries and receiving inquiries from poet groups who had heard about the project through conferences and social media. Criteria for selecting the sites involved

- the identification of an individual willing to spearhead the establishment of the library in the country in question and willing to either staff the library themselves or find volunteers to do so;
- locating a venue that was open, secure, and accessible to everyone interested in using the facility and accessing the books and journals (the venue had to be capable of shelving up to 1,500 titles and include a space to allow for reading); and
- identifying a core of individuals and organizations on the ground willing to, and capable of, making the library sustainable for the long-term.

Partners were to be connected to the poetry groups in their area and have the capability to work with volunteers to maintain and manage the library collection. Five key regions in Africa were targeted, and poets with connections to APBF or the *Prairie Schooner* editor were contacted to see if they (or any other poets) would be interested in piloting a library. The response was encouraging, and five countries were selected. All libraries were located in established facilities: two in established libraries—Botswana and Ghana—and three in arts cultural centers—Uganda, The Gambia, and Kenya. These different locations have created an eclectic array of community libraries, all having unique advantages and challenges that have contributed to their success and impact.

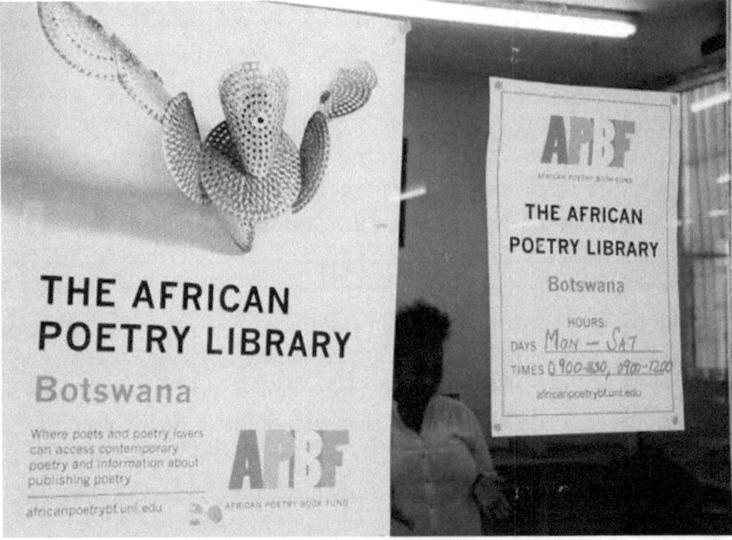

Figure 23.1. Botswana Library

All libraries were spearheaded by renowned poets and academics. A published poet based in London and the Gambia, Kadija Sesay George, acquired the location arranging for the collection to be housed in an unused annex of the National Center of the Arts and Culture in the Greater Banjul area. The location was easily accessible with a spacious reading room, computer workspace, a small workshop/presentation area, and an outside grounds area that provides room for events and seating. Poet TJ Dema in Botswana made contacts and arranged with Keleapere Makgoeng, a public librarian at the Botswana Public Library, to host the Botswana library. Poet Beverley Nambozo Nsengiyunva in

Uganda collaborated with Fred Batale at the 32° Ugandan Arts Trust, and in Kenya, poets Michael Onsando and Clifton Gachagua were instrumental in setting up the library, first with Eliphas Nyamogo at the Goethe-Institut and then arranging for it to be moved to its final destination at Kwani Trust. In Ghana, Dr. Helen Yitah, a professor at the University of Ghana, made the necessary contacts and arrangements for the George Padmore Research Library in Accra to host the library, where Gheysika Agambila and volunteers from the Ghana Association of Writers manage the day to day operations of the library.

The Collections: US and International Publishers

Recognizing that many poets in Africa have limited access to contemporary poetry due to poor distribution and the high costs of books, the libraries are supplied by the African Poetry Book Fund through its partnership with various organizations around the US and the UK. Each year, the APBF sends approximately three hundred titles to each library. The books are new, and although an important part of the project's goals is to build a list of African titles, the collections currently represent contemporary world poetry and are comprised of donations from more than thirty-six publishers, presses, foundations, and individuals. Books that are not donated directly from publishers arrive from the "review copies" stacks of partnering literary journals across the US. Books are distributed randomly to the libraries, taking into consideration special subject requests and cultural or religious concerns. All libraries are guaranteed books for the first three years, depending on their ability to accommodate the collection, and managers are encouraged to make connections with publishers in their region for additional donations. This initial partnership with the UNL libraries requires minimal monetary investment and is based on the global exchange of information and consultation and networking with scholarly communications departments and publishers. Personal donations of books have also been received, and in 2015, Elizabeth Alexander, chancellor of the Academy of American Poets, donated fifty copies of her new book, *The Light of the World*, to each library to be used as prizes and book club readings.

The Libraries: Administration and Programming

These libraries are managed by volunteers and poets who may not have any experience working with collections, so the UNL librarians made the decision for the libraries to be non-circulating collections during the first three years while they were in their infancy. This would ensure the security of the collection, allow the libraries to become established, and give the coordinators the time to find and train volunteers and work through any management issues before making any circulation loaning decisions. The UNL librarians work with the APBF and serve as library consultants and liaise with the libraries managers. They are available to answer questions pertaining to the management of day-to-day operations and serve as technical advisors and coordinators of the libraries. The librarians also work with the *Prairie Schooner* staff and student volunteers to organize the shipment and distribution of the books. The donated books are received by the *Prairie Schooner* office, where they are cataloged, stamped with the library APBF logo, and packaged by student volunteers using instructions from the African Poetry Library Manual,[14] a thirteen-page manual written by the UNL librarians. The manual provides directions for the receiving, unpacking, labeling, and shelving of the books in addition to containing instructions on how to set up the library, manage the daily operations, and search and print from the catalog. The books are cataloged before shipping in the APBF Libraries Union Catalog on *LibraryThing*, an open access catalog, that allows each library to view the collections in all the APBF Poetry Libraries and accommodates the cataloging of each library as a separate entity within the larger APBF collection.

The initial shipment of books was accompanied with a copy of the manual, publicity flyers and postcards, printed catalogs (author/title and alphabetical list), book spine labels, a visitor's sign-in book and a records book. To help with the setting up of the libraries, the manual also contained suggestions on how to arrange the library space, publicize the library, and how to manage the daily workflow. The librarians thought it was important to encourage the libraries to keep records and numbers of their daily activities and event participants; they included a records book in their shipment for this purpose. Periodically and at the end of each year, the libraries are required to submit a report to the APBF before the new shipment is sent off. This ensures that the libraries are still operational and allows the librarians to deal with any lingering issues before new books are shipped.

Programs and Events

The libraries all hosted extensive launch events, inviting local poets, academics, and government officials involved in the arts to participate and attend the events. After the first two years, there is evidence of the development of established programs and events at each location. It is obvious that the most valuable indicator of library success and impact is the presence and vitality of an established community of poets in the area.

The library in The Gambia provides an example of this success. The African Homecomer's Collective, a community poets group, provides the volunteers for staffing the library and together with SABLE Litmag have taken responsibility and ownership of the collection. The commitment of these volunteers to their poets group and the magazine has been the main impetus of this library's vibrancy. The Gambia library hosted opening events that spanned the weekend with seventy-five people attending, engaging adults, youths, and children in open-mic performances, workshops, and poetry readings. In the last two years, the library collection has been used to support several poetry workshops for local schools and is used extensively by a new poetry group, The Cloud, that now organizes regular poetry events in the library. The volunteers in this library continue to organize poetry readings and competitions and are very proactive as they endeavor to make new connections with other local groups of poets. The library has begun an outreach to the schools that involves hosting several workshops and has now requested more children's books to support this endeavor. Poet Kadija Sesay George was very instrumental in making this library visible. Her involvement with poets in The Gambia is remarkable. "The dream that the library will be a focal point, where young poets can develop their writing but also exchange ideas about how the Gambian people can get access to poetry, through books and readings" is her goal for The Gambia Poetry Library as she continues to publicize and garner support for poets and the library, *Ping*.[15]

At the launch of the Botswana Public Library, the site manager and public librarian, Keleapere Makogoeng, engaged primary school children in some creative writing workshops. These initial connections with the community were extremely effective in gaining support for the libraries and increasing usage. This opening event was attended by representatives from the Ministry of Youth, Sports, and Culture in addition to officials from the Botswana National Library Services and celebrated the poetry library and shared a vision of celebrating the spoken word through workshops for youth. In her keynote speech, poet TJ Dema announced that the existence of the poetry books was in line with the Botswana National Library Policy of 2013, and emphasized that the purpose of the collection was to "foster growth of a knowledge society through facilitating access to relevant, current and good quality information that supports lifelong learning and enhance the quality of life for all."[16]

The advantage of having the libraries adopted by established poetry groups is also evident in the caliber of the events at the Uganda library. In September 2014, the launch event was scheduled to be a part of the 32° Ugandan Arts Trust regional festival, and this allowed the event to feature the short-listed poets from the prestigious Babishai Niwe Poetry Awards in addition to the members of Uganda Women Writers Association, Makerere University Literature Students, and Kampala's Poetry In Session members. The Babishai Niwe Poetry Foundation also donated books to the library and committed to organize at least two readings a year. In addition to providing spaces for poets to gather and learn, the presence of these dedicated libraries has propelled critical conversations around poetry and its place in the society.

The Kenyan library launch at the Goethe-Institut, in addition to an eclectic selection of poetry readings and performances, hosted a panel discussion that explored the importance of libraries in the evolution of the poet and the negative impact of Kenyan educational and political systems on the production and publication of Kenyan poetry anthologies. Due to the generosity and commitment of Eliphas Nyamogo, the head of Information and Library Department at the Goethe-Institut, the Kenya library was housed at this location temporarily for one year and in June 2017, returned to its permanent home at Kwani Trust, now managed by Angela Wachuka and the new director, Velma Koome.

The Ghanaian Library is located in the George Padmore Research Library on African Affairs and is a part of the public library system. It is managed by the library staff and the Ghana Association of Writers volunteers but is the least active of all the poetry libraries. This may be due to the research nature of this special library that may not be highly used by poets and writers. The UNL librarians will continue to focus on this library after the initial three-year commitment, to explore ways to make this collection more accessible and beneficial to the local poets and writers.

The Future: Challenges, Opportunities, and Sustainability

In only three years, there is evidence that the African Poetry Libraries have been successful in hosting an eclectic assortment of events, actively supporting the community, and gaining the involvement of local poets, committed volunteers, and the library staff. The communities have taken ownership and created libraries that are unique to their cultures and cities. The most successful libraries have dedicated local poets and volunteer staff that organize events and manage the collection, facilitate the creation of new poetry groups, and support established writer's groups in the community. They have hosted poetry workshops in the schools, poetry competitions, scholarly discussions, and open-mic readings for children and adults, making new connections and establishing networks among poets, academics, and the community.

As the number of libraries increase and the first libraries are released from the initial three-year APBF support, other academic libraries, publishers, or literary organizations in the US and UK will be approached to adopt these libraries, to continue helping and advising the managers, and use their own networks to solicit and bolster the existing poetry collections. The partnership with *Prairie Schooner*, APBF and UNL Libraries will continue as new libraries are planted and these already-established libraries advise and help new libraries in other parts of the continent. The APBF is currently working on requests from Nigeria, Zimbabwe, and South Africa for the next round of libraries that will be launched in 2018. In 2016, APFB received an Honorable mention in the National Book Foundation Innovators Award,[17] and there is no doubt that this type of publicity will generate more support and publisher donations to the libraries.

One major challenge centers around issues related to space limitations and the need to find more public and accessible spaces to house the libraries. To date, volunteers have been very successful negotiating for such spaces, and this is important if the libraries are to be sustainable. The availability of such buildings with adequate space and suitable facilities may be difficult in other countries and so may require financial support in the future. The acquisition of permanent locations is important, but because these spaces need to be free and accessible to the public, this poses additional challenges that need to be addressed.

Recruiting and managing volunteers to work with a permanent collection can be very difficult. When poets or individuals partner to open a library, they commit to finding and managing volunteers, and the hours of operation and sustainability of the library is predicated on the availability of these volunteers. The recruitment, retention, and training require time and commitment that can be extremely challenging. When libraries are set up in already-established spaces—i.e., libraries and community centers—the volunteers assist the center staff, resulting in more structure in the management and more regular opening and closing hours; however, the volunteers may lack the autonomy they need to plan innovative events and have access to the collection after work hours. On the other hand, when volunteers alone manage libraries, regular hours may be difficult, but this independence may allow for more unconventional events and more community involvement. Finding a balance between the two organizational models is difficult to achieve.

The manual has been extremely helpful to the volunteers as they set up, organize, and manage the collections. The decision to catalog and process the books before shipping proved to be welcome and very successful and ensured a consistency in the catalog that would have been very difficult to achieve with the volunteer staff model that is at the core of these libraries. Although the libraries are initially set up as reading rooms only, after the first three years, each library will make its own decision on circulation policies. The UNL librarians determined this to be the best approach in order to give the libraries time to become established and to give the collection the opportunity to expand to a substantial size before opening the collection up for circulation. All of the libraries are encouraged to develop their own acquisition network, and it is the hope, especially if they are adopted by other academic organizations, that they will continue to add to their collection, acquiring donations from local African publishers and writers. The UNL librarians will be committed to consulting with these libraries as they develop and grow, working with them to select lending models and develop policies that are suitable for their unique library community. The libraries, once established, will be autonomous.

Communication with the libraries can be difficult. Although email is used, the internet access in some of the libraries can be expensive or absent, and this, together with time zone differences, can impede communication. Skype and Facebook messaging proved to be helpful to all but one of the libraries, although all the libraries mentioned their need to use social media more effectively to communicate and publicize events to the community. This is something that can be addressed by APBF and the UNL librarians through regular internal e-newsletters to all the libraries, which would include news and happenings from each site and other information to encourage a sense of community between the library managers and volunteers. A community cloud-sharing space would also be a welcome addition and would allow sites to upload images and videos more easily.

Gaining Support

These libraries are dependent on philanthropic donations and community support, and integral to their success is their ability to solicit and retain this support by demonstrating the impact they have on the community and the value they bring to the literary arts. Libraries have traditionally struggled with evaluation measures and have moved from internal measurements that support the strength of their collections to outward performance indicators that support the strength of their services to the community.[18] The Free Library of Philadelphia implements a pallet of tools and strategies to evaluate and communicate its impact in the city,[19] some of which are relevant and could be very effective in the African Poetry libraries. Closter suggests connecting programs with larger societal literacy issues and articulating these clearly in the library strategic plan as an avenue for communicating value and soliciting funding.[20] As the UNL librarians continue to mentor the library managers, a more purposeful approach to evaluation will be taken to try to help the managers measure and document their impact based on their goals and the needs of the communities they serve. It will be important to spend some time with each library manager developing one or two achievable goals that they can focus on during each year. They may also coordinate with academic libraries sponsors to communicate with APBF and possibly organize the digital scholarship of the poets. University presses and libraries can host symposia for the poets to increase visibility for the projects.

What makes the African Poetry Book Libraries unique is the poetry community. It's a poet's library that inspires the written and spoken word in a specialized community library. Opportunities for sustainability lie in the creative outputs, awards, and partnerships with other academic institutes to share avenues for publishing and support for literary awards. For the future, there is a desire to collect non-English titles, understanding that such spaces that support print and oral traditions encourage the development of a reading culture and indigenous knowledge.[21] International library organizations, such as International Federation of Library Associations and Institutions (IFLA), are in place so that librarians can work together to meet the national library policies and initiatives as noted by the Botswana library organizer. These libraries are determined to meet the cultural needs of the community and not only incorporate the Western values or traditions.

Academic libraries as a collaborative partner gently wraps around the African libraries' needs and provides a structure and collection based on the literary partners. In many ways, academic libraries can build bridges between poets, reading culture, scholarly networks, African librarians, and information specialists. Agyemang draws attention to the struggle and survival of community libraries in Ghana. These African libraries, now supported, may continue to develop and connect with larger public libraries or cultural arts networks for survival.[22]

The goal of this project was not only to create dynamic resources centers but to create sustainable physical and virtual spaces to inspire poets and encourage the writing of poetry. The path to establishing a sustainable collection will not be complete in three years, so the partnership will continue, and future directions for this project will entail the continued consultant support for the management of the collections, enhancing the accessibility of open education resources for the arts and the planting of new libraries in other parts of the continent. The APBF will attempt to investigate how the poetry libraries impact the African poets' scholarship and publishing record, as this was one of the initial goals of the project. Academic libraries can play a vital role by first aligning strategic goals with campus entities and global efforts that enhance teaching and learning, and by actively promoting and contributing their expertise to non-academic libraries of this nature.

This case study highlights strong partnerships between a literary magazine, a faculty initiative, and an academic library that has shaped a global connection of outreach to African communities by linking them to scholarly, community, and literary exchanges fulfilling the values of the university community.

Notes

1. The African Poetry Book Fund, the brainchild of founding editor and director Dr. Kwame Dawes, promotes and advances the development and publication of the poetic arts through its book series, contests, workshops, and seminars, and through its collaborations with publishers, festivals, booking agents, colleges, universities, conferences and all other entities that share an interest in the poetic arts of Africa.
2. Peter E. Sidorko and Tina T. Yang. "Knowledge Exchange and Community Engagement: An Academic Library Perspective," *Library Management* 32, no. 6 (2011): 386.
3. Jack Hang Tat Leong, "Community Engagement—Building Bridges between University and Community by Academic Libraries in the 21st Century," *Libri: International Journal of Libraries & Information Services* 63, no. 3 (September 2013): 220.
4. Elizabeth Greyling and Sipho Zulu, "Content Development in an Indigenous Digital Library: A Case Study in Community Participation," *IFLA Journal* 36, no. 1 (March 1, 2010): 31.
5. B. J. Mostert, "Community Libraries: The Concept and Its Application—with Particular Reference to a South African Community Library System," *International Information and Library Review* 30 (1998): 76–77.
6. J. C. du Plessis, "'From Food Silos to Community Kitchens'—Retooling African Libraries," *International Information and Library Review* 40, no. 1 (2008): 49.
7. The Library as Incubator Project, http://www.libraryasincubatorproject.org/?page_id=9.
8. Sandra D. Sjollema and Jill Hanley, "When Words Arrive: A Qualitative Study of Poetry as a Community Development Tool," *Community Development Journal* 49, no. 1 (2014): 55.
9. Ibid., 64.
10. Jane Preston, Institute of Museum and Library Services (US), and Poets House (Firm). *The Language of Conservation* (New York: Poets House, 2013), xvii.
11. Ibid.,16.
12. Poets House. "About Poets House."

13. Kwame Dawes, "African Poetry Book Fund Libraries," email, February 3, 2014.
14. Lorna Dawes and Charlene Maxey-Harris, "African Poetry Book Fund-African Poetry Library Manual: How to Manage and Set up the Library," University of Nebraska-Lincoln Digital Commons, 2014, http://digitalcommons.unl.edu/libraryscience/346/.
15. Ingela Hofsten, "Library Paves the Way for African Poetry," *Ping* 1, no. 3 (2016): 46.
16. Kea Leboga, "Poetry Corner Launch at the Gaborone Public Library, Botswana," presented at the Gaborone Public Library, Botswana, November 14, 2014, 1.
17. Jennifer Baker, "National Book Foundation Celebrates Innovators of Reading Encouraging Philanthropy for More Literacy," *Forbes Magazine*, February 14, 2016.
18. Matthew Closter, "Public Library Evaluation: A Retrospective on the Evolution of Measurement Systems," *Public Library Quarterly* 34, no. 2 (2015): 2.
19. The Pew Charitable Trust, "The Library in the City: Changing Demands and a Challenging Future," http://www.pewtrusts.org/en/research-and-analysis/reports/2012/03/07/the-library-in-the-city-changing-demands-and-a-challenging-future.
20. Closter, "Public Library Evaluation," 113.
21. Franklin Gyamfi Agyemang, "Community Libraries in Ghana: The Struggle, Survival, and Collapse," *International Information & Library Review* (2017), 6.
22. Ibid.

Bibliography

Agyemang, Franklin Gyamfi. "Community Libraries in Ghana: The Struggle, Survival, and Collapse." *International Information & Library Review* (2017), 1–12.

Baker, Jennifer. "National Book Foundation Celebrates Innovators of Reading Encouraging Philanthropy for More Literacy." *Forbes Magazine*. February 14, 2016.

Closter, Matthew. "Public Library Evaluation: A Retrospective on the Evolution of Measurement Systems." *Public Library Quarterly* 34, no. 2 (2015): 107–23.

Dawes, Kwame. "African Poetry Book Fund Libraries." Email. February 3, 2014.

Dawes, Lorna, and Charlene Maxey-Harris. "African Poetry Book Fund-African Poetry Library Manual: How to Manage and Set up the Library." University of Nebraska-Lincoln Digital Commons, 2014. http://digitalcommons.unl.edu/libraryscience/346/.

du Plessis, J. C. "'From Food Silos to Community Kitchens'—Retooling African Libraries." *International Information and Library Review* 40, no. 1 (2008): 43–51. doi:10.1080/10572317.2008.10762761.

Greyling, Elizabeth, and Sipho Zulu. "Content Development in an Indigenous Digital Library: A Case Study in Community Participation." *IFLA Journal* 36, no. 1 (March 1, 2010): 30–39. doi:10.1177/0340035209359570.

Hang Tat Leong, Jack. "Community Engagement—Building Bridges between University and Community by Academic Libraries in the 21st Century." *Libri: International Journal of Libraries & Information Services* 63, no. 3 (September 2013): 220–31.

Hofsten, Ingela. "Library Paves the Way for African Poetry." *Ping* 1, no. 3 (2016): 40–47.

Leboga, Kea. "Poetry Corner Launch at the Gaborone Public Library, Botswana." Presented at the Gaborone Public Library, Botswana, November 14, 2014.

The Library as Incubator Project. "About." *Library as Incubator*. May 25, 2011, http://www.libraryasincubatorproject.org/?page_id=9.

Mostert, B. J. "Community Libraries: The Concept and Its Application—with Particular Reference to a South African Community Library System." *International Information and Library Review* 30 (1998): 71–85.

The Pew Charitable Trust. "The Library in the City: Changing Demands and a Challenging Future." http://www.pewtrusts.org/en/research-and-analysis/reports/2012/03/07/the-library-in-the-city-changing-demands-and-a-challenging-future.

Poets House. "About Poets House." *Poets House*. May 27. 2017, https://www.poetshouse.org/about.

Preston, Jane. Institute of Museum and Library Services (U.S.), and Poets House (Firm). *The Lan-*

guage of Conservation. New York: Poets House, 2013.

Sidorko, Peter E., and Tina T. Yang. "Knowledge Exchange and Community Engagement: An Academic Library Perspective". *Library Management* 32, no. 6 (2011): 385-397.

Sjollema, Sandra D., and Jill Hanley. "When Words Arrive: A Qualitative Study of Poetry as a Community Development Tool." *Community Development Journal* 49, no. 1 (2014): 54–68.

CHAPTER TWENTY-FOUR

Undergraduate Education Abroad in Community Settings:

Pedagogical Opportunities for Librarians

Laurie Kutner

Introduction

As undergraduate possibilities for study and service abroad increase and develop strategically to address local community needs in settings in the Global South,[1] there is greater opportunity for academic librarians to contribute expertise in supporting and facilitating student learning and engagement with research and information concepts and processes. Education abroad experiences are considered high-impact educational practices[2] and, as such, provide excellent vantage points from which to consider contextualizing engagement with the expanded construct of information literacy as described in ACRL's Framework for Information Literacy for Higher Education.[3] Utilizing a case study of a pilot project, this chapter focuses on initial work to incorporate critical information literacy concepts into international applied learning settings. The setting for this case study is the Monteverde Institute (MVI) in Costa Rica, a Costa Rican non-profit organization that provides a teaching and learning setting and essential infrastructure for North American education abroad programs.

Throughout this chapter, the term "education abroad" is used predominantly to describe American student learning experiences abroad that happen in a variety of venues. Consistent with the most recent iteration of the ACE (American Council on Education) national survey entitled "Mapping Internationalization on U.S. Campuses,"[4] the term "education abroad" is favored over the term "study abroad" to reflect the range of American student international experiences that may include research, service-learning, internships, and other activities that all contribute to student learning and development.[5] The Monteverde Institute hosts a variety of research-based and service-based education abroad programs of varying durations, as well as student internships and shorter-term travel study programs.

This chapter focuses on work done on-site in the summer of 2017, when the author participated in activities in two education abroad programs at the MVI and subsequently presented and facilitated a one-hour long discussion in each program entitled, "Equity Issues in Scholarly Access and Production: A View from Latin America." At the beginning of the discussion, students were given a directed reflective question to consider during the course of the presentation and asked to form a written response that was handed in at the end of the session. The content of the presentation, a summary of student reflective responses, and the author's reflections on the experience are presented below.

Background/ Literature Review

There are several trends in higher education that set the context for this work and demonstrate that a timely opportunity exists for academic librarians to leverage their skill set to make meaningful pedagogical contributions to education abroad programs. By considering the interrelationships of these disparate trends, new possibilities emerge for librarian contributions to education abroad instructional content, including

- pedagogical opportunities created by engaging with the ACRL Framework for Information Literacy, with a focus on the external social, contextual aspects of information;
- increased emphasis in higher education on high-impact practices such as global education, undergraduate research, and service;
- increasing numbers of students in education abroad programs;
- expansion of education abroad locations to include more community settings in the Global South;
- impacts of international service-learning and research activities on host communities and the need for equitable distribution of benefits; and
- academic library contributions to campus internationalization efforts.

According to the latest Open Doors Report released by the Institute of International Education in 2016, the number of American students studying abroad has continued to increase. Students engaging in education abroad experiences have more than tripled in the past ten years, though more recently the rate of growth is slowing. Destinations for education abroad in Latin America are also increasing, and Costa Rica is leading the way with a growth rate of 8 percent in the past year, hosting approximately 9,300 students.[6] The Monteverde Institute alone hosted approximately 500 students participating in community-based education abroad programs in varying capacities in their most recent fiscal year.[7]

In 2008, American Association of Colleges & Universities published George Kuh's seminal study entitled, "High Impact Educational Practices: What They Are, Who Has Access to Them, and Why They Matter."[8] Based on decades of research, he substantiated that "participating in certain high-impact educational practices correlates with higher levels of student performance."[9] In his study, Kuh identified ten high-impact practices, including diversity/global learning, service-learning, community-based learning, undergraduate research, internships, and capstone courses and projects,[10] all of which fall under the realm of MVI programmatic offerings. Though these practices are not new, after the publication of Kuh's research, there was an effort to systematically document the impact of these practices and view multiple high-impact practices as important elements of an undergraduate education.[11]

A 2013 study done by Riehle and Weiner examined incorporation of information literacy competency development into five specific high-impact educational practices and confirmed that these are excellent vantage points from which to engage students in information literacy-related themes. Through the literature they examined, they provide substantial evidence of this occurring within the context of high-impact educational practices, though they note that the term "information literacy" is not necessarily used in disciplinary literature to describe the set of abilities and habits of mind that our profession refers to as IL.[12] Their research was conducted before the adoption of the current ACRL Framework for Information Literacy, which provides potential for further articulations of intersections of information literacy with high-impact learning practices.

While the theme of student learning is a predominant focus of the education abroad literature, there is a growing body of literature which focuses on impacts of education abroad and international service experiences, both positive and negative, on host communities in the Global South.[13] Increasingly, there is recognition that education abroad experiences should not only be evaluated from the student learning perspective, but also from home and host institution programmatic perspectives, and as well from the host community perspective.[14] An unexplored theme in the education abroad literature is the potential value of new information and knowledge generated by students that can make long-term contributions to a host community knowledge-base, particularly in community-based settings. This theme was explored in the library literature in an article that discusses the importance of providing open access to student research-based information generated through local community research in Monteverde, Costa Rica.[15]

The ACRL Framework for Information Literacy for Higher Education, formally adopted in January, 2016, provides six "interconnected core concepts," or frames, that are a set of "conceptual understandings" with which to develop in students the increasingly complex understandings of our information ecosystem, both as consumers of information and as active knowledge producers.[16] While the previous ACRL Information Literacy Standards for Higher Education focused on the development of individual, reproducible skills, developing an understanding of the larger external social context of information is inherent in the new framework.[17] The importance of the social contextual aspect of information to the pedagogy behind the framework additionally encourages consideration of critical questions to develop a nuanced understanding of our information environment that preferences some and marginalizes others.[18]

The framework represents engagement with the growing area of critical information literacy. Early critical information literacy proponents elucidate the importance of developing a criticality in teaching about information by engaging with its larger, socio-political contexts.[19] "Critical information literacy …looks at the cultural, social, and economic structures that underlie all of information production and dissemination" and asks students to critically reflect on this larger underlying context of information, both as information producers and consumers.[20] As critical information literacy has developed, the literature demonstrates both an increasing depth and breadth of engagement with its constructs, both from theoretical and practitioner perspectives.[21]

When conversations ensued surrounding development of the framework, proponents of creating a separate frame on social justice elucidated the importance of engagement with underlying issues of "unequal distribution of power, privilege, and authority" in developing a complex, critical understanding of our place in the information universe.[22] Though the framework ultimately emerged without social justice as a separate frame, opportunities for engagement with related concepts that are woven into it may be considered a result of those conversations, and the case study presented below is reflective of this.

As colleges and universities have become increasingly engaged in internationalization-related initiatives, library support and participation has been documented across all library functions.[23] Though the largest body of related literature focuses on supporting and working with international students,[24] there is a small body of literature on the roles of librarians supporting and interfacing with students in education abroad programs. Themes explored in this literature include provision of library resources and services for students in education abroad programs, ways in which to improve student awareness of utilizing their home institution libraries from abroad, opportunities for librarians to directly interface with students at all phases of their experience through both face-to-face and electronic means, and support for the dissemination of education abroad students' work.[25]

Librarians have also had the opportunity to partner with disciplinary faculty to lead education abroad programs[26] and to lead their own international service-learning programs.[27] More recently, there has been an emerging recognition of the potential for engaging with the ACRL Framework for Information Literacy in the context of high-impact educational practices such as education abroad experiences.[28] However, there has been no evidence to date of specific ways this has been accomplished at the time of student active engagement in education abroad. The case study outlined below begins to fill that gap.

Setting

The Monteverde Institute is located in Monteverde, Costa Rica, an area with a population of roughly 7,000 that is situated on the continental divide in the province of Puntarenas.[29] Monteverde is a rural Costa Rican community and a small North American Quaker community. Best known as an international eco-tourist destination due to its spectacular natural beauty, easily accessible high elevation cloud forest ecosystem, and extraordinary biodiversity, Monteverde sees about 250,000 tourists pass through each year.[30] Because of the area's unique history, its biodiversity and multiple tropical ecosystems, an early commitment to conservation and sustainability, as well as challenges associated with being both a small, rural community and a significant eco-tourist destination, it has additionally become an area that hosts a high number of international education programs.

The Monteverde Institute is the largest of three institutions that support education abroad programs in the area. Since its inception in 1987, the MVI has hosted almost 10,000 students, with a client base of over approximately 130 universities, high schools, and study programs.[31]

Study, research, and community are the three cornerstones of the MVI mission, and it is the interplay of these three facets that facilitates pedagogical opportunities for incorporating interaction with the information literacy frames elucidated in ACRL's Framework for Information Literacy. There is a commitment on the part of the MVI to share with the local community the results of research conducted under its auspices. Additionally, the MVI is home to a small library that supports its educational programs, and the author has worked closely with that library for over ten years.[32]

The author's strong connection with the MVI and a history of successful initiatives there enabled further opportunities to engage more directly with their courses and programs. In Summer 2016, the author proposed to MVI administration ideas and opportunities for utilizing her instruction librarian skill set to contribute more directly to MVI course content, pedagogy, and assessment. There was much support of the idea and, at the time, a decision to host a pilot project in Summer 2017.

The unique opportunity to be directly involved with international applied learning experiences at the time of active student engagement has provided an initial opportunity to participate in activities, listen to students, lead discussions, and provide reflective exercises to reinforce engagement with information literacy concepts for two courses. The remainder of this chapter focuses on the information literacy aspect of this pilot project.

The Courses

As a pilot project, the MVI staff and the author collectively decided which two courses would be best suited for incorporation of active information literacy engagement, based on course content and itinerary, the willingness of university instructors, and timing. The MVI staff were instrumental in facilitating the logistics involved in adding this into the courses, scheduling, and communication. The names of the courses and associated home institutions are not identified here due to the nature of this work as a pilot project. Instead, they are identified as Course A and Course B.

Course A was an international service-learning program with contextual activities and a research component incorporated into it, coming out of a private internationally known US research university. Participants were twelve undergraduates who had to go through a competitive application process in order to be selected for participation. The duration of the program was almost two months.

In Course A, the author participated in a number of learning activities with the students before leading an information literacy-focused activity, including an interpretive naturalist-led cloud forest ecology hike and two participatory lectures, one delivered by the resident expert naturalist educator and the other by an internationally known local scientist. Students were required to keep reflective journals and after these activities were asked to write a reflection about their preferred learning styles for active engagement with new information, considering the different ways that information was delivered to them in the first couple weeks of the course. Students were told that responses would be anonymously shared with the librarian. Their reflections were very helpful when considering how to best deliver the information literacy-related presentation and additionally framed the expectation that the librarian was an active participant in the course content.

Course B was a one-month program focused on learning about tropical ecology, collecting ecological field data, engaging with contextual and cultural Costa Rican background information, and creating a final presentation based on data collected in order to teach the processes involved in conducting ecological field research in an international setting. Interestingly, the course participants included fifteen undergraduates from the home institution, a small, private undergraduate university in the US, and three Costa Rican students who were selected to receive scholarships to participate in the course. The course was an upper-division biology course. In Course B, the librarian initially met the students by attending one participatory course activity focused on understanding Costa Rican cultural context. Because the duration of Course B was shorter than Course A, this was the only opportunity to engage with students before delivering the information literacy-related presentation to them. In retrospect, it was a sufficient opportunity to establish a connection to the program before leading the IL-related presentation and discussion with them.

Engaging Students at the MVI in an "Information Conversation"

The ACRL Framework for Information Literacy provides increasing recognition by our profession that there are important critical learning processes related to developing an understanding of information access and production processes from broader social, cultural and historical perspectives.[33] Concurrently, there is recognition that high-impact learning practices create excellent opportunities for engagement with information literacy concepts.[34] With this in mind, a program was created for students in the two MVI courses described above to consider questions related to equity issues in access to scholarly information as well as in scholarly production. Approaching these issues from the perspective of being actively engaged in experiential learning in Latin America, the hypothesis was that "a rich and timely pedagogical opportunity existed for students to engage with information social justice issues from a different perspective than when they are at their home institutions. International education programs, particularly in community-based locations in the Global South, provide excellent vantage points for impactful conversations regarding global and local inequities in access and production of scholarship."

Students in both courses participated in a one-hour long presentation and discussion, entitled, "Equity Issues in Scholarly Access and Production: A View from Latin America," that focused on consideration of the following overarching questions:

- Is the production of scholarship and access to information equitable across the world?
- Who benefits?
- Who loses?
- Why should we care?

Three basic learning outcomes were established which both guided development of the presentation and were driven by background research for the presentation:

1. Students begin to understand the economics of access to scholarly information and their privileged vantage point as North American university students. Concurrently, they develop an understanding of the implications of non-access to the body of proprietary scholarly resources.
2. Students begin to understand that production of scholarship is impacted by complex societal forces and consider this from a Latin American and global perspective, specifically with regard to advancing knowledge of complex global issues such as global climate change.
3. Students begin to understand the potential and importance of open access resources in the advancement of scholarship from a Latin American and global perspective.

See the Appendix 24A for a list of frames from the ACRL Framework and the connected knowledge practices and dispositions that were touched upon in the sessions. Additionally, in the Appendix, the three learning outcomes listed above are mapped to these knowledge practices and dispositions. A strength of the ACRL Framework for Information Literacy is that it is not meant to be prescriptive; the relationship between the learning outcomes and the framework developed organically through engagement with the presentation content.

Presentation Content

After presenting a brief introduction, context, and background information, the intent was to have a participatory conversation that would allow for collectively grappling with complex questions. We would frame and consider the issues from a local perspective, using local examples wherever possible.

Additionally, students were asked at the beginning of the session to consider themselves as the next generation of researchers that have the potential to work toward changing the way scholarship is produced and disseminated into the future. They were each given a copy of the following question on a slip of paper and were asked to write down two ideas that emerged for them during the session and hand them in upon leaving at the end as a reflective and reinforcing exercise.

> As future potential contributors to the scholarly information universe as the next generation of researchers ...what can the next generation of researchers do to work toward leveling the global information playing field?

Responses were compiled and are discussed in detail at the end of this section.

The first slide presented to the students was a screenshot of a Web of Science search using the keywords "monteverde costa rica" with search results arranged by "Times Cited." The search yielded 264 results; we noted that 263 of them were in English and one in Spanish, and 242 results were not in open access publications. A lively discussion immediately ensued as we deconstructed the search results and students made observations about language, accessibility,

journal titles represented, and the inherent irony in a highly cited author from whom they had received a lecture, who, by virtue of lack of a university affiliation, does not have the ability to afford a subscription to the journal in which he had published. We discussed ballpark figures for journal costs and for access to core scholarly databases such as Web of Science. We discussed local researchers losing the ability to access locally based research when the scholarship is exported and published in cost-prohibitive publications. But because of the vantage point from which we were discussing this, this was not an objective academic exercise. There was a personal connection to the place, the research, and the local researchers who students had met through various lectures and presentations. We then looked at a visual depiction of what major North American universities pay for Springer, Wiley, and Elsevier journal bundles. We turned to the local researchers present in the room to ask what they do when they need to get access to a journal article that they do not have the ability to access. Not surprisingly, local researchers make use of their social networks to individuals associated with Northern institutions to acquire the information they need.

The next question that we explored was where the researchers are coming from that are contributing to these core scholarly, peer-reviewed journals, and we looked at data presented in a 2017 article that was published in *Nature Climate Change* entitled, "Steps to Overcome the North-South Divide in Research Relevant to Climate Change Policy and Practice."[35] Close to 90 percent of the researchers included in this study came from OECD Northern countries, indicating a striking North-South divide in climate change research published in what has been established as the core scientific journals. This led to examining in some detail the question of what the implications are for Northern researchers clearly dominating the research arena of a truly global issue. What gets left out? How does this affect research priorities? How does this affect climate change policy? And what are the underlying societal forces that result in Southern countries' capacities to do research? With large international collaborative research projects, Southern countries may be represented but, almost without fail, lead authors tend to be from Northern countries. What are the overall effects of this unequal flow of information?

We looked at a couple of other studies that provided more support for these main themes and turned our discussion to implications of English being the dominating language of global scholarship.[36] We discussed questions of who is favored in a competition-based model of scholarship, what research questions are not being addressed, and thought about the range of good science that is potentially being missed and the implications of this. Throughout the discussion, which was supported with Latin American examples, students were actively engaged and recognized that these were important and compelling issues that they had never before considered.

The conversation then took a more positive turn as we moved on to discuss the possibilities afforded by an open access model of journal publication. Latin America has more open access journal publications than any other region of the world, and we discussed reasons for this.[37] We focused on the regional Latin American repository approach to providing a common platform for housing open access journals and discussed the two large regional repositories, ScieLO and Redalyc. We considered the potential implications of a sub-set of ScieLO journals that are now searchable through the Web of Science interface. We finished by looking at world internet access statistics and noting that in Latin America and the Global South, price is only one obstacle in the ability to access research and scholarship. The discussions were vibrant with wide student participation; if it were not for our time constraint, we could have continued in both presentations. At the end, students took a few minutes to compose their written responses to the prompt:

> As future potential contributors to the scholarly information universe as the next generation of researchers …what can the next generation of researchers do to work toward leveling the global information playing field?

Student Reflective Responses

The reasons for incorporating an exercise for students to create written suggestions to this prompt were multi-fold:

- It provided an opportunity for students to reflect on and critically apply information they had engaged with during the session.
- It provided a scenario that was relevant to them, particularly from being present

in the Latin American vantage point and allowed them to consider their defined priorities and verbalize them.

- It enabled students to provide an active voice for their opinions regarding shaping the future of the way scholarship gets produced and disseminated on a global scale.
- It provided an immediate reflective assessment tool for the instructor and the Monteverde Institute staff to understand how students engaged with the topics discussed.

A total of twenty-six responses were collected. Many of the responses at least partially focused on the importance of open access publications for the widest dissemination of scholarship. But they went beyond articulating a passive importance to playing a direct, more active role:

- "Submit work to open access journals. Try to convince institutions to submit articles to open access."
- "Contribute as peer-reviewer for open access journals."
- "Help with the language barrier by doing some translation work."
- "Work within open access publications. As editor? As translator?"

There was also a strong theme of the importance of making research available in multiple languages:

- "Publish articles in languages in addition to English."
- "Translate into more languages."
- "As a Spanish speaker, make sure that my research is available in more than one language."
- "Publish in a way that can be translated easily into other languages."

Finally, a strong concern for inclusion of local researchers and for making results of research available to local populations was articulated:

- "Share it with the community where the research takes place. Implement programs at schools and high schools to share with them all this info."
- "Requirement for open access publication in [the] country that research study is being done in."
- "Publish research in the country in which it was conducted, not just the country where your university is."
- "Collaborate with local researchers."
- "Rely more on local workers for research assistants; try to keep research local so it can maintain a local presence."
- "Science that is conducted abroad needs to be published abroad first."
- "Publish new findings in [the] local newspaper using local high schoolers to rewrite what was found in a fashion that locals would be able to comprehend. Take local students into the field when collecting data."
- "Researchers (should) do more to present and contextualize their work for the populations under study."

Reflections/Future Plans

ACRL's Framework for Information Literacy has provided the pedagogical basis for engaging in conversation with students about inequities of access to and production of scholarship from a Latin American perspective. The unique vantage point and willingness on the part of program instructors provided an excellent opportunity to engage students in a focused, critical discussion of the broader contextual aspects of the global scholarly information ecosystem in ways that would be extremely challenging, if not impossible, to replicate while at their home institutions during the course of a regular semester. An overarching theme of information social justice permeated the discussion but with an additional experiential, place-based connection.

The reflective responses presented above demonstrate that students processed the information presented and discussed and were able to synthesize and further articulate ideas for working toward future greater equity in access to and production of scholarship. Based on oral feedback from course instructors, students, and staff at the Monteverde Institute, this small pilot project has supported the initial hypothesis that "international education programs, particularly in community-based locations in the Global South, provide excellent opportunities for impactful conversations regarding global and local inequities in access and production of scholarship." It has confirmed the value in further and wider subsequent engagement with the presented content.

The Monteverde Institute staff member present at the second session has since adapted the content for her own presentation to the summer internship students at the MVI. She plans on continuing to foundationally present it to other student groups at the MVI. From her perspective, the context provided in this presentation creates important meaning for students who are asked to leave the final products of their research behind so that the MVI can make it openly accessible in its digital library collections. An important intent of this conversation has been for students to further understand that the research they conduct while in the area is potentially valuable to the host community, and that access to the information they generate and dissemination of that information is their lasting contribution.

The success of the pilot project was impacted by the author's previously existing relationship with the MVI and the resulting confidence with which the MVI enabled and facilitated its logistics. The digital library projects that the author directed at the MVI over the years were focused on creating greater accessibility to locally based research through open access venues and were framed with an information social justice perspective that the MVI leadership was familiar with. Therefore, they recognized the importance and relevance of discussing this with students. MVI staff that attended the presentations were active, engaged participants that brought important perspectives to the discussion.

Current plans are to expand and update the content next year when the author is again on-site and to deliver it to an increased number of programs during that time. More formal mechanisms of assessment of the session's learning outcomes, as well as related wider programmatic outcomes, will also be further discussed next year as part of a larger project to develop systematic assessment strategies for determining long-term impacts of MVI programs.

In conversations thus far, an information literacy lens from which to contribute to programmatic content and assessment efforts has proven to be relevant and valued. From a librarian perspective, it has been extremely heartening to hear instructors and administrators of education abroad programs refer to "information literacy" as something relevant to what they do. Though this chapter presents one case study in a unique location with a unique set of circumstances, it hopefully points to further possibilities for unique librarian pedagogical contributions to education abroad.

Appendix 24A: ACRL Framework knowledge practices and dispositions addressed in the session with associated learning outcomes

Frame: Information has Value

(Knowledge practices). Learners who are developing their information literate abilities

- understand how and why some individuals or groups of individuals may be underrepresented or systematically marginalized within the systems that produce and disseminate information (learning outcomes 1, 2);
- recognize issues of access or lack of access to information sources (learning outcomes 1, 2, 3); and
- decide where and how their information is published (learning outcomes 1, 3).

Frame: Information Creation as a Process

(Knowledge practices). Learners who are developing their information literate abilities

- articulate the capabilities and constraints of information developed through various creation processes (learning outcomes 2, 3);
- recognize that information may be perceived differently based on the format in which it is packaged (learning outcomes 1, 2, 3); and
- monitor the value that is placed on different types of information products in varying contexts (learning outcomes 1, 2, 3).

Frame: Authority is Constructed and Contextual

(Dispositions). Learners who are developing their information literate abilities

- develop awareness of the importance of assessing content with a skeptical stance and with a self-awareness of their own biases and worldview (learning outcomes 1, 2);
- question traditional notions of granting authority and recognize the value of diverse ideas and worldviews (learning outcomes 1, 2); and
- are conscious that maintaining these attitudes and actions requires frequent self-evaluation (learning outcomes 1, 2, 3).

Frame: Scholarship as Conversation

(Dispositions). Learners who are developing their information literate abilities

- recognize that systems privilege authorities and that not having a fluency in the language and process of a discipline disempowers their ability to participate and engage (learning outcomes 1, 2, 3).

Notes

1. The term "Global South" is used here to refer to the lower income, more impoverished areas in the world that lie predominantly in Africa, Asia, Latin America, and Oceania. It is used as an alternative to the stigmatized terms "developing countries" and "Third World." For further discussion about the term, see: Nour Dados and Raewyn Connell, "The Global South," *Contexts* 11, no.1 (2012): 12–13; United Nations Development Programme, "Forging a Global South: United Nations Day for North-South Cooperation" (2004), accessed October 4, 2017, http://www.undp.org/content/dam/china/docs/Publications/UNDP-CH-PR-Publications-UN-Day-for-South-South-Cooperation.pdf; "North and South, The (Global)," in *International Encyclopedia of the Social Sciences*, ed. William A. Darity (Detroit: MacMillan Reference U.S.A., 2008), 5: 542–44.
2. George D. Kuh, *High-Impact Educational Practices: What They Are, Who Has Access to Them, and Why They Matter* (Washington, DC: Association of American Colleges & Universities, 2008).
3. Association of College and Research Libraries, "Framework for Information Literacy for Higher Education" (2016), accessed July 19, 2017, http://www.ala.org/acrl/standards/ilframework.
4. American Council on Education, "Mapping Internationalization on U.S. Campuses," (2017), accessed July 20, 2017, http://www.acenet.edu/news-room/Pages/Mapping-Internationalization-on-U-S-Campuses.aspx.
5. Robin Helms, "Mapping Internationalization 2016: Updates, Improvements, and What We Hope to Learn," *Higher Education Today: A Blog by ACE*, February 12, 2016, http://www.higheredtoday.org/2016/02/12/mapping-internationalization-on-u-s-campuses-2016-updates-improvements-and-what-we-hope-to-learn/.
6. Institute of International Education, "Open Doors 2016 Executive Summary" (2016), accessed July 20, 2017, http://www.iie.org/en/Why-IIE/Announcements/2016-11-14-Open-Doors-Executive-Summary.
7. Monteverde Institute, *Executive Director's Report 2016*. (unpublished).
8. Kuh, *High Impact Educational Practices*.
9. George D. Kuh, "Why Integration and Engagement are Essential to Effective Educational Practice in the Twenty-first Century," *Peer Review* 10, no. 4 (2008): 27.
10. Kuh, *High Impact Educational Practices*.
11. Susan Albertine and Tia Brown MacNair, "Seeking High-Quality, High-Impact Learning: The Imperative of Faculty Development and Curricular Intentionality," *Peer Review* 14, no. 3 (2012), accessed July 20, 2017, http://www.aacu.org/publications-research/periodicals/seeking-high-quality-high-impact-learning-imperative-faculty.
12. Catherine Fraser Riehle and Sharon A. Weiner, "High-Impact Educational Practices: An Exploration of the Role of Information Literacy," *College & Undergraduate Libraries* 20, no. 2 (2013): 127–43.
13. Robbin D. Crabtree, "The Intended and Unintended Consequences of International Service-Learning," *Journal of Higher Education Outreach and Engagement* 17, no. 2 (2013): 43–66; Jennifer Kozak and Marianne Larsen, "ISL and Host Communities—Relationships and Responsibilities," in *International Service Learning: Engaging Host Communities*, ed. Marianne Larsen. (New York: Routledge, 2016), 263–76.
14. Margaret Sherraden, Benjamin J. Lough, and Amy Bopp, "Students Serving Abroad: A Framework for Inquiry," *Journal of Higher Education Outreach and Engagement* 17, no. 2 (2013): 7–40.
15. Laurie Kutner, "Study-Abroad Programs as Information Producers: An Expanding Role for Support of Our Students Studying Abroad," *Journal of Library Administration* 50, no. 7/8 (2010): 767–78.
16. Association of College and Research Libraries, "Framework for Information Literacy for Higher Education."
17. Nancy M. Foasberg, "From Standards to Frameworks for IL: How the ACRL Framework Addresses Critiques of the Standards," *portal: Libraries and the Academy* 15, no. 4 (2015): 699–717.
18. Kevin Seeber, "This Is Really Happening: Criticality and Discussions of Context in ACRL'S Framework for Information Literacy," *Communications in Information Literacy* 9, no. 2 (2015): 157–63.

19. James Elmborg, "Critical Information Literacy: Implications for Instructional Practice," *The Journal of Academic Librarianship* 32, no. 2 (2006): 192–99; Heidi LM Jacobs, "Information Literacy and Reflexive Pedagogical Praxis," *The Journal of Academic Librarianship* 34, no. 3 (2008): 256–62.
20. Annie Downey, *Critical Information Literacy: Foundations, Inspiration, and Ideas* (Sacramento, CA: Library Juice Press, 2016), 18.
21. Nicole Pagowsky and Kelly McElroy, eds., *Critical Library Pedagogy Handbook*, 2 vols. Chicago: Association of College and Research Libraries, 2016; Eamon Tewell, "A Decade of Critical Information Literacy: A Review of the Literature," *Communications in Information Literacy* 9, no. 1 (2015): 24–43.
22. Andrew Battista, Dave Ellenwood, Lua Gregory, Shana Higgins, Jeff Lilburn, Yasmin Sokkar Harker, and Christopher Sweet, "Seeking Social Justice in the ACRL Framework," *Communications in Information Literacy* 9, no. 2 (2015): 111–25.
23. Steven Witt, Laurie Kutner, and Elizabeth Cooper, "Mapping Academic Library Contributions to Campus Internationalization," *College and Research Libraries* 76, no. 5 (2015): 587–608.
24. Amanda B. Click, Claire Walker Wiley, and Meggan Houlihan, "The Internationalization of the Academic Library: A Systematic Review of 25 Years of Literature on International Students," *College & Research Libraries* 78, no. 3 (2017): 328–58; Steven Witt, Laurie Kutner, and Elizabeth Cooper, "Mapping Academic Library Contributions to Campus Internationalization"; Karen Bordonaro, *Internationalization and the North American University Library* (Lanham, MD: Scarecrow Press, Inc., 2013).
25. Ann Lindell, *Library Support for Study Abroad* (SPEC Kit 309) (Washington, DC: Association of Research Libraries, 2008); Kayo Denda, "Study Abroad Programs: A Golden Opportunity for Academic Library Engagement," *Journal of Academic Librarianship* 39 no. 2 (2013), 155–60; Kutner, "Think Locally, Act Globally: Understanding Home Institution Library Engagement among Study-abroad Students," *College & Research Libraries* 70, no. 2 (2009): 158–76; Virginia Connell, "Getting to Know the Neighbors: Library Support for Study Abroad Programs," *Library Philosophy & Practice* (2009): 1–12; Sarah F. Cohen and Andy Burkhardt, "Even an Ocean Away: Developing Skype-based Reference for Students Studying Abroad," *Reference Services Review* 38, no. 2 (2010): 264–73; Laurie Kutner, "Study-Abroad Programs as Information Producers: An Expanding Role for Support of Our Students Studying Abroad," *Journal of Library Administration* 50, no. 7/8 (2010): 767–78.
26. Lily Griner, Patricia Jean Herron, and Susan White, "Study Abroad Partnerships: Librarians, Business Faculty, and in-Country Facilitator Develop an Innovative Experiential Learning Program," *Journal of Business & Finance Librarianship* 20, no. 3 (2015): 189–208.
27. Lily Griner and Patricia Herron, "Preparing Global Citizens: Librarians Connect Students with a Learning Service Opportunity in Nicaragua," *Electronic Journal of Academic and Special Librarianship* 10, no. 3 (2009): doi:10.13016/M2C905.
28. Elizabeth L. Black, "Engaging Second Year Students in Transformational Learning Experiences," in *ACRL Conference Proceedings* (Chicago: Association of College and Research Libraries, 2015): 244–50; Laurie Bridges, Kelly McElroy, and Kenya Juarez, "A Little About a Short Study-Abroad Course in Barcelona, and Everything You Always Wanted to Know about US Librarians," presentation in Oregon State University Study Abroad Program, Barcelona, Spain, http://hdl.handle.net/1957/59827.
29. Monteverdeinfo.com, "Monteverde Area Maps, Facts, and Links" (2011), accessed online July 21, 2017, http://www.monteverdeinfo.com/facts.htm.
30. Costa Rica Information, "Monteverde," accessed online July 21, 2017, http://costarica-information.com/destinations/destinations-of-puntarenas/monteverde.
31. Monteverde Institute, *Executive Director's Report 2016*.
32. The author's affiliation with the Monteverde Institute began in 2007 and has included two six-month sabbaticals, developing the library's digital presence, directing three digital library projects utilizing Syracuse University MLIS student interns for on-site internships, developing library policies and writing library administrative documents, and running an ALA travel/service trip to Costa Rica in 2014 that included MVI lectures and volunteer work at the MVI library.

Publications based on the MVI-related work include: Laurie Kutner, "Think Locally, Act Globally: Understanding Home Institution Library Engagement among Study-Abroad Students," *College and Research Libraries* 70, no.2 (2009): 158–76; Laurie Kutner, "Study-Abroad Programs as Information Producers: An Expanding Role for Support of our Students Studying Abroad," *Journal of Library Administration*, 50. No.7/8 (2010): 767–78.

33. Association of College and Research Libraries, "Framework for Information Literacy for Higher Education."
34. Catherine Fraser Riehle and Sharon A. Weiner, "High-Impact Educational Practices."
35. Malgorzata Blicharska, Richard J. Smithers, Magdalena Kuchler, Ganesh K. Agrawal, Jose M. Gutierrez, Ahmed Hassanali, Saleemul Huq, et al, "Steps to Overcome the North-South Divide in Research Relevant to Climate Change Policy and Practice," *Nature Climate Change* 7, no. 1 (2017): 21–27.
36. Luis F. Gomez, Leonardo Rios-Osario, and Maria Luisa Eschenhagen, "Agroecology Publications and the Coloniality of Knowledge," *Agronomy for Sustainable Development* 33, no. 2 (2013): 355–62; Hebe Vessuri, Jean-Claude Guedon, and Ana Maria Cetto, "Excellence or Quality? Impact of the Current Competition Regime on Science and Scientific Publishing in Latin America and Its Implications for Development," *Current Sociology* 62, no. 5 (2014): 647–65.
37. Juan Pablo Alperin and Gustavo Fischman, eds., *Made in Latin America: Open Access, Scholarly Journals, and Regional Innovations* (Buenos Aires: CLACSO, 2015).

Bibliography

Albertine, Susan, and Tia Brown MacNair. "Seeking High-Quality, High-Impact Learning: The Imperative of Faculty Development and Curricular Intentionality." *Peer Review* 14, no. 3 (2012). http://www.aacu.org/publications-research/periodicals/seeking-high-quality-high-impact-learning-imperative-faculty.

Alperin, Juan Pablo, and Gustavo Fischman, eds. *Made in Latin America: Open Access, Scholarly Journals, and Regional Innovations*. Buenos Aires: CLACSO, 2015.

American Council on Education. "Mapping Internationalization on U.S. Campuses." 2017. http://www.acenet.du/news-room/Pages/Mapping-Internationalization-on-U-S-Campuses.aspx.

Association of College and Research Libraries. "Framework for Information Literacy for Higher Education." January 11, 2016. http://www.acrl.org/acrl/standards/ilframework.

Battista, Andrew, Dave Ellenwood, Lua Gregory, Shana Higgins, Jeff Lilburn, Yasmin Sokkar Harker, and Christopher Sweet. "Seeking Social Justice in the ACRL Framework." *Communications in Information Literacy* 9, no. 2 (2015): 111–25.

Black, Elizabeth L. "Engaging Second Year Students in Transformational Learning Experiences." In *ACRL Conference Proceedings*, 244–50. Chicago: Association of College and Research Libraries, 2015.

Blicharska, Malgorzata, Richard J. Smithers, Magdalena Kuchler, Ganesh K. Agrawal, Jose M. Gutierrez, Ahmed Hassanali, Saleemul Huq, et al. "Steps to Overcome the North-South Divide in Research Relevant to Climate Change Policy and Practice." *Nature Climate Change* 7, no. 1 (2017): 21–27.

Bordonaro, Karen. *Internationalization and the North American University Library*. Lanham, MD: Scarecrow Press, Inc., 2013.

Bridges, Laurie, Kelly McElroy, and Kenya Juarez. "A Little About a Short Study-Abroad Course in Barcelona, and Everything You Always Wanted to Know about US Librarians." Lecture presented to Catalonian librarians in Spain, Summer 2016. http://hdl.handle.net/1957/59827.

Click, Amanda B., Claire Walker Wiley, and Meggan Houlihan. "The Internationalization of the Academic Library: A Systematic Review of 25 Years of Literature on International Students." *College & Research Libraries* 78, no. 3 (2017): 328–58.

Cohen, Sarah F., and Andy Burkhardt. "Even an Ocean Away: Developing Skype-based Reference for Students Studying Abroad." *Reference Services Review* 38, no. 2 (2010): 264–73.

Connell, Virginia. "Getting to Know the Neighbors: Library Support for Study Abroad Programs." *Library Philosophy & Practice* (2009): 1–12.

Costa Rica Information. "Monteverde." Accessed July 21, 2017. http://costarica-information.com/destinations/destinations-of-puntarenas/monteverde.

Crabtree, Robbin D. "The Intended and Unintended Consequences of International Service-Learning." *Journal of Higher Education Outreach and Engagement* 17, no. 2 (2013): 43–66.

Dados, Nour, and Raewyn Connell. "The Global South." *Contexts* 11, no.1 (2012): 12–13.

Denda, Kayo. "Study Abroad Programs: A Golden Opportunity for Academic Library Engagement." *Journal of Academic Librarianship* 39, no. 2 (2013), 155–60.

Downey, Annie. *Critical Information Literacy: Foundations, Inspiration, and Ideas.* Sacramento, CA: Library Juice Press, 2016.

Elmborg, James. "Critical Information Literacy: Implications for Instructional Practice." *The Journal of Academic Librarianshi*p 32, no. 2 (2006): 192–99.

Foasberg, Nancy M. "From Standards to Frameworks for IL: How the ACRL Framework Addresses Critiques of the Standards." *portal: Libraries and the Academy* 15, no. 4 (2015): 699–717.

Gomez, Luis F., Leonardo Rios-Osario, and Maria Luisa Eschenhagen. "Agroecology Publications and the Coloniality of Knowledge." *Agronomy for Sustainable Development* 33, no. 2 (2013): 355–62.

Griner, Lily, and Patricia Herron. "Preparing Global Citizens: Librarians Connect Students with a Learning Service Opportunity in Nicaragua." *Electronic Journal of Academic and Special Librarianship* 10, no. 3 (2009). http://hdl.handle.net/1903/16392.

Griner, Lily, Patricia Jean Herron, and Susan White. "Study Abroad Partnerships: Librarians, Business Faculty, and in-Country Facilitator Develop an Innovative Experiential Learning Program." *Journal of Business & Finance Librarianship* 20, no. 3 (2015): 189–208.

Institute of International Education. "Open Doors 2016 Executive Summary." 2016. http://www.iie.org/en/Why-IIE/Announcements/2016-11-14-Open-Doors-Executive-Summary.

Jacobs, Heidi LM. "Information Literacy and Reflexive Pedagogical Praxis." *The Journal of Academic Librarianship* 34, no. 3 (2008): 256–62.

Kozak, Jennifer, and Marianne Larsen. "ISL and Host Communities—Relationships and Responsibilities." In *International Service Learning: Engaging Host Communities*, edited by Marianne Larsen, 263–76. New York: Routledge, 2016.

Kuh, George D. *High Impact Educational Practices: What They Are, Who Has Access to Them, and Why They Matter.* Washington, DC: Association of American Colleges & Universities, 2008.

———. "Why Integration and Engagement are Essential to Effective Educational Practice in the Twenty-first Century." *Peer Review*, 10, no. 4 (2008): 27.

Kutner, Laurie. "Study-Abroad Programs as Information Producers: An Expanding Role for Support of Our Students Studying Abroad." *Journal of Library Administration* 50, no. 7/8 (2010): 767–78.

———. "Think Locally, Act Globally: Understanding Home Institution Library Engagement among Study-abroad Students." *College & Research Libraries* 70, no. 2 (2009): 158–76.

Lindell, Ann. *Library Support for Study Abroad* (SPEC Kit 309). Washington, DC: Association of Research Libraries, 2008.

Monteverde Institute. *Executive Director's Report 2016*. Unpublished.

Monteverdeinfo.com. "Monteverde Area Maps, Facts, and Links." https://www.monteverdeinfo.com/monteverde-area-maps-facts-and-links.

"North and South, The (Global)." In *International Encyclopedia of the Social Sciences*, Vol. 5. edited by William A. Darity, Jr., 542–44. Detroit: MacMillan Reference U.S.A., 2008.

Pagowsky, Nicole, and Kelly McElroy, eds. *Critical Library Pedagogy Handbook.* 2 vols. Chicago: Association of College and Research Libraries, 2016.

Riehle, Catherine Fraser, and Sharon A. Weiner. "High-Impact Educational Practices: An Exploration of the Role of Information Literacy." *College & Undergraduate Libraries* 20, no. 2 (2013): 127–43.

Seeber, Kevin. "This Is Really Happening: Criticality and Discussions of Context in ACRL'S Framework for Information Literacy." *Communications in Information Literacy* 9, no. 2 (2015): 157–63.

Sherraden, Margaret, Benjamin J. Lough, and Amy Bopp. "Students Serving Abroad: A Framework for Inquiry." *Journal of Higher Education Outreach and Engagement* 17, no. 2 (2013): 7–40.

Tewell, Eamon. "A Decade of Critical Information Literacy: A Review of the Literature." *Communications in Information Literacy* 9, no. 1 (2015): 24–43.

United Nations Development Programme. "Forging a Global South: United Nations Day for North-South Cooperation." December 19, 2004. http://www.undp.org/content/dam/china/docs/Publications/UNDP-CH-PR-Publications-UNDay-for-South-South-Cooperation.pdf.

Vessuri, Hebe, Jean-Claude Guedon, and Ana Maria Cetto. "Excellence or Quality? Impact of the Current Competition Regime on Science and Scientific Publishing in Latin America and Its Implications for Development." *Current Sociology* 62, no. 5 (2014): 647–65.

Witt, Steven, Laurie Kutner, and Elizabeth Cooper. "Mapping Academic Library Contributions to Campus Internationalization." *College and Research Libraries* 76, no. 5 (2015): 587–608.

CHAPTER TWENTY-FIVE

Successful American-Russian Partnership Through Education Abroad

Yelena Luckert and Lindsay Inge Carpenter

Over the past almost ten years, the University of Maryland has been developing a four-way partnership among the University of Maryland Libraries, the University of Maryland College of Information Science (iSchool), the Library of Russian Academy of Sciences (BAN), and the Library and Information department at the St. Petersburg State University of Culture and Arts (SPbGIK). It began with the development of a single course for the College of Information Science: LBSC 729: International Opportunities in Information Studies; Libraries and Cultural Heritage Institutions of St. Petersburg, Russia, later renumbered INST729R. This course was initially developed in a partnership between an iSchool faculty member, Trudi Hahn, and a subject librarian for Slavic Studies, Yelena Luckert, who was the initiator for the course. This chapter provides a history of the course as well as reflections on its success from both the course leader and a student participant.

A Faculty Perspective

It took about four years to develop this course before the first class went to St. Petersburg in 2012.[1] The first cohort consisted of thirteen students, the two instructors who developed the course, and another librarian who was invited to assist with the class because none of the students spoke Russian or had any cultural familiarity with the country. This trip was followed in 2014 by the second class with five students, the same principal librarian, but another iSchool faculty member, Ann Weeks. The goals and curricula for both classes were principally the same, but some adjustments were made for the second class that will be discussed later.

At the time the course was being developed, the University of Maryland iSchool was very interested in international education, particularly in study abroad classes. Several courses already had been given in Nicaragua, England, South Africa, and India. Thus, adding Russia to this portfolio was met with great interest by the college. It is easy to understand the motivation behind the iSchool's drive to internationalize their students' education, which was rooted in its desire to fulfill the strategic goals of the university. We live in an increasingly global society where information travels with great speed across political, cultural, religious, and geographical divides. There is an interest in academic communities to develop conscientious citizens—i.e., people who can function in the increasingly global environment. As in the case of many other institutions, globalization of all aspects of the university's life has become an integral part of the strategic goals of the University of Maryland, which trickled down to all of the university's departments and program. This has since manifested in a variety of different activities, including education abroad.

The study abroad classes to Russia presented additional opportunities for the library and information program at Maryland that few other destinations offered. Russia and the US, two global superpowers much at odds with each other, compete in the world arena for moral and political superiority and information control. Russia's recent tampering with the American political process is an acute example of this. Yet most Americans are unfamiliar with Russian culture, history, politics, and the very policies and institutions that made them what they are. Even less understood and properly valued are Russian libraries and Russian readership, which are crucial factors in this information exchange. Both countries have very different information and library systems anchored in their political differences, and so are not fully apparent to each other. Historically closed to freedom of information, after the Glasnost' i Perestroika, Russian cultural institutions, including libraries and archives, have become more open to readers and researchers, both homegrown and international. However, this openness is rather fragile, discriminatory, and fluctuates over time, as it is often used for political gains of the state. All that had to be accounted for when planning this course.

The main goals for the course were to introduce our students of information sciences—future American library professionals—to the Russian library system by showing them different types of libraries, including those for the general public, children, and academic and specialized audiences. They would get a firsthand sense of how they work, have opportunities to communicate with library professionals and library users, see library processes, get a glance of Russian-held indescribably rich collections, have conversations and develop relationships with students and faculty of a library school, better understand the exchange and management of information, the network of the library system, issues of readerships, and above all learn from each other. St. Petersburg was chosen for several strategic reasons. Among them, St. Petersburg is one of few cities in Russia that could provide the students with all the opportunities mentioned above within a relatively small geographical area. The city is rather compact and easily walkable, which makes things easier logistically. St. Petersburg boasts some of the best and oldest libraries in Russia, with fabulous collections and the oldest and most prestigious library program in the country. St. Petersburg also is one of the most beautiful cities in the world with lots to do for all types of interests. The summer short-term study abroad course, rather than other possible variations, was also chosen with care and thought for financial and logistical reasons. For example, these courses do not go through the regular registrar; thus, it is easier to organize payments, include non-UMD students, decide on the length and structure of the course, time of travel, and monitor cost.

Organizational logistics of this course were excruciatingly difficult. Developing contacts and finding people in St. Petersburg willing to work with the course was challenging. There is a general mistrust in Russia of everything that is new and unfamiliar. To break through this barrier required recommendations from known individuals, in-person meetings, numerous letters with signatures from the top administrators of both sides—in all, a very lengthy process. Securing permissions was different for various libraries. For example, getting access to the Mayakovsky Central City Library, the main public library of the city, was rather easy and required just a few signatures. They were also very interested in working with us and were amenable to all our ideas; they even organized a meeting with their readers during our first trip. (It did not work as well as we hoped, and we decided not to repeat it during the second trip.)

To visit the Library of the Hermitage Museum required a personal introduction to the head librarian and then the approval from the director of the Hermitage. Getting to know faculty at the St. Petersburg library program was more challenging until, by chance, we were introduced to Dr. Valerii Leonov, director of BAN, who, as it turned, out studied at the University of Maryland iSchool as a foreign exchange student in the 1970s during the Cold War. Dr. Leonov was able to open those doors to us. In Summer 2011, the Slavic Librarian traveled to Russia to secure final approvals and work out all details of our visits and to develop logistics for the trip—housing, food, excursions, transportation—with a goal to make it affordable for students. All of this had to be done by us since we were not successful in getting funds to develop the course and could not hire outside help. Of course, the fact that the Slavic librarian was born and raised in St. Petersburg and knew the city, its history, and culture were enormously helpful in all these negotiations and arrangements.

The issue of resources, or lack of them, was challenging to overcome. The team applied to several grant opportunities to develop this course, including several on campus that provide seed money to develop innovative courses, and a few outside, such as the Likhachev Foundation, the U.S.-Russia Peer-to-Peer Program, Open World, and several others. Many of these organizations expressed a strong interest in our project, and several times it felt like the course, and even the partnership at large, would receive some granting, but in the end it did not happen and we had to rely on our own resources and student tuition to make it happen. Keeping the cost down for the students was very important to ensure the success of the trip—and for a very good reason: Russia is an expensive country to travel to and could be completely unattainable on a student budget. Here, the librarian's knowledge of the city was the key factor in ensuring that the cost for each student did not exceed the cost of an average study abroad class, a major achievement. Lodging, food, transportation, sightseeing, and other components of the trip had to be meticulously developed ahead of time. Visas were another daunting and costly issue that required careful planning. To allow ample time to get them, the university's Education Abroad office made an exception for us by allowing an early registration, several months ahead of schedule. However, it should be noted here that dealing with our own campus bureaucracy, including the Education Abroad office, was at times painfully slow and with many issues.

The course consisted of three components. Before both departures, the class met to prepare for the trip and get to know each other. Harold Leich and Angela Cannon, two

Russian specialists from the Library of Congress, presented lectures on the Russian library system and network as well as on the development of Russian collections in the US, specifically at the Library of Congress. This gave the background framework for the class. The first time around, we also had a security specialist on Russia, who was particularly familiar with St. Petersburg, providing students with information of what not to do to stay safe. To provide them with further background information, the students were assigned several articles on the topics related to Russian libraries, including a couple of articles by Dr. Leonov since they were to meet him during the trip, and were asked to watch several movies that the instructors felt might help them better understand the places we will visit.

Once in St. Petersburg, we visited libraries of different types to provide students with an array of experiences. All students had to keep a detailed daily reflection journal that later was graded. They also had to take turns to write in our blog, to which all friends and families were invited as observers to follow adventures of their loved ones. We visited the Library of the Russian Academy of Sciences, the National Library of Russia, the Presidential Yeltsin Library, the Mayakovsky Central City Library, the Pushkin Central Children's Library, the Library of the Hermitage Museum, and Pushkinsky Dom, which is the main and best-known literary archive in the city. Each visit was different, exciting, meaningful, full of information, and affected different students in different ways, often based on their own specializations and interests. Some could not get enough of the public children's library, while others were mesmerized by the accounts from the Pushkinsky Dom of selfless and courageous acts by curators preserving materials of doomed individuals during turbulent times. The visit to the Hermitage library, so seldom visited by patrons outside the museum staff, also included a guided tour of the museum; individuals were then allowed to wander around for the remaining time, which all students were very excited about. We were met as old friends at BAN, and meeting Dr. Leonov, the author of the articles the students read, was another highlight of the trip. At the start of the trip, we also visited and had activities with the St. Petersburg State University of Culture and Arts School of Library and Information Services (SPbGIK). Students' comments in their diaries and course evaluations attested to many different emotions these visits evoked, from strong, admiring, appreciative, and exciting to questioning and even, at times, disappointing. We did a lot of sightseeing of other cultural institutions, such as parks, churches, palaces, and other iconic activities, including seeing the Bolshoi Theatre performances and the opening of the bridges over Neva during White Nights. Upon return home, the students had to write a final paper detailing an aspect of Russian librarianship of their choosing.

Although most of the course remained the same in both years, the work with SPbGIK progressed and improved over time. In 2012, when we came to Russia for the first time, SPbGIK was not clear on their own goals for this program. Thus, most of the work was done on our side, with our students preparing short, two-slide presentations each to our Russian friends on the important topics of American librarianship. Topics included services to patrons with disabilities, green libraries, storytelling, and others, which proved to be new to Russia at that time. We were shown around, looked in on their classes in session, saw their promotional videos, and talked to the dean. It was a very nice visit but missing was one of the most important things that we desired—more interactions between the students of the two countries.

In 2014, things changed dramatically with the new dean, Valentina Brezhneva, and with the support of Dr. Leonov and American Consulate in St. Petersburg. Conversations about student participation began months ahead of the trip. More important this time around, the Russian side came up with the idea of the International Library School (ILS), a two-part program, with both parts completely different from each other in their intent and goals and run consecutively not simultaneously. The first part of the ILS was designed for students and the second for professionals already in library employment in Russia and its former republics. For the ease of explaining, I will call them ILS1 and ILS2. As instructors of INST729R, we got to participate in both, which was a very special opportunity for us. The students of INST729R participated only in ILS1.

Early in the spring 2014 semester, twenty students were selected from the Russian side to participate in ILS1. All five students enrolled into INST729R were automatically included. As soon as INST729R was given the final OK and we got the names of participating students, we created a joint reflector where both Russian and American students could start communicating about things that interested them, including but not limited to librarianship. We were somewhat disappointed that participation in this reflector was not as robust as we hoped for and was usually initiated by the American students, which might give an insight on the pedagogical differences of both countries. Once in St. Petersburg, the program itself consisted of tours, lectures, presentations, discussions, a joint program with BAN, a fun marketing SPbGIK program called Bibliofest, and even a concert, where all students were participating together.

Comments on the joint program from both sides were quite interesting. One of the more unexpected comments was expressed by some of the Russian students. They felt that without our presence, they might not have been exposed to the treasures of BAN. Some independent socializing between the students of the two countries occurred, but not as much as American students wanted, particularly in discussions about librarianship. It is important to note that all our students were graduate students; however, library education in Russia is undergraduate, so our students were older, in a few cases by quite a bit. American students also observed that their Russian counterparts were more reserved, less willing to speak up, start conversations, or share opinions, especially in a classroom setting. This can be explained by the pedagogical differences of the two countries, the young age of some students within a multigenerational student group, cultural differences, and the language barrier, although all the Russian students spoke fairly good English; in contrast, many Russian faculty did not. A good number of Russian students also expressed a desire to come to the United States to further their education but, unfortunately, our iSchool could not establish any special scholarship to help them do so. Despite some difficulties, this was a great start, and students of both countries much appreciated the interactions and exchanges and were hoping for more.

ILS2 was designed for library professionals from all over Russia and former Soviet republics and took place immediately after ILS1 was over. One of its main supporters was the American Consulate in St. Petersburg. Staff from BAN, faculty of the SPbGIK, the two INST729R instructors, and the associate dean for collections at the University of Maryland, who flew in just for this session, were invited to participate as instructors and mentors for ILS2. Forty-three professional librarians from places such as Cheliabinsk, Karaganda, Perm, Kazakhstan, Volgograd, and St. Petersburg participated in ILS2. In the absence of well-developed post-MLS professional training for librarians, as it is the case in the United States, this program was innovative, experimental, and valuable to its participants. Although this program was about four weeks long, the guests from America participated only in a small portion of the program, providing our insights on libraries, library profession, and the future.

Once back in the United States and after grading the papers, we were able to assess the course based on student work and their course evaluations. Whether in 2012 or 2014, the results were similar. The students found the course interesting and appropriately challenging. They related that they learned a lot and all of them found it to be a trip of a lifetime. They also commented on getting a better understanding and appreciation of library and information fields both home and abroad. Here are some of the random comments from both classes:

- "Russian students have more fun."
- "American students are less shy in classrooms."
- "Russian librarians are very dedicated and work in [a] difficult environment."
- "Huge discrepancy on how [Russian] libraries are funded, have and have-nots."
- "Russian libraries do a lot for their users, but there is still a need for better information sharing."

In the past several years, the relationship between the United States and Russia has deteriorated dramatically. Getting visas have become even more expensive and difficult. Grants to support academic work in Russia have also dried up, some due to budget instabilities in higher education as a whole, some because of political reasons. Thus, maintaining relationships, even more so the partnerships, are more difficult than ever. Yet it is important to persevere. Although at this time a third study abroad trip to Russia is on hold, I am not losing hope to do it in a very near future, perhaps after this book is finished. In the meantime, I am still constantly corresponding with my Russian contacts at BAN and SPbGIK and have contributed to their conferences in absentee, provided live webinars to their students, and have welcomed some of their faculty to the University of Maryland—Dr. Leonov in 2013 and Albina Krymskaya in 2017.

A Student's Perspective

The study abroad trip to St. Petersburg had a tremendous impact on my education as a librarian, in ways that could not be replicated in a domestic course. At the time of the 2014 trip, I was pursuing dual degrees in library science and Russian/Soviet history. I was about halfway through my program and was struggling to decide whether to pursue librarianship or further graduate work in history after completing my program. This trip illustrated the opportunities librarianship could provide for exploring international history and politics, cultural exchange, and rigorous scholarly work, and cemented my decision to pursue academic librarianship as a career.

From the perspective of someone fascinated by rare books and Russian history and culture, the trip was an absolute dream. To go behind the scenes of the Hermitage, one of my favorite places in the world, was truly a once-in-a-lifetime opportunity. Viewing rare books and manuscripts at BAN (including a gorgeous manuscript celebrating the ascendency of Peter the Great) was almost like entering a time machine. What made these experiences even more exciting was the obvious pleasure that the Russian librarians took in sharing these treasures with us. Their enthusiasm was infectious and was especially appreciated by students.

The trip offered sobering moments as well. Speaking with Russian librarians and archivists about historical collecting practices led to conversations about the intersections of politics, government, and libraries. Hearing stories of collections preserved in times of war, political upheaval, or natural disasters demonstrated to us the lengths to which

Russian librarians have gone to protect their collections. These conversations inspired my cohort to reflect on how politics shape American cultural institutions and have continued to provide me with food for thought as I navigate my role as an academic librarian.

Meeting fellow library sciences students was a wonderful experience. After the official tours and formal presentations and discussions concluded, we were able to connect with the Russian students more informally. My cohort took a group of students out to a restaurant where we treated them to pizza and beer. (They were fascinated by all things American, so we thought this would be a welcome gesture!) We had so much fun that evening. We talked casually about American entertainment (the students loved *How I Met Your Mother* and wanted to know if we really do say "cheers" each time we drink) and about their experiences growing up in St. Petersburg. Another night, a smaller group of us met for an evening picnic. We brought along snacks to share, and in a lovely gesture, one of the students brought me a crossword puzzle book in Russian. (I had told her before that I was learning Russian and was hoping to find one during my visit!) Once, in the smaller group, and now having become better acquainted with each other, we asked each other more frank questions about Russian-American relations and perceptions of our cultures. I tentatively asked them what they thought about the busts of Lenin that still adorned the main readings rooms in the National Library of Russia. They cocked their heads and laughed, telling me, "It's not so weird." For their part, they were clearly dying to ask us about stereotypes of Americans but were too well-mannered to do so outright. Once we assured them they wouldn't offend us, they eagerly ran through a list of questions for us about Americans. By the end of the evening, we were all bent over laughing. I think anyone who has had the privilege of traveling abroad and interacting with locals knows this feeling of fast friendship; it is one of those unusual situations where it is sometimes easier to speak more freely with almost-strangers than with the people we see every day.

The immersive experience of traveling abroad not only deepens your understanding of a culture, it also deepens your relationship with your travel companions. This trip presented me with an opportunity to work closely with Yelena, whom I had briefly met while working on a group project for an earlier course. My library science courses were primarily taught by research faculty and, despite my classrooms being located just a few minutes away, I had only rare occasions to interact with academic librarians at my institution (outside of regular patron-librarian interactions). This was one of my first times interacting with an academic librarian as a librarian-in-training myself. Study abroad programs such as this one present students with an opportunity to learn more about the breadth and diversity of the work that academic librarians engage in and to speak in-depth with academic librarians about their professional experiences and career paths. Courses co-taught by MLS faculty and academic librarians offer students a chance to connect with mentors in the field, something that can be difficult for new professionals just starting to engage with the field.

The experiences I had on this trip were not something I could have coordinated on my own. Thanks to Yelena's tireless work in building relationships and coordinating visits, I was able to meet people and visit places I would have never had access to as an independent traveler. Incorporating this international component into my coursework strengthened my interest in international and academic librarianship and heightened my awareness of the importance of international and domestic politics in our work. Despite how labor-intensive these programs are, I think that MLIS programs would be doing a true service for their students by coordinating short-term education abroad opportunities. I strongly encourage MLIS students (as well as practitioners!) to take advantage of opportunities like these and to consider how these types of cultural exchange can enhance our librarianship.

Conclusion

The authors believe the work described in this article to be very important, particularly in view of the global political climate of today. The more we understand each other, the less there is a likelihood of unintended misconceptions and consequences. Whether good or bad, whether we agree or don't, we must understand what lays behind our differences so that we can come up with meaningful solutions. Libraries, especially academic libraries in the United States, are an integral part of such efforts, no matter how small each of these individual efforts appears to be. Libraries are cornerstones of our democracy. It is our mission to ensure the flow of free and reliable information and to encourage meaningful discourse. As academic librarians, we have an obligation to our communities to enable open dialogue and help raise globally responsive citizens, even if one at a time. To do that, we need to be an integral part of the educational mission of our institutions and participate in helping to raise individuals who can understand and follow all sides of debates.

Notes

1. Yelena Luckert, "Globalizing Librarianship: A Study-Abroad Class in Russia," *Slavic & East European Information Resources* 15, no. 3 (2014): 175–81, doi:10.1080/15228886.2014.928846.

Bibliography

Luckert, Yelena. "Globalizing Librarianship: A Study-Abroad Class in Russia." *Slavic & East European Information Resources* 15, no. 3 (2014): 175–81. doi:10.1080/15228886.2014.928846.

CHAPTER TWENTY-SIX

Serving Students Across the Globe:

Establishing Library Outreach and Instructional Services for an International-US Dual-Degree Program

Mary K. Oberlies

The creation of inter-university partnerships can enhance the course offering of universities by filling programmatic gaps, increasing student and faculty diversity, and building institutional reputations. Universities can take advantage of many types of partnerships—domestic and international. Domestic partnerships might be with another university or a specific organization. For example, George Mason University collaborates with the Smithsonian Institute to offer intensive, hands-on conservation programs. International partnerships might take the form of creating a type of "branch campus," a study abroad collaboration, or departmental partnerships with faculty exchanges. This chapter focuses on a dual degree master's program between George Mason University's School of Conflict Analysis and Resolution (S-CAR) and the University of Malta's Mediterranean Academy of Diplomatic Studies (MEDAC). This unique departmental partnership is a truly international program, uniting departments from two institutions, where faculty, staff, and students exchange ideas and research. While this international partnership provides students with a unique opportunity to gain knowledge and experience from the faculty of two reputable universities, supporting the research and information literacy needs of the program is not always easy. The inclusion of the library in the development of inter-university partnerships is essential to improve the overall experience for students, faculty, and staff and contributes to the success of the program. This chapter offers a case study of a successful partnership, including implementing information literacy instruction, research, and collection support to an international-US dual-degree program.

The S-CAR/MEDAC Partnership

Established in 2010, the S-CAR/MEDAC international master's program created an opportunity for George Mason University (GMU) and S-CAR to participate in global education, expand the program to students outside the United States, and foster relationships with international colleagues.[1] Through the work of Dr. Richard Rubenstein, who had a relationship with the University of Malta (UM), where he taught in 1994 and served as a Fulbright Specialist, the partnership joined two programs with decades of experience in diplomacy and conflict resolution.[2] Based at the University of Malta's Valletta Campus, students in the program benefit from the location due to its proximity and connections to the Middle East, North Africa, Europe, and the Mediterranean. Malta's history of hosting peace negotiations and conferences provides an opportunity for students to engage in practice.[3]

The S-CAR/MEDAC dual-master's program is intense and fast-paced, lasting thirteen months. Students apply directly to the program through George Mason, if American or Canadian, or the University of Malta, if from any other country. Anyone who meets the admission requirements may apply, no matter their nationality. The entire degree is completed at the University of Malta's Valletta Campus, with faculty from George Mason traveling to Malta to teach classes. Students are required to reside in Malta for the duration of the program, which includes fifteen courses, each two weeks long, spending four to five hours in the classroom from Monday through Thursday. The summer is spent completing a thesis. During the program, students may also participate in research programs in Malta and nearby locations in the Mediterranean. These research programs tend to be short and are scheduled to be conducted during breaks between classes. Upon completion, students receive a master of arts degree from UM and a master of science degree from GMU.[4] The curricula of the program include course requirements from both S-CAR and MEDAC's home programs, with faculty sharing teaching duties, so students accomplish the requirements established by GMU and the UM. A benefit for students within the program is learning from the diverse experiences and perspectives of faculty in Malta and the US, as well as the diverse experiences of their cohort-mates.

Now in its sixth year, typical student cohorts are between fifteen and twenty students and represent a group of diverse and highly motivated scholars who become closely knit over the course of the program. On average, student cohorts include students from Western and Eastern Europe, Malta, the United States, Africa, and the Middle East.[5] Beyond the academic experience provided to students within the program, they also gain experience adapting to different cultures and educational experiences. Half of the courses are taught by European faculty who focus more on lecture and less on student-led discussions; the other half are taught by American faculty who place more emphasis on student participation. This requires students to be flexible and gain skills applicable to their work within conflict resolution and diplomacy.[6]

Research and library involvement

Students participating in the S-CAR/MEDAC international master's programs are dual enrolled at GMU and the UM. This allows students access to the research collections of both university libraries, including electronic resources, interlibrary loan, and research assistance. There are limitations on the type of materials students can access from George

Mason. For example, the physical materials, like books, cannot be shipped to Malta from the George Mason University Libraries. Students are restricted to electronic resources and electronic interlibrary loan (book chapters and articles). Similarly, there are restrictions on the Malta side with library resources. The student must cover the costs of interlibrary loan requests, and ordering books from Amazon can become expensive. Overall, however, students do benefit from the combined collections of the two universities and have access to a departmental library through MEDAC.

While students can access materials from both university libraries, they can have trouble navigating the different library interfaces and maintaining awareness of what they can access. Pival and Johnson found during their study of a joint-international program that "it can be challenging for students to learn how to interact with more than one library in terms of how to access different systems, resources and support."[7] Over the years, I have found this to be true for students in the MEDAC/S-CAR program. Students lack experience with the UM Libraries because they are not located on the main campus in Msida. The Valletta campus does have a small library but its hours vary, the space is very small, and the permanent book collection is not always relevant to the needs of students. The journey to the main library or the MEDAC library in Msida takes about thirty minutes by bus, but there is little reason to go to the main campus aside from these trips. The lack of interaction with the main campus leaves many students within the program unaware of all the resources available at the UM.

In terms of librarian support, at this time, students within the program do not receive library instruction from the UM librarians. The program coordinator, generally an S-CAR PhD student residing in Malta, arranges for the S-CAR subject librarian to provide virtual instruction in the fall term during a week when S-CAR is teaching. Beyond this instruction session, students in the program are encouraged to contact the S-CAR librarian for individual research assistance with their theses.

Library Services and International University Partnerships

Library literature about supporting joint international programs, international branch campuses, or study abroad and distance education courses is limited; however, it does highlight similar experiences and difficulties.

Knowledge of remote library resources

The adage "out of sight, out of mind" comes to mind when surveying the joint experiences of librarians serving students and faculty in international academic partnerships. Learning how to interact with multiple library systems and knowing about all the resources available is challenging for students and faculty. Alleyne and Rodrigues collaborated to provide instruction and reference support for the Bermuda College and Mount Saint Vincent University (MSVU) joint international program and found that students rarely made use of the MSVU electronic resources. Students within the program began in Bermuda and finished the program in Nova Scotia. While students have access to the resources at both institutional libraries, Alleyne and Rodrigues discovered that students lacked knowledge about the resources available to them at the remote library.[8] Students studying in inter-university programs experience similar issues. Pival and Johnson relate that students within the tri-institution distance education program offered by three Canadian institutions struggled with interacting with more than one library system and found it challenging to learn the different systems, resources, and support available from each of the library systems.[9] Librarians supporting students at international branch campuses reported similar experiences, where students often did not realize they had access to the remote "home" institutional library in the United States.[10] As I have worked with the students within the S-CAR/MEDAC, I have found they experience a similar disconnect with library resources at both institutional libraries. The location of the program at a branch campus of the UM make the libraries of both the UM and GMU remote for students. Without continuous outreach to students about the resources available to them and providing assistance and instruction on navigating the different library systems, students miss a benefit of international partnerships—expanded access to research resources.

Limited physical collections

For many students and faculty, the tradition of a "strong" library focuses on its physical space and collection of resources. Depending on the international partnership, the experience level of staff, the size of the physical space, and depth of the print collection vary. Rochester Institute of Technology's (RIT) branch campuses in Kosovo, Croatia, and Dubai each have a small campus library but they are not staffed by librarians, making access to the RIT librarians and e-resources important for student research.[11] Librarians supporting international branch campus library programs through the University of Nottingham and Long Island University had similar experiences. Long Island University's international site library resources vary from location to location with some sites having very limited resources and others having partnerships with other universities or embassy resources.[12] Access to qualified librarian assistance, especially those trained as librarians, varies from site to site. Coombs and Green found library staff at the international branch campuses sometimes needed training on teaching information literacy to better support student needs.[13] The library at the University of Malta's Valletta campus is staffed by two librarians and has a small physical collection that does not necessarily support the research needs of students in the S-CAR/MEDAC program. This leads many students to believe they do not have access to a library in Malta. Alleyne and Rodrigues found that joint international programs on the organizational level are often created to enhance each other's course offerings. The implications for libraries in this scenario is that the collection of the library of the institution where the program is based likely cannot fully support the research needs of the joint program, making access to the partner institution's library important for student success.[14] Addressing this challenge needs more than just outreach from the remote institution's library but also, ideally, collaboration and partnership between the libraries.

Virtual instruction and the "human link"

Providing virtual instruction and creating a human link to a remote library is difficult for a variety of reasons. Virtual instruction requires the development of trust and partnerships with the international institution's faculty or librarians before beginning anything. These partners advocate for carving out a chunk of time for the session and ensuring that students join the session. On the other side, the remotely based librarian must figure out time zone variances and adjust to giving instruction virtually to students who are not always native English speakers and have their own cultural understandings of what a librarian does.[15] When providing instruction virtually, it is difficult to gauge student understanding or difficulties with language. Pival and Johnson and Alleyne and Rodrigues found that collaborating with the librarian at the international campus helped overcome the challenges of language barriers and assessing student understanding. In both cases, the librarians collaborated to set up a session where one librarian in the US taught the session virtually while the librarian at the international campus sat in on the session to assist students with questions.[16] Wang and Tremblay decided to provide an information literacy session before students left for the international sites and supplemented knowledge by creating tutorials.[17] Creating a human link back to the US library for students at the international campus is difficult but possible through tutorials, collaboration with partners at the international campus, and continual outreach. For the S-CAR/MEDAC students, they are introduced to the S-CAR librarian within the first month of the program through a virtual instruction session. Prior to the session, I work with the on-site S-CAR program coordinator to learn about the students in the program and any areas I should focus on, including English-language experience. Following the session, students are continually reminded by the faculty and coordinator about me and the library to develop the "human link" to the George Mason University Libraries.

Developing Library Services for the S-CAR/MEDAC Program

I joined the GMU Libraries in May 2012, almost two years after the S-CAR/MEDAC partnership began. My introduction to the program came almost two months later when I received a reference question from a student trying to use our interlibrary loan system for an article request. Having never heard of the program, the request came as a surprise. As I worked to troubleshoot the student's issue by talking with colleagues within the libraries, it quickly became apparent that few really knew about the program. Some library staff believed the students started the program at Mason and finished it in Malta while others thought the UM Libraries were supposed to provide all research support for the program. The lack of information about the program, the obligations of each partner, and the role of the partner institutional libraries in how they would support the program hindered the development of library services. Figuring out the responsibilities of each library, what access students had to resources, and how to best support the students and faculty of the program became my first goal.

Step 1: Offer virtual assistance and learn the program

My interaction with the program began by establishing contact with the students in the Malta program via Skype. The Arlington Campus Library used Skype to communicate between our reference and circulation units, and it was easy to share my details with students in the program and remain logged in during work hours. I enlisted the help of the student who first contacted me to share this information with her cohort mates—not the most effective way of communication, but with no other method of contact, it worked. From my discussion with students, figuring out the process of requesting articles via interlibrary loan was the most essential task. Contacting faculty in S-CAR, I began by learning about the Memorandum of Understanding (MOU) between GMU and UM—in particular, the provision of library services. In talking with faculty within S-CAR about the program, I learned that the costs for interlibrary loan through UM Libraries was covered by students and that GMU Libraries should provide basic library services. This gave me the go-ahead to begin finding a way to ensure that students in the cohort could place electronic interlibrary loan requests. At the time, our system required students to enter the barcode from their student IDs to submit requests, so students needed a way to get a student ID. Luckily, our ID office was more than happy to work with the students in Malta to create and ship IDs, going so far as to provide the barcode electronically until the ID arrived. My student contact shared this information with others in the program. After establishing basic contact methods for reference assistance, the next obstacle was finding a way to contact the cohort as a whole so I could proactively assist them rather than provide "Band-aids" to issues.

Assistance came in the form of a previous Arlington Campus Library graduate research assistant who was a doctoral candidate in S-CAR. He was asked to serve as the first program coordinator, assisting students and faculty with navigating the program. Through him and an S-CAR faculty member who wanted library assistance, I began offering a virtual instruction session in the fall via Skype. It took time to set up, including testing of software, finding a time that would work for all with the time difference, and determining what to cover. The first session went well, but the following year, internet issues made it impossible for me to lead the session. I was also beginning to receive more questions from students that were difficult to answer without knowing anything about the UM side of the program. It became obvious that an on-site visit was needed.

Step 2: Plan an on-site visit

A five-day on-site visit was planned in March 2013 so I could provide in-person instruction and individual consultations with each student and meet with the MEDAC faculty and the UM librarians at the Valletta campus. Before leaving for Malta, the program coordinator worked with me to set up the student appointments and instruction session and provided me with contacts with MEDAC. While I was able to arrange for a meeting with faculty, all attempts to set up meetings with the UM librarians failed. Fortunately, one of the MEDAC faculty was able to arrange for a quick tour of the Valletta campus library, which provided me with an opportunity to see the space and speak with the librarian about resources. From these meetings, I discovered that students and faculty really relied on the electronic resources from GMU to supplement collection gaps at the UM libraries. The information I gathered allowed me to help set up a LibGuide for Malta students, advocate for Malta faculty to receive Mason NetIDs so they could access our electronic resources, and work toward continuing one-on-one meetings with students.

On-site visits are expensive and take a lot of planning, but even a single visit can prove essential in successfully assisting international programs. Beyond the value of being able to work with students and faculty in-person, on-site visits provide orienting information. Seeing where students meet for classes, the resources available to them on-site, the problems students and faculty experience (for example, maintaining a wireless internet connection is a struggle), and the information they have readily available provides valuable details that inform practice. I spent a majority of my time at the Valletta campus but also visited the MEDAC offices on the Msida campus, providing me a complete picture of the students' experiences and how I can assist them.

Step 3: Improve virtual reference and instruction to international and ESL students

Supporting an international inter-university partnership requires flexibility, creativity, and continual assessment. Outside of the single on-site visit, providing reference and instruction services to students within the S-CAR/Malta program is virtual. This student population requires some additional thought when providing assistance. It is necessary to consider time zones, cultural references and other "Americanisms," access to information and cost of resources, internet stability, and ESL students.

When teaching international and ESL students, it is necessary to adjust normal methods of instruction. Being cognizant of how quickly you are speaking is not enough; when leading instruction for ESL students, it is important to speak clearly and pause between groupings of ideas to assist with comprehension.[18] This is difficult in face-to-face sessions and even more so for virtual sessions when it is not possible to see if students are following. I have found having either the professor for the session or the program coordinator present during the session to help with this. The coordinator informs me when the internet connection breaks out, if I am speaking too quickly, or am not clear enough for students, and helps ensure the session runs relatively smoothly on the Malta side. While little can be done about internet connections, we have found being connected via Ethernet cable rather than relying on wireless connectivity greatly improves the experience. In addition to speaking clearly and grouping ideas, the instructor should avoid idioms, jargon, or other cultural references because international students often do not have a point of reference to help them understand.[19] For example, when covering controlled vocabulary, I often make a reference to the words used to describe the size of a coffee when ordering at Starbucks and Dunkin Donuts. This works well in the United States because these coffee shops are abundant. However, it does not work for many international students, especially the Maltese, since there is not a single Starbucks in Malta. (Who needs Starbucks when you have Italian-inspired coffee everywhere you turn?) I did not know this American analogy was falling flat until my on-site visit, so getting feedback from partners at the international site about cultural references is important.

Step 4: Develop a plan for the future

Working with the S-CAR/MEDAC program requires continual adjustment, not only because library services and technologies evolve over time but also because new opportunities arise to improve student experiences. The S-CAR Malta program coordinator and I have explored various instructional technologies from Skype to Blackboard Collaborate to Go To Meeting, trying to determine what would provide the best experience for students. At the start of each new year, the coordinator gets to know the students and evaluates what information literacy skills I should focus on, and we brainstorm new intervention methods, particularly one-on-one assistance.

Maintaining the human link between the students and GMU libraries is not easy. Students, especially highly motivated ones attracted to such a high-demand program, are inclined to try navigating all obstacles with their research. Building student trust and the kind of relationship that encourages them to contact me for virtual appointments is difficult, particularly when it is necessary to navigate a six- or seven-hour time difference and troubled internet connections. This is where building the relationships with the program coordinator and the faculty is essential. Students in the cohort know they can rely on the program coordinator—he is their constant link, so he serves as my advocate. Being proactive and working with him to brainstorm ideas of what I can offer is important. This year, we decided to try requiring students to set up individual appointments with me after they finish their spring methods course. The idea here is that this first touchpoint will encourage them to talk with me throughout the summer as they complete their theses.

Recommendations for the Future

Reflecting on the literature about library international partnerships and experiences with the Malta program, there are several recommendations for the future that need further exploration.

1. Integrate multiple information literacy instruction sessions into the program. Studies on the information literacy acquisition of international students found that international students are better able to understand and apply information literacy concepts if they are introduced in multiple sessions. By beginning with an overview and then having one or two follow-up sessions, students gain stronger understandings about the application of these skills in their own research. Finding a way to encourage student involvement with these virtual sessions also needs further exploration.[20]
2. Establish a joint-lending partnership between GMU and UM. At the moment, I allocate a portion of my collection development budget to acquiring ebooks and streaming media for S-CAR's distance education degrees and the Malta program. I work with faculty to identify what books they will need for their courses at the start of each semester and do my best to get ebook licenses. This is a great remedy but is not sustainable. Creating a joint-lending partnership between GMU and UM would allow for the lending of the physical collection between our universities, which would greatly improve library services. I have started discussions with S-CAR's Malta Committee but this will require the involvement of library leadership, and potentially university leadership, to proceed. Falling back on the relationships built within the program will likely be key to achieve this type of goal.
3. Create multiple touch-points throughout the year to further develop "human link." Multiple touch-points with students and faculty can help overcome the "out of sight, out of mind" scenario when relying on virtual library services and partnerships to lay the foundations of research support. Expanding relationships to include faculty within MEDAC and the UM library system could create access to more touch-points with students. Currently, I rely on an S-CAR network to reach the students, which limits my outreach. Gaining the trust and support of Maltese faculty in addition to S-CAR might assist with

establishing a program where students interact with me and library services from both GMU and UM multiple times throughout the year.

4. Embed tutorials and guides within Blackboard/Learning Management System. The S-CAR/MEDAC program recently moved to using Blackboard for courses. I currently work with distance education courses to embed content including tutorials, LibGuides, discussion boards, and other content to link students to library resources and services. This is an area of opportunity for the Malta program which needs further investigation.

Recommendations for Librarians with Similar Programs

Taking the experiences and lessons learned with my work establishing library outreach and instructional services to an international-US partnership, I have the following recommendations for anyone working with similar programs.

1. **Start small.** Focus on learning about the program, the content of the Memorandum of Understanding (MOU), and the types of services/support the library is required to provide. What type of support is the library able to *actually* provide? You do not have to do everything in the first year; it could take several years to build up services.
2. **Make friends.** Identify people or groups within the program that you can build relationships within the other country. It will be very difficult to create a connection with the program without someone on the other side. This will assist you in setting up virtual instruction and reference, guide you on the needs of students, and create a first touch-point to the students. I have found having a contact in Malta to be essential to developing library services with the S-CAR/MEDAC program.
3. **Be flexible, creative, and persistent.** Be prepared to hear the words "no" or "we can't do that" and troubleshoot from there. While it is important to have a big picture of what you would like to do with the program, set simple goals for each year and work toward them. Stretch the goals if needed.
4. **Do not be afraid to ask for the impossible but have a fallback plan just in case.** I recently asked a member of the S-CAR Malta Committee if they would be re-negotiating the MOU with Malta soon and how we can build the library into that. While I do not expect to have more on-site visits, it does not hurt to ask and advocate for this. A single on-site visit will help establish library services because it provides a baseline understanding of what is available to students and faculty and gives you something to work from.
5. **Consider how you can utilize current technology and tools, especially those used for distance education, for the international partnership.** As you work with faculty within the partnership, highlight these tools and how you can use them to assist students with research and applying information literacy skills.

Notes

1. Richard Rubenstein, "Path-Breaking International Masters: Forging a Partnership Between ICAR and the University of Malta," *S-CAR News* 4, no. 3 (April 2010), activity.scar.gmu.edu/newsletter-article/path-breaking-international-masters-forging-partnership-between-icar-and-universi.
2. James Grief, "Mason Offers Conflict Resolution Degree with University of Malta," *University News: George Mason University*, August 9, 2010, https://news.gmu.edu/articles/3781.
3. Ibid.
4. Rubenstein, "Path-Breaking International Masters"; Buzz McClain, "Two Degrees, Two Schools, One Year: Mason and Malta," *University News: George Mason University*, March 7, 2014, https://scar.gmu.edu/news/171.
5. McClain, ""Two Degrees, Two Schools, One Year"; Richard E Rubenstein, "Study Conflict Resolution at University of Malta in 2016–17: The George Mason/U of Malta Dual Degree Program," *Rich Rubenstein's Blog*, May 26, 2016, http://www.rich-rubenstein.com/2016/05/study-conflict-resolution-at-university-of-malta-in-2016-17-the-george-masonu-of-malta-dual-degree-program/.
6. McClain, "Two Degrees, Two Schools, One Year."
7. Paul R. Pival and Kay Johnson, "Tri-Institutional Library Support," *Journal of Library Administration* 41, no. 3–4 (January 25, 2004): 353, doi:10.1300/J111v41n03_01.
8. Jiselle Maria Alleyne and Denyse Rodrigues, "Delivering Information Literacy Instruction for a Joint International Program: An Innovative Collaboration Between Two Libraries," *College & Undergraduate Libraries* 18, no. 2–3 (April 1, 2011), doi:10.1080/10691316.2011.577697.
9. Pival and Johnson, "Tri-Institutional Library Support."
10. Harriett Green, "Libraries Across Land and Sea: Academic Library Services on International Branch Campuses," *College & Research Libraries* 74, no. 1 (January 1, 2013): 9–23, doi:10.5860/crl-259; Susan Mee, "Outreach to International Campuses: Removing Barriers and Building Relationships," *Journal of Library & Information Services in Distance Learning* 7, no. 1–2 (January 1, 2013): 1–17, doi:10.1080/1533290X.2012.705173.
11. Mee, "Outreach to International Campuses."
12. Zhonghong Wang and Paul Tremblay, "The Global Library: Providing Resources and Services to International Sites," *College & Undergraduate Libraries* 16, no. 1 (March 30, 2009): 26–52, doi:10.1080/10691310902754239.
13. Jenny Coombs, "Delivering Information Literacy Support Internationally: A Report of a Visit to the University of Nottingham's Overseas Campuses," *Journal of Information Literacy* 7, no. 1 (May 26, 2013): 90–92, doi:10.11645/7.1.1814; Green, "Libraries Across Land and Sea."
14. Alleyne and Rodrigues, "Delivering Information Literacy Instruction for a Joint International Program."
15. Mee, "Outreach to International Campuses"; Green, "Libraries across Land and Sea"; Alleyne and Rodrigues, "Delivering Information Literacy Instruction for a Joint International Program."
16. Pival and Johnson, "Tri-Institutional Library Support"; Alleyne and Rodrigues, "Delivering Information Literacy Instruction for a Joint International Program."
17. Wang and Tremblay, "The Global Library."
18. Dawn Amsberry, "Talking the Talk: Library Classroom Communication and International Students," *The Journal of Academic Librarianship* 34, no. 4 (July 2008): 354–57, doi:10.1016/j.acalib.2008.05.007.
19. Ibid.
20. Selenay Aytac, "Use of Action Research to Improve Information Literacy Acquisition of International ESL Students," *New Library World* 117, no. 7/8 (June 30, 2016): 464–74, doi:10.1108/NLW-03-2016-0017; Miriam E. Conteh-Morgan, "Empowering ESL Students: A New Model for Information Literacy Instruction," *Research Strategies* 18, no. 1 (2001): 29–38, doi:10.1016/S0734-3310(02)00064-2.

Bibliography

Alleyne, Jiselle Maria, and Denyse Rodrigues. "Delivering Information Literacy Instruction for a Joint International Program: An Innovative Collaboration Between Two Libraries." *College & Undergraduate Libraries* 18, no. 2–3 (April 1, 2011): 261–71. doi:10.1080/10691316.2011.577697.

Amsberry, Dawn. "Talking the Talk: Library Classroom Communication and International Students." *The Journal of Academic Librarianship* 34, no. 4 (July 2008): 354–57. doi:10.1016/j.acalib.2008.05.007.

Aytac, Selenay. "Use of Action Research to Improve Information Literacy Acquisition of International ESL Students." *New Library World* 117, no. 7/8 (June 30, 2016): 464–74. doi:10.1108/NLW-03-2016-0017.

Conteh-Morgan, Miriam E. "Empowering ESL Students: A New Model for Information Literacy Instruction." *Research Strategies* 18, no. 1 (2001): 29–38. doi:10.1016/S0734-3310(02)00064-2.

Coombs, Jenny. "Delivering Information Literacy Support Internationally: A Report of a Visit to the University of Nottingham's Overseas Campuses." *Journal of Information Literacy* 7, no. 1 (May 26, 2013): 90–92. doi:10.11645/7.1.1814.

Green, Harriett. "Libraries Across Land and Sea: Academic Library Services on International Branch Campuses." *College & Research Libraries* 74, no. 1 (January 1, 2013): 9–23. doi:10.5860/crl-259.

Grief, James. "Mason Offers Conflict Resolution Degree with University of Malta." *University News: George Mason University*, August 9, 2010. https://news.gmu.edu/articles/3781.

McClain, Buzz. "Two Degrees, Two Schools, One Year: Mason and Malta." *University News: George Mason University*, March 7, 2014. https://scar.gmu.edu/news/171.

Mee, Susan. "Outreach to International Campuses: Removing Barriers and Building Relationships." *Journal of Library & Information Services in Distance Learning* 7, no. 1–2 (January 1, 2013): 1–17. doi:10.1080/1533290X.2012.705173.

Pival, Paul R., and Kay Johnson. "Tri-Institutional Library Support." *Journal of Library Administration* 41, no. 3–4 (January 25, 2004): 345–54. doi:10.1300/J111v41n03_01.

Rubenstein, Richard. "Path-Breaking International Masters: Forging a Partnership Between ICAR and the University of Malta." *S-CAR News* 4, no. 3 (April 2010). activity.scar.gmu.edu/newsletter-article/path-breaking-international-masters-forging-partnership-between-icar-and-universi.

———. "Study Conflict Resolution at University of Malta in 2016–17: The George Mason/U of Malta Dual Degree Program." *Rich Rubenstein's Blog*, May 26, 2016. http://www.rich-rubenstein.com/2016/05/study-conflict-resolution-at-university-of-malta-in-2016-17-the-george-masonu-of-malta-dual-degree-program/.

Wang, Zhonghong, and Paul Tremblay. "The Global Library: Providing Resources and Services to International Sites." *College & Undergraduate Libraries* 16, no. 1 (March 30, 2009): 26–52. doi:10.1080/10691310902754239.

CHAPTER TWENTY-SEVEN

Globalized Collecting:

Building special collections at NYUAD

Nicholas Martin and Justin Parrott

Background

Special collections at New York University Abu Dhabi (NYUAD) began as a rare and unique opportunity to build a globally minded collection in the United Arab Emirates (UAE) at the crossroads of Africa, Europe, and Asia. At the outset, librarians and faculty collaborated on serving two broad objectives of the University: first, to serve the standard academic goals of teaching, learning, and research, and second, to augment the collections of local institutions such as the National Library and National Archives by building a discoverable and openly accessible repository of special collections materials within the UAE. In terms of academic programs, NYUAD faculty often utilize primary sources in special collections to meet the curricular needs of their students. At the same time, the collection has been built to be an asset to the UAE and the region in general while not being in direct competition with other local institutions.

The term "special collections" can be defined quite differently by research libraries based on a variety of criteria, sometimes distinguished by time (the age of an item), format (analog, digital, archival), and so on. This makes the term rather flexible and contextual.[1] At NYUAD, special collections is envisioned as a space for patrons, including students, faculty, and visiting scholars, to examine and utilize primary sources relevant to the study of Arab heritage, the Middle East and Indian Ocean regions, and the standard American liberal arts curriculum.[2] Items are selected for the collection based on a combination of their relevancy to these ends, rarity, and/or value.

NYUAD itself was the result of an agreement between NYU New York and the government of Abu Dhabi to create a liberal arts educational and research institution committed to preparing students to be "citizens of the world," in the shared belief that amicable interaction among people of different backgrounds and perspectives is inherently valuable and necessary in our increasingly globalized world. NYUAD is part of a global network university system consisting of main degree-granting campuses in Abu

Dhabi, New York, and Shanghai, as well as eleven additional "study away" global sites. Students and scholars move seamlessly through the network while making use of a single integrated library system; through global delivery services and shared online resources, NYU Libraries has pioneered the exchange of international scholarship in the twenty-first century.[3]

NYUAD draws top students from all over the world to prepare them for the mutual challenges and opportunities that lie ahead, as well as attracts new ideas and talent to enrich the country as a beacon and model of progress within the Middle East. In this environment, NYUAD Library is selecting and acquiring materials for special collections to meet the university's broad and specific goals. The collection as a whole is divided into several projects, each with its own unique value and corresponding set of challenges.

Collections

The main special collections at NYUAD contain historic and contemporary materials related to the Arabian Peninsula, the broader geographic region commonly known as MENASA (Middle East, North Africa, and South Asia), and the historic trade hubs surrounding the Indian Ocean. A major goal of the collection is to situate and contextualize the Arabian Gulf within these two significant arenas of economic and cultural exchange. Items in this wide-ranging collection include early printed editions on Islamic science, twentieth-century plays and novels in Arabic (many of which are out of print), Western colonial and orientalist travel narratives and memoirs, and more. This collection draws active interest from NYUAD students and faculty, particularly those in the interdisciplinary Arab Crossroads Studies program, which focuses on the importance of the Gulf region as an historical crossroads connecting Europe, Asia, and Africa. In addition to serving a real institutional need for accessible primary sources, it is the library's hope that this collection will offer a unique and valuable local resource for scholars located in the region. NYUAD Special Collections are open to all interested researchers, regardless of credentials or institutional affiliation.

One of the most important ways that the collections directly support the undergraduate curriculum is by providing raw primary sources for use in classroom teaching and student research and writing. The ability to distinguish between primary and secondary sources is a key outcome of ALA's Information Literacy Guidelines and Competencies for Undergraduate History Students.[4] Primary sources are the "raw data" used in the construction of new information and scholarship. Supporting undergraduates in their use of primary sources within the special collections requires skills involved in accessing, using, interpreting, and evaluating paper documents—everything from the use of finding aids and physically handling rare and fragile materials with proper care to simply knowing the collections exist.[5] Faculty in the classroom often point their students to the collections for examples of primary sources. For instance, a major research topic in history and humanities among faculty has been the global slave-trade and particularly its manifestations at the economic crossroads of the Middle East. To this end, instructors make use of such documents as nineteenth-century British government reports on the slave trade in Zanzibar, or the eighteenth-century Portuguese text *Sucinta relaçam do ultimo naufragio e fim que teve o famozo baxá de Rhodes,* which deals with the slave trade in Malta. Historical documents like these make tangible for students the distinction between primary and secondary sources, between an eyewitness account of slavery and a book about slavery after the fact.

The concept for NYUAD's Global Shakespeare Collection, another major special collections effort, arose in close concert with the University's Arts & Humanities division. NYUAD has engaged actively in Global Shakespeare Studies since its founding and hopes to position itself as an international hub for the field. The Theater and Literature departments host annual Shakespeare-related performance festivals and academic conferences on campus. To add value to this pursuit, the library is collecting early, rare, and contemporary editions of Shakespeare works, mostly in translation. At this point, the Global Shakespeare Collection contains more than 500 volumes in more than thirty languages and offers a perspective on the poet and his works as global cultural commodities. It also provides a unique opportunity to attract research work from our diverse student body, many of whom read and speak English as a second, third, or even fourth language.

Other collections have arisen in collaboration with individual faculty members at the university. Faculty contributions to collection development can be a great boon to building special collections, as long as concepts for new collections are robust and serve the larger mission of the university. Particularly in a library with a small staff, allowing faculty members to act as curators for new library collections enables more rapid collection growth. Such circumstances led to the founding of the Abu Dhabi Film Festival Collection (ADFF) and the Photobook Collection, created in collaboration, respectively, with film and new media professor Dale Hudson and arts and literature professor Shamoon Zamir. In both cases, the faculty members carry a share of collection-development responsibility, alerting the library to potential acquisitions and using their expertise to steer the collections in appropriate directions. Professor Zamir has even been able to raise funds for new acquisitions to expand the Photobook Collection more quickly. Most important, both collections engage with areas of great interest to the university and the UAE: the Abu Dhabi Film Festival is now defunct and therefore begs for documentation, and historical photography is a significant area of study in the UAE and across the MENASA region.

What began as a project to collect, document, and preserve the ADFF films has grown to include original short films, feature films, and documentaries relevant to the region, including some presented at the Dubai International Film Festival and other regional productions. Film is not only of interest locally in the UAE but is also valued as a medium to spread humanizing art, globally minded consciousness, and build bridges between cultures. The primary aim of the film collection is to support the immediate curricular needs of the Film and New Media major as well as related programs such as Arab Crossroads. In particular, ADFF films and other Emirati films have been used as supplementary material for the Arabic-language learning program.[6] The secondary aim of the collection is to serve the university's broader mission of promoting advanced research and intercultural communication and understanding. Beyond the ADFF project, the criteria for acceptance into the special collections—as opposed to the main multimedia collection—is a combination of cost, rarity, relevance, and licensing restrictions (if applicable). The library has established and continues to seek out new relationships with independent filmmakers and producers in the Middle East, Europe, and elsewhere, with the goal of building a rich collection of an international scope and character. As the research interests at NYUAD are as diverse as the student population, selections have been purchased in a variety of languages if English subtitles are provided, since English is the official instructional language of the university. Occasionally, some films were deemed important enough to acquire even without subtitles. The ambition moving forward, at the encouragement of the Film and New Media faculty, is to develop the collection even further to include other film festivals in the MENASA region.

The Photobook Collection developed as a complement to an already-existing research and archives initiative. NYUAD's Akkasah Center for Photography, which has its headquarters in the NYUAD Library, "explores the histories and contemporary practices of photography in the Arab world from comparative perspectives."[7] Akkasah acquires, preserves, and digitizes photograph collections from the Arab world, making them accessible online via its website. The center also hosts conferences and invites visiting researchers to examine its collections. Once digitized, the original photographic prints, negatives, and slides from the Akkasah collections are housed and made accessible through the NYUAD Special Collections reading room. These collections are described archivally in order to become discoverable via NYU's special collections search tool. The Photobook Collection was partially conceived as a complement to the archival collections the Akkasah staff were collecting. The Akkasah collections are rich in vernacular photography, including personal and studio portrait photography. The Photobook Collection, which tracks the medium from a global art-historical perspective, provides a contextual counterpart to the archival collections; visitors to the reading room can explore the development of photography from its inception through the lens of studio photographers, artists, and everyday people in the Arab world and around the globe.

Challenges

The global nature of special collections at NYUAD presents unique challenges related to acquisitions, processing, and cataloging. These challenges, however, should not be a reason to limit the mission, scope, and access to the collections. The approach has been to focus primarily on the needs and wants of users; any difficulties in the processing of materials are of secondary importance and solutions are sought on a case-by-case basis.

Funds for special collections are built into the structure of the library's annual budget, providing a baseline for acquisitions alongside budget lines for general collections, electronic resources, and operating costs. If additional funds remain near the end of the fiscal calendar from other budget lines, and the library has no other purchasing priorities, this surplus is often allocated for special collections materials. Occasionally, the library also receives funds from donors to acquire specific materials for the collection. Due to this relative fluidity in the budget, curators take a conservative approach to purchasing over the course of the fiscal year, often revisiting potential acquisitions as new funds become available later.

Purchasing materials from a variety of sources requires the use of multiple methods of payment and shipment. University guidelines stipulate standard payment by a mailed USD (US dollars) check as the preferred option, with wire transfers in USD (within a certain threshold cost) as a secondary option. This allows for necessary tracking of expenses on the special collections budget. Standard payments through normal channels may also take some time to process. Predictably, smaller vendors and unique outlets often have different preferences, sometimes asking for payments in a local currency or by another irregular route, such as Western Union. Negotiation is often needed to arrive at a resolution acceptable to both parties, the vendor, and the financial policies of NYU Division of Libraries.

When standard payment is not an option, the library's third preferred option is to use a purchasing card or another reliable service like PayPal. If a credit card purchase is unavailable, then it has been possible for staff, librarians, and faculty to purchase items from their own funds and receive a reimbursement from the collections budget. The reimbursement method has been used often to acquire films, books, and other materials, particularly by faculty and students visiting foreign countries that have access to materials and markets unavailable elsewhere.

Besides payment, films present another challenge of licensing access to the materials. Filmmakers and documentarians, especially those from the Abu Dhabi Film Festival, sometimes do not offer their work commercially. They may be reluctant to sell their films to a library in an effort to protect their work from copyright violations. Hardly any emerging filmmaker, for example, wants their work to show up on YouTube or Vimeo and therefore lose revenue from screenings or sales. In such a case, the library offers them payment along with a clearly worded legal agreement stipulating that the film will be held in the non-circulating collection and will be viewed only on campus in a controlled, academic setting. Most of the time, filmmakers readily agree and are pleased to receive exposure to faculty and students, yet the library still must remain sensitive to their legitimate concerns as content-creators.

The effort to acquire unique materials for the collections results in the constant need for original catalog records. Films, rare books, maps, and other multimedia require distinct cataloging expertise in each particular format. For example, an Arabic-language film requires a cataloger with expertise in both Arabic and multimedia cataloging. It is not possible, due to staffing limitations, for the NYUAD Library to have all the expertise needed on-site to catalog every item acquired. For this reason, the library relies heavily on the expertise of colleagues based at NYU in New York.[8] Films and other items are cataloged by "surrogate," a process in which digital images or copies of an item are shared with colleagues for cataloging purposes and are discarded later.

Sometimes, as is the case with the Global Shakespeare Collection, the library acquires items in languages that neither staff in Abu Dhabi nor New York can read. For instance, the library acquired a batch of Shakespeare translations in Armenian and Tagalog, both of which no staff member can read. One option is to outsource cataloging to services such as OCLC TechPro; however, the cost of such services is often prohibitively high for the number of items in need of cataloging. When an item cannot be fully cataloged, brief partial records are created to represent the item to patrons as best as possible.

Preservation concerns for items in the NYUAD Special Collections are another real challenge to the library. Since collection materials are cataloged in person by special collections catalogers on the NYU New York campus, identifying concerns and planning actions remotely can be difficult. To that end, NYUAD librarians rely upon various sources, from bookseller's descriptions to advice from on-site catalogers, for clues to an item's disposition. If an item seems like it will require treatment, it can be assessed by NYU Libraries' conservators and treated before shipment to Abu Dhabi. NYUAD does not employ any trained conservators, so when items arrive in need of treatment, only basic, non-invasive actions can be taken, such as fabricating phase boxes or clamshell enclosures made of archival board.

Special collections materials are often desirable fodder for digitization projects, and the NYUAD Special Collections have been no exception. Projects in digital humanities are pursued with increasing frequency at NYUAD, and faculty often wish to engage directly with rare materials in the library. This presents similar problems to those surrounding preservation: NYUAD has, to date, lacked the resources to invest in preservation-level digitization equipment and expertise. The university is still able to pursue digital preservation and access projects in collaboration with NYU New York, but librarians are reluctant to send rare, typically fragile materials from Abu Dhabi to New York for digitization. Digitizing materials on campus would also be preferable from an instructional standpoint, giving students a window into the complexities involved in the process.

To explore those complexities, even in the absence of state-of-the-art digitization facilities, the library worked with digital humanities professor David Wrisley to design a workshop in map digitization to take place in the special collections. The goal of the workshop was to attempt to capture usable digital images of folding maps from the collections. Some of these were bound into rare books; others were exceedingly large. The workshop, then, focused on the difficulty of capturing high-resolution digital images of these materials without damaging the materials in the process. In that way, the collections still offered a valuable teaching tool, despite the lack of resources at hand.

Conclusion

The mission of special collections at NYUAD involves multiple layers and audiences; an imperative to support the immediate learning outcomes of the undergraduate curriculum, to act as a repository of original documents (including films) for advanced research, to attract world-class scholars with its offerings, to build unique collections that augment (without competing with) the local national archives, and to become an asset to the global academic community. Acquisitions in each of the sub-collections were initiated with these specific and broader goals in mind. Librarians at NYUAD perform outreach on behalf of the collections as part of their regular subject liaison duties, knowing well the value of the collections to teaching and research, both locally and internationally.

Nevertheless, creating collections of international and multilingual scope presents formidable challenges for librarians. A limited amount of subject, language, and technical expertise is available among the staff—even with the help of New York-based colleagues—to meet the procedural and logistical challenges of such efforts. Librarians must come up with innovative solutions to satisfy the users first and foremost, while at the same time balancing staff resources with the administrative standards of NYU's Global University Network.

But as it is said, "If you aren't in over your head, how do you know how tall you are?"[9] A great collection with an international vision is not built from inside a librarian's comfort zone. It does not consist of merely the safe acquisitions—easily purchased, easily cataloged, easily accessed. Rather, the uniqueness and value of an acquisition are proportional to the challenges it raises; as the cost of an investment is higher, the potential payback is even greater. Students, faculty, and visiting scholars are exposed to exceptional teaching, learning, and research opportunities with the capability of transmitting their findings, knowledge, and insights into diverse languages and cultures across the world. The way forward is beset by more obstacles from a librarian's perspective, to be sure, yet any difficulties are offset by the excitement of contributing to a worthwhile venture, pushing the limits of just how far the institution and profession can go.

Notes

1. Alice Prochaska, "Special Collections in an International Perspective," *Library Trends* 52 (2003): 138–139.
2. Virginia Danielson and Michael Stoller, "Creating Special Collections: A Case Study from NYU Abu Dhabi," in *Bridging Worlds: Emerging Models and Practices of U.S. Academic Libraries Around the Globe*, ed. Ray Pun et al. (Chicago: Association of College and Research Libraries, 2016), 107.
3. Beth D. Lindsay et al., "Creating Global Delivery Strategy: Services, Systems and Practices," in *Bridging Worlds: Emerging Models and Practices of U.S. Academic Libraries Around the Globe*, ed. Ray Pun et al. (Chicago: Association of College and Research Libraries, 2016), 27.
4. "Information Literacy Guidelines and Competencies for Undergraduate History Students," last modified May 28, 2013, http://www.ala.org/rusa/resources/guidelines/infoliteracy.
5. Peter Carini, "Information Literacy for Archives and Special Collections: Defining Outcomes," *portal: Libraries and the Academy* 16, no. 1 (2016): 197–200.
6. Nasser Isleem and Hajar Madi, *al-Lughah al-□Arabīyah fī al-aflām al-Imārātīyah: Nāfidhah lughawīyah wa-thaqāfīyah □alá al-aflām al-Imārātīyah = Arabic language in the Emirati films: linguistic and cultural window on Emirati films* (S.l.: Createspace, 2016), i.
7. "Akkasah: Center for Photography," accessed May 1, 2017, http://nyuad.nyu.edu/en/research/faculty-research/akkasah.html.
8. Justin Parrott, "Communication and Collaboration in Library Technical Services: A Case Study of New York University in Abu Dhabi," *New Review of Academic Librarianship* 22 no. 2/3 (2016): 297–300.
9. Attributed to T.S. Eliot, but it seems to be a paraphrase of his quote, "Only those who will risk going too far can possibly find out just how far one can go," in Preface to Crosby, Harry, *Transit of Venus: Poems* (Paris: Black Sun Press, 1931).

Bibliography

"Akkasah: Center for Photography." Accessed May 1, 2017. http://nyuad.nyu.edu/en/research/faculty-research/akkasah.html.

Carini, Peter. "Information Literacy for Archives and Special Collections: Defining Outcomes." *portal: Libraries and the Academy* 16, no. 1 (2016): 191–206.

Crosby, Harry. *Transit of Venus: Poems*. Paris: Black Sun Press, 1931.

Danielson, Virginia, and Michael Stoller. "Creating Special Collections: A Case Study from NYU Abu Dhabi." In *Bridging Worlds: Emerging Models and Practices of U.S. Academic Libraries Around the Globe*, edited by Ray Pun, Scott Collard, & Justin Parrott, 105–12. Chicago: Association of College and Research Libraries, 2016.

Freire, Manuel Tomás da Silva. *Sucinta relaçam do ultimo naufragio e fim que teve o famozo baxá de Rhodes, primeiro, e o mais perfido autor da conspiraçaõ ideada contra toda a ilha de Malta*. [Lisbon]: [Joze da Silva da Natividade], 1749.

Great Britain. *British Government reports: a collection of eight reports and correspondence on Zanzibar, its trade and commerce, slavery and the slave trade presented to the Houses of Parliament between 1887 and 1919*. London: His Majesty's Stationery Office, 1887.

Isleem, Nasser, and Hajar Madi. *al-Lughah al-□Arabīyah fī al-aflām al-Imārātīyah: Nāfidhah lughawīyah wa-thaqāfīyah □alá al-aflām al-Imārātīyah = Arabic language in the Emirati films: linguistic and cultural window on Emirati films*. S.l.: Createspace, 2016.

Lindsay, Beth D., and Kristina Rose, Sydney Thompson, Shoshannah Turgel. "Creating Global Delivery Strategy: Services, Systems and Practices." In *Bridging Worlds: Emerging Models and Practices of U.S. Academic Libraries Around the Globe*, edited by Ray Pun, Scott Collard, and Justin Parrott, 27–40. Chicago: Association of College and Research Libraries, 2016.

Parrott, Justin. "Communication and Collaboration in Library Technical Services: A Case Study of New York University in Abu Dhabi," *New Review of Academic Librarianship* 22 no. 2/3 (2016):

294–303.

Prochaska, Alice. "Special Collections in an International Perspective." *Library Trends* 52 (2003): 138–50.

Pun, Ray, Scott Collard, and Justin Parrott, eds. *Bridging Worlds: Emerging Models and Practices of U.S. Academic Libraries Around the Globe.* Chicago: Association of College and Research Libraries, 2016.

Reference and User Services Association (RUSA), and American Library Association (ALA). "Information Literacy Guidelines and Competencies for Undergraduate History Students." Last modified May 28, 2013. http://www.ala.org/rusa/resources/guidelines/infoliteracy.

SECTION V

Career & Professional Development

CHAPTER TWENTY-EIGHT

International Academic Librarianship:

Meeting Our Professional, Institutional, and Personal Goals

John Boyd and Elizabeth Cramer

Introduction

What is an "international librarian?" A librarian that is globally aware, who travels and experiences the traditions and cultures of other countries. A librarian that liaises with international students and scholars and domestic students studying abroad. A librarian whose research or service agenda spans outside of their home country. For the authors, our experience as international librarians includes all the above, with travel to fourteen countries for research, service, and librarian exchanges. We are experiencing other cultures while creating scholarship and service agendas that serve our university, our profession, and the international library community. Consider this chapter a "how-to" for building an international research and service record: obtaining institutional support; developing expertise and professional connections to advance your scholarship and service; building cultural competencies at home and abroad; obtaining funding; and, ultimately, achieving professional and personal fulfillment.

In this chapter, we share our experience on how we fulfilled our dream to be international academic librarians. For readers to understand our experience, we provide background about our careers, including our research and service records. We have worked most of our careers (over twenty years each) at Appalachian State University Libraries, located in Boone, North Carolina. Beth has worked on the Resource Acquisition and Management team as a cataloger and coordinator and in collection management as a liaison for the Department of Languages, Literatures, and Cultures (DLLC). She obtained a masters in French in 2005, allowing her to teach French in the DLLC as an adjunct instructor. In 2012 she completed her doctorate in educational leadership, focusing on international library aid for developing countries. Beth is active in the American Library

Association's International Relations Round Table (ALA IRRT), serving as chair 2016–2017 and past editor of *International Leads*. Her research interests include international library development and the ALA Sister Library Initiative. Recent site visits include travel to Ghana, Zambia, Central America, Nepal, and India.

John has worked on the Library and Research Services team as a traditional Reference Librarian, known at Appalachian State University Libraries as an Information Literacy Librarian. He works with undergraduate and graduate students in all disciplines, but his first love is helping first-year students navigate the library and the research process. Much of his time is spent teaching in the classroom and in coordinating the library's Research Advisory Program (known as RAP Sessions at Appalachian), whereby students meet individually with a librarian for research help. His research interests also include international library development and the influence of libraries in communities. He has always been active in supporting campus internationalization efforts, including hosting international students and visiting scholars in the library, participating in the university's International Education Week, presenting to study abroad students on library services and resources, co-organizing the Global Film Series, and getting involved with programs through Appalachian's Office of International Education and Development (OIED).

Institutional Support

One of the most important factors in becoming an international librarian is to find an institution that will support a librarian in achieving this goal. Likewise, a librarian must work to support the goals of their institution. This match between personal, professional, and institutional goals is critical. However, libraries and universities vary widely in their support for internationalization and the role of the librarian in these endeavors.[1] To find a good match, one can review the mission, vision, and strategic directions of universities and their libraries. After browsing more than thirty universities' mission statements, we found the following terms that signal a commitment to internationalization: global learning, intercultural skills, global community, world scholars, global society, interconnected world, and cultural enrichment, among others. One can also review library annual reports or individual librarians' vitaes, if they are made available to the public, for evidence of internationalization support.

At Appalachian State University, librarians are tenure-track faculty members with expectations for research and service. One reason both authors have worked at Appalachian for over twenty years is the tremendous support librarians receive in terms of funding, release time, and choice of scholarly agendas. As individuals with shared passions for travel, libraries, and new experiences, we craft research and service agendas that allow us to pursue our interests while addressing two strategic directions of Appalachian State University: sustainability and global learning. Both directions are emphasized in the first sentence of the university's mission statement: "Appalachian State University prepares students to lead purposeful lives as global citizens who understand their responsibilities in creating a sustainable future for all."[2] Our research and service agendas acknowledge and support these directions by focusing on relevant topics: the sustainability of libraries created by international non-governmental organizations (INGOs) in developing countries, library services to international students and students studying abroad, and international partnerships and exchanges among university libraries.

Building International Research and Service Agendas

In our careers at Appalachian State University, we have had the opportunity to develop multiple research agendas. While we have both published within our specializations (technical services and library instruction), we have also published journal articles, book chapters, and news pieces on international topics. On some occasions, our specializations and internationalization were combined, one example being an article one of the authors co-wrote about building ties between serials librarians at Fudan University (China) and Appalachian State University Libraries.[3] So, whether you are a liaison librarian, a technical services librarian, or an information technology librarian, all areas of library specialization can include an international angle. With some creative thinking and institutional support, all librarians can establish an international research agenda.

Our service agendas were developed at three levels: library, university, and professional. As with our scholarship, we followed our interests while meeting the needs and expectations of Appalachian State University. At the library level, we both served on the Diversity Committee for over a decade. As members of this committee, we helped with the library reception for new international students, interviewed small focus groups of international and study-abroad students about the library's services and collections, and created the Global Film Series. The Series screens six international films each year, each film co-sponsored by a student language, ethnic, or culture club. The student clubs help to select a film, advertise the screening, and promote their club to the film audience.

At the university level, we work closely with the Office of International Education and Development (OIED). We have served on the International Education Week Planning Committee, the Global Engagement Council, and OIED search committees, plus we collaborate with OIED to screen the Global Film Series and arrange library tours and other hosting functions for international students and scholars. Building a positive relationship with OIED has benefited us in many ways. They have made introductions for us to partner universities in France and England and provided travel funds for establishing ties with libraries in Mexico and China. Most recently, OIED has procured host invitations from two partner universities in India in support of a future Fulbright application.

At the professional level, we have been involved with the American Library Association's International Relations Round Table (ALA IRRT). Both authors have served as volunteers at the IRRT International Visitors' Center, presented posters and papers at IRRT programs, and attended IRRT lunches and receptions. Through their participation in IRRT, they networked with other international librarians, discovering ideas and opportunities that helped them to craft their research and service agendas.

In crafting their international research and service agenda, the authors began by recognizing their love of languages, cultures, and travel. Beth established her first service and research agenda around the Spanish language, a topic that connects with her role as library liaison to the Department of Languages, Literatures, and Cultures (DLLC). The evolution of this agenda serves as an example of how one opportunity leads to additional research, service, and funding opportunities. For example, the authors' attendance at the NCLA Conference in 2002 led to numerous such opportunities and eventually to obtaining travel funding:

- 2002—While attending NCLA (North Carolina Library Association), volunteered to help establish the Carolina Chapter of REFORMA (National Asso-

ciation to Promote Library & Information Services to Latinos and the Spanish-Speaking)
- 2003—Applied for and received the ALA-FIL Free Pass Program to attend the Feria Internacional del Libro in Guadalajara, Mexico, for six days
- 2006—Presented a paper, "ESL and SSL: English and Spanish as Second Languages Collection Development," at the First Joint Conference of Librarians of Color, in Dallas, Texas; the paper was published in the conference proceedings
- 2006—Obtained a $1,500 travel grant through the University's Appalachian Fellows Foundation Grant, a grant that supports faculty members' career development; Beth used the money to study Spanish in Guatemala for one month
- 2006–2009—Presented at six additional conferences on the topic of REFORMA and library services for speakers of Spanish
- 2008—Published "Servicios para la Comunidad: Sharing the Experience of Three Hispanic Services Librarians in North Carolina," in *North Carolina Libraries*

Another way in which a research and service agenda evolves is through professional connections. This is particularly the case with finding opportunities to present at conferences or institutions. The following are some examples of making serendipitous connections:

- While leading a tour of the Appalachian State University Libraries for visiting officials from Université d'Angers (France), we made contacts that later led to spending our 2012 sabbatical at the Université d'Angers. During that semester, we presented three times at l'Université and were invited to attend many campus and social activities.
- Through service in ALA IRRT, we met William Middleton, a US Department of State Information Resource Officer (IRO). William was serving as the IRO for Nepal and India and helped us to establish contacts and arrange speaking and publishing opportunities in 2015–2016.
- While attending a campus presentation about Sister Library initiatives, we met Gabi Vallejo, founder of la Biblioteca Th'uruchapitas, the first children's library in Bolivia. Following the lead of Appalachian faculty member Linda Veltze, we became involved in supporting la Biblioteca, an endeavor that led to two trips to Bolivia, two published articles, a poster session, and three program presentations (ALA Annual 2012, Library 2.0 2012, and the IX Congreso Nacional del IBBY in Cochabamba, Bolivia, 2015).

Figure 28.1. Gaby Vallejo, John Boyd, students, and volunteers at la Biblioteca Th'uruchapitas in Cochabamba, Bolivia.

Opportunities to Build Cultural Competencies at Home

As librarians at an institution of higher education, we are uniquely positioned to engage people from all over the world.[4] At home and abroad, through interactions with international guests visiting our university and through our travels, we have developed a degree of cultural competency that allows us to successfully engage with students, faculty, scholars, and librarians from around the world, to learn from them, and to share stories and ideas with them. This engagement has become an important part of our work and personal lives. The Association of College and Research Libraries (ACRL) in their document, "Cultural Competency for Academic Libraries," defines cultural competence as "the process by which individuals and systems respond respectfully and effectively to people of all cultures."[5]

At Appalachian, we have taken advantage of many opportunities to interact with students and visitors from around the world. For six years, Appalachian State University has hosted hundreds of international teachers through the Teacher Excellence and Achievement (TEA) Program, funded by the US Department of State's Bureau of Educational and Cultural Affairs. This program brings teachers (Teaching Fellows) from other countries to our campus and to our local schools for four weeks of interactive workshops to enhance their teaching skills. Their visits include seven scheduled visits to the University Libraries as well as a two-week teaching experience with a partner teacher in an area secondary school. During their time at the libraries, they receive library instruction from the Instructional Materials Center (IMC) librarians and are given access to the Idea Factory in the IMC, which provides resources for them to create classroom displays and teaching materials.

Each year, the Office of International Education and Development (OIED) offers faculty, staff, and community members the opportunity to serve as host families to the TEA Fellows. Through this program, we have hosted TEA Fellows from Egypt, Cote d'Ivoire, Tunisia, India, China, Pakistan, and many more countries. We invite TEA Fellows to our home to share a meal, spend the weekend, enjoy a picnic and hike along the Blue Ridge Parkway, or go to a local festival. As volunteers for the TEA Fellows program, we serve as an additional source of information about the community, the university, and the United States. We have made many friends throughout the world and continue to keep in touch through Facebook and LinkedIn.

A second example of hosting international visitors is the Legislative Fellows Program for South Africans, a collaborative program between Appalachian State University and the Africa Governance Transformation, funded by the US Department of State's Bureau of Educational and Cultural Affairs. The goals of this two-year program are to strengthen South Africa's democracy, assist in the development of mid-level government professionals, and to enhance the skills of South African legislative professionals. Each South African Fellow participates in a four-week individualized internship program, visiting a location within the US that corresponds with the size of their governmental unit in South Africa.

Once again, the OIED puts out a call for volunteers to host a South African Legislative Fellow in their home, but for Fellows in this program, it was for a month-long stay. So, for two consecutive years, we hosted a Legislative Fellow from KwaZulu-Natal Province in our home. This gave us ample time for nightly dinner conversations about that day's events and what was going on in the world around us, both locally and globally. Those two months were very special and rewarding and gave us time together to gain a greater understanding and appreciation for each other.

Each academic year at Appalachian brings new opportunities to support internationalization efforts on campus and in the library. Other opportunities have included giving a library tour to new international students, hosting a library table during International Education Week, or giving presentations on library services and resources to Appalachian students planning to study abroad. Seek out opportunities within your university and community that offer the possibility of enriching your understanding and appreciation of other cultures and peoples through direct interaction. We choose to participate in these activities not only because we get to meet people from all over the world but because it also provides us with service opportunities that reflect our personal goals, the goals of the University Libraries, and the goals of Appalachian State University. To learn about the wide array of programs, activities, and funded international projects at Appalachian State University, visit the website of the Office of International Education and Development at https://international.appstate.edu/.

Opportunities to Build Cultural Competencies Abroad

Our travels to other countries, often including library visits, have helped strengthen our cultural competencies as well as demonstrate our own commitment, the library's commitment, and the university's commitment to global learning. As faculty on campus, we serve as an example and (hopefully) inspiration to students and fellow faculty about the benefits of breaking out of your comfort zone to experience what the world offers. Establishing global connections has enabled us to share ideas and cultural perspectives with others that enhance understanding and knowledge about each other's cultures. Below are some examples of our international travels that have enhanced our cultural competencies, broadened our global perspectives, and helped us to strengthen a global community within our university.

The University Libraries have established two programs in China—the American Culture Center (ACC) at Northeastern University in Shenyang and a formal librarian exchange program with Fudan University in Shanghai. The ACC was established in 2013 when two library colleagues, Xiaorong Shao and Allan Scherlen, received an initial $100,000 grant from the US Department of State to establish an American Culture Center at Northeastern University.[6] The ACC is jointly operated by Appalachian State University and Northeastern University and is one of nineteen Centers established in China. The ACC houses approximately 8,200 books in English, 3,500 books in Chinese, films, CDs, and periodicals. The ACC sponsors programs and activities throughout the year, including film screenings, American culture lectures, student leader programs, faculty development and exchanges, arts and music performances, and Fulbright lectures.

Each year, Xiaorong and Allan select a topic for the ACC programming, such as sustainability and academic writing. Selected faculty from Appalachian travel each year to Shenyang to present workshops and programs, an opportunity extended to us in 2015. Along with Xiaorong and colleagues from Appalachian's Department of Anthropology and the Sustainable Development Department, we presented lectures and film discussions on the topic of sustainability. Presentations included: US Literature and the Environment;

US Environmental Justice and Sustainable Development; Film Discussions: *Food Inc.* and *No Impact Man*; and Higher Education and Graduate Studies in the US. Our visit also included scheduled meetings with librarian counterparts at Northeastern University and two Appalachian partner universities, the University of Shanghai for Science and Technology and Beijing International Studies University. These visits included tours of the libraries, discussions of recent trends, opportunities, and challenges in Chinese and American academic libraries, and each day ended with the sharing of gifts and a fabulous meal.

The second program—the Fudan-Appalachian Librarian Exchange Program—was initiated in 2009 to exchange librarians between Fudan University Library and Appalachian University Libraries. Each librarian is in residence at the others' institution for one to four months. Beth, along with library dean Mary Reichel, Xiaorong Shao, and Allan Scherlen, traveled to China in 2008 to establish this program. The initial agreement was for four years and was renewed for an additional three years in 2015. Workshops and presentations conducted by visiting Appalachian librarians to Fudan University have been on a wide range of topics, including user experience research in academic libraries, research by students in 3D environments, embedded librarianship, delivering library content for course management systems, information literacy and why it matters, and the role of an Instructional Materials Center in supporting student teacher education.

As librarians with faculty status, Appalachian State University librarians are eligible for sabbaticals, officially referred to as an Off-Campus Scholarly Assignment, or OCSA. After getting approval from our library colleagues for an OCSA, the authors decided to spend the 2012 fall academic semester at one of our university's partner institutions, the Université d'Angers in Angers, France. Our initial plan was to finish researching and writing two articles, one on the sustainability of Reicken Community Libraries in Guatemala and Honduras and the other on bicycle tourists and public libraries. We did complete these projects, but our stay became much richer by making connections with students and faculty at the university and with people from the city of Angers. These connections allowed us numerous opportunities to engage with the local community, including lectures to students from the university's Library Science program and Archival Science program, multiple presentations to librarians at the university, and each Thursday morning throughout the semester we led an English conversation group for native French speakers at the Bibliothéque Anglophone (English-Language Library) in Angers.

Figure 28.2. The authors with the library staff of the Bibliloteca Riecken Library in Tatumbla, Honduras.

Acquiring Funding

The first question other librarians ask when we tell them about our international endeavors is, how did we pay for them? We answer by saying it is a combination of our own money and funding from our library, the university, and external sources. When we began our careers, we requested funds from the library travel budget and our library's innovation grant, the Martha and Nancy Lee Bivens University Library Fund Grant. We progressed to applying for university travel and research grants, and more recently we have begun applying for external grants. And as we write more grant proposals, our grant-writing skills improve.

Funding from our library has come through two sources, the library travel budget and the Bivens Grant. We have received funding through the library travel budget by presenting a strong rationale of how our research and service will impact students, faculty, and the profession. Examples of support from the library travel budget include travel to Bolivia to present at an IBBY (International Board on Books for Young People) Conference, air travel in support of Beth's doctoral dissertation work in Ghana and Zambia, and air travel to France for our OCSA. We have also received funding from the Bivens Grant to visit partner universities in England to discuss potential librarian exchanges and to supplement a University Research Grant to travel to Nepal in 2014.

As faculty librarians at Appalachian, we have been fortunate to be eligible for a wide variety of university research grants. Funding received from our university includes an Appalachian State University Research Council Grant received in 2014 to investigate the sustainability of libraries supported by two INGOs in Nepal, Room to Read and READ Global. As previously mentioned, one of the authors has also received a professional development grant, the Appalachian Fellows Foundation Grant, for improving her Spanish language skills in Guatemala.

Figure 28.3. Elizabeth Cramer with teachers and library staff at the Rajratna Primary School and Library in Nawalparasi District, Nepal.

At the national and professional level, Beth received in 2015 the Harold Lancour Scholarship for Foreign Study from Beta Phi Mu International Honor Society to investigate the sustainability of libraries in India supported by INGOs. She is currently investigating applying for a Fulbright Scholar's Grant to teach and perform research in India with support from the Office of International Education and Development. Several ALA IRRT colleagues have received Fulbright grants from the US Department of State in the past, assuring her that Fulbright is looking for a variety of scholars. Librarians are very well situated to have a grant proposal accepted for travel to another country to either teach or conduct research.

In locating funding opportunities and writing grant proposals, we offer the following advice:

- Investigate funding opportunities. One excellent source is to connect with your university's grants resources and services office. Upon our request, we receive an email every month from the office with library-related grant opportunities.
- Write your grant proposal/application to directly address the scope of the grant. If it is a university grant, how does your proposed research intersect with stated strategic campus directions? How does your research directly impact students, faculty, and the profession?
- Do not be modest when it comes to the impact of your research. You must convey your confidence in your research in order to convince others of its importance.
- Include a statement from your dean or supervisor that supports your grant application. Even better, secure a pledge of library financial support to supplement your grant proposal.
- Find an experienced grant writer to proofread your proposal and to offer advice for improvements.
- Make contacts with individuals and institutions abroad to support your grant proposal. For example, in our investigation of INGOs working in developing countries, we needed to show that the INGOs had agreed to allow us access to their libraries for site visits and to interview their librarians.

Achieving Professional and Personal Goals

To close this chapter, we share our reflections on how our experience traveling and working with international partners has impacted our librarianship, teaching, and personal lives. For John, internationalization changed his approach to library instructions sessions by consciously incorporating research from around the globe. Students would too often dismiss research from other countries as either not relevant to their own work or seen somehow as inferior. Sometimes they were not even aware of their pro-Western bias in the choice of resources. He learned to emphasize that in this day of instant global connectivity, scholars, teachers, and students are easily able to collaborate with others from around the world. Students often expressed surprise when a paper was authored by researchers from two or more different countries.

For Beth, traveling has given her a much broader scope of knowledge and experience with which to develop the language and non-English literature collections and to serve as liaison with the DLLC. When one is planning travel to another country, that geographical region becomes more of a reality. You begin to understand a bit about the culture, people, and lives of people upon your investigation. The actual travel to the place makes that understanding even deeper and more personal. We have now traveled to countries that speak Chinese, French, Spanish, German, and Arabic, plus numerous local languages. Through immersion in non-English and non-Western cultures, we now understand more about the challenges in language acquisition and adaptation experienced by many of our international students and scholars.

Sharing our experiences with colleagues gives them a greater understanding of the libraries' and university's strategic efforts for internationalization and global learning. It may spark their interest in spending two months in China as a visiting librarian at Fudan University or applying for a university international research grant. We work toward building their confidence to venture outside of their comfort zone. The number one regret of older people is not what they did do, it is those things that they did not do.

And our last bit of advice: Never undervalue the worth of meeting your personal goals while also being able to fulfill your professional goals and expectations. At times, people lose sight that there are ways to combine your life's passions with your career. By following your passion in some segment of your duties, you are adding to the scope of librarianship. Chances are, others share your passion and appreciate you forging new territory, whether it be travel, physical fitness, popular culture, or other interests. For us, combining travel with research resulted in experiences outside the general tourist realm. We traveled by tuk-tuk, bicycle, and jeep on treacherous back roads to visit libraries in small villages in Guatemala and Nepal, attended a librarian social in Delhi with more than 100 local librarians, lived in a small fishing village in Ghana, and have been invited into the homes of fellow librarians in several countries. We have more courage, empathy, curiosity, and enthusiasm for future travels. We are deeply grateful for these experiences and realize they have forever changed us.

Notes

1. Steven W. Witt, Laurie Kutner, and Liz Cooper, "Mapping Academic Library Contributions to Campus Internationalization," *College & Research Libraries* 76, no. 5 (2015): 587–608, https://doi.org/10.5860/crl.76.5.587.
2. "Mission, Vision and Values," Appalachian State University, accessed April 24, 2017, http://www.appstate.edu/about/mission-values/.
3. Allan Scherlen, Xiaorong Shao, and Elizabeth Cramer, "Bridges to China: Developing Partnerships between Serials Librarians in the U. S. and China," *Serials Review* 35 no. 2 (June 2009): 75–79.
4. Maria P. Cantu, "Three Effective Strategies of Internationalization in American Universities," *Journal of International Education and Leadership* 3, no. 3 (Fall 2013): 1–12, accessed *Education Source*, EBSCO*host* (accessed August 11, 2017).
5. "Diversity Standards: Cultural Competency for Academic Libraries," Association of College and Research Libraries, 2012, http://www.ala.org/acrl/standards/diversity.
6. "Appalachian Opens American Cultural Center at China's Northeastern University," Appalachian State University, accessed July 15, 2017, http://newsarchive.appstate.edu/2013/07/15/northeastern-university-china/.

Bibliography

Appalachian State University. “Appalachian opens American Cultural Center at China’s Northeastern University.” Last modified July 15, 2013. http://newsarchive.appstate.edu/2013/07/15/northeastern-university-china/.

Appalachian State University. “Mission, Vision and Values.” Accessed April 24, 2017. http://www.appstate.edu/about/mission-values/.

Association of College and Research Libraries. “Diversity Standards: Cultural Competency for Academic Libraries.” 2012. http://www.ala.org/acrl/standards/diversity.

Cantu, Maria P. “Three Effective Strategies of Internationalization in American Universities.” *Journal of International Education and Leadership* 3, no. 3 (Fall 2013): 1–12. Accessed *Education Source*, EBSCO*host* (accessed August 11, 2017).

Scherlen, Allan, Xiaorong Shao, and Elizabeth Cramer. “Bridges to China: Developing Partnerships between Serials Librarians in the U. S. and China.” *Serials Librarian* 35, no. 2 (2009): 75–79.

Witt, Steven W., Laurie Kutner, and Liz Cooper. “Mapping Academic Library Contributions to Campus Internationalization.” *College & Research Libraries* 76, no. 5 (2015): 587–608. doi:10.5860/crl.76.5.587.

International
Peer-Mentoring

CHAPTER TWENTY-NINE

Virtual Peer-Mentoring Programs:

Building Global Professional Connections Through the International Librarians Network

Kelsey Corlett-Rivera and Pirjo Kangas

Introduction

This chapter focuses on the International Librarians Network (ILN) peer-mentoring program and the opportunities it provided to build a global professional network. The chapter will be of interest to librarians who are interested in expanding their network internationally while developing as professionals through a well-run, informal, virtual peer-mentoring program. We will present a case study of our experience as ILN program participants in spring 2016. Our aim is to explore the effectiveness of the ILN program, in part to determine how long-distance peer-mentoring programs like these can help build international connections between libraries and librarians and contribute to our professional development.

We first present background information and details regarding the practical implementation of the ILN program. Then we move on to review research about virtual mentoring, peer mentoring, and informal mentoring, all of which are components of the ILN's approach. In the evaluation section, we discuss the ways in which the ILN's implementation of best practices recommended in the literature contributed to the program's effectiveness, as evidenced by the authors' experience and other participants' positive evaluations. Finally, we conclude the chapter with possible directions for a similar program and suggestions for future research.

Background

The International Librarians Network (ILN) was a facilitated peer-mentoring program designed to help librarians build international connections. The first ILN round was launched as a pilot project in 2013, and the program was administered twice a year until the end of 2016. Altogether, there were eight program runs with more than 5,500 participants from more than 130 countries.[1] During its existence, the program grew rapidly: in three years, the number of participants in a single round grew from ninety-two to 1,162 (see figure 29.1). The program was run by volunteers, first informally and later as a non-profit association.[2] The program was discontinued in 2017 when the founders of the ILN concluded that running the program on a volunteer basis was not sustainable in the long term. The processes used to run the program will be documented and shared under a Creative Commons license.[3]

ILN round	Participants	Countries
Pilot (2013)	92	18
2013B	391	39
2014A	764	76
2014B	630	73
2015A	820	79
2015B	862	85
2016A	1,162	95

Figure 29.1. ILN participants by program round[4]

The ILN was started in 2012 by three Australian librarians, Kate Byrne, Alyson Dalby, and Clare McKenzie. The idea behind the program was to offer librarians a chance to meet fellow professionals from other parts of the world without the expense of international travel. The founders developed the ILN concept of a semi-structured peer-mentoring program by borrowing elements from different professional development formats. The ILN also regularly surveyed participants since the program's founding, and the ILN model evolved over time in response to that feedback.[5]

Applications to the program were made online via a form on the ILN website. Applicants were asked to provide information about their interests, career stage, and the library sector in which they work. It was also possible to indicate some wishes about the partners' interests or work background. ILN administrators formed mentor pairs based on their applications by matching successful applicants with someone outside their country. The ILN model did not require the participants to be at similar career stages or to work in the same library sector. This enabled the ILN to draw from a wider pool of participants and avoid the problem of an insufficient number of mentors. The ILN participants seemed to be open-minded about their prospective partners—approximately half of the applicants did not list any specific requests for potential partners[6]—probably partly due to the global nature of the program.

The ILN primarily facilitated the program by sending suggested discussion topics to participants every other week. For example, in the 2016A round, they distributed nine topics ranging from library spaces to management and leadership, library advocacy, and professional development. Ultimately, the mentor pairs naturally decided on the topics they wanted to discuss. The use of discussion topics to structure conversation grew during the existence of the program: in the early rounds of the program, only half of the participants were using discussion topics, whereas in later rounds, the figure was closer to 90 percent.[7] It seems likely that with the growth and development of the program, the topics, or their introduction, had been refined and thus became more useful to participants.

The main communication method used in the ILN program was email, which was preferred by the program administrators as well. Surveys conducted by the ILN show that almost all participants used email to communicate with their partners.[8] The ILN encouraged the mentor pairs to discuss platforms and then choose the communication methods most suitable for them, but also to try different methods, such as Skype meetings in addition to e-mail discussions. The ILN also arranged open discussions on Twitter and Facebook. The participants were often in different global time zones, which partly explains the popularity of asynchronous communication methods such as email.

The authors participated in the second-to-last ILN program round, 2016A, which took place between February and May 2016. Most of the examples mentioned in the article are based on this program round and on our individual experiences. For example, the discussion topics and methods of participation may have been different in other rounds or even for other mentor pairs within the same program round. For both authors, this was the first and only time we participated in the program. We mostly communicated by email but also had a few online meetings via Adobe Connect. Neither of us participated in the public Facebook or Twitter chats arranged by the program, so our program experience is based on direct communication within the mentor pair, which we feel was the core of the program.

Literature Review

The general topic of mentoring has received significant attention in the library and information science literature, but several aspects of the ILN program made the mentoring relationship unique, such as:

1. Mentor pairs were usually peers rather than a senior librarian paired with a junior librarian.
2. The relationship was entirely virtual and involved no in-person contact.
3. While the program operated very professionally, mentor relationships were informal and flexible.
4. Partners were from very different institutions in different positions and, of course, came from all around the globe.

This literature review is focused on virtual mentoring, peer mentoring, and informal mentoring, which are all components of the ILN's approach and are well-represented in the literature. While little investigation of the ILN's specific brand of international, virtual, and informal peer-mentoring programs has been conducted thus far, their methods have a strong theoretical and practical basis, as seen in the literature and detailed in the ILN's 2016 report.[9]

The literature provides a significant corpus of best practices and lessons learned that, along with being invaluable for those who are developing a mentoring program, can also be utilized to evaluate the ILN's approach. We reviewed key works that are applicable to the ILN model in order to determine whether our experience was in part due to the ILN founders' adherence to best practices.

First, electronic, or virtual, mentoring in libraries goes back to the early days of email, and several more recent articles discuss virtual mentoring programs in detail.[10] As mentioned in the 2016 ILN report,[11] these all predate the ubiquitous use of social media, smartphones, and other systems that facilitate communication at a distance, but many of their recommendations stand. In a 2007 article, Samantha Hines describes founding an online career-mentoring program in 2004, during her term as co-chair of the American Library Association's New Member Roundtable (NMRT).[12] New professionals were matched up with experienced colleagues based on input provided via an online form. Monthly discussion topics were distributed to mentor pairs, who were asked to communicate at least twice a month. Hines provides numerous suggestions for developing a virtual mentoring program, such as providing a contact for technical concerns, communicating to participants that mentor pairs may not necessarily be "soulmate relationship[s]" but can still be valuable and informative, and expressing that both partners need to dedicate time to the relationship.[13]

In another 2007 article, Hilbun and Akin describe efforts to establish an e-mentoring program for school library media specialists in a very large school district. While this example varies greatly from both the ILN and NMRT contexts, their recommendations are similar: ensure a formal structure is implemented, establish specific goals between mentor and protégée, and provide technical and administrative support.[14]

The more recent Finlayson article describes a narrower program in which mentors were assigned to protégées to support their completion of a specific project during a set time frame after a library merger.[15] That said, recommendations were again rather similar: more training should be provided for mentors, as well as more time dedicated to the relationship by both parties, with the support of administration.[16]

The ILN employs a peer-mentoring approach that moves away from the senior colleague mentoring a junior librarian model of the preceding articles. Peer mentoring has also received significant attention in the literature, with several articles demonstrating its effectiveness.[17] While Mavrinac primarily discusses values-based transformational change, the learning culture necessary to achieve it, and how peer mentoring can contribute to those efforts, this article lists numerous positive aspects of peer mentoring, such as its democratic nature, distribution of mentorship across boundaries, mutual benefits, and the ability for multiple mentors with different perspectives to support a single protégée.[18] In fact, "research indicates that mentoring relationships between peers provide similar benefits to traditional mentoring in the areas of psychosocial support such as confirmation, emotional support, and career development, as well as providing feedback, information sharing, and career planning."[19]

In a 2005 article, Level describes a peer-mentoring group formed to bring tenure-track librarians together to discuss the tenure process. The program was specific to one institution and operated alongside a formal one-on-one mentoring program employing more traditional senior/junior mentor pairs. Administrative support was mentioned as a key requirement, so librarians felt comfortable taking the time to participate. Other recommendations include maintaining flexibility, making involvement purely voluntary, and allowing time for open discussions.[20]

Another peer-mentoring program established within the City University of New York (CUNY) brought together junior library faculty from twenty different libraries of various sizes. Cirasella and Smale explain that communication took place online and in-person, and meeting topics and discussions typically focused on research, scholarship, and professional development concerns specific to early career library faculty members. This experience can be applied more directly to the ILN, as the disparate tenure requirements of each library precluded official discussion of the process itself and meant that the program has served primarily to unite pre-tenure librarians into a community of scholars with similar concerns.[21] Assessment data, primarily in the form of member surveys, was key to shifting programming and communication to better meet participant needs as the program progressed.

While his work is primarily focused on the ability of virtual peer mentoring (VPM) to support evidence-based practice in librarianship, Jonathan Eldredge contends that a model combining the virtual mentoring approach with the less-traditional peer-mentoring approach allows information professionals to be more productive in their organizations. Eldredge shares two recommendations for successful VPM programs. First, it is important to establish a social presence, which he defines as "avenues for presenting VPM participants as lifelike, trustworthy, and authentic as possible at a distance in order to approximate face-to-face communication."[22] He also emphasizes the importance of employing cultural sensitivity when building mentor relationships.

Finally, the third well-studied aspect of the ILN program is informal mentorship, which has received positive treatment in the literature like that of peer mentorship.[23] James, Rayner, and Bruno surveyed Illinois academic library employees to determine if they were participating in informal mentorship arrangements and, if so, whether those were valuable. The results contributed to several recommendations for successful approaches: initiative and openness is required on the part of the mentor, as are "two people who are willing to work together in a mutually acceptable way to address the concerns of the mentee, and to share relevant knowledge, expertise, and wisdom."[24]

Appleton also obtained feedback, by conducting case studies of three high-performing employees in a British information resource center, to determine how their informal mentorships contributed to their success. He determined that "an informal framework, where the organization has had no input into the mentorship, is far more likely to result in professional development and career progression."[25] Informal mentorship also encourages reflective practice, as the mentor inspires the mentee to reflect on their own work, rather than giving specific guidance to the mentee as to how to approach a challenge. Having someone to bounce ideas off allows mentees to gain professional insight and inspiration. As with peer mentoring, multiple informal mentors can each provide individual insights.[26]

Evaluation

Both authors had extremely positive experiences with the ILN mentoring program. In a 2016 newsletter article, we both recommended the well-structured program as an excellent way to build more in-depth relationships than is possible in a conference setting, without the time and expense of travel.[27] Through this mentor relationship, we were inspired to consider alternative approaches to our work and professional development. The program also gave us perspective on the many similarities and differences in academic librarianship as practiced in different countries. The ability to ask questions back and forth during one-on-one discussions helped create a more thorough understanding of the other person's institution and working context than would be possible through just reading an article or listening to a presentation.

The broad discussion topics shared by the ILN program directors contributed to our positive experience, as librarians in different positions at different institutions could relate to them more than narrower topics that might only apply to one type of library. We found that these suggested topics frequently led us to further discussion. For example, the first suggested topic was space. After sharing photos of our respective offices, Kelsey learned that Pirjo works from two different campuses, switching back and forth depending on the day of the week. That led us to a discussion about the many different responsibilities that a solo librarian in a small institution must handle, such as database management, library usage reporting, library instruction, collaborating on research projects, etc. While Kelsey's position is much more specialized, we agreed that we both enjoy the fact that you never know what a day is going to be like and it is therefore it is difficult to get bored over time.

These discussions, especially those regarding management and leadership in libraries, led to some of the most fascinating observations for us about how things are done in other countries. The University of Maryland (UMD) Libraries are, of course, much larger than the Humak University of Applied Sciences and so is far more hierarchical in structure. Kelsey was surprised to learn that Pirjo is the only librarian at her campus and her supervisor has no library background. Her librarian colleagues are distributed around Finland, so only meet in person a few times a year and conduct all other business virtually. From a Finnish perspective, Pirjo was surprised the learn that the recruitment process for faculty positions at American university libraries was so in-depth, with twelve-hour interview days, including presentations. The concept of a leased collection (UMD leases a popular reading collection that circulates at a high rate) was new to Pirjo as well. Overall, we both learned a great deal about how other libraries operate and we were able to incorporate new ideas into our work.

ILN participant survey results reflect our rewarding experiences. Respondents report a satisfaction rate of 80 to 90 percent and mention benefits such as "a widening of their professional awareness," "encountering new ideas," and "an increase in professional confidence" in their responses.[28] Along with the survey results, the 2016 ILN report features a case study of a repeat participant,[29] Jenny Mustey, who has published a glowing personal evaluation similar to our newsletter article,[30] as have several other participants. One early participant, Renee Mason, who began her career in librarianship at a remote library in China, remarked, "For those of us who work in environments where it can sometimes feel like we are isolated from the world, [our networks] can often be the only source of validation."[31] The benefits of the ILN, especially the ability to forge international connections without the need for travel funds, were also touted by Shaharima Parvin in her article describing the operations of the East West University Library in Bangladesh.[32]

In reviewing the literature, it became apparent that the ILN participants' positive experiences can be attributed to the program founders having implemented the best practices and recommendations found therein. A strong structure, specific information about how to rectify any technical issues, clear expectations for participant time commitment, and an emphasis on staying open-minded about how you might benefit from a non-traditional mentor pairing, were key factors recommended by multiple authors investigating virtual mentoring programs.[33] The authors' experience substantiates the research that shows the benefits of a non-traditional peer-mentoring arrangement,[34] in that two librarians at the same points in their careers, working at very different institutions, had a successful relationship and learned many things from each other. Another mentor pair,

Pan and Robinson, also "found that despite very different backgrounds and training, the essence of our roles was not disparate."[35] The ILN's willingness to adjust the program based on feedback between each round of mentoring was also recommended in the literature and certainly contributed to the program's success, as did the voluntary nature of the program.[36] Only truly interested librarians sought out the opportunity and signed up to participate.

Two slightly more abstract concepts set forth in the literature also directly contributed to the success of the ILN program: social presence and reflective practice.[37] Social presence, recommended by Eldredge to insert the human component into a virtual relationship, was also fostered by the ILN program. Their suggestion that mentor pairs try technologies, such as Skype or Adobe Connect, for face-to-face communication and to share social media accounts, etc. enriched the authors' experience, built trust, and amplified the human connection at a distance. Reflective practice, as discussed by Appleton, was the primary mode in which the authors' discussions benefited their work and provided an avenue to incorporate disparate experiences in very different settings into our work. While neither of us was trying to teach or guide the other, hearing how we approach different challenges made us think about how we could do our work differently. Inspiration, also cited by Appleton as a benefit of informal mentorship, was another vehicle through which we translated our discussions into our work.

Conclusion

As this chapter was being written, the authors were disappointed to learn that the founders of the ILN had decided to discontinue the program, as we had both planned to participate in another round of the mentoring program to further grow our international networks and meet librarians in different countries. The ILN had been run entirely on a volunteer basis, and the founders concluded that it could not be sustained long-term.[38] The ILN founders indicated that they will document the processes used to run the program and share the documentation under a Creative Commons license in order to make it possible for others to build on their efforts.

The popularity of the program, with more than 5,500 participants from more than 130 countries in four years shows that there is strong interest in international librarianship in the form of a global peer-mentoring program. It would be interesting to see a program like this run by an international organization with better support and infrastructure, such as the International Federation of Library Associations and Institutions (IFLA). The program could also be organized in other widely spoken languages, such as French or Spanish.

The ILN model of a virtual peer-mentoring program could also be adapted to work in more finite contexts—for example, within a nation such as the United States. Individual elements of the program could be adapted to different settings, rather than attempting to resurrect and run a full version of the program. That said, the ILN program's successful strategies should not be ignored, as they are well-supported by the literature. That literature could be bolstered through investigating more recent virtual mentoring programs conducted in libraries. Technological advances mean that the authors could have a face-to-face conversation via smartphone while walking around campus, which was simply not possible when the earlier virtual mentoring programs discussed herein were implemented.

Notes

1. Kate Byrne, Alyson Dalby, and Clare McKenzie, "The Future of the ILN," *International Librarians Network*, March 27, 2017, http://interlibnet.org/2017/03/27/the-future-of-the-iln/.
2. Kate Byrne, Alyson Dalby, and Clare McKenzie, "Introducing the International Librarians Network Incorporated," *International Librarians Network*, March 24, 2015, http://interlibnet.org/2015/03/25/introducing-the-international-librarians-network-incorporated/.
3. Byrne, Dalby, and McKenzie, "The Future of the ILN."
4. Data sourced from Kate Byrne, Alyson Dalby, and Clare McKenzie, "Rethinking Mentoring: Online, International Peer-Mentoring with the International Librarians Network," June 14, 2016, https://figshare.com/articles/Rethinking_Mentoring_Online_International_Peer-Mentoring_with_the_International_Librarians_Network/3413632, 4.
5. Ibid., 4, 7.
6. Ibid., 5–6.
7. Ibid., 7.
8. Ibid., 7.
9. Ibid., 4–6.
10. Samantha Schmehl Hines, "Adventures in Online Mentoring: The New Member's Roundtable Career Mentoring Program," *Journal of Web Librarianship* 1, no. 4 (October 2007): 51–65, doi:10.1080/19322900802111411; Janet Hilbun and Lynn Akin, "E-Mentoring for Librarians and Libraries," *Texas Library Journal* 83, no. 1 (Spring 2007): 28–32; Avenal Finlayson, "Electronic Mentoring and Academic Librarians: A Case Study," *Innovation*, no. 39 (December 2009): 58–72.
11. Byrne, Dalby, and McKenzie, "Rethinking Mentoring," 4.
12. Hines, "Adventures in Online Mentoring," 52.
13. Ibid., 59.
14. Hilbun and Akin, "E-Mentoring for Librarians and Libraries," 31.
15. Finlayson, "Electronic Mentoring and Academic Librarians," 58–72.
16. Ibid., 71.
17. Allison V. Level and Michelle Mach, "Peer Mentoring: One Institution's Approach to Mentoring Academic Librarians," *Library Management* 26, no. 6/7 (September 2005): 301–10, doi:10.1108/01435120410609725; Jill Cirasella and Maura Smale, "Peers Don't Let Peers Perish: Encouraging Research and Scholarship Among Junior Library Faculty," *Collaborative Librarianship* 3, no. 2 (April 2011): 98–109; Mary Ann Mavrinac, "Transformational Leadership: Peer Mentoring as a Values-Based Learning Process," *Portal: Libraries & the Academy* 5, no. 3 (July 2005): 391–404.
18. Mary Ann Mavrinac, "Transformational Leadership: Peer Mentoring as a Values-Based Learning Process," *portal: Libraries & the Academy* 5, no. 3 (July 2005): 398–99.
19. Ibid., 398.
20. Level and Mach, "Peer Mentoring," 309–10.
21. Cirasella and Smale, "Peers Don't Let Peers Perish," 106.
22. Jonathan D. Eldredge, "Virtual Peer Mentoring (VPM) May Facilitate the Entire EBLIP Process," *Evidence Based Library & Information Practice* 5, no. 1 (April 2010): 9.
23. Julie James, Ashley Rayner, and Jeannette Bruno, "Are You My Mentor? New Perspectives and Research on Informal Mentorship," *Journal of Academic Librarianship* 41, no. 5 (September 2015): 532–39, doi:10.1016/j.acalib.2015.07.009; Leo Appleton, "Informal Mentoring in Library and Information Services," *Impact: Journal of the Career Development Group* 7, no. 3 (October 2004): 54–58.
24. James, Rayner, and Bruno, "Are You My Mentor?," 537.
25. Appleton, "Informal Mentoring in Library and Information Services," 55.
26. Ibid., 57.
27. Pirjo Kangas and Kelsey Corlett-Rivera, "Making Connections Abroad through the International Librarians Network," *WESS Newsletter*, Fall 2016, https://wessweb.info/index.php/Making_Connections_Abroad_through_the_International_Librarians_Network.

28. Byrne, Dalby, and McKenzie, "Rethinking Mentoring," 8–9.
29. Ibid., 10.
30. Jenny Mustey, "ILN: A Meeting Place for Librarians from Around the World," *inCite* 36, no. 9 (September 2015): 22–23.
31. Renee Mason, "Reach Out to Real People," *inCite* 35, no. 1/2 (February 1, 2014): 23.
32. Shaharima Parvin, "The East West University Library: Sharing My Personal Experiences," *International Leads* 30, no. 3 (September 2016): 1–5.
33. Hines, "Adventures in Online Mentoring," 51–65; Hilbun and Akin, "E-Mentoring for Librarians and Libraries," 28–32; Finlayson, "Electronic Mentoring and Academic Librarians," 58–72.
34. Level and Mach, "Peer Mentoring," 301–10; Cirasella and Smale, "Peers Don't Let Peers Perish," 98–109; Mavrinac, "Transformational Leadership," 391–404.
35. Connie Pan and Shannon Marie Robinson, "Pen Pals," *inCite* 36, no. 3 (March 2015): 33–33.
36. Cirasella and Smale, "Peers Don't Let Peers Perish," 98–109.
37. James, Rayner, and Bruno, "Are You My Mentor?" 532–39; Appleton, "Informal Mentoring in Library and Information Services," 54–58.
38. Byrne, Dalby, and McKenzie, "The Future of the ILN."

Bibliography

Appleton, Leo. "Informal Mentoring in Library and Information Services." *Impact: Journal of the Career Development Group* 7, no. 3 (October 2004): 54–58.

Byrne, Kate, Alyson Dalby, and Clare McKenzie. "Introducing the International Librarians Network Incorporated." *International Librarians Network*, March 24, 2015. http://interlibnet.org/2015/03/25/introducing-the-international-librarians-network-incorporated/.

———. "The Future of the ILN." *International Librarians Network*. March 27, 2017. http://interlibnet.org/2017/03/27/the-future-of-the-iln/.

———. "Rethinking Mentoring: Online, International Peer-Mentoring with the International Librarians Network." June 14, 2016. https://figshare.com/articles/Rethinking_Mentoring_Online_International_Peer-Mentoring_with_the_International_Librarians_Network/3413632.

Cirasella, Jill, and Maura Smale. "Peers Don't Let Peers Perish: Encouraging Research and Scholarship Among Junior Library Faculty." *Collaborative Librarianship* 3, no. 2 (April 2011): 98–109.

Eldredge, Jonathan D. "Virtual Peer Mentoring (VPM) May Facilitate the Entire EBLIP Process." *Evidence Based Library & Information Practice* 5, no. 1 (April 2010): 7–16.

Finlayson, Avenal. "Electronic Mentoring and Academic Librarians: A Case Study." *Innovation*, no. 39 (December 2009): 58–72.

Hilbun, Janet, and Lynn Akin. "E-Mentoring for Librarians and Libraries." *Texas Library Journal* 83, no. 1 (Spring 2007): 28–32.

Hines, Samantha Schmehl. "Adventures in Online Mentoring: The New Member's Roundtable Career Mentoring Program." *Journal of Web Librarianship* 1, no. 4 (October 2007): 51–65. doi:10.1080/19322900802111411.

James, Julie, Ashley Rayner, and Jeannette Bruno. "Are You My Mentor? New Perspectives and Research on Informal Mentorship." *Journal of Academic Librarianship* 41, no. 5 (September 2015): 532–39. doi:10.1016/j.acalib.2015.07.009.

Kangas, Pirjo, and Kelsey Corlett-Rivera. "Making Connections Abroad through the International Librarians Network." *WESS Newsletter*. Fall 2016. https://wessweb.info/index.php/Making_Connections_Abroad_through_the_International_Librarians_Network.

Level, Allison V., and Michelle Mach. "Peer Mentoring: One Institution's Approach to Mentoring Academic Librarians." *Library Management* 26, no. 6/7 (September 2005): 301–10. doi:10.1108/01435120410609725.

Mason, Renee. "Reach Out to Real People." *inCite* 35, no. 1/2 (February 1, 2014): 23–23.

Mavrinac, Mary Ann. "Transformational Leadership: Peer Mentoring as a Values-Based Learning Process." *Portal: Libraries & the Academy* 5, no. 3 (July 2005): 391–404.

Mustey, Jenny. "ILN: A Meeting Place for Librarians from Around the World." *inCite* 36, no. 9 (September 2015): 22–23.

Pan, Connie, and Shannon Marie Robinson. "Pen Pals." *inCite* 36, no. 3 (March 2015): 33–33.

Parvin, Shaharima. "The East West University Library: Sharing My Personal Experiences." *International Leads* 30, no. 3 (September 2016): 1–5.

CHAPTER THIRTY

Myanmar Librarians' Research and Study Tour at the Rutgers University Libraries:

A Report

Triveni Kuchi

Introduction and Background

Change was imminent in Myanmar. Initiatives led by President Thein Sein since March 2011 brought reforms: political prisoners were being released, the country was opening up to international observation of elections, and foreign investment was being welcomed to help rebuild Myanmar. Most notably, charismatic Aung San Suu Kyi, a Nobel Peace Prize winner and political prisoner under house arrest since 1989, was finally released. Her party, the National League for Democracy of Myanmar (NLD), re-registered for elections and gained a major victory in April 2012. Considering all these transformational changes that were propelling Myanmar toward democracy, the United States undertook significant steps to encourage Myanmar's efforts toward positive change. In a show of strong support, United States Secretary of State Hillary Clinton visited Myanmar in November 2011, and in November 2012, President Obama became the first sitting United States president to visit Myanmar. The United States and other countries lifted sanctions on Myanmar and significant foreign investment flowed into Myanmar.[1] Through all these changes, Myanmar's endeavor has been to establish itself on a path of progress and development. One of the significant reform movements in Myanmar was aimed specifically at higher education, which was in a state of disrepair from decades of neglect. A thorough and complete review to make higher education stronger and "independent" was pledged through national committees that were set up for "drafting a new higher education law" and for the "revival of the University of Yangon."[2]

In the summer of 2012, two new faculty members from the Rutgers University School of Arts and Sciences' history and religion departments began conversations about a Rutgers University Myanmar Studies Initiative (RUMSI). The initiative's mission was "to foster Myanmar-related scholarship and teaching at Rutgers and to strengthen collaborative research and intellectual exchange among Rutgers faculty and academics in Myanmar."[3] During the fall of 2012, the professors coordinated several meetings in collaboration with the Centers for Global Advancement and International Affairs (GAIA Centers)—the Rutgers administrative unit responsible for "facilitating collaborative projects and strategic partnerships around the world."[4] Along with the mission, they also circulated a brief background document describing the history and current state of Myanmar among participants of the initiative. The group also reviewed and planned to apply for an USAID/Burma call for concept papers. This call encourages "university-private sector partnerships involving US businesses and US and Burmese institutions of higher education to address Burma's critical short, medium and long-term development needs."[5]

Around this time, the Institute of International Education (IIE) also put out a call for a Myanmar Initiative. With the momentum gained from activities of RUMSI and the GAIA Centers, the opportunity to participate in IIE's International Academic Partnership Program (IAPP) with Myanmar was ideal to advance academic relations in a country transitioning into the new era. In February 2013, the chair of RUMSI and the Vice President of the GAIA Centers from Rutgers University, along with representatives from other universities, took part in a historic delegation by ten universities to Myanmar. This delegation, co-led by IIE and a representative from the United States Department of State, visited various higher education institutions in Yangon, Mandalay, and Naypyidaw as "part of a broader IIE Myanmar higher education initiative which seeks to help the country rebuild its higher education capacity."[6]

The purpose of the delegation was to observe and learn about the state of higher education in Myanmar. Higher education reform became one of the several priorities for Myanmar government, for which the Myanmar government specifically announced its support. The delegation noted multiple challenges for re-energizing higher education arising from lack of existing capacity in physical buildings, technology, academic curriculum, and faculty education. The delegation determined that urgent investment in infrastructural development to support both undergraduate and graduate students as well as sustain advancement in curriculum design and faculty development was required. In particular, they observed:

> One other area that requires revitalization and upgrading are university libraries; most lack access to the world of electronic databases and digital publications. The majority of libraries do not have adequate funds for subscribing to the most important journals and magazines. And the books, textbooks, and other publications that already are in hand have been updated three or four times since the 1980s in most university libraries abroad. The modernization of library facilities is badly needed to encourage students and faculty to view their university libraries as reservoirs of new, relevant information, data, etc.[7]

The delegation members further discerned that development of the infrastructure for university libraries was one of the essential foundations that would move Myanmar's higher education forward. In light of this context, they suggested a training tour for Myanmar librarians in the United States as a first step toward modernizing Myanmar university libraries' resources and services:

> As an example of helping to inform the vision of Myanmar higher education, we recommend a study tour from Myanmar librarians to the United States. This study tour would allow librarians to visit multiple sites in the United States, spending a few weeks at each. Arizona State University, Northern Illinois University, Rutgers University and the University of Washington have volunteered to host such a study tour, provided funding can be identified for transportation and related costs.[8]

Planning and the Proposal

The libraries were abuzz with the news by the time the Rutgers members of the delegation returned from Myanmar in March 2013. The vice president of information services and the university librarian of Rutgers University were debriefed on discussions that occurred in Myanmar and were asked to help in determining the feasibility of hosting a librarian study tour at the libraries. Several conversations took place among RUMSI faculty, the vice president of the GAIA Centers, and the university librarian. Many questions were raised in these initial discussions and an internal team within RUL was formed consisting of the university librarian, associate university librarian, and the librarian for South Asian studies (the author) to brainstorm and address the potential for the study tour. The university librarian also held conversations with her counterparts collaborating in this venture viz., Arizona State University (ASU), Northern Illinois University (NIU), and the University of Washington (UW) to study the feasibility and gauge RUL's role in this effort. Moreover, the leaders of the four universities consulted with Cornell University library to gather information about Cornell's ongoing participation in a project for Myanmar through the Open Society Institute (OSI).[9] At each of the four institutions, South/South East Asian studies or international studies librarians were selected as primary contacts for planning this study tour. Thus, the libraries of the four institutions formed a Myanmar Library Consortium within the United States (USMLC).

During May 2013, the librarian representatives from the four libraries set up an initial telephone conference to discuss each library's approach for hosting the Myanmar librarians. Most agreed that their libraries would be able to provide overall library-wide rather than collections-specific training, given the relative weakness of their collections in Myanmar or South East Asia materials. NIU was the only institution within this consortium that was unique with a Center for Burma Studies and strong collections in that area. During the discussions, all agreed that the Myanmar librarians should at the very least have some ability to communicate in English. This was important because three of the four libraries did not have Burmese language expertise, nor could they arrange for translation services required for training and hosting non-English-speaking international librarians. Despite unclear budget availability at this point, the librarian representatives were asked to go ahead with the planning for the study tour. The consortium determined that spring or fall of 2014 would allow sufficient time to make all the arrangements to host Myanmar librarians for the study tour.

The chair of RUMSI and vice president of information services and the university librarian at Rutgers drafted a proposal for a Department of State grant for funding international travel and other related costs for the study tour. USMLC also participated in the preparation of this proposal. In addition, during July of 2013, the librarian from ASU visited Myanmar and held conversations with the Myanmar Library Association and heads of Myanmar libraries to determine their needs. He presented the idea that a "program focusing on library management and services" was feasible for USMLC.[10] With all these various processes in motion, as well as the discussions that faculty and administrators had during the February 2013 IAPP IIE study tour, a model of a "one-month internship" program for Myanmar librarians began to emerge. There was further discussion about different types of study tour models and the feasibility of implementing them at various locations. Given that the consortium planned to host librarians in either the spring or fall of 2014, and not having heard information from the Department of State grant yet, the librarians from ASU and UW visited Myanmar in early 2014 to continue and push forward the conversation. They held preliminary discussions with librarians (including contacts at the Myanmar Library Association), determined the Myanmar librarians' communication abilities in English, then interviewed and selected participants for the program. This helped consolidate the study tour and training program plans for the USMLC.

In January 2014, after further discussions via email, the program to bring six Myanmar librarians to the United States was decided. Of the six librarians, a set of two would spend a month at one of the three USMLC libraries and then all would gather at the fourth library, NIU, for an additional ten days for collections-specific training and workshops. Based on librarian and staff availability and arrangements they could make at their universities, ASU, UW, and NIU librarians were planning to bring over the Myanmar librarians during May 2014. However, this date did not work out for RUL because housing arrangements were impossible to make on short notice, and the month of May being the end of the semester was not ideal for the Myanmar librarians to observe the dynamic activities of the library with users. Finally, USMLC determined that four Myanmar librarians would come in May 2014 and two would arrive in October 2014. The split in the arrangements also worked for the two Myanmar librarians, one of whom had a dissertation defense and could not travel during the month of May.

By this time, it was already March 2014. With the dates decided, USMLC libraries quickly confirmed the proposal for the study tour, which was sent for approval to the Myanmar Ministry of Education. In addition, each of the USMLC libraries created an institution-specific profile and training program for inviting the Myanmar librarians to the United States. At Rutgers libraries, the internal team for Myanmar discussed availability, priorities, and possibilities for training the two librarians during October. The university librarian and associate university librarian created the institutional and library profile for Rutgers University while the author created an outline of the curriculum for training at Rutgers libraries.[11] UW collated all the proposals on behalf of USMLC, included the list of the six Myanmar librarians and the criteria used for their selection, and described an overall study tour plan in a letter addressed to the Myanmar Ministry of Education. The overall curriculum included areas within library management and leadership, library services, digitization and preservation, and management of e-resources. USMLC sent the letter by mid-March 2014 and the Myanmar Ministry of Education approved the study tour proposal around early April 2014.

ASU, UW, and NIU now only had a few weeks to get the paperwork, visas, housing, and other arrangements done before the Myanmar librarians' visit in May 2014. Rutgers was advised to start the visa process early along with the others since these processes have deadlines and can take an unusual amount of time. The RUL internal team, along with the head of Human Resources, formulated a budget required for the Myanmar librarians' study tour that included costs for training materials, lodging, meals, stipend, travel, and other incidentals. Since the Department of State grant had not come through, the university-wide collaboration made up of the GAIA Centers, RUMSI, and RUL collaboratively funded this project. It was decided that RUL would conduct all the training as well as provide for housing on the Rutgers New Brunswick campus, and the GAIA Centers and RUMSI would cover the rest of the expenditure.

Next, the RUL vice president of information services and the university librarian sent out invitation letters offering a paid study tour and training for the two Myanmar librarians by email and by postal mail. Soon after this, RUL human resources began conversations with Rutgers Global services offices and international staff contacts at UW and NIU to determine the type of visa required for the month-plus-ten-day stay of the Myanmar librarians. Even though RU began the visa process early for the October visit, a constant uncertainty of whether this project would take place was felt throughout the summer months as the process moved slowly into September without any final confirmation. Several follow-ups later, finally on September 17, 2014, visas for the two Myanmar librarians were approved. So, within the last two weeks of September, all plans for the Myanmar librarians' visit that had started nearly two years earlier materialized.

Implementation

At the end of a long flight from Yangon, the Myanmar librarians arrived at Rutgers mid-week on the afternoon of October 1. After brief introductions, the author drove the librarians to the two-bedroom housing arranged on campus and gave them a brief rundown of the next day's itinerary. The tentative study tour schedule was a detailed list of daily activities, events, and meetings for each week, based on the broad curriculum outlined by USMLC's proposal for the study tour. To the extent possible, the schedule was kept fluid, leaving space for Myanmar librarians' expectations, plans, and any unforeseen appointments.

An informal reception was held on October 2 on the New Brunswick campus of RUL. During the first few days, the Myanmar librarians learned to travel on campus buses across different campuses, acquired their Rutgers identity cards, set up login information for wireless access, did some banking, and a few other activities that were necessary to begin campus life at Rutgers. An office in the library was assigned for the two librarians and they were given laptops and storage devices to record and organize information for their study tour at Rutgers. During this week, the librarians were also introduced to the overall organizational structure of RUL with information and brochures about the campuses, departments, committees, and so on. With some preliminaries taken care of, the two librarians planned a trip to Washington DC for their first weekend for a tour of the Library of Congress (LOC).

During the second week, GAIA Centers and RUMSI organized a faculty meeting to welcome the Myanmar librarians. There was a brief discussion about needs and availability of resources and archives in Myanmar. They compared some ideas and methods to consider for use and implementation upon their return. In the next few days, the content of the Rutgers library website, access and availability of resources, reference and information services, and the library's consortial arrangements for borrowing and sharing collections were discussed. In addition, they observed different types of library instruction classes, including a seminar-style course taught by a librarian. This informed them about the variety of ways information literacy is adopted for a course or curriculum often taught in collaboration with professors at Rutgers.

On October 14, the Myanmar librarians visited the Rutgers School of Communication and Information and held conversations with professors. The following day, they attended the Rutgers Teaching and Technology Conference about the transformation of information and education. After the conference, the librarians participated with Rutgers students in a special and fun event at the Kilmer Library Pumpkin Decoration—a mid-term stress buster—where they painted pumpkins and shared conversations with students.[12] Next, the librarians attended the Library Resources Council meeting for system-wide collections management information. This teleconference meeting helped the librarians interact with library representatives from all campuses online and in-person. The librarians then toured most of the libraries on New Brunswick campus and squeezed in a tour of the Health Sciences Libraries, Dana Library, and the Institute of Jazz on the Rutgers Newark campus. Also, during the weekend, a Rutgers librarian treated them to a whirlwind tour of the New York Public Library and some of New York city's renowned museums.

Throughout the week of October 20, the librarians heard presentations from several RUL departments, including the Scholarly Communication Center, Integrated Information Systems, Central Technical Services, Acquisitions, Distributed Technical Services, and Cataloging including East Asian cataloging. At the end of all these meetings, they shared their impressions of American libraries and provided an overview of their experiences with Myanmar libraries. Despite their packed agenda, they further squeezed in a meeting of the User Services Council where system-wide public service issues are discussed and policy updates and changes recommended. Their next stop was at the Special Collections and University Archives, where they spent an entire day with rare books, digital projects, archives and manuscripts, and state and regional historical collections. The librarians were also able to observe activities of RUL administration, Human Resources, and the Planning and Coordinating Committee.

GAIA centers hosted an international scholars' reception, where the Myanmar librarians were guests of honor and the mission and spirit of the study tour at RUL were highlighted. The Rutgers student newspaper wrote: "This year is the first time Rutgers welcomed scholars from Myanmar to Rutgers.... They came to study the advanced library system at Rutgers.... A scholar from Myanmar said, 'There is a lot to learn from Rutgers.'"[13] On October 28, a forum entitled "Conversations with Myanmar Librarians" was held to celebrate the completion of the study tour, share the librarians' impressions and experiences, and discuss plans for future collaborations. The librarians gave a presentation about Myanmar libraries, history, collections, archives, and services and discussed what they learned during the study tour. After the presentation, RUL awarded certificates to the Myanmar librarians for their effort and participation. Subsequently, a discussion took place about library partnerships, higher education in Myanmar, and potential collaborations with Rutgers. This program was well attended by librarians and staff from various departments of RUL, faculty from several disciplinary departments, RUMSI, and the GAIA Centers, and guests from the Center for International Partnerships in Higher Education at IIE, New York.

The Myanmar librarians concluded their study tour by visiting several local public libraries, which provided them with a glimpse of how local public libraries (of different sizes) serve their community's needs. The author and the librarians then had a wrap-up conversation to discuss impressions, exchange feedback, and share future contact details. The Myanmar librarians left for NIU to continue their training and tour for another ten days and then returned to Myanmar on November 10, 2014.

Lessons Learned

The research and study tour of the Myanmar librarians at Rutgers University libraries was part of a unique and valuable undertaking carried out by four university libraries that formed the United States Myanmar Library Consortium, as well as by Rutgers University partners. The objective of this study tour at Rutgers was to provide the Myanmar librarians with an opportunity to observe the complex operations and management of a large American academic library system. RUL was also a perfect example for the librarians to experience the environment and workings of a large, multi-campus, multi-site library that caters to the needs of more than 68,900 students.[14] Specific presentations and programs to engage the Myanmar librarians were arranged alongside regularly planned RUL meetings to not only provide them with specific training but also allow for an immersive experience of activities as they occur during the semester.

Given the geographic distances between Rutgers campuses, it was a challenge to balance meetings, programs, and objectives of the study tour across the four campuses. For instance, to accommodate meetings on the New Brunswick campus and the Myanmar librarians' plans, the tour of the library on the Camden campus was difficult to fit in along with the other events on the New Brunswick or Newark campuses. Although not quite the same, Myanmar librarians were still able to interact with some of the librarians from the Rutgers Camden library, when the latter attended meetings through video teleconference or in-person on the New Brunswick campus. However, for future iterations of such study tours, obtaining a balance in the tours among locations is an important factor to consider for even representation of the different locations of the libraries. In this regard, it is worth pointing out the significance of providing apartment-style housing for the librarians to live on campus, which enabled them to have a "home" to go back to at the end of the day's events, to entertain guests, and to review or make plans with each other. In addition, although not connected across all the campuses, the librarians were able to ride the University's campus buses for meetings on different New Brunswick campuses to derive a taste of academic life at Rutgers.

The various partners involved in bringing together the Myanmar Study Tour were proud to have been able to participate in a program that hosted the international librarians. The IIE mentioned the significance of the first historic delegation of universities from the United States to Myanmar and the important and much-needed commitment by United States libraries for training librarians.[15] Rutgers GAIA Centers promoted the significance of the Myanmar librarian's study tour saying, "Rutgers is hosting its first

Myanmar scholars for the first time—in library studies." More significantly, they noted that "a meet and greet presentation that allowed the Myanmar librarians to exchange knowledge and ideas with Rutgers faculty" was organized by the libraries.[16] In addition, RUL administration announced that they "were pleased to host this intensive research tour and cultural encounter" with the Myanmar librarians.[17] Generally, there was agreement that the Myanmar Study Tour was a successful program that created new partnerships, strengthened relationships, and promoted goodwill across several national and international entities—namely, Rutgers libraries, Rutgers University, partner libraries in the United States, and the Myanmar libraries and universities.

The study tour required comprehensive planning, time commitment, and understanding in order to successfully organize activities. It involved considerable effort from several RUL staff and library faculty, who generally felt that the experience was rewarding because it gave them an opportunity to view their roles outside-in while answering the Myanmar librarians' questions. The interactions, communication, and care needed to engage and ensure that the Myanmar librarians felt at ease during their month-long stay were undoubtedly intense, but the librarians and staff at RUL participated with enthusiasm and warm hospitality. Some went out of their way to give the Myanmar librarians a tour of the area, parks, and shopping centers. In fact, one was thrilled to make the librarians' acquaintance because he was planning a visit to Myanmar and now had access to knowledgeable tour guides. Several RUL librarians and staff commented how much they enjoyed making contact with the Myanmar librarians and hoped to continue those connections via email. One of the heads of the department said they "were delightful and we really enjoyed their visit… [and at lunch] they told us although the food was good, the company and conversation were better."[18] The numerous photos and videos that the Myanmar librarians took as they traveled through RUL interestingly revealed their perspective of the complex network and structure of RUL's functions and departments.

This report serves as a practical example for planning and implementing a broad training and experiential program for international librarians at a large academic library system. The Myanmar librarians' study tour at RUL represented an important opportunity to enhance intercultural understanding between American and Myanmar librarians. Despite some difficulty experienced due to weak communication in English, it was gratifying to see the positive effort that went into preparing, anticipating, and collaborating to make the research and study tour a success at RUL.

Soon after the study tour ended on October 31, 2014, several events and personnel changes occurred concurrently within Rutgers, prompting a temporary pause in international librarian training programs and tours. The leadership that promoted, funded, and brought together this partnership changed. The vice president of the GAIA Centers left Rutgers, key RUMSI faculty members were away on sabbatical, and the vice president for information services and the university librarian retired. In addition, RUL's New Brunswick Libraries were undergoing reorganization.

Despite the temporary hiatus of international exchange programs at RUL, some faculty from RUMSI have continued activities by teaching courses, hosting workshops, and participating in other types of academic and educational engagement with the academics at Myanmar.[19] In fact, an important change after the RUL New Brunswick reorganization took place was the formation of the Global Experience Team. This team made up of librarians and staff was created to continue serving and supporting international students, study abroad, and visiting scholars programs at Rutgers. This setup would likely help the future hosting of international exchange, training, and tour programs. In addition, USMLC successfully pursued funding for future training programs for Myanmar librarians through a Henry Luce Foundation grant for 2016 and 2017.

The success of the planning, organization, and implementation of the Myanmar librarians research and study tour can be attributed to the strong collaboration, communication, and resolve maintained by various individuals at multiple levels of the libraries, university, and external institutional partners. The commitment and responsibility of so many individuals to bring this project to fruition in such a large geographically spread-out organization as Rutgers is truly a matter of pride and achievement. The RUL participation has indeed been a valuable experience, and the bonds established with the Myanmar librarians remain a source of fulfillment. The Myanmar librarians keep in touch every so often, reporting excitedly about new projects they are embarking on, such as teaching library research and information literacy for their first-year students.[20]

Notes

1. "Thein Sein: A presidential timeline," *Frontier Myanmar*, April 24, 2016, accessed February 26, 2017, http://frontiermyanmar.net/en/thein-sein-presidential-timeline; Steven Lee Myers, "In Myanmar, Government Reforms Win Over Some Skeptics," *New York Times*, November 29, 2011, http://www.nytimes.com/2011/11/30/world/asia/in-myanmar-government-reforms-win-over-countrys-skeptics.html; Steven Lee Myers, "New York Times: U.S. rewards Myanmar, Easing Ban on Investments," *BurmaNet News*, May 17, 2012; Steven Lee Myers and Thomas Fuller, "U.S. Moves Toward Normalizing Relations with Myanmar," *New York Times*, April 4, 2012, accessed February 19, 2017, http://www.nytimes.com/2012/04/05/world/asia/myanmar-sanctions.html; Tin Maung Maung Than, "Myanmar's 2012 By-Elections: The Return of NLD," *Southeast Asian Affairs*, (2013): 204–19, http://www.jstor.org/stable/23471145.
2. John Morgan, "Hope in Myanmar," *Inside Higher Ed*, July 25, 2013, accessed February 22, 2017, https://www.insidehighered.com/news/2013/07/25/signs-home-higher-education-myanmar.
3. "The Rutgers Myanmar Initiative," *South Asian Studies Program (SASP), Rutgers School of Arts and Sciences*, accessed February 25, 2017, http://southasia.rutgers.edu/initiatives.
4. As the Director of SASP, Rutgers School of Arts and Sciences, the author was invited to participate in these discussions. During 2010–2013, the author served as both the director of SASP and the social sciences/instructional services & South Asia librarian at Rutgers University libraries; "About Us," The Centers for Global Advancement and International Affairs (GAIA Centers), accessed June 5, 2017, http://global.rutgers.edu/about/about-gaia-centers.
5. United States Agency for International Development (USAID), "Concept Paper on Public-Private Alliances in Burma: Higher Education Partnerships to Support the US-Burma Commitment to Democracy, Peace and Prosperity," November 26, 2012, accessed February 20, 2017, https://www.usaid.gov/sites/default/files/documents/1861/USAID_Burma_GDA_APS_Addendum_2012.pdf.
6. Rutgers Centers for Global Advancement and International Affairs, "Myanmar," *Global Relations*, accessed February 18, 2017, http://global.rutgers.edu/programs/iapp/myanmar.
7. Institute of International Education, *Investing in the Future: Rebuilding Higher Education in Myanmar* (New York: Institute of International Education, 2013), accessed February 19, 2017, https://www.iie.org/-/media/Files/Corporate/Publications/Rebuilding-Higher-Education-in-Myanmar.ashx?la=en&hash=517AA4A5D7134E1EA86F94D1BF6DD99BBBA8F578, 19.
8. Ibid., 26.
9. RUL University Librarian email correspondence to author, April 9, 2013.
10. ASU librarian's email correspondence to author, October 15, 2013.
11. The Rutgers University Libraries comprise twenty-six libraries on New Brunswick, Newark,

Camden, and Rutgers Biological and Health Sciences (RBHS) campuses that operate as a unified library system with coordinated public, technical services, and collection development programs. More information is available from https://www.libraries.rutgers.edu/. The Rutgers University New Brunswick campus is the largest of the four regional campuses of the university. Located in central New Jersey, it is one hour from New York City and two hours from Philadelphia. Supporting over 33,000 graduate and undergraduate students in approximately 100 undergraduate programs, it has more than eighty graduate/professional programs and sixty doctoral programs as a Carnegie Classification Research University (very high research activity) campus. The Myanmar librarians were housed on this campus for the study tour. Rutgers Newark campus is about forty minutes or so north of the New Brunswick campus. It is considered to be the "most diverse university" in the nation and has more than 12,000 students and nearly 1,300 faculty and staff. RBHS is New Jersey's academic health center with eight schools, six centers and institutes, and a behavioral health network. In addition to being located in New Brunswick and Newark campus, it has several other locations across New Jersey. Rutgers Camden is located about an hour and half south of the New Brunswick campus. It is a smaller campus but offers more than forty majors, fifty minors, and twenty-nine graduate programs, plus special programs. More recent information about all the four campuses is available from http://www.rutgers.edu.

12. Kilmer Library on the Rutgers New Brunswick Livingston campus is popular library used heavily by undergraduates for study. The library's gate counts during mid-semester have often nearly reached 4,000 per day.
13. Jeff Hammond, "Reception Helps Scholars Make Global Connections," *The Daily Targum*, New Brunswick, NJ, October 27, 2014, accessed March 3, 2017, http://www.dailytargum.com/article/2014/10/reception-helps-scholars.
14. "Facts and Figures," Rutgers, The State University of New Jersey, accessed February 15, 2017, http://www.rutgers.edu/about/facts-figures.
15. Clare Banks and Daniel Obst, "Myanmar: What a Difference 2 Years Can Make" (blog), June 2, 2015, https://www.iie.org/Learn/Blog/2015-June-Myanmar-What-A-Difference-2-Years-Can-Make.
16. "From Delegation to Education: Rutgers Hosts Myanmar Scholars for First Time," Centers for Global Advancement and International Affairs (GAIA), *News*, October 31, 2014, https://global.rutgers.edu/delegation-education-rutgers-hosts-myanmar-scholars-first-time.
17. "RU Libraries Share Expertise with Myanmar Librarians," Rutgers University Libraries, *News*, November 14, 2014, https://www.libraries.rutgers.edu/news/ru-libraries-share-expertise-myanmar-librarians.
18. RUL librarian's email correspondence to author, July 9, 2015.
19. "About Connecting with the World," *Institute for International Education*, accessed March 15, 2017, https://www.iie.org/Programs/Myanmar-Higher-Education-Initiative/Connecting-with-the-World.
20. Myanmar librarians' email correspondence to author, Dec 31, 2014.

Bibliography

"About Connecting with the World." *Institute for International Education*. Accessed March 15, 2017. https://www.iie.org/Programs/Myanmar-Higher-Education-Initiative/Connecting-with-the-World.

Banks, Clare, and Daniel Obst. "Myanmar: What a Difference 2 Years Can Make" (blog). June 2, 2015. https://www.iie.org/Learn/Blog/2015-June-Myanmar-What-A-Difference-2-Years-Can-Make.

"Facts and Figures." Rutgers, The State University of New Jersey. Accessed February 15, 2017. http://www.rutgers.edu/about/facts-figures.

Hammond, Jeff. "Reception Helps Scholars Make Global Connections." *The Daily Targum*. New Brunswick, NJ. October 27, 2014. Accessed March 3, 2017. http://www.dailytargum.com/article/2014/10/reception-helps-scholars.

Institute of International Education. *Investing in the Future: Rebuilding Higher Education in Myanmar.* New York: Institute of International Education, 2013. Accessed February 19, 2017. https://www.iie.org/-/media/Files/Corporate/Publications/Rebuilding-Higher-Education-in-Myanmar.ashx?la=en&hash=517AA4A5D7134E1EA86F94D1BF6DD99BBBA8F578.

Morgan, John. "Hope in Myanmar." *Inside Higher Ed.* July 25, 2013. Accessed February 22, 2017. https://www.insidehighered.com/news/2013/07/25/signs-home-higher-education-myanmar.

Myers, Steven Lee. "In Myanmar, Government Reforms Win Over Some Skeptics." *New York Times.* November 29, 2011. http://www.nytimes.com/2011/11/30/world/asia/in-myanmar-government-reforms-win-over-countrys-skeptics.html.

Myers, Steven Lee. "New York Times: U.S. rewards Myanmar, Easing Ban on Investments." *BurmaNet News.* May 17, 2012.

Myers, Steven Lee, and Thomas Fuller. "U.S. Moves Toward Normalizing Relations with Myanmar." *New York Times.* April 4, 2012. http://www.nytimes.com/2012/04/05/world/asia/myanmar-sanctions.html.

Rutgers University Libraries. "RU Libraries Share Expertise with Myanmar Librarians." *News.* November 14, 2014. https://www.libraries.rutgers.edu/news/ru-libraries-share-expertise-myanmar-librarians.

Than, Tin Maung Maung. "Myanmar's 2012 By-Elections: The Return of NLD." *Southeast Asian Affairs* (2013): 204–19. http://www.jstor.org/stable/23471145.

The Centers for Global Advancement and International Affairs (GAIA Centers). "About Us." Accessed June 5, 2017. http://global.rutgers.edu/about/about-gaia-centers.

The Centers for Global Advancement and International Affairs (GAIA). "From Delegation to Education: Rutgers Hosts Myanmar Scholars for First Time." *News.* October 31, 2014. https://global.rutgers.edu/delegation-education-rutgers-hosts-myanmar-scholars-first-time.

The Centers for Global Advancement and International Affairs (GAIA Centers). "Myanmar." *Global Relations.* Accessed February 18, 2017. http://global.rutgers.edu/programs/iapp/myanmar.

"The Rutgers Myanmar Initiative." South Asian Studies Program (SASP), Rutgers School of Arts and Sciences. Accessed Feb 25, 2017. http://southasia.rutgers.edu/initiatives.

"Thein Sein: A Presidential Timeline." *Frontier Myanmar.* Accessed Feb 20, 2017. http://frontier-myanmar.net/en/thein-sein-presidential-timeline.

United States Agency for International Development (USAID). "Concept Paper on Public-Private Alliances in Burma: Higher Education Partnerships to Support the US-Burma Commitment to Democracy, Peace and Prosperity." https://www.usaid.gov/sites/default/files/documents/1861/USAID_Burma_GDA_APS_Addendum_2012.pdf (access date).

Global partnership to bring visiting librarians / sending librarians abroad

→

CHAPTER THIRTY-ONE

From Visitors to Friends[1]

Margaret Law

In 2010, the University of Alberta's president asked that all academic units within the university develop and implement an international strategy to support the university's strategic plan and goals. Her overarching goal was to move the university from an excellent national university to one that would be recognized globally as a leading research-intensive university. The initial implementation was to promote research partnerships with leading institutions in other countries. Each of the Faculties was to establish these partnerships, often with visiting faculty. The success would be measured in several ways, including increased enrollment of international graduate students and postdoctoral fellows and changes in global ranking.

The University Libraries is considered to be an academic unit rather than a service unit, so the president's direction applied here as well. Discussions between the chief librarian and the president focused on the libraries' difficulty in developing sufficient research partnerships and the challenge of developing an international strategy that would align with the rest of the university's directions while staying true to the libraries' own goals and values.

The University of Alberta Libraries developed their international strategy with three overall programs: Sharing Collections, Sharing Staff, and Sharing the Future. The Sharing Collections goal was initially a program that set up book exchanges to meet the libraries' goals of developing a broad and deep research collection that incorporated material from different parts of the world, and in different languages, that supported the research and teaching areas of the university. It eventually evolved to include discussions of shared open access and online developments. Material that was shared with international academic library partners originally supported Canadian studies programs and Canadian literature programs, with material that was difficult for our partners to locate and acquire. It later included material to support partner libraries in developing countries, with a focus on those where there were existing research partnerships with University of Alberta faculty members.

The Sharing the Future goal was to develop partnerships with libraries globally to develop new shared programs that would benefit both partners. Many of these turned out to be either collections or staff development goals. This provided an opportunity for

University of Alberta librarians to travel to a variety of countries to provide training or hands-on support. For example, a Canadian librarian supported the development of a website for a library in Nepal. Shared development also included library guides, strategic planning, and library evaluations.

The Developing Staff goal was realized through the implementation of a Visiting Librarian program. One of the objectives of the Visiting Librarian program was to introduce our own staff to the backgrounds of our increasingly diverse students and faculty members. As the university community became more international, library staff were very conscious of the need to be inclusive and sensitive to the differing needs of the community.

Because the development and implementation of international activities were so critical to the president's goals, responsibility was assigned to one of the libraries' associate university librarians, with the intention that it would be approximately half of the total job assignment. The determination was made by the chief librarian based on skills, experience, interest, and workload. As the programs developed, other staff members were invited to volunteer to take a role as contact people for individual libraries. They had to work with their own supervisors to determine how this fit with their other responsibilities. For example, one librarian took the lead role in hosting the visit of a Nepalese librarian, helping to develop the website and then staying in contact with the visiting librarian after he returned home.

Over time, various librarians took over different roles in the international activities but none of them were formally assigned to these initiatives, except for the coordinator. Librarians hosted visiting librarians from many countries, did book selection for international partner libraries in Ghana and Uganda, provided online support for assessing information literacy programs in Pakistan, and provided professional training in India. Librarians were able to volunteer for one project, for one partner, or to be the contact person for one part of the globe for as long as they were interested or able to balance it with the rest of their workload. Supervisors throughout the University of Alberta Libraries were more or less supportive of their staff participating.

The Paperwork

The University of Alberta already had a Visiting Professor program, which provided a great deal of the background information needed to develop a Visiting Librarian program. It helped that librarians at the University of Alberta are considered to be academic staff, so there was a strong logic in adapting an existing faculty program. Nonetheless, it took a considerable amount of effort to help both the university and the libraries staff to understand both the value of the program and the procedures and structures needed to support it.

The first step was working both with the university's International Office and the university's human resource specialists to figure out the mechanics of getting the necessary paperwork so that potential visitors could procure visas to visit Canada. The Canadian government has many categories of visitors, and the correct paperwork was crucial to the success of the program. After many discussions and meetings, we determined that the category of "self-funded researcher" was likely to have the most success. This required a carefully written description of the activities to be undertaken by the visiting librarian as if they were coming to do research. We needed to be clear that they were not falling into any other categories—in particular, categories that might imply that they were coming as learners (interpreted by the government as students and therefore subject to different regulations) or coming to do any kind of work (interpreted by the government as employment). One of the side benefits of this step was the opportunity to promote the libraries and their work to these departments in the university, who were not typical targets for library promotional activities. Several strong and enduring professional relationships developed.

Describing the activities as those of a "self-funded researcher" turned out to have other benefits when it came time to promote the program to the libraries' staff. It was clear that this person was coming to meet their own needs, and that the responsibility of the University of Alberta staff was limited to providing assistance rather than specific training or orientation. Additionally, it helped the visiting librarians understand that they needed to determine ahead of time what they wanted to learn and be active in their own success.

The research descriptions were developed jointly by the University of Alberta organizer and the visiting librarian and served to help structure the visit. Typical descriptions of the research that was being conducted and that were used on visa applications included:

- observation and analysis of best practices in the delivery of health sciences information services in a modern academic research library;
- critical observation of best practices in delivering networked library services in a geographically dispersed academic research library; and
- analysis of marketing options and programs to support the special collections unit of a modern academic research library.

To navigate the visa process, we learned to avoid words such as "experience" and "learn." This turned out to be true not only for visas to visit Canada but also for those countries where people needed exit visas or other government documentation to leave their home country.

By using the same language on the letters of invitation, visa applications, and project proposals, as well as any funding applications submitted by the candidates, we learned to establish a consistent approach that worked well in moving the program forward.

Finding Candidates

Once we had a structure in place, it was time to find our first candidate. The University of Alberta had a longstanding partnership with the Aga Khan University in East Africa and Pakistan, so that seemed like a logical place to start. The chief librarian was a Canadian and was familiar with the University of Alberta Libraries, and that provided an opening for the invitation. He was enthusiastic about the idea and was able to get support and funding for our first candidate, from Tanzania. This visit was so successful that the Aga Khan University Library made it an annual commitment and over time sent candidates from their other campuses.

This led to a strategy of contacting the libraries at any university where the University of Alberta had an existing agreement. With the assistance of the university's International Office, a list of all these partnerships was developed. As the program coordinator, I began the process of visiting the departments at the university that had agreements in place, to discuss the value of training librarians at their partner institutions. Predictably, some of the agreements were no longer active, and some faculty members couldn't see any advantage of a library component to their work.

Once again, this was an opportunity to promote the libraries in a different way across the university, and in particular to talk about the need for constant training and upgrading of library staff to meet the needs of a changing information and technological environment. Some departments saw immediate advantages and were happy to support the libraries' initiative. They wrote letters to their colleagues, introducing the Visiting Librarian program and offering their support. These letters of introduction proved to be invaluable and provided immediate validity to the program. This led to candidates from several universities in China and the University of the West Indies participating as visiting librarians.

Through the development of relationships internally and many discussions with faculty members who were involved in international programs, we became aware of the importance of addressing sustainability. We were able to suggest that the development of the library in the partner institution, particularly in developing countries, was a component of sustainability as it allowed the institution to continue with the research or teaching programs that had been developed in partnership with University of Alberta faculty. The inclusion of this into funding applications led to visiting librarians from Nepal and Somalia, both from institutions where the University of Alberta faculty of medicine had development projects.

Participation in international conferences also led to a number of visiting librarians. Candidates from Zimbabwe, South Africa, Korea, and the Democratic Republic of the Congo resulted from this kind of personal contact. A Facebook site recorded the visits, and photographs appeared on the libraries' website. Eventually, it seemed that word of mouth began to spread, leading to candidates from India and Israel, as well as many inquiries from other parts of the world. Finding candidates was no longer a problem.

Funding

Like most libraries, the University of Alberta had very little money to put into this program, so it needed to be close to self-funded. The available budget paid for the coordination of the program, including supplies and a small amount for hosting. The stated expectation was that the home institution of the candidate would pay for all travel, accommodation, and expenses, and the University of Alberta would contribute the training and hosting.

In general, this worked well. As the program coordinator, I also took on the responsibility of looking for outside funding and was somewhat successful. Within the university, there were small amounts of money that were available for different kinds of programming. Since the cost of the visits was relatively low in comparison with other projects, the libraries were successful in getting small grants of approximately $5,000 to fund some visits. The relationships within the university also led to some other funding options, including a scholarship fund from the Canadian government that was adapted to funding candidates from the Caribbean.

Additionally, some of the Faculties were willing to contribute money to support librarians from international institutions where they had ongoing projects. From their perspective, the small amount of money needed to fund a visiting librarian left a legacy to the sustainability of their projects.

Once again, it required considerable discussion with the Finance Office and the Human Resource Office of the university to figure out how to pay for the visiting librarians without jeopardizing their status as self-funded researchers. In many cases, we were able to give them some funds as speaker's fees. In some cases, we also had to figure out how to give people cash, as they needed the funds to pay their expenses during the visit, and not all banks operate internationally.

Organizing Visits

After the program was established, the process for organizing visits was streamlined. The initial contact was an email to the program coordinator requesting a visit. This led to considerable back and forth to determine the specific area that the candidate wanted to learn about, the timing of the visit, and to start to manage expectations. When this was settled, the coordinator began the internal university process to issue a letter of invitation. Using the wording that the Human Resource department had developed for other visitors was straightforward, as it addressed issues such as risk management, responsibilities, and other matters that the visa department might be concerned with. No planning of the visit was started until the candidate had a visa. This was learned the hard way after several visits were delayed or canceled due to visa difficulties.

Each visiting librarian was hosted by a particular library unit, depending on their area of interest. Over time, visitors were hosted by all the public service units of the libraries as well as by the information technology department and the cataloging department. The process of selecting a hosting unit and working with the staff of that unit was the responsibility of the program coordinator.

It became clear that it was important to meet with all the staff of the hosting unit, not just the manager. The most successful hosting experiences were ones in which all staff members were involved, and the visitors reported that this helped them understand the work of different types of staff members as well as the interaction between them. Most importantly, our staff wanted our visitors to be comfortable while they were learning about Canadian libraries and Canadian culture.

In each unit, one person was assigned the responsibility of managing a calendar for the visitor and setting up meetings. In general, we aimed to schedule half days, leaving the rest of the time for the visitor to set up further meetings or use our library collection to work on their own projects. Depending on the interests of the visitor, the following meetings were set up for them:

- meeting with the chief librarian or other senior management staff
- meeting with staff responsible for particular strategies, such as the indigenous services librarian
- tours of all library units
- tours of other area libraries, including tours of consortium offices

The structure of the visit was essentially one of job-shadowing. The visitors followed library staff throughout their day, including any teaching commitments, committee meetings, training activities, desk time, meetings with faculty or students, or other work. By shadowing different staff members, visitors began to understand not just the nature of the work but how it was organized through the libraries' committee structures and interactions with members of the university community. Support staff often played a valuable role in walking with visitors to locations where they had meetings. This accomplished two things: visitors made their way safely across a complex campus, and support staff members were included in the hosting and were able to contribute to a successful visit.

The only formal requirement of our visitors was that they make at least one presentation. They were asked to prepare a presentation for staff at the beginning of their visit on the situation of libraries in their home country. This gave our staff some background information about the visitor and enabled some interesting and useful conversations. As the program evolved, we began asking them to do a second presentation at the end of their visit on what they had learned. This resulted in a great deal of learning by our staff as we began to understand what we looked like to others. Several staff members commented that this helped them provide service to our increasingly diverse student and faculty community.

At the end of the visit, participants were presented with a nicely framed certificate. Subsequent visits to people's offices in many different parts of the world found them displayed proudly, and they became an important part of encouraging other people to apply to the program. We also learned that most visitors bring gifts, and we had to figure out what to give them in return. Our criteria for gifts was that they be identifiably Canadian and made in Canada. We learned this after the embarrassment of giving a Chinese visitor a university mug that was made in China!

In addition to the formal program, staff members were encouraged to think about informal activities that guests would enjoy. Visitors were invited to dinner and barbeques at people's homes, on shopping expeditions, and to sports and arts events. Not surprisingly, some long-lasting friendships grew out of this, resulting in return visits, both professional and personal. One of the unintended side effects was a new appreciation of our own area after seeing it through the eyes of a visitor. Mountains and parks that we took for granted were seen as awe-inspiring by people from other places, causing us to look at them with new eyes. Many visitors got their first exposure to ice hockey through attending university games, although none of them could be induced to try it.

Units were provided with a very small budget for hosting their visitor. Most units used it to have some kind of social function, often with faculty invited, or for a welcome or goodbye party. Many also used it to buy a transit pass so that visitors could travel freely around the city.

Through trial and error, we learned to restrict the visit to a period between two weeks and four weeks. Shorter than two weeks did not give any opportunity for a relationship to develop and felt more like someone was just coming to tour around. Longer than four weeks meant that it was too difficult to sustain the level of energy needed. Most visitors stayed for four weeks—long enough to engage with different approaches to library service but short enough to manage being away from home.

Impact of the Program

At the end of 2016, after the program had been running for five years, a review was completed. At that time, fifteen visiting librarians from ten different countries had participated in the program. They were all from academic libraries and came from a range of roles, including technical services, cataloging, special collections, and many levels of management, including two chief librarians.

The review of the program also asked participants if they would recommend it to friends and colleagues, what changes they had made as a result of their time with the

University of Alberta, and what changes we could make to improve the program. Universally, participants were happy to recommend the program to friends and colleagues, and, indeed, several of our candidates came through these recommendations.

We were amazed by the number of new initiatives that were fostered by participation in the program. Many visiting librarians went home to provide training or workshops in their home library in such disparate areas as pre- and post-testing of information literacy students, digital preservation, metadata, and library guides. Even more impressive was the number of new programs started. These included

- one-on-one consultations for graduate students;
- opening a copyright office within the library;
- implementation of an open access journal;
- on-site librarian service with a librarian offering office hours in various faculties;
- a digital repository; and
- off-campus access to library resources.

Additionally, several participants reported that they made administrative changes when they returned home, based on what they had observed at the University of Alberta Libraries. Some were straightforward, such as implementing collection development plans, but some required significant shifts in organizational culture, such as "changes with regards to meetings and the way in which decisions are being recorded." One librarian reported that the visit had given him the confidence to completely reorganize the special collections at his institution, integrating several collections, which eventually led to a new and much bigger space.

Perhaps the changes in attitude were best summarized by one participant, who reported that "I changed my perception of library work from the traditional rules I was used to and became a very good advocate for change."

The changes in the staff at the University of Alberta Libraries, while perhaps less dramatic, were also significant. After hosting visiting librarians, staff members became much more engaged in library issues outside the University of Alberta, and many retained ongoing relationships through their international networks. This has resulted in a much broader awareness of the conditions at the institutions that many of our international students come from, which has set the stage for more inclusive service. Once you have heard firsthand about the difficulties in accessing electronic resources in countries where electricity is unreliable, it is easy to understand why some students have a great deal of anxiety about database searches.

Both the participants and the hosts talked about the relationships that were developed and the importance of spending time together. As one participant described it, "It was about observing, and for that you had to be there. One informal conversation led to another. It was totally different than reading about something and experiencing it firsthand. I saw things in context as it is." One of the things that we stressed to our staff members who were hosting visitors was that they should share anything that wasn't confidential (in our case, this means matters related to individuals). Visitors were not there just to see the things we do well but also to learn from our less successful experiences.

As a result of the program, several of our staff members had opportunities to travel to other countries to provide training on-site. Librarians traveled to Barbados, Vietnam, China, India, and Kenya to work with their new colleagues on resolving problems. Each one of these came home with a better understanding of the global nature of information and the unevenness of information technology worldwide.

Things That Went Wrong

So, was it all perfect? Of course not. Some of the things that didn't work out very well led us to make changes in the program as it evolved. After each visit, there was a follow-up discussion about what went right and what could have been improved. Overall, the visits were surprisingly successful, with the positives considerably outweighing the problems.

One of the things we learned to watch out for was dubbed "academic tourism" by a colleague in the university's international unit. It was a relief to discover that the libraries were not the only part of the university to be affected by this and to discuss with colleagues in other units various approached to prevent it. Academic tourism occurs when people use the university to get a letter of invitation and get a visa and then go on vacation. There are few things more frustrating than to develop a calendar for a visitor and then have them inform you that they can't attend any meetings because they have booked a trip to the mountains. To prevent this, we began asking candidates if they had any other obligations that we needed to include in their calendar. Some of them, of course, fell within the framework of their visit, such as visiting colleagues at other institutions. We didn't expect our visitors to spend all their time with us, but it was important to remember that we were investing considerable time and expertise into the program and that we were making a commitment to the immigration department about their activities while they were in Canada.

A second problem that arose—and that we learned to manage—was when a candidate was sent by their employer but actually had no real interest in being with us. This only occurred twice but it was clear that it was important to correspond with the potential visitor and not just their supervisor. Being sent led to lack of enthusiasm and very little engagement, which was not only a waste of everyone's time but disheartening to the hosting unit.

We learned as we went along to assess the skill level of participants before they arrived, through asking about their current responsibilities and background. Because of different qualifications in different countries, and different expectations of librarians, we learned that people arrived with very different expectations. If we knew this ahead of time, we were able to deal with it. For example, a recently appointed chief librarian from a university that was being rebuilt after it had been destroyed by war had no library experience or training at all. Knowing this, we were able to scale the program to a level that would be useful and not overwhelming. Similarly, we learned that in many Asian countries, chief librarians at universities were not professional librarians; rather, they were faculty members who were appointed for a limited term as part of their administrative progression in the university.

A faulty assumption that we made, since all participants were librarians, was that they would have done some research before they arrived. After some false starts, we learned to provide information about our working language (English), our electricity (110 volts, compared to 220 volts in much of the world), and our money (Canadian dollars, not US dollars). We also learned to explain our weather, which we took for granted. It is very changeable and somewhat unpredictable, so we provided links to weather sites. We also learned to keep various electrical plugs available and learned which banks provided currency exchange.

Finally, there were candidates who were refused visas, often for reasons that we were not able to discover. In some cases, we simply needed to write a new letter of invitation with more detail or a change of dates, but in some cases, there was no explanation. Visits to Canadian embassies in countries that issued visas didn't add any clarity to this, and we responded by not planning visits until the visitor reported that their visa was in hand.

It was also important to meet visitors at the airport and take them to their accommodation. Many wrinkles occurred at this point. Visitors arrived late at night having not eaten, and some of the accommodations had no food service. Twice we had visitors arrive with a letter indicating that their institution had paid their hotel bill in advance but the hotel had no record of it. Someone local can find solutions to these problems much better than someone who has just arrived in a strange country suffering from jet lag.

We learned that we needed to limit the number of visits. Because we are a large distributed library with nine service points, it was possible to host visitors in different locations. Even so, there is a lot of work in arranging the visits and we discovered that we were not able to host more than three visitors each year.

During the review process, we asked participants what changes they would recommend. Those that were possible were implemented, including more visits to other libraries and co-ordinating the visit with a local library conference whenever possible. Providing the visitor with one person to contact throughout the visit for any questions was something we learned early in the process.

Conclusion

This program not only contributed to the development of academic libraries in many countries, it led to the establishment of worldwide professional networks and friendships. Learning that we all had the same challenges, although they varied in scope, was a liberating and refreshing experience. The extended network grew into opportunities for sharing knowledge in other ways: through phone calls, email, and meeting up at conferences. How else would you know who to call when you need some reading material in KiSwahili suitable for a beginning reader?

Staff members and visitors alike discovered that library service was more the same than different across the globe. No matter how big the budget or how developed the information technology infrastructure, we all struggle with the best way to serve a changing population in a changing environment. A program that was started in response to a need for the University of Alberta Libraries to align with the University of Alberta's plans and goals turned out to be a rewarding professional and personal experience for participants.

Notes

1. All material quoted in this chapter is from personal communications with participants or from their responses to the evaluation survey.

CHAPTER THIRTY-TWO

The Horner Fellowship:

An Exchange Program for Arizona and Japan Library Personnel

Jeanne L. Pfander, Alexandra Humphreys, and Smita Joshipura

The Horner Fellowship program was established in 1989 with an endowment generously provided by Dr. Layton "Jack" Horner and his wife, Marian Horner. Under the auspices of the Arizona Library Association (AzLA), this unique program was created to foster cultural understanding and to facilitate informational exchanges between library personnel from Arizona and Japan, many of whom have been academic librarians. Over the years, the Horner Fellowship exchange has created goodwill and opened doors to new experiences and minds to new ideas that benefit the profession on both sides of the Pacific.

About Jack and Marian Horner

Layton (Jack) Horner was born in rural Pennsylvania in 1914. He attended Bethany College in West Virginia, graduating in 1937 with a bachelor of arts degree in history. He subsequently obtained a master's degree from Yale Divinity School in 1938. While at Yale, he roomed with Saburo Matsuyama from Kyoto, Japan and the two became lifelong friends which inspired Horner's respect and affinity for the Japanese culture.

Although in 1940 Horner initially declared his intention to refuse to register for the draft because, as he stated, he was "totally and unconditionally opposed to war and hence to military conscription," in 1942, following the attack on Pearl Harbor on December 1941, he enlisted in the US Navy[1] and served during the war on the east coast of the United States as well as in Alaska and East Asia.

While stationed in Japan after the war ended, Horner was assigned to the Shizuoka Military Government Team as a Civil Education and Information Officer, where he helped implement a decentralized, reformed education system. He led the establishment of local school boards in many areas and directed deliveries of protein supplements to Japanese children suffering from nutritional deficiencies. The influence and the respect accorded to him by Japanese educators is evidenced by the inclusion of his first name in the book titled *Jack and Betty: English Step by Step,* written by Horner's colleagues and friends, Kyohei Hagiwara, Matsuo Inamura and Keiichiro Takezawa, and first published in 1948.[2] This book is still known by many English-language learners in Japan and it continued to be used for many years.

In 1946, Horner married Marian Johnsen in Bremerton, Washington, and after their post-war years in Japan, they returned briefly to his home in Pennsylvania, where he began to buy and sell farms. However, he soon re-enlisted in the Navy and subsequently served in the Korean War and later in the Philippines and other Pacific islands.

Following his Navy career, Horner completed a doctorate in Oriental Studies at the University of Arizona in 1973. He became a professor of oriental studies with a focus on Japanese history and culture and taught at Western Carolina University in Cullowhee, North Carolina and at Pacific Lutheran College in Tacoma, Washington. Horner wrote two insightful books on the intersections of Japanese and American cultures entitled *The Japanese and the Americans* (1986)[3] and *On Both Sides of the Pacific* (1989).[4]

Jack and Marian Horner made more than twenty trips to Japan during their life together, maintaining ties with Japanese friends and colleagues. With his Yale roommate, Matsuyama, Jack Horner established the International Student Exchange Service and served as the first chairman. The organization provided financial aid to US students to travel to Japan to teach English while providing Japanese students with opportunities to study in the United States. The Horners also hosted Japanese friends, colleagues, and students over the years at their homes in the United States.

Jack and Marian Horner were world travelers, often taking university students on study trips to South America and China. As a result, in addition to the Japan-focused fellowship in Arizona,[5] they established (also in 1989, the same year as the Arizona endowment) a Horner endowment with the Oregon State Library to sponsor library staff exchanges between Fujian Province in China and Oregon.[6]

On top of their commitment to librarian exchange programs, Jack and Marian Horner established scholarships at colleges and universities such as Rice, Bethany, Yale, and the University of Arizona. As further evidence of their kindness and compassion, the Horners generously provided a monthly stipend for a Chinese scholar who had been persecuted during the Cultural Revolution in China. They were clearly committed to supporting education and literacy at multiple levels.

Dr. Horner died in Tucson on September 9, 1990 at the age of seventy-five. Marian Horner, his wife and partner in bringing diverse cultures together, died in 2002. They both are remembered and honored for their kindness, generosity, and dedication to promoting libraries, literacy, and international cultural exchanges. Their legacy has continued through the Horner Fellowship.

The Horner Fellowship Committee

The Horner Fellowship program is administered through the Arizona Library Association's (AzLA) Horner Fellowship Committee. The purpose of the committee is to facilitate reciprocal exchanges between Japan and Arizona and to oversee the administration of the Horner Fellowship, in cooperation with the AzLA president and executive board and the International Relations Committee of the Japan Library Association (JLA). The committee bylaws[7] serve as operational guidelines for its members. The leadership of the committee consists of the chair, vice-chair/chair-elect, and immediate past chair with other members coming from different types of libraries, such as academic, public, school, and special. The committee meets quarterly, submits regular reports to the AzLA executive board, and organizes a business meeting during the AzLA annual conference. The agenda at the business meeting includes presentations from the current and/or most recent Horner Fellow from Arizona or Japan, who share their travel and learning experiences with attendees. The Horner Fellowship Committee has a strong presence on the AzLA website, with a Horner Fellowship web page. Committee members submit frequent contributions regarding fellowship activities to the AzLA newsletter and social media outlets (Facebook, etc.). In addition, the Horner Fellowship Committee works closely with AzLA's International Interest Group to organize webinars or conference programs supporting international librarianship.

Horner Fellow Selection Process: Criteria and Procedures

The Horner Fellowship is awarded annually, with the Arizona and Japanese committees selecting Fellows in alternating years. Typically, the awardee visits occur during the months of October or November. Criteria for the selection of Horner Fellows are similar for the AzLA and JLA committees. However, despite the similarity of the criteria, the selection process differs between the two associations due to differences in the practice of librarianship in the two nations as well as differences in the two organizations.

The selection process for an Arizona Horner Fellow typically begins in February (in alternating years) when the committee meets to review the timeline, selection criteria, and procedures. The committee chair distributes a call for applications to AzLA members, with a deadline approximately one month later. The fellowship opportunity is promoted through various outlets, such the AzLA newsletter, an email blast to all AzLA members, announcements posted on the AzLA website and social media accounts, as well as postings by individual committee members to their respective institutions or other relevant listservs.

The application packet consists of an application letter, current résumé, letter of recommendation from the applicant's supervisor, and contact information for three professional references. The application letter must address the purpose for the candidate's interest in the exchange, what the applicant hopes to gain from the fellowship, and how the experience will benefit Arizona libraries and the library patrons he or she serves. The letter of support from the applicant's supervisor should describe the administrator's confidence in the applicant's ability to fulfill the role of a Horner Fellow, a willingness to support a leave of absence for the exchange, and a willingness to welcome the visit of a Japanese Horner Fellow at the supervisor and applicant's library in the following year.

The application packet also requires that candidates must confirm they are willing to sign the following forms: (1) Release of Liability, (2) Emergency Information Sheet, (3) Copyright Release, and (4) Memorandum of Understanding.

The Release of Liability form is a contract between the Horner Fellow and AzLA Horner Fellowship Committee requiring Fellows to release the AzLA and the fellowship from legal liabilities incurred from accidents, health incidents, hotel/flight cancellations, and other incidental expenses. This form also requires that the Fellow carries appropriate health and travel insurance.

Through the Copyright Release Form, the Horner Fellow grants AzLA and the Committee permission to publish the Fellow's report and any other narratives on the AzLA and JLA websites and print publications, while the Memorandum of Understanding requires the Fellow to write a report, serve on the committee for at least a year, and, among other requirements, to take responsibility for any accompanying family members during the fellowship trip to Japan.

Once the deadline for applications has been reached, the Horner Committee chair collects and shares the application packets with committee members. Each committee member evaluates all applicants based on established selection criteria, as documented in the Horner Fellowship Committee Bylaws.[8]

Applicants must

- be an AzLA member in good standing;
- be currently employed in an Arizona library doing the work of a librarian;
- have a minimum of three years library experience;
- have strong references;
- be willing to share their exchange experience with AzLA members in the form of a digital report, to be published in the *AzLA Newsletter* and posted to the AZLA website;
- be willing to make a presentation at the annual AzLA Conference; and
- be willing to actively serve on the Horner Fellowship Committee.

Following evaluation and ranking of applicants, committee members submit their rankings to the chair and a meeting is scheduled to discuss their evaluations and select the top three candidates to be interviewed. Depending on the physical locations and the ability to travel of both the candidates and committee members, the candidate interview process may be virtual (e.g., via Skype, Google Hangout, etc.) or in person. Interview questions pertain mainly to the candidate's purpose for their exchange visit, how they plan to share their travel experiences and learnings with AzLA colleagues, their ability, based on a relevant example they share with the committee, to deal with challenges associated with travel in a foreign country, as well as practical questions confirming their commitment to represent the AzLA in Japan, and their willingness to serve on the AzLA Horner Fellowship Committee for at least a year after the exchange, etc.

The selection of a Horner Fellow is usually completed by the end of May or beginning of June, after which the committee notifies the JLA International Relations Committee about the individual selected. In years with especially strong applicant pools, the AzLA committee may also designate a Special Project Horner Fellow. To date, there have been only three Special Project Horner Fellows from Arizona.

The selected Horner Fellow is responsible for making their own travel arrangements and for working with the JLA International Relations Committee to finalize their in-country itinerary. The Horner Fellow communicates with the JLA committee about their professional and personal interests for their fellowship visit, which, in turn, helps the JLA committee make arrangements with Japanese libraries, museums, and other places of interest. The AzLA Horner Fellowship reimburses the Fellow for their travel-related expenses, including air travel, lodging, meals, transportation in Japan, health/travel insurance, and incidentals. The JLA also receives a stipend from the Horner Fellowship to facilitate the stay of the AzLA Fellow, including the provision of translator/interpreter services for Arizona librarians who do not speak Japanese.

The application process for a JLA Horner Fellow also takes place in the spring in alternating years. The JLA International Relations Committee issues a call for applications in the library trade publication *Toshokan Zasshi*. Applicants must be members of the JLA and have worked in a library for a minimum of three years or studied library information science. They also must provide a letter of recommendation from their supervisor and a letter of approximately 1,300 words in Japanese in which they explain their motivations for applying for the fellowship. The applicants are required to show enthusiasm for the Horner Fellowship program and agree to continue to support it after their visit to Arizona is completed. The deadline for JLA applications is the beginning of June, and the International Relations Committee selects a JLA Horner Fellow by the end of June.

Once the JLA Fellow accepts their appointment, they sign documents similar to those signed by AzLA Horner Fellows. For example, a Letter of Commitment requires insurance in case of cancellation so that the JLA incurs no compensation obligations. The Fellow is also required to write a report to be published in *Toshokan Zasshi*.

Members of the Arizona Horner Fellowship Committee, in preparation for the JLA Fellow's visit, begin correspondence with that individual to plan an itinerary to accommodate their professional and personal interests. For most Japanese Horner Fellows, one of the highlights of their visit is the AzLA Annual Conference, usually held in late October or early November, where they deliver a short presentation at the Horner Fellowship Committee business meeting and receive recognition at the AzLA Awards luncheon. In addition, a trip to the Grand Canyon is usually part of the itinerary for most visitors from Japan. The conference, the visits to libraries, places of interest, and homestays (if requested) provide a unique opportunity for Japanese librarians to become familiar with American librarianship and ways of life in the American Southwest.

History of Arizona and Japanese Horner Fellow Visits

In the years since the Horner exchange visits began in 1989 and up through 2017, there have been a total of seventeen AzLA members who have traveled to Japan as Arizona Horner Fellows[9] or Special Project awardees.[10] From the other side of the Pacific, ten JLA members have visited Arizona as Horner Fellows.[11]

The first Arizona Horner Fellow to visit Japan was Cathy Chung, a librarian at the Phoenix Public Library, who traveled to Japan for three weeks from September 25 to October 13, 1989. The focus of her visit was to learn about Japanese cataloging practices, library automation, Romanization standards, special collections, and recording technologies. She visited libraries, attended a vendor conference, and a bookbinding and repair class, and she spoke briefly at the Nippon Library Association Technical Processing Study Group.[12]

In 1990, Junko Matsui, Faculty of Arts at Osaka University of Arts, was the designated Horner Fellow from Japan. To mark the importance of this first year of exchange, Junko Matsui was accompanied by Dr. Tsutomu Shihota, a professor at St. Andrew's University and a founding member of the Library and Information Science Society in Asia and the Pacific, along with twelve other colleagues.[13]

The same year, Carol Elliott, a law librarian at the University of Arizona, traveled to Japan as the second Horner Fellow from the state. From October 15 to November 5, 1990, she visited seven libraries with legal collections, including several at different universities in Osaka and Tokyo, the Ministry of Justice, and the Tokyo Bar Association.

During the first ten years after the establishment of the Horner Fellowship endowment, the process and timeline for exchanges between Arizona and Japan had not been established, so the pattern of visits was somewhat irregular. After the visits in 1989 and 1990, librarians from Arizona traveled as Horner Fellows to Japan in 1992, 1995, 1997, and 1998. Only one other librarian from Japan visited during that first decade, when, during three weeks in January and February 1996, Mr. Fumiyoshi Kiuchi, director of the Inzai Public Library in Chiba Prefecture (a suburb of Tokyo) traveled throughout Arizona, visiting twenty-three public, academic, and school libraries as well as the Grand Canyon and several notable museums. It was reported that he even attended a cowboy wedding in Prescott![14]

During her three-week visit to Japan in October–November 1998, the sixth Arizona Horner Fellow, Charlotte Cohen, a reference librarian at the Arizona State University Libraries, had, as one of her desired outcomes, the goal "to facilitate the establishment of an informal reciprocal exchange agreement between librarians from Japan and Arizona." Her efforts came to fruition when in April of 1999 JLA's board approved and accepted an invitation from AzLA president Caryl Major to establish a partnership.

Beginning in November 2000 with the visit of Noriko Motoyama, a school librarian from Tokyo, exchange visits became more frequent, if not regular. Arizona librarians visited Japan in 2002, 2005, and 2008, and librarians from Japan traveled to Arizona in 2006 and 2008.

On September 18, 2008, the relationship between AzLA and JLA was further strengthened and formalized with an agreement signed by AzLA president Angie Creel-Erb and JLA chairman Shiomi Noboru.[15]

Since that time, the number of exchange visits has increased and the alternate year pattern has been established, with seven librarians from Arizona traveling to Japan between 2009 and 2016, either as Fellows or special project awardees. In May 2017, the AzLA Horner Committee selected the next Arizona Fellow, an academic librarian from the University of Arizona, who traveled to Japan in October 2017. In return, four librarians from Japan have visited Arizona as Horner Fellows in 2010, 2012, 2014, and 2016.

Arizona and Japanese Horner Fellows: Characteristics and Impact

Over the years, the types of librarians traveling from Arizona have been divided among public librarians (eight), academic librarians (seven), one state government librarian, and one school librarian. Their areas of interest have ranged widely. The public and school librarians have often focused on services to children and youth, frequently seeking to learn more about Japanese anime and manga. Academic librarians often focus their visits on learning about Japanese approaches to collection development and management and services for students and faculty. Most librarians from all categories (and, in fact, from both countries) have been interested in learning how the internet and new technologies are employed in providing content and services to library users.

The impact of the Horner Fellowship experience on individuals has been significant. Carol Elliott, former law librarian at the University of Arizona and the second AzLA Horner Fellow to visit Japan, commented on how much her experience as a Horner Fellow affected her life:

> The Horners made a constructive investment: they hoped that the Fellows would forge relationships that would continue to flourish, that Fellows would want to return to Japan, and that it would be a great experience personally and professionally. And for me all of this has happened. I have returned to Japan with family members and have had my hosts while in Japan as a Fellow visit me. I have also had professional visitors and, with others, was able to assist Mr. Shihota with his sabbatical in Tucson at the School for Information Resources and Library Science. Having visitors from Japan in our home has had a tremendous impact on my family and has given us a new perspective on our own lives.[16]

David Brown, Youth Services Librarian at Casa Grande Public Library in Casa Grande, Arizona, was the 2015 Horner Fellow from Arizona. His goals in visiting Japan included to

- explore library/museum services for children in Japan;
- learn Japanese puppetry and storytelling techniques and practices; and
- study the architecture and design of children's spaces as well as the interactive elements for education and play.[17]

Mr. Brown has described the impact of his experiences as follows:

> The most unexpected professional impact of my trip was in witnessing Kamishibai storytelling, a kind of picture book theater where storytellers act out stories written on the back of oversized pictures. While most of the youth programs that I witnessed during my fellowship were calm and quiet, Kamishibai was loud, silly, and dramatic (something that translates really well to an American audience). I managed to purchase a Kamishibai theater and several Kamishibai stories at a Bookstore in Tokyo and have utilized them in my story times in Casa Grande ever since. I have created a video demonstrating Kamishibai performance techniques for other Librarians in Arizona and have presented on the art and craft during the AZLA annual conference in 2015. I plan to personally continue seeking out other forms of storytelling for youth, and have learned from my fellowship that we can always adapt and evolve based on the practices of our colleagues overseas.[18]

As an example of a recent AzLA Horner awardee from an academic library, Sarah Kortemeier, at the time library assistant at the University of Arizona (UA) Poetry Center and graduate student in the UA library science program, visited Japan in January 2016 as a Special Project Horner Fellow. The purpose of her visit was to study Japanese collections of traditional and contemporary poetry and learn how Japanese libraries participate in the work of dissemination and promoting poetry and their preservation standards and techniques.[19] In writing about her experience as a Horner Special Project Fellow and the impact it has had on her life, Ms. Kortemeier says:

> The most powerful impact of the Horner Fellowship for me was both personal and professional: I was able to have detailed conversations with colleagues in Japan that revealed the depth of some of the phil-

> osophical differences between library practice in our two countries (there are many similarities too, of course!). I listened hard, and I came away from the experience thoroughly convinced that there are multiple "right" ways to do librarianship. I had some core assumptions about preservation and access challenged in the course of those conversations, and I'm so grateful. We should never lose our curiosity, never stop being open to new ideas.... As a result of what I saw in Japanese cultural heritage institutions, I have begun exploring ways to intensify outreach around exhibitions and web content in my home institution. I'm specifically interested in increasing the interactive potential of our library exhibits, both in person and online.[20]

Characteristics of Japanese Horner Fellows have followed a similar distribution as those from Arizona, with four from academic libraries, three public, one school librarian, and one special librarian. Their interests are also similar to those of the Arizona Horner Fellows but often take a more general approach, wanting to visit a broad range of Arizona libraries to see how they provide services, programming, and resources for library users.

In 2010, Ms. Motoko Hori, librarian at the Japan Society of Civil Engineers, traveled to Arizona as the JLA Horner Fellow.[21] She visited twenty public, special, and academic libraries throughout the state and attended the AzLA Annual Conference, making special note of the special collections and archives at Northern Arizona University and the statewide Arizona Memory Project, a web-based initiative supported by the Arizona State Library, Archives and Public Records to make available the archives of libraries, museums, and cultural institutions. In describing the impact of the fellowship, Ms. Hori reports that the Horner Fellow experience changed the direction of her life both personally and professionally.[22] In 2012, she returned to the United States, subsequently earning an associate degree in library information technology. She is now employed as a cataloging assistant at the University of California, Berkeley and is planning to return to university to earn a master's degree in library science to further her career.

The most recent Horner Fellow from Japan was Ms. Masako Iwashita, a librarian and professor at Shigakukan University in Kagoshima, who came to Arizona in October 2016. Because she teaches library science courses in Japan, Ms. Iwashita wanted to visit a wide range of types of libraries to learn about library management, library design, and the relationship of teachers and students in Arizona classrooms. She met with librarians and campus faculty at the University of Arizona and Arizona State University and visited a community college library, several public libraries, a school library, and some specialized libraries. During her visit, she shared her experiences with her university students back in Japan by way of email and blog posts. Some of the things that most impressed Ms. Iwashita during her visit were the maker spaces at the university libraries, the friendly and open nature of Arizona librarians and libraries, and the services in public libraries for different age groups (children, teens, seniors, etc.). She also enjoyed the opportunity to attend the 2016 AzLA Annual Conference, where she gave a presentation during the combined Horner Committee/International Interest Group meeting. At the AzLA Awards luncheon, Ms. Iwashita was presented with a Horner Fellow commemorative plaque. She gave a brief and well-received thank-you speech and later said that she felt like she was a winner at the Academy Awards![23]

Following her return to Japan, Ms. Iwashita recounted her experience in a presentation to colleagues at Shigakukan University who demonstrated an intense interest in

American academic librarianship. In her talk, she especially focused on the equipment lending (laptops, cameras, etc.) at the university libraries, study spaces (including group study rooms) for students, and US approaches to information literacy and critical-thinking instructional services. She wrote an article about her Horner Fellowship experience for the JLA monthly publication and has also written a series of articles about her Arizona travels for a Kagoshima newspaper.

Additional library services that have inspired other Japanese librarians visiting Arizona include Finals Study Break activities (including therapy dogs) at universities, "Read to a Dog" activities in some Arizona school and public libraries, "Bi-Folkal" memory kits,[24] and Little Free Library installations (https://littlefreelibrary.org) in Arizona communities. The bond and level of support between the local community and libraries in Arizona have been noteworthy to many Japanese Horner Fellows.

Conclusion

New expertise in haiku poetry, puppet theatre, manga books, graphic novels, comics, ebooks, digitization, preservation, library design and services, and teaching literacy skills are only some of the outcomes resulting from the Horner Fellowship visits. The Horner Fellowship has offered rewarding learning experiences on both professional and personal levels for librarians in Arizona and Japan. These librarians have applied their newly acquired knowledge in their professional positions to benefit their clientele and have shared their experiences with their communities through presentations, newsletters, journal articles, blogs, social media, and other venues.

For Horner Fellows from both countries, the interactions with their foreign counterparts have revealed the differences but also the similarities between library practices in the two countries, showed them multiple ways of practicing librarianship and made them more receptive to new ideas. Over the years, Horner Fellows have succeeded in fulfilling Jack and Marian Horner's original purpose in establishing the Horner Endowment—to build bridges between Arizona and Japan based on knowledge, understanding, and respect for our different library practices and cultural heritages.

Notes

1. "First Objector Serves in Navy," *Altoona Mirror*, Altoona, PA (February 11, 1942): 4.
2. Kyohei Hagiwara, Matsuo Inamura, and Keiichiro Takezawa, *Jack and Betty: English Step by Step* (Tokyo: Kairyudo Shuppan K.K., 1948).
3. Layton Horner and Otani Yasuteru, *The Japanese and the Americans* (Tokyo, Japan: Seibido, 1987).
4. Layton Horner, Yukio Sakamoto, and Otani Yasuteru, *On Both Sides of the Pacific* (Tokyo, Japan: Asahi Press, 1989).
5. "The Horner Fellowship and Horner Fellowship Committee," Arizona Library Association, accessed August 17, 2017, https://www.azla.org/page/hornerfellowship.
6. "Sister Libraries: 30 Years of International Friendship and Exchange," State Library of Oregon, accessed on August 17, 2017, http://www.oregon.gov/osl/Pages/ExhibitOnDisplay.aspx.
7. "Horner Fellowship Committee Bylaws," *AzLA Handbook*, accessed August 17, 2017, http://azlahandbook.pbworks.com/w/page/8817435/HORNER%20FELLOWSHIP%20COMMITTEE.
8. Ibid.
9. "Horner Fellows: AzLA/JLA Fellowship," Arizona Library Association, accessed August 17,

2017, http://www.azla.org/?page=HornerFellows#AzLAJLA.
10. "Special Project Program," Arizona Library Association, accessed August 17, 2017, http://www.azla.org/?page=HornerFellows#SpecialProjectProgram.
11. "Horner Fellows: AzLA/JLA Fellowship."
12. Ibid.
13. Ibid.
14. "Horner Fellows: AzLA/JLA Fellowship."
15. "AzLA and JLA Sign an Official Horner Fellowship Reciprocal Exchange Agreement," *AzLA Newsletter* (March 29, 2009).
16. "A Tale of Libraries: October 15–November 5, 1990," accessed October 4, 2017, http://c.ymcdn.com/sites/www.azla.org/resource/resmgr/Horner/HornerReports/1990_Carol_Elliott.pdf.
17. "Library Youth Services, the Design of Youth Spaces, and the Puppetry of Japan," accessed October 7, 2017, http://c.ymcdn.com/sites/www.azla.org/resource/resmgr/Horner/HornerReports/2015_David_Brown.pdf.
18. David Brown, email communication to authors, June 20, 2017.
19. "Special Project Program."
20. Sarah Kortemeier, email communication to authors, June 14, 2017.
21. "My Experience with the Horner Fellowship Library Study Tour," accessed October 7, 2017, http://c.ymcdn.com/sites/www.azla.org/resource/resmgr/Horner/HornerReports/2010_Motoko_Hori_Report_.pdf.
22. Motoko Hori, email communication to authors, June 5, 2017.
23. "Report from Masako Iwashita, 2016 Horner Fellowship Recipient," *AzLA Newsletter* (May–June 2017), accessed October 7, 2017, http://newsletter.azla.org/article/report-from-masako-iwashita-2016-horner-fellowship-recipient/.
24. BiFOLKal kits (http://www.bifolkal.org) can be checked out from several public and county libraries in Arizona. They include photographs, videos, music, and things that can be touched to remind seniors of experiences and to invite them to share their stories with others. Each kit designed to elicit memories and knowledge focuses on a specific time or era.

Bibliography

"AzLA and JLA Sign an Official Horner Fellowship Reciprocal Exchange Agreement." *AzLA Newsletter*. March 29, 2009.

"First Objector Serves in Navy." *Altoona Mirror*, Altoona, PA. February 11, 1942.

Hagiwara, Kyohei, Matsuo Inamura, and Keiichiro Takezawa. *Jack and Betty: English Step by Step*. Tokyo: Kairyudo Shuppan K.K., 1948.

"Horner Fellows: AzLA/JLA Fellowship." Arizona Library Association. Accessed August 17, 2017. http://www.azla.org/?page=HornerFellows#AzLAJLA.

"Horner Fellowship and Horner Fellowship Committee." Arizona Library Association. Accessed August 17, 2017. https://www.azla.org/page/hornerfellowship

"Horner Fellowship Committee Bylaws." *AzLA Handbook*. Accessed August 17, 2017. http://azlahandbook.pbworks.com/w/page/8817435/HORNER%20FELLOWSHIP%20COMMITTEE.

Horner, Layton, Yukio Sakamoto, and Otani Yasuteru. *On Both Sides of the Pacific*. Tokyo, Japan: Asahi Press, 1989.

Horner, Layton, and Otani Yasuteru. *The Japanese and the Americans*. Tokyo, Japan: Seibido, 1987.

"Library Youth Services, the Design of Youth Spaces, and the Puppetry of Japan." Accessed October 7, 2017. http://c.ymcdn.com/sites/www.azla.org/resource/resmgr/Horner/HornerReports/2015_David_Brown.pdf.

"My Experience with the Horner Fellowship Library Study Tour." Accessed October 7, 2017. http://c.ymcdn.com/sites/www.azla.org/resource/resmgr/Horner/HornerReports/2010_Motoko_Hori_Report_.pdf.

"Report from Masako Iwashita, 2016 Horner Fellowship Recipient." *AzLA Newsletter*. May–June 2017. Accessed October 7, 2017. http://newsletter.azla.org/article/report-from-masako-iwashi-

ta-2016-horner-fellowship-recipient/.
"Sister Libraries: 30 Years of International Friendship and Exchange." State Library of Oregon. Accessed on August 17, 2017. http://www.oregon.gov/osl/Pages/ExhibitOnDisplay.aspx.
"Special Project Program." Arizona Library Association. Accessed August 17, 2017. http://www.azla.org/?page=HornerFellows#SpecialProjectProgram.
"A Tale of Libraries: October 15–November 5, 1990." Accessed October 4, 2017. http://c.ymcdn.com/sites/www.azla.org/resource/resmgr/Horner/HornerReports/1990_Carol_Elliott.pdf.

CHAPTER THIRTY-THREE

Internationalization and Global Engagement in LIS Education:

Programs for International Master's Students at the University of Wisconsin-Milwaukee Libraries

Shana R. Ponelis, Ewa Barczyk, and Johannes J. Britz

Introduction

In 1951, Ranganathan stated that "the library profession is international"[1] and librarians "belong to the world and not merely to any particular country."[2] International engagement of library and information science (LIS) professionals leads to benefits for individuals and communities through the exchange of experience and ideas.[3] Libraries are one of the primary providers of access to different cultures, ideas, and knowledge and meeting places for people from various communities, thereby facilitating social and cultural interaction among people from different backgrounds. Thus, "international and intercultural opportunities are essential components in educating and training library and information professionals."[4]

Internationalization is a process of exchange and mutual influence among actors from different countries. The purpose of international collaboration and engagement in higher education is "to enhance the academic excellence and the relevance of institutions' contribution to their respective societies."[5] Internationalization can take various forms, depending on the degree of involvement of an institution in one or more destination countries. Activities can include faculty and student exchanges, international research collaboration, cross-border delivery of education through online education, offering joint degrees, establishment of campuses by universities outside of their home countries, mutual recognition of qualifications between countries, harmonization of qualification systems, and increased inclusion of an international, intercultural, and global dimension in the home institution's curriculum.

The internationalization of higher education has intensified over the past two decades, largely as a result of globalization and the development of information and communication technology (ICT) that enables online education. Over the past few decades, ICT has also impacted significantly on library and information services, the LIS profession, as well as higher education. It has given libraries greater connectivity and access to international resources and facilitated the sharing of information across the world through, among other things, co-operative cataloging and globalized resource discovery. In essence, borders are no longer boundaries that block information sharing and collaboration.

It is increasingly crucial to promote international engagements that are innovative, multifaceted, and attuned to the ever more complex globalized landscape of internationalization in higher education.[6] In this chapter, the authors discuss the goals, expectations, resources, challenges, outcomes, and impact of two programs coordinated by the University of Wisconsin-Milwaukee (UWM) Libraries for international master's students in LIS from the perspective of the library, LIS faculty, and university administration after providing contextual background on UWM. We also discuss the benefits to the host institutions and how these programs strengthen UWM's reputation as a globally engaged university.

Contextual Background

UWM is a public university located in Milwaukee, Wisconsin, in the United States. With just under 27,000 students and 190 degree programs, UWM is the largest university in the Milwaukee metropolitan area, the second largest university in Wisconsin, and one of two doctoral degree-granting public universities in the state. In terms of research activity, the university is categorized as an R1 institution in the *Carnegie Classification of Institutions of Higher Education*. According to the university's vision, UWM "will be a top-tier research university that is the best place to learn and work for students, faculty and staff, and that is a leading driver for sustainable prosperity" that will be accomplished through "a commitment to excellence, powerful ideas, community and global engagement, and collaborative partnerships."[7]

UWM's progress toward becoming a globally engaged university is assessed according to criteria stipulated for an internationalized university by the *Association of Public and Land-Grant Universities*.[8] The criteria include the following:

- Internationalization is included as an integral part of the institution's vision, mission, and strategic plan.
- Academic and administrative leadership provides a strong commitment to international engagement.
- International content is infused into the teaching, research, and engagement programs of all schools and colleges.

- Faculty, staff, and administrators with an international outlook are employed across all schools and colleges.
- Evaluation and promotion guidelines strongly encourage international involvement to assist with the internationalization of people and programs.
- Faculty are encouraged to engage in international research, teaching, and leading study abroad programs.
- International linkages or partnerships that support regular faculty and student exchanges, visits, shared use of field sites, use of technology in teaching, jointly sponsored workshops, performances, and research partnerships are maintained.

Internationalization encompassing all the above criteria is a strategic initiative to strengthen UWM's reputation as a globally-engaged university in the *UW-Milwaukee Strategic Plan 2020.*

The UWM Libraries, consisting of the Music, Curriculum, Media, and internationally recognized American Geographical Society Libraries, which are centrally located, house more than five million items and serve more than 1.3 million visitors in the main buildings with more than three million visits to the libraries' extensive online resources. The professional staff are actively engaged in teaching, research, are deeply involved in campus governance and leadership, and present papers and participate in numerous international conferences.

The UWM Libraries play an important role in UWM's strategic initiative through globally focused academic, research, and outreach programs to increase students' international learning and understanding. The Libraries are members and contributors of materials to the World Digital Libraries portal, a UNESCO/Library of Congress initiative. The American Geographical Society Library annually provides fellowships to international researchers to support their research utilizing our unique collections. An inter-institutional agreement with the University of Zululand (Unizulu) in South Africa includes a component for librarian exchanges, resulting in the UWM Libraries hosting two librarians and the Director of the Libraries, and UWM faculty visiting Unizulu for multiple presentations and discussions with staff. A recently signed agreement with the Rwandan Ministry of Education was an outcome of library staff participating in a Peace Corps-sponsored program to train community librarians. Thanks to the rich global scope of the libraries collections, the UWM Libraries has hosted international conferences, exhibits, dignitaries, and speakers, thus providing the campus with more global contacts. This, in turn, has led to some particularly unique and important global initiatives. In 2006, the library director, along with a history faculty, facilitated the return of a dozen medieval documents to the State Archives of Wroclaw, Poland, which were found by a local soldier during World War II and, after his death, were turned over by his family to find their rightful repository (figure 33.1). Thanks to international researchers, the UWM Libraries and staff also helped solve an international riddle of an unidentified seventeenth-century scroll that had been acquired by the Libraries in 1917. The large "Tira de Santa Catarina Ixtepeji," dating from the seventeenth century, was translated from an extinct dialect to discover that it was the history of the mountain village near Oaxaca, Mexico. An exact facsimile on linen was made and delivered in person for the village's anniversary celebration, linking the UWM Libraries with the history of this remote village (figure 33.2).

Figure 33.1. Medieval document repatriated from Milwaukee on display at State Archive of Wroclaw, Poland.

Figure 33.2. Presentation by UWM Libraries of reproduction of the Codex of Santa Catarina Ixtepeji to the village depicted on the scroll.

The instructional programs and research by the School of Information Studies (SOIS) blend UWM's mission with the school's information focus, international scope, and interdisciplinary mindset. SOIS offers several undergraduate- and graduate-degree programs, one of which is an MLIS degree program accredited by the American Libraries Association (ALA) with various transcript-designated concentrations, including information technology and digital libraries, and coordinated degree programs, including history and anthropology. The culturally diverse faculty at SOIS fosters a multifaceted approach to the curriculum and encourages involvement in activities from Wisconsin, across the United States, and beyond. SOIS has partnerships with thirteen universities in seven countries, including the National Taiwan Normal University and the University of Pretoria in South Africa. These international partnerships enable a range of study abroad programs, student and faculty exchanges, and research collaborations that support students developing the skills necessary to succeed in the global information society.

Programs at UWM Libraries

In this section, the goals, expectations, resources, challenges, outcomes, and impact of two very different programs at UWM for international master's students in LIS are discussed.

Program 1: National Taiwan Normal University internship program

MOTIVATION FOR PROGRAM AND CONTEXT OF PARTICIPATING STUDENTS

The Graduate Institute of Library and Information Studies (GLIS) at the National Taiwan Normal University (NTNU) was established to nurture talents for library information services in Taiwan to meet the needs of a knowledge-based society. NTNU launched a doctoral program in 2009. Concomitantly, NTNU wanted to provide their master's students with an opportunity for international exposure in response to the trend of globalization in the profession and academy and to give graduate students a diverse learning experience. Libraries in Taiwan are well-financed and maintained with cutting-edge technology incorporated into their operations.

OVERVIEW OF THE PROGRAM

This collaborative international program was initiated with an agreement in 2009 between UWM Libraries, UWM SOIS, and the Graduate Institute of Library and Information Studies at the NTNU (figure 33.3). Funding for the interns was secured by NTNU from their Ministry of Education and the National Chinese Association. In recent years, NTNU was able to expand the program to six interns rather than the initial four.

UWM Libraries
NEWSLETTER
Milwaukee, Wisconsin 53201 ■ uwm.edu/Library ■ Volume No. 65 Fall 2014

Internship Program Brings Taiwanese Students to Campus for Fifth Consecutive Year

The UWM Libraries hosted four of eight graduate students selected to receive scholarships from their school, National Taiwan Normal University, and from the Taiwanese government, to participate in an eight-week program this summer at UWM and the School of Information Studies. The other four students interned with Milwaukee Public Library and Marquette's Raynor Library. Pictured here are all the interns on a field trip to the Wisconsin Historical Society in Madison. Front row, from left: Wang Yun-Chiao, Michael Edmonds (WHS Deputy Administrator of the Library-Archives Division), Lin Yi-Ting, and Wu Chia-Chen; back, from left: Hsieh Yu-Hsin, Chang Chia-Lin, Wa Yang, Chou Ting-yu, Chang Ju-Fang. Photo by Linda Kopecky.

UWM Libraries Newsletter • Spring 2014 9

Figure 33.3. NTNU Internship program shared UWM campus and community.

The students are selected by NTNU and are highly-motivated with excellent grades and a strong desire to expand their global awareness of librarianship. Each summer, the interns come to UWM Libraries for eight to ten weeks. These are generally second- or third-year graduate students who must pass the TOEFL language exam with high marks and demonstrate good academic standing. Prior to their arrival, the selected interns get two-month training at Taiwan e-Learning Digital Archives Program (TELDAP). The UWM Libraries identifies areas to place the interns where they can gain practical experience in technical applications in libraries, strengthen their skills in leadership by managing a project, gain greater fluency in English, make meaningful contributions to the overall library operations, and experience professional enrichment. The interns are told of their assignment prior to arrival and are connected with their supervisors. They also select a SOIS class to attend while in residency, which can be an online class.

We host a welcome lunch for the students to meet all the staff and SOIS faculty. The first weeks involve a general orientation to the campus and city, meeting staff, and getting an overview of each unit and their work. The interns spend twenty hours a week working in the libraries under the supervision of a librarian, but during their stay, they are encouraged to attend library lectures, all staff meetings, and major campus events to give them a good understanding of academic library and campus life in the US. One librarian is their main contact to assist with any practical issues as well as being a resource for activities in the city for their leisure time.

To provide in-depth training and expand the student's opportunities for learning, we expanded the collaboration to include a large public library system, the Milwaukee Public Library, and a private Catholic university, Marquette University, with rotation so that the interns gain experience in each of the different libraries. Each intern has their home unit and project, but they have the opportunity to visit all the libraries and learn the differences in their missions and services. During their summer stay, the interns attend the ALA Annual Conference at which they often present a poster. The UWM Libraries arranges field trips to other major libraries in the region. They visit UW Madison Libraries and the newly renovated Madison Public Library and get tours of the Wisconsin State Capitol building, where the highlight is to sit in the governor's chair (figure 33.4). Chicago Public and Newberry Libraries have been other field trips.

Figure 33.4. Visit to the Wisconsin State Capitol in Madison, Wisconsin.

At the end of their stay, the interns give a presentation to our staff in which they talk about their experiences, what they learned, about similarities and differences between their libraries and those in the US, and their overall impressions. Since the students come with great media skills, most of them choose to make a wonderful video presentation, which is greatly enjoyed by the staff. The students are formally presented with certificates of completion of the internship program signed by the provost (figure 33.5). It is a wonderful finale to a mutually beneficial summer experience.

Figure 33.5. Official welcome with the provost and farewell with certificates of recognition.

ACTIVITIES UNDERTAKEN IN COLLABORATION WITH UWM AND RESOURCES REQUIRED

Coordination with NTNU, SOIS, Marquette University, and Milwaukee Public Library are required to facilitate the interns' stay. The libraries work with SOIS and campus foreign student office to provide appropriate letters of invitation for their visas. The libraries coordinate assignments for each student and create a training rotation around SOIS courses the students attend (figure 33.6).

We meet the students upon their arrival in Milwaukee to help smooth the move into the dormitory rooms. Since the students choose not to eat in the dorm dining hall, due to cost and type of food provided, the students prepare their own meals, so our staff members put together a handy box of basic kitchen utensils, dishes, and pots and pans. This box gets saved from year to year and is given to the next cohort. Library staff also provide groceries and cooked meals on their first days to ease their transition.

Figure 33.6. NTNU interns working with staff on digitization skills, creating posters, and with mentors at Milwaukee Public Library.

We felt it helped the students adapt and learn about our culture better through social events, so we took them around the city, to shopping, baseball games, museum outings, festivals, and invited them to staff houses (figure 33.7). Staff are encouraged to invite the students to share activities with them and let them know of activities in the city for them to attend. These costs are mainly personal contributions, not funded by the libraries. However, the library did organize the field trips and paid for all transportation costs.

Figure 33.7. NTNU students enjoy summer in Milwaukee with Library staff.

CHALLENGES EXPERIENCED

The biggest challenge was to identify meaningful and valuable work for each intern without knowing the depth of their abilities. Because this is a summer internship, a period when staff take vacation time, some librarians were concerned about providing adequate training and ongoing supervision. The main challenge was the commitment of time necessary to make each summer cohort a successful learning experience. This included training and supervision but also a social and practical connection to provide a full cultural experience for the students. Because every student participant thus far was so eager to learn and came with very high technical skills, it was such a positive and enriching experience to work with each summer cohort.

In terms of teaching, NTNU students are not accustomed to fully online classes, and some have found it difficult to adjust to this mode of delivery and derive full benefit from their selected class. Students are often surprised by the level of interaction in online classes, for example, between the students themselves in discussion forums and the extent of group work.

Figure 33.8. UWM libraries director invited to lecture at NTNU and meet other library directors in Taipei.

OUTCOMES AND IMPACT

The interns provide valuable contributions to the libraries by helping to build our digital collections, indexing Asian cultural and heritage materials, translating library tutorials into Chinese (which serves our growing Chinese student population), metadata creation of Chinese language maps, and organizing and managing archival slides and photographic projects. They learn how American students use the libraries and the staff as a resource for research. Our Learning Commons is always a surprise to them because we permit food and drink and our policies are more flexible.

The internship is truly an integration of library science theory and philosophy with experiential learning in a library setting. The cohort leaves with practical technical skills in digitizing, data curation, and cataloging, as well as the provision of services to users. All participants, hosts, and interns gain improved intercultural competencies and a broader understanding of similarities and differences between both countries. An unanticipated outcome was a closer engagement between the local libraries in building a three-pronged inter-institutional internship program. Because of this international partnership, NTNU invited the Director of the Libraries to come to Taiwan to lecture to their graduate program classes and the library staff. This visit provided professional and personal enrichment while enhancing understanding of cultural differences (figure 33.8, figure 33.9). In turn, this helped the director to reshape future internships to be even more fruitful for the interns and our staff. A good way to summarize the impact is this quote from an NTNU intern in the 2012 cohort:

> I think it is an opportunity for me to put what I've learned into action, to obtain an overall understanding of the differences of the trends and developments of library and information science among different countries.

Figure 33.9. Presentation of NTNU Internship Program at IFLA in Singapore.

Program 2: Master's in IT degree program in collaboration with University of Pretoria and others

MOTIVATION FOR PROGRAM AND CONTEXT OF PARTICIPATING STUDENTS

LIS schools in sub-Saharan African (SSA) countries face several challenges pertaining to ICT-related education. For example, in Uganda, located in East Africa, there were inadequate educators, especially at the postgraduate level and in ICT-related courses, coupled with poor technology infrastructure at LIS schools.[9] Furthermore, continuing education for LIS school lecturers is problematic.[10] To help address these challenges and exploit opportunities for LIS education in Africa, LIS schools are advised to, among other initiatives, partner with other schools to work collaboratively in areas such as staff exchanges, curriculum development, distance teaching, and research supervision.[11,12] To this end, a master's degree program was jointly conceived by faculty at UWM and the University of Pretoria under the auspices of an existing inter-institutional agreement to contribute to ensuring that "libraries and other information services will take their rightful leadership role in the development of Africa."[13]

OVERVIEW OF THE PROGRAM

The Master's in Information Technology (M.IT) degree program is a collaboration among the Department of Information Science at the University of Pretoria, South Africa, the East African School of Library and Information Science (EASLIS) at Makerere University in Kampala, Uganda, the Mortenson Center for International Library Programs at the University of Illinois at Urbana-Champaign (UIUC), and UWM. The degree-granting institution is the University of Pretoria (UP).

The objectives of the M.IT degree program are two-fold:

1. To empower the next generation of library and information professionals and LIS educators with the knowledge and skills to apply modern information and communication technologies (ICTs).
2. To build capacity in library and information professionals managing ICTs or working in ICT-intensive environments in all types of libraries, and in LIS education, to support all library users, including researchers, academics, and students.

The two-year program is comprised of ten compulsory coursework modules of which seven are year-long modules and three are semester-long modules, and a mini-dissertation based on research conducted at the student's institution supervised by one or more of the coursework instructors. Coursework modules include The Knowledge Society and International Librarianship, IT Systems in Libraries, Digital Repositories, Web Trends in the Library, Facilitating Information Retrieval and Information Use, Knowledge Management, ICT Project Management, Strategic ICT Management, Organizational Behavior and Leadership, and Research Methodology (preparation for mini-dissertation research). Syllabi for courses were jointly developed by faculty from the participating institutions to give students a broader international perspective while ensuring content is relevant to the students' local context. The courses are delivered using a blended learning methodology with technology-mediated synchronous distance education on the learning management system (LMS) of UP combined with face-to-face lectures and site visits to the participating universities during study abroad trips. In total, four trips are undertaken during the two-year program: the first to UP in February of year one for orientation, lectures, and site visits, the second to the US in September of year one for site visits and lectures, the third to Uganda in June of year two for a methodology workshop and site visits, and the final trip to UP in August of year two to complete the write-up of mini-dissertations. Selected staff from the participating universities accompany students on these visits (figure 33.10).

Figure 33.10. SOIS faculty with students on study abroad trips in the US (2014), South Africa (2016), and Uganda (2017).

Between 2011 to 2016, there were two types of intake—funded and non-funded. Prospective students could apply for either the funded or the non-funded intake, depending on their country of origin. Academic librarians and LIS faculty in Ghana, Kenya, Nigeria, South Africa, Tanzania, Uganda, and most recently Kenya were eligible to apply for admission to the intake fully funded by the Carnegie Corporation of New York (CCNY). Funding covered books and other academic expenses, flights, accommodation, and a daily stipend while visiting participating campuses in South Africa, Uganda, and the US, as well as full sponsorship to present accepted research papers at the annual International Federation of Library Associations and Institutions (IFLA) World Library and Information Congress (WLIC) to three students from each intake. From 2017 onward, the program offers the non-funded option only. Due to the prohibitive expense of travel and the ever-increasing difficulties for many of the African students to obtain visas to travel to the US, the program will no longer include any study abroad trips. Lectures are presented synchronously and asynchronously via web-based conferencing tools only. Recordings made during the 2016 study abroad trips, including the site visit to UWM, will be used to supplement future instruction.

ACTIVITIES UNDERTAKEN IN COLLABORATION WITH UWM AND RESOURCES REQUIRED

Since 2011, UWM has hosted a one-week annual visit in September by a cohort of approximately twenty mid-career LIS professionals enrolled in their first year of the M.IT program, accompanied by faculty from UP. The visit forms part of a three-week visit to the US that includes stops in Washington, DC to visit the Library of Congress, a Smithsonian Institution library, and the University of Illinois at Urbana-Champaign (UIUC) (figure 33.11). Activities during the visit to UWM comprised lectures presented by faculty from SOIS, on-campus exchanges with UWM Libraries staff, and site visits to other academic and public libraries in the state.

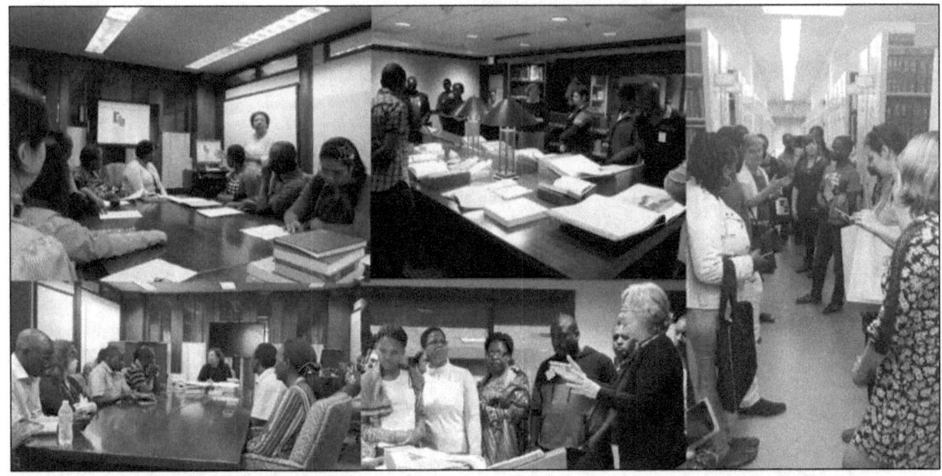

Figure 33.11. Students from 2013–2015 intakes visiting the Library of Congress African and Middle Eastern Division, the Smithsonian Libraries' rare books collection in the Cullman Library, and the University Library at UIUC.

The students and faculty are welcomed with a lunch at which library staff join the students and where they have opportunities to interact and invite the students to their area for further discussions (figure 33.12). This is followed by a general in-depth tour of the libraries lasting several hours. Additionally, students are invited to meet for more focused discussions and follow-up questions in units of interest to them. We facilitate meetings with archival staff, digitization specialists, or our IT experts for meetings after their classes. To give them a broader understanding of American libraries, we arrange tours of specialized libraries in the State Capitol; the students meet librarians at the University of Wisconsin Special Collections, Wisconsin Historical Society Library, Madison Public Library, Undergraduate Library and Research Commons (figure 33.13). In Milwaukee, tours are arranged at Milwaukee Public Library and Marquette University. During their stay in Milwaukee, the accompanying librarians and faculty meet with library staff to discuss research and trends in the libraries.

Figure 33.12. Welcome lunches hosted at UWM Golda Meir Library for the students with library staff, SOIS faculty, the provost of UWM, as well as staff from the University of Pretoria and University of Makerere.

Figure 33.13. Students visiting the State Capitol in Madison and the University of Wisconsin Special Collections.

CHALLENGES EXPERIENCED

At the inception, SOIS took a leading role in arranging to host the students. Over the years, however, there were several leadership changes that resulted in less involvement and commitment in arranging and hosting the annual visit. Initially, five faculty members of SOIS were involved in teaching in the program, but the number of faculty members presenting lectures also declined steadily due to lack of leadership support, staff turnover, time pressures, and communication frustrations. Communication frustrations are due not only to differing language abilities on the part of faculty (several from outside of the US themselves) and students but also a lack of understanding by faculty of the context of many students that differ dramatically from students in the US: lack of internet access at home and even at work, high cost of data, limited bandwidth, lack of reliable power supply, and lack of electricity at home (for example, one student would take her work laptop home and work on her assignments by candlelight until the battery was flat), and widely varying levels of preparedness for scholarly work at a master's-degree level. At the time of writing, two SOIS faculty members taught in the program.

The face-to-face lectures in the US were impacted by several students being unable to obtain visas (between 10 to 25 percent of students' visa applications were declined annually), requiring faculty to record lectures for these students. Where in-class discussions or presentations were made, synchronous technology had to be used to allow the students outside the US to participate. Fortunately, the time difference was not a problem since the lectures were always scheduled in the morning when it is afternoon in most of the affected students' countries.

OUTCOMES AND IMPACT

The purpose of the M.IT degree program is to enhance IT skills to enable research in African universities and to contribute to making accessible and expanding Africa's knowledge base. The outcomes of the program in this regard have been three-fold. First, specialized skills and expertise for library staff to use ICT to manage and disseminate research and local knowledge to faculty, researchers, and students at universities were developed as well as the capacity to keep up-to-date with technological developments and evaluate the relevance thereof for local contexts. Second, the program increased ICT capacity among LIS faculty at African LIS schools and enabled some of these faculty members to be promoted to more senior positions at their institutions. Through ongoing interaction in a private group on social media, all graduates, current students, and faculty can continue to share and discuss information about emerging ICT trends, upcoming conferences, local and web-based training opportunities, and recent relevant publications, share their experiences regarding ICT in LIS, and ask for technical assistance. Third, research students writing mini-dissertations contributed to the LIS body of knowledge and to training the next generation of scholars. Students co-authored papers with their supervisors and presented their research at regional and international conferences (such as the Standing Conference of Eastern, Central and Southern African Library and Information Associations (SCECSAL) and IFLA's WLIC) and were published in peer-reviewed journals.[14] In some instances, students and SOIS faculty continued to collaborate on research on new topics after graduation.[15] Several graduates have subsequently enrolled in and/or completed doctoral degrees and received prestigious bursaries, relying on, among other things, letters of recommendation from participating SOIS faculty.

In terms of the impact on UWM, the collaboration and participation in this program has engendered mutual understanding and promoted cultural exchanges. Faculty and library staff were able to learn from African students about their experiences in their workplaces, both academic libraries and/or LIS schools, and share their knowledge and experiences to support initiatives. It also enabled participating faculty members to expand the international and global dimension in the curriculum of UWM's MLIS degree program. Interaction with the students made faculty and library staff more aware of the limitations some libraries experience to provide library services and access to information for their user communities. At the same time, several students commented that they were impressed by what librarians in the US were able to accomplish with constrained budgets and limited staff—which they didn't realize was the case—and were inspired and motivated to accomplish more with the resources they do have. It is testimony to the impact of the program on UWM that several Libraries staff expressed dismay that the visits would not continue beyond 2016.

Conclusion

The two master's-level programs described in this chapter, involving the library, faculty, and administration of UWM, are examples of innovative and multifaceted programs that are attuned to the respective participating institutions' and students' objectives and needs within the ever more complex and changing landscape of internationalization in higher education. The programs offer opportunities for intercultural and international interactions pertaining to LIS practice and education to the visiting students and participating staff and faculty from UWM. Finally, both programs have contributed to UWM meeting several of the criteria for an internationalized university as stipulated by the *Association of Public and Land-Grant Universities* criteria and have contributed to UWM executing its strategic plan in accordance with its vision of global engagement through collaborative partnership.

Notes

1. Herbert Coblans, *Librarianship and Documentation: An International Perspective* (London, United Kingdom: Deutsch, 1974), 25.
2. Coblans, *Librarianship and documentation*, 25.
3. Alan Hopkinson, "International Librarianship: One Librarian's Experience in Reducing the Digital Divide," in *Collaboration in International and Comparative Librarianship* (IGI Global, 2014), 51–62.
4. Ismail Abdullahi, Leif Kajberg, and Sirje Virkus, "Internationalization of LIS Education in Europe and North America," *New Library World* 108, no. 1/2 (2007): 8.
5. Abdullahi, Kajberg, and Virkus, "Internationalization of LIS education," 13.
6. Paul T. Zeleza, "Engagements between African Diaspora Academics in the US and Canada and African Institutions of Higher Education: Perspectives from North America and Africa" (New York: Carnegie Corporation of New York, 2013).
7. "UWM's Vision, Values, and Mission Statements | UW-Milwaukee," University of Wisconsin-Milwaukee, accessed November 23, 2017, http://uwm.edu/mission/.
8. UWM Task Force on Internationalization, "Advancing Internationalization at UWM: Fostering Success, Facilitating Growth and Expanding Horizons in the 21st Century University," University of Wisconsin-Milwaukee, 2009, accessed November 23, 2017, http://www4.uwm.edu/planningportal/v1/docs/Intl_Task_Force_Report.pdf.
9. Constant Okello-Obura and Isaac M. N. Kigongo-Bukenya, "Library and Information Science Education and Training in Uganda: Trends, Challenges, and the Way Forward," *Education Research International* 2011 (2011), http://dx.doi.org/10.1155/2011/705372.
10. Okello-Obura and Kigongo-Bukenya, "Library and Information Science Education."
11. Peter Burnett, "Challenges and Problems of Library and Information Science Education in Selected African Countries," presentation at 79th IFLA World Library and Information Congress, Singapore, August 17–23, 2013, accessed November 23, 2017, http://library.ifla.org/175/1/199-burnett-en.pdf.
12. Dennis Ocholla and Theo Bothma, "Trends, Challenges and Opportunities for LIS Education and Training in Eastern and Southern Africa," *New Library World* 108, no. 1/2 (2007): 55–78.
13. Johannes J. Britz, Peter J. Lor, and Theo J. Bothma, "Building Library Leadership in Africa: A Proposed Education Initiative," *The International Information & Library Review* 39, no. 2 (2007): 107.
14. Robert S. Buwule and Shana R. Ponelis, "Perspectives on University Library Automation and National Development in Uganda," *IFLA Journal* 43, no. 3 (2017): 256–65, https://doi.org/10.1177/0340035217710539.
15. Philliam Adoma and Shana R. Ponelis, "Open Source Integrated Library Systems in Academic

Libraries in Uganda: Initial Results," presentation at IFLA WLIC IT section satellite meeting, Stellenbosch, South Africa, August 13–14, 2015.

Bibliography

Abdullahi, Ismail, Leif Kajberg, and Sirje Virkus. "Internationalization of LIS Education in Europe and North America." *New Library World* 108, no. 1/2 (2007): 7–24.

Adoma, Philliam, and Shana R. Ponelis. "Open Source Integrated Library Systems in Academic Libraries in Uganda: Initial Results." Presentation at IFLA WLIC IT section satellite meeting, Stellenbosch, South Africa, August 13–14, 2015.

Britz, Johannes J., Peter J. Lor, and Theo J. Bothma. "Building Library Leadership in Africa: A Proposed Education Initiative." *The International Information & Library Review* 39, no. 2 (2007): 103–08.

Burnett, Peter. "Challenges and Problems of Library and Information Science Education in Selected African Countries." Presentation at 79th IFLA World Library and Information Congress, Singapore, August 17–23, 2013. Accessed November 23, 2017. http://library.ifla.org/175/1/199-burnett-en.pdf.

Buwule, Robert S., and Shana R. Ponelis. "Perspectives on University Library Automation and National Development in Uganda." *IFLA Journal* 43, no. 3 (2017): 256–65. https://doi.org/10.1177/0340035217710539.

Coblans, Herbert. "Librarianship and Documentation: An International Perspective." London, United Kingdom: Deutsch, 1974.

Hopkinson, Alan. "International Librarianship: One Librarian's Experience in Reducing the Digital Divide." In *Collaboration in International and Comparative Librarianship*, 51–62. IGI Global, 2014.

Ocholla, Dennis, and Theo Bothma. "Trends, Challenges and Opportunities for LIS Education and Training in Eastern and Southern Africa." *New Library World* 108, no. 1/2 (2007): 55–78.

Okello-Obura, Constant, and Isaac M. N. Kigongo-Bukenya. "Library and Information Science Education and Training in Uganda: Trends, Challenges, and the Way Forward." *Education Research International* 2011 (2011). http://dx.doi.org/10.1155/2011/705372.

UWM Task Force on Internationalization. *Advancing Internationalization at UWM: Fostering Success, Facilitating Growth and Expanding Horizons in the 21st Century University*. 2009. http://www4.uwm.edu/planningportal/v1/docs/Intl_Task_Force_Report.pdf.

Zeleza, Paul T. "Engagements between African Diaspora Academics in the US and Canada and African Institutions of Higher Education: Perspectives from North America and Africa." New York: Carnegie Corporation of New York, 2013.

Author Biographies

Ahmed Alwan (ahmed.alwan@csun.edu) is a tenure-track faculty at California State University, Northridge (CSUN) and a research, instruction, and outreach librarian in the Oviatt Library. In the most recent years leading up to his appointment at CSUN, Ahmed was the information literacy librarian at the American University of Sharjah in the United Arab Emirates. Ahmed has a bachelor of arts in history and religious studies from York University, a master of information science from the University of Toronto, and he is currently working on a master's in educational technology through Michigan State University.

Dawn Amsberry is a reference and instruction librarian at Penn State University Libraries, University Park campus. She has a master's in library science from San Jose State University, California and an MA in teaching English to speakers of other languages from Hunter College, New York. She has been a children's and reference librarian in public and academic libraries, and has taught English as a second language and writing to adults. She is the author of several articles and book chapters on academic library services to international students.

Susan Avery is the instructional services librarian and an associate professor in the Undergraduate Library at the University of Illinois at Urbana–Champaign. In this position she manages the library instruction program for those courses that fulfill the Composition I requirement and trains and mentors graduate assistants who teach library instruction sessions. This program provides library instruction to more than 4,500 first-year students each year, making it the largest library instruction program at the university. She has presented and published on the assessment of library instruction focused on both the student experience and teaching effectiveness, investigating the role of teachable moments in the classroom and at the reference desk, international students in the instruction classroom, and building effective faculty/librarian relationships. She is active in the ACRL Instruction Section.

Ewa Barczyk is associate provost and director of libraries, University of Wisconsin-Milwaukee, USA (emerita, retired May 2016). Ewa led the expansion of international initiatives in the Libraries involving many partnerships. She oversaw the implementation of agreements with NTNU and the University of Pretoria and has presented on these initiatives at various international venues.

Laura Bohuski is a database project specialist at Western Kentucky University where she fixes human and computer errors that develop in the libraries ex-libris database. She received her bachelor's in history and social studies from WKU before receiving her master's in library science from Indiana University Bloomington in December of 2010. Ms. Bohuski has started work on her master's in history from WKU, is a new member of the American Library Association, and looks forward to interacting with the academic community.

Karen Bordonaro is a liaison librarian at the James A. Gibson Library. Her work includes library instruction, collection development, and research consultations with students and faculty in applied linguistics, classics, modern languages, literatures and cultures, history, Canadian studies, and medieval and Renaissance studies. In addition, she also serves as the liaison librarian for ESL Services, the Office of International Services, and the Confucius Institute. Prior to working at Brock, Karen was a reference librarian at Canisius College in Buffalo, New York. Karen works full time as a librarian and part time as an ESL instructor. Karen holds a BA in Spanish and German, an MA in German, an MLS, an EdM in TESOL, and a PhD in foreign and second language education. Her research areas of interest focus on the intersection of library use and language learning by international students.

Steve Borrelli is the head of assessment at Penn State University Libraries, University Park campus. He has a master's in library science from the University at Buffalo. Prior to his time with the Penn State University Libraries, he led assessment efforts at the Washington State University Libraries in Pullman, Washington. He has authored several articles on the assessment of library services and library instruction.

John Boyd is an associate professor and information literacy librarian at Belk Library and Information Commons at Appalachian State University in Boone, North Carolina. John obtained his MLS from Kent State University and an EdS in adult education from Appalachian State University. His research interests include international library development and the roles of libraries in communities. He has visited libraries across the United States, Central and South America, Europe, and Nepal.

Johannes J. Britz is provost and vice chancellor for academic affairs, University of Wisconsin-Milwaukee, USA. He is the former dean of the School of Information Studies at the University of Wisconsin-Milwaukee, and before that was a research associate in the department of information science at the University of Pretoria, South Africa.

Megan Browndorf is the East European studies liaison and reference librarian at Georgetown University in Washington, DC. She has previously served as the history librarian at Towson University in Maryland, and social sciences librarian at North Dakota State University in Fargo, ND. She holds a BA in Russian area studies from Dickinson College and an MA in Russian and East European studies as well as an MLS from Indiana University. Her research interests include library history, particularly in Soviet Ukraine.

Osman Celik is international acquisitions coordinator and head, gifts and exchanges section at the UCLA Library.

Yao Chen is the librarian for East Asian studies, linguistics, and ESL at the University of Minnesota. Her liaison departments include Asian Languages and Literatures, Linguistics, and Minnesota English Language Program. She received her master of library science from the University of Oklahoma, and master of linguistics from Xi'an Jiaotong University, China. Her research interests include information literacy, East Asian librarianship, data management in arts, humanities, and social sciences.

Janet Clarke is associate dean of research & user engagement at Stony Brook University Libraries. She holds a PhD in Asian American literature and an MLS in library science.

Kelsey Corlett-Rivera completed her undergraduate studies in Romance languages at Harvard University in 2005, which led to a five-year career as a project manager in the language services industry, and later, after obtaining her master of library science in 2012, a return to academia as the librarian for the School of Languages, Literatures, and Cultures at the University of Maryland. In 2014, she was promoted to head of the newly formed Research Commons. In that role, Kelsey is responsible for the majority of the University Libraries' initiatives targeting faculty members, graduate students, and researchers on campus. This includes campus partnership-building, program development, and space planning, along with coordination among internal library divisions providing services to this population. Kelsey has published research on ebook usage by academic library patrons and is the site designer and editor of *A Colony in Crisis: The Saint-Domingue Grain Shortage of 1789.*

Laura Costello is the virtual reference librarian at Rutgers University. She formerly served as the head of research and emerging technologies at Stony Brook University Libraries and as the head of library materials and acquisitions at EdLab at Teachers College, Columbia University. She received her MLIS from the University of Wisconsin and BA in English literature from the University of Minnesota.

Elizabeth Cramer is the coordinator of bibliographic services at Belk Library and Information Commons at Appalachian State University. Elizabeth has an MLS from Kent State University, an MA in French from Appalachian State University, and a doctorate in educational leadership from Appalachian State University. Elizabeth is active in the American Library Association (ALA) International Relations Round Table (IRRT), serving as Chair 2016-2017 and past editor of International Leads. Her research interests include international library development and the ALA Sister Library Initiative. Recent site visits have included travel to Ghana, Zambia, Central America, Nepal, and India.

Linda Daniel is a librarian at Duke University and coordinator of Duke Libraries' support for the Duke Kunshan University Library. She set up the Duke Kunshan University Library, fall 2014, and served as the associate university librarian at Duke Kunshan, 2015–2016. She received her BA in history from Duke University and her MSLS from the University of North Carolina at Chapel Hill. Her research interests include the development of critical thinking and information literacy skills. Linda's efforts focus on using interactive learning techniques to enable students to master skills needed to successfully use information to improve their research and enhance their life goals. Her desire is to use education to create global citizens who can live intelligently and act ethically in an increasingly digital world.

Kimberly Davies Hoffman is the River Campus Libraries' head of outreach, learning, and research services at the University of Rochester (UR). She has leveraged many lessons learned from 20 years in the field—focusing on librarian-faculty collaborations, active learning pedagogies, instructional design (in person and online), and professional development training—to strengthen staff capacity and programs at UR. She holds an MLS from the University at Buffalo and a BA in French and international affairs from the University of New Hampshire.

Marian G. Davis is institutional repository librarian at the University of Central Missouri. Her professional career began in academic medical libraries, including University of Kansas Medical Center, Washington University Medical Library in St. Louis, and St. Louis University Medical Library. She became the manager of library services at Marion Laboratories; this pharmaceutical company then merged with Merrell Dow to become Marion Merrell Dow. After the merger, she was the health education program coordinator at the American Academy of Family Physicians.

Lorna Dawes is an assistant professor and the first-year experience/learning communities librarian, and liaison for the Teacher Learning and Teacher Education department at the University of Nebraska Libraries. She also works closely with UNL Programs for English as a Second Language teaching and preparing international students for college research. Her research and practice focus on the scholarship of teaching and learning, and student and faculty experiences with information literacy. Her current research on faculty conceptions of information literacy and its impact on informed learning will be published in January 2017. For the past three years she has served as the primary consultant for the African Poetry Libraries Project.

Molly Des Jardin is the Japanese studies librarian and liaison for Korean Studies at the University of Pennsylvania Libraries, where she has worked since 2013. She is also an amateur digital humanist: co-founder of the text analysis interest community WORD LAB at Penn Libraries, Mellon Research Fellow at the Price Lab for Digital Humanities in 2016-2017, leader of a workshop on Japanese text mining at Emory University, and instructor of a course on East Asian digital humanities at Penn. Her research, not as digital, largely focuses on late nineteenth-century Japanese book history, publishing, and authorship practices. Molly authored *Inventing Saikaku: Collectors, Provenance, and the Social Creation of an Author* (Book History 2017) and has written for *Dissertation Reviews.*

José Díaz is associate curator for special collections and Latin American and Iberian studies librarian at The Ohio State University, Columbus, Ohio. In that capacity, José is responsible for special collections in all areas of American history and for activities such as reference, public programming, and collection development. He is also responsible for the acquisition of Latin American and Iberian materials for the library's general collection. Dr. Díaz is the special collections' liaison to the history department, teaches courses in public history and American fraternalism, and serves on the Latin American Studies Center's advisory board. Jose's research interests include nineteenth century American history, fraternalism, modern Latin American history, and public history. He just concluded a three-year term on the University Senate and one year as chair of the Senate's Diversity Committee. He currently serves on the Senate's Rules Committee and on the Council on Libraries and Information Technology (COLIT).

Joy Doan (joy.doan@csun.edu) is a tenure-track faculty at California State University, Northridge (CSUN) and a research, instruction and outreach librarian in the Oviatt Library. Prior to joining the faculty at CSUN, Joy held a position at the University of

California, Los Angeles (UCLA), where she served as the music inquiry and research librarian. Joy holds a bachelor of arts in English literature and music from the University of Michigan, an MA in music history from Case Western Reserve University, and a master of library and information science degree from San Jose State University.

Gabriel Duque is an associate librarian at the Shapiro Undergraduate Library at the University of Michigan. He obtained an MS in information science from the University at Albany in 2007. Duque has a BA in sociology and has a background in English as a second language instruction. His duties comprise creating and providing library support for undergraduate learning, library instruction, reference services, and he specializes in services for international students and scholars as well as study abroad programs at the university. He is also the head of the Michigan Library Scholars, an undergraduate internship program with a global focus.

Pamela Espinosa de los Monteros is the current Mary P. Key Resident Librarian in Latin American Studies at The Ohio State Libraries. As a bilingual/bicultural information professional she has supported international research initiatives, instructed bilingual digital literacy classes, and coordinated inclusive library programs for youth and adults. She was the recipient of a Fulbright Garcia Robles Binational Business Fellowship to Mexico City, Mexico (2010-2011), a program initiated after the signing of NAFTA to promote binational business relations between Mexico and the United States. She holds an M.S. in library and information science from Syracuse University and a B.A. in interdisciplinary humanities from the University of San Diego. As a resident librarian Pamela serves as a liaison to the Spanish and Portuguese department, Max M. Fisher College of Business, and the Center for Latin American Studies.

Kirsten Feist works in the Undergraduate Library's Instructional Services department at the University of Illinois at Urbana-Champaign. In this role, she primarily teaches library instruction sessions for courses that fulfill the Composition 1 requirement on campus and creates online learning content. She also mentors graduate assistants training to become professional librarians, which she immensely enjoys. Her research interests currently include student learning and research readiness in first-year and international student populations. She is active in ACRL's Instruction Section and the Library Instruction Round Table.

Liangyu Fu is the Chinese studies librarian at the Asia Library and faculty associate at the Lieberthal-Rogel Center for Chinese Studies, University of Michigan. She holds a PhD degree in communications from the University of Pittsburgh and an MLS degree from Nanjing University. Her research focuses on the intersection of print culture, visual rhetoric, and translation studies. She has published in *Translation Studies*, *Papers of the Bibliographical Society of America*, and leading Chinese journals in library science among other fields. Fu is responsible for collection development, reference service, instruction, and public service in Chinese studies at the University of Michigan Library. She serves a large community of Chinese studies faculty, students, and scholars from highly diverse academic and cultural backgrounds. She collaborates extensively with library colleagues in teaching classes related to Asian culture and globalization, offering workshops for improving intercultural competence on campus, and conducting events that reach out to the university's international community and non-traditional users of the Asia Library resources. The library orientation in Chinese is one of these collaborative projects.

Alia Gant is a diversity resident librarian at Penn State University Libraries. Prior to this position she attended the University of Texas at Austin to pursue a graduate degree in information studies focusing on academic libraries. She also has an undergraduate degree from American University and a graduate degree from the University of Iowa in international studies.

Eric Garcia (eric.garcia@csun.edu) is tenured faculty at California State University, Northridge (CSUN) and a research, instruction and outreach librarian in the Oviatt Library. Eric holds a bachelor of arts from Loyola Marymount, an MA in history from Pepperdine University, and a master of library and information science degree from San Jose State University.

Dr. Kenneth Haggerty received his PhD from the iSchool of Information Science and Learning Technologies at the University of Missouri, Columbia in July 2016. He also has an MLIS from the University of Alabama. Dr. Haggerty joined the University of Memphis Libraries in November 2016. His responsibilities include providing leadership and direction for the design, development, and implementation of the various online interfaces that provide access to the resources and services of the University Libraries. As a member of the University Libraries' faculty, he participates in the collection development program, the user instruction program, staffing of the research and information services (RIS) desk, and also serves as liaison librarian to three academic departments.

E. Haven Hawley, PhD, is chair of Special and Area Studies Collections Department at the University of Florida. She is an historian of technology and science and specialize in issues of technological access, especially regarding how this affects the production and preservation of historical materials. She frequently works as a community-institution liaison, connecting donors and underrepresented communities with repositories, or otherwise advising on preservation of materials. She also provides consultations regarding identification of print and papermaking processes related to authentication of, preservation of, and instruction with historical print and manuscripts. She has been associated with Rare Book School for more than a decade, helping to teach descriptive bibliography courses and historical printing practices. Her recent research and writing have focused on the different meanings of objects for creators and those encountering artifacts in an institutional setting.

Megan Hodge, in her position as teaching and learning librarian at Virginia Commonwealth University (VCU), has been the library liaison to VCU's Global Education Office since 2014. In this role, she provides course-integrated library instruction to VCU's English language program, which helps students who have not passed the TOEFL improve their English skills so they can enroll in an American institution of higher learning upon successful completion of the program. She also gives specialized library tours for English-language learners and maintains LibGuides devoted to international students/scholars, English language learners (as well as one for their faculty), and students studying abroad. She is an IRRT member and a member of the ACRL Academic Library

Services to International Students Interest Group. She is a current member of the International Relations Committee, Near East and South Asia Subcommittee, and in 2015–2016 served as a member of RUSA's Reference Services Section (RSS) Committee on Multilingual Library Services. In 2013 and 2014, she participated in two separate rounds of the International Librarian Network's peer mentoring program. She is also currently enrolled as a doctoral student in educational research, and as a result of her experiences teaching information literacy to English-language learners, is hoping to write her dissertation on international students' perspectives on plagiarism and methods for introducing the concept of academic integrity to students whose educational backgrounds prize memorization and do not use citation.

Alexandra Humphreys is an instruction and education librarian at Arizona State University (ASU), Downtown Phoenix campus. She immigrated to the United States after living and in various European countries. Her international involvement includes a presentation at the 100th All Japan Library Conference in Tokyo (2014) and other foreign appearances, service as Chair of the Horner Fellowship Committee (2014-15), President of the Arizona Chapter of the Fulbright Association (2011-15), and Co-chair of the ALA Sister Libraries Committee (2015-present). At ASU she provides library support to Fulbright Foreign Language Teaching Assistants and international teachers from the ASU Teachers College.

Lindsay Inge Carpenter is the pedagogy librarian at the University of Maryland, College Park, where she supports undergraduate research and provides leadership in the areas of online learning and open educational resources. She also co-directs the UMD Libraries Research & Teaching Fellowship, a three-semester teacher training program for MLIS graduate students. Lindsay's research interests include international librarianship, mentorship, critical librarianship, and critical pedagogies.

Rebecca J.W. Jefferson, PhD, is head of the Isser and Rae Price Library of Judaica. She has degrees in Hebrew language and literature (with minor studies in Aramaic, Yiddish and Jewish history and culture). Her doctoral thesis, *Popular Renditions of Hebrew Hymns in the Middle Ages* (University of Cambridge, 2004), concentrated on a corpus of medieval Hebrew poetry manuscripts and analyzed scribal speech patterns and codicological practices.

Smita Joshipura is a director of the e-resources & serials management unit at Arizona State University (ASU), where she is responsible for managing the life cycle of e-resources from acquisitions to access, as well as overseeing print serials management. She is an incoming chair of the Arizona Library Associations' (AzLA) Horner Fellowship Committee (2016-17), standing committee member of IFLA's Serials & Other Continuing Resources Section, serves as a committee member of ALA's Asian & Pacific Library Association's Mentor & Membership Committees, and is a member of North American Serials Interest Group's Communication & Marketing Committee. She is a great supporter of diversity in libraries and has served as a chair of the Diversity Initiative Team at ASU, and currently serves as an active member of AzLA's International Interest Group. She has library and information science master's from India and University of Arizona, USA, and has rich experience for more than 30 years in research, academic, and public libraries in India and the USA.

Pirjo Kangas completed her master of arts degree in English philology at the University of Turku, Finland in 2008. Pirjo has also studied information studies at Åbo Akademi University to become a credentialed librarian, and completed a teacher training diploma at HAMK University of Applied Sciences in 2013. Pirjo works as an information specialist in Humak University of Applied Sciences and her responsibilities include for example information literacy teaching and work with the library system and e-resources. Pirjo has published articles in Finnish higher-education library journals *Signum* and *Kreodi*.

Triveni Kuchi is the head, Learning & Engagement Department, and social sciences/instructional services librarian at New Brunswick Libraries, Rutgers University. She works with the team leaders for the instruction and information literacy, global experience, and undergraduate experience teams. As a subject specialist librarian for sociology, criminal justice, South Asian studies, and Middle Eastern studies, she provides reference, instruction, research consultations, liaison services, and is responsible for collection development in these subject areas. She is a member of the graduate & faculty services team and the global experience team at New Brunswick Libraries. During 2010–2013, Triveni served as the director of the South Asian Studies Program at Rutgers School of Arts and Sciences, managing the programming, planning, and hosting of events and lectures, and advising undergraduate minors and graduate students in their course selection and research. She continues as an executive committee member of the program. In 2012, as a member of the Rutgers University IAPP Institute for International Education study tour, Triveni traveled to India for developing higher education contacts and partnerships. She is an affiliate faculty member in the African, Middle Eastern, and South Asian Languages and Literatures (AMESALL) Department at Rutgers. She is also engaged in graduate programs such as sociology's "Culture and Cognition" workshop, the Middle Eastern studies graduate students forum, and the South Asian studies faculty-research working group. All these experiences have assisted her in representing the library and strengthening relationships with Rutgers faculty and students. Triveni received her MLIS from Rutgers—The State University of New Jersey and has a master's degree in economics from the University of Bombay, Mumbai, India. Her research interests include communication, self-presentation, information literacy, liaison interactions, and collaboration and partnership-building in the context of libraries. She has a number of publications, reports, and presentations to her credit and is the recipient of several awards, including the 2006 Leader in Diversity from Rutgers University, and Special Recognition Awards for extraordinary contributions in advancing the mission and goals of ALA-Association of College and Research Libraries' Asian, African and Middle Eastern Section (2006–7, 2010–11, and 2011–12). She is active in ACRL sections and interest groups and is currently the co-chair of ACRL Anthropology and Sociology Section's Liaison Committee (2017–2019), and the convener for ACRL Asian, African and Middle Eastern Interest Group (2018–2019).

Laurie Kutner is an information and instruction librarian, library associate professor, at the University of Vermont, with liaison responsibilities in the following departments, programs, and schools: global and regional studies; environmental program; Rubenstein School of Environment and Natural Resources; anthropology; geography. She has ten years of experience working in international settings with students, faculty, and librarians, mostly in Costa Rica, and recently in Peru. She ran an ALA trip to Costa Rica in

2014, where they engaged as a group of librarians in 200 hours of library community service in small, rural settings. Previous to that, she coordinated an on-site internship program for Syracuse University MLIS students in Monteverde, Costa Rica, for five years, developing digital libraries of locally based research.

Margaret Law is currently director, external relations for the University of Alberta Libraries in Edmonton, Canada. In this role, she is responsible for implementing and managing external partnerships, including those with international partners. The Visiting Librarian program was developed as part of her portfolio and is the basis for this chapter. She has also implemented several development projects with academic libraries throughout the world. She holds a doctor of business administration with a focus on organizational behaviour, in addition to an MLS and MBA. She is a frequent speaker internationally, providing workshops on marketing and advocacy, intellectual property and human resource management issues in many locations, including Africa and Asia. Her most recent book, *Cultivating Engaged Staff*, was published by Libraries Unlimited in 2017.

Yelena Luckert is the director of research & learning at the University of Maryland Libraries. In this role, she provides leadership for the library's subject-liaison services, general reference, instructional services, and the development of Research Commons. She is also a subject liaison librarian for Jewish and Slavic studies and has served in this role since she first started at the University. During this time, she has been very fortunate in building extensive Judaic and Slavic collections for the Libraries, deep ties with faculty and departments, and a unique exchange program with partners in Russia, including several study abroad classes to St. Petersburg. Ms. Luckert has been very active in the professional service to her library, university and nationally, and has presented and published on topics related to area studies librarianship and library administration.

Deborah J. Margolis is Middle East studies and anthropology librarian at Michigan State University (MSU). Her position includes liaison to MSU's Muslim Studies and Jewish studies programs. Deborah received her MLS from Syracuse University and an MA from Hebrew College in Newton Centre, Massachusetts, and has worked in a variety of academic and public libraries. At Michigan State, Deborah was project director for two National Endowment for the Humanities/ALA "Muslim Journeys" grants and has continued to organize the "Muslim Journeys" series. Deborah is active in ACRL's Anthropology and Sociology Section (ANSS). She has published in *ANSS Currents* and *MELA Notes: Journal of Middle Eastern Librarianship*, a chapter on community partnerships in *Children's Services: Partnerships for Success* (ALA Editions), and *Reaching Your Community via Social Media: Academic Libraries and Librarians Using Facebook and Twitter for Outreach* (with Emily A. Treptow) forthcoming from Springer. Deborah has curated exhibits at the MSU Libraries, including (with Kirsten Fermaglich) the online exhibit, *Telling Family Stories: Jews, Genealogy and History.*

Nicholas Martin is librarian for archives and special collections at New York University in Abu Dhabi. Prior to joining NYUAD, he worked as a processing archivist at New York University's Fales Library and Special Collections. Nicholas holds a master's in library and information ccience from Pratt Institute, and an MA in humanities and social thought from NYU. His latest essay, "An Action Painter Manque," about the artist Larry

Rivers, is available at http://www.tate.org.uk/research/publications/in-focus/parts-of-the-face-french-vocabulary-lesson-larry-rivers/an-action-painter-manque.

Kristen Mastel is an outreach and instruction librarian at the University of Minnesota. Her liaison areas include the College of Continuing Education, Extension, and Agricultural Education. She received her master of library science from Indiana University, master of liberal studies from the University of Minnesota, and her bachelor of arts from the University of Minnesota-Morris. Her research areas of interest include instruction, information literacy, outreach, and instructional design. Kristen is a past president of the Minnesota Library Association. She also is a director of the United States Agricultural Information Network.

Charlene Maxey-Harris is the associate professor and chair of the research and instructional services department at the University of Nebraska Libraries. As a scholar practitioner, her research focuses on diversity and multicultural issues in academic libraries and library instruction for first generation college students. Maxey-Harris published ARL's *Diversity Plans and Programs*, Spec Kit 319, in 2010. Her most recent article was "Diversity Initiatives Still Matter" in ARL's *Synergy*, issue 13, July 2016.

Claudia McGivney is coordinator of assessment at Adelphi University, cmcgivney@adelphi.edu. In her previous role as the head of academic engagement at Stony Brook University Libraries, she believed it imperative that academic librarians are prepared to navigate the delivery of information instruction in a globalized forum. She was thrilled to be able to co-teach the pilot session for the university's Korean campus, to create materials to support international instruction, and to facilitate a survey to assess their instruction methods.

Lana Munip is an analysis and planning consultant at Penn State University Libraries. She has an MEd in Higher Education from Penn State with a focus on institutional research. Prior to joining Penn State, she worked as an education journalist in Malaysia, covering the private higher education sector.

Daniel Necas, as archivist for the Immigration History Research Center Archives (IHRCA) at the University of Minnesota, Minneapolis, has in the past fifteen years worked with collections documenting immigrant and refugee experiences in the United States of the last 150 years. Since 2009, he has been on the team developing the Digitizing Immigrant Letters project. This project involves international collaborations with archives, museums, and libraries in several European countries as well as scholars in the United States and Canada. The latest phase of this effort explores the possibilities of working with the Europeana Digital Library and the Digital Public Library of America.

Mary Oberlies is the conflict and peace studies librarian at George Mason University and has worked with the School of Conflict Analysis and Resolution and the dual-degree program with the University of Malta since 2012. She currently works with faculty and librarians at both institutions to facilitate access and cultivate awareness of library resources and provide research and instruction services. Having completed a master's degree at Queen's University at Belfast in the United Kingdom, Mary has first-hand experience conducting research within an international library system and understands how the differences between library systems may be navigated more successfully with librarian and faculty assistance.

Erin Pappas is currently a liaison librarian at the University of Virginia Libraries. Prior to that she was librarian for European languages and social sciences at Georgetown University. She holds degrees in anthropology from Reed College and the University of Chicago, and in library science from the University of Kentucky. Her research focuses on linguistic anthropology, semiotic mediation, and textual representations of talk.

Justin Parrott is acquisitions and research librarian at New York University in Abu Dhabi. He is the co-editor of *Bridging Worlds: Emerging Models and Practices of U.S. Academic Libraries Around the Globe* (ACRL 2016).

Jeanne Pfander is an associate librarian at the University of Arizona (UA), working as liaison to the UA College of Agriculture and Life Sciences and providing orientation and instructional support to international students and visiting scholars across campus. Her education includes a BA in biology (Stephens College), a MA in library science (University of Missouri), and a graduate certificate in digital information management (University of Arizona). Her current professional activity includes service as chair of the Arizona Library Association's Horner Fellowship Committee (2016) and service on the Online Education Committee for the American Library Association's Sustainability Round Table. Ms. Pfander has presented at international meetings such as the International Federation of Library Associations Conference (IFLA 2016), the Japan Library Association Conference (2014), and the International Association of Agricultural Information Specialists Conference (IAALD, 2010). Born in El Paso, Texas, she has lived in Taiwan and Germany and traveled in North America, Asia, Europe, and Oceania (Australia and New Zealand).

Shana R. Ponelis is assistant professor, School of Information Studies, University of Wisconsin-Milwaukee, and research associate, Department of Information Science, University of Pretoria, South Africa. Shana taught a class in the master's in IT degree program, IT systems in libraries, and taught several NTNU students in her summer classes.

Cheryl Riley has worked at the University of Central Missouri since 1985. She has been active in the Faculty Senate for much of that time, including serving three terms as Faculty Senate vice-president and three terms as Faculty Senate president. She has been a lifelong advocate for the underdog. She has had many different titles and duties during her tenure at UCM but is most proud of her advocacy work—for disabled students when she served as accessibility librarian and for various disadvantaged groups during her ten years teaching race, class, and gender as an adjunct professor for the women's studies program. When budget constraints meant she could no longer teach race, class, and gender, she turned her teaching to the information literacy class being developed by the library. This endeavor provided her the opportunity to work with classes predominantly composed of international students taking courses within the industrial management program. Subsequently, she was offered the opportunity to work as a liaison librarian at a satellite location where she found that most of the industrial management courses and all of the computer science courses are offered. She has been in the liaison position at the satellite campus for two semesters and is very happy with the relationships she has developed with the industrial management program faculty and the services provided to the students at this location. Her advocacy efforts are now aimed at serving this student population and helping the classroom faculty who work with this population.

Kristine N. Stewart is an assistant professor and information literacy coordinator at Zayed University in the United Arab Emirates. She received her MA in library and information science and PhD in information science from the University of Missouri. Her research interests explore information literacy in relation to issues such as public policy, multiculturalism, and social justice. She may be contacted via email at Kristine.Stewart@zu.ac.ae.

Chao SU is a graduate assistant in the library assessment department. She is pursuing a dual master's degree in comparative international education and educational theory & policy studies. Prior to her time at Penn State she earned dual bachelor's degrees in English and finance from China Agricultural University.

Yukako Tatsumi is East Asian studies librarian and curator of the Gordon W. Prange Collection at the University of Maryland Libraries. As East Asian studies librarian she provides education, research, and collection support for multidisciplinary studies related to the languages, literatures, cultures, and history of China, Japan, and Korea. As curator of Gordon W. Prange Collection, she assists with research and course-integrated instruction focusing on the Allied occupation of Japan.

Margarita Vargas-Betancourt, PhD, is the Caribbean Basin librarian and Latin American and Caribbean special collections curator at the University of Florida. She has contributed to numerous major grant projects and international initiatives at the University of Florida, including the integration of the Panama Canal Museum Collection with the University of Florida Libraries. She received the Society of American Archivists' Diversity Award as a co-founder of an international webinar series bringing archivists throughout the Americas into communication with one another, and has been active in diversity service at the University of Florida and archival profession. Vargas-Betancourt is from Mexico, and grew up in an environment shaped by indigenous and European cultures. Her research and publications study the encounter of these cultures and the resulting conflicts. She recently received her PhD from Tulane University in Latin American Studies, with a dissertation studying conflicts over land and water faced by an indigenous community during the sixteenth and seventeenth centuries: the Tlatelolca from Santiago Tlatelolco, one of the two indigenous communities located in Mexico City.

Michael P. Williams is the library specialist for the Japanese and Korean collections at the University of Pennsylvania Libraries. He received his MSLIS in library and information science from Drexel University. He also serves as associate editor for Boss Fight Books, a Los Angeles-based independent press specializing in nonfiction books about video games, and he has authored *Chrono Trigger*, the second volume in the press's eponymous anthology series. His shorter work has appeared in diverse publications including *The Journal of East Asian Libraries* (JEAL), *The Appendix*, and *The Atlantic*.

Kathy Leezin Wu is the government information and economics librarian in the outreach, learning, and research services department at the University of Rochester (UR). Kathy also chairs the River Campus Libraries' UR international community team. Throughout her professional career, Kathy has been devoted to enhancing international students' learning and research experiences through library services. She earned her MLS from the University at Buffalo and a BS in history from SUNY, the College at Brockport.

Yi-Chin Wu, PhD, is a research analyst with the Center for the Study of Student Life at The Ohio State University. She has been a passionate advocate for enhancing international students learning experiences and promoting intercultural education. Her principle responsibility is working with multiple divisions in student affairs develop various programs to improve students' engagement, retention and graduation rate. She earned her PhD in higher education from The Florida State University (2016), her MEd in learning and instruction from National Central University, Taiwan (2007), and her BS in social psychology from Shih-Hsin University, Taiwan (2005). Dr. Wu's research interests include international education, mentoring in higher education, and evaluation and assessment. She has published two book chapters, "Exploring Excellent Teaching: A Narrative Approach" (2010) and "Supporting Learning Flow Through Integrative Technologies" (2007). Her research has appeared in many international and local conferences, such as "International Doctoral Students' Self-Regulation and Culture Influence: A Pilot Study" at the Comparative and International Education Society conference, and "Senior Scholars on Early-Career Professional Development for Black Women Emerging Scholars" at the American Educational Research Association conference. She has worked with numerous organizational settings across the United States and abroad to enhance teaching and learning programs, as well as conducted substantial research on examining learning process and outcomes. She has also received many honors and scholarships including Outstanding Thesis in the Global Chinese Conference on Computing in Education, Outstanding Academic Award, W. Hugh Stickler Memorial Scholarship, and Taoist Tai Chi Society of the USA Scholarship.

Mary Jo Zeter is Latin American and Caribbean studies bibliographer and coordinator for area studies at the Michigan State University Libraries. She has a secondary assignment in the Libraries' special collections unit that includes selection of Latin American studies-related materials and extensive work with donors. Mary Jo is active in SALALM, the Seminar on the Acquisition of Latin American Library Materials, and currently chairs the review group for a new line of awards established in 2015, the SALALM Dan C. Hazen Fellowships. She has served as an elected member of its executive board and as co-editor of the organization's newsletter. Mary Jo has created many exhibits in the MSU Libraries and in 2016 curated a large exhibit, "Latin American Comics: Selections from Special Collections," in the gallery of the Residential College in the Arts and Humanities to coincide with MSU's annual Comics Forum. Mary Jo holds an MS in Library and Information Science from the University of Illinois at Urbana-Champaign.